Event Tourism
Concepts, International Case Studies, and Research

Donald Getz, Ph.D.
Professor, School of Tourism,
The University of Queensland, Australia
Affiliated with the Norwegian School of Hotel Management
at the University of Stavanger, Norway
Donald Getz resides in Calgary, Canada

Cognizant Communication Corporation

Where
Knowledge
Resides

PO Box 37•18 Peekskill Hollow Rd. Putnam Valley NY 10579
www.cognizantcommunication.com

Event Tourism
Concepts, International Case Studies, and Research

Cognizant Communication Offices:

U.S.A.   18 Peekskill Hollow Road, Putnam Valley, NY 10579

Library of Congress Cataloging-in-Publication Data

Getz, Donald, 1949-
   Event tourism : concepts, international case studies, and research / by Donald Getz, Ph.D.
      p. cm.
Includes bibliographical references and index.
ISBN 978-1-882345-60-1 (alk. paper)
1. Tourism–Research. 2. Tourism–Planning. 3. Special events–Planning. I. Title.
G155.A1G4385 2013
910.68'4–dc23

                         2013007980

Printed in the United States of America

Printing: 1 2 3 4 5 6 7 8 9 10 Year: 1 2 3 4 5 6 7 8 9 10

Contents

i

List of Photos

List of Tables

Acknowledgments

My special thanks are offered to the following contributors:

Aaron McConnell and the TransRockies team
Alan Clarke and his team at Northern Ireland Tourist Board
Anders Nordvall, Mid-Sweden University
Bo Svensson, Mid-Sweden University
Brendon Downey, Tourism Victoria
Brent Moyle, Southern Cross University
Cameron Hart, Gold Coast Events
David Gration, University of the Sunshine Coast
David McGillivray, University of the West of Scotland
Dominic Moran, Moran Tourism Group, New Zealand
Gayle McPherson, University of the West of Scotland
Harald Dolles, Molde University College
Heather Gibson, University of Florida
Heather Bell, University of Florida
Holger Preuss, Johannes Gutenberg-University
Ian Patterson, The University of Queensland
Joe Goldblatt, Queen Margaret University
John O'Sullivan, Events Queensland
Judith Mair, Monash University
Kerin Weber, Hong Kong Polytechnic University
Marco De Iaco and his team at Calgary Sport Tourism Authority
Matt Lamont, Southern Cross University
Millicent Kennelly, Griffith University
Ossian Stiernstrand, Goteborg and Co.
Paul Bush and his team at EventScotland
Reidar Mykletun, University of Stavanger
Richard Scharf and the Visit Denver team
Rob Davidson, University of Greenwich
Robert Peterssen, Mid Sweden University
Tommy Andersson, University of Gothenburg
Xin Jin, Griffith University

Appreciation is offered to my colleagues at the School of Tourism, The University of Queensland. Special thanks to publisher Bob Miranda for continued support, over many years.

Preface

This book is the direct descendent of *Event Management & Event Tourism*, which was published by Cognizant in 2000, and the second edition in 2005. Since then numerous texts on all aspects of event management have become available, and indeed that literature has exploded. But Event Tourism as a topic has somewhat languished. In my mind there has always been a need for a separate book on Event Tourism. It should fit well into tourism programs, especially those that have added event management or event studies. And I think it is important to be taught within event management programs because of the numerous links to tourism—especially at the policy and industry strategy levels. If you look into my other book, Event Studies, you can also find many of the connections between event management and event tourism. In that book I explain the three discourses of event management, event tourism, and the classical (or discipline-based) approaches to the study of planned events. These are also covered here, specific to festival tourism.

My approach is to bring all aspects of Event Tourism together, whereas there are already available books on sport tourism (in which events figure prominently), festivals and tourism, and convention and exhibition tourism. There is no other integrative book available that covers all of these, especially from the policy and strategy perspectives. I also have several big new ideas, or challenges, to put forward in this book, especially the portfolio approach. Most of the research and literature has been focused on single events, and mostly large or mega-events, whereas the trend (and the necessity for competitive advantages) is clearly towards the creation and management of balanced portfolios.

Key Objectives of the Book

1. Provide a textbook for students of events and tourism, and a reference for practitioners of Event Tourism.
2. Challenge the "industry" and students with five major areas for advancing knowledge and competitive advantages.
3. Explain and illustrate the key concepts of Event Tourism, both in the context of the study of tourism and its professional practice.
4. Employ case studies, expert opinion, and professional profiles in order to illustrate how Event Tourism works in the real world.
5. Connect readers to the research literature and encourage its consultation through use of Research Notes and provision of additional readings.
6. To provide a comprehensive, systematic study of event tourism as a social, cultural, economic and environmental phenomenon and as an important aspect of international business.
7. To provide students with the knowledge and skills for event tourism careers.
8. To explain the nature and importance of event tourism, and how to employ events in destination planning and marketing.

9. To use case studies of successful events, cities, and destinations in demonstrating effective event tourism policies, strategies, and actions, including impact assessments and triple bottom line evaluation of event tourism.

This book is dedicated to my family, and especially the newest member, grandson Joshua (born July 1, 2012 to Audrey and Jody Bailey).

How to Use This Book

Instructors

It is always problematic to know at what level a book fits into any given curriculum. When I wrote *Event Studies* I thought it would be best used for research students, including postgraduate courses, or during the final year of a full degree program. But it turns out that many instructors prefer it at an introductory level, as their emphasis is on academics (i.e., studies) rather than application (i.e., management).

This new Event Tourism book could be used in both studies and management-oriented programs, depending on the emphasis given to "how-to" (as in how to plan and develop Event Tourism) versus an emphasis on understanding what the nexus of events and tourism is all about and the issues it raises. Those are more like end-points on a continuum, and of course a blending is ideal.

I can recommend two specific roles for this book. In tourism degree programs Event Tourism should at least be an option, but given the ascendency of planned events—a trend likely to continue—as policy instruments and travel motivators, I think it deserves to be part of the required curriculum. Of course there are tourism and hospitality programs that already feature business events as an industry, and in those programs this book offers a much broader and integrative approach.

Within event management degree programs there is definitely a need for at least acquainting students with all the tourism-related issues. At a minimum, most event producers and managers will have to consider tourists as a market segment. But beyond this, I think it has become impossible for professionals in the events sector to avoid all the tourism- and development-related policy and strategy connections. Government at all levels bid on, create, facilitate, and market (even exploit) events for many purposes, so professionals must be able to work comfortably in this environment. *Event Tourism* can therefore be used in a full course within event management, or used as a complement to other required readings.

Students

Leading each chapter are Learning Objectives, which should inform you on what the chapter covers and the knowledge you should be gaining through reading and discussion. At the end is a summary, and study questions, which I always write as possible exam questions. Your instructor might have a different approach, but I think if you can thoroughly and accurately answer all the study questions you will have mastered the chapter contents.

There are a number of major themes running through the book that you should also pay attention to, particularly as they are summarized in the final chapter. Major essay questions could be based on these themes. Therefore, pay attention to the Five Major Challenges outlined in Chapter 1, developed throughout the book, and finally as summarized in Chapter 11.

There are a number of features particularly aimed at enhancing the student's enjoyment and value gained from reading this book. First, the industry and some academic colleagues have kindly provided a number of Case Studies. These are fairly detailed accounts, written by or with the cooperation of external experts and agencies. In contrast, the many Research Notes are much shorter, intended to link readers to the research literature and encourage further research. My selection is not necessarily of the best on every topic, as that would require a lot of judgment, but they are all recommended readings. Mostly they consist of the author's abstract, or excerpts from the article.

A number of academics have contributed Expert Opinion pieces, with references. Again, these provide gateways to important literature, and ideas, especially for students in need of research projects or references for papers.

Several Professional Profiles are included in Chapter 1, and those professionals are directly connected to the case studies. They provide an example of careers specific to Event Tourism, as opposed to event management.

At the end of the chapters are Additional Readings. Mostly theses are books that are cited in the text. Readers will find a lot of additional pertinent material in these texts.

The photos have all been provided by contributors and they illustrate events that are profiled or at least mentioned in the text.

Practitioners

Although this book has been written primarily for students, as a textbook, practitioners will find the contents of considerable value—particularly because there is no other book available that integrates all aspects of Event Tourism. In particular, the five big challenges represent new ways of thinking about Event Tourism strategy and policy. Leaders in this sector are already putting into practice some or all of these ideas. Consider that competitive advantages are not going to accrue from doing the same old things. The marketplace is crowded and new strategies are required. You will find it challenging, but rewarding, to implement many of these ideas.

Chapter 1

Introduction to Event Tourism

Learning Objectives

Upon completion of this chapter the student should understand and be able to explain the following:

1. The meaning and importance of the academic subfield, and the professional practice of Event Tourism.
2. Why Event Tourism is one of three major discourses related to planned events.
3. How Event Tourism connects to other applied fields including leisure, hospitality, and sport.
4. Career paths available within Event Tourism.
5. How Event Tourism relates to other forms of special interest travel.
6. Demand and supply-side definitions, as well as demand and supply-side approaches to planning and development of Event Tourism.
7. The instrumentalist nature and societal importance of Event Tourism, including its main economic and place-marketing roles.
8. Types and roles of stakeholders.
9. Justifications for public sector intervention in Event Tourism (policy and development).
10. Categories of planned events, and typologies of events based on form and function.

Introduction

Event Tourism has become established as a major social phenomena and big business at a global scale. People travel for many reasons, and planned events figure prominently in many travel decisions. Just about every city, destination, and country wants to employ events for a multitude of strategic and political reasons, with tourism at the fore. Competition has never been fiercer, and it will increase. Why? The limits of mass tourism have been reached in many places, and it might very well decline owing to a variety of constraints. Competitive advantages can be realized only through aggressive niche marketing and events constitute a prime area for attracting special interest segments. Furthermore, events can contribute greatly to branding and place marketing and generate numerous social, cultural, economic, and environmental benefits for residents.

In this book I present an integrated and strategic approach to Event Tourism, with no attempt made to cover the actual production and management of events nor the facilities that are often required to support them. I argue that Event Tourism is not only a distinct discourse within the academic literature (i.e., having its own terms and concepts and line of theory development) but is a strategic domain within tourism or destination development and marketing. What's more, Event Tourism is now inextricably linked to a variety of other policy domains, ranging from urban development and renewal to social and cultural policy.

Perhaps the greatest evidence of the ascendency of Event Tourism is the range of career paths now open to professionals. While they might have to understand the basics of tourism and event management, they can focus on event tourism in a number of ways: bidding; hosting; relationship management; provision of services; media management, etc. These are discussed in the text, with examples.

The future of tourism and hospitality does not lie in mass tourism, but in niche marketing. If climate change, energy costs, or financial crises do not halt the growth we have seen in international travel, thereby forcing change, then ever-more intense competition will cause the industry and destinations to focus more on people who have to travel, and those who have very compelling reasons for travel—not to mention the means to do so. This means that Event Tourism will become more important even as constraints on mass tourism take hold. This is the basic premise of the book.

Events motivate a great volume of travel, generating demand for all the venues and services associated with tourism and hospitality. But more importantly, events can attract high-yield tourists, and in particular give people very specific (and often non-substitutable) reasons for visiting particular cities and countries. Furthermore, the range of events that attract tourists is enormous, and in fact ever-expanding. While business events and sports are already very well developed in many places, the new and growing opportunities are within leisure, attached to lifestyle, and very much part of the experience economy. Here are virtually unlimited possibilities for new events and ever-more refined target marketing—all of which requires market intelligence and research. Oh, and some theory.

Five Big Challenges

These five big challenges are presented as themes through book, and they each require a short introduction here.

Moving From a Supply-Side to a Demand-Side Approach

A major innovation in this book is the switch in emphasis from supply-side to a demand-side approach to Event Tourism. This represents a paradigm shift that will necessitate adjustments on the part of many practitioners. Yes, we still need venues and they have to be marketed. There will always be events wanting to attract tourists. And bidding for one-time events will undoubtedly remain important. But the demand-side approach opens up numerous avenues of development and marketing that have little if anything to do with the prevailing emphasis on sports and business events. Destinations looking for competitive advantages will have to get started soon before they are left behind.

From Top-Down to Bottom-Up Planning (Liberating Innovation)

In keeping with the demand-side approach is the necessity for more bottom-up, as opposed to top-down, planning. A top-down approach is typical, and is associated with one agency (say, a government tourism department) or organization [e.g., a destination marketing organization (DMO)] preparing strategies and expecting everyone to implement them. It seldom works that way; it is far too simplistic. We do not want to abandon strategic thinking, including visioning exercises, but top-down initiatives have to be in balance with, and support, bottom-up initiatives taken by the numerous entrepreneurs (social and private), organizations, events, and other stakeholders in Event Tourism who are much more likely to adapt quickly, to innovate, and to see new opportunities.

In a highly competitive world, liberating innovation is the key to success. By definition we cannot say what the next great idea will be, or how competitive advantages will be found in the future. Any strategy that attempts to move all the stakeholders in one direction is doomed to failure.

From Single Events to Portfolios

Here is another relatively new idea developed in this book, and it is already being picked up by leading destination marketing and event development agencies. The focus has always been in single events, selling venues to them, bidding on them, developing and marketing them. The future lies in portfolios of events, all managed together as assets achieving multiple goals for the host cities and destinations. If you think it is a challenge to organize or market one event, imagine the complexity involved in managing dozens or hundreds of events to satisfy numerous stakeholders! Within this new portfolio approach it becomes quite evident that the highest value assets are events anchored in the destination or city, particularly Hallmark Events with long-term, institutional status, and Iconic events that attract niche markets. One-time events, usually won through sales and bidding, come with higher costs and sometimes dubious value. This especially applies to one-time mega-events that can incur enormous costs. Therefore, sustainability enters the picture as a major theme.

Create Your Own Destination Events

The destination perspective dominates in this book, as that is where most of the Event Tourism action takes place (by that I mean strategy, policy, funding), but the book also covers single events and how they can be developed and marketed as tourist attractions. And we deal with entrepreneurial possibilities as well, featuring in a case study one company that creates and markets destination events—events you have to travel to. In this context, the book presents new ideas on developing and marketing Hallmark and Iconic Events. These two special categories of planned events represent some of the best potential for creating long-term, sustainable benefits and for tapping into the virtually unlimited potential within the sport and leisure markets.

An Integrated, Sustainable Approach

The fifth big idea, or challenge, is to move from a narrow, supply-side approach stressing sports and business events (both heavily dependent upon expensive venues) to a fully integrated and sustainable development model. Principles of sustainability can best be applied when portfolios of events and related facilities are managed together, and when the emphasis is broadened to include other types of events and venue-free strategies. This incorporates festivals and celebrations more fully, and also encompasses the basic ideas behind the demand-side, bottom-up approach. One new way of thinking is to avoid the traps presented by gigantism (venues and events getting bigger and bigger) and constant bidding on mega-events.

While sustainable events are a hot topic, sustainable Event Tourism presents us with a fundamental quandary. How can any activity or industry be "sustainable" when it depends so heavily on energy consumption, built facilities, and the luxury of spending great sums of money on nice trips to faraway places? Is that sustainable? Academics and activists go on and on about sustainability, yet the "industry" and government continuously collaborate to develop tourism and push the Event Tourism agenda to the fore. It is a truly global phenomenon. Are they all going in the wrong direction? I do not try to answer this question, but green events and sustainability are mentioned in many places. It will be up to the policy makers and professionals to come up with solutions. A starting point is for everyone to consider this simple proposition: *It is far better (in both competitive and sustainability terms) to motivate and facilitate a few people to travel for very specific reasons, with high yield to the industry and destinations, than to continue developing mass tourism. The more focused on niche markets you become, the more sustainable will be the outcomes.*

Events *and* Tourism

We first need to talk about *events and tourism*. When two fields of study combine like this, something unique happens. First, we apply concepts and theories from the two contributing fields (which in turn draw upon many foundation disciplines)—event studies and tourism studies—and then we undertake interdisciplinary research and theory building to explore the unique aspects of events and tourism combined. Academics and practitioners both want to know what is unique, and why this justifies separate treatment—otherwise event management would merely consider tourism as one market, and tourism management would simply recognize events as one form of attraction.

It is the unique, new dimensions of Event Tourism that justify separate treatment within an academic context, and these are explored in this chapter and throughout the book. Ontologically (i.e., concerning what we claim to know) Event Tourism has its own concepts and terminology, with new theories emerging such as the event travel career trajectory and a theory of Hallmark and Iconic events. These exist only when events and tourism are combined, with input from other fields and disciplines. Furthermore, if one becomes interested in the study of Event Tourism, by definition you have to understand fundamentals of both event and tourism studies, and that kind of synergy is always helpful to theorists and practitioners.

This issue has been considered in other fields, notably sport and tourism. An overall summary of the debate can be found in the book *Sports Tourism: Participants, Policy and Providers* (Weed & Bull, 2009). Those authors (p. 31) suggest that to be legitimate, sport tourism (and by implication Event Tourism) must demonstrate a body of research (and researchers devoted to the subject), quality, peer-reviewed journals, and texts on the subject. So far there is no specific Event Tourism journal (there should be!) but both event and tourism journals cover the field.

In my review of the Event Tourism literature and discourse in "Event Tourism: Definition, Evolution, and Research" (Getz, 2008) I noted that tourism dominated the discourse, reflecting the instrumentalist approach to events as tools for development and marketing. It was, and remains, my conclusion that "Event tourism is both a sub-field within established academic streams, in realty at the nexus of tourism and event studies, and an area of destination management application", and that "It can be concluded that event tourism studies and related research are still in the early stage of development and there is great scope for theoretical advances" (p. 421).

Another important conclusion from that review was that "A broad range of methodologies and methods drawn from foundation disciplines and closely related professional fields are appropriate and necessary for creating knowledge and developing theory in event tourism" (p. 422). Much of the content of this book draws from and elaborates upon material in that article, but many new ideas are presented, and theoretical advances can be claimed.

What Is Event Tourism?

Throughout this book I use Event Tourism as an integrating concept. It is capitalized wherever I mean the integrative study of events and tourism (which is in large part a social phenomenon) and the business practice of using events as instruments of policy, corporate and industry strategy, and in development. Consequently, three subdefinitions of Event Tourism are required. The first two can be called supply-side definitions because they stress the importance of events to attract tourists. The third is a demand-side definition because it focuses on tourist demand for events.

Event Tourism as a strategy or policy is instrumentalist—that is, events are viewed as tools to achieve economic and other goals. Here is definition from the point of view of cities and destinations wanting to develop it: *Event Tourism at the city or destination level is the development and marketing of planned events as tourist attractions, catalysts, animators, image makers and place marketers. This process includes bidding on, facilitating and creating events, and the management of portfolios of events as destination assets.*

Many event managers get involved with marketing to tourists, so Event Tourism from the individual event's perspective is that of marketing to a specific segment—those who will travel to get to the event. And there are many purpose-built facilities that have to attract and host events, as that is their core business; there are many other facilities and even parks that want events and tourists to help realize their goals. If you are operating any kind of venue, you are automatically in the events business—and tourists might very well be an essential or important client segment. So this is also a definition of Event Tourism: *For individual events, Event Tourism means taking a marketing orientation to attract tourists, sometimes as an additional segment and sometimes as the core business. When tourists are the core business we can refer to "destination events."*

Event Tourism must also have a demand-side definition related to the strong propensity of people to travel to events, and because of events. We need to study why people travel to events, their patterns and preferences, and their impacts. To events and destinations, this is essential market intelligence. *Event Tourism is travel to attend events, both on the part of dedicated event tourists who are motivated to travel for specific events, and other tourists who attend events while away from home.*

Further consideration must be given to media reach, as those who get exposed to, or informed about planned events might be influenced to travel.

Examples of Event Tourism in Practice

These examples are all elaborated upon later in the book, and they cover all levels of Event Tourism practice from local through national, individual events to portfolios, and both public and private sector initiatives.

- TransRockies Challenge: This private, for-profit company produces two "destination events," one in Alberta and the other in Colorado, that attract national and international mountain bikers and runners (respectively) to compete at the highest level. Manager and part-owner Aaron McConnell is interviewed.
- Visit Denver: This DMO and convention bureau promotes the "Mile-High" city as an international destination famous for its events, produces several events of its own, and markets the Colorado Convention Center.

- Melbourne, Australia: An events capital globally, and awarded the best Sport City in the world! We look at how the convention center boosts attendance and leverages events for maximum local benefits, and in detail at the impacts of business event tourism.
- Calgary Sport Tourism Authority: Their roles, strategy, and successes are examined, how they bid on events, and technical details of feasibility, risk assessment, and event tourism capacity building. Vice-President Marco De Iaco is interviewed.
- EventScotland: Scotland has a degree of autonomy within the UK and considers events and tourism to be of utmost importance. The case study covers their mandate, overall roles and strategy, and some success stories. Key staff members are profiled and CEO Paul Bush is interviewed. Details from a major study of festivals and their impacts in Edinburgh are presented.
- Individual events and their tourism orientation are profiled, including the Whitebait Festival in New Zealand, Woodford Festival in Australia, and Seniors Games in Florida.
- Belfast and Northern Ireland celebrated a "Titanic" year in 2012, featuring a new Titanic visitor center and Titanic Festival, all as part of their repositioning and rebranding strategy.
- Detailed research findings on the nature and impact of music festivals and concerts in the UK; the nature and impacts of business events, festival and sport tourism in US, UK, and Australia.
- New theory development on the Event Tourist Career Trajectory, supported by research on running and mountain biking events.
- Trends and issues pertaining to arena and stadium development, as you cannot have events with venues.
- Queensland Events Corporation, Australia, represents state-level policy and programs to promote events sector and event tourism, including events owned and produced by its subsidiary, Gold Coast Events.

These examples illustrate the breadth of Event Tourism studies and the diversity of applications in the real world.

Why Study Event Tourism?

One obvious reason for studying Event Tourism is the opportunity to develop a professional career or set up a business of the types mentioned above. But there are broader reasons. Within a tourism curriculum, events constitute such an important element of strategy and supply that a course on event tourism is certainly justified. Often it is subdivided, particularly into the three components that are given emphasis in this book: business events; sport events; festivals and other cultural celebrations, entertainment, and private functions. This is the first book that integrates these major components, but more importantly this book provides a rationale and guidelines for fully integrated policies and strategies towards developing and marketing event tourism for destinations and for individual events.

Event Tourism also belongs in event management degree programs, given the importance of tourism to many events. It is more than just one market segment, because a goal to attract tourists or be a tourist attraction requires considerable change to the typical event marketing mix. An event cannot simply say we want tourists! It has to start with a marketing or consumer orientation. Furthermore, tourism policy and strategy will impinge on the operations of many events whether they like it or not, and they will increasingly have to operate and compete within a managed portfolio of events, or within a population of events that are expected to generate many different benefits. Therefore, event managers have to understand tourism and related policy.

Event Tourism and Event Studies

There is a very interesting thing about tourism: you can place numerous adjectives before the word and (apparently) create new subfields of study and niche markets. I also study food and wine tourism, for example, and there is virtually unlimited potential for this kind of subdivision. But is this process, which is quite evident in both the popular and academic research literature, actually necessary? Do we really need a book devoted to Event Tourism?

For starters, it is clear that Event Tourism is both a distinct subfield that merges events and tourism, and there are a variety of strategic reasons why it should be dealt with professionally by destination planners and marketers. What's more, Event Tourism is increasingly generating its own professional career paths.

Figure 1.1 (from my book *Event Studies: Theory, Research and Policy for Planned Events*) (Getz, 2012) illustrates how Event Studies encompasses event management and Event Tourism. It makes equal sense to show how tourism studies encompasses events, but that diagram would also have to include all the other tourism subfields that connect to real-world phenomena, like agricultural tourism, parks tourism, urban tourism (i.e., tangible things that attract tourists) as well as numerous experiential realms of tourism such as food tourism, cultural tourism, ecotourism. What is of importance here is the fact that events make many aspects of tourism tangible: for example, urban and agricultural

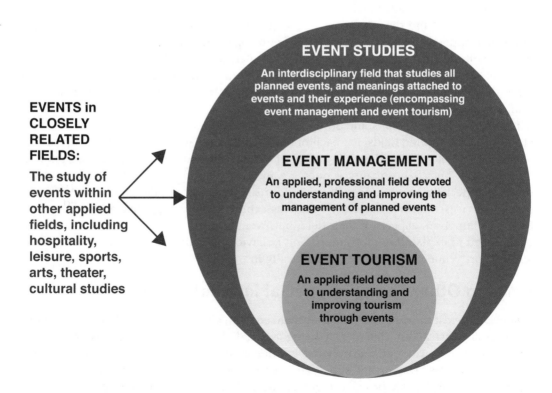

Figure 1.1. Event Studies, Event Management, and Event Tourism (from Getz, 2007, 2012).

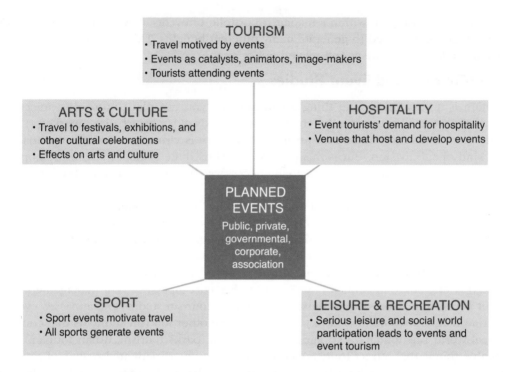

Figure 1.2. Linking events to closely related fields.

tourism are manifested through numerous celebrations, while desired ecological or cultural experiences are also made tangible through a variety of events in parks and cities.

As indicated in the diagram, there are important connections between event studies and other applied fields in which events figure prominently: hospitality, leisure, sport, theater, cultural, and arts management in particular. Event Studies attempts to unify the study of planned events, which means relating them to these other fields and drawing upon those fields for theory and methods. All of these fields are in turn dependent upon foundation disciplines for theory and methodology.

Figure 1.2 elaborates on some of the specific connections between Event Tourism and closely related, applied fields. For each of these links the diagram suggests the topics that help define Event Tourism. Hospitality studies focus on hotel and catering restaurant/catering management, but all hospitality venues are in the events business and want to attract tourists (especially resorts). As well, event tourism generates additional demand for hospitality services. Sports management students cannot avoid competitive and recreational events as important aspects of their field, but Event Tourism is also of relevance because of the need to explain fan motivations and behavior including sport event tourism. And again, sport venue managers are automatically in the events business.

Links to Other Forms of Special Interest Travel

Special interest tourism can be conceptualized from either the demand or supply sides; however, Trauer (2006) argued that being "special" lies in the experiences of tourists, and is not necessarily defined by what is offered to them. There are broad categories of special interest travel that subsume events, such as cultural, business, sport, or leisure travel. But such broad categories mean little when it comes to pinpointing motivations and travel behavior—we have to be more refined. For example, within sport tourism a large subcategory is sport event tourism, which can then be broken down by participant versus spectator, followed by types of sport, different settings and formats, etc. The whole idea behind "special interest" is that we should identify very specific, personally meaningful motivators that lead to particular patterns and forms of travel. We do that in Chapter 2 by examining serious leisure, social worlds, and event travel careers. In each of Chapters 5 through 8 we examine very specific motivations and forms of leisure and business travel.

What exactly might a special interest tourist be interested in? Most commonly it will be an activity—that is, the conative dimension of experience, such as fishing, spectating, eating, or viewing. But it can equally be a learning experience (e.g., I am interested in learning more about wine making and cooking) or an emotional experience (e.g., I am interested in sharing my beliefs, and celebrating with others who are part of my community). All experience dimensions can apply. A person might also want to have a special experience in a particular setting (wine tourism in France), or among particular company (friends at a marathon, family at a reunion, others in the community of dancers at a festival). The combinations of special interests, experience dimensions, settings, travel, and events are endless, literally. The term "affinity group" comes into play here, as many people chose to travel (some or all of the time) with a preexisting group such as a club or association, or the events they go to are aimed at such groups.

The broad relationships of Special Interests, Tourism, and Events are indicated in Figure 1.3. Special interest travel occurs because of either intrinsic or extrinsic motivation (or combinations), the key point being that specific benefits/experiences are sought. Benefits can be at the personal or group level, and in the case of extrinsic motivators they can be personal or corporate. In terms of the seeking–escaping model of Iso-Ahola (1980, 1983), special interest travel is mostly about seeking, but we can assume there are underlying escapist tendencies, and it relates to both personal and social motivators because people are often influenced by the needs of family, friends, and affinity groups who want to do things together.

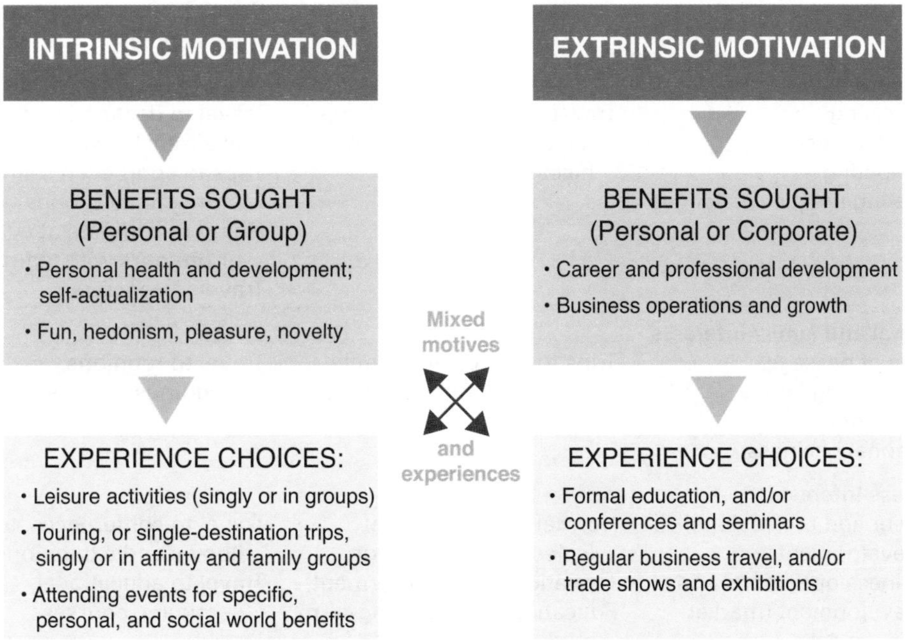

INTRINSIC MOTIVATION

▼

**BENEFITS SOUGHT
(Personal or Group)**
• Personal health and development;
  self-actualization
• Fun, hedonism, pleasure, novelty

▼

EXPERIENCE CHOICES:
• Leisure activities (singly or in groups)
• Touring, or single-destination trips,
  singly or in affinity and family groups
• Attending events for specific,
  personal, and social world benefits

Mixed
motives

and
experiences

EXTRINSIC MOTIVATION

▼

**BENEFITS SOUGHT
(Personal or Corporate)**
• Career and professional development
• Business operations and growth

▼

EXPERIENCE CHOICES:
• Formal education, and/or
  conferences and seminars
• Regular business travel, and/or
  trade shows and exhibitions

Figure 1.3. Special interests, tourism, and events.

There are a range of experience and setting options to meet these motivators, and some are planned events; the event can be part of, or the focus of, the travel. There are also many event trips motivated by mixed reasons, leading to combinations of experiences, such as family holidays tied to a conference, or personal business added to participation in a sport event.

Table 1.1. Specific Forms of Special Interest Tourism and Events

Interest Categories and Examples	Related, Normal Tourism Activity	Travel to Events
Cultural interests The arts Religion Spiritualism Ethnic and racial connections	Visit museums and galleries, heritage sites and shrines Visit homelands ("roots pilgrimages") Tours to explore exotic places Live abroad	Attend special art exhibits Religious pilgrimage events Ethnic and multicultural festivals
Lifestyle Food, wine, design, shopping Entertainment (artist and musical preferences) Hobbies (photography, models, games)	Secular pilgrimages to sites of importance Tours or destination-specific trips for related activities (e.g., taking photos) Taking pictures while on holidays; traveling to famous/special sites for painting	Food and wine classes, demonstrations, competitions, festivals Shopping festivals Concerts and award ceremonies Game/hobby conventions and competitions Hobbyist conventions and exhibitions Special sales or markets for collectibles
Sport interests Exercising Serious training Competing Meeting unique challenges	Travel to places for individual activity (e.g., fishing, hiking)	Travel to destination events like TransRockies Trips to sport events singly or in affinity groups Going to compete at events, or on tours with teams Travel to spectate
Personal and family interests Rites of passage Maintaining family relations Personal business	Trips to friends and family Trips for personal business	Travel to reunions, weddings, parties
Business Interests Career and professional development Business operations and development (marketing, trade) Job obligations	Normal business travel (sales, small meetings, relationship management) Educational travel (long-term study)	Travel to conferences, trade shows and exhibitions Travel to educational seminars, courses

Almost any kind of travel and event fits into this model, which is both a strength and weakness. How special does the benefit or trip purpose have to be? Presumably what is excluded is mass tourism for generic reasons such as relaxation or visiting friends and relatives, yet even these motivators can include events.

Specific forms of special interest tourism are described in Table 1.1, and this is closer to what tour companies might offer as "special interest" travel.

Careers in Event Tourism

The most generic career related to Event Tourism is marketing and sales, because all events, venues, and destinations are constantly selling their space and services. As well, there are a variety of generic, event-related jobs in these venues, ranging from coordination to actual event production. What differentiates Event Tourism careers from others in event and tourism management are the unique, focused, and dedicated careers that are necessary for the planning, delivery, and management of Event Tourism. These are related to the need for professionals to plan and manage Event Tourism within DMOs, event development agencies, and at events or venues.

A dramatic rise in the number and variety of professional careers specifically tied to Event Tourism has become evident. There is no one landmark date or development I can identify as a starting or turning point; it has been more of an evolution. Certainly the pioneering work of event development corporations in Australia can be cited, and these had their origins in the 1980s, but elsewhere the trend can be seen in progressive destination marketing organizations or tourism agencies around the world. The case study of Calgary Sport Tourism Authority (see Chapter 6) shows how recent the surge in Event Tourism

Table 1.2. Event Tourism Career Paths

Typical Functions	Major Tasks
Event facilitator/ coordinator	Work with events in the destination to help realize their tourism potential (funding, advice, marketing) Liaison with convention/exhibition centers and other venues; liaison with sport and other organizations that produce events
Event tourism producer	Create and produce events specifically for their tourism value Stakeholder management (with numerous event partners)
Event tourism planner	Develop a strategy for the destination Integrate events with product development and image making/branding
Event tourism policy analyst and researcher	Work with policy makers to facilitate event tourism Conduct research (e.g., feasibility studies, demand forecasting, impact assessments and performance evaluations)
Event bidding	Bid on events Develop relationships leading to winning events for the destination Conduct risk assessments and feasibility studies for each potential bid
Event services	Provide essential and special services to events (e.g., travel and logistics; accommodation and venue bookings; supplier contacts)
Event sales	Convention and exhibition sales (i.e., attracting events) Other venues selling event spaces and services (hotels, resorts, etc.) Selling to exhibitors and the public (for exhibition companies)
Meeting planner	Assess potential venues and destinations; negotiate with suppliers; arrange services for events; organize and produce events

initiatives has been, although Calgary previously hosted the 1988 Winter Olympic Games and in 2012 celebrated 100 years of the famous destination event, the Calgary Stampede. This shows that Event Tourism is not an invention; it is a progression towards more sophisticated and competitive marketing and development.

Once the preserve of marketing professionals, now numerous DMOs and special purpose event development agencies are employing event tourism professionals who understand the roles events can play in destination development and marketing. A background in tourism, events, and marketing is ideal, but increasingly there will be specializations within event development agencies and DMOs. Table 1.2 presents a number of positions and key associated tasks. Note that sales is not really specific to tourism, but is a large part of what DMOs, convention centers, and venues have to do.

As well, event coordinators in venues are not necessarily engaged in tourism-related work, but are essential to the event tourism process. Meeting planners deal with venues and destinations, therefore they require some knowledge of tourism-related issues.

Research on Careers

Very little has been published specifically on Event Tourism careers. In the mainstream of event studies, Baum, Deery, Hanlon, Lockstone, and Smith (2009) edited a book entitled *People and Work in Events and Conventions: A Research Perspective*, and this was the first to cover research on HR issues in the events sector. In that book, Jago and Mair (2009) discuss career theory applied to major events, pointing out a number of important trends and issues. They referred to McCabe's (2008) identification of a career pattern called "butterflying," at least applicable in convention and exhibition professionals (see the Research Note). And they noted the difficulties associated with "pulsating" event organizations and one-time events. Many event professionals, out of preference and necessity, do not stay long in one job, and full-time, traditional careers are in short supply (this might not hold true for festivals, however). One consequence is the rotating of key staff between major events, and a career pattern that is described as "episodic"—moving from one major event to another, in sequence. In this way, expertise from the Olympics, for example, gets transferred to the next one. Another trend is for private firms to provide staff to multiple events, or to produce many events professionally, for profit.

Careers related to meetings, conventions, and exhibitions have been studied the most, presumably because they are usually associated with major venues. Similar research on festivals and sport event careers is needed.

Research Notes on Event Careers

McCabe, V. (2008). Strategies for career planning and development in the Convention and Exhibition industry in Australia. *International Journal of Hospitality Management, 27*(2), 222–231.

This article examines the career planning and development strategies of individuals in the Convention and Exhibition industry in Australia. Through a structured questionnaire career information was received from a sample of individuals (*n* = 126) employed within the industry. The exhibition sector is dominated by well educated, career mobile females who follow a strategy of "butterflying" between jobs and subsectors of the industry. They also use a range of personal career planning and development strategies that may be affected by their age but not their gender.

Ladkin, A., & Weber, K. (2010). Career aspects of convention and exhibition professionals in Asia. *International Journal of Contemporary Hospitality Management, 22*(6), 871–886.

The article reviews the key literature relating to life and work history research, career profiles, and human capital, which is followed by a discussion of findings of an online survey of C&E industry professionals in Asia. Findings indicate that there is no specific career route/path into the industry, with experience being generated in a wide variety of sectors, and primarily gained in management, sales variety of challenges relating to environmental, customer and job demands.

One study specific to Event Tourism operations was conducted by Krysztof and Davidson (2008). They examined the educational and career backgrounds of professionals in destination marketing organizations with a focus on those charged with attracting events.

Research Note on Event Tourism Professionals

Krysztof, K., & Davidson, R. (2008). Human resources in the business events industry. In J. Ali-Knight (Ed.), *International perspectives of festivals and events—paradigms of analysis* (pp. 241–252). London: Elsevier.

The extent to which any city or country may be successfully branded, positioned, and promoted as an events destination depends largely on the availability of a wide range of resources within the destination itself. These may include infrastructural, natural, and cultural resources. However, increasingly, attention is focusing on human resources as a critical success factor in the events industry in general and the business events sector in particular. The dedication, expertise, and creativity of all events professionals operating in any destination are clearly of great importance in determining that destination's level of success in this industry. But while this has been widely acknowledged in the case of the men and women who conceive, plan, and deliver the actual events (with job titles such as events managers, events planners, and events coordinators), far less attention has been paid to the human resources element represented by those professionals who are responsible for marketing their destinations as attractive places in which to hold events. As competition to "win" events of all types intensifies worldwide, it is becoming clear that the degree of success of any city or country in attracting such events depends partly on recruiting and retaining professionals of the right caliber into these key destination marketing positions. Destinations that are eager to succeed as places that host highly lucrative business events such as conventions and incentive trips need to attract and retain professional staff capable of using their initiative and innovative skills to secure these types of events for their particular city or country.

Nevertheless, despite the widely acknowledged importance of the role played by marketing professionals in attracting events to their destinations, very little is known about how these vital stakeholders are educated and trained for, as well as recruited into, such positions. This chapter therefore explores the issue of the education and careers backgrounds of professional staff in destination marketing organizations, with particular emphasis on those who are responsible for attracting business events to their destinations. It examines the extent to which the educational community is contributing to preparing young people for employment in these organizations and investigates the career paths that currently lead to this particular occupation.

Educational Programs Related to Event Tourism

Currently there are very few programs of study that are called Event Tourism, but there are many that blend Event Tourism with event management, or subsume aspects of it (such as a specialization in conventions and meetings) under tourism or events. Current practitioners probably came from generic marketing and communications, or from tourism, hospitality, leisure, sport, event management, or business backgrounds.

The following are examples from universities offering pertinent degrees, undergraduate or graduate, beginning with the only one I could find that is actually called Event Tourism.

- *Master of Science in Event Tourism: Indiana University, IU School of Physical Education & Tourism Management.* The MS in Event Tourism builds on the state's rich reputation around the attraction of events to stimulate economic development and image enhancement. Graduates will have a practical and theoretical understanding of the events and experiences created by expositions, fairs, sports, festivals, conferences, meetings, and cultural destinations. The program culminates in a thesis such that graduates are well equipped to conduct research as a means to inform and improve decision making. Graduates will be prepared for positions in public, private, and nonprofit organizations related to event tourism experiences.
- *Tourism, Conventions and Event Management: Indiana University, IU School of Physical Education & Tourism Management (Bachelor of Science).* The possibilities are numerous for TCEM graduates. Once students identify specific interest areas, they may become meeting/event professionals or managers of sports venues, conventions centers, conference centers, or hotels. International, national, state, and local associations employ planners for meetings and conventions, as do association management companies. Convention and visitors bureaus and destination management companies are a good fit for many of our graduates. Attractions and cruise lines are also options.
- *Master's Degree in Event Management for Tourism: Universidad Europea de Madrid (Spain).* The market for conference meetings and event organization continues to grow. Nowadays it is a major market that generates considerable profits and employment for both companies and tourist destinations. The growth of this sector has led to a notable increase in the demand for professionals who are familiar with the key elements of the industry in all its forms. These key elements range from the presentation of a candidacy to an international medical conference to managing meetings and conferences for corporate executives, as well as managing meeting rooms and conference halls at hotels, promoting venues to attract business tourism, etc. In response to this high demand and market needs, for the last nine years IEDE Business School has offered a Master's Degree in Event Management for Tourism.
- *BBA program in Sport, Event and Tourism Management: University of Texas at San Antonio.* The purpose of the new degree is to provide students with an opportunity to obtain a general business background and to specialize in sport, event and tourism management by taking specific courses that focus on sports and events, or tourism. Students who obtain this degree can pursue jobs in all business and operations areas in the following industries. *Sports*—professional sport franchises (e.g., MLB, NFL, NBA, USTA, PGA/LPGA, and minor leagues), amateur sports (collegiate, high school, AAU, etc.), nonprofit organizations (e.g., sports councils, YMCAs, and other organizations that produce sporting events), sports facilities (e.g., stadiums and arenas), and recreational sports (e.g., fitness centers, golf courses, tennis centers, country clubs, etc.). *Events*—hotels and other event facilities/venues (e.g., convention centers, country clubs, etc.), nonprofit organizations (e.g., arts councils, historic groups, charitable organizations, etc.), event management companies, corporate meeting planners, sports groups, attractions, etc. *Tourism*—destination management and marketing organizations (e.g., convention and visitors bureaus, tourism bureaus, etc.), convention centers, attractions, resorts, etc.

Profiles of Professionals

Connected to the case studies, several practitioners kindly agreed to provide profiles and mini-interviews. Read these again in conjunction with the cases found in later chapters. There are also several additional professional profiles contained in the EventScotland case study in Chapter 3.

Paul Bush is Chief Operating Officer of EventScotland. In August 2007 Paul was appointed Chief Operating Officer of EventScotland and is responsible for the delivery of Scotland's Major Events Strategy and managing relationships with a diverse range of public and private sector partners and international federations. Prior to this role Paul was Deputy Chief Executive of EventScotland. In 2007 he was awarded an OBE (Order of the British Empire) in the New Years Honors List for services to sport. In 2006 Paul served as Chef de Mission, Scottish Commonwealth Games Team, and in 2002 was General Team Manager, Scottish Commonwealth Games Team. Prior to that he held positions as Chief Executive for Scottish Swimming and Team Manager for Great Britain Swimming Team and the England Swimming Team.

> Q: What is it about your background that prepared you for this position as Chief Operating Officer?
>
> A: Being so heavily involved in sport and taking part in and preparing other athletes in major sporting events gave me a valuable insight into what makes a successful event. As well as seeing how an event runs from the point of view of the audience it is vital to understand how they work for athletes and performers and this helps enormously when working with International Federations who need to know that a national event agency understands why their world cup or world championship is so important.
>
> Q: Are you personally involved with events, or is being the CEO a purely administrative or political position?
>
> A: I believe it is important to get as close to an event as you can. I make a point of getting out to even the smallest events that EventScotland supports so I can understand and experience the occasion for myself. That way I can make informed decisions about future funding opportunities and identify links across the industry to help keep the industry developing.

Marco De Iaco is Vice President, Sales, Sport and Major Events within Tourism Calgary, and is in charge of the Calgary Sport Tourism Authority operations. He is a graduate of the Bachelor of Hotel and Resort Management degree program of the University of Calgary. Upon graduating, Marco approached Tourism Calgary with a proposal to create a strategy for attracting sport and major events. In 2005, the plan was advanced by working with business leaders in the community and the Mayor to create the Calgary Sport Tourism Authority (CSTA). Since 2005, Tourism Calgary has seen production growth within the segment of event tourism, 6 out of 7 years. A new department of sport tourism was formed at Tourism Calgary and the CSTA model is now widely considered as the best practice for sport event tourism in Canada.

His path to Vice President was relatively quick, paralleling the growing recognition of the importance of events and reflecting increasing sophistication and successes in bidding on events. When he started in Tourism Calgary, convention sales was the only event-specific area of significance. When Marco was hired by Tourism Calgary in 2003 there was no strategic investment made in the proactive pursuit of sport and major events.

Today, sport tourism is a key pillar of the organization and recognized as one of the most important strategic priorities and growth segments for the industry. Further, the segment has produced arguably the most significant return on investment and incremental benefit for key tourism stakeholders in the city of Calgary over the past 7 years.

Q: What do you mostly do in the VP role?

A: I work with leaders in business and tourism to bring sport, culture, and major events to Calgary and lead a team of sales professionals that deliver an event bidding and hosting strategy for the city of Calgary. Since 2005, the organization has supported more than 130 national and international events, generating over 160,000 hotel room nights, producing well over $250 million in gross economic activity in the city of Calgary. In 2011, Tourism Calgary posted its most successful year in the segment of sport event tourism, supporting or leading bids for 36 events, resulting in 44,000 hotel room nights.

Q: How have you made an impact in this short period of time?

A: We have led and supported numerous successful bid campaigns for high-profile events and initiatives, including the 2012 IIHF World Junior Championship, 2012 Canadian Track & Field Championship, 2011 Cavalia, 2009 World Water-Ski Championship, 2009 CN Canadian Women's Open, 2008 JUNO Awards, and the national relocation bid for Canada's Sport Hall of Fame. The 2012 IIHF World Junior Hockey Championship was a highlight, as Calgary and Edmonton successfully co-hosted a major international event for the first time, setting the stage for the potential of future international co-initiatives between the two cities. We were very proud to help unite the Province and two cities to achieve the collective delivery of this world-class event. Serving as the bid director for 5 years, I was also a member of the executive host committee and chairman of the legacy committee.

Q: What do you think are the benefits of Event Tourism for Calgary?

A: The events we help bring to Calgary have stimulated economic activity, extended the profile of the city and improved quality of life in the community. For example, as a result of the 2009 CN Canadian Women's Open (golf), the Alberta Children's Hospital received a donation of $1.6 million benefiting children and their families across the Province. Our effort to bring the 2009 World Water Ski Championship to Calgary attracted competitors, families, and officials from 35 countries and helped develop the facilities at Predator Bay into a world-class water-ski venue. The 2012 IIHF World Junior Championship has a produced a legacy for grass roots sport across Canada with a record profit of $21 million and over $1 million invested directly into Alberta-based programs. As well, fans, volunteers, and officials across the Province were engaged and enthusiastic about the experience. In fact, 1,155 volunteers and 14 communities across Alberta formally participated in the event, hosting a record 11 exhibition games and 3 selection camp games. Over 25,000 tickets to the event were donated to community groups and charities across Alberta. And the event set a new attendance record of 443,000 spectators with a new average attendance of 14,300 per game.

Aaron McConnell, President TransRockies Challenge. Before joining TransRockies in 2004, Aaron already had a long history with the Sport of Mountain Biking in Western Canada. Most notably, he organized the UCI Mountain Bike World Cup in Canmore from 1998 to 2000, which was awarded the World Cup "Event of the Year" trophy in its inaugural year. In 2002–2003 he was Event Director for 24 Hours of Adrenalin series, then in 2005 Aaron received his MBA from the Haskayne School of Business at University of Calgary and immediately started with TransRockies. A major initiative was the 2007 launching of the GORE-TEX® TransRockies Run in Colorado. Most recently, the company has expanded to encompass the management of events.

Q: How did you progress from an amateur mountain biker to an event organizer and now to a manager, producer, and part-owner?

A: I always had an interest in organizing and making things happen for the sport. For many years I was involved in grass roots things like coaching, volunteer committees, club and team management, and smaller events. When I got into larger events it was a natural progression.

Q: What special skills or personality traits are useful for being successful in this business?

A: One of the great things about event management (depending on your perspective) is that the deadlines are fixed, so you know for sure the date you have to deliver a finished product. To thrive in this environment, you need to be organized and detail oriented, but also flexible enough to adjust on the fly and not to get too hung up on unimportant details.

Q: Did your MBA help in any way?

A: Yes, the MBA was helpful in providing the concrete business skills I needed, but more importantly the strategic sense to adjust to quickly changing environments and finding ways to scale the business.

Q: It seems to me that your whole business model is based on a deep understanding of niche markets. How do you stay on top of the trends and how do you continue to attract and satisfy these target segments?

A: It's one of the biggest challenges that we face. There is a lot of fluidity within the market between sports, distances, formats, etc. A format that might be popular one year could be replaced by a totally new format the next year, creating major shifts in participation patterns. We try to gather as much feedback as possible from our participants, and also benchmark against other events to see what is gaining momentum.

Q: I call your main owner-produced events "destination events" because to participate you must become a tourist, and long-distance tourism is generated. Does that enable you to deal more effectively with important stakeholders?

A: In some cases, we have partnered with tourism marketing organizations to produce destination events. These events may generate tourism as well as destination awareness through media coverage of an event. Being associated with DMOs definitely lends legitimacy and makes stakeholder relationships easier.

Q: What are the biggest challenges facing your events business?

A: The biggest challenges we face are around unpredictable swings in participation. Sometimes events can grow rapidly and a quick adjustment is required. At other times, events may get smaller, creating a need to reduce costs or replace the revenue through other events. Shorter events also typically have a lot of last-minute registration, or weather-dependent participation, where people wait to see the forecast before registering. Sponsorship is another major challenge, mainly in that it requires a major time commitment to recruit and service sponsors, and many sponsors, especially in the sport industries, prefer to provide in-kind value instead of cash. This makes it difficult to justify the time required to build sponsorships.

Integrating the Elements of Event Tourism

There are several integrative ways of looking at Event Tourism that both justify its teaching as a subfield (or at least as a unified subject) and that introduce the various elements of Event Tourism that have to be brought together for effective development and management. The first framework is taken from my approach to Event Studies.

A Framework for Understanding and Creating Knowledge About Event Tourism

Figure 1.4 shows the framework for understanding and creating knowledge about event studies (from Getz, 2007, 2012), which has been adapted to Event Tourism. You can start thinking about Event Tourism anywhere in this system (e.g., with Personal Antecedents and Decision Making). Why do people travel, and therefore what benefits/inducement to offer them is the basic Event Tourism marketing question. But we also want to understand economic, cultural, and social factors that shape interest in, and demand for, events—not to mention constraints that act against Event Tourism.

"Outcomes" refers to the goals of policy and strategy for Event Tourism, especially the economic benefits desired by events and destinations, but we also need knowledge and theory on the personal, social, and ecological impacts. Some outcomes will be negative and unpredictable, so we cannot assume the Event Tourism is always good.

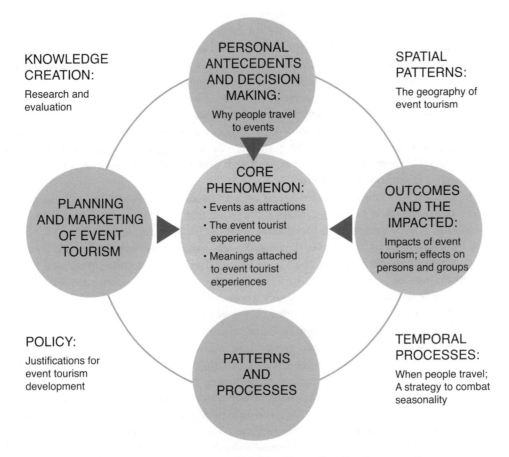

Figure 1.4. Event Tourism within the Event Studies framework (adapted from Getz, 2007, 2012).

The "Planning and Marketing of Event Tourism" is conducted principally by individual events and venues (like convention centers and sport arenas), by DMOs (destination management or marketing organizations) and increasingly by event-specific development, marketing, and bidding agencies. Many other stakeholders are involved, as will be discussed. What do they all want? Are all their goals the same? How do they collaborate? These are essential concerns in the study of Event Tourism.

The Core Phenomenon really defines a field of study. For this subfield, located at the nexus of event and tourism studies, it is events serving as attractions that defines the core. All else in Event Studies follows from this basic phenomenon—events attract people and generate travel. Related to that is our concern for why people travel to events and this requires us to focus on event–tourist experiences: not just the event itself, but the event as part of travel and even event–tourist careers. Finally, experiences have meanings, and Event Tourism has personal meanings to the tourists but the phenomenon has economic, societal, cultural, and environmental meanings that have to be considered.

The rest of the system consists of dynamic patterns and processes shown as connections on the model. Tourism is a spatial–temporal phenomenon (i.e., people travel from home to destinations, covering specific routes, at particular times). Events are shapers of tourism, and are especially useful in attracting tourists outside the usual peak seasons, and to places where they would not otherwise go. Policy is always shaping Event Tourism, and we pay particular attention to policy contexts in this book, and to how policy and strategy are evolving. Finally, the model includes knowledge creation, both market intelligence for strategists and event operators, and research to advance general and theoretical knowledge of this subfield.

Management System (Resources, Stakeholders, Networks, Collaboration, Evaluation)

Figure 1.5 is a different kind of system model (adapted from Getz & Frisby, 1988). In this framework the developers and marketers are at the center. They are engaged in a transforming process, turning various inputs into desired outcomes. When a specific event is at the center (as discussed in Getz, 2005), tourism is merely one of the outcomes desired by organizers. If we place a DMO or Event Tourism development agency at the core we expand the scope considerably to include various tourism, place marketing, and urban development goals.

An important concept in Event Tourism is that of events in a managed portfolio. They are transforming processes intended to fulfill a range of goals pertaining to the various roles of events in economic and place marketing policy. The community, and specific stakeholder groups, will, however, have more expectations from their events, so that a triple-bottom line approach becomes inevitable. The portfolio can be "managed" to various degrees, depending on intervention by government, industry, and others.

The advantage of looking at Event Tourism this way is that you can easily visualize how resources must flow, what stakeholders are involved, the nature and evaluation of outcomes—all as an integrated system. A system is a set of interdependent or interacting elements, and all conceptual systems (or policy domains) like this are "open systems" that depend on, and influence, the environment around them.

Inputs consist of all those things needed to develop and market Event Tourism, including: tangible resources, such as money, equipment, and facilities; venues; human resources, both volunteers and staff; political and moral support; information, including feedback from evaluation processes and market research. Inputs for local Event Tourism agencies come mostly from local government and the tourism hospitality industry

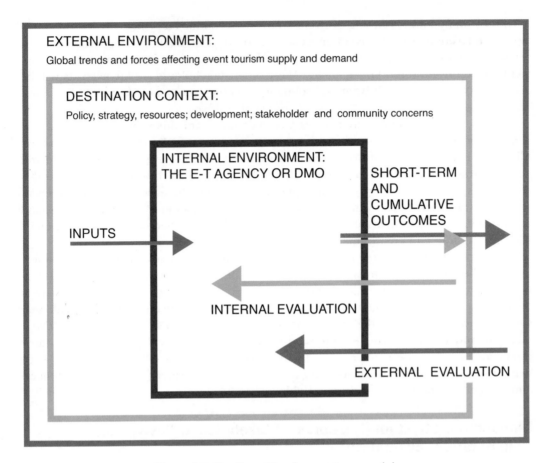

Figure 1.5. The Event Tourism system model.

(often as members of a DMO). For state or national Event Tourism agencies the inputs additionally come from state or central governments.

The diagram also shows a general "environment," which can be thought of as the global context as it influences supply and demand, especially competition and economic conditions, but in fact all the forces discussed later in this chapter. It is essential to develop networks and alliances with government agencies, professional associations, tourist industry groups, or other special interests in order to monitor and understand the various trends and forces impacting upon tourism and events. It is a very complex environment.

An internal evaluation system is usually concerned with efficiency and effectiveness of this Event Tourism system. The agency responsible will measure how well resources were utilized and calculate various return on investment measures (this is the efficiency part), and the degree to which goals have been obtained (i.e., effectiveness). But it has to be remembered that outcomes are not always going to be as expected, or positive. An evaluation system must include the means to uncover unintended outcomes, and to report on negatives. Feedback should change the way things are done. One key goal is to continuously improve the portfolio and its outcomes.

External evaluation is undertaken by stakeholders, including the politicians, industry, residents, and special interest groups, all of which have different perspectives on Event Tourism and its impacts on them. While outcomes include everything changed by the system, impacts are what people and groups feel happens to them! They might be unhappy, so the system has to be responsive to their legitimate claims.

Various external stakeholders evaluate outcomes differently than managers and owners, unless they have agreed-upon, common goals. When events take money and other support from external stakeholders, such as tourism, then an obligation to account for Return on Investment is introduced. Social, cultural, environmental, and ecological watch-dog groups will also be evaluating, employing their own criteria.

A system model is more than a theoretical framework—it can be used to systematically evaluate the organization or an event, and to diagnose specific problems. The model helps identify the flows and uses of resources, including money and information that are the life blood of all events and development. It helps identify key stakeholders who have to be brought into decision making. And systematic evaluation helps the manager keep the whole picture in mind, whereas the natural tendency is to get lost in daily problem solving.

The Specialized Marketplace Perspective

This perspective is strategic in nature, viewing Event Tourism as a specialized marketplace occupied by buyers and sellers. This marketplace requires specialized expertise and separate policy and strategy to be successful.

On the one side are suppliers, namely events that want tourists, cities/destinations engaged in place marketing and event tourism, and all sorts of event-specific venues and other facilities that require events. On the other side are the main markets of leisure, sport, and business events. Some selling goes on all the time, plus lots of bidding, but ongoing relationships must be sustained and reputation building and branding must be strong.

Approached from the point of view of a DMO, or a national tourism organization (NTO), all of which seek to foster competitive advantages in attracting tourists, the development and marketing of events is a major and growing part of their business—so much so that many cities, regions and countries have already established event development agencies or major event units within tourism bodies. In other words, event tourism is a unified subject from the supply side of tourism. It makes sense to treat events as one area of competitive advantage requiring specific policies, strategies, funding, and staff. Of course, it is not necessary to compete in all the subareas of event tourism, and many cities, for example, stress conventions and exhibitions; others focus on sports or festivals. Most engage only in strategy and marketing, while some (see the Visit Denver case study) produce their own events.

An illustration is contained later in the book (Figure 4.3) for the specific, specialized marketplace associated with bidding on events. That model shows how destinations must engage in relationship marketing and intelligence gathering with, and about the organizations that own events. Event tourism agencies must also decide what events they need and want, and their capacity to win and host these events. When bidders and owners interact, it will often result in formal bid processes, but sometimes other transactions will occur, such as when a venue is sold to a meeting planner, or an event owner decides there is only one destination that meets its needs.

The marketplace analogy implies an open market, and of course that is not always the case. Some deals are done through a closed process. In these cases the public does not find out what the real costs are, and the bidding agency probably does not want them to learn about all the impacts either. While that might be an efficient way to do business, it certainly cannot be justified in otherwise open and democratic nations. It will change, but only when enough stakeholder power is martialed to convince governments.

The Place Marketing Perspective

This perspective is broader than that of tourism and events management as it starts with a corporate or community vision for the town, city, or destination and progresses to describe goals and strategies that will incorporate events and tourism. This approach also ties in with urban planning/renewal and economic development. Quality of life is an important component, as is efficiency and other economic/financial consequences of government spending and policy making.

Both facility and event needs are articulated, leading to considerations of the event portfolio and its specific relationships with facilities. City branding implications flow from the visioning. A key question has to be: Who can participate? If it is done just by the corporate elite, public reaction might be hostile and many important opportunities could be missed.

What is really important about the place marketing perspective on Event Tourism is that it elevates the process, including inputs, goals, outcomes, and evaluation, to a much higher policy domain—in fact, to a set of interrelated domains. Elsewhere I have argued (Getz, 2009) that events-related policy must be better integrated with many other policy fields, and this includes urban renewal and development, social and cultural, leisure and recreation, environment and community. Events and tourism both gain in recognition and importance when they are affiliated directly with other policy domains.

A Demand-Side Perspective (the Event Tourists)

Event tourism is less unified from the demand side, given the enormous differences in motivation and behavior between groups holding a convention and individuals competing in marathons, or celebrants at a festival versus exhibitors at a trade show. Despite these differences, it is still logical to view all event tourists together as opposed to lumping them in with demand for built attractions (such as theme parks and art galleries), or with other forms of special interest tourism such as those based on setting (e.g., nature based), lifestyle pursuits (e.g., gastronomy), or very general categories like "cultural tourists." Events overlap with all of these, as will be discussed in this book, but events are developed and marketed in a number of unique ways.

In Chapter 2 various theoretical approaches to studying and explaining event tourist motivation and behavior are explored. The one I am personally trying hardest to advance is called the Event Tourist Career Trajectory, and it applies to anyone who becomes sufficiently involved with a particular leisure or lifestyle pursuit that they start attending events and develop "careers" that generate more and more event tourism. It can also apply to professionals, but that has yet to be tested.

Reactive Perspectives

Event tourism initiatives can arise from the desire of existing events to market themselves to tourists, or simply to expand their revenue-generation potential, and this might spur tourism and destination agencies to at least assist in the process. A similar reactive approach to event tourism is to simply assist local organizations, businesses, and diverse interest groups to organize and bid on events that suit their specific purposes. Over time, the effectiveness of an ad hoc approach to event tourism pales in comparison to the results achieved by destinations aggressively pursuing this business.

Portfolio Approach

This book covers the portfolio approach in detail, with a number of models presented in later chapters. The idea is to develop and manage events as destination assets, although the same concept applies to a venue, company, or an agency. The key is to expand one's thinking from single events in an ad hoc approach to multiple events managed strategically. A full portfolio will consist of various types of events, for different target markets, held in different places, and at different times of the year, in pursuit of multiple goals. Obviously it is a big task, and undoubtedly requires the systems approaches described above. There are any number of specialized marketplaces to consider.

Equally important is the pursuit of synergies, with the portfolio achieving much more than a mere sequence of uncoordinated events. Synergies can arise in several areas, which will be examined in greater detail later: economic benefits; social and cultural capital; stability and sustainability of events; environmental sustainability. In a portfolio approach the types of events, and their host or owners, will often be of less importance than the cumulative effects.

Stakeholders

Common to any perspective on Event Tourism, or any strategy and development plan, are stakeholders. The term comes up again and again in this book, so here is a good place to define and explain the term. *Stakeholders are people or organizations that can influence events and Event Tourism, and those impacted by events and Event Tourism.* The degree to which they are consulted and supportive can determine your success, so proactive stakeholder management is vital. Consider a possible list of key stakeholders for a single event:

- the customers;
- volunteers and staff;
- suppliers, venues, performers, and other participants;
- agencies providing grants;
- corporate sponsors;
- participating organizations (i.e., partners and allies);
- the media;
- the local community/residents;
- social and environmental lobby groups;
- potential customers;
- regulators: governmental agencies at all levels.

There are additional stakeholders for Event Tourism, starting with the tourism and hospitality sectors through their collective associations. "Internal stakeholders" include owners, directors, staff, volunteers, and participants. "External stakeholders" might have power to influence you, or can become allies, while others will be impacted by your actions. These groups have to be managed differently. For general references on stakeholder theory see Freeman (1984) and Jawahar and McLaughlin (2001). Applied to events, there are several research articles available (Larson: 2002, 2009).

Research Note on Event Stakeholders

Larson. M. (2009). Joint event production in the jungle, the park, and the garden: Metaphors of event networks. *Tourism Management, 30*(3), 393–399.

This article argues that actors in different event networks experience different dynamics in terms of the joint organising of the event. The Political Market Square (PSQ) model is used to describe, analyse and compare the interactions and dynamics going on in three event networks. The purpose is to categorise different kinds of PSQs in terms of actors' interactions and network dynamics, which, in turn, contributes to knowledge on how events are produced using a network perspective. An analysis of the different event networks resulted in three different categories of Political Market Squares—the jungle, the park, and the garden, representing a tumultuous, a dynamic, and an institutionalised event network. The institutionalised PSQ (the park) is often prescribed in literature on event organising. Therefore, more research focused on understanding tumultuous and dynamic event networks (the jungle and the park) is needed.

"Legitimacy" is a term of importance in stakeholder theory. Some persons or groups will want to be consulted or will seek to influence your actions, but you do not see them as being "legitimate." What is to be done with them? In some cases, it is wise to accept their self-defined legitimacy, in others to ignore them. There are no hard and fast rules about this, but perhaps it is wise to be as inclusive as possible and not shut out too many potential stakeholders.

Now consider those who are likely to be impacted by any planned event or tourism in general, and those who will want a say in how it is developed. These stakeholders should

Table 1.3. Event Tourism Stakeholders, Queensland, Australia

Strategies	Partnership Agencies
Stadiums strategy	Queensland Events Stadiums Queensland Tourism Queensland Department of Sport and Recreation
Sport strategy: Substrategies for growing existing events to their optimum potential and identifying and securing new events	Queensland Events Department of Sport and Recreation
Cultural strategy: Substrategies for film, exhibitions, festivals	Queensland Events Arts Queensland Department of the Premier and Cabinet Major Brisbane Festivals Pacific Film and Television Commission Queensland Art Gallery Gallery of Modern Art Tourism Queensland Asia Pacific Screen Awards
Business events strategy covering: Incentive travel, association meetings, tradeshows, and exhibitions	Queensland Events Department of the Premier and Cabinet Department of Tourism, regional development and industry Tourism Queensland Convention Centers Convention Bureaus
Regional events strategy	Queensland Events Tourism Queensland Department of the Premier and Cabinet Arts Queensland Department of Sport and Recreation Department of Tourism, Regional Development and Industry

be consulted, although perhaps they do not require permanent, formal links of the kind you need with those on whom you are dependent. For issues such as environmental quality or community support you might have to deal with elected officials and special interest groups that feel they represent those perspectives, so stakeholder management can be a very political process.

Stakeholders for Event Strategies in Queensland

In 2008 a review was completed by consultant David Williams who compiled the information in Table 1.3, referred to as the "strategic partnership framework for developing a major events strategy." Notice the overlapping of agencies related to various strategies, all of which are necessary for the bidding on, and production of, major (i.e., tourism-oriented) events in the State of Queensland. Also observe how events interconnect with other development strategies including film and culture. How these strategies and agencies interrelate and the role of the lead agency can determine how effective the overall strategy will be. As identified in this Queensland review, the degree to which the agency and the strategy hold political credibility, and the priority given to these interrelated strategies, are also of critical importance.

Events as Instruments of Policy and Strategy

Events are sometimes organically grown, literally springing from the needs and desires of communities and interest groups. But in the modern world most are produced—or

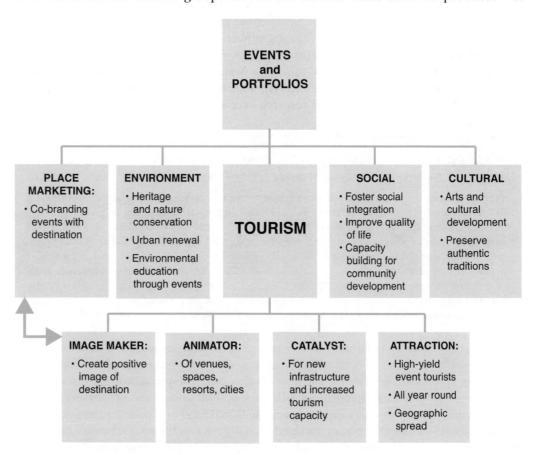

Figure 1.6. Major and Secondary Roles of Events as Instruments of Policy and Strategy.

at least subsidized and marketed—as instruments of public policy or the strategies of industries (like tourism) and the corporations that sponsor or produce them.

These roles are illustrated in Figure 1.6, placing the tourism-related role of events alongside environmental, social, cultural, and place marketing goals, then showing specific, secondary roles of Event Tourism below. This is a complex destination or city environment into which events and tourism must fit.

There are two sides to "Environment," which will be discussed throughout the book, one pertaining to ecology and the resource base, the other to the built environment. Tourism and events impact upon both. Social policy encompasses the roles of events in establishing civic pride, as social integrators, and as sport/leisure/entertainment outlets that enhance quality of life. As creators of social capital, events can expand community development capacity. Within cultural policy, events provide a means for preserving authentic traditions and boosting interest or participation in the arts. "Place marketing" entails a bunch of interrelated strategies and actions that overlap Event Tourism, as events are often viewed as ways to enhance a city's image for tourists, investors, and residents, and to improve its quality of life.

Events as Attractions

Although many tourism organizations stress international tourism, there is no doubt that most festivals and events are dependent upon local and regional audiences. But whether events are true tourist attractions (i.e., motivating overnight or nonlocal travel), or a reason for visitors already in an area to stay longer, they can have tourism value. Events can also have the effect of keeping people and their money at home, rather than traveling outside the region. Event "drawing power" or "attractiveness" to tourists is discussed in detail in Chapter 2. A particularly important goal is the spreading of tourist demand over time (to overcome the tourist seasonality problem) and space (to spread demand throughout a country or region). The following research note is a classic, being (as far as I know) the first published research article clearly about Event Tourism.

Research Note on Events and Seasonality

Ritchie, J. R. B., & Beliveau, D. (1974). Hallmark events: An evaluation of a strategic response to seasonality in the travel market. *Journal of Travel Research, 13*(2), 14–20.

Cyclical demand in the leisure, recreation, and travel markets is a major factor contributing to low productivity and low returns on investment among the suppliers of goods and services to these markets. One strategic response to "the seasonality problem," which has had varying degrees of success in different regions, is termed the Hallmark Event. Such events, built around a major theme, serve to focus tourism and recreational planning on a particular period of the year. The present research provides both an in-depth, cross-sectional study of one such activity (The Quebec Winter Carnival) as well as a longitudinal analysis of the event's evolution over its 20-year history. Finally, the social and economic implications of the findings are discussed with a view to aiding persons interested in developing such events.

The tourism industry is in many places preoccupied with overcoming traditional "seasonality problems"—that is, demand is concentrated in one or more "peak seasons" rather than being spread uniformly over the year. Events have unique advantages in overcoming seasonality. They can capitalize on whatever natural appeal the off-season presents, such as winter as opposed to summer sports, seasonal food and produce, and scenery or wildlife viewed in different places and under changing conditions. Or events can ignore the climatic differences altogether and concentrate on indoor activities. Also, in many destinations the residents prefer the off-season for their own celebrations, and these provide more authentic events for visitors. Of course, if this strategy is too successful, there will be no off-season.

Certain tourist segments have a natural preference for off-peak travel, either because of potential cost reductions or a desire to avoid crowds of other tourists. Retired persons and upper-income segments with more than one holiday opportunity a year are the key targets. Events can pull them for short breaks or even main holidays. Dedicated music lovers, athletes, sports fans, and other special interest travelers will potentially attend events at any time of the year to satisfy their desire for special experiences. These target markets might be smaller, but also more loyal and easily reached through targeted promotions. Meeting and convention travel often favors off-peak seasons, both to secure lower costs for participants and to ensure sufficient space in facilities.

Despite the advantages events have in creating off-peak demand, festivals and sports events tend to adhere to the tourism peak season—generally summer. Janiskee (1996) examined a large database of American community festivals and determined that January was the least popular month and July the most popular. He concluded: "The first weekend in May can be regarded as the unofficial start of the high season for festivals" (p. 131). The numbers dropped dramatically after mid-October. Regional variations related to climate were observed, and it became clear that certain periods of time were congested with events.

A study of event demand in the American Midwest (Wicks & Fesenmaier, 1995) proved that summer was most popular, followed by fall, for attending events. The dearth of participation in spring and winter could, of course, reflect supply, but it also suggests the need for caution when planning off-peak events. Wicks and Fesenmaier recommended identification of a market niche that was prepared to travel at off-peak times for specific events.

Events as Animators

Resorts, museums, historic districts, heritage sites, archaeological sites, markets and shopping centers, sports stadia, convention centers, natural parks, and theme parks all develop programs of special events. Built attractions and facilities everywhere have realized the advantages of "animation"—the process of programming interpretive features and/or special events that make the place come alive with sensory stimulation and appealing atmosphere. The potential benefits of animation through events are of major importance to facility and attraction managers:

- to attract people who might otherwise not make a visit because they perceive the facility or attraction itself to be uninteresting;
- to encourage repeat visits by people who might otherwise think that one visit is enough;
- to attract visiting friends and relatives who might ask their hosts what is going on;
- to attract publicity for the site or facility, including the highlighting of historical events associated with the site;
- to encourage longer stays and greater spending;
- to target groups who need a venue for private functions.

Research Note on Animation

Axelsen, M. (2006). Using special events to motivate visitors to attend art galleries. *Museum Management and Curatorship, 21*(3), 205–221.

The contemporary directions of art galleries worldwide are changing as social patterns and demands, as well as visitor expectations of their experiences at art galleries, change. New programs and strategies are being developed in galleries to make these institutions more appealing to people who would not normally visit them, and one such strategy is the staging of special events. However, because galleries are staging an increasing number of special events, the factors motivating visitors to attend these institutions are changing. Visitors hope to have different experiences and encounters in the gallery during special events. This paper presents the findings from a study in Australia about visitors' motivations to attend special events in galleries. It highlights the different factors that motivate visitors to attend the gallery specifically for a special event in comparison to visiting the gallery's permanent collections.

Events as Image Makers

It is apparent that major events can have the effect of shaping an image of the host community or country, leading to its favorable perception as a potential travel destination. With global media attention focused on the host city, even for a relatively short duration, the publicity value is enormous, and some destinations will use this fact alone to justify great expenditures on attracting events. For example, Wang and Gitelson (1988) observed that the annual Spoleto Festival in Charleston, South Carolina does not appear to be economically justifiable, "but the city holds it every year to maintain a desirable image" (p. 5). Cameron (1989) noted the role of festivals and events, and cultural tourism in general, in altering the image of the Lehigh Valley in Pennsylvania.

Longitudinal studies of the impact of hosting the 1988 Winter Olympic Games on Calgary (J. R. B. Ritchie & Smith, 1991) showed how a definite positive image boost grew, peaked, and started to decline afterwards, so there is a life cycle related to the "halo effect" of one-time events. But additional gains in tourism infrastructure and the legacy of enhanced tourism marketing and organization can potentially sustain the effect.

What happens when negative publicity strikes a destination? To a degree, bad news events can be managed—both to minimize the negative impact and to fight back. Ahmed (1991) argued that negative images can be turned into positive ones by organizing festivals and commemorations of the event, although this is restricted mostly to natural disasters and entails the risk of stirring up unhappy or controversial memories. Gwinner (1997) proposed that an event's image is a function of the type of event (e.g., sports, festival, arts), the event characteristics (e.g., size, professional status, history, venue, promotional appearance), and individual factors (e.g., meanings associated with the event, strength of meanings, and history with the event).

Research Notes on Image Effects of Major Events

Kim, S. S., & Morrison, A. (2005). Change of images of South Korea among foreign tourists after the 2002 FIFA World Cup. *Tourism Management, 26*(2), 233–247.

This research examined changes in the images of Korea over two points in time among Japanese, Mainland Chinese and US visitors to South Korea. Between October 4 and November 10, 2002, about 3–4 months after the 2002 World Cup ended, 223 tourists from Japan, 143 from Mainland China and 173 from the US completed the survey instrument. According to the results of paired t-tests, the visitors from all three countries had more positive images after than before the World Cup. The findings from the ANCOVA tests indicated that the image changes due to the World Cup were different among the three nationalities. The correspondence analyses results also showed that the image changes after the World Cup varied according to nationality, educational level, age and occupation. Collectively, the study suggests that an internationally significant event can change the image of a tourism destination in a short time period.

Green, B. C, Costa, C., & Fitzgerald, M. (2008). Marketing the host city: Analyzing exposure generated by a sport event. In M. Weed (Ed.), *Sport and tourism: A reader* (pp. 346–361). London: Routledge.

This research in San Antonio, Texas, attempted to add to the limited research on the media impacts of hosting events. The researchers studied the 2002 NCAA Women's Final Four Basketball Championship through content analysis of ESPN's television coverage. They measured how many times San Antonio was mentioned, and images of the city shown in the broadcasts. "Overall, the findings question the value of the exposure generated by events as a tool for place marketing. However, three key findings have practical implications for potential implementation of event-based place marketing strategies: (1): the minimal exposure obtained for the host city via event telecasts; (2) relative exposure obtained by the event logo and by actual host city images; and (3) the need for cities to differentiate themselves from their competitors." Logos for events should ideally incorporate city images, or be linked to them, and athletes and event personalities should be featured in city-showcase settings. Relationships have to be built with the media, especially event announcers, and materials provided to them.

Events and Place Marketing

Kotler, Haider, and Rein (1993), in their book *Marketing Places*, identified the value of events in enhancing the image of communities and in attracting tourists. They demonstrated how places compete for investments, quality people, and tourists, all in pursuit of more livable and prosperous communities. Place marketing provides a framework within which events and event tourism find multiple roles, as image makers, quality of life enhancers, and tourist attractions. More traditional approaches to economic development stressed industrialization, provision of physical rather than cultural infrastructure, and downplayed the economic value of tourism.

One key feature of place marketing is its attention to cultivating a positive image. Thus, events produced or assisted by economic development departments, mayor's offices, tourist agencies, or convention and visitor bureaus all must attract media attention, portray the place in the best possible light, and be tangibly linked to other promotional campaigns. This can, of course, distort event goals and lead their managers into potentially difficult political territory.

Research Note on Place Marketing and Events

Gotham, K. (2002). Marketing Mardi Gras: Commodification, spectacle and the political economy of tourism in New Orleans. *Urban Studies, 39*(10), 1735–1756.

Recent urban scholarship on the rise of the tourism industry, place marketing, and the transformation of cities into entertainment destinations has been dominated by four major themes: the primacy of 'consumption' over 'production'; the eclipse of exchange-value by sign-value; the idea of autoreferential culture; and, the ascendancy of textual deconstruction and discursive analyses over political economy critiques of capitalism. This paper critically assesses the merits of these four themes using a case study of the Mardi Gras celebration in New Orleans. The analytical tools and categories of political economy are used to examine the rise and dominance of tourism in New Orleans, explore the consequences of this economic shift and identify the key actors and organised interests involved in marketing Mardi Gras. 'Marketing' is the use of sophisticated advertising techniques aimed at promoting fantasy, manipulating consumer needs, producing desirable tourist experiences and simulating images of place to attract capital and consumers. The paper points to the limitations of the 'cultural turn' and the 'linguistic turn' in urban studies and uses the concepts of commodification and spectacle as a theoretical basis for understanding the marketing of cities, the globalisation of local celebrations and the political economy of tourism.

Events as Catalysts

Mega-events, such as World Fairs and Olympics, have been supported by host governments in large part because of their role as catalysts in major redevelopment schemes. The Knoxville World's Fair was conceived as a catalyst for urban renewal through image enhancement and physical redevelopment, and left a legacy of infrastructure, a convention center, private investments, a better tax base, and new jobs for the Tennessee city (Mendell, MacBeth, & Solomon, 1983). Dungan (1984) gave a number of examples of the indirect and direct physical legacies of major events, including improvements to the Los Angeles airport, Montreal's subway system, Knoxville's freeways, fairground renovations in Oklahoma City, parks in Chicago, and various urban renewal schemes. He also pointed out that physical structures, particularly those created for World Fairs, such as the Eiffel Tower in Paris or Seattle's Space Needle, have become valuable permanent symbols for their cities.

Atlanta's 1996 Summer Olympic Games generated $2 billion in construction projects in Georgia, including sport facilities, an urban park in central Atlanta, housing improvements, and educational facilities (Mihalik, 1994). In particular, the Games were a catalyst for achieving a $42 million federal housing grant to revitalize a low-income housing project next to the Olympic village. The Olympic Park, funded privately, was said to be valuable in restoring a blighted area next to the city's convention center.

Major events tend to attract investment into the hospitality sector, especially hotels and restaurants. Sometimes these additions have been brought forward in time, while others represent new infrastructure related to expected longer term increases in demand. Sport events generally lead to new or improved facilities that can be used to attract events in the future, and improvements to convention or arts centers can have a similar effect. In this way a community can use the event to realize a "quantum leap" in its tourism development, accelerating growth or jumping into a higher competitive category.

The concept of an event legacy has been expanded substantially to include many social, cultural, or environmental benefits, and indeed these can be more profound and sustainable than economic and tourism gains—at least in the minds of residents. In this context, events can be the catalyst for augmenting participation in the arts or sports, for increased volunteering and skills acquisition, or for capacity building at the community level (i.e., heightened competence and commitment to solving their own problems).

Research Note on Events as Catalysts

Bergsgard, N., & Vassenden, A. (2011). The legacy of Stavanger as Capital of Culture in Europe 2008: Watershed or puff of wind? *International Journal of Cultural Policy, 17*(3), 301–320.

When studying the impact of cultural mega events, researchers tend to scrutinise their economic benefits, cultural identity, competitive advantage in attracting the attention of important stakeholders or the effect on regional development and urban regeneration. The impact on the field of cultural production has received less attention. In this article, the authors highlight the latter. Stavanger, Norway, was the 2008 European Capital of Culture. We present an analysis of the impact of this mega event on the cultural sector in the Stavanger region. Using Bourdieu's notions of social field and social capital, this article explores the interplay between this mega event and the structure of the local field of culture. The authors analyse (1) the impact on the field itself; and (2) how it affected different parts of the sector differently. The article concludes that the field was 'lifted.' At the same time, the larger and most institutionalised producers—the core arts institutions—gained the most, especially by increasing their social capital.

Justifications for Public Sector Intervention

It is possible that the industry and especially DMOs could completely plan and develop Event Tourism, but public sector (i.e., governmental) involvement is widespread and perhaps necessary. How can governments at all levels justify their interventions, especially when it comes to investment and planning to promote and develop Event Tourism?

The Public Good Argument

The key to this powerful argument is to demonstrate important benefits from events and facilities that accrue to society as a whole—or to the economy (which should clearly benefit us all), and to the environment (everyone supports a healthier, safer, more sustainable environment). When backed by research, expert testimony, and public opinion surveys showing support for sport and events, the "public good" argument cannot easily be refuted.

But in order to make the "public good" argument valid and convincing, the following criteria have to be met:

- facilities and events must fit into accepted policy domains including culture, health, and the economy;
- public benefits have to be substantial (i.e., it is worth our while to get involved), inclusive (everyone gains), and they can be demonstrated or proved;
- there must be rules and accountability for money spent and other actions taken.

Social Equity

The "social equity" principle is really a part of the "public good" justification. In the context of facilities and events it can be stated this way: subsidies to venues and event are justified in order to ensure that everyone has the opportunity to participate . . . OR . . . direct provision of events is justified to fill an important gap in opportunities that are deemed essential for the public good (e.g., health, culture, jobs creation) but are, in the free market, not equitably provided.

"Social equity" literally means that access to a public good or service, and to the benefits of public investment, is based on principles of fairness, justice, and need. This is not the same as "equality," wherein everyone gets exactly the same thing. For example, "equal access" to events or the benefits of events would mean that everyone gets the same, but that principle is not widely held to be feasible or desirable.

Failure (or Inadequacies) of the Marketplace

This economic justification for public involvement rests on the premise (or ideological belief) that economic development in general is best left in the hands of the private sector, but in some cases the "free market" does not provide sufficient incentive or reward to stimulate entrepreneurial activity or to generate public goods and services. Accordingly, giving money to tourism marketing organizations, participating in joint ventures with the private sector, or providing tax incentives or subsidies to investors (including facilities and events) can all be justified as a necessary means to achieve public policy aims.

Mules and Dwyer (2006) and Burgan and Mules (2001) argued that fewer sporting venues would be built and fewer events would occur without public support, because market forces will not support them. Yet many of the direct benefits accrue to the hospitality and travel industry, so why should the public sector intervene? The supply of events would eventually reach equilibrium with demand (i.e., what consumers are willing to pay) only if a completely free market existed. At that equilibrium point there would theoretically exist the number and types of events that were "demanded" by paying customers. But a relatively "free market" really only exists for certain types of events, namely those produced by for-profit corporations for companies or consumers that are looking for specific entertainment, learning, or marketing opportunities that can only be met by these types of events. This might apply to weddings or private parties. But most event entrepreneurs have to compete with subsidized events and event venues in the public or nonprofit domains, which distorts the marketplace.

Return on Investment and Economic Efficiency

Numerous studies have shown that governments at all levels realize substantial tax gains from tourism in general and event tourism in particular. Events stimulate consumption of goods and services that are heavily taxed. Purely on a profit basis, public sector investment is thereby justified. However, there has to be proven feasibility, accountability, and professional management in place.

Efficiency is also gained when events with surplus capacity are marketed to tourists, and when events are held in public facilities and spaces that both have surplus capacity and need additional revenue. In these cases, spending a little on events can realize important benefits for residents.

Justifications Based on Intangible Benefits (Psychic and Existence Values)

"Psychic benefits" accrue to people when they value something more than its related costs, as was calculated in the landmark event impact study by Burns, Hatch, and Mules (1986). This is similar to "consumer surplus," meaning that people are willing to pay more than the actual cost to them.

Researchers might also be able to show that people value events even when they do not attend, because it leads to pride in their community or they anticipate indirect benefits. This "existence" value can be given weight through use of "contingent valuation methods." Andersson (2006) concluded that researchers have generally found citizens to approve of public expenditure on culture, whether or not they are users.

In Chapter 10 we examine use and nonuse values more carefully, the intent being to place an economic value on some of these psychic benefits.

Definitions and Typologies

More detailed examination of definitions and classifications is found in *Event Studies* (Getz, 2007, 2012), with the following discussion providing a summary. The emphasis is placed on relevance to Event Tourism, and with a view to clarifying terminology used in later chapters.

Planned Events

For our purposes in this book, we are only interested in planned events. Yes, a riot or protest or spontaneous celebration is of interest within event studies, and might affect tourism, but these events are not what we want to include in portfolios and strategies.

All planned events have the following characteristics:

- a beginning and an end (they are scheduled; they only occur once);
- a given place (in a venue or marked space);

- a special set of circumstances or experiences available to customers and participants that constitute a value proposition from the organizers, and sometimes also from the destination;
- they are unique and cannot be replicated;
- they are live and social in nature (i.e., they bring people together).

However, what we call planned or special events are social constructs. If a DMO wants to call a year-long packaging of events and promotions an event, such as Visit U.S.A. Year, then it's an event. Some aspect of setting, people, and program will ensure that events are always tangibly different, and this uniqueness makes them attractive, even compelling. Cultivating a "once in a lifetime" image for an event is the marketer's goal. All the planned events we talk about in this book are social events. They are for people, and not merely events in our own, personal lives.

Virtual Events

While online or teleconferenced events have their place, they are not replacements. In this book we talk about virtual events in several places, but they are not the object of, nor at the core of, Event Tourism. Online communications, or social media, can augment the appeal and reach of live events.

Destination Events

Marketers want people to travel to events because of the allure of the event itself, and many events are in fact produced mostly or completely with tourists as the target market. We call these "destination events." Several of the case studies are of destination events, and it is an important part of the event travel career. "Hallmark" and "Iconic" events (defined later) are special cases of destination events.

Participatory Events

Some events do not exist without participants, including meetings, conferences, sport competitions, performing arts, etc. Others provide opportunities for different kinds of participants, including volunteers and officials. Observers, such as media people and sponsors, are not really "participants" in this sense. Spectators might be present, but they also are not participants in this context. Because every special interest and social world stimulates a desire for its own events, in part to be with others sharing their interests, the scope for participation events is virtually unlimited.

Spectator Events

Professional sports and major competitions like the Olympics require spectators, usually as paying customers. Spectator events also include the theater and festivals—wherever you find an audience. We usually associate the term spectator with sports and entertainment and it implies passivity rather than activity or participation. However, there are many events that blend opportunities for participation, action, and spectating. A special case is that of the "fan," or fanatic, as that label implies a high degree of involvement or identification with the sport or pursuit.

Cause-Related Events

Numerous events are held for the purpose of raising money or generating awareness and support for a cause. These are also called "charity events" or "fund-raisers." And there are events held for the purpose of "social marketing," as in antismoking campaigns, that aim to change attitudes and behavior. These worthwhile events are not necessarily tourist attractions, but they could be. Those with big-name celebrities have the potential to generate travel.

Media Events

Some events might never attract large numbers, but still generate enormous exposure through media coverage. These "media events" are gaining in popularity, based especially on the power of television and Internet coverage to reach global mass audiences or very targeted segments. Examples are sport events in which spectating is impractical but television appeal is high, such as cross-country ecochallenges. Media events are created primarily for live and/or delayed broadcast (television and Internet) as opposed to those held for large spectator audiences.

Created solely or mainly for TV or online audiences, media events do not need spectators, but they do require participants. A remote ecorace or a surfing event can be held primarily for later broadcast packaging. On the other hand, any event can have media appeal.

One-Time Versus Periodic Events

"Periodic events" occur regularly, as with festivals held every year in the same place, or events that are held regularly but in different locations each time. "One-time events" are completely unique, such as a never-to-be-repeated exhibition. But the term is also used to describe events that move around and seldom, if ever, return to the same place. Countries, tourist organizations, and venues systematically bid on such events, including meetings, exhibitions, World Fairs, and sport competitions, and they are considered to be one-time events from the perspective of the hosts.

Typology of Planned Events and Venues

Figure 1.7 combines the major categories of events with venues/facilities that are most connected to them, and clusters the events in four broad categories. For a detailed

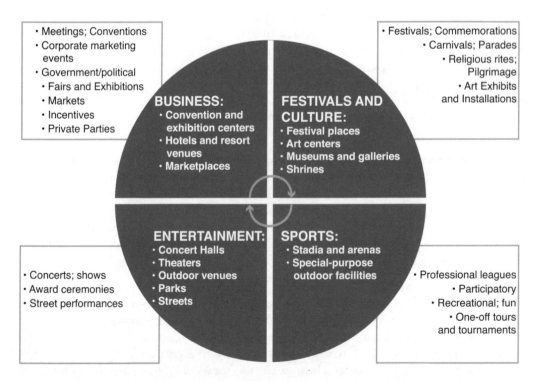

Figure 1.7. Typology of planned events and venues: A portfolio approach.

discussion of each type and subtype see *Event Studies* (Getz, 2007, 2012). The four broad categories are elaborated upon in subsequent chapters.

The universe of events is amazingly diverse, and any classification is bound to be incomplete. This one is based on the form of events, being a social construct describing their expected form and programming, and even the venues they are usually located in. But keep in mind that different cultures and subcultures might have a different view as to what a festival means, or what a fair should contain. Also, it has to be emphasized that people can have any kind of experience at any kind of event, depending in large part on their expectations, what they bring to the event in terms of mood, experience, and friends/family, and what they decide to do.

The need for business events is as old as commerce and trade, whereas the other three clusters are dependent upon the rise and democratization of leisure and travel and therefore can be considered modern phenomena. True, ancient Greeks traveled to see, and take part in, the Olympic Games, but this was leisure for an extremely small, privileged class; probably every society throughout history has similar examples. We did not see large-scale travel to sport events until the age of steam trains began and fans could move between cities. Travel for cultural and entertainment events is an even more recent trend.

Business Events and Venues

Sometimes referred to as the MICE sector (for Meetings, Incentives, Conferences, and Exhibitions) this is without question the best established component of Event Tourism—at least in terms of venues, professional associations, and agencies devoted to selling space in convention/exhibition centers. Most DMOs are fully into this sector. Numerous hotels, resorts, and other facilities are also in this business, as there is plenty of demand for unique places in which to hold a meeting, convention, exhibition (trade and consumer shows), or retreat. "Corporate" events include the usual meetings, but also marketing and PR events such as product launches and publicity stunts and business-to-business hospitality. "Incentives" fit here as they often combine tours and meetings as rewards to employees or salespersons. Government and political parties also hold business events, while international summits and academic conferences typically require the same facilities as conventions and exhibitions.

The term "fair" can be confusing, as it is sometimes applied wrongly to festivals or carnivals. In this book it is used as a synonym for "exhibition" (see the example of the Canton Fair), and for state fairs (which are more like festivals and exhibitions rolled into one). A "world's fair" (or expo) falls into this cluster. Similarly, "exhibition" is a term that gets applied to different types of events, but in this book it refers to trade and consumer shows (which are generally lumped together and called the exhibition industry).

Private parties and other small-group functions are part of this cluster, mainly because they tend to use commercial accommodation and hospitality services, such as weddings in hotels (or special-purpose chapels). Most of this work is sales (both venue and services being offered) while many larger business events demand competitive bidding.

Sport Events and Venues

There are endless varieties of sports, and more appearing all the time. Any sport can be subdivided, and any recreational pursuit can conceivably be elevated into a sport—complete with rules and regulations, hierarchical organization, and sanctioned events. Today, cities build huge sports arenas and special-purpose stadia that are well beyond the needs of residents alone—they are catering to professional teams and many different types of one-time events.

However, these sport-specific criteria do not matter all that much when it comes to event tourism strategy and development. It might be more important to consider the relative advantages and costs of spectator versus participant sports and the special venues required by different sports and event formats. Indeed, a supply-side approach could begin with determination of what venues a destination has and the events it could feasibly host. Venue capacity and quality very much restricts the Event Tourism "league" cities play in, whether it is regional, national, or international in scale.

A demand-side approach starts with an assessment of the markets for various sports and sport event formats. Many sport events attract a variety of tourists, each with different spending patterns. Professional athletes might get paid to attend, or win prize money; therefore, leakages to the area occur. Amateur participants on marathons often come in groups or bring spouses and families. Spectators, including the friends and relatives of participants, are valuable tourists who will likely stay in commercial accommodation.

From an event tourism perspective a different kind of classification makes sense, as advocated by Gratton, Dobson, and Shibli (2000) and Gammon (2012). It combines the notion of an event hierarchy (from mega-events like the Olympics and World Cup of Football down to international, national, and local championships) with various tourism and event-related criteria (e.g., media interest, tourism potential for spectators or competitors, sport development opportunity).

There are different kinds of hierarchies that should be considered. Size is an obvious one, but size has to be measured in terms of one or more of these variables: cost, tourist demand, media impact, venues required, etc. For the leisure markets a social world hierarchy could be more important, with internationally iconic events at the top (e.g., Boston Marathon) and locally important events at the bottom. In the social world frame, "iconic" events stand for the biggest, best, most unique, most prestigious or challenging.

The concept of *Destination Sport Events* is important in this context. These are sport events that are fixed in place and anyone wanting to participate or spectate has to go to the event, when and where it is held. In other words, they are tourist attractions. Some of these are moveable (they can be bid on, or the owners can relocate them) and some are permanently attached to venues and destinations (like professional sports). While most cities recognize the value of hosting professional sport teams with this drawing power (not to mention image boosting), not all destinations have realized the potential of other types of destination events. To be successful they have to be iconic within particular social worlds and/or very well marketed.

Festivals and Cultural Celebrations

This category is dominated by festivals, but also includes carnivals and Mardi Gras, heritage commemorations, religious rites and pilgrimages, and many parades. Parades and processions are common elements in festivals, but those that are held on their own also display many celebratory elements. Here is my simple definition of festival: *A festival is a public, themed celebration.*

For a fuller definition and discussion of the social and anthropological meanings of festival and festivity see Getz (2011, 2012), and as summarized in Chapter 8.

To many young people, "festival" has come to mean outdoor music, either one concert or a whole program of them. The term is rather overused and often misused. A real festival has a theme, something to be celebrated or commemorated. Festival-like programming, including spectacle and entertainment, are frequently added to sports and other types of event to make them more appealing. Some call this process "festivalization" or the "carnivalesque."

Galleries, museums, and other art facilities are formally in the exhibition business, but their normal displays of art are sometimes replaced by "touring exhibitions" or one-time-only exhibits. These can have major drawing power, generating substantial income for the producers and hosts, and for destinations.

Many outdoor fields and city streets or plazas are utilized as festival/parade venues, but cities have in many cases constructed event districts and festival places in order to host large assemblies. This can be an important advantage in the Event Tourism marketplace. Places with indoor theaters and arts centers have advantages when it comes to limited seating, ticketed concerts, and shows. It is no longer unusual for cities to advertise sport, entertainment, and cultural districts or precincts.

Entertainment

Although it is often said that there is a huge "entertainment industry," this is misleading. People can find anything to be entertaining (even solemn, religious ceremonies or political speeches), and entertainment is generally a part of all sport and cultural events. Most conventions and exhibitions also provide entertainment. What are included in this cluster are the stand-alone events such as concerts and award shows that are clearly not part of something else. In terms of venues, entertainment generally utilizes sport and culture facilities, both indoors and out; there are huge financial savings in building multipurpose facilities. The private sector is most associated with entertainment (as opposed to festivals) because of the profits realized, from music in particular. Later we will look at the UK music concert sector as an example.

In Chapter 8 entertainment events are considered in more detail, and for convenience private functions (like parties) are included. Many such functions are indeed of the entertainment variety, although others are solemn and ritualistic.

Typology Specific to Event Tourism Portfolios

We can also classify events on the basis of their functions within an Event Tourism context, connected explicitly to the portfolio concept illustrated later. This typology combines size, drawing power, and value considerations, all of which are relative—in other words, there is no absolute measure of mega or hallmark, local or regional, they are defined contextually. I argue that the most value comes from permanent Hallmark Events, and the related concept of Iconic Events, and not from occasional mega-events.

Mega-Event

"Mega" means large or huge, or more precisely "1 million" in the metric system. Marris (1987), summarizing a conference of the International Association of Tourism Experts (AIEST, 1987) that was themed on the subject of mega-events and mega-attractions, noted that mega-events can be defined by reference to their volume of visitors, their cost, or by psychological criteria. Their volume should exceed 1 million visits, their capital cost should be at least $500 million, and their reputation should be that of a "must see" event. Marris thought the key to getting mega-events through the political approval process was the prestige factor. Others might prefer a definition that stresses the economic impacts of the event, rather than its costs, size, or image. Vanhove and Witt (1987), in the same conference, stressed that a mega-event must be able to attract worldwide publicity. So an event can be a mega-success if it generates exceptional levels of coverage or fosters a strong positive image among key target segments.

If we equate "mega" with large size, then it usually refers to World Fairs, Olympics, and other international sport events. But even a small music festival can have mega-impacts on a small town in terms of tourists, economic benefits, or disruption. It can also refer to media coverage and impacts on image. Accordingly, I define them this way: *Mega-events, by way of their size or significance, are those that yield extraordinarily high levels of tourism, media coverage, prestige, or economic impact for the host community, venue, or organization.*

The definition of mega-events will therefore always remain subjective. It is really more a question of the relative significance of an event, rather than any particular measure of size. In general, there has been a trend towards "gigantism" in the events world, and in my opinion this is a big mistake. So-called mega-events have been glorified, and it is mistakenly believed by many that they generate mostly positive, long-term legacies. This view has been perpetuated by several elite groups in society that directly benefit, even while the public often pays an immediate and long-term cost well in excess of any tangible benefits.

Hallmark Event

The earliest reference to hallmark events in the research literature was by J. R. B. Ritchie and Beliveau (1974) who succinctly defined the seasonality problem and the event's function in these terms: "Cyclical demand in the leisure, recreation, and travel markets is a major factor contributing to low productivity and low returns on investment among the suppliers of goods and services to these markets. One strategic response to "the seasonality problem," which has had varying degrees of success in different regions, is termed the Hallmark Event. Such events, built around a major theme, serve to focus tourism and recreational planning on a particular period of the year" (p. 14). A decade later, J. R. B. Ritchie (1984) elaborated on hallmark events by addressing their economic, physical, socio-cultural, psychological and political impacts, and by defining them as follows: "Major one-time or recurring events of limited duration, developed primarily to enhance the awareness, appeal and profitability of a tourism destination in the short and/or long term. Such events rely for their success on uniqueness, status, or timely significance to create interest and attract attention" (p. 2).

In Ritchie's perspective, events were instruments of strategy to solve the seasonality problem. The type of event, and its permanent or periodic status, was not of principle concern. However, C. M. Hall (1989) defined hallmark events this way, incorporating the key consideration of international stature: "Hallmark tourist events are major fairs, expositions, cultural and sporting events of international status which are held on either a regular or a one-off basis. A primary function of the hallmark event is to provide the host community with an opportunity to secure high prominence in the tourism market place" (p. 263). In his subsequent book on hallmark events, C. M. Hall (1992) added: "Hallmark events are the image builders of modern tourism," but he also equated the term with "mega or special events" (p. 1).

What remains consistent in the events and tourism literature is an emphasis on how hallmark events, as attractions, can help in overcoming seasonality, and how they can attract attention and enhance the destination's image. There has been no agreement on types of events or periodicity as defining variables. Indeed, the term "hallmark" can hold a variety of other connotations. For example, Graham, Goldblatt and Delpy (1995, p. 69) referred to hallmark sport events as being those that mark an important historical anniversary. According to Westerbeek, Turner, and Ingerson (2002), size is a major factor, but their definition is more akin to mega-events, as they give the Olympics as a prime example.

Getz (1991, p. 51) turned to a dictionary, where "hallmark" refers to a symbol of quality or authenticity that distinguishes some goods from others, or pertains to a distinctive feature. An event, therefore, can aspire to be the hallmark of its organizers, venue, or location, thereby placing the emphasis on permanent, recurring events. In 2005 he defined them this way: "The term hallmark event is used to describe a recurring event that possesses such significance, in terms of tradition, attractiveness, image or publicity, that the event provides the host venue, community or destination with a competitive advantage. Over time, the event and destination can become inseparable" (p. 5).

More recently, in the context of working with Swedish colleagues to help a small resort town develop a new hallmark event, greater elaboration of the concept resulted in this three-part definition (from D. Getz, Bo Svensson, Robert Pettersson, and Anders Nordvall, unpublished).

Hallmark Event refers to the function of events in achieving a set of goals that benefit tourism and the host community, namely: attracting tourists; creating and enhancing a positive image that is co-branded with the destination/community; and delivering multiple benefits to residents.

Over time, the Hallmark Event as a tourist attraction also becomes an institution and its permanence is taken for granted. Its traditions generate a stronger sense of community and place identity. The event and city images become inextricably linked.

Hallmark Events can also exist within the context of social worlds and for special-interest groups as iconic tourist attractions that facilitate communitas and identity building.

In Chapter 4 a planning and marketing process for Hallmark Events is detailed, with additional considerations for Iconic Events provided in Chapter 5.

Local and Regional Events

Every city and destination contains many one-time and permanent events, the majority of which typically hold little or no drawing power for tourists—nor are they produced with tourism in mind. Some have the potential to grow, if assisted, and some could be developed into major destination events if that was an agreed-upon goal. Over time, some local, resident-oriented events will naturally evolve into permanent institutions and Hallmark Events. And others might take on that role within specific social worlds, becoming iconic for a particular community of interest.

Even if they do not attract tourists or generate much in the way of cobranding, the population of local and regional events is likely to perform two vital functions that should be recognized and facilitated. They help animate the city or destination, giving it cultural and social life, providing outlets for residents to take visitors, and giving people reasons to visit or revisit otherwise static attractions.

Second, they are important in place marketing, not for the image-boosting, cobranding effects desired by marketers, but in terms of making the place more attractive for residents and especially contributing to creative cities. This is usually thought of as a cultural or social policy domain, but it is of equal importance to all forms of tourism and economic development. You cannot satisfy tourists if residents are unhappy and bored.

Olympic and Mega-Event Studies

Although mentioned frequently in this book, it is not specifically about the Olympics, nor other mega-events such as World Fairs and the largest international sport competitions. The Olympic movement has its own culture and Olympic Games are also accompanied by much politics, debate, and dissent. I consider them to be atypical of the events world, and of only secondary interest in the context of Event Tourism. Consider the infrequency of hosting the Olympics or other mega-event in any one place, the enormous cost, the relatively few tourists who can obtain or afford tickets, and you can easily understand why they do not fit into my portfolio approach. Instead, think more about permanent (anchored) Hallmark and Iconic events.

Weed's book *Olympic Tourism* (2008a) notes that research on the Olympics has burgeoned, with various themes being politics, impacts, history, and ideology. This is in addition to the literature on Olympic sports and athletes. In his assessment of Olympic tourism, Weed covers pre- and post-Games activity, as well as halo or legacy effects for the host destination. With regard to the Beijing Summer Olympics of 2008, Weed notes how the event helped Beijing position itself as a "global city" and was part of a global campaign to open up China for tourism. Indeed, it seems likely that only world cities can now host the Games, and their reasons for doing so will have little to do with immediate, event-specific tourist flows.

Debate about the costs and impacts of the Olympics and other mega-events will continue; indeed, I expect it to get very intense. On the one hand are those who stand to gain (see the research note by Morse) and on the other are a large number of critics (count me in this camp) who believe such gigantic events cannot be justified on any grounds (see the e-journalist Commentary on Athens, which also takes a stab at London 2012).

Research Note on Olympic Tourism

Morse, J. (2001). The Sydney 2000 Olympic Games: How the Australian Tourist Commission leveraged the Games for tourism. *Journal of Vacation Marketing, 7*(2), 101–107.

This paper outlines the key strategies used by the Australian Tourist Commission (ATC) in leveraging the Olympic Games to boost tourism to Australia. In 1995, the ATC established its Olympic Games Business Unit. The key elements of the pre-Games strategy were in developing joint-promotions, the establishment of a major media programme, working with TV broadcasters, and the setting up the Business Development Programme. Following the success of the Sydney 2000 Olympic Games, a twelve month post-Games strategy was operationalised. It has included tactical advertising in key markets, the use of direct marketing, working with key market segments such as the business tourism sector, and developing research to monitor the success of the strategy and tactics. The ATC strategy has also been recognised by the International Olympic Committee (IOC) as a benchmark on how to maximise the benefits for both the Games and the host country.

Commentary on the Athens Olympics

Gatopoulos, D. (2010). *Greek financial crisis: Did 2004 Athens Olympics spark problems in Greece?* Retrieved from http://www.huffingtonpost.com/2010/06/03/greek-financial-crisis-olympics_n_598829.html

While many factors are behind the crippling debt crisis, the 2004 Summer Olympics in Athens has drawn particular attention.

If not the sole reason for this nation's financial mess, some point to the games as at least an illustration of what's gone wrong in Greece.

Their argument starts with more than a dozen Olympic venues—now vacant, fenced off and patrolled by private security guards. Stella Alfieri, an outspoken anti-Games campaigner, says they marked the start of Greece's irresponsible spending binge.

The 2004 Athens Olympics cost nearly $11 billion by current exchange rates, double the initial budget. And that figure that does not include major infrastructure projects rushed to completion at inflated costs. In the months before the games, construction crews worked around the clock, using floodlights to keep the work going at night. In addition, the tab for security alone was more than $1.2 billion.

Six years later, more than half of Athens' Olympic sites are barely used or empty. The long list of mothballed facilities includes a baseball diamond, a massive man-made canoe and kayak course, and arenas built for unglamorous sports such as table tennis, field hockey and judo.

London's main Olympic budget now stands at $13.3 billion. Last week, Britain's new coalition government announced $38 million in Olympic budget cuts as part of efforts to slash the nation's budget deficit.

Summary and Study Guide

This chapter introduces key terms and concepts related to the study of Event Tourism, and in particular explains why an integrated approach to Event Tourism is desirable and how it can be framed. Several systems models were presented to specify the elements of Event Tourism and how they are connected, both in terms of the stakeholders involved and the flows of information and resources necessary to make it happen. Justifications for public sector involvement were examined, as these are the bases for policy and for public–private partnerships to plan and develop events and tourism.

Potential career paths were illustrated with profiles and interviews with professionals. The main roles of events and tourism were introduced, along with a discussion of how and why Event Tourism links with other fields, and other important policy domains. Event Tourism is considered in the context of special interest tourism, and it is argued that every special interest you can think of translates into demand for planned events.

Five key challenges, or big ideas are introduced, and these are developed throughout the book. While the dominant approach to Event Tourism right now is what I call a "supply-side approach," based on marketing events and venues and focusing on sales and bidding, for competitive advantage cities and destinations will have to move towards more "demand-side" development, based on detailed understanding of target markets. This should be accompanied by a bottom-up approach to planning and development that engages all the stakeholders, liberates innovation, and generates new, emergent strategies. Destinations will have to move from a focus on single events to a portfolio approach, including ownership of their own hallmark and iconic events. A sustainability theme runs through the book, and this applies both to sustainable event and portfolio management. Each of these key challenges is developed in multiple locations throughout the book, and they make for potential essay questions or term paper themes. They are summarized in the final chapter.

Study Questions

Start studying with the learning objectives, which tell you what is really important in each chapter. The study questions are possible exam questions, so writing out full answers is the best way to prepare.

- Define Event Tourism and explain it both as a business and an academic subfield.
- What is special interest tourism? Is Event Tourism a special interest?
- Explain the differences between supply-side versus demand-side definitions and development approaches.
- Are there career paths specific to Event Tourism? What knowledge is required?
- Explain event typologies by form and function, with particular emphasis on a portfolio approach.

- What are the four main sectors of Event Tourism in terms of venues and events?
- What are the main tourism and economic roles of events? Define the key terms (e.g., catalyst).
- What other policy fields involve events and tourism? Give examples and describe key stakeholders outside Event Tourism.
- Can you justify public sector involvement in Event Tourism? What are the main justifications?
- Use the "public good" justification to explain government subsidies for Event Tourism.
- Outline the five big challenges or ideas introduced in this chapter (you will need the full book to give complete answers; see the summaries in Chapter 11).

Additional Readings and Resources

- *Event Studies: Theory, Research and Policy for Planned Events* (Getz, 2012); *The Routledge Handbook of Events* (Page, & Connell, 2012); *Host Cities and the Olympics: An Interactionist Approach* (Hiller, 2012).
- Event-related research journals: *Event Management*; *Journal of Convention and Event Tourism*; *International Journal of Event and Festival Management*; *International Journal of Event Management Research* (online at: www.ijemr.or).
- Some introductory Tourism texts: *Tourism: Principles, Practices, Philosophies* (12th ed.) (Goeldner & Ritchie, 2012); *Tourism Management: An Introduction* (4th ed.) (Page, 2011).
- Some introductory Event Management texts: *Special Events* (5th ed.) (Goldblatt, 2011); *Festival and Special Event Management* (5th ed.) (Allen, O'Toole, Harris, & McDonnell, 2011); *Events Management* (3rd ed.) (Bowdin, Allen, O'Toole, Harris, & McDonnell, 2011).

Chapter 2

Demand and the Event Tourist

Learning Objectives

Upon completion of this chapter the student should understand and be able to explain the following:

1. The demand-side approach to event tourism and how it relates to service-dominant logic.
2. Classification of various types of event tourists, and the significance of each.
3. Direct and induced demand.
4. Propelling and constraining forces shaping trends in Event Tourism.
5. Festivalization and legitimation processes.
6. Basic human needs and how these generate leisure, work, and travel motivations.
7. Intrinsic and extrinsic motivation and how this relates to seeking and escaping theory.
8. Generic and targeted benefits that influence event demand.
9. How serious leisure, ego-involvement, and social world theory relates to event demand.
10. The mediating effects of social networking on event tourism.
11. The motivation of being a fan and highly involved participants, and how these connect to the event travel career trajectory.
12. The theory and practical implications of the decision-making process for event attendance and travel, including the nature of constraints and substitution.
13. How event marketing can influence demand and repeat visits.

Introduction

Does supply lead demand? Sometimes it does, as with new destinations like the Emirates and their enormous investment in venues, events, and marketing. They have literarily created Event Tourism destinations from nothing. Other destinations have taken the "instant attractiveness" approach to building the infrastructure and filling it with events to compete at the global level. This trend has put additional pressure on all established destinations, venues, and events.

Overall, supply and demand interact at macro- and microlevels to influence the growth of Event Tourism around the globe, and how event-specific patterns emerge and evolve.

While it is evident that demand for all types of events has been increasing, there are certainly potential limits at the global scale, and most definitely it can be said that when new destinations succeed they are taking some market share from others.

Supply and development strategies and methods are considered in detail in subsequent chapters, while here we focus on the demand side and how a demand-side strategy has the potential to revolutionize Event Tourism. This approach is explained and illustrated, and theoretically connected to the service-dominant paradigm from the marketing literature. Basically, I argue that only so much can be accomplished through traditional approaches to selling events and venues and bidding on available events, while future competitive advantages must come from deeper understanding of, and catering to, the myriad possible sources of demand for events. This leads to new strategies like creating your own events and, in particular, matching events with the needs of special interest groups.

We also examine in this chapter trends in, and forces shaping, demand. Various aspects of globalization are discussed. Both propelling and constraining forces are at work, and the growth-propelling forces have been dominant. This leads to a general discussion of the event tourist and various types of event tourists.

Theory pertaining to needs, motivation, and decision making is presented. It is shown how marketing to event tourists depends on detailed understanding of serious leisure, involvement, and social worlds. The event travel career trajectory is a theoretical construct that helps explain how, as involvement increases in a sport, hobby, lifestyle, or artistic pursuit (any serious leisure), participants tend to seek out events and develop travel careers built around events.

Later, in Chapters 6 through 8, greater detail is provided on motivation, demand, and impacts in each of the four major event clusters (sport, business, festivals, arts and entertainment).

The Demand-Side Approach

Start with the four main markets already discussed: (1) business events, (2) sports, (3) festivals and cultural celebrations, and (4) arts/entertainment and private functions (Figure 1.7). In the demand-side approach we start with markets and work back towards events and venues. That process might lead to the same venues and events, or to new ones. Most certainly it will lead to the identification of new opportunities—especially in the leisure markets defined by intrinsic motivation and communities of interest with their own social worlds.

Many destinations have realized that a supply-side approach is very expensive, particularly in terms of venue development and operations. And many have also realized that constantly pursuing more tourists and events is not always affordable or effective, because more tourists require more facilities, impose many costs on the community, and over time mass tourism can move downwards in terms of yield per visitor. By "mass tourism" I mean large-scale, undifferentiated tourism, generally associated with sightseeing, beach tourism, city breaks, and a few events (like global parties) aimed at very large audiences. Instead, it is generally wiser to focus on higher yield, and therefore niche market segments. Events are sometimes aimed at large audiences, but most are highly targeted. The spending associated with many event tourists is much higher than for mass tourism.

Research and other sources of market intelligence must accompany Event Tourism planning, and in fact should lead it. Looking for competitive advantages, destinations should be spending more time and money on this task, with particular interest in learning about new trends and potential changes in leisure, sport, the arts, business, and trade that might suggest opportunities.

The logic of this approach is simple: competitive advantages will accrue from a better understanding of the markets for event tourism, then matching supply with demand. Right now many cities and destinations are fixated on selling the venues and events they have, or on bidding on the available pool, rather than looking for new possibilities. That situation will be changing fast, in response to market pressures. This trend can be seen in destinations that are already engaging in niche market event promotion and direct creation of new events. It requires a sophisticated approach to market intelligence and development, and to matching supply with demand. This approach might very well lead to infrastructure requirements, but the need for them arises from the events being created or promoted to meet identified demand.

One starting point is to evaluate the current portfolio of events in terms of the market segments they attract, and then identify potential for attracting new segments. Because there is virtually an unlimited number of niche markets out there, a hierarchical approach will be required, as illustrated in Figure 2.1. In this illustration the main potential sources of demand for events are examined. Each of these categories already generates many events, and they are readily observable on the internet or within your own destination.

A precise definition of "market" is not really needed, nor is it essential that these five major markets be mutually exclusive. What counts is the logic of demand-side Event Tourism planning and development. The starting point is the potential and existing event

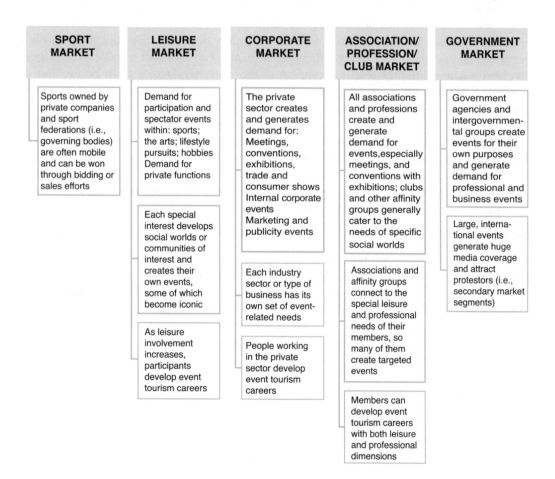

Figure 2.1. Demand-side approach to Event Tourism.

tourists—not venues, not whatever limited knowledge exists about current markets and obvious trends, and not what everyone else is doing.

This is an aggressive approach to identifying market segments and attracting them to destinations and events, plus the realization that new events are needed to cater to various segments. Event ideas suggest themselves when these markets are examined in detail, aided by theory, and when comparative SWOT analysis is conducted against competitors to identify gaps.

Let's look first at the broad leisure and sports markets, because I believe that is where the greatest opportunity lies for growth and competitive advantage. Also in the leisure market are hobbies (e.g., gardening, game playing), lifestyle pursuits (like wine and food), and the arts (from ballroom dancing to fine-art appreciation), all of which generate special interests, social worlds, and event travel demand. These social worlds develop their own events, and destinations can get into the business of catering to them with new ones. Some are very undeveloped this way, and new special interests are constantly emerging.

The business events category has in this diagram been separated into corporate and association markets as they behave quite differently. Again, you can identify submarkets here such as corporate meetings and exhibitions/trade shows, or under associations you could separate professional from academic, or clubs from other affinity groups that hold meetings. We will discuss how both intrinsic and extrinsic motivations apply, as there are often mixed leisure and business motives for making particular trips. The fifth market is government, and not every city will want to compete for these—especially the large, international congresses or summits that nowadays generate so much controversy and protests or riots.

In every market, events are either essential or highly desirable, and this fact generates event tourism demand. Out of this emerges the concept of an event travel career. Highly involved amateur athletes tend to compete in more events, farther from home, and to combine holidays with events. Yoga practitioners and ballroom dancers have ever-growing opportunities for attending events aimed specifically at their interests. Professionals want to advance their careers through learning and networking events, while corporations need to reach their potential customers and conduct business-to-business relationships at events. Even academics develop event travel careers, as we have a need to constantly learn, meet like-minded people, and sustain relationships. Within these social worlds some events stand out as being Iconic; that is, they hold symbolic meaning because of their prestige, reputation for quality, size, or uniqueness.

Service-Dominant Logic and Cocreation of Value

There has been a revolution in marketing theory in recent years, and it applies to Event Tourism; it is closely linked to the demand-side, bottom-up logic being advocated in this book. "Service-dominant logic" (see: www.sdlogic.net), as articulated by Lusch and Vargo (2006), Lusch, Vargo, and O'Brien (2008), and Vargo and Lusch (2008a, 2008b), provides a set of principles that can guide all marketing. It starts with the premise that the traditional distinctions between goods and services are invalid; that all marketing is concerned with the exchange of service.

Here are the key principles (adapted from Lusch and Vargo) in italics, with my own interpretation of implications for Event Tourism.

1. *Service is the fundamental basis of exchange; goods derive their value from the service they provide to users.* Events are services with value to users, and the value is defined by the users. Event venues exist to provide service (as benefits or measured value) to specific user groups. In Event Tourism, service is the basis of all exchanges.

2. *Service is the application of knowledge and skills; these are the source of competitive advantage.* Not venues, not comparative destination advantages, but knowledge and skill lead to success in Event Tourism.

3. *Complex combinations of goods, money, and institutions provide service, which can make the nature of service difficult to perceive.* Event Tourism as a system is complex, involving many stakeholders and interactions, but the entire process is intended to provide valued service to customers (being corporations, associations, event owners, and event tourists).

4. *Service is exchanged for service; all markets exist for the exchange of service; a customer-centered view is essential.* Customers in Event Tourism are sometimes individuals, and at other times corporations, associations, or government agencies. A demand-side approach to Event Tourism incorporates the customer-centered principle.

5. *Cocreation: the customer is always a cocreator of value; it is an interactional process; firms offer value propositions, they do not deliver value on their own.* In Event Tourism the value propositions are crucial: venues and events offer the potential to satisfy customer needs and give event tourists rewarding experiences; it is the job of suppliers to work with customers to ensure the experience is rewarding, even memorable; close and on-going relationships are essential.

6. *Value is determined by beneficiaries; it is idiosyncratic, experiential, contextual, and meaning laden.* This principle of SD logic is identical to the core phenomenon of Event Tourism and event management, as explained in Event Studies (Getz, 2007, 2012). This is why interdisciplinary theory is essential.

7. *The context of value creation is networks of networks, or resource integrators.* Event Tourism as a system requires that resources are devoted to venues, events, infrastructure, marketing, skill development, and knowledge creation. DMOs know this is their job, to be team leaders in getting the resources and applying the knowledge.

Value and Experience Design

There is value in use, which we define as "consumption," but in the experiential realm of events there is much more of a socially constructed value to consider, such as the *communitas* of shared experiences within groups that meet because of their common interests (i.e., social worlds) or even among crowds that enjoy the same event or entertainment. In this context, value is more difficult to measure, as is the nature of the cocreation process.

Experience design therefore becomes a key topic. In line with SD logic, designers do not actually generate, nor can they guarantee or deny, certain experiences—all of which are personal and social constructs. Experience and event designers are therefore, by definition, cocreators who offer value propositions to their guests and customers. A number of authors take this "value-in-experience" perspective, arguing that only customers can make sense of their internal, subjective experiences (Helkkula & Kelleher, 2011; Helkkula, Kelleher, & Pihlström, 2012). See also Holbrook (1999, 2006) and Holbrook and Hirschman (1982) for a discussion on the hedonistic and experiential dimensions of marketing.

Bottom-Up Logic

Top-down planning and policy making is the norm, just as supply-side marketing is most common in events and tourism. Those in charge of the process have specific goals and limited knowledge of potential, so they tend to sell what they have, and to pursue strategies that reflect their own values and biases. What results is typically more of the same, or preserving the status quo.

Demand-side logic requires more of a bottom-up approach in which all stakeholders participate, drawing on their own needs, goals, strategies, and intellectual capital to formulate emergent, flexible strategies. The process has to tap into the energy of many, and not try to impose a uniform strategy on them, from the top down. This does not say a vision, policy, and strategy are not required (such as by the DMO), only that the approach seeks to liberate and not constrain entrepreneurship, innovation, and competition. How is this in line with service-dominant logic? Ask: Who is best equipped to satisfy customer needs? Which organizations (including events) understand best how to service the needs of niche markets?

Trends and Forces

Trends are changes, measured over time. The popular practice of social network "trending" relates to the sudden popularity of a topic, but this is a very short-term phenomenon compared to what we are interested in.

Only in their early stages are trends difficult to detect, and that is a place where entrepreneurs can find opportunity. It explains why there are so many "trend spotters" looking for the hottest, most explosive fads or fashions, because big profits can be made through first entry into new markets.

"Forces" are the underlying causes, and in order to make forecasts, or future scenarios, we have to have knowledge of the major forces shaping supply and demand. First we will consider some of the big, measureable trends in Event Tourism, and then have a look at underlying forces.

Event Tourism Trends

These are obvious, important trends at the global level, both for tourism in general and Event Tourism in particular.

- We have experienced long-term growth in international tourism, and this has been projected by the World Tourism Organization to continue through 2020 (see details below).
- There continues to be major changes in the patterns and distribution of international tourist arrivals, with Asia on the growth curve, while in many mature destinations both international and domestic tourism has been flat or declining.
- Although largely unmeasured, there has been a huge increase globally in the number and variety of events (accompanied by many events increasing in size and impact) and in event venues.
- Ever-increasing competition for events and tourists is quite evident, at all levels (local, regional, national); more cities and destinations are entering this marketplace with huge expenditure on infrastructure and events.
- I have observed global legitimation of the idea that festivals and events are public goods, leading to their exploitation as instruments of government policy in a variety of policy domains.; this process has often been called "festivalization."
- There has been widespread legitimation of the idea that events are powerful branding and marketing tools for corporations, leading to the term "live communications."
- More and more event-specific development, bidding, and marketing agencies are appearing; most tourism agencies now recognize the critical importance of events.
- Diversification of the "product" is occurring, from a traditional emphasis on business events and sports towards all-encompassing event portfolios that also feature arts, cultural, and lifestyle events.

The World Tourism Organization (WTO) has documented the growth in international arrivals, showing an average annual growth rate of 6.5% to 2005—a year in which 806 million arrivals were recorded. They project this growth will continue to 2020, in which there is to be 1.6 billion arrivals.

> Tourism 2020 Vision is the World Tourism Organization's long-term forecast and assessment of the development of tourism up to the first 20 years of the new millennium. An essential outcome of the Tourism 2020 Vision are quantitative forecasts covering a 25 years period, with 1995 as the base year and forecasts for 2010 and 2020. (www.unwto.org/facts/eng/vision)

WTO monitoring demonstrates that tourism demand follows from economic growth and especially growth in private, disposable incomes. There is latent demand for tourism, so once people's basic needs are satisfied they tend to very quickly get involved in leisure and travel pursuits. In this context, events are not a secondary consideration; rather, they are frequently the means by which people meet their leisure and travel preferences.

Of course, when economic conditions change for the worse, demand will fall. But periodic recessions have resulted in short-lived plateauing, not a permanent curtailing of overall growth. Economic, health, social, or political problems do, however, shift demand between regions as people avoid trouble spots. Events are often the first things canceled when troubles arise, but they are also used by destinations to fight back after trouble—to change people's perceptions about the health or safety of a visit.

Europe and the Americas were the main tourist-receiving regions between 1950 and 2000, but much of the growth has shifted to the Middle East and Asia, and in particular China (both in and outbound, as it has the largest population on the planet). Mature destinations in Europe and North America are having a more difficult time maintaining demand, necessitating that destinations work hard (and intelligently) to be more competitive, and that is a factor leading to increased emphasis on Event Tourism.

Legitimation

One can easily observe how festivals and events have become accepted as instruments of government policy, not just economic and tourism policy, but also social and cultural. This process of "legitimation" has clearly led to a proliferation of festivals and events around the world, and it is in part an innovation that diffuses through space and time as examples of successes get reported or observed. This process applies to the corporate world as well, as it is now legitimate for companies to sponsor and produce their own events as "live communications" with their target audiences—not to mention for business-to-business relationship management.

Legitimation is not faddish, it is a process of institutionalization of an idea, or value set, so that events have become permanent manifestations of policy and strategy. Legitimation also applies (in the context of organizational ecology) to new forms of organization, or in our context, new forms of events and Event Tourism (see Hannan & Freeman, 1977) that serve to meet important social and economic goals.

Festivalization and Eventful Cities

Festivals, usually located in the public and nonprofit domains, have come under increasing pressure to serve as instruments of public policy, sometimes for social and cultural reasons, but equally for tourism and place marketing purposes. And in many cities festivals have been the preferred tool in development, renewal, repositioning, and branding. So much so that the term "festivalization" has been coined to describe the trend for cities in particular to exploit the image and attraction power of their cultural sectors. Hitters (2007) stated:

The concept of festivalization is a fairly widely accepted phenomenon among analysts of urban policy and cultural trends. . . . It refers to the increasing use of flagship festivals and large cultural events as a means to market major cities. Furthermore, I will argue that festivalization is not just limited to city marketing objectives but is becoming a new policy paradigm in the field of urban culture. (p. 282)

In the book *Eventful Cities*, Greg Richards and Robert Palmer (2010) elaborated on the concept. They observed that cities are increasingly promoting themselves as being "eventful" or "festival cities," and this is part of being a "creative city." As festivalization progresses, said Richards and Palmer, it embraces "new forms of animation, including edu-tainment and shop-a-tainment" (p. 29), and requires "performative spaces" for interaction, theater, and sensory experiences. They also concluded that "The notion of festivalization reflects much more than an increase in the number of events being held in cities: it echoes a qualitative change intimately linked to the spatial and economic restructuring of cities" (p. 30).

Richards and Palmer compared three models of how cities have used culture and events for competitive advantage in a postindustrial world. The "entrepreneurial city" represents a shift from management to entrepreneurial action, including place marketing and proactive Event Tourism. Funding of culture and festivals is typically linked to performance such as tourism gains, and public–private partnerships are the norm. In this context, events generate "symbolic capital" (p. 12). In the "creative city" importance is given to "creative industries" (including design and culture) and the "creative class" (as popularized by Richard Florida, 2002). Festivals in particular are valued for their contribution to creativity and as innovation generators. An attractive lifestyle for residents and visitors alike is a key element. Creative cities supposedly adapt better to changing environmental conditions.

In the "intercultural city," Richards and Palmer (2010) argue that globalization and increased mobility (or diaspora) has transformed most cities, giving rise to intercultural events that deliberately bring people together. This should generate a "diversity advantage" (p. 17). Furthermore, "The intercultural approach moves beyond equal opportunities and respect for existing cultural differences ('multiculturalism') to the use of dialogue and exchange between people of different cultural backgrounds to facilitate the transformation of public space, civic culture and institutions" (p. 17).

Propelling Forces

Without an understanding of the underlying forces, we cannot confidently project trends very far into the future. Forces can act to propel or constrain growth in Event Tourism, and that is the way the ensuing discussion is organized, with Figure 2.2 providing a summary.

Most commentators attribute profound changes in the leisure, tourism, and events sectors to "globalization." We can think of globalization as a collection of forces resulting in greater integration of economies and cultures. Global communications, transportation advances, capital flows, migration, and freer trade are major contributing factors.

Page and Connell (2012) in *The Routledge Handbook of Events*, provide the following summary:

Events reflect a range of established and emergent social, economic, political and cultural transformations. One of the most profound social changes affecting tourism and leisure (including its worldwide commodification and analysis as a form of consumption under the aegis of events) is the process of

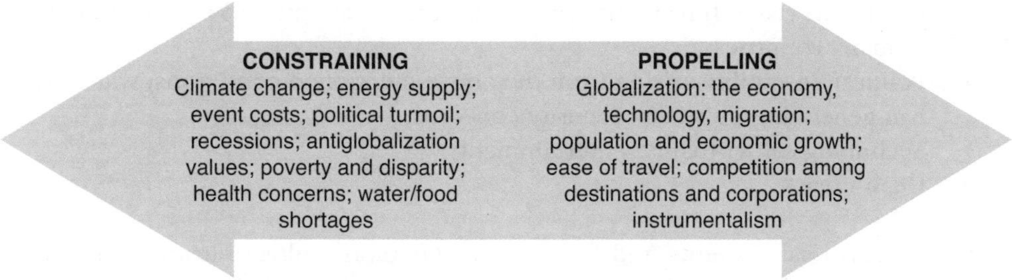

CONSTRAINING	PROPELLING
Climate change; energy supply; event costs; political turmoil; recessions; antiglobalization values; poverty and disparity; health concerns; water/food shortages	Globalization: the economy, technology, migration; population and economic growth; ease of travel; competition among destinations and corporations; instrumentalism

Figure 2.2. Forces propelling and constraining Event Tourism.

globalisation. Globalisation has created a world stage for events through the growth of event destinations and internationalisation of events via enhanced media and digital forms of transmission, sometimes resulting in audiences (actual and virtual) of millions. (p. 5)

In addition to global communications and the rise of new media as significant forces for change, Page and Connell (2012) refer to rising education levels, affluence, and positive attitudes towards the roles of culture, leisure, and travel. The rise of the so-called "experience economy" (Pine & Gilmore, 1999) has emerged from these forces, marked by "serious leisure" and the amassing of "cultural capital." Economic globalization has resulted in a borderless world for information and many goods or services, while large corporations can exploit events for global impact. People are better connected than ever, giving rise to the "network society." All this reinforces the need for a demand-side approach.

In examining globalization and sport tourism, Higham and Hinch (2009) said "The first general characteristic of globalization is the accelerated compression of time and space" (p. 18). This is followed by growing interdependence, but with marked inequalities of its costs and benefits. These forces are reflected in the "spectacularization" of sport mega-events like the World Cup and Olympics. Fans can travel easily to numerous events, internationally, but favoring highly developed economies with modern transport. Both teams and fans are more mobile than ever. They go on to say: "Sport is ubiquitous as a form of popular culture while maintaining its significance as a form of place-based local culture" (p. 26).

Constraining Forces

Just as tourism has grown internationally, Event Tourism will continue to expand as long as the underlying forces do not shift suddenly or in unexpected directions. The constraining forces might very well increase in power and act to check growth, particularly in some regions. More likely, however, in the short term the constraining forces will heighten competitive tensions and force more and more destinations to question why and how they are developing and marketing events and tourism. The age of relying on mass tourism is probably coming to an end, and hereafter niche marketing will prevail.

C. Jones (2012) reflected on the period of sustained growth in the festivals and events sector over recent decades, but cautioned that a number of factors threaten event viability and might force a retrenchment. These are the main constraining factors he identified:

- Environmental: resource and especially fossil fuel depletion; regulations stemming from climate change;
- Social: travel might become socially unacceptable, given the costs;

- Economic: rising travel costs (peak oil); the sovereign and personal debt crisis in many countries;
- Political: instability arising from the above-mentioned conditions; war or terrorism generating increased security concerns;
- Technological: virtuality; entertainment;
- Health fears.

C. Jones (2012) said "events and festivals are far more vulnerable than most activities, partly because they usually involve a high degree of travel consumption, and personal cost (and often community and national level infrastructure development), but also because the event sector is badly placed to respond to rapidly changing environmental conditions (in the widest sense)" (p. 108).

From the Australian State of Queensland review in 2008 of their events policy a number of particular threats and issues were identified. The report is available online. The consultant noted:

> Queensland has enjoyed a healthy share of the Australian business events market over the last decade but there are signs the state's business events market is starting to plateau and market share is starting to decline, particularly in the international marketplace. Queensland's share of the international meetings market against other leading Asia Pacific destinations has been static, despite overall growth in the number of international conventions and the number of participants over the last 10 years. Meanwhile, other destinations in the region have seen significant increases in delegates attending international association events. The growth of the business events industry internationally is enormous. Australia's close neighbours China, India and Singapore are investing huge sums in constructing numerous world-class convention and exhibition centers as are Middle Eastern destinations such as Dubai and Bahrain. Further compounding the declining international market share, the Australian industry is facing new issues that pose threats to future growth:
>
> - concerns over the strength of the US and world economies
> - continuing emergence of new international destinations in Eastern Europe and North Asia
> - increasing strength of the $A
> - fuel cost, surcharges and other taxes associated with long haul travel
> - carbon emission issues
> - investment by new destinations and reinvestment by mature destinations (D. Williams, 2008)

The balance between constraining and propelling forces constantly shifts, and from region to region, so for strategic planning purposes it is a matter of monitoring, forecasting, and scenario making. While the long-term future is unknowable, and people fall into both optimistic and pessimistic camps, there is no doubt that cities and destinations will have no choice but to continuously adapt. Taken all together, constraints and propelling forces, I foresee a continued, substantial period of time in which Event Tourism reigns above most other forms of tourism development and marketing. In 2013 Event Tourism is still in its ascendency.

The Event Tourist

Remember that event tourism is defined on the demand side by reference to those who travel specifically for events, and those who can be motivated to attend events while traveling. Event Tourism developers and marketers need "destination events" that generate incremental, or new, demand. Events themselves will also want to market to residents and to visitors already in the area. This distinction gives rise to the following discussion of various types of event tourists, and to the important concept of "direct and induced demand."

Basic Categories of Event Tourists

Start with the fact that some people who go to events are traveling because of the event, and others are not. This gives rise to two important categories:

Dedicated event tourists: they travel specifically because of an event; it is the main purpose of their trip, so their spending in the area can be counted as an economic benefit of the event.

Casual (and accidental) event tourists: They are already in the area and attend accidentally or because it is something to do; often they are taken to events by their hosts, such as family and friends. The event has not motivated their trip, so their total spending cannot be attributed to the event; but if it can be shown they spent more because of attending an event, then a portion of their tourist spending could be attributed to the event. They might constitute a good target audience, especially during peak tourist seasons when cities and resorts are normally busy.

Now we have to distinguish between types of involvement in the event.

Spectators: those who watch a sport competition, and the audience for an entertainment production; highly involved spectators are also called "fans" or "enthusiasts"; spectating is largely a passive experience, but there are exceptions; "spectator events" are often also "media events."

Participants: all those who are the object of the event, including athletes in sport competitions, delegates at meetings and conventions, and amateur performers in shows and festivals (staff, paid performers, volunteers, and officials represent "direct demand" for an event if they travel because of it, but it is not held because of them, it is held with their help, so I do not call them participants). In Event Tourism "participation events" are often "destination events" that generate travel.

It is also useful to distinguish between those who attend an event as participants, and those who accompany the attendees.

"Accompanying" event tourists: those people, usually family and friends, who accompany dedicated event tourists to the event and/or the destination. They constitute a potentially substantial additional source of economic benefits through extended stays and tours/activities beyond the event itself.

Case Study: Seniors as Event Tourists

The seniors market should never be underestimated. Many aging baby boomers are remaining active and have already developed event tourist careers.

Senior Games Participation in Florida (Heather J. Gibson—Dr. Heather Gibson is an Associate Professor in the Department of Tourism, Recreation and Sport Management at the University of Florida and an Associate Director of the Eric Friedheim Tourism Institute)

While the number of amateur sports events continues to grow in communities across the US, the number of participants over the age of 50 years has also increased. In Florida, this may not be surprising as the state is a haven for retirees and what we have called the "Florida Factor" (H. Gibson, Ashton-Shaeffer, & Sanders, 2002) may encourage mid- and later-life individuals to participate in physical activity. While the summers are hot and steamy, for 6 months of the year the climate is conducive to being outside and the concentration of retirement communities offering a range of leisure activities to those in their 50s and older may encourage more individuals to be physically active, and even to participate in the many amateur sports events on offer in the state. Over the past decade, we have been studying participants in the Senior Games, a competitive multisport event for athletes aged 50 and over. We have collected both quantitative survey-based data and qualitative in-depth interview data from Senior Games' participants, exploring their experiences, sport history, and their evaluations of the various events.

Our research started with our local Senior Games Competition organized by the Gainesville Sports Commission as one of their signature events held in October of each year. This event draws around 300 participants from all over the state and is a qualifying event for the state level competition held annually in December. Senior Games competitions have been held throughout the US since 1985 to encourage individuals aged 50+ to adopt active and healthy lifestyles and include local-, regional-, state- national-, and international-level competitions. The Senior Games include a variety of activities including a parade of athletes, communal meals, medal ceremonies, and of course a range of sports such as track and field, basketball, swimming, table tennis, and at some events even arts and crafts. In our most recent survey in 2007, the participants indicated that 84% lived outside of the community and traveled to attend the event and so for many communities the Senior Games is part of their sport tourism portfolio (Kaplanidou & Gibson, 2010). Many of the participants tend to participate in the

Photo 2.1. Senior Games, Gainesville, Florida
(Credit: Photo courtesy of Heather Bell).

Senior Games on a regular basis, with 84% reporting they had taken part in our local event an average of 2.56 times over the past 5 years, 57% had taken part at the state level an average of three times, and almost 30% had participated at the national level.

These participation patterns are quite common in the various studies we have conducted over the years. For example, in our qualitative study we found that while six of our participants were first-timers, the rest had taken part in the Senior Games anywhere from 2 to 7 years (H. Gibson, Ashton-Shaeffer, Green, & Kensinger, 2002). In fact, when asked about the role of sport in their lives, over half of the participants reported that sport "It's my number one leisure" interest (Don, 52) and Mary an avid tennis player explained "it's meshed right in to my everyday life." Many participated in sport on a daily basis from golf and tennis to lifting weights at the gym. Others also competed in organized events such as triathlons, road races, and US Masters swimming, in addition to the Senior Games. When asked about the physical benefits of staying active, they all spoke about improved health, longevity, and quality of life. However, there was also an awareness of the mental benefits of sport participation, whether it helped them deal with the stresses of everyday life or as Joyce a 57 year old retired lawyer said "I got smarter by doing this, believe it or not." She talked about being burned out from her job and that taking part in sport and the senior games in particular had enabled her to focus on learning new things and regain her mental sharpness.

Traveling to different locations and meeting new people were also cited frequently as reasons for participating in the Senior Games. "Experiencing new places" was a major part of the senior games experience. In a survey of 260 senior athletes, 59.6% combined senior games with other tourist activities [visiting family/friends (35.3%), attractions (26.8%), nature (24.6%), and culture/arts (15.6%)] (H. Gibson, Chang, & Ashton-Shaeffer, 2007). Others talked about developing friendships through the people they had met at different Senior Games events, even friends from different countries at the national and international competitions. The longer time participants were great advocates for the Senior Games movement and lamented that they wished more older adults would take part, as Mary said "it's never too late to be an Olympian" (H. Gibson, Ashton-Shaeffer, Green, et al., 2002). Indeed, in examining the social world (Unruh, 1979), involvement (Bricker & Kerstetter, 2000) and their motivations (Beard & Ragheb, 1983) to take part in the Senior Games we found that among participants surveyed at four different Senior Games events in Florida, the athletes exhibited the full range of social world membership in the Senior Games from the relative outsiders (Strangers) to the Regulars and the ultracommitted (Insiders) (S. Chang, Kang, & Gibson, 2007). Not surprisingly, the Insiders had significantly higher levels of Social Identity Involvement when compared with those less committed to the Senior Games social world and also tended to more motivated by fitness and intellectual stimulation than other participants. Understanding that event participants have different needs is something that event organizers should pay attention to, thereby increasing participant satisfaction levels and encouraging repeat participation (Kaplanidou & Gibson, 2010).

In terms of recommendations for organizers of Senior Games competitions and other similar events for older athletes, many of the same recommendations for athletes of all ages should be followed. For example, many of the participants are highly experienced and skilled in their particular sports and so get very distressed when competition venues are perceived as substandard or officiating (refereeing) is of poor quality, or even the signage to the different competitions within a community are poor. All of these issues can be alleviated by the event organizers by paying particular attention to the facilities, officials, and general organization of the event. Some of the event qualities that may be more unique to this age group and the Senior Games competitors in general are that they describe a level of competition that is not as "antagonistic" and aggressive as that of younger participants (H. Gibson, Ashton-Shaeffer, Green, et al., 2002). There is still competition, but there is much more emphasis on the fun of taking part and the camaraderie among the participants. There is also a sense of inspiration about seeing the older participants in particular compete. Thus, elements of the event such as the celebration of athletes' parade, communal meals, and medal ceremonies are integral parts of the event for these participants and should not be ignored or marginalized by event organizers. Indeed, Green and Chalip (1998) urge event organizers to program time into their events so that the participants can socialize and celebrate their sporting subculture. Certainly, these lessons should be headed by communities wishing to host sporting events such as the Senior Games for the increasing number of mid and later life athletes.

Direct and Induced Demand

Dedicated event tourists are what destination events need to survive, and are often the target of event managers looking for additional demand. Local residents might represent the primary source of direct demand for an event, but in this book we are mostly interested in the tourist demand. Here we can include sponsors, officials, staff, volunteers, paid performers, media, and other observers who would not travel except for the event:

> **Direct demand:** All the people who traveled because of an event are "event tourists," consisting of participants, exhibitors, suppliers, officials, sponsors, the media, producers (staff and volunteers), paid performers, and of course spectators. This is called "direct demand" because their attendance and travel are generated specifically by the event; they are the key target segments.

If an event generates sufficient media coverage and interest there is a good likelihood that people and groups will be attracted to the venue, host city, or destination before, during, and after. It has been observed that conference demand picks up in the years before and after the Olympics. Tours come to see Olympic facilities and museums. Years after a World Fair, monuments live on to attract visitors. During an event it is now common to host larger crowds in fan zones or outside stadia, creating a festive atmosphere for those not lucky enough (or unable to afford!) tickets. And it is every host city's aim to realize a quantum leap in demand overall for tourism because of the combined tangible legacy and improved destination image. Some people refer to these impacts as the "halo effect."

> **Induced demand**: Events, and in particular large, one-time events, can generate a positive image of a destination that leads to additional visits before, during, and after; this is "induced demand." It occurs more for mega-events because of enormous media coverage; the "halo effect" is similar to the image-enhancement and branding roles that an event tourism portfolio aims to generate.

There is often a need for event owners, organizers and others (such as suppliers) to visit venues and destinations before and after an event to do business, including site inspections. This can also be thought of as "induced demand," but it is usually invisible and not measured in impact studies.

Kang and Perdue (1994) examined the long-term impact of the 1988 Seoul Olympics on tourism flows to Korea and drew several important conclusions. These researchers felt that any increase in Korea's global tourism market share could not be estimated, but that the mega-event did have a positive effect in increasing long-term visitation to Korea. Because the host country was an emerging destination, the impact might be greater than for mature destinations. Consumer reaction to the image enhancement created by the event was judged to be lagged and protracted, or what others have called the "halo effect." It was apparently greatest the year following the Olympics and might extend as long as 10 years.

We return to direct and induced demand in Chapter 10 when economic impacts and multipliers are discussed. Note that in the context of event impact assessment, economists have a different meaning for "induced"—as tertiary effects of incremental income.

A Demand-Side Classification of Events

Most attraction and event typologies are from the supply perspective, whereas a marketing orientation suggests a consumer or demand-side classification should be developed. How do potential customers of events view them? What criteria do they use? Securing the opinions of the tour industry is one important step. Researching consumers is another. To a limited extent this has been done by Getz and Cheyne (2002) through focus groups that covered event trip motivations, benefits sought, and related behavior and experiences.

Results suggested that a number of factors were important when people consider an event-related purchase or trip, and these can be utilized in a classification system:

- uniqueness: opportunities to experience something different (e.g., major entertainers or international sports celebrities);
- socializing: opportunities for family outings; meeting and seeing people; party atmosphere;
- learning: opportunities for authentic experiences; interpretation provided;
- packaging the event with a wider social and travel experience;
- participating in an event; viewing friends and relatives who are participating.

The demand-side classification could therefore include the types of events shown below, with dichotomies or ranges possible within each:

- once-in-a-lifetime opportunities (as opposed to periodic);
- celebrity events (see/meet the stars or VIPs);
- participatory events (versus spectator);
- public, festive events (as opposed to private parties);
- learning events (including authentic cultural experiences);
- leisure events (featuring relaxation, fun, health);
- family- or friend-oriented event outings;
- event-related tour packages (self-assembled or all-inclusive).

Once such a system is established—and more research is required to determine its applicability to different consumer segments under varying circumstances—communications could stress the relevant messages in a variety of media. While supply-side classifications might be of value in planning, demand-side typologies will have greater applicability in marketing.

It has to be cautioned, however, that experiences are personal and social constructs, occurring within and among people, and they are not designed (in the sense that they can be guaranteed). Calling an event "entertaining" gives a powerful clue (and is a "value proposition"), but it is not the same as a person "being entertained." Consider this issue again when we talk about Iconic events that hold special symbolic meanings.

Why People Travel to Events

Marketers must understand the needs, motives and expectations of potential customers in order to influence decisions and satisfy patrons. But according to research undertaken by Mayfield and Crompton (1995), many festival organizers do not undertake thorough customer-oriented research, believing in their own ability to know what their customers want, or lacking the resources to do it. The culture of organizations often leads to product rather than a marketing orientation, in which case market research is undervalued.

Figure 2.3. Consumer decision-making process for Event Tourism.

Figure 2.3 conceptualizes the consumer decision-making process for events. Underlying the desire to travel, pursue a leisure activity, or specifically attend an event are basic human needs that lead to behavioral motivations. People expect that certain activities or experiences will provide the desired benefits to meet their needs and wants, but of course many choices are available. Events must compete with other forms of leisure and other events. As well, there are many constraints or barriers to possible participation, some personal (time, money, social influences) and some related to the event (location, accessibility, cost). Even if the consumer decides to attend an event, there can be good reasons why the desired experience never occurs.

Having enjoyed (or not) the event experience, future intentions will be influenced, including the possible development of an event-related "career." All these elements and processes are discussed more fully below.

Needs and Motivation

Do people need events? They are so well established in all civilizations that we have to conclude the answer is yes, but only in general terms—for celebration, leisure, socializing, business. There is seldom a need for a particular event, although in some social worlds there are Iconic events that members feel compelled to attend. In religions, there are sometimes required pilgrimages. Professionals might feel the need to attend specific seminars or congresses as part of their career advancement.

Almost all motivational theory rests on the belief that humans have basic needs that motivate behavior. In discussing the psychology of events, Benckendorff and Pearce (2012, p. 168) referred to needs theories by Maslow (1954) and others who identified basic physiological needs (e.g., food, safety, health), social and esteem needs, and higher order self-development or self-actualization needs. They used this definition of motive from Iso-Ahola (1980): "an internal factor that arouses, directs and integrates a person's behavior" (p. 230). Knowledge of motives is crucial when designing attractive event experiences, and also in monitoring satisfaction, understanding the decision-making process, giving insights to behavior, and outcomes of event attendance or participation.

Many festival motivational studies have demonstrated the specific relevance of seeking–escaping theory to explain event attendance and related travel. Iso-Ahola (1983) and Mannell and Iso-Ahola (1987) argued that leisure and travel behavior is stimulated by both a desire to escape undesirable conditions and, simultaneously, to realize desired experiences. Underlying this concept is the belief that people seek levels of "optimal arousal," or a balance between under- and overstimulation in their environments and personal lives. Marketing people often refer to "push and pull" factors (i.e., motivators to get away from and attractions to move towards), but it is wrong to think of them as always acting independently.

This seeking–escaping behavior operates within both personal and interpersonal dimensions. It can therefore be said that a trip to an event is motivated both by the desire to escape and the desire to seek out new experiences, relative to the person's interpersonal and personal needs. Note that this is leisure theory, and might not apply to people attending business events or those doing business at events.

"Intrinsic" motivation relates to one's own needs and desires, not what others want. By contrast, "extrinsic" motivation occurs when a behavior or activity is done to please someone else, meet obligations, or for a reward. Attending an event might be done for reasons of personal development (e.g., to learn something new; for aesthetic enjoyment), or because the family or friends expect it. Often a combination of intrinsic and extrinsic motives will be found.

At any given event we might find people who came because they felt a need, others who were obligated in some way, and still more who were just curious or looking for diversion. This gives rise to the marketing concept of "generic versus targeted benefits," as discussed next.

Benefits: Generic and Targeted

"Benefits" are what people believe they will obtain from consumption or participation, and these are generally expressed in terms related to need fulfillment. For example, of all the benefits provided by leisure services and sport, improved health has to be near the top of the list. People "want" many things or experiences, but that is not necessarily the same as needing them. Only the individual can decide when a want becomes a need, although society often makes judgments as to what is a basic need. Often potential substitution comes into play, because many needs and wants can be met through different means.

M. Morgan (2009) reviewed the literature and concluded that event motives fall into three groups, namely: (1) the personal benefits of hedonic enjoyment (e.g., novelty, escape, fun) and achievement (through meeting challenges); (2) social interaction with family, staff, other visitors, and (3) wider symbolic meanings derived from shared cultural values. Most of these are generic, and not at all related to the theme or activity of the event. So the question becomes, which of these benefits depends on the exact theme, nature, activities, or marketing appeal of the event?

Being together as a family, meeting people, and doing things with friends are generic motives. Some events are better than others at meeting these needs, especially festivals and celebrations. Acting out of curiosity or escaping boredom are generic—you do not need a particular event, and the event could easily be substituted by other forms of entertainment or diversion. There is also hedonism, reflected in partying, eating, and drinking, which is often expressed as "having fun" or "looking for thrills"—these are facilitated by certain types of events, but are not event dependent.

Pursuit of higher order needs, as in self-development (most importantly: learning, aesthetic appreciation, personal and group identity building, mastery and meeting challenges) normally motivates "seeking" behavior (i.e., looking for very specific events that can meet one's needs). This leads members of special interest groups and various social worlds to events created for them, or events with "targeted benefits."

Any given event can provide a mix of generic and targeted benefits to motivate travel by different groups. When sport events add festivity to their program they are deliberately expanding the range of benefits in order to attract wider audiences. If organizers add meetings and exhibitions, they are really targeting those with special interests. This is also what I call "convergence." The power of events to motivate, satisfy, and meet multiple aims is greatly enhanced when multiple forms of event and "elements of style" are combined (for a detailed examination, see Getz, 2012).

Now if we look at business events, the targeted benefits are necessarily different. Association members attend conventions because of their involvement in the association, or commitment to its purpose, so what motivates them can be a combination of generic benefits (e.g., the joy of travel, a desire for socializing) and the very focused benefits related to the particular association (often this is learning and networking). For some association members there will be an obligation to attend, either because they have duties to perform or it is expected of them. In other words, a mix of intrinsic and extrinsic motivations can easily apply.

As to corporate events and exhibitions, it might be that only extrinsic motivators apply to attendance at the actual event (i.e., it is required by the boss, or "I have to do business there"), whereas the rest of the trip might include a family holiday or short break for pleasure. Mixed motives are very common in this way. It also applies to competitive sports when accompanying event tourists expect more from the trip than just the event itself.

Expectations of the benefits that can be obtained through an event or a travel experience are shaped in three major ways: previous experience, word of mouth, and marketing. Loyal consumers are those that have had a satisfying experience, and they typically share their opinions with others, fueling higher demand in the future. Marketing seeks to convey attractive imagery and messages about the event or destination, and the more targeted it is the more likely it will influence potential event tourists.

Case Study: Voss Extreme Sports Festival

The following case is from Norway and describes the Voss Extreme Sports Festival, an annual event that was once the "space" only of a few outdoor enthusiasts who used a remote mountain environment to pursue a variety of challenging activities. This event can be viewed in the context of "the landscapes of sport" as described by Bale (1994) and reproduced in Hinch and Higham (2011, pp. 122–124). To Bale, sport landscapes can have aesthetic meaning and unique place characteristics, and these certainly apply to the extreme sport enthusiasts. But when such an event goes mainstream the sport landscape takes on economic value as a generator of tourism and corporate activities. Also view this case in the context of subcultures and rural development.

Voss Extreme Sports Festival (Professor Reidar Mykletun, Norwegian Hotel School, University of Stavanger)

The case is the Ekstremsportveko (The Extreme Sports Week), or "Veko" for short, held annually since 1998 in Voss, Norway. From a modest start, it has developed into the largest annual extreme sports festival worldwide, currently attracting 1,200 active sports participants. A hybrid mix of sports and cultural expressions are presented in the festival program as being about music, playfulness, and extreme sports in the amazing nature of Western Norway. The 2012 program announces the 15th year of the event as: "*For one whole week national and international athletes compete and challenge themselves in the elements. However, competitions are not always the main focus for the athletes. The sharing of knowledge, when hundreds of top athletes are gathering this last week of June, is just as important. . . . The music program has become an important part of the total festival experience. The last three days of the event, national and international artists spice up the festival with their vibrant music within the genres; pop, rock, funk and reggae!*" (http://ekstremsportveko.no/about). The activities of the event are partly in and around the festival tent, nicely placed in a public park area on the bank of lake Vangsvatnet, 2 minutes' walk from the Voss town centre; and around in the nature according to the unique features of each sport.

The event usually hosts competitions in kayaking, rafting, MTB, BMX, skydiving, paragliding, hang-gliding, multisport (Horgi Ned), free-ride, big air, climbing, BASE and long-boarding. Each year one or two new activities are included. For one whole week national and international athletes compete and challenge themselves in the elements, and they are generally very satisfied with the event. Some come earlier or stay longer to use the opportunities of practicing their sports in these feasible environments. They appreciate especially the social aspects of the event, the stunning nature of the area and the opportunities to learn and develop their sportsmanship.

The event attracts about 10,000 visitors to Voss and about 20,000 spectators to participate in evening activities in the festival tent and concert halls and to watch amazing extreme sports in the daytime. The unique Try-it concept is a 4-day adrenaline program for people with little or no experience in the different sports represented at Ekstremsportveko. This very popular initiative offers opportunities to try selected extreme sports activities under the guidance of athlete club members. New in 2012 for the public was the *SUP Sessions* (upright standing while paddling on surfboards), the strenuous but fun exercise of *One Call Challenge*, a *Photo Workshop with Pål Hermansen* in cooperation between Voss Kunstlag (Visual arts organization), the photographer Tom Hatlestad's exhibition *Tracing Freedom,* an ongoing photographic documentation project that aims to explore the concept of freedom, the *Power Yoga Classes* (in nature) by Sheri Trellevik, and *Capoeira Workshops* and *Capoeira Fun For Kids Day* (anAfro-Brazilian art form that combines elements of martial arts, music, and dance) facilitated by capoeiristas from KolibriCARF in Brazil. In addition a special program for children and youngsters is offered.

Evening entertainments in the festival tent offer sales of food, beverages, and a limited choice of souvenirs. A main attraction is "Today's video." which presents stunning scenes from each day's sports activities seasoned with humor and street music. A varied concert and entertainment program in the tent is offered at the end of each day. A Cashless Card Payment System applies in the Festival Tent. A prepaid Festival Pass gives access to the festival tent, while watching the sports may be done for free. Accommodation may be at the festival camp at Bømoen, 3 kilometers away from the festival tent, or at the local hotels, camping grounds and B&B facilities.

The interest in the Extreme Sports Festival may rest on a rising fashion trend of enjoying the thrills of adventure, a "Zeitgeist" of excitement, activity and play in travel, sports and other "serious leisure," because everyday life has become safe and predictable. It is also likely that participants and spectators flock to the event to share and celebrate their own subcultures. Spectators may come to seek self-actualization and self-demonstration (Gyimóthy, 2009) and may patronize the festival as ways to define themselves and construct their social identities (Gyimóthy & Mykletun, 2009).

The Launch of the Festival: Entrepreneurship and Ownership

"Once upon a time four men put their brilliant heads together and came up with a unique idea. Little did they know that their idea would turn out to become an annual highlight for hundreds of enthusiastic extreme sports athletes" (Festival Program, 2007, p. 4). These four friends with central positions in four different extreme sports organizations—the Voss Rafting Centre, the Voss Kayak Club, the Voss Hang- and Paragliding Club, and the Voss Skydiving Club—were talking about their clubs' plans at the small pub "Minigolfen" on the bank of Lake Vangsvatnet. The Voss Rafting Centre and the Voss Hang- and Paragliding Club planned to arrange national competitions at their branches in 1998 and at a planned Norwegian Army Cup in Woodland Racing.

"The idea was simple and brilliant. . . . I suggested that we should cooperate and make a festival out of it, instead of organizing two separate competitions. Moreover, we wanted to get in touch with each other's sports activities and maybe try more of the sports that were not our own. We did have great luck, too. One day in September 1997, I mentioned the idea to some clients at the Rafting Centre, preparing their rafting trip on the Strandaelva. One of them, a sales manager in the Ringnes brewery, liked it and promised to support the project with 70,000 NOK, which then became the budget for the first Extreme Sports Week 1998."

Voss may be conducive to the festival theme and the lifestyles it advocates. The area has hotels, cabins for rent, and camping areas. It is easily accessible by train from Oslo and Bergen, and Bergen Airport, Flesland is 90 minutes away. Voss is connected to surrounding areas by four main roads (www.visitvoss.no). It contains wide lowland valleys surrounded by mountains rising 1,500 meters above sea level and partly covered with snow until the end of July or later. The rivers, wide valleys, and mountains constitute a unique natural venue for extreme sports, and some rivers are accessible by car, facilitating transport of equipment and athletes.

The Extreme Sports Week remains unique regarding its basic idea, size and content. A competing but smaller event is the Nissan Outdoor Games by Colombia arranged annually since 2005 in Chamonix in France (4 days of winter games), and in Interlaken in Switzerland (2 days of summer games with competitions in mountain biking, kayaking and climbing, air shows with BASE jumping and paragliding acrobatics, and finally professional film and photo competitions).

Extreme Sports Week has become successful for several reasons. It is a unique hybrid niche festival that has matched market demands and prospered in a competitive festival climate. It is rooted in local values while also reflecting "Die Zeitgeist" or the spirit of the time with a search for adventure, extreme activities, and celebration of their subcultures; hence, saturation of demand is currently not an issue. It is embedded in seven capitals local to the region and has developed a positive balance in relation to six of them, which are the human, the social, the cultural, the natural, the financial, and the physical capitals. This balance should support the continuation of the festival as it demonstrates sustainable relationships between the festival and the capitals employed in its creation and operation. Interestingly, local financial capital has to a very little extent been involved in the creation of the event. This indicates that the other local capitals may be more important for the success of festivals than access to local financial capital, and the balance over time with these other capitals seems to be main factors in making the festival sustainable. This case also demonstrates the relevance of the seventh capital, the administrative capital, as a "new" capital construct among analysis of festivals in context. This capital is constituted of the public regulations, laws, and the local, regional, and national policies and administrative routines. The event complains about lack of understanding and various difficulties with this type of capital.

The management of this event has changed and adapted flexibly to changing demands as the festival has undergone different challenges and crises. After the fourth year, the leader has taken proactive stands to overcome upcoming challenges including bankruptcy threats, thus exemplifying that improved management may be the solution to a crisis that on the surface appears with another label. The new management resources were found in the social and human capital and rest on the cultural capital of Voss.

Demand, and the Attractiveness of an Event

"Attractiveness" is clearly related to the benefits people expect to derive from traveling to an event. In tourism, it is normally expressed as a measure of the relative strength of attractions, in terms of the number of people drawn, the geographic spread of the market area, or its appeal compared to the competition. Mill and Morrison (1985) used the term "drawing power" and linked it to the distance people are willing to travel to experience the attraction. They distinguished between local, regional, and national or international market areas. Event tourism must therefore seek to enhance the attractiveness of individual events and festivals and to use them to enhance destination attractiveness.

S. Lee and Crompton (2003) researched the drawing power of three events in Maryland, as indicated in the ensuing Research Note.

Research Note on Event Drawing Power

Lee, S., & Crompton, J. (2003). The attraction power and spending impact of three festivals in Ocean City, Maryland. *Event Management*, 8(2), 109–112.

Ocean City is a traditional resort community stretching for 10 miles along a barrier island on the coast of Maryland. Tourism is the basis of the town's economy and the reason for the community's existence. It is estimated that more than 8 million people visit the resort each year. The full-time resident population of the town is approximately 7,000. However, visitors and part-time residents swell this number to 300,000 in the height of the summer season.

The resort community hosts three annual major festivals: Springfest, Sunfest, and Winterfest. The primary goal of the festivals is to stimulate the local tourism economy during the shoulder and off-season months. The study reported here compares and contrasts the geographic and economic spending profiles of visitors to the three different festivals. The research question investigated was, "Do major festivals held at different times of the year in the same community exhibit similar attraction power and generate similar economic impacts?"

"Demand" is often equated with how many people will come to an event, or what they are willing to pay for it. More correctly, in economic terms, it is a function of the relationship between price and the quantity "demanded" for an event in particular circumstances. For each price the demand relationship tells the quantity the buyers want to buy at that corresponding price.

Consider other related factors. Usually price is a monetary cost, as in how much an admission ticket costs, but you might also want to put a value on the consumer's time and energy expended, especially if travel is involved. What about "free" events? For these it is common to measure demand in terms of attendance, but organizers have to be cautious about interpreting this. Many people might not pay anything for an event that is currently free. Research on "willingness to pay" is then required.

In the context of economic "demand," attractiveness could be equated with "market potential" and measured by "penetration rates." That is, within a given market area, how many purchases can be expected, expressed as a percentage of the population? (if half the people come twice, that is considered to be 100%). Different market areas also have to be considered, such as local, regional, national, and international zones.

Alternatives and Substitution

Just about every leisure and travel pursuit can be substituted. We do not absolutely need to go to a specific destination or participate in a specific event, and (this is assuming free choice) there are always alternative ways to meet our leisure needs. If extrinsic motivations to attend an event apply, substitution takes on a different meaning. We might be able to learn what we need to know from different trade shows, or meet the necessary contacts at different conventions, but these choices are less common than in the leisure realm. Many event attendees go to a specific event because it is the only one, or the best one, to satisfy their purposes.

The theory of "leisure substitution" suggests that if a person cannot do one thing, he or she will choose another that provides similar psychological experiences, satisfactions, and benefits (Brunson & Shelby, 1993). This appears to be very true for primarily social experiences where the activity, setting, or event is of secondary concern. Events offering "targeted benefits" for highly involved persons are less substitutable than those offering only "generic benefits."

Constraints or Barriers

Even if we decide we want to attend an event or go on a trip, there are normally many constraints. Leisure researchers Crawford, Jackson, and Godbey (1991) identified three general categories of constraints to participation: "structural, personal, and interpersonal." They are not necessarily hierarchical, and might be interactive. We can adapt these to our model of the Event Tourism decision-making process.

The first and foremost of the "structural constraints" is accessibility, which stems from the location and timing of events of all kinds—they are simply not always available, convenient, or known by all potential participants. All aspects of supply analysis come into play here, as does marketing and communication. For example, it has long been observed that there is a huge gap between tourists' interest in attending cultural events in other countries and actual participation. Why? Because they have imperfect knowledge of what is available, and are most likely to be in an area when the events are not held. This is also why we are so interested in the "dedicated event tourist" who travels specifically because of events.

Time and cost are always structural constraints. On the one hand we need to identify who is left out of the arts, or sports, or any other type of event because they are unable to afford it or cannot make the necessary time. On the other hand, "not enough time or money" are convenient excuses, and might often mean the person does not assign any priority to a given opportunity. The first is a constraint issue, the second pertains more to preferences. Age and health are obvious factors to consider. In youth we cannot get about on our own, and until we have income we cannot do what we want. With advancing age and declining health (or at least specific health problems) interest and participation in many leisure and work-related events will likely decline. For events, there is a need to combine both life cycle and work/career evolutionary approaches.

"Personal constraints" are individual psychological conditions, including personality and moods, that hold us back from participating. Some people are predisposed to social activities, others to introversion. Sometimes we want to mix, at other times we need to be left alone. Personality, values, attitudes, and lifestyle are important factors. Risk perception, and tolerance for risk, enters into many leisure and travel decisions. Do we want to have a thrill if it means assuming personal risks, or can we afford to spend time and money on an event that might not satisfy us? How preferences are first formed for events or event experiences has not been researched, but for ongoing participation there are explanations within the concepts of "serious leisure," "commitment," and "involvement" (discussed later in this chapter).

"Interpersonal constraints" arise within social contexts, taking into account the influence of others. This might take the form of letting significant others make decisions for us, being influenced by peer pressure (e.g., fear of ridicule), or being subjected to discrimination. Social isolation is often a limitation, especially for certain types of events—after all, who wants to go to a party or celebration alone? On the other hand, events are often great places to meet people.

Because constraints almost always exist, how do people who do participate or attend events overcome them? "Negotiation" of constraints is the individual process of finding ways to do what we want to do. If we really want to attend a concert, how do we get the money, make the time, find someone to go with, book the tickets, etc.? E. Jackson, Crawford, and Godbey (1993) discussed generic strategies for negotiating constraints. "Cognitive" strategies are the internal, psychological ways we deal with constraints. For example, the theory of "cognitive dissonance" can be applied by suggesting that if we cannot attend a concert because of high costs we will devalue the artist or type of music and do something else that we perceive to provide equal benefits. In this sense, when people say they do not like certain types of event, they might mean they cannot afford them. We all want to feel good about the choices we make, even if they were influenced by constraints.

"Behavioral" strategies include better time management, learning new skills, earning more money, or modifying our routines in order to do what we want to do. Some people turn leisure into work, or vice versa. For "serious leisure" one generally has to acquire knowledge to get the most out of the experience, and this applies to many volunteers at events. In order to think of oneself as an expert or connoisseur, say for the purpose of getting the most from a wine festival, advanced wine knowledge is essential. Similarly, to really be satisfied with your performance at the next Masters Games or X Games, you need to advance your skills through training and competition. To even compete in many sport events you have to qualify through lower level competitions. It seems paradoxical, but the most constrained people sometimes are the most active! How do they manage to engage in preferred leisure pursuits when others give up? The fact is that many people find innovative ways to overcome or negotiate through constraints.

Decision to Attend or Participate

Wanting to attend, even planning to, is quite different from going to an event. At some point commitment is made, perhaps money spent on travel or tickets, but something might still intervene to prevent attendance. Researchers therefore seek to discover the links between levels of awareness, interest in attending, forming a specific intention to go, and actual attendance.

Decision making occurs in stages, with feedback called "postpurchase evaluation." There is an awareness and opinion-forming stage, which might be combined with information gathering (even if it is no more than asking for someone's advice), during which the consumer forms an intent, rejects the opportunity, or waffles indecisively. Marketers seek to influence the decision-making process in many ways. First, the event and destination have to be perceived to be appealing, safe, accessible, and affordable. Potential problems associated with costs and accessibility need to be confronted and the whole experience made more convenient and affordable, usually through packaging. It must always be kept in mind that those seeking generic benefits (to be entertained, to socialize, to have fun, try something new) have different information search behavior, and respond to different messages, compared to potential event tourists who want specific (targeted) benefits and are therefore typically more involved in the decision-making process.

Event and Postevent Considerations

Was the event experience as expected? Was it merely satisfactory, or in some way exceptional, even surprisingly pleasant? Presumably people who have disappointing event experiences are less likely to become loyal customers or to spread positive word-of-mouth recommendations. However, novelty seekers might very well seek out new events regardless of the quality of a given event, simply because they get easily bored or constantly need new experiences. By contrast, do loyal event goers necessarily have a low level of need for novelty?

If events are memorable, assigned profound personal and social meanings, or somehow transform the individual, then surely this will encourage loyalty or development of an event career. The "event careerist" might be constantly engaged in evaluation and planning for new events. One leads to another, until some point of diminishing returns is reached (i.e., "satiation") or certain constraints (perhaps health) become insurmountable.

Loyalty in the events sector is a tricky concept—it is not at all similar to being loyal to a car brand or a favorite restaurant. For one thing, except for professional sports and regular theatrical productions, most events are unique opportunities. Numerous event-related decisions are never exactly repeated. As well, it is known that many people engage in novelty seeking in travel and leisure, generally preferring something new each time a decision is made.

But event loyalty does exist in some forms. Loyalty to periodic conferences exists, both because of the business or professional advantages and the enjoyment of socializing with friends who always meet there. Many people do go to the same festivals year after year, especially those that have become traditions in their home communities. Hypothetically, event loyalty is likely to result from obtaining specific benefits, especially those related to special interests. Loyalty might also be a lifestyle factor stemming from events that fit one's work life and social calendar.

Serious Leisure, Social World, and Involvement

Leading to a discussion of the event tourist career trajectory, several important theories have to be explained. Combined, they provide a powerful tool for examining and marketing to the most sought-after event tourists, those who travel to many and specific events because of their interests.

Serious Leisure

"Serious leisure" is "the systematic pursuit of an amateur, hobbyist, or volunteer core activity that is highly substantial, interesting, and fulfilling and where, in the typical case, participants find a career in acquiring and expressing a combination of its special skills, knowledge, and experiences" (Stebbins, 1992, p. 3). Pursuing the three forms of serious leisure that Stebbins identified "amateurs, hobbyists, and volunteers" can lead to deep self-fulfillment. Stebbins described it as being similar to pursuing a career, but without the remuneration. Stebbins further argued that serious leisure is distinguished from "casual leisure" by six characteristics: need to persevere in the activity; availability of a leisure career; need to put in effort to gain and utilize specialist skill and knowledge; realization of various special benefits; a unique ethos and social world; and an attractive personal and social identity. Serious leisure is seen as the systematic pursuit, for deep satisfaction that participants find to be substantial and interesting; many devote a major part of their lives to acquiring and expressing the special skills, knowledge and experiences of their serious leisure activity. For many people it brings them great pleasure and satisfaction, as well as providing "personal expression, self-identity enhancement, and self-fulfillment" (Stebbins, 1992, p. 253).

Competitors found in largely nonprofessionalized sports often meet these criteria. The serious leisure career consists of evolving stages and includes turning points, and it is logical to extend the construct to an investigation of the role of events and travel in serious leisure careers. Serious leisure also stresses the "ethos" that members of a given social world share and develop over many years (Stebbins, 2007, p. 12). According to Unruh (1980), and cited by Stebbins, social worlds have characteristic groups, events, routines, practices, and organizations. Stebbins also stressed that "the lifestyle of the participants in a given serious leisure activity expresses their central life interest there and forms the basis for their personal and communal identity" (Stebbins, 2001, p. 53).

Involvement

With regard to leisure, travel, and lifestyle pursuits, it has often been suggested that consumer preferences, behavior, and satisfaction are affected by one's level of involvement with products and pursuits. Havitz and Dimanche (1997) defined "ego-involvement" as "an unobservable state of motivation, arousal or interest toward a recreational activity or associated product, evoked by a particular stimulus or situation and it also has drive properties" (p. 246). How one actually becomes involved is another question, and more difficult to answer. Havitz and Dimanche's (1999) conclusion that strong support has been found for involvement as a mediator of purchases and participation was based on a meta-analysis of 53 leisure involvement studies. The evidence they cited contained little about the link between recreational involvement and travel.

Research evidence supporting the link between involvement and travel includes the study by S. Kim, Scott, and Crompton (1997) of birdwatchers attending a festival. They found that behavioral measures of involvement were substantially more useful in predicting intentions than social-psychological measures of involvement and commitment. Behavioral measures can include frequency of participation, money spent, miles traveled, ability or skill, ownership of related equipment and materials, memberships in clubs, extent of information, and product search.

"Commitment" is a social-psychological construct used to explain consistent behavior. In the context of leisure, it has been defined by S. Kim et al. (1997) as "those personal and behavioral mechanisms that bind individuals to consistent patterns of leisure behavior" (p. 323). Those authors sought to explore commitment in terms of dedication, inner conviction, centrality, costs, and social considerations. According to S. Kim et al., involvement is likely an antecedent of commitment and might be at the root of serious leisure.

The multidimensional view of involvement dominates the literature, and there is strong support for the following three facets of leisure involvement: *attraction,* or the combined enjoyment, interest and importance associated with the activity; *centrality,* or how central the activity is to the individual's lifestyle, and *sign,* or the self-expression value or level of symbolism that the activity represents. Risk is sometimes included in involvement scales, such as those employed by Getz and McConnell (2011) to test participants' level of involvement with mountain biking. The risk element deals with the fact that highly involved event tourists place a higher value on well-run events because they invest so much of themselves (and their money and time) in making event and travel decisions. They really hate it when events are poorly run, and this presumably applies to the risks associated with any of their decisions. To someone less involved the risk of a bad experience might be the same, but not the psychological consequences. Kyle and Chick (2002) developed and tested a widely used, mutidimensional scale, and Kyle, Absher, Norman, Hammitt, and Jodice (2007) later revised their scale to give much greater emphasis to the social aspects of "enduring leisure involvement". Based on research, their new scale included dimensions of attraction, centrality, social bonding, identity expression and identity affirmation.

As another example of the application of involvement theory to travel and events, the chapter by Ryan and Trauer (2005) is noteworthy. They studied a major participant-based, multisport event, for which they believe location is a secondary consideration to the sport tourists. Masters Games attract a large core of sport "enthusiasts" who invest heavily in their athletic pursuits—including travel—and also those who only participate at the local level. They talked about a "career" that leads from local to international competitions. "It can be hypothesized that participants form a degree of involvement with games participation that in part is a confirmation of self-identity as an exponent of a particular sport" (p. 179). The highly involved participants who are willing to travel may be critical for the success of events.

Social Worlds

Unruh (1979, 1980) explained the nature of a social world, including aspects of individual involvement, structural features, and levels of analysis. He acknowledged earlier works of various theorists for his understanding of the "unique character of social worlds as a unit of social organization" (Unruh 1980, p. 276). These social worlds occur without a powerful centralized authority structure and are seen as "amorphous and diffuse constellations of actors, organizations, events, and practices which have coalesced into spheres of interest and involvement for participants" (Unruh 1979, p. 115).

Within social worlds there are four kinds of social actors, each identified by their relative closeness to the activities and knowledge that are vital to the continuance of the social world. Closest in proximity are the insiders who organize the activities and hold the knowledge that is central to their social world. Nearby to the insiders are the regulars who are the consistent participants committed to the continuation of their social world. Further out are the tourists who limit their involvement in the social world to entertainment, profit, and diversion. Finally, at the periphery, are the strangers who influence some aspect of the social world; however, they are not involved in the interests of the social world (Unruh, 1979).

Events are personal occurrences that are important to people who are involved in a social world, such as their first or most prestigious race. However, these can also be events that participants attend, including those planned specifically to attract members of a social world. It is also clear that events are produced by the insiders themselves, as in the case examined by Green and Chalip (1998) with regard to the subcultural identity of female flag footballers.

Members of social worlds meet, participate in clubs, correspond, travel to events, and buy and sell items of value. There is also a symbolic and ritualistic dimension to their practices, reflecting the values or ethos of the social world. This includes signs of membership and status, and prescribed or desired ways of speaking and doing things. Subcultures and other communities of interest tend to develop their own language or to adopt jargonistic terminology that can be an indicator of insider status.

Many organizations can play roles in shaping social worlds and facilitating networking among members: governing bodies and associations that are often hierarchical in nature; corporations that are intent on building brand communities for their own marketing purposes; clubs and teams; tourist organizations attempting to attract groups; events catering to special interests; and publications focused on special interests.

Unruh also produced an analysis of the different levels of social worlds. A local or regional social world might have boundaries, but that is not what defines them—it only shapes their scale and scope. Globally dispersed social worlds have grown enormously since Unruh's treatise, facilitated by travel, a proliferation of planned events (periodic and one-off), and the power of the Internet and other forms of social media that bring like-minded people together.

Research Note on Social Worlds as Generators and Mediators of Event Tourism

Ian Patterson, Ph.D., Associate Professor, and Donald Getz, Ph.D., Professor, School of Tourism, The University of Queensland (with special thanks to Xiang Ying Mei)

In this study we searched specific blogs on the Internet for people who were engaged in serious leisure and lifestyle pursuits, as well as analyzing related websites where information pertaining to these interests was found. The following three serious leisure pursuits were selected: marathon runners, ballroom dancers, and food lovers. Long-distance runners were selected as it was a sport that had previously been researched from the perspective of event tourism and involvement. Ballroom dancing was selected as it is a participatory art form enjoyed both socially and competitively around the world; while food lovers are people who have an ardent or refined interest in food, which has become an important lifestyle pursuit.

For each of the selected pursuits, Google searches revealed a range of websites that were scanned for their relevance, resulting in the selection of 20 sites for each serious leisure pursuit. The researchers used these as the basis for their on-line searches, constructing a grid that was based on Unruh's elements of actors, practices, events, and organizations. Within each of the elements the aim was to discover any evidence of social world activity and the hypothesized links to events and tourism.

The process involved reading and rereading websites to gain a general sense of the themes in the data. This was followed by manual coding: identifying, marking out, and making notes on interesting and recurrent ideas. As a result, the researchers were able to use a comparison method to demonstrate the interactions between bloggers on the sampled sites.

We discovered that there are substantial differences between leisure pursuits and Event Tourism in terms of whether or not competition is essential or optional, and related to pursuits that were normally social versus solitary, yet all pursuits could lead to an event tourism career. Social worlds both generated an interest in events through communications and provided specific opportunities by a variety of actors and organizations. This process is illustrated in Figure 2.4. Although this study was exploratory, it points to potentially unlimited creation of events for an ever-growing number of special leisure interests. Planned events figure prominently in all social worlds and for many involved participants travel becomes an important, and possibly essential, expression of identity within the social world.

The Event Tourist Career Trajectory

In his initial formulation of the "travel career ladder" (later renamed "trajectory"), Pearce (1993) argued that through travel experiences one's motivation and satisfaction will tend to shift from basic relaxation to stimulation/novelty, to relationships, to self-esteem and development, and ultimately to personal fulfillment. In other words, experiences transform travelers so they become more motivated to seek fulfillment of the higher order needs, as theorized in Maslow's (1954) hierarchy of needs. In a more recent article, Pearce and Lee (2005) reexamined the concept and concluded that there exists a core of

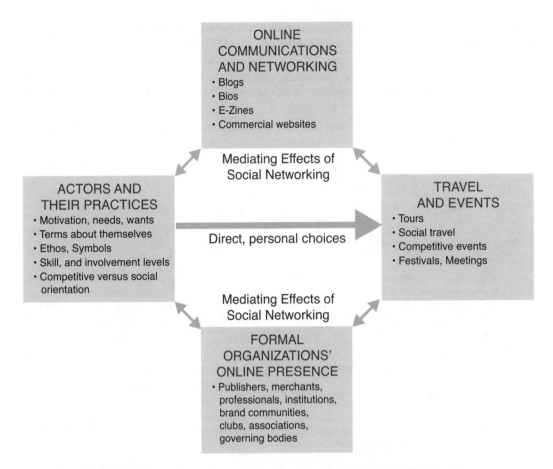

Figure 2.4. The mediating effects of social networking on Event Tourism.

travel motivation factors that include escape, relaxation, relationship enhancement, and self-development that apply to all tourists.

Combining the ideas of serious leisure careers with the notion of a travel motivation trajectory, Getz (2008, p. 416) argued that a travel career trajectory should be more applicable to those with special interests as they become more involved over time; this should especially apply to event tourism. Six dimensions are hypothesized (see Table 2.1). The first dimension is motivation, both the underlying drive to travel and precise motives for specific event experiences. A shift towards pursuit of higher order benefits, corresponding with higher involvement, is hypothesized. Second, travel styles should evolve, as indicated by mode of transport, travel group, length and number of trips—especially to events. It is possible that there will be an increase in mixed-motive trips as involvement progresses, as family holidays get combined with trips to events.

Temporal patterns are expected to change, as event-oriented travel requires adherence to the dates of desired events. The travel of highly involved persons therefore should be less seasonal.

Fourth, it is hypothesized that geographic preferences and patterns should also display a trajectory, such as a progression from local to national and ultimately international travel. This relates mostly to the hierarchical nature of competitive events aimed at special interests. As one gets more involved in a pursuit, the desire to attend bigger, more challenging, unique, or prestigious events also might increase. Variety and novelty seeking

Table 2.1. Dimensions of the Hypothetical Event Tourist Career Trajectory and Empirical Evidence

Dimensions and Hypothetical Trajectory	Possible Measures	Evidence From the TransRockies Study
Motivations: the more involved participants become in a serious leisure pursuit, the more they will pursue higher order benefits	Determine the participants' benefits sought and needs met in terms of relaxation, stimulation/novelty, relationship, self-esteem, and personal development or fulfillment	The most important motives for these mostly highly involved mountain bikers were athleticism and excitement. The top individual motivator was challenge. Social motives and extrinsic rewards were not as important. They take great pleasure in competing and spend huge amounts of time and money on their sport.
Travel style: there should be an increase in event tourism incorporating family and destination vacations, resulting in more long-distance travel by air	Transport mode, travel group, length of event trips, event-specific or mixed-motive trips	TransRockies Challenge participants were mostly males traveling without spouses or families. The nature of this event, being in remote and rugged terrain, makes it quite different from the majority of sport events.
Temporal: higher involvement should be reflected in greater frequency of event participation, and less seasonality of demand (because events are the attraction)	Measure the frequency and timing (seasonality) of participation in events	Participants in this event were frequent competitors and attended many events, including, for many of them, a portfolio of similarly challenging pursuits.
Spatial: there should be a progression from local to international; distance traveled to events should increase	Local, regional, national, and international events traveled to	About half were long-distance tourists, many from outside the country. They traveled because of this event.
Event types: variety/novelty seeking should become more apparent, along with a higher emphasis on uniqueness, challenge, and prestige	Assess events in terms of their level of competition, uniqueness, branding, quality	Their motives indicated they were novelty seekers. They hate poorly organized events and seek out challenge.
Destination criteria: destination choices are increasingly made because of their events; attractive destinations have a comparative advantage	Where events are held and their overall attractiveness for holidays as well as events; the uniqueness or iconic appeal of the event host destination; packaging of events, or "bundling"	Participants selected this uniquely positioned event, but in combination with attractive mountain scenery.

would particularly apply to the most highly involved and travel experienced. Finally, the choice of travel destination should increasingly reflect the previous five dimensions, with some destinations being selected because of events, and attractive destinations being more successful with their events when compared to less attractive host areas.

Testing and refinement of this theory-in-development will require multiple methods and comparative studies, including longitudinal research over the careers of persons engaged in serious leisure and sport tourism. As well, comparisons of highly involved and the lesser involved will be very useful. In the first TransRockies Challenge research (Getz & McConnell, 2011) it was found that mostly highly involved athletes were surveyed, thereby providing a limited but valuable assessment of the six hypothetical stages. Subsequent research on amateur distance runners (Getz & Andersson, 2010) has confirmed the existence of event travel careers and the value of employing the trajectory construct. Other researchers are using the career trajectory concept to examine different sports (see the ensuing research profile of triathletes by Lamont, Kennelly, and Moyle).

Expert Opinion on Triathlon Event Travel Careers and Leisure Constraints

Dr. Matthew Lamont is a Lecturer in the School of Tourism and Hospitality Management, Southern Cross University, Australia. Aside from his Ph.D. research, Matt has also worked as a research consultant and project manager with the Australian Regional Tourism Research Centre.

Dr. Millicent Kennelly is a Lecturer in the Department of Tourism, Leisure, Hotel and Sport Management at Griffith University, specializing in event and project management. Millicent has been researching and teaching in event management, with a specific focus on sport events, since 2004.

Dr. Brent Moyle is a Postdoctoral Research Fellow in the School of Tourism & Hospitality Management, Southern Cross University.

Triathlon is a burgeoning sport in many developed nations. Its popularity is congruent with a boom in mass participation sporting events such as distance running, cycling, ocean swimming, and adventure racing. The growth of triathlon is demonstrated by the Noosa Triathlon, held in Noosa Heads, Queensland, Australia, which is regarded as the largest triathlon in the Southern Hemisphere. The Noosa Triathlon first attracted 180 competitors in 1983 and by 2011 had grown to 8,500 competitors, (USM Events, 2011). As a result of this increased growth specialist travel agencies (such as TriTravel in Australia, Endurance Sports Travel in the US, and Sports Tours International in the UK) now exist, specifically catering for triathletes traveling to events around the globe. However, despite this exponential growth, little research exists that explains this boom in travel to mass participation events such as triathlon.

Triathlon combines the three sports of swimming, cycling, and running into a single event. Participants must sequentially and seamlessly "transition" between each discipline to complete an event. It is a physically demanding sport requiring high levels of aerobic fitness, necessitating sustained physical training to develop and maintain the required conditioning. Participants who commit to competing in triathlons on an ongoing basis typically accept a significant lifestyle shift as they integrate training sessions into their day-to-day routine (McCarville, 2007). Atkinson's (2008) study of amateur triathletes in Canada found that athletes trained between 4 and 6 days per week, spending on average 14.5 hours weekly training for competition.

There is scope for amateur triathletes to engage in an event travel career (ETC) because there are a wide range of triathlon event formats, events of varying "status" within the triathlon social world, and there is a global calendar of events. For example, short, high-intensity "sprint" triathlons can be as short as a 400-m swim, 20-km cycle, and 5-km run. At the other end of the spectrum, the Ironman triathlon consists of a 3.8-km swim, 180-km cycle, and 42.2-km (full-length marathon) run leg. A plethora of event distances exists between sprint and Ironman triathlon. The difficulty of events may also vary due to course terrain and prevailing weather conditions. As most individual triathlon events are held only on an annual basis, supply of events is limited and geographically dispersed. Thus, it is often necessary for triathletes to travel extensively within the course of a season if they wish to compete regularly, or if they are targeting particular race formats (Lamont & Kennelly, 2011).

Pursuing an ETC in triathlon can be resource intensive and can consume an individual's personal resources such as time, money, and energy (Lamont, Kennelly, & Wilson, 2012). Some ETCs may consume more personal resources than others, to the point where the ETC adds an additional and significant element to an individual's life and social identity. Individuals also require personal resources to satisfy other day-to-day priorities and obligations (such as at work or within their family). Therefore, research investigating the constraints faced by participants is important, not only for theory development around ETCs, but in informing key stakeholders (particularly event organizers, triathlon coaches, and clubs) about the circumstances surrounding people's participation in triathlon events. Implications may be drawn regarding how events are timed, delivered, and priced. Further implications may be drawn for the way individual athletes go about managing busy lifestyles to sustain their participation.

A study conducted in 2010 examined amateur triathletes' perceived constraints to ongoing participation in a triathlon ETC. Qualitative interviews were conducted with 21 amateur athletes pursuing an ETC in triathlon. Interviews were conducted in northern New South Wales and South East Queensland, Australia. The study found that these athletes faced a range of "competing priorities," or conundrums in effectively distributing their personal resources (e.g., time, money, energy) between their day-to-day obligations (such as work, family, personal care, etc.) and their ETC. These competing priorities were experienced in the domains of familial relationships, domestic responsibilities, sociability, finances, leisure, well-being, and work/education (see Lamont et al., 2012).

Space precludes a detailed discussion of these competing priority domains, however, to illustrate this concept a brief example will suffice. "Kate," a committed amateur triathlete, is married with two young children. She described the challenges of arranging childcare to enable her to train and attend events. Kate also noted difficulties in having only limited leisure time, which needed to be apportioned between training for/attending events and spending quality time with her husband and children. She also explained that the expenses associated with equipment, training, and travel to triathlons meant that her limited financial resources could not extend to other luxuries such as family holidays.

Broadly, this study found that amateur triathletes make significant sacrifices in various parts of their life to pursue an ETC. Some key implications for event managers and stakeholders in host communities can be drawn from these findings, such as:

- Triathlon event organizers should educate host community stakeholders about the participant base an event is likely to attract. For example, it is common for accommodation providers to impose minimum stays well in excess of an event's duration. This study found that triathletes travel to and participate in events on the basis of limited resources, and excessive minimum stays can conflict with athletes' needs for only short-term accommodation. Failure to cater to these needs may result in negative destination image and stifle repeat visitation for an event, especially if a destination develops a reputation for price gouging or unreasonable accommodation booking conditions.
- Event organizers should acknowledge that promoting events that consume significant personal resources to participate in can also impact upon participants' significant others. Participation often occurs as a result of compromises and/or sacrifices that participants' family members may or may not be amenable to. Consequently, efforts should be made to ensure the event experience is enjoyable not only for participants, but also for their entourage. Designing an event to include and engage athletes' family members may involve simple measures such as ensuring easy access to food and beverages and providing adequate shelter. Providing access, and possibly transport, to on-course vantage points may also help entourage see their athlete more frequently throughout the event and ameliorate long intervals of waiting. Further, event organizers might liaise with local tourism bodies to identify means of keeping athletes' entourage entertained at the destination while participants are occupied preparing for, and competing in the event.

Summary and Study Guide

A shift towards the demand-side approach in Event Tourism requires some background theory and lots of market intelligence. Compare Figures 1.7 and 2.1. The first diagram illustrates the four main sectors of Event Tourism as it is normally practiced, with venues in the core and types of events to the outside. This can be used as a starting point to think about portfolios, Event Tourism development, and where demand comes from. In the supply-side approach the emphasis will be placed on marketing and selling existing venues and events, plus ad hoc bidding. In an integrated, demand-side approach the markets are what counts, and that is the starting point in Figure 2.1. However you define the markets (the figure suggests five, but they can all be subdivided), you have to learn as much as you can about them, then translate that knowledge into creation of an integrated strategy and balanced portfolio of events. The need for new events, bidding, and venues arises from this knowledge. Of course, in reality, a combination of both approaches will coexist.

Forces and trends were examined, with the conclusion that those forces propelling growth in event tourism will continue for a substantial period of time. In strategic planning it is always necessary to scan environmental forces and understand trends. Opportunities for competitive advantage arise for those who detect trends early on.

Since there is virtually unlimited potential for catering to the needs and preferences of an ever-growing number of special interests in sports, hobbies, arts, and lifestyle pursuits, destinations seeking competitive advantages must understand how to go about catering to their needs. The results can lead to creating events that are Iconic within social worlds, or bidding on events that appeal to known segments. The starting point is to understand the different types of event tourists, and direct versus induced demand. We come back to these essentials when considering evaluation and impacts in later chapters.

A consumer decision-making model was presented, beginning with a theoretical discussion of needs and motivation. There are differences between events that appeal to intrinsic motives (freely chose, for leisure and self-development benefits) and extrinsically motivated travel that stems from obligation or rewards tied to business and work. Yet they can overlap and mix, as when business travelers extend their trips for holidays, or bring families along. Event designers also know that they have to satisfy the social and entertainment needs of all attendees, regardless of the event type. This model also introduces the concepts of constraints and substitution.

In the rest of this chapter theory and research are presented, with examples, to illustrate how knowledge of serious leisure, involvement and social worlds can reveal much about why and how people travel to events. The event tourist career trajectory can help explain why some events are destination events for interest groups, and why some become Iconic. Social networking mediates the process, as people with common interests are constantly interacting with each other and with organizations (including events and destination) that link to them in meaningful ways.

Pay particular attention to the contributions, first of Senior Games by Heather Gibson, then the Voss Extreme Sports Festival by Reidar Mykletun, and the Expert Opinion piece by Matthew Lamont, Millicent Kennelly, and Brent Moyle.

These all provide detailed understanding of quite different segments of amateur athletes as target markets. Event developers and marketers need exactly this kind of insight to create and sell their "destination events." The fact that they are all sport examples reflects the dominance of sport-related research, not importance. The contribution by Ian Pattersson and myself on social networking demonstrates the importance of social worlds as mediators of Event Tourism in all serious leisure pursuits.

Study Questions

- Explain the "demand side approach" and contrast it with the traditional supply-side approach.
- What are the five main "markets"? How would you break down the leisure and business event markets into subsegments?
- How does "service-dominant logic" relate to the demand-side approach? Where does "cocreation" fit? Give an example of a "value proposition."
- Give examples of "propelling and constraining forces," within the general concept of "globalization."
- What are "festivalization" and "legitimation" processes and how do they shape Event Tourism?
- In the context of explaining "direct and induced demand," give examples of different kinds of event tourists (start with "dedicated").
- Illustrate and explain the consumer decision-making model for event tourism; define all key terms. Explain why constraints and substitution are important. What makes events "attractive"?
- Discuss motivational theory, including seeking–escaping, and the relevance of intrinsic versus extrinsic motivators.
- What needs are met by attending events? Are they different for spectators and participants?
- Explain how serious leisure, involvement, and social world theory shape our understanding of event tourism demand.
- Show how social networking mediates leisure and event tourism.
- Explain the event tourist career trajectory and illustrate the key hypotheses by referring to actual research findings (e.g., triathletes).

Additional Readings

- *Eventful Cities* (Richards & Palmer, 2010).
- *Consumer Behaviour in Tourism* (Swarbrooke & Horner, 2007).
- *The Tourism and Leisure Experience: Consumer and Managerial Perspectives* (Morgan, Lugosi, & Ritchie, Eds., 2010).
- *Marketing of Tourism Experiences* (Scott, Laws, & Boksberger, 2010).
- *Serious Leisure: A Perspective for Our Time* (Stebbins, 2007).

Chapter 3

Planning for Event Tourism:
The Destination Perspective

Learning Objectives

Upon completion of this chapter the student should understand and be able to explain the following:

1. Who is making policy and formulating strategy for events and tourism, and why.
2. Possible roles and strategic options of DMOs, tourism, and event agencies.
3. "Bottom-up" versus "top-down" planning and development.
4. "Comparative and competitive advantages" and how they lead to strategy.
5. The "supply-side approach" and generic strategies.
6. Event Tourism strategic planning process including vision, goals, and objectives.
7. Research to support planning and strategy, including "SWOT" analysis.
8. Stakeholder input.
9. Capacity building.
10. How cities, regions, and nations plan and develop Event Tourism.

Introduction

Our focus in this chapter is on destination-level planning for Event Tourism, and this includes individual cities, regions and countries. The first issue is that of who does it, namely the DMOs and event development or bidding agencies that are at work on some aspects of Event Tourism. Normally the responsibility lies with a DMO, but their mandates are typically too narrow to achieve the full potential of an integrated approach. Bidding agencies are similarly limited in their mandate, usually focusing on either/or conventions and sport events. Some event development agencies are comprehensive, but even those will have to reconsider their roles and priorities when it comes to creating and managing balanced portfolios.

A part of the discussion on who does what is the issue of top-down versus bottom-up planning and development. Top-down is the usual, and often it is conducted in secrecy or without full public accountability. What is being advocated in this book is a bottom-up approach that engages all the stakeholders, liberates innovation, and provides full accountability. This too requires a major change in the way things are usually done.

We then examine the possible roles of government, DMOs, or event development agencies in the planning and development process. These include venue development and sales, bidding, creating and owning events, sponsorship and taking equity in events, or assistance to the events sector, which can involve anything from passive moral support to aggressive financial assistance.

Sources of comparative and competitive advantages are introduced, with the argument that destinations cannot rely on their legacy, or what they have inherited. It is essential in a competitive world to invest in professionalism, market intelligence, venues, bidding, and marketing for Event Tourism. New forms of organization might very well be required, and new adaptive, strategies. An integrative, sustainable approach featuring portfolios is a growing necessity. As part of this discussion of who does what, and potential roles, the supply-side development approach is elaborated upon, including some generic strategies that can be pursued.

The chapter then turns to the strategic planning process, starting with vision, goals, and objectives, then strategy development. Stakeholder input and capacity building are stressed as is the research needed to support planning. A major case study of EventScotland demonstrates in detail how Event Tourism is being planned and developed at the national level. In the next chapter we shift to an emphasis on actual development actions, including the sales and bidding processes, venue development, and marketing and branding.

Who Does Event Tourism Planning and Development?

Most Event Tourism planning and development occurs at the city and local level, as this is where destination marketing organizations do their sales and bidding, events are held, venues are built, and the event tourism experiences mostly occur. The exceptions are state- or national-level events development corporations, and there is a growing number of them active in Event Tourism planning and development. However, most senior levels of government and their development or bidding agencies play support roles. For mega-events, the national government will have to participate in terms of investments and underwriting potential losses. Events can be awarded to nations, but appropriate local hosts must be found.

Heeley (2011) categorized city tourist organizations in Europe, and these pretty much define the global situation as well. There are city leisure tourism bureaus, convention bureaus, and marketing boards, which are differentiated on the degree to which they are responsible for attracting and servicing one or both of the leisure and business event forms of tourism. In addition, Heeley points to the existence of city marketing organizations, including city branding authorities, those seeking inward investment and dealing with business development, all-purpose marketing agencies, and combinations of these.

In this book DMO is a generic term that refers to any organization or agency with marketing responsibilities, and this might include events development, whereas event development agency is used for those event-dedicated agencies that bid, facilitate, and produce events for tourism and place-marketing purposes.

Top-Down Versus Bottom-Up

Top-down planning and policy-making and development strategy is the norm in many countries and destinations, relying on one central or powerful authority to set the vision, make the plans, and try to ensure they are implemented. This state of affairs reflects the dominant role that governments have played in tourism development and the fact that cities typically leave tourism marketing to industry bodies or industry–public partnerships (the DMO). Although no research has been done on this, I would say that most countries, states, and cities have not gone beyond an ad hoc approach to Event Tourism, so when we talk about top-down versus bottom-up it might be irrelevant in many places.

Traditional, top-down planning and decision making has a number of serious flaws, including:

- it is increasingly viewed as being unresponsive to changes in the marketplace;
- is relatively ineffective when it comes to realizing the competitive potential of private enterprise;
- is based on the belief that tourism can be controlled and predictable;
- is ineffective in stimulating innovation and entrepreneurship;
- actors conduct business in isolation, avoiding cooperative strategies and encouraging potential growth to identify new target markets;
- ineffective actions and/or money being used for actions that they should not;
- ignorance and neglect of local and small entrepreneurs or the visitor experience;
- competition occurs over money and duplication, or overlapping actions between different tourist organizations;
- a lot of bureaucracy and resulting dissent among stakeholders.

Tourism plans do not always work, simply because tourism is too complex for the deterministic model implied by a strategic plan. Does this mean there should not be top-down planning?

In contrast is the bottom-up approach, in which many stakeholders participate, decision making is diffuse, strategies emerge from successful innovations and practices, and no one presumes to know exactly what is best for everyone else. It is characterized by the following (some of which might represent wishful thinking, as research evidence is slim):

- it is more attuned to a demand orientation and niche marketing;
- rapid adaptation to market conditions at the local/regional and network levels;
- liberating of innovation processes among entrepreneurs and organizations;
- emergent strategy, not control;
- open communication, widespread participation, and tolerance;
- networking and learning system;
- clusters form around competitive advantages, in particular places;
- local product clubs enable innovation and sharing;
- visitor experiences are given priority, not the sale of products.

It is not so much a program as a philosophy, so whatever the existing framework for tourism policy, planning, and development, a more bottom-up approach can be implemented to some degree. There are steps that need to be taken, but it is not a regimented system. It should be research driven, with market intelligence to suit the needs of innovators. Most innovation will come from the local level, from new networks and collaborations, from entrepreneurs. New experiences, not existing products, have to be created.

While a national-level tourism strategy is useful, especially for establishing the importance of tourism in the economy and society, and more particularly for creating funding and research/information programs, in a bottom-up approach the emphasis shifts towards strategies that emerge from successful initiatives. This recognizes that it is difficult or impossible to predict what will work in the future, or what new opportunities can be seized by an innovative, dynamic tourism sector. For Event Tourism, the top-down initiatives should include:

- policy, planning, strategy as support platforms, not mandates;
- funding (various forms of financial assistance);
- research to support special interest, demand-side initiatives;
- national- and regional-level event bids;
- support for local bids and other initiatives;
- enhance learning networks;
- foster globally competitive clusters where potential is high;
- pursue special interest segments; form product clubs.

Development Roles of Government, DMOs, and Event Development Agencies

Assuming the government wants to intervene for various policy reasons (see the discussion of justifications in Chapter 1), what are its options? They range from direct involvement, acting as an entrepreneur and event producer (potentially at a huge cost), to merely providing advice and moral support (at little or no cost). Entering into public–private partnerships is increasingly popular, especially to pay for expensive infrastructure. Combining facility development with urban renewal schemes often makes intervention more justifiable, and crouching it in terms of economic development helps sell the argument that some degree of public investment is needed and wise. We consider these arguments more fully when discussing venues in the next chapter.

More and more public agencies and DMOs are engaging in entrepreneurial activities when it comes to tourism and economic development, including venue construction and event development/ownership. Setting up a marketing body or events development unit within government is a clear indicator of entrepreneurship in the public sphere, whereas the same initiatives within a DMO might appear to be purely an industry operation. There are five major roles that an agency can play in the development of the events sector, and it is likely that some combination of these will be implemented (see Figure 3.1).

Venues and Sales: These actions dominate in supply-side development, especially with regard to sports and business events. Venues are considered in each of the chapters dealing with sports (Chapter 6) and business events (Chapter 7), while the sales process is considered in Chapter 5.

Producing and Owning Events: For a DMO or city to become an event owner and producer (see the cases of Visit Denver and Gold Coast Events) has certain advantages:

- control of the theme, timing, program, and setting;
- relieving the burden from community groups;
- raising money; controlling admission prices;
- enhancing the agency's image;
- ensuring professionalism and quality.

Sponsoring or Taking Equity in Events: A degree of ownership, or equity, can be taken in events while still leaving the production and management mostly or entirely to a partner. This kind of joint venture most likely will arise when either the agency or event organizers lack the resources to produce an event on their own, and where the agency believes its own goals can be met without exercising total control. A contract should stipulate exact obligations, risks and potential benefits

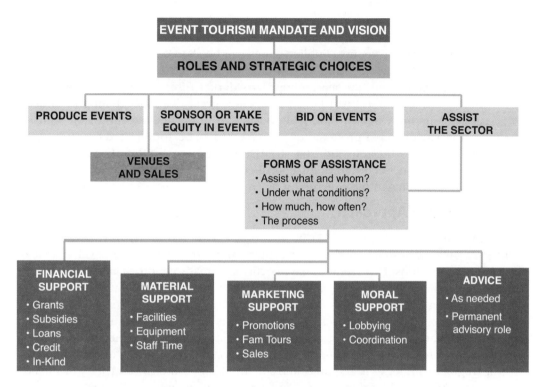

Figure 3.1. Roles and strategic choices in developing Event Tourism
(adapted from Getz & Frisby, 1991).

(especially of costs and revenues) accruing to each party. Sponsorship is similar, but like any corporation, the city or destination agency merely gains exposure and certain other rights, without control (or responsibility). Tourist agencies and local authorities can realize substantial benefits through selected sponsorship in events by helping organizers financially. A tourist organization can exhibit at events, boost its profile through promotions and imagery, and capture the event database for future targeted promotions.

Bidding on Events: A separate agency for bidding is not essential, but does enhance professionalism and the likelihood of success. We explore bidding in detail in the next chapter, including its role in creating a balanced portfolio.

Assisting the Events Sector (Facilitation): A number of forms of direct and indirect assistance can be provided to the events sector: financial, material, marketing, moral, and advice. Financial assistance, beyond ownership and sponsorship, can include grants, subsidies (e.g., free use of facilities), loans, lines of credit, and in-kind donations. Other forms of material assistance can include the provision of equipment, staff persons (as volunteers, or seconded to events) and the use of offices. There are some cities that charge events for services like police and inspection, and others that consider these costs to be important subsidies to the event and tourism sectors. What's the reason for this split? It is partly ideology, sometimes a lack of resources, and maybe ignorance. The industry has an obligation to educate the public and politicians. Political leadership and expressed support for Event Tourism can be useful, especially as a starting point for future action. Often local and senior levels of government are directly involved with DMOs so support is at least implicit. Facilitation could include support for the sector through such means as doing research, joint marketing efforts, organizing festival and event networks, or coordination of schedules and use of public venues. Public venues can be shared, and marketed as tourist attractions. Marketing support can take the form of joint or free promotions, and assistance with the marketing plan. Market research and the provision of timely, useful reports will help managers a great deal. Moral support should, at a minimum, extend to lobbying on behalf of events and the Event Tourism sector. The giving of professional advice will also be appreciated by many event managers and the tour industry. Tourist agencies or local authorities can also aid the events sector through coordination, ranging from the production of event schedules to the overseeing or creation of an event association.

An Evolutionary Approach

William O'Toole (2011, pp. 10–11) in his book *Events Feasibility and Development: From Strategy to Operations*, outlined an evolutionary approach to the development of events policy in nations. This seems to have occurred in many countries including Canada, Scotland, Australia, and South Africa. In Stage 1, which he called "disparate event growth," events develop in a haphazard way because there is no strategy. However, existing events will likely meet resident and business needs. Stage 2 is "national event support," and with the establishment of a national strategy and facilitation, expertise and quality should improve, signature events get created, and goals become aligned with national priorities. Next, a "regional strategy" is required and an "industry" established. This will include events associations, bidding on events, and training programs. An "industry" like this should be able to support itself, and will be accompanied by university-level education, professional standards, and development opportunities.

It appears that a number of countries have deliberately implemented an events "industrialization" process, starting with very little on the ground and aiming to grow Event Tourism as quickly as possible—in effect creating instant event destinations. Massive investment is required in venues and other infrastructure, and as O'Toole (2011) points out, this has to be accompanied by investment in expertise and professionalism.

An example of event and Event Tourism support is that of the Province of Alberta, Canada. Assistance programs are typically hierarchical, and in Canada the national government is concerned primarily with international mega-events that it must underwrite and sanction. Cities have policies and programs that mix culture, social and economic goals.

Government of Alberta: Tourism, Parks, and Recreation (2012): Festivals and Events Tourism Growth Program (www.tpr.alberta.ca)

The Festivals and Events Tourism Growth Program aims to increase tourism revenues and visitation in Alberta by investing in established festivals and events demonstrating potential for tourism growth.

Organizations will be selected through a competitive application process to receive funding of $25,000 to $40,000 each to hire a third-party consultant. The amount will be determined by the scope and location of the festival or event. The consultant will work with the organization and its stakeholders to evaluate the event, identify tourism growth opportunities, and develop a Festival/Event Tourism Growth Plan.

As result of the program, Alberta festivals and events with high tourism growth potential will commit to meeting targets, for the following year, to increase attendance by 10%, increase revenues by 10%, and enhance the quality and quantity of programming by 20%.

Expert Opinion

Event Policy and the Creative Place: A Case Study From Scotland (Dr. David McGillivray and Professor Gayle McPherson, University of the West of Scotland)

In our book *Event Policy: From Theory to Strategy* (Foley, McGillivray, & McPherson (2011) we argued that over the last century events have moved from being somewhat "unplanned"—or at least not as clearly "created" for a specific purpose—to the point where they are planned by "experts" with intended outcomes in mind. These outcomes are so powerful that they can alter the very fabric of the event, as originally conceived. This is important, because, from the point of view of local and central government officials in an urban entrepreneurial policy environment, events are increasingly deemed unsupportable unless they achieve economic, social, cultural, and environmental goals. In the 1980s and 1990s the civic boosters created fantasy cities investing in iconic architecture, festival marketplaces, cultural quarters, convention and exhibition centers alongside a renewed focus on the value of sporting and cultural events. The function and form, temporal and spatial dimensions of events supported by city leaders also changed fundamentally. Unique features of existing festivals and events were marketed to attract the global tourist and cities started to compete to host peripatetic sporting and cultural events—often with little or no resonance with the host city. Externalities reigned—events were worth growing or creating if they could contribute to economic development, cultural vibrancy, quality of life, image making, or even health (e.g., sporting events). If they were not, then public investment (whether in the form of direct delivery or subsidy) was unlikely.

In the agrarian, preindustrial period, events were inseparable from the rhythms of the calendar, occurring on a cyclical basis (e.g., feasts, fairs, rituals, holidays). The events of the day were ritualistic celebrations of the impending harvest, of the arrival of summer, or of the passing of time. In this sense, events played an important collective social role, linking communities (e.g., farmers) together in important symbolic celebrations and commemorations. There existed an abundance of fairs and festivals, invested with significant localized *meanings* and, in the main, free of external governance. In place of the relatively unplanned, episodic and amorphous fairs and festivals comes the *disciplined spontaneity* wrought by modern planning, turning "symbolic spaces into functional spaces for maximising consumption and facilitating transit" (Edensor, 1998, p. 213). Events now play a multitude of functions, some demonstrating continuity with the past (e.g., celebration, commemoration, community cohesion, and control) and some intimating a new role (e.g., image enhancement, economic regeneration or development, media expansion, and social cause promotion). There exists a shift from events that were ritualistic in nature, fixed in time and space, and deriving their importance from that stability, longevity, and continuity to events conceived and exploited for regenerative imperatives that venerate the new, the transitory, the contrived, the nomadic and moveable nature of celebrations to secure a plethora of social, political, and economic externalities. Many events are now spatially and temporally decontextualized, infinitely portable to new locations and times in the name of securing planned outcomes. They are, like other areas of cultural life, administratively planned.

In policy terms, a cursory glance at recent developments in Scotland provides an illustration of the changes afoot. In Scotland, two quasi nongovernmental bodies, EventScotland and Creative Scotland, have played a significant role in attracting event-based tourism visitation to the country. EventScotland was established in 2003 with the aim of strengthening and promoting Scotland's events industry, attracting, generating and sustaining a portfolio of world-class events in Scotland, helping this small nation to compete successfully in an increasingly international market place and aligned with its strategy "Scotland The Perfect Stage." This strategy was designed to attract international visitation and investment around a calendar of sporting, cultural and business events. It emphasizes the importance of working collaboratively with other governmental and nongovernmental agencies to develop a strong event portfolio, across different genres and to invest to grow the existing product as well as securing new events. Furthermore, Creative Scotland, the national arts and creative agency, has also set out its stall to position Scotland as a Festival Nation by 2020, playing a crucial role in developing the cultural events product in collaboration with EventScotland, VisitScotland, and the Scottish government to make sure the nation's cultural assets are exploited to attract international visits and, crucially, to foster a culturally vibrant nation containing places rich in artistic activity. Although using events to attract higher value international visitors, both EventScotland and Creative Scotland have also shown a commitment to developing the existing, home-grown product to sustain the wider cultural and sporting infrastructure. Their aim is to export this talent, further showcasing the highlights of Scottish talent internationally. EventScotland has a national and regional events investment program and Creative Scotland has supported the development of Creative Places (many of which are built around a festivals and events agenda) to celebrate the unique cultural heritage and contemporary artistic value of Scottish towns and cities.

In event terms, the Scottish case at one level exemplifies an international trend towards the exploitation of events and festivals to generate economic value in a postindustrial environment. However, on another level, Scotland's investment in regional and national programs can be viewed as a response to the threat of *diminishing uniqueness*, which "places" across the world face as event competition intensifies. The globalized ubiquity of festivals for food and drink, comedy, music, arts, gay pride, and, of course, sport means that "distinctiveness gets reduced to a formula" (Hassan, Mean, & Tims, 2007, p. 35). While there remain many examples of predominantly "local" festivities across the world, in intense interurban competition, cities share formats and often bid for events not because of some intimate connection or "roots" to the locality but out of an economic necessity to draw media coverage and mobile capital in the form of tourism. The challenge for proponents of events as meaningful social entities is that spaces dripping with meaning are, in the name of regenerative and consumerist logic, surveyed, monitored, and normalized to secure the sort of policy outcomes that public investment demands. Perhaps by investing in the unique cultural (and sporting) assets of the nation, locality and distinctiveness, marked by the nature of the celebration, who organized it and who attended it can be reenergized to the benefit of the Scottish nation.

Comparative and Competitive Advantages (see Table 3.1)

In their book, *The Competitive Destination: A Sustainable Tourism Perspective*, J. R. B. Ritchie and Crouch (2003) explain how both comparative and competitive advantages must be cultivated. This is a useful starting point for thinking about Event Tourism planning and policy as it requires the planners and policy makers to undertake some research, make comparisons, and formulate strategies to gain advantages and move forward. While comparative advantages pertain to a destination's legacy, or heritage of assets and resources, competitive advantages stem from what destinations consciously do to improve their position.

Comparative advantages accrue from what you inherit; they include location, geography, climate, natural resources, or events and organizations that have evolved along with historical development of an area. Culture is included, and for Event Tourism cultural resources are a major source of authenticity and therefore can yield an advantage.

Probably the most important competitive advantage will come from a concerted effort to develop plans and policy for event tourism. Many cities and destinations pursue occasional bids in an ad hoc manner, while others develop infrastructure for events without a coordinated plan involving all the stakeholders. In Australia, competitive advantages have been gained at the international scale through organizational development, as each Australia State has an event development corporation.

Note that every comparative advantage listed in the figure implies a disadvantage if you do not have it. When doing a competitive SWOT analysis (strengths, weaknesses, opportunities, and threats) these have to be taken into account. It should also be emphasized that some disadvantages can be dealt with, but some cannot be overcome or reversed—you

Table 3.1. Comparative and Competitive Advantages

	Comparative Advantages: What Destinations Inherit	Competitive Advantages: How Destinations Compete
Location and accessibility	Large resident population. Proximity to major market areas. Easy accessibility by road, water, air to the destination. Easy movement for visitors within the city/destination.	Investment in transport infrastructure. Cultivation of resident demand for events. Research on nearby markets, including benchmarking.
Climate	A climate attractive to tourists and favorable for certain activities and events.	Investment in indoor venues. Emphasize winter or summer sports/activities.
Accommodation	Adequate for major events, and simultaneous events. International standard. Attached or close to major event venues.	Encouraging private sector investment Facilitating complexes of venues with accommodation (e.g., event districts).
Built attractions	A diverse portfolio of built attractions for all-year demand and as venues for events. A concentration of attractions and event venues (event or entertainment or sport districts).	New attractions with international appeal. Flexible, multiuse design.
Culture	Friendly and hospitable for visitors. A tradition of volunteering. Authentic traditions expressed through events.	Arts and cultural venues. Programs of financial assistance. Technical and marketing assistance.
Economy	Cost advantages; low inflation. Strong local businesses.	Yield management. Overcoming seasonality of demand. Capitalizing on local business strengths. Low taxes. Packaging events for cost saving and perceived value.
Social conditions	A healthy, open resident population. Strong civil society (the voluntary sector). Political support for events. Strong participation rates in sports and other leisure pursuits.	Education of residents as to the benefits of Event Tourism. Permanent volunteer programs and a related training legacy. Participation incentives for sports, arts, leisure.
Health conditions	Healthy residents. Ability to deal with health emergencies and scares, including at events.	All venues co-managed for resident use. Educational programs at events. Foster healthy lifestyles through events. Position the destination for healthy living.

(continued)

Table 3.1. Comparative and Competitive Advantages (continued)

	Comparative Advantages: What Destinations Inherit	Competitive Advantages: How Destinations Compete
Professionalism	Education/training available for event management and event tourism. Professional associations and standards.	Industry–education linkages strengthened. Mentorship and apprenticeship programs.
Prosperous and supportive businesses	Successful for-profit events. A legacy of philanthropy and event sponsorship. Established tradition of public–private partnerships.	Leveraging events for maximum local benefits. Incentives for private investment and for-profit events.
Events	Existing Hallmark events that are popular with residents and tourists alike. A healthy portfolio of permanent local and regional events. A tradition of organizations organizing and bidding on events. A successful track record in bidding and hosting one-time events.	Build on local strengths to create Hallmark events. Sophisticated portfolio creation and management. Learning organizations employing market intelligence.
Event venues	Indoor and outdoor venues for high-quality events of many types, all-year round. Good use of venues by residents.	Justified as public goods and supported by local institutions, businesses, and residents.

cannot easily turn from a winter to a summer destination. This suggests that in some areas it is best to make do with what you have and build on it.

The list of competitive actions can be summarized as follows, and strategies are suggested by each of these:

- organization and professionalism: DMO or event development agency; leadership, vision, partnerships, collaboration, strategic approach, creativity;
- investment: venues, infrastructure, bidding, research, feasibility tested; balanced portfolio for animation and all-year benefits; bidding and owning events; leveraging events; legacies;
- marketing: branding and positioning; effective, targeted communications;
- intelligence through research and evaluation; learning organizations; planning for sustainability; benchmarking
- expertise and professionalism, competence, innovation, quality.

Supply-Side Approach and Strategies

We have already established that supply-side approaches are the norm, and I have advocated a demand-side emphasis for new, competitive advantages. Now let's look more closely at supply-based strategies, particularly as they follow from the discussion of comparative and competitive advantages. In Figure 3.2 existing facilities, venues, and events are the starting point, and each has to be marketed to Event Tourists. The marketing includes both sales and bidding. The general aim is to make efficient use of facilities and

Figure 3.2. Supply-side approach.

add value to existing events through tourism. Inevitably, consideration will periodically be given to expansion of the supply of events and venues as a city or destination decides it needs growth or renewed competitiveness—or in response to the fact that facilities age and grow obsolete. Even the needs of residents, as populations grow, require constant planning for changes in the system.

In Table 3.2 the fundamentals of supply-side management and strategies are shown, emphasizing facilities, sales, bidding, and marketing of what you have. As soon as the destination decides this is insufficient, it either has to expand its supply or progress to more of a demand-side approach.

Supply-Side Strategies

Community-Based, Sustainable Event Tourism

This particular strategy is considered by many to be more sustainable than all the others. It consists of a low-cost emphasis on community events, the marketing of existing events, and efficient utilization of existing venues. There will be no large-scale events or venues built for one-time events. Probably this is a wise option for many small towns and rural areas, or for parks and sensitive environments.

Events as Core Attractions

Events can be used by cities and destinations as their primary attractions, around which theming, image building, and packaging are created. This will likely be most appropriate at the community level, as many towns and cities have fashioned themselves as "tournament capitals" or "festival cities." It can also be a good strategy for rural areas lacking major tourist infrastructure. In effect, the destination's positioning strategy is shaped by one or more event attractions and the theming that surrounds them. One or more

Table 3.2. Fundamentals of Supply-Side Strategies and Management

Main Categories	Requirements
Sport events	Requires dedicated sport facilities, often sport specific; ideally these will be shared with residents and mainly meet their needs; tourism can increase efficiency. Bidding on major sport events can require heavy investment in new or improved venues. Cities compete on size and quality of arenas and stadia so it is necessary to determine what "league" you are playing in (regional, national, international?). Professional teams require the biggest and best venues; their tourism impact can be low but image effects can be high. Numerous local sport clubs generate demand for facilities, but also aid in generating and attracting events.
Business events (MICE)	Cities compete on size, quality, convenience, and cost of dedicated venues for meetings, conventions, and exhibitions. Resorts and hotels often provide venues at a smaller scale. A wide range of other facilities provide unique or special-purpose venues, including zoos, heritage and arts facilities, parks, and museums. Permanent sales effort is required. City-wide business events usually require bidding and coordination by the DMO. Convention/exhibition centers and nearby hotels have different priorities when it comes to tourism and event development.
Festivals and other cultural celebrations	Large-scale tourism is usually linked to major, existing (i.e., Hallmark) events, including carnivals, festivals, and parades; "global parties" might lack authenticity and local support. Establishing new Hallmark events can require heavy investment, if not in capital costs then in marketing. Numerous local and regional events help animate the destination; some can be developed into tourist attractions.
Entertainment and private functions	All facilities can be a venue for small- to medium-scale private and corporate functions, including restaurants, wineries, shopping centers. The trend is for public facilities to be built as function/event venues, primarily to generate additional revenue (this is the efficiency justification). DMOs can aim to facilitate this sector through marketing support.

Hallmark events will be desirable—that is, events with such profile that the image of event and destination become inseparable and mutually reinforcing. At a minimum, the destination will require media-oriented events to attract substantial publicity. Substantial event venues are also desirable, and might be a prerequisite for hosting major events and bidding on others. Even the smallest community can adapt its recreational and cultural facilities for events and seek to be known for its quality events. At the other end of the size spectrum are "world cities" that compete for the biggest and most prestigious mega-events, and attempt to be competitive in all types of Event Tourism.

Events as Supplements or Complements to Other Forms of Tourism

Events can supplement other forms of tourism, as in the case where theme parks predominate, or winter sport resorts are the main attraction, and events help fill the slow seasons. In some cases it is more appropriate to view events as being complimentary to other forms of tourism, in order to round out a portfolio of attractions, and in these instances Event Tourism has equal status with cultural or sport tourism.

Focus

It will often be impractical to develop a full portfolio of events, giving equal weight to business, sports, cultural, and entertainment events. Being a sport capital or festival city might imply a focus, and investing mainly in one type of venue will definitely result in a focused strategy.

Theme Years

This has become very popular through the spread of "cultural capital" years in many countries. The idea is to package a host of events and generate mega-publicity, without the cost of a single mega-event. It could be accompanied by new investments, or simply enhanced marketing. The primary consideration is the legacy, and clear goals have to be specified in the beginning. If it is a cultural theme then festivals will likely prevail, but there are more generic themes such as "Visit Us Year."

In the profile of Northern Ireland's Strategy, note how Event Tourism is positioned within their overall tourism and place marketing strategies, with a focus on events that can generate positive images and create demand for short, city breaks.

Draft Tourism Strategy for Northern Ireland

Tourism is now seen as a sector that can make a significant contribution to the economy of the country. Currently NI welcomes in the region of 3.3m visitors, spending £500m into the economy, and supports 40,000 jobs.

The vision is to "create the new Northern Ireland Experience and get it on everyone's destination wish list," in turn to increase employment supported by tourism to 50,000 jobs, the number of visitors to 4.5 million and double the revenue generated to £1 billion by 2020.

Events have a key role to play in driving this ambition. Event-led short breaks is one of the key market segments. Events, whether home grown local events or major one off international events, have the capability of showcasing the people and place on a global stage. Major events in particularly are able to fulfill the objective of showcasing Northern Ireland as a unique destination to live, work, invest, and visit.

Events can drive visitor numbers and spend and also provide platforms for the visitor to interact with the local culture, people, and place.

NITB's vision for a sustainable events future is to have a progressive, diverse, cohesive events industry, successfully attracting significant tourism revenue to the economy of Northern Ireland. As well as supporting existing Northern Ireland events we also have a vision to bid for and attract new events to Northern Ireland.

2012 saw a number of new international-scale events developed specifically for the year. We have also been successful in bidding for a number of major events such as the MTV EMA's in November 2011, which generated £10m into the economy and a further £10m in positive PR, as well as the Irish Open in June 2012, the first time the event had been staged in Northern Ireland in 60 years and the only European Tour event to ever sell out with over 130,000 people attending across the 5 days.

Going forward we have a vision, through the new Events Plan for NI, to bid for major events which showcase Northern Ireland on a world stage as a great place to invest, work, live and visit, which showcase our people and place and our unique tourism assets and products and which ultimately create a legacy for the future of tourism.

Strategic Planning Process for Event Tourism

All planning is future oriented, and very political. Even within organizations, like DMOs or event development corporations, there will be discussions and perhaps conflicts over goals and strategies, which is a political process. But when politicians are involved, as in the spending of public money, ideology and party politics can easily intervene to make it a messy and unpredictable process.

This section covers a rational, strategic planning process for Event Tourism at the destination level, although much of the logic also applies to single events. But it has to be remembered that politics are often not rational. As well, events and tourism have to learn how to work with politicians and government agencies, whether they like it or not. In fortunate circumstances, governments favor events and tourism and make it easy, but in many cases the political environment is not so friendly.

Planning has to be ongoing and cyclical. No plan can survive very long without changes, and strategies have to be adaptable. The process illustrated in Figure 3.3 is intended to be cyclical, with no particular starting point and certainly no finishing point. You can start the process at resource evaluation, with a marketing plan, or research into niche segments, it does not really matter. In larger, sophisticated event and destination organizations all these tasks can occur simultaneously. Although a specific type of plan is often the end product, the planning process itself is often more important. After all, the future

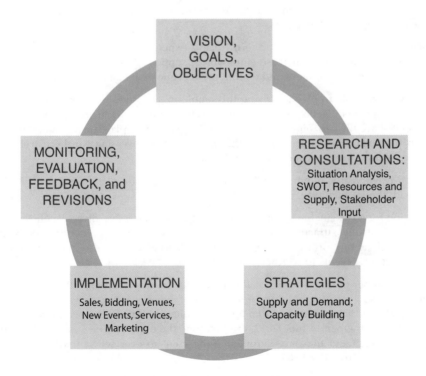

Figure 3.3. Strategic planning process for Event Tourism.

cannot be predicted nor can its shape be guaranteed. Whatever plans humans formulate, adaptation and revisions are always going to be needed.

Conceptually it does not make sense to separate supply and demand development, as in theory supply is developed to match demand and vice versa. In reality, however, we always have existing supply that requires selling, improvement, or expansion, and we have existing markets that we have measured and hopefully can expand. In many destinations numerous, uncoordinated actors pursue development and undertake marketing, and it becomes a huge task to coordinate them.

Planning and leadership are closely related. This role is generally played by the lead organization, with a strong mayor or tourism minister pushing the agenda. Often it is a partnership of politicians, industry executives, and professional destination mangers. If there is no will to change or to compete at a higher level, Event Tourism will not likely get much attention.

"Policies" are best expressed as formal rules to guide the diverse actions of organizations and government, but they can also be unwritten guidelines that are understood by everyone, or programs of action that make foundation policies implicit. Policies implement the mission and goals of the organization by showing what actions are desirable, permissible, or forbidden. Within each policy field, procedures will be formulated to regulate routine actions.

Vision, Goals, and Objectives

Mintzberg (1994, p. 209) proclaimed that "visioning" is at the heart of strategic planning. It is a process of setting the broad outline of a strategy, or identifying elements of a desired future. Every Event Tourism organization should have not only have a mandate, or statement of its purpose, but a vision statement that can motivate and foster unity of purpose among all stakeholders.

A good vision statement is one that reflects the organization's mandate or mission, is broad and general enough to attract widespread support, and sufficiently inspired and forward-looking to stimulate innovation in its pursuit. Consultations with stakeholders will be important in shaping the vision, especially if they will be asked to support the strategies and goals that flow from it. Without a clear vision and goals, Event Tourism initiatives are likely to become ad hoc and ineffective.

J. R. B. Ritchie and Crouch (2003) explained how a vision statement should reflect the philosophy and values of tourism development in a destination, and establish "the more functional and the more inspirational portrait of the ideal future that the destination hopes to bring about" (p. 154). A key big question is the importance or centrality of events: Are they a supporting element or one of the major platforms of tourism development and place marketing? In the case of Calgary, documented by Ritchie and Crouch, events figured prominently in helping to achieve the central concept of the city becoming "host, consultant and educator to the world." Specific facilities and types of events were identified as means to help realize the vision, including world class sports events and winter sport facilities.

Goal statements are needed to help translate the general direction of the organization into more tangible, results-oriented efforts. Goals can be of three general types. "Input goals" concentrate on what is required to get the job done, including resource acquisition, organizational structure, and processes that convert inputs into outcomes. "Outcome goals" focus on what is to be accomplished, and generally should be accompanied by performance measures and action plans. "Process goals" pertain to how the planning and development process is to be undertaken, including stakeholder consultations, research needs, and monitoring/feedback. You can also state goals in the negative, as things to be avoided.

Table 3.3. Sample Goals and Objectives for Event Tourism

Major Goals	Sample Objectives
Create a favorable image for the city Co-brand events with the destination	Attract and win through bidding, or create high-profile events to maximize positive media exposure. Develop one or more Hallmark events. Develop Iconic events for specific target markets. Animate the city/destination through a program of events, including local and regional. Use themes and theme years to capture attention.
Attract foreign visitors and increase their yield	Favor events that attract foreign visitors. Leverage all events for maximum local benefit.
Expand the tourism season and spread demand throughout the area	Develop and manage a full portfolio of events by type, target market, value, and season. Attract or create new events during winter and autumn, especially where none exist.
Use events as a catalyst to expand and improve tourism infrastructure	Ensure that events contribute to efficient, multi-purpose event facilities. Occasional mega events hosted to obtain a boost in infrastructure and capacity to host future events.
Stimulate repeat visits	Maintain effective relationships with key stakeholders (e.g., event owners, meeting planners, tour operators, venue managers). Establish quality control standards and process. Measure customer and client satisfaction. Seek expert advice and utilize research. Produce and market a program of events at all attractions and facilities.
Develop and improve the infrastructure and management necessary to create, attract, and sustain events	Provide assistance and advice. Foster the pooling of resources. Create cooperative marketing and promotions.
Foster development of the arts, sports, culture, heritage, and leisure.	Assist all types of events. Link events to other policy areas.
Ensure maximum benefits to the host community Ensure public and political support	Conduct cost–benefit studies. Follow community-based planning process. Implement full stakeholder and resident consultations for meaningful input. Be fully open and accountable; justify public investments.
Create and manage Event Tourism in a sustainable manner Avoid negative environmental effects Foster conservation	Green certification imposed. Stimulate ecotourism through events. Require comprehensive impact evaluations with costs and benefits.

Sample event tourism goals and objectives are provided in Table 3.3. These are mainly outcome goals, being worded as intended benefits. The sample objectives are more specific statements of how the goal is to be implemented, and each of them should include measurable key results or performance criteria.

Consultations

There has to be a circular process established for consultations that influence visions, goals, and strategy formation—it cannot be neatly slotted into a specific time period. Residents, the industry, politicians will all have much to say about the process, its implementation, and perceived impacts.

Stakeholder input should at least address the following general issues:

- the extent to which existing events are to be developed and promoted as tourist attractions;
- the extent to which support will be given to develop or assist the creation of new events and bidding for events;
- the roles events are to play in extending tourist seasons and the geographic spread of tourism;
- the role events are to play in creating and enhancing images, particularly a destination area or attraction theme, and in correcting negative imagery;
- the roles events are to play in fostering the arts, cultural goals, sports, fitness, recreation, nature and heritage conservation, and community development;
- attitudes toward, and the perceived worth of, events;
- perceived impacts of Event Tourism;
- the acceptable costs associated with development, and who is to pay for them;
- the means to identify, prevent, ameliorate, or remove negative impacts;
- the need for organizational development at the level of interest groups, communities, destination areas, and government agencies/departments to support event tourism.

Public input to tourism or Event Tourism planning and development is rare, as it is often seen as an industry function ("just marketing"), or is considered by politicians to be the business of semipublic or public–private agencies that lack the legal requirement for full accountability. This situation is not sustainable, as the more aggressive or successful it becomes, the more Event Tourism will attract media and public attention. Not all of that attention will be favorable.

Research for Event Tourism Planning

Market intelligence was considered in Chapter 2, as demand analysis, but there are a number of other types of research needed for effective Event Tourism planning and development.

Resource and Supply Appraisal

"Resources" in this context are the human, financial, physical, political, and technological factors that can be used in developing and marketing Event Tourism. It is useful to think of resources as "potential," while "supply" defines the existing infrastructure of the tourism and event sectors. Many events have the potential to become tourist attractions, but are not actually developed or marketed for tourist consumption. Venues have potential but must be sold, and organizations have potential to create or bid on events, but might need assistance.

Not all resources should be exploited. It is not legitimate, and might actually be counterproductive, to attempt to promote all events as attractions, or to encourage all communities and organizations to produce events. Accordingly, there is much more to resource and supply appraisal than simply listing and classifying events. Judgment and stakeholder input is called for when assessing such issues as classifying events as to their tourism potential.

It is both a technical and evaluative process, as judgment is required in a number of areas:

- what to include or exclude (e.g., all events? all venues?);
- evaluation of resource potential (e.g., what can be done with existing human resources?);
- obtaining quality input from research and stakeholders;
- assessing the data in meaningful ways;
- developing rating systems of tourist attractiveness;
- conducting portfolio, capacity, and SWOT evaluations;
- formulating strategies.

Resource Analysis

Financial resources: These include the means to plan, bid on, and produce events, including development of event venues. Much of the capital for events comes from the private sector, especially sponsors, and from nonprofit organizations. Public–sector investments have to be openly justified.

Natural resources: Events can be used to interpret, protect, and enhance parks and protected areas, so a general resource inventory should be evaluated to determine existing and potential linkages. The natural resource base can also suggest themes, such as agricultural or other resource-based industries, and the community's interdependence with other environmental factors (such as wildlife, scenery, climate). Potential venues should be considered, including parks and open spaces. An activity analysis can be formed using a natural resource inventory and data base of maps. All recreational activities, including wildlife viewing and nature interpretation, are potential event themes. Questions of capacity and compatibility will have to be evaluated.

Cultural resources: Many event themes are derived from the cultural makeup of communities, including their history, ethnicity, traditions, and folklore. Built heritage is also important in suggesting event venues (like historic districts). Arts and crafts activities will be included, as will entertainment and performing arts. Consideration of cultural uniqueness and authenticity is important. Religious and educational institutions should be covered, as they are both sources of events and potential stakeholders or supporters of events.

Human resources: Organizations and their memberships should be covered, leading to identification of event producers, potential facilitators, and volunteer pools. Who are the community leaders? What groups are most involved in activities that could become event attractions? What are current levels and patterns of volunteering? Who has the expertise to bid on events or produce them? An assessment of training and education needs for events might be important, but should be covered under general tourism and hospitality labor evaluations. Are there any event-specific training opportunities in the area? What institutions or associations could provide them? If there is little event management experience in the area some outside advice and assistance will be required.

Physical resources: This category covers the built environment, particularly venues for events. All attractions and public facilities should be examined as to their potential for hosting various types of events, and their management invited to suggest ideas and state requirements for developing the events sector.

Political resources: Is there support for tourism and events? Is there a bias towards one type of event, or one event in particular? Who can exert leadership in favor of an event funding policy? Examine interorganizational linkages, the degree of cooperation among organizations, and the roles of various political persons or parties in getting things done. In other words, allying with "movers and shakers" in a community is a good way to initiate Event Tourism plans.

Technological resources: Are there technological themes that could be developed through events, such as inventions, transportation heritage, or communications innovations? What technological resources exist to help produce or market events? Is there a computerized ticket reservation system in place? What is the state of local and regional media, especially in terms of covering and promoting events?

Supply Analysis

Supply is tangible and can be measured. How many events, venues, and sponsors are there in the destination? What are the trends in numbers, size, location, seasonality, and demand? It is useful to examine past events as well, and failed bids. Event organizations and sponsors should also be counted and scrutinized for possible contributions to an expanded events sector. Tourism services, including event-related packages, should also be inventoried and assessed.

The inventory is a quantitative exercise intended to accurately describe the nature and size of the event sector. Many destinations and communities do not have adequate data, and even if there is a directory or calendar of events it will likely be reliant on voluntary submission of information—and therefore incomplete. Research will be needed to complete the inventory and to assemble a permanent database useful in planning and impact assessment. The usual starting point will be whatever calendar or listing is available, followed by telephone calls and interviews to update and refine the data base.

This analysis cannot be done without first establishing a classification system, as well as criteria to determine what exactly constitutes a "festival" as opposed to, say, a "fair" or "party." A degree of interpretation will likely prove necessary, so it is best to acquire information on the event program and goals to assist in classification. The scope and detail of the inventory will depend on resources available to do the job, and the ultimate uses of data. Enlisting the help of the events themselves is a wise tactic, especially if they have an association or other means of regular communication.

Components of an event inventory:

- name or description of the event;
- main theme(s);
- the organizers (a profile or cross-reference to another inventory);
- dates, times, venues, locations;
- frequency or periodicity;
- indicators of professionalism (e.g., business plan, budget, staff);
- key contact persons and addresses;
- visitor/guest profile; target market segments;
- estimated attendance; growth; percent local versus tourist;
- tourist orientation (e.g., reflected in goals, marketing, attendance);
- activities (i.e., the program);
- goals and objectives of the organizers;
- historical background (e.g., date of origin; development);

- major sponsors (any "title" sponsor?)
- staff and volunteer numbers; staff positions; full- or part-time?;
- total operating budget;
- economic impact;
- operating surplus or loss;
- grants or other support received (amounts; sources);
- sponsorship revenue (amounts; in-kind);
- other revenue (amounts; sources);
- any strategic plan? marketing strategy?;
- support requested or needed (link to SWOT evaluation).

Policies and Programs

Particular attention should be paid to government policies and programs at all levels. What is the current and potential future level of support for tourism in general, and for events? Do policies stress one type of event, such as the arts or sports, over others? What regulations, such as licensing, apply specifically to events? Are the tax, labor, and safety laws a deterrent to events tourism development? More subjectively, is the political mood favorable?

This latter question raises the need for compiling a database of all stakeholders, including groups and individuals who could support or threaten event tourism. The planning process must involve all these stakeholders in order to identify problems and opportunities, and to ensure collection of all pertinent information.

Classification

Within a resource and supply appraisal, classification is a useful tool, whether for types of event, themes, programs, activities, venues, organizations, or services available. In the portfolio models there is an implicit classification based on the scale of events and their tourist attractiveness: local events; small regional; regional events with above-regional importance; Hallmark events (permanent institutions). Event development agencies tend to focus on events with national and international levels of attraction.

In a study for the Province of Ontario, consultants (Economic Planning Group and Lord Cultural Services, 1992) recommended a six-level classification based on five criteria: size and scale of the event; uniqueness of the product; quality of the experiences offered; image established in the marketplace; reputation in the marketplace. Although such classifications (they are really rating systems) are useful, there are many potential problems in determining where any given event fits, and the more important issues of whether existing conditions or the event's potential should form the basis of the evaluation. As all events have tourism potential, focusing on one or more of these five criteria could impair future development of the sector, especially if financial assistance is linked to a high rating. Would it not be better to use the criteria in a self-diagnosis or marketing audit to look for ways to improve each event?

Benchmarking

Benchmarking is a formal process of learning from the best, and is always a good idea, even if the "best" is rather uncertain. It depends on finding a cooperative player in the Event Tourism business, and one that does not mind sharing. That could be a challenge, so benchmarking often gets done more informally through surreptitious "scouting," "secret shopping," or other forms of obtaining intelligence about competitors. Some things simply will not be shared (typically what goes into an event bid) while others are posted on the Internet (a general policy or strategy, without much detail). The cases and examples in this book and in the recommended readings constitute a starting point.

One purpose of joining associations and going to conferences is to share and learn. Event Tourism practitioners need this contact as much as anybody in the corporate sector. Bodies such as the National Association of Sports Commissions (www.sportscommissions.org) and The Canadian Sport Tourism Alliance (canadiansporttourism.com) exist to give all their members good information.

SWOT Analysis

You know you are being out-competed when:

- your destination's market share is decreasing (e.g., your percentage of national and international congresses);
- your city's bidding success is declining (fewer and fewer bids are winners);
- your brand is lost among the crowd; recognition values are low; perceived image is that of a boring, unappealing place;
- your events are old and stale;
- your venues are third rate.

All that is obvious, but it actually cannot be determined unless a SWOT or situation analysis is being conducted regularly. A SWOT analysis consists of a summary of the destination's strengths, weaknesses, opportunities, and threats pertaining to Event Tourism, and relative to competitors. It can be done in isolation (i.e., without benchmarking and other forms of comparisons), but the results could easily be misleading. For example, one city might have a good international airport, which they consider to be a strength, but their chief competitor for events has plans for a newer, larger international airport that will handle more flights. SWOT needs a frame of reference in time and space.

Strengths, in the context of resource and supply evaluations, are resources, events, or related services and packages considered to be of high quality, high attractiveness, or strong in terms of numbers and/or variety. Tourism strengths should be identified for individual events (on the basis of an audit) and the portfolio of events in a destination. They might consist of any or all of these:

- unique themes and settings;
- top-quality venues;
- large venues (national or international is scale);
- a track record in bidding, winning, and hosting one-time events of significance;
- Hallmark events: one or more, co-branded positively with the destination;
- Iconic events with specialized appeal (a social world orientation);
- a large and diverse portfolio in terms of program, activities, target segments;
- existing large audiences, many of whom are regulars;
- a good reputation outside the area and internationally;
- high-quality event programs and service delivery;
- a captive tourism audience (at resorts, convention centers, staying with friends and relatives, at second homes);
- a range of complementary attractions and services in the area;
- widespread promotion through media coverage;

- sponsors with national or international interests;
- existing packages and services for tour groups;
- solid support from the community, including volunteers and political support;
- organizational and management capability (to expand, improve and innovate);
- a high ratio of benefits to costs demonstrated through valid research.

Tourism *opportunities* are anything that can be taken advantage of to enhance tourist attractiveness, such as:

- new/developing tourist attractions in the area;
- newly emerging target markets;
- opportunities for joint promotions and packages;
- potential addition or improvement of new event activities/attractions.

As already stressed, a demand-side approach will reveal more and more opportunities, especially within leisure and sport markets.

Threats are emerging or potential obstacles to achieving goals, including the following examples:

- competition (assume it is always increasing! but identify the toughest competitors);
- markets are changing to favor other types of event or attraction;
- declining quality of the event product due to age, or poor management;
- inability of event management/volunteers to adapt and innovate;
- loss of community and volunteer support if benefits are not obvious or costs/problems grow;
- lack or support and promotion from tourist organizations.

SWOT Criteria

When conducting a SWOT evaluation several important criteria should be considered: variety; quality; drawing power (attractiveness); image; and reputation. *Variety* is a measure of the breadth of resources such as events, by type, size, location, or whatever. There can be no measure of variety without an inventory and classification of all events in the area. Are certain types over- or underrepresented?

Some resources display higher *quality* or potential than others. How this is determined is open to debate and experimentation, but quality can be evaluated in three general ways: by reference to external conditions; through customer feedback and consumer research; and by expert evaluators. For example, determining whether the destination has high-quality human or cultural resources for event tourism is likely to be answered by experts and through input from many stakeholders. To determine if the area has high-quality events requires a different approach. Almost everyone has experienced a variety of events and can apply that experience to the evaluation. Input from event managers and sponsors will add a great deal to the evaluation. Comparing local events with external ones will be improved by obtaining an outside expert's judgment.

Are events currently drawing tourists? From what distance and for what length of time? Strengths derive from existing events with tourist *drawing power*, from organizations that produce or sponsor these events, and from high-quality event venues that appeal to tourists. There might be high-quality events in the area that, for lack of promotions, do not have current drawing power. This conclusion leads to an opportunity to be exploited.

Threats are likely to come from competitors, but also from internal factors that could, for example, change domestic demand for local events. Is size a factor in determining attractiveness? There is little doubt that large events generate publicity, excitement, and repeat visits, but small events can be just as important for particular market segments. In fact, it may be that many consumers will seek out the small events, associating them more with authentic cultural experiences.

Image and reputation are also key criteria. Surveys of the tour industry and media can determine if events have a good reputation. However, it is more important to find out reasons and to use this knowledge for improving events.

Core Competency (What Do We Do Best?)

Arising from the forgoing evaluation should be a statement on "core competency." This statement identifies what the destination does best in the events sector. In part this is a direct output of the portfolio and SWOT exercises. One school of thought holds that a business should stick to what it does best, shunning temptations to continuously add new products or cater to different markets. Hence, a community that has a strong base of sports venues, clubs, and related events would not stray into arts festivals even if potential demand and local interest existed. A contrary strategy would be to hold onto and develop the core competency while at the same time expanding the variety or market appeal of its events. I have to recommend the latter, but only where the expertise and resources are available to support broader portfolios.

Capacity and Fit

When appraising the resource base certain limitations will become evident. For example, there is likely to be a limit to the number of volunteers a community can muster, or to the number of event venues. And each venue will also likely have a fixed capacity in terms of crowd size or the range of activities it can support.

As much as possible, the analysis should identify these limits and translate them into strengths, weaknesses, opportunities, or threats. Each should be quantified, such as by making an estimate of the maximum number and types of sports events and area can accommodate by fully utilizing its existing supply. A resultant statement of strengths might be: "This destination can accommodate a wide range of high-quality sporting events," with a directly related weakness being: "but only at the scale of local and regional competitions."

A more difficult issue is that of determining the community's or destination's capacity to absorb tourism, or a specific type of tourism like events. *Fit* is a related concept. An area might be able to host a major sporting event, but is there compatibility (or good fit) between the community's capabilities, strengths, and weaknesses and the needs of the event or the potential impacts of the event? Part of the evaluation will be the issue of capacity, and part concerns other factors such as management capabilities and goodwill towards events and tourists.

Situation Analysis and Environmental Scanning

A "situation analysis" is equivalent to taking stock of the organization and its environment. It has several major components. "Environmental scanning" seeks to identify conditions and underlying forces shaping events and event tourism. Existing and potential markets must be identified, and competitors and complimentary events and event tourism products evaluated, leading to identification of threats and opportunities. "Future scanning" extends trends into the future to assess the probability and potential impacts of future conditions. "Resource appraisals" examine the availability of human, financial, political, and material support to meet the event's goals. An "organizational audit" should be part of this scanning, to ask where have we been and where are we headed? What are our organizational strengths and weaknesses?

Every manager has to conduct ongoing environmental scanning to stay current, but especially when engaged in strategic planning. The basic elements and methods of environmental scanning include the following:

- determine what information is needed for ongoing event management or Event Tourism and for related strategic planning;
- locate the best sources and obtain the information regularly (e.g., from magazines and journals) or periodically (e.g., new census data);
- establish relationships with other organizations and experts (such as consultants or academics) to ensure you learn from them;
- establish a system suitable to your style and the organization's capabilities to acquire and use appropriate information;
- become a "learning organization" devoted to continuous improvement.

Distinguishing trends from fads is one challenge, and applying global forces to local and event-specific planning is another. Obviously, the more experience managers have, the better they should be at obtaining and using the most important information. Professional associations, conferences, and publications can be a big help in this process.

This stage should ideally involve a great deal of research, but at a minimum can be done through expert consultations and discussion among the leaders or planners. Stakeholder input is vital. Consider that the most knowledgeable people are often already on top of trends and issues. Sharing information and research among events, professional associations, and with educational establishments is desirable. Also, tourism and economic development agencies will have pertinent data that they can provide and interpret.

Public input, either through formal surveys, focus groups, or public forums, will be useful. Consult the public on their attitudes towards the organization and towards events and tourism in general; also measure the current and potential market for events.

Implementation

Numerous plans and strategies have found their ultimate role to be that of dust collector on a shelf. To avoid this fate requires early attention to implementation methods, the viability of the strategy, and action plans that will motivate the key people. Failure to involve all stakeholders will also affect implementation. Feasibility studies and cost–benefit evaluations should be used to determine the viability of a strategy, especially if it requires a great deal of resources and advance planning.

To ensure that plans will be implemented, the following principles should be followed:

- develop a shared vision that all stakeholders can accept;
- maximize shareholder involvement in the entire process;
- develop strategies, rather than detailed blueprints;
- focus on results and how to attain and evaluate them;
- develop action plans with time lines and assigned responsibilities.

Management Systems

In addition to the crucial research efforts mentioned above, a comprehensive evaluation system must be established. Are goals being reached? At what costs? Can the strategy be made more effective or efficient? What unexpected outcomes or impacts have been generated? This analysis is fed back into the system for purposes of both accountability and improving the strategies.

A number of management support systems are required to implement the strategies:

- technological support: computer and communication systems;
- databases (accounting and finance; customers; stakeholders; resources and inventories; events and competitors);
- ongoing research and evaluation instruments and standardized measures of performance;
- external audits and evaluations (e.g., by experts and stakeholders);
- training and professional development.

Strategic choices often require modification to the organization, such as its committee structure or leadership roles, to ensure implementation. There is little point in changing the structure unless it will serve a broader strategy or solve a specific, serious problem.

Evaluation, Learning, and Refinement

Strategic planning is an ongoing process. Indeed, some people believe it is a waste of time to actual write a plan because it will either get out of date quickly or it will serve to stagnate the organization. When too much effort is expended on implementing the plan, opportunities and threats might be missed. Nevertheless, managers have to at least *think strategically*, and they must have the planning, research, and evaluation tools at their disposal.

All plans have to be refined and adapted as environmental forces change. This can be done formally, every year or two, or through ongoing changes in direction. "Emergent" strategies are those that evolve out of the day-to-day operations of the organization and at some point will have to be evaluated and possibly abandoned or formalized.

Case Study of EventScotland

To begin the case is this short interview with Paul Bush, Chief Operating Officer of EventScotland, which expands on the material presented in the Chapter 1 profiles of professionals.

Q: What is it about your background that prepared you for this position as Chief Operating Officer?

A: Being so heavily involved in sport and taking part in and preparing other athletes in major sporting events gave me a valuable insight into what makes a successful event. As well as seeing how an event runs from the point of view of the audience it is vital to understand how they work for athletes and performers and this helps enormously when working with International Federations who need to know that a national event agency understands why their world cup or world championship is so important.

Q: Are you personally involved with events, or is being the CEO a purely administrative or political position?

A: I believe it is important to get as close to an event as you can. I make a point of getting out to even the smallest events that EventScotland supports so I can understand and experience the occasion for myself. That way I can make informed decisions about future funding opportunities and identify links across the industry to help keep the industry developing.

Q: How do politics affect your strategy or operations? Specifically, with a plebiscite coming in 2014 on Scottish independence, are you feeling any pressure? There has been controversy over Homecoming—how did EventScotland deal with that?

A: Major events provide legitimate platforms for politicians. Everyone involved in the industry appreciates that, and for many countries that is why events are so important. For Scotland, with a rich and diverse event portfolio, political support is important but politicians from all parties understand why Scotland needs a world-leading events industry so whilst there may be disagreement around levels of funding there are no fundamental differences as to why events exist—namely to drive economic impact and international media profile. 2014 will be a year like no other for Scotland with the Commonwealth Games, The 2014 Ryder Cup, and Homecoming Scotland all taking place. Whilst the referendum on independence is likely to take place in this year, EventScotland is clear on our role. Namely to ensure the successful delivery of these major events.

Q: How does EventScotland compare to other event development agencies around the world? Do you benchmark against any of them?

A: Whilst we don't directly benchmark ourselves against other agencies we are very well aware of the competition—their strengths and the challenges they face. In some instances some of these are the same as EventScotland faces. Each agency is slightly different in the way it operates, which can make direct comparisons more difficult. For us the comparisons really come when we are going up against another country for the same event. At that point we're able to see their strategy and approach first hand. Whilst I respect our competitors and their work I know that EventScotland, with our successful partnership approach, is able to match and beat the bigger players on winning bids.

Q: Can you comment on how events are co-branded with Scotland's overall brand?

A: The Team Scotland approach is a vital element of our success in winning event bids and in promoting the country's own events, ensuring we get all we can from staging them. Events will always carry EventScotland's Scotland the perfect stage brand, but equally too the tourism message VisitScotland.com. For an event like The 2014 Ryder Cup the approach will be about putting a central Scotland message out there, clearly visible to a wide range of audiences around the word. Working in a smaller country allows us to harness partnership support and have everyone working with a common purpose.

Q: How do you evaluate a large portfolio of events, as opposed to single events, across the seven impact criteria?

A: EventScotland reports back on the success of the portfolio each year in our Annual Review. This allows us to tell the story of the economic success, the overall return on investment, and the geographic and date spread of the portfolio. We're looking at extending this annual work to include analysis of trends in visitor numbers, the involvement of local communities and trends in sustainability.

Context

Scotland is a small country, with a population of just over 5 million, but with a very large tourist organization (about 750 staff). Scotland is different from the rest of the UK; it has its own education system, separate judicial and legal systems, but it is not an independent state. In 1999, the UK government devolved limited authority and power to the new Scottish Parliament, including judicial authority, education, health, and industrial development—including tourism. The main public sector body with responsibility for tourism in Scotland is VisitScotland (previously the Scottish Tourist Board), with a net spend of about £50 million annually.

According to Frew and Hay (2011) public sector intervention in tourism in Scotland is usually justified in terms of a number of issues:

- a low level of knowledge by the purchasers of services, in this case tourists, of the range of available products, particularly those that lie outside the main tourism destinations in the country;
- because tourism is a fragmented industry with many players, there is a need for somebody or organization to take an overview of the marketing and development opportunities, of which few individual businesses could be fully aware;
- there is a real need to counteract the seasonality peaks and troughs of capacity underutilization of the tourism stock, if businesses are to not only survive, but to thrive;
- there is a poor geographical spread of the benefits of tourism, resulting in some regions not obtaining their fair share of the tourism cake;
- quality is now seen as a "hygiene issue" (i.e., it is a given factor), but there is a real need for tourism businesses in Scotland to drive up their quality, because standards in other countries continue to improve.

History and Organization of EventScotland

EventScotland was started in 2003 as a joint venture between the Scottish Executive and VisitScotland, the national tourism organization. At that time it was felt that Scotland was not achieving all that it could, particularly in terms of bidding for and winning major events and so, following a consultant's report that recommended the creation of a dedicated expert agency, in 2007 EventScotland became a full directorate within VisitScotland. EventScotland has an annual budget of £5 million provided by the Scottish government and a team of 20 specialist event, marketing, and communication practitioners.

Selected Staff Profiles

Stuart Turner: Position of International Events Director—Sport. Stuart is responsible for EventScotland's major sporting events portfolio and joined in December 2007. He has responsibility for managing the work of the events team, in relation to all sports events, and also of leading the agency's strategic approach to sports events. Prior to EventScotland, Stuart was Performance Director with the Scottish Golf Union. In addition he has also worked with the Commonwealth Games Council for Scotland on the last three Commonwealth Games, with the British Curling Association in the build-up to the 2002 Salt Lake City Winter Olympics, and was part of the Great Britain Holding Camp team for the 2000 Sydney Olympics.

Gayle Wilson: Position of Special Projects Communications Manager. EventScotland has recently established its Special Projects Team, who are responsible for the delivery of funding programs and initiatives that are not covered by the established International and National Events programs. Gayle manages the delivery of the PR and marketing for Special Projects, and prior to this role was PR Manager for Homecoming Scotland 2009. Prior to EventScotland, Gayle worked for 6 years as a Senior PR Executive in the UK Consumer PR team at VisitScotland. She has won a variety of CIPR awards including the CIPR Gold award for Best Campaign and Best Overall Campaign in 2007 for her work on the White Campaign. She has also been a regular contributor to *The Scotsman* newspaper with her Nature Diary column.

Marie Christie: Position of International Events Director—Culture. Marie is responsible for EventScotland's cultural events portfolio and has responsibility for managing the work of the events team, in relation to all cultural events, and also of leading the agency's strategic approach to cultural events. Joining the EventScotland team at its creation in 2003, Marie set-up and ran EventScotland's successful Regional Events Programme and is also the coauthor of the agency's popular events management manual, *Events Management: A Practical Guide.* Marie led the delivery of Homecoming Scotland 2009—a year-long celebration of Scotland culture and heritage that aimed to motivate Scots to come home in 2009, which was delivered by EventScotland and VisitScotland. Prior to EventScotland Marie was General Manager and Producer with UZ Events.

Vision and Strategy

In 2009 EventScotland launched the national events strategy, "Scotland The Perfect Stage," which will lead Scotland's events industry into and beyond 2020 and outlines a clear mission and vision to further establish Scotland as a world leading event destination. These are excerpts:

Our 2020 vision for Scotland: Scotland established as the perfect stage for events.

Our mission to deliver this vision: To develop a portfolio of events that delivers impact and international profile for Scotland.

Our strategy for delivering the vision and fulfilling our mission is to utilise and develop the assets that Scotland has that make it "The Perfect Stage" for sporting and cultural events:

Our cultural identity and heritage—Scotland's culture and heritage is a strong differentiating factor that we can use to attract major events. This includes our rich history, our world-famous food and drink, our reputation as a leading nation in the fields of education and innovation, our iconic poets, artists, writers and musicians and the vibrant contemporary cultural scene in today's Scotland. It also includes the diversity of language in Scotland, including of course, Gaelic and Scots.

Our people—Scotland is known for the friendliness of the welcome and the passion of our people. The people of Scotland are proud and have a strong sense of their identity. Our people are ideal ambassadors for Scotland and for Scottish events both at home and abroad. We also benefit from large numbers of people across the world with an affinity for Scotland, as well as a strong business community with excellent international links. Our people are also at the heart of strong communities within Scotland, which not only benefit from events but also support and deliver them.

Our natural environment—Scotland has a rich array of beautiful and dramatic landscapes ranging from mountains to lochs to beaches and magnificent islands. Our landscapes are both diverse and unique and are a key asset in attracting major events to Scotland.

Our built facilities—Scotland has a long history and tradition in architecture, including castles, public buildings and cityscapes incorporating historical and contemporary design. In short, Scotland has iconic buildings in and around which to stage events. We also have a range of excellent sports facilities and indoor arenas including those being developed for the Glasgow 2014 Commonwealth Games.

Our signature events—Scotland has a range of signature events which are so large and iconic that they form the heart of our strategy for retaining our status as a world-leading international events destination. Events such as Edinburgh's Festivals, the Glasgow Commonwealth Games and The Ryder Cup in 2014, our winter festivals and Homecoming Scotland 2009 will form the backbone of our events portfolio. We will aim to develop the portfolio of signature events by attracting further major scale events and by developing our own events to this level alongside other events of great significance to Scotland such as The Open Championship.

Photo 3.1. Edinburgh Jazz and Blues Festival (Credit: photo courtesy of Professor Joe Goldblatt).

Photo 3.2. Edinburgh Festival Fringe, high street performer
(Credit: photo courtesy of the Edinburgh Festival Fringe Society).

Operations

EventScotland aims to influence, lead, coordinate, support, and bring together people and organizations in order to deliver the events strategy. EventScotland is the lead agency for public sector engagement and investment in events. This lead role is at a national strategy and policy level while other agencies will provide leadership on a geographical or event sector basis.

The portfolio of events supported by EventScotland will be those of national and international significance, which will be complemented by other events supported at local level. EventScotland works to three core principles which guide all work:

1. Working in partnership both with event organizers and deliverers and with other funding partners as EventScotland is not a deliverer of events and will always seek at least one funding partner.
2. National significance of work undertaken. This has two important consequences. First, support and investment will only be directed to events which have a national significance in their ability to deliver the seven impacts. Second, EventScotland will aim to support events in every local authority area over each 4-year period, ensuring that the benefit reaches all of Scotland.
3. Additionality brought by the input of EventScotland. This could be in terms of adding specific value to an event by funding activity that has not taken place previously or could be using funding to secure an event that would not otherwise come to Scotland.

EventScotland leads work on events in Scotland by:

- devising and implementing strategy;
- developing and sharing methodology for measurement;
- gathering and sharing best practice examples and information;
- assessing, evaluating, and publicizing the impact of events on other key policy areas;
- building its international reputation and expertise in relation to events;
- capitalizing on the opportunities presented by Homecoming Scotland 2009 and the Commonwealth Games and The Ryder Cup in 2014, including the development of the new and upgraded facilities;
- coordinating public sector support that is being invested to achieve differing outcomes;
- identifying legacy opportunities from events and taking action to ensure that resource commitment is made to planning and maximizing these legacies;
- using staff expertise to assess which events will be supported and at what levels;
- monitoring and evaluating all events supported;
- working with partners to ensure high-quality delivery.

For every event supported or considered for support, EventScotland will conduct a thorough assessment, including an evaluation of how the event could deliver against the seven impact areas. This will always include a preevent economic impact assessment and the attribution of a media index to an event. These figures will be reported annually against the portfolio of events supported.

EventScotland will operate programs of support to deliver against "The Perfect Stage." The range and scope of the programs operated will be regularly reviewed and adjusted to ensure they maximize delivery against the desired impacts. EventScotland will put details of current programs at any given time on its website. Programs will always be designed to engage partners in delivering maximum impact.

EventScotland will seek and coordinate input from all other public agencies, including local authorities. EventScotland will also look to proactively engage the business community in events. This may involve working with chambers of commerce or, where these do not exist, other relevant business-focused groups to fully engage Scottish businesses. The support of this sector is vital to the economic success of events. Many local authorities can also play a key role in supporting this work.

Types of Events

EventScotland will not normally consider support for conferences; the Business Tourism Unit at VisitScotland already covers this function. Exhibitions may be considered as events, but will be required to demonstrate the potential to deliver the same level of impact as other supported events.

Sports events are classified by EventScotland in three categories: 1) Fixed events that happen annually at the same location in perpetuity; 2) Recurring events that happen annually at the same location for a number of years; 3) One-off events that are usually bid for and brought in for a single staging.

EventScotland's approach will be to balance the three different categories, ensuring there is a strong base portfolio of fixed and recurring events, while pursuing opportunities to secure one-off events. EventScotland will look to grow and provide additionality to fixed events, seek to retain and develop recurring events, and research, seek, and influence the bidding for and allocation of one-off events that will deliver impacts for Scotland. These one-off events must fit with the priorities of the sport at UK and Scottish levels, be winnable, and be able to be delivered in our built or natural facilities with resources currently or potentially available.

EventScotland will work closely with UK Sport as many of the one-off events that will be sought will be bid for by UK governing bodies. This work will align priorities and ensure that, wherever possible, events that are being sought for Scotland are identified as such in UK-level plans.

Cultural events are in the main either fixed or recurring. There are very few one-off cultural events available to be attracted or bid for in the international market. This necessitates a different approach to supporting and setting objectives for cultural events.

EventScotland will treat many fixed cultural events in the same way as sports events by looking to provide additionality and help them grow. Some events will be specifically identified as having significant growth potential and, where the ambition to achieve this growth is shared by event organizers and other partners, a long-term and proactive approach will be taken by EventScotland.

EventScotland will also seek to engage with existing cultural events to identify areas where EventScotland could provide additionality and also to identify and possibly exploit growth potential. EventScotland will also research and proactively seek cultural events that can be attracted to Scotland or bid for.

Training and Networking

EventScotland recognizes the needs of partners for more training and development opportunities for those working in the events industry and will take a proactive role in this. EventScotland will also seek to provide opportunities for networking and exchanges between those involved in events. This will include a national events conference.

EventScotland will produce an annual report that will lay out in greater detail its retrospective operation, including details of events supported, case studies, and economic impacts. Below are two recent initiatives.

Event Team Scotland (www.eventteamscotland.org) is a new web-based portal that matches volunteers across Scotland with exciting sporting and cultural events.

Delivered by EventScotland and Volunteer Development Scotland, Event Team Scotland will provide volunteers with varying levels of experience with the opportunity to participate in sporting, cultural, and charity events taking place across Scotland. For event organizers, the volunteering database will provide a bank of potential volunteers in local areas, regionally, and across Scotland who can provide general or more specialist event support.

As part of a games legacy for Scotland programme, Event Team Scotland will provide a platform for the development and training of an experienced volunteer workforce in the years leading to Scotland hosting both the Ryder Cup and the Commonwealth Games in 2014. The Games alone will require around 15,000 volunteers, and it is hoped they will go on to form part of a sustainable workforce for Scotland's events industry in the years to come.

Volunteer Development Scotland, Scotland's center for volunteering excellence, will host the database, which will allow event organizers to advertise their event and associated opportunities and also target volunteers by geographical area or specific skills and experience. Once registered, volunteers will be connected to a network of opportunities and event contacts across Scotland.

The Festivals Forum was established by the City of Edinburgh Council, Scottish Government, Scottish Arts Council/Scottish Screen, Event Scotland, Visit Scotland, Scottish Enterprise and Festivals Edinburgh in March 2007. It is a high-level, strategic commission bringing together representatives of those with a stake in maintaining the global competitive advantage of all Edinburgh's Festivals.

Legacy

Legacy is a vitally important aspect of events, which is well understood in the events industry. A truly successful event not only delivers an immediate impact but also leaves a footprint of benefits for years to come. Legacy can be defined as long-term impact. A key legacy of all events will be their delivery against the seven impact areas.

Events offer a platform to create impact and achieve legacy. To achieve this there must of course be resources for the event, but core funding of event facilities, built and natural, is also essential. There is also a need for resources to be allocated specifically to developing legacy. Further, there is a strategic need for desired legacy to be planned at the outset of an event. Methods of evaluating whether this has been achieved also need to be established at this stage. The objectives of an event are directly related to the legacy it can and will achieve. This could be in terms of economic benefit, facilities, or an increase in the personal and community capacity of those involved.

Event objectives, impacts, and legacy should be central to the plans of event organizers at all levels, although it is recognized that the size, scale, and ambition of these will vary according to the scale and resources of the event. The aim of achieving a lasting legacy from events can be supported by ensuring that government agencies agree on their common objectives regarding legacy and pursue working practices that achieve a united sense of direction, an efficient approach, and effective results. The goals and results should be explicit from the start, and communicated to the wider Scottish community. This is true of all events and is a key aim of "The Perfect Stage."

Aspects such as volunteering and sports development are key aspects of legacy, which can arise from events. It is the role of relevant agencies to utilize the platform provided by events to maximize these legacies.

Impacts

EventsScotland's strategy is based on the belief that events generate economic growth, both through a positive impact and subsequent legacy. Seven key impact areas were identified: tourism; business; image and identity as a nation; media and profile; participation and development; environment; social and cultural benefits.

An evaluation of the overall benefit to Scotland of any event can be made by assessing its level of impact in each of the seven key areas (two examples are appended). The level of impact can then be used to assess whether a given event should receive support from the public sector and whether this should be at a national or local level. In all cases, impact will include both immediate impact and long-lasting legacy. Different organizations will have their own criteria for decision making, emphasizing differing impacts to a greater or lesser extent. It is acknowledged that events at all levels contribute to the overall events industry in Scotland. Those that have significant national impact will inevitably have a greater relevance to a national strategy, but the value of smaller events run at a local community level or in specific interest groups, such as a branch of the creative industries or a specific sport, is acknowledged. These events have the potential to deliver significant impact at a local level or in a specific area of interest.

The seven key areas of impact identified can also be used postevent in assessing the overall level of impact of the event and the return on investment of any public support.

In addition the seven key areas of impact will be used by EventScotland when building rationale for future or enhanced public investment or demonstrating impact of previous public investment.

Partnership will be central both to the delivery of events and perhaps more significantly to the planning and maximizing of impact and legacy from events. In order to effectively and efficiently maximize delivery of impact there is a need to ensure a geographical spread of events and to support a portfolio of events across the calendar year. Impacts related to tourism, in particular, can only be maximized if this geographical and seasonal spread is achieved.

EventScotland will invest the budget allocated by Scottish Government to develop a portfolio of events and as overriding measures will seek:

- a return on investment through estimated economic impact of at least 8:1;
- a media index, using its own assessment, of 8, 9, or 10/10 for events where media exposure is the main driver for investment;
- a clearly demonstrated level of partners funding for events of at least 1:1.

EventScotland will invest in events relative to the levels of all seven of the identified impacts they can bring; however, there will be a greater emphasis on the economic and media benefits in order to reflect the core measures above.

Impact Measurement

The success of this strategy will be measured by the level of achievement of the mission. Specifically, this will involve the levels achieved in each of the seven key impacts. These will be looked at in relation to the amount that was or is proposed to be invested, with set levels of return on investment expected. EventScotland will be responsible for establishing methods for measuring each of the seven key impacts and also then for measuring them for identified events which are supported by EventScotland. It is not cost-effective to carry out full evaluations on all events.

Major progress in event impact evaluation has been made through the collaboration of EventScotland and UK Sport, Visit Britain, the London Development Agency, the North West Development Agency, Yorkshire Forward and Glasgow City Marketing Bureau (see: www.eventimpacts.com). The eventIMPACTS Toolkit is intended to provide organizers and supporters of public events with some key guidance and good practice principles for evaluating the economic, social, environmental, and media-related impacts associated with their event. Practical advice plus case studies are provided on this website, covering the following topics:

- **Attendance:** capture the number of total attendances, unique spectators and the numbers in various subgroups; profile event spectators and attendees using a range of different demographic categories; consider the effect of an event experience on the likelihood of people attending future events.
- **Economic impact:** capture headline spectator and attendee numbers, as these are a strong indicator of likely economic impact; survey work to calculate the "direct economic impact" figure from the event; consider adjustments to the "direct economic impact" figure, usually to measure the subsequent effects of increased spending in the host economy (i.e., the multiplier effect).
- **Environmental impact:** measuring how attendees have traveled to an event, their perceptions of the event's environmental credentials, and their intent to change their environmental behavior; number and type of environmental management plans in place (systems should include the identification of environmental impacts to be measured); considers long-term change in people's environmental behavior, especially linked to any changes in participation.

- **Social impact:** the impact of peoples' experience of attending an event (i.e., satisfaction); changed perceptions of the host city/region as a place; the impact of engaging with an event to bring about a change in people's interest in participating in a certain activity; the impact of acquiring new skills or experiences through working or volunteering at an event; impacts on children and young people.
- **Media impact:** measures fit with message; volume and type; tone.

Communication

Events will be used to promote Scotland, with "The Perfect Stage," drawing on the national assets identified in section one: our cultural identity and heritage; our people; our natural environment; our built facilities; our signature events.

This will be achieved through worldwide television coverage of events, international web-based and print media, and through direct promotion to the audiences/spectators and participants at events. It is also vital that successes are communicated through Scottish media channels at both a national and local level to ensure that the general public is aware of why events are important and where Scotland stands in the world. The level and nature of media coverage that can be secured for or offered by an event is one of the seven key impacts and will therefore be a crucial aspect of decision making in the level of support to be offered.

Critical Success Factors

If the Scottish events industry, with leadership from EventScotland, is successful in delivering the vision, the following will characterize the Scottish events scene in 2020:

- Scotland will be recognized worldwide as a leader in the delivery of events.
- Events will take place in Scotland across each calendar year and throughout the country.
- The events industry will be a significant contributor to Scotland's economy.
- The portfolio of events delivered annually will be made up of a core of events that are unique to Scotland and are embedded in Scottish culture, covering all aspects of arts, sport, culture, and heritage.
- The core portfolio will be complemented by a range of high-profile one-off and recurring events that have been attracted to Scotland by its unique appeal as a destination and international reputation as a country that delivers high-quality events.
- The roles of all agencies, public, private, and voluntary, within the Scottish events industry will be clearly identified and understood with partnership being a recurring theme.

There are a number of factors that will prove critical in successfully achieving this vision. Obviously the primary factor will be successfully delivering the identified impacts.

The other critical success factors are:

- The ability and credibility of EventScotland as a national agency to lead the implementation of this strategy and the expertise and network of key contacts of EventScotland staff.
- The credibility and capability of Scottish and UK event partners as agencies and of their individual staff members.
- The engagement of proactive involvement from Scotland's business community.

- A high level of political support for events and their impact, and their contribution to the wider agenda.
- Positive media coverage in Scotland and around the world that delivers the desired messages.
- Vision to anticipate market changes in the events industry and flexibility to adapt plans and working practices to meet new challenges.
- Resources from all sources that match the level of ambition.
- A well-trained and motivated volunteer workforce in the events industry to drive developments from local level.
- A track record of delivery and success at international, national and local level.
- International standard venues and good accessibility.
- Identifying, developing, and utilizing Scotland's unique selling points.

EventScotland will review these critical success factors in its internal risk register and will report on them as part of its annual report.

Examples of Events in Scotland

Commonwealth Games 2014 (Glasgow)

EventScotland contributed £1.5 million in support of the Commonwealth Games 2014 bid and has since worked to attract and secure a range of events for the city.

From the 10th World Team Badminton Championships—Sudirman Cup to the FISA World Rowing Under 23 Championships, sporting events showcase Glasgow as a world leading events destination and reinforce the city's credentials as the best candidate city for the 2014 Games.

EventScotland continues to work with local partners to invest in test events to promote Glasgow's profile as an international event destination. And in December 2008 EventScotland announced its intention to lead a bid to host a stage of the UCI's prestigious track cycling World Cup at the future Glasgow velodrome. Working with Culture and Sport Glasgow and British Cycling the agency's aim is to secure the event for the winter of 2012/2013.

Hebridean Celtic Festival 2010

Based in the Outer Hebrides, the Hebridean Celtic Festival is a flagship Scottish cultural event that has earned an international reputation for quality and cutting-edge programming. The music festival features major international performers from across the Celtic nations and beyond, and local, emerging artists.

The success of the festival is due in part to the unique setting of the Outer Hebrides, in particular the main festival arena within the grounds of Lews Castle overlooking Stornoway Harbour. Loyal audiences and the support of hundreds of volunteers each year also contribute to the success of the festival. The distinctive island Gaelic culture creates an event of exceptional quality and character attracting tourists each year.

The festival has now firmly established itself as an international event providing invaluable economic and cultural tourism benefits, but also providing a platform for artists from the Highlands and Islands to showcase the cultural wealth of the Hebrides. EventScotland has previously supported the festival in 2005 and 2006.

The Festival, which was attended by crowds of over 16,000 in 2010 and doubled ticket sales from 2009, is a key driver for tourism in the Hebrides. A survey showed that 41% of visitors traveled to the area specifically to attend festival while 62% of visitors said they would be likely to return to the Islands due to their festival experience.

The festival also drives tourism into other areas of the Hebrides with 41% of visitors staying for 10 days or more, taking in all that the Islands have to offer. Promotion of the Outer Hebrides and its rich culture are fundamental to the Hebridean Celtic Festival marketing campaign.

The event is crucial to many local businesses and, in particular, the catering and hospitality industries; almost 50% of festival attendees are visitors to the island.

The festival collaborated with several local producers—Harris Tweed artisans produced a unique festival tweed; a 15th anniversary whisky was produced and sold at the festival; and Hebridean Chocolates produced a Festival Whisky Truffle that was retailed before and after the festival.

The festival cites community involvement as a major player in the success and attraction of the festival. In 2010, the event welcomed 76 staff and 452 volunteers.

The festival places an emphasis on participative programming encouraging confidence in aspiring musicians and providing a platform to showcase their talent. The organizers aim to develop the festival through participation opportunities and education. Youth groups from Orkney, Shetland, Lewis, and Harris participated in workshops and music sharing. The outreach program ensured that the festival reached more remote locations from North of Lewis to South of Harris with workshops, concerts, and ceilidhs.

The festival has aims to strengthen the core activity of the event and broaden the program by introducing a second stage within the main festival arena. Improvements to on-site catering and bar facilities are also being planned. In 2011, the event is being funded through Scotland's Island's as the flagship event.

The Festival furthered efforts in 2010 to reduce environmental impact by increasing recycling of glass, tin, and plastic with the support of a Waste Aware team. In 2009, the festival introduced compostable cornstarch "glasses" that could be disposed of through the local authority anaerobic digester. Building on the success of this, the festival supplied subsequent local events with these materials to foster a more responsible environmental approach.

The festival has created firm roots in the community by operating a partnership approach. The festival is a champion of social enterprise and works closely with local groups, organizations, individuals, and the wider community. Committed to developing the skills of local people, the festival recruits a number of volunteers to assist in running the festival who often return to volunteer year on year. However, the most important legacy that the festival can provide is by assisting the cultural aspirations of the future music makers, fostering new, local talent and providing a platform for established performers.

The festival also achieved extensive coverage in print and online media and BBC Scotland, GMTV, and STV all ran news pieces on or related to the festival. BBC Radio nan Gaidheal broadcast live from the festival while BBC Radio Scotland broadcast interviews with the Festival team preevent. The festival team produced two 60-minute music programs for BBC Alba with four further 15-minute shorts broadcast later on the same channel.

Key outcomes:

- a flagship event that showcases the unique Gaelic culture to an international audience;
- focus on participation particularly from local people;
- 100% increase on ticket sales since 2009;
- 16,000 attendances;

- high level of community involvement;
- extensive media coverage across all mediums.

Mountain Bike World Cup, 2010

The Mountain Bike World Cup at Fort William is one of several locations on the UCI World Cup series that take place between April and August. The Fort William event has been successfully held from 2002 to 2010, with EventScotland supporting from 2003. In 2007 the venue hosted the UCI Mountain Bike & Trials World Championships instead of the World Cup. Nevis Range, where the competition is held, is the only venue in the UK to have hosted all three key disciplines of the World Cup: Downhill, 4X, and Cross Country. For both spectators and participants, the Mountain Bike World Cup at Fort William is a thrilling, fast-paced event enhanced by the party atmosphere. In a 9-year period (2002–2010) the Fort William World Cup (and World Championship in 2007) has established itself as one of the premier events and venues on the international mountain bike circuit. It has a reputation for innovation, big crowds, and a great atmosphere—a true showcase event for the sport. The event consistently runs impressive marketing campaigns. Incorporated into the 2010 "Downhill Rock n Roll" marketing campaign, Leith Records hosted a Battle of the Bands contest. Over 11,000 online votes were cast in advance of the event and 40 bands entered. EventScotland works closely with organizers, Rare Management, and has secured the World Cup event for Fort William up to and including 2013.

This high-profile international event is hosted in a semirural area of Scotland, which ensures a consistent influx of tourism year on year. In 2010, the Mountain Bike World Cup attracted 285 competitors from 24 nations across the two disciplines, with 171 accredited media reporting on the event. Visitor numbers in 2010 remained high for the event, averaging at 17,300 over the 3 days, of which 8,500 were unique visitors; 13% of these were overseas visitors who stayed on average for 3.5 nights, while all visitors on average returned to the event for a second day.

The event works with Highland Council, SportScotland, and Scottish Cycling to introduce local children to mountain biking. Highland Council and Scottish Cycling have created a regional development center in Fort William and, in 2009, a Highland-wide schools development program culminated in the Youth XC Sprint event at the World Cup. Meanwhile, the youth-level event, Scottish Cycling Youth Dirt Crit, is used by Highland Region as the culmination of a qualification series inspiring riders from all over Scotland to pursue competitive mountain biking. Organizers aim to develop similar initiatives from 2010 onwards to create a comprehensive plan for local schools in the build up to the London Olympics and Glasgow Commonwealth Games, developing local riders at elite level and developing Fort William as an elite training center. 2011 saw new developments around the Downhill course, which follows a ferocious track straight down the face of Aonach Mor, the ninth highest mountain in the UK. The competition ensures spectators are at the forefront of the event with the incredibly exciting 4X format where riders battle it out down a custom-built course of berms, jumps, step-ups, and other testing features.

The event organizers take environmental management seriously with standard plans in place for the Mountain Bike World Cup. Organizers have improved year on year with increased efforts in recycling and waste separation. Nevis Range, an area of natural beauty, is protected within Nevis Range and Forestry Commission's environmental policies.

The event has assisted in engaging and developing local businesses, individuals, and schoolchildren. The event has provided training for local volunteers since 2002, many of which have gone on to work in the events or mountain bike industry. The event reinforces

Photo 3.3. Mountain Bike World Cup, Fort William, Scotland (Credit: photo by phunkt.com).

and validates Fort William's status as Outdoor Capital of the UK and has created a facility in the area that is now used year round by local riders and clubs, as well as tourists.

The event attracts significant TV coverage, both in Scotland and internationally across every continent, providing a strong platform to promote Scotland's natural assets and facilities for mountain biking and adventure tourism. Welcoming 171 accredited media, the 2010 Mountain Bike World Cup increased its PR and media value to £846,000 compared with £508,000 in 2009. Eurosport broadcast both live and highlights programs of the event while Freecaster broadcast live across the Internet. BBC2 Scotland featured the Mountain Bike World Cup on the Adventure Show.

Key outcomes:

- best Downhill Event by the UCI; "Event of the Year" at the Sunday Mail Scottish Sport Awards; finalist for "Best Event Look" at the International Sports Management Awards; Singletrack Best UK Event;
- attendance of over 17,000;
- widespread media coverage at home and abroad valued at £846,000 and showcases Scotland's natural facilities for mountain biking;
- development of Nevis Range and Fort William as the Outdoor Capital of the UK;
- direct economic impact to the Highland;
- sporting legacy in the creation of permanent World Class facilities.

Summary and Study Guide

Destination-level planning was the focus of this chapter, covering the organizations responsible, policies, and planning process. Of particular importance are the options available for policy and action, including direct investment and facilitation. "Top-down" versus "bottom-up" planning and development were contrasted, and while they are likely to be complementary in practice, I believe innovation is fostered mostly by a bottom-up approach that involves facilitation and stakeholder engagement. There are many potential actors involved in Event Tourism and the typical supply-side approach is rather limited in scope. Certain generic strategies are association with the supply-side approach, mainly the selling of venues, venue development, and bidding on events.

"Comparative and competitive advantages" were explained, showing how strategies flow from analysis (including SWOT). The strategic planning process was illustrated, with emphasis on visioning and formulating goals and objectives. Research is needed to support the process, including situation, supply and resource analysis, and environmental scanning. Several related concepts are important, including "capacity" and "fit."

Scotland was featured, both in the Expert Opinion piece on policy and in the detailed case study of EventScotland. These provide valuable, detailed insights on the actual practice of Event Tourism at the national level, particularly with regard to policy (and politics), planning, strategy, and operations. Make an effort to compare all the cases in the book involving planning and development, including Calgary, Northern Ireland, and Queensland. In particular, look for evidence of leading-edge research, target marketing, portfolio development and management, and evaluation and impact assessment.

Study Questions

- Discuss the potential conflicts and complementarities among Event Tourism and other policy domains affecting events.
- What types of organizations have responsibilities for Event Tourism planning and development? What are their limitations?
- What are the advantages of "bottom-up" planning and development?
- Discuss the potential development roles of governments and DMOs regarding Event Tourism, with emphasis on facilitating and growing the "industry."
- Differentiate between "comparative and competitive advantages" and explain how analysis, including SWOT, leads to strategies.
- What are the generic "supply-side" strategies; be sure to differentiate supply and demand-side approaches.
- Outline the Event Tourism strategic planning process, including the importance of vision, goals and objectives, and stakeholder input.
- What does "capacity building" mean in the context of Event Tourism planning? Give examples of how to do it; also explain the concepts of "capacity" and "fit."
- What kinds of research are needed to support planning and strategy? Connect scanning and situation analysis back to forces and trends.
- Use the EventScotland case to specify goals and methods of Event Tourism at the national level.

Additional Readings

- *Inside City Tourism: A European Perspective* (Heeley, 2011).
- *The Competitive Destination: A Sustainable Tourism Perspective* (Ritchie & Crouch, 2003).
- *Events Feasibility and Development: From Strategy to Operations* (O'Toole, 2011).
- *Event Policy: From Theory to Strategy* (Foley, McGillivray, & McPherson, 2011).

Chapter 4

Development of Event Tourism

Learning Objectives

Upon completion of this chapter the student should understand and be able to explain the following:

1. The meanings of "development" and "capacity building."
2. "Sustainable Event Tourism development."
3. The development process for Event Tourism.
4. Marketing and branding.
5. Co-branding of events and destinations; management of media, image, reputation, brand.
6. Development methods:
    *   bidding on events;
    *   creating and owning your own events; hallmark events;
    *   facilitating and growing the events sector;
    *   venues;
    *   leveraging and boosting events;
    *   servicing events;
    *   the legacy;
    *   portfolio creation and management.

Introduction

The previous chapter discussed planning and policy making, plus general supply-side strategies, and in this chapter we go into detail on the meaning of development and specific methods of Event Tourism development. Figure 4.1 illustrates an integrated development process for Event Tourism that summarizes this content.

We start with a discussion of "development," including the issue of whether or not tourism and Event Tourism can be considered an "industry," and then how Event Tourism is related to urban development and rural development. Principles of sustainable development are discussed here, but a more thorough examination is provided in the final chapter.

Branding and marketing are essential, ongoing components of Event Tourism development. A model is provided and explained of the important interrelationships between the brand, co-branding, positioning, image, and reputation, and how these are managed.

Most of this chapter consists of sections on each of the development methods (or action areas), with the most material provided on portfolio creation and management. It is important to also include feasibility study and risk assessment/management, which are covered in Chapter 5, and sales, which is covered in Chapter 7.

What Is Development?

The simplest dictionary definitions refer to development as growth (of something) and also to the process of developing (something). To many people in the tourism industry this means sustained growth of tourist numbers and of profitability, as they take the bottom line approach. Events, in this context, are to generate room nights, especially in non-peak times. Governments count on the process to create and maintain jobs. We can call this "economic development."

Some people think of development in physical terms, specifically new facilities for sports, exhibitions, conferences, and festivals. These are tangibles that can be seen, names are put on them (corporate sponsors, rich donors, and politicians like this a lot), and many years of use follow. In this way Event Tourism connects directly to urban development (or renewal), often with the aim of using the power of events and facilities to reshape and reimage entire districts.

The link to "social and cultural development" is less tangible, relying on events to foster social integration, intercultural understanding, healthier lifestyles, or increased capacity for communities to solve their own problems. Fostering skills through volunteering is a form of social development, and bringing the arts to people is a form of cultural development that events can implement.

"Sustainable development" is a complex concept, as to many people it means the "greening" of events, and to others it is completely incompatible with tourism! Whatever the definition (explored more fully in the final chapter), it is really a process of *becoming* more sustainable. That is because there is no single state of affairs that can be called sustainable, and nothing we do is completely reversible. Everything to do with tourism consumes energy and other resources, generates lots of waste, changes or damages the environment in some way, and contributes to climate change. So, all we can accomplish is to always try to be more green and sustainable, in a triple bottom line context. If we could find alternative energy sources for travel, that would go a long way to becoming a more sustainable industry.

Development of Event Tourism in this book means a process of growth, but not necessarily in more physical/venue development or more tourists by volume. It is far better to think in terms of growing yield, capacity to compete, sustainable events, and specific benefits for industry and residents. Viewed this way, the emphasis should not be placed on more, more, more, but on better, better, better. This has direct implications for the concept of managing event portfolios, as the portfolio is designed to realize many sustainable benefits. When you begin to look at Event Tourism this way, an entirely different development paradigm is possible.

Research Note: Events and Urban Renewal

Carlsen, J., & Taylor, A. (2003). Mega-events and urban renewal: The case of the Manchester 2002 Commonwealth Games. *Event Management, 8*(1), 15–22.

With the decline of traditional economic activities in postindustrial cities such as Manchester, mega-events linked with urban renewal programs are becoming increasingly important. The hosting of large international events is not only beneficial for the tourism industry but it is linked to all aspects of economic and social development. Manchester has actively sought a program of tourism and cultural events as a means of showcasing the city as well as accelerating the process of urban renewal. This article examines how the management structures, policies, and programs for the Manchester 2002 Commonwealth Games were linked with existing efforts to achieve long-term urban renewal.

Research Note on Events and Rural, Social and Cultural Development

Lade, C., & Jackson, J. (2004). Key success factors in regional festivals: Some Australian experiences. *Event Management, 9*(1–2), 1–11.

The state of Victoria, Australia, suffers from a scarcity of iconic natural advantages, to attract both domestic and international visitors, relative to those possessed by other Australian states, such as the Great Barrier Reef in Queensland or Uluru in the Northern Territory. As a result, event tourism based on cultural activities becomes a key differentiator for tourism in Victoria. Regional events now play a significant role in the Victorian tourism product with the state hosting over 60 regional tourism events and festivals each year. The contribution of these events and festivals to regional and state economies is important, as is the contribution they make to social and cultural development in regional Victoria. However, they are often developed and planned in a manner that may not lead to the success originally anticipated by organizers. Hence, any means developed to enhance their chances of success may be considered valuable. This article studies the development of two regional Australian festivals and the range of factors that contributed to their success, including the degree of market orientation, analyzed within a framework suggested by Mayfield and Crompton. A heightened awareness of underlying key success factors for these two festivals is likely to assist organizers of other festivals in prolonging their destination's life cycle and to maximize the potential benefits associated with staging the festival.

Capacity and Capacity Building

The term "capacity" is used in many places, and in different ways throughout this book. These are the common usages of the word:

- **Absolute or legal capacity of a site or venue:** how many people can it hold legally, safely, or comfortably, for different purposes?
- **Design capacity:** in event design the producers want to ensure a safe and enjoyable experience, and this must be translated into a specification of maximum or desired numbers of visitors; it also means what number of patrons a facility is designed to hold.
- **Community capacity:** does the community have the overall ability to host tourism or events in broad terms, including venues, accessibility volunteer numbers, infrastructure, sponsorship, and political support?
- **Capacity to absorb tourism:** including the two definitions above, but with the additional consideration of impacts and legacy, using sustainability criteria (see Getz, 1983).
- **Surplus capacity:** hotels and venues almost always have times when they are not fully utilized, resulting in "surplus capacity." Event Tourism is often pursued specifically to overcome seasonality of demand, and to make business and venue operations more efficient; there can also be surplus capacity within an event portfolio, when there are too many events for all of them to attract sufficient customers.

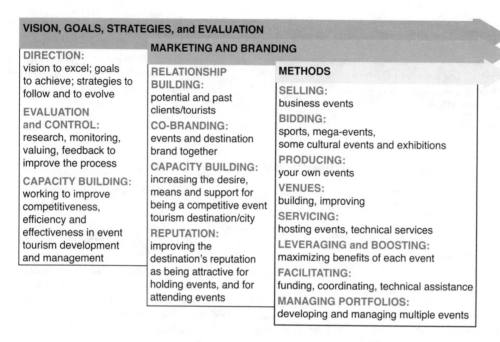

Figure 4.1. Event Tourism development process.

"Capacity building" is a process for increasing the capacity of something to hold more people, do more activities, or be more successful. It is used in several ways in this book. In the context of social and cultural goals we speak of "community capacity building"— that is, using events and tourism as instruments of social and cultural policy, so that the residents acting together are better able to achieve their goals and realize the potential of the community (the concepts of cultural and social capital are relevant here). For Event Tourism in general, "capacity building" is the process of improving the destination's ability to realize its goals and specifically to successfully compete in the marketplace; this might require infrastructure development or any of the other development methods discussed below.

Event-Tourism Development Process Model

A strategic planning process has already been described, as a continuous process. That has been incorporated into Figure 4.1, which shows three ongoing processes: (1) planning for Event Tourism (visioning, etc.); (2) marketing and branding, and (3) a set of development methods, or Event Tourism actions, that implement strategies. The bulk of this chapter is devoted to the specifics of the methods shown in the diagram, namely: sales, bidding, producing events, servicing, leveraging/boosting, facilitating the events sector, and creating and managing portfolios.

The planning and strategy-formulating process was described in Chapter 3, so we can go straight into Marketing and Branding, then a section on feasibility and risk assessment which describes factors that must be considered before undertaking any form of investment or development.

Marketing and Branding

Destination marketing organizations (DMOs) are created primarily to promote and sell the destination, and to assist members in their marketing efforts. Most are also in the convention sales and bidding business, and many are also bidding actively on sports. Few engage in integrated Event Tourism development or in event portfolio creation and management. But organizations created especially to develop events and Event Tourism have a different approach to marketing, as their primary concern is with one sector of tourism. In this section several key components of Event Tourism marketing are examined.

Capacity Building

In a marketing context, capacity building means to increase the desire, means, and active support for Event Tourism and the events sector. This is partly accomplished through strong relationships, but also through political lobbying, publicity (showing what events can do to benefit the public and particular stakeholders), and being accountable. Strong local support for events and Event Tourism will translate into sustainable development.

A destination also employs experience (in addition to tangible investments) from hosting events to increase its marketing effectiveness. In the learning organization each event presents an opportunity, through formal evaluations, to improve its bidding capabilities and marketing effectiveness. Part of this process relates to enhanced relationships and networking.

Relationship Management

This task is of critical importance to the overall functioning of DMOs and event development agencies, so much so that it is also often incorporated into the job descriptions for people in convention sales, event bidding, and working with coach and tour companies. Relationship establishment might not be easy, as with a small city attempting to connect meaningfully with international governing bodies or multinational corporations, and belonging to a sport tourism or destination marketing association might help. Joining professional associations [e.g., Meeting Professionals International (MPI)] is also a standard way to enter a larger, international network.

At the local level, relationship management with key stakeholders is also an ongoing job. Evidence of this is found in the case studies, demonstrating the necessity for strong linkages with local organizations that produce, host, and bid on events, corporations that can sponsor events, volunteer recruitment agencies, venue owners, academic and research institutions, and so on.

Destination Branding and Co-Branding With Events

The individual event's brand is considered in the following chapter with particular reference to Hallmark events, and then again for Iconic events in Chapter 5). Here we are focused on destination branding, and co-branding with events.

According to John Heeley (2011), author of the book *Inside City Tourism: A European Perspective*, a city brand is not the same as its image, identity, or reputation, which all exist in the minds of potential visitors or investors. He said "a brand seeks to challenge and change 'received' image, identity and reputation . . . branding is a business discipline" (p. 121). Branding starts with core values and how to communicate them, typically includes a logo and slogan, design themes, and messages (see the Belfast/Northern Ireland case), and official images or "signature shots" (p. 129). Nevertheless, it can be difficult to change perceived image, or reputation, despite efforts to shape attitudes and beliefs about a destination.

Heeley documented how the cities of Gothenburg, Sweden (Göteborg) and Barcelona, Spain, employed event-led branding strategies. For Barcelona, the 1992 Summer Olympic Games are viewed as the starting point, or perhaps catalyst, for the city's repositioning as a cultural capital and world-class tourist destination—what Heeley (2011) called its "post-industrial re-invention" (p. 44). Heeley believes that the Olympic success boosted the city's image, demonstrated competence in the events sector, and ignited public–private partnerships. Its legacy was "profound, as the city harnessed the Olympics impetus and investments to create sustained tourist growth and to fashion a new image for Barcelona: an identity characterized by urbanism, culture and style" (p. 45).

Gothenburg is a contrasting example, as it is a much smaller city (about a 0.5 million compared to 2 million for Barcelona) and it has never hosted the Olympics or similar mega-event (but it has been a successful host of World and European Athletics Championships). Its branding as an "events capital" depends on sustained cooperation among all the key stakeholders: "a collaborative platform for committed and active partnership across the local public and private sectors to implement a long-term strategy designed to position Gothenburg on the world stage and to maximize tourism revenues" (Heeley, 2011, p. 52).

It is widely accepted that major events can have the effect of shaping an image of the host community or country, leading to its favorable perception as a potential travel destination. With global media attention focused on the host city, even for a relatively short duration, the publicity value is enormous, and some destinations will use this fact alone to justify great expenditures on attracting events. For example, Wang and Gitelson (1988) observed that the annual Spoleto Festival in Charleston, South Carolina does not appear to be economically justifiable, "but the city holds it every year to maintain a desirable image" (p. 5).

The somewhat limited research on media impacts suggests that enhanced image is difficult to obtain, let alone prove (Mossberg, 2000). A study by Boo and Busser (2006) concluded that the festival under study did not contribute to a positive destination image among participants. Indeed, it appeared to have a negative impact owing to poor marketing and quality. The researchers pointed out the necessity for further research on the imputed connections between events and image enhancement.

Logically, permanent events have much more opportunity than one-time events to generate and manage media coverage, with the resultant potential for enhanced image. The very fact that a Hallmark event has become a tradition and a permanent attraction is in itself sometimes newsworthy. As well, Hallmark events will have an additional role in place marketing, to help attract residents and investment, and this leads to branding effects.

"Co-branding" refers to the efforts of two or more partners to associate their individual brands for mutual gain. Events with their own image and appeal can be "co-branded" with the destination, assuming they are both positive. Researchers in Australia have paid particular attention to these relationships (Brown, Chalip, Jago, & Mules, 2001; Jago, Chalip, Brown, Mules, & Shameem, 2003). Workshops with tourism marketers and event managers were held in several Australian cities, revealing a number of important themes that both stakeholder groups must collaborate on. Community support for events was viewed as being the most important criterion for successful co-branding, as the absence of strong support will hurt the event and its image. A closely related factor is the event's "fit" with the destination, both in terms of values, culture, and use of infrastructure, as this will affect local support. In repositioning a destination, the way in which the community wants to be perceived must be taken into account. Recurring events probably have a better chance of a close fit than do one-time events. On the other hand, hosting a once-only mega-event can help develop a profile and establish new traditions. Participants in the Australian workshops also believed that uniqueness was important, to the degree that events help differentiate the destination. If all places host the same kinds of events, or events providing the same benefits sought by consumers, little is gained.

Having an attractive and diverse portfolio of events was perceived to be important in destination branding (Jago et al., 2003). Large events might attract the greatest media attention, but small events can help support larger ones while developing community support and event management skills. The researchers concluded that hosting quality events is a necessary condition for effective co-branding, but there is also the need for integrating events into destination marketing and communications.

Image and Reputation Management

A number of closely interrelated terms and processes have to be sorted out and clarified here (see Figure 4.2). The brand is put in the middle, although it is really an integral part of a larger identity building and communications process that includes co-branding with events, positioning, image, and media management.

Crompton (1979) defined destination images as "the sum of beliefs, ideas and impressions that a person has of a destination" (p. 18). Hunt (1975) emphasized that a person's image of an area might have more to do with how the media projects the area or its attractions than with its tangible resources, and Goodall (1988) stressed that a destination image is conditioned by available information. People develop "preferential images" of ideal holidays or experiences, according to Goodall, and this determines how they react to actual experiences.

An "image" may be formulated by any person or public about a destination or event without regard to its branding or communications, but that is an ill-informed perception (which could be favorable or hurtful). Organizations, cities, and destinations engage in communications and media management with a view to creating a desirable image or "controlled viewpoint," through consistent advertising and messaging. The "brand identity and values" must be reinforced, plus "positioning" relative to the competition.

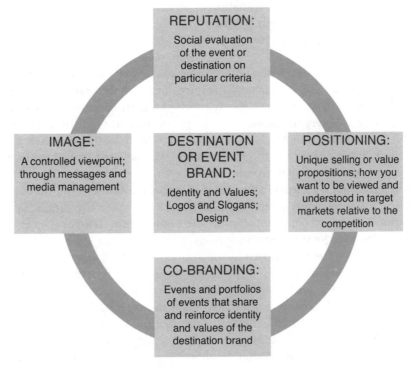

Figure 4.2. Interrelationships of image, reputation, branding, and positioning.

"Positioning," as a strategy employing the full marketing mix, manages how an event or destination wants to be viewed and understood by specific target markets (or "publics") relative to competitors. This entails "unique selling propositions" that differentiate you from competitors. Obviously, this strategy (or set of strategies in terms of marketing to specific interest groups) must also reflect brand identity and values.

A "reputation" is a social evaluation of the event or destination on specific set of criteria (e.g., that is a great city for festivals and conventions because of its facilities) or in more general terms (e.g., the city has a reputation for being safe and friendly). A positive reputation, or being "held in high esteem" is desired by every event and destination, and it constitutes "social capital" with potentially long-term benefits. As stated elsewhere in this book, a Hallmark event or Iconic event MUST have a strong, positive reputation to be effective in those roles.

Reputation management is the realm of public relations. Reputation has to be based on knowledge, so key target groups (such as meeting planners, event owners, social worlds) must be given a firm basis for forming an evaluation. This is the work of ongoing "public relations" at the broadest level, and "relationship and media management" in a more focused context.

Media Management of Events to Promote the Destination

Many DMOs seek to obtain specific promotional and image-building benefits from media coverage of events. To make this work requires an understanding of consumer decision making, how destination images are formed, and of managing the media to ensure that they communicate desired images and messages to their audiences.

Getz and Fairley (2004) examined the media management of a number of sport events in Gold Coast, Australia. While there were some notable efforts being made to promote the destination, it was concluded that a lot more could be achieved through better planning and in particular through coordination of all the stakeholder actions. Table 4.1 lists the major actions that can be taken by event organizers, DMOs, corporate sponsors, the travel trade, media, and sport organizations for the joint goal of promoting the destination as a tourist attraction.

Destinations want to get informative, exciting, and emotionally engaging stories into print and online media, and similar visual features inserted into broadcasts and rebroadcasts of events. They are designed to showcase the attractiveness of the host destination: its people, culture, scenery, or attractions. If the event is owned by a destination, the inclusion of destination promotion can be ensured, whereas in many cases it is a matter for negotiation. Sport events are often a problem for the host city or country as sport event owners require that visual prominence be giving to their sponsors, and broadcasters will then have their own advertisers. As well, sport journalists (and the media in general) usually have to be given incentives (and material to make their job easy) to feature the destination instead of concentrating on the competition. Longer events have much more opportunity to meet these media management goals than short ones.

The visual impressions of a host city or country can be packaged in a number of ways, including very short "postcards," longer stories or "vignettes," and full features. This is where familiarization trips and media hosting becomes essential. Shibli (2002) provided a good description of a "postcard" used in the 2002 Embassy World Snooker Championship held in Sheffield, England. One feature shown on television included Steve Davis, seven-time world snooker champion, starting the 2002 Sheffield Marathon and included images of the Don Valley Stadium. The idea was to promote the city as a National Centre of Sport.

Table 4.1. Stakeholder Roles in Media Management to Promote the Destination

Stakeholders	Actions
Event organizers	Utilize media relations professionals, photographers, and videographers. Develop long-term media relationships. Secure media sponsorship. Use the event website to feature the destination and link to tourism sites; incorporate potential visitor experiences (stories and packages). Employ imagery consistent with the destination. Co-brand through use of the destination name (e.g., Gold Coast Airport Marathon). Place destination signs at event. Provide destination information to all participants and visitors.
Destination marketing organizations	Require assisted events to adopt destination promotional goals and actions. Prepare video "postcards" and feature stories. Build an integrated branding campaign around major events. Develop and assist events that reinforce desired images or help repositioning (i.e., co-branding). Arrange "fam" tours for events.
Corporate sponsors	Co-marketing should include destination imagery. Sponsors should use event and destination-related material (e.g., videos) in their own promotions and B-to-B contacts.
Travel trade	Create packages for events to sell in target countries/regions. Sponsor events and incorporate destination imagery in all promotions. Travel agents to promote the event and destination together.
Media	Sponsorship deals with media should specify destination promotion goals and methods. Media will sell advertising spaces to DMOs. Media will purchase coverage in some cases. News coverage can be improved through cultivation of media (e.g., "fam" tours; hospitality).
Sport organizations	Participating sport organizations should promote the destination as well as the event. Sports and their governing bodies should be long-term allies of the DMO.

Venues

Venues as spaces must be sold (filled with events). Venues are also symbols of what a city or destination believes itself to be, manifestations of its self-image, branding, and positioning. Convention and exhibition centers, sports stadia and arenas, and festival places all invite the world to visit, to meet with residents, to enjoy and do business. Event venues are as old and necessary as events themselves, as they facilitate economic and social exchanges.

Most Event Tourism venues are shared spaces, with both residents and visitors having access. The balance of use, between residents and tourists, is a major component of the impact of Event Tourism, as visitors generate bed-nights and much more expenditure. Yet justifying public investment in these palaces and halls demands that residents have good and full access, or at least see the tangible benefits.

Events vary in their degree of place dependence and attachment, from completely footloose to completely embedded as permanent institutions. But all facilities for events are permanent within the host community, and are integral parts of its structure and character—so much so that event venues figure prominently in urban renewal and growth. Even the smallest communities need them, and want the best venues they can afford.

Amazingly, and this is a topic for theorists and researchers in many disciplines, the roles and basic forms of event venues have never changed, through all of history. We have indoor and outdoor places for assembly (i.e., meetings), arenas for sport and spectacle, spaces designed for exhibitions and sales, streets and plazas suitable for parades and demonstrations, routes for running and sailing, and large and small venues for all kinds of entertainment. Perhaps the first and most enduring event places are those for rituals and rites of passage. These generic event settings exist in all societies, and probably always will. So, we need the venues as much as we need the events—but to what scale and at what cost?

Justifying Public Investment in Event Venues

The justifications are basically the same as for intervention in the events sector (see Chapter 1), but they are complicated by several factors:

- many sport venues are primarily built for, and used by professional teams, for private profit;
- sport facilities built for mega-events are seldom used efficiently afterwards (the white elephant legacy);
- residents have no particular use for venues designed to meet international event demand (raising the issue of what scale is justified);
- tourism events can make many resident-oriented facilities more affordable;
- there are constant pressures on public authorities to increase the number, scale, or quality of tourism-oriented venues (by the groups that benefit most, raising the equity issue).

Issues specific to each type of venue are discussed more fully in Chapters 6 through 8.

Bidding on Events

Selling and bidding constitute two different marketplaces in Event Tourism. Seldom is the "purchase" decision solely based on price, but in a buyer–seller marketplace price is always an issue, and sometimes it is the primary consideration. What good salespersons understand is that they have to focus on service and value for money, not price alone. But consider this axiom of free enterprise: when customers have many choices, and they are all perceived to be equal in their potential to satisfy needs, then price (i.e., the lowest cost) will usually prevail.

Now let's consider the event bidding marketplace. In Event Tourism a "biddable event" has an owner who is willing, and often needing, to find a temporary or one-time host, and that is to be decided through a competitive bidding process. In this marketplace we have owners and bidders, and the bidders are generally DMOs, event development corporations, sport commissions, or special purpose companies put together especially for the purpose of making a major bid. Private citizens do not get the opportunity, and governments seldom bid on events directly—they employ the above-mentioned as their agents, but are often required to underwrite the bid (i.e., take responsibility for implementing the plan and paying for any financial losses).

If there are many competitors for an event the price will climb. And that in fact is what has happened with numerous biddable events, starting with the Olympics and international sport championships like World Cup, and progressing all the way down to fine art exhibitions or bringing pandas to your local zoo. What if there are no competitors? That changes the dynamics of the marketplace a lot, but the owner still has the right to refuse the awarding of the event, so in all cases there is at least the potential for every bidder to fail in their effort to secure the event (or pandas). In some cases, when the owner needs to find a host and there is little or no competition, then the process will end up being a negotiation. This is a stronger position for the sole bidder, and a weaker one for the owner.

In the selling marketplace the event owner is a paying customer who looks for the best possible deal, considering cost and many other variables. In the end, they pay for the privilege, but the venue or authority might in fact sweeten the deal, and might negotiate costs and other terms. But in the bidding marketplace the event comes with a price and whoever wants it has to meet conditions and pay the price. It has become common practice on the part of highly demanded events for the owners to require cash payments upon receipt of the award.

Catherwood and Van Kirk (1992) wrote from experience about bidding on special events, particularly in the sports sector. Most sports have governing bodies responsible for sending out requests for proposals to host their events. For the coveted Superbowl, huge lists of specifications and demands are made, and typical bids are 100 pages long. Site selection committees are typical, and this group visits competing destinations or venues. Escalating competition to obtain events in the US has led to the offering of cash guarantees by destinations. In other words, regardless of event attendance or sales, the organizers are guaranteed a certain amount of money. This practice tends to overcome some of the risks of holding an event in unproven locations.

The highest bids in monetary terms are not always winners. According to Catherwood and Van Kirk (1992), international governing bodies also want tangible benefits and excellent treatment for athletes, trouble-free management, and the best venues and hospitality. The potential for popularizing and expanding the influence of their sport is another important bid determinant. These authors provided a seven-point list of rules to follow in making bids, including the making of a unique selling proposition.

Bidding Strategy and the Comfort Zone

In many places event bidding is an ad hoc process, lacking clear direction and controls. That is simply too expensive and inefficient to be tolerated for very long. More appropriate is a bidding philosophy and strategy in tune with the management of a portfolio of events for the destination.

What exactly are one-time events to accomplish? How is their value to be measured against that of permanent events? Are they filling in gaps or simply being pursued for prestige reasons? Do small elite groups benefit at the expense of residents overall?

Ideally, destinations bid on events to achieve clear-cut objectives that cannot be met in other ways; otherwise why spend the money on such a risky venture? These are the main justifications for making bids:

1. bidding can obtain prestige or large-scale events that: (a) the city/destination cannot develop (otherwise, do it yourself!); (b) are highly valued in their own right for known, positive impacts (compared to events that do not have to be "bought");
2. bidding can obtain events that fill gaps in the portfolio, such as (a) specific events types appealing to desired target segments; (b) seasonality considerations (filling the off-peak); (c) specific benefits not otherwise attainable (e.g., substantial bed-nights, filling specific venues).

The principle is to make certain you know exactly why bids are being made, and how to evaluate costs and benefits. Also note that this is not the same as sales for venues that have to be used more efficiently—it is a complimentary process in that context. Major conventions and exhibitions, for example, might have to be won through competitive bidding, whereas many small events can be "sold" to meeting planners.

Another guiding principle is that of the "comfort zone" (see Figure 4.3). Each bidding organization has to determine what it values most, how much it can spend, and how much risk it can afford, thereby establishing its own comfort zone—which is likely to shift over time. Valuing events is discussed in detail in the section on portfolios, and again in Chapters 9 and 10.

Bidding on mega-events (with presumed high value) is an expensive and risky business, with failure to win being very likely. The bigger the event, the more it will cost and the riskier bidding becomes. As well, capacity is a major limitation, and if new infrastructure is needed the costs could get out of control. On the other hand, cities often want mega-events to help them boost their capacity. These bids should be rare. Many destinations have learned the hard way that mega-events end up costing way more than predicted, and residents are afterwards left with the burden. Others have been promised numerous and lasting benefits, but they only accrue to the elite groups who wanted the event in the first place.

If due diligence is performed through feasibility and risk assessments, many potential bids will be revealed to be too risky or too costly to justify, unless someone else shares

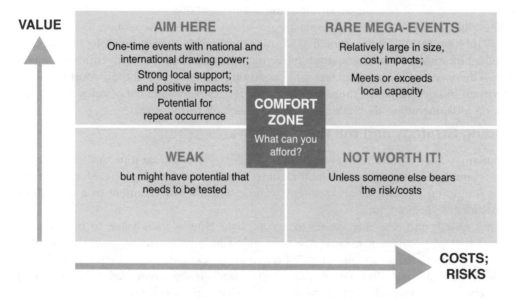

Figure 4.3. Event bidding strategy and the comfort zone.

the costs and the risks (i.e., helping with the bid and underwriting potential losses from the event itself). This quadrant is labeled "not worth it." Experience should teach bidding agencies how to detect these events, and lasting relationships plus professional networking will assist.

The "weak" area in the model is low in cost/risk but also on potential value. Perhaps deliberate "leveraging" strategies can elevate the value of these events, or maybe a number of them together can increase their value and justify the effort. Maybe this is a starting point for inexperienced bidding groups.

The target zone, "aim here," should encompass events with high value and reasonable costs and risks. Bidding here should be comfortable and easily justifiable. Most destinations want national and international-level events, although this goal is not necessarily for small towns. A bonus is the potential for repeat visits, or even turning the one-time event into a permanent, locally owned event. Strong long support is usually a good signal that the bid is within the comfort zone.

Critical Success Factors in Bidding

Ingerson and Westerbeek (2000) compiled a list that experts felt was important in winning sport event bids. "Primary criteria" were considered to be political support and stability, potential economic impact and ability to fund the event, media support and exposure to produce a positive image, accessibility and necessary infrastructure, technical expertise and communications, and city image plus community support. Also of primary importance are relationship building, reputation and professionalism of the bidders, commitment to the project, a positive slant on the event, composition of the bidding team, and guarantees for value adding and producing a legacy.

Westerbeek et al. (2002) later concluded that owners were looking for much more than the mere ability to host the event; they also wanted political support, adequate infrastructure, communications and exposure, accountability, and relationship marketing.

Research Note on Bidding for Events

Westerbeek, H., Turner, P., & Ingerson, L. (2002). Key success factors in bidding for hallmark sporting events. *International Marketing Review, 19*(3), 303–322.

Hallmark sporting events often are commercially driven entertainment entities which represent an economically important part of the overall sport industry. Because of the high popularity of international sporting contests, hallmark sporting events attract significant commercial, media and consumer attention. Cities around the world are beginning to understand the potential of using these events to draw attention to the host city, which is why the market for hallmark sporting events is becoming increasingly competitive. In order to award the hosting of the event to the most suitable organizer, event owners often require potential hosts to bid. The most important elements in this process have been largely based on logical assumptions rather than empirical data. This study focused on the bid process in order to ascertain the important elements essential in achieving a successful bid. Using an international sample of 135 event owners and organizers, principal components analysis delivered eight factors that were deemed critical in the process of bidding for hallmark sporting events.

Emery (2002) described the process of bidding through local, national, and international sport governing bodies and examined why cities in the UK bid on major sport events. It was concluded that cities needed to develop relevant professional credibility, know their strengths and weaknesses compared to the competition, learn about the decision-making processes, and do not assume that rational criteria are always employed in awarding events.

Research Note

Emery, P. (2002). Bidding to host a major sports event: The local organising committee perspective. *International Journal of Public Sector Management, 15*(4), 316–335.

Major sports events have the potential to offer significant benefits to any city, but at the same time are likely to entail immense resource utilisation and enormous risk. Focused at the organising committee level, and drawing upon general management and project management literature, aims to collect empirical data to identify current management practice used in the bidding process, and determine key factors in successful bidding. A self-administered postal questionnaire was sent to 220 randomly selected major sports event organisers from ten different countries. Targeted at the chief executive officer level or equivalent, the questionnaire provided general contextual detail and focused on present sports event management practices and processes. To gain more in-depth understanding of successful applications, three semi-structured interviews were administered in England. The findings reveal that the primary motivations behind local authority involvement are heightening area profile and sport promotion. Successful public sector applications were found to use bounded rational decision-making, driven largely by political reasoning rather than detailed objective analysis. Specifically identifies and discusses five key factors behind successful national and international governing body approval.

Destinations can also gain competitive advantage by improving the quality of services offered to event owners and by improving the events. This requires improvement of event management and marketing, fostering a hospitable resident population, and investment in staff and services aimed at both event owners and managers. Getz (2004) also sought to determine critical success factors for winning events of all kinds by surveying experts.

Research Note

Getz, D. (2004). Bidding on events: Critical success factors. *Journal of Convention and Exhibition Management, 5*(2), 1–24.

This research obtained information on event bidding from Canadian Visitor and Convention Bureaus. A variety of goals were identified pertaining to both intended outcomes (e.g., economic impacts) and the process of event bidding. Goals pertaining to economic impact dominated, including maximizing economic impacts, filling beds, and increasing tourist numbers. Overcoming seasonality problems and enhancing destination exposure or branding are also important goals. Of the "process" goals, the most frequently mentioned were concerned with winning events (e.g., the success rate), and making better bids. Critical success factors for event bidding were also identified: have strong partners in the bid process; make excellent presentations to the decision makers; treat every bid as a unique process; promote the track record of the community in hosting events; assist other organizations to make better bids.

Controversy Over Bidding Strategies

Very seldom is event bidding open to public or academic scrutiny, as many bid agencies prefer to go about their work with some degree of secrecy—especially when it comes to accountability for taxpayers' money. However, a review of event strategy and bidding in South Australia was conducted by Pomfret, Wilson, and Lobmayr (2009) and has been presented as a conference paper and made available online.

These economists sum up the available evidence on the effectiveness and impacts of bidding on and hosting sport mega-events, most of which fails to demonstrate any positive, lasting social value. In other words, how are authorities justifying their strategy, and are they really accountable? This controversy will only increase as the public gets more information about the huge costs of mega-events, the failure to deliver on promised benefits, and the matter of just who benefits and who pays.

> **Research Note: Controversy on Sport Mega-Event Bidding**
>
> Pomfret, R., Wilson, J., & Lobmayr, B. (2009). Bidding for sport mega-events. Proceedings of SERC 2009 (pp. 1–19). Retrieved from http://trove.nla.gov.au/work/156366894?selectedversion=NBD47729750.
>
> Sport mega-events such as the Olympic Games and FIFA World Cup, or on a smaller scale the Commonwealth Games or regional events, attract competing bids from nations or cities. These bids are mostly made at tax-payers' expense and spending is often large and non-transparent. Our paper addresses the question of why large sums of public money are spent in an attempt to secure uncertain rights to host events which, according to ex post studies, often yield few gains. The paper analyses the economics of the bidding process, emphasising public choice aspects of mega-event bidding to identify the interaction of potential beneficiaries and policymakers' interests. We do not directly enter debates about legacies of hosting mega-events, but ask why public money is spent on a bidding process which is even less likely to realize net social benefits. The empirical part of the paper uses past bids from the state of South Australia, a demonstrated bidder for various sports mega (or not so mega-) events with a mixed record of success, as a case study of the economics of bidding.

Convention Bidding

Most of the literature is on sport events, as this is where the media and public tend to focus. Little has been done to study convention or exhibition bidding, and perhaps this is related to the fact that so much of the business event tourism is generated through selling rather than bidding.

McCabe, Poole, Weeks, and Leiper (2000), in their book on the convention business, provided a case study on event bidding by the Sydney, Australia, Convention and Visitor Bureau. Sydney is ranked as the world's top international convention city, and no doubt the 2000 Summer Olympics helped to secure that enviable position by adding to the city's already attractive image. The Sydney CVB makes bids on behalf of the city, competing internationally. The bureau "promotes itself as a not-for-profit organization which provides a free and unbiased service to put conference organizers in touch with the best Sydney has to offer" (p. 168). They develop customized bids, obtain written endorsements from key political and industry representatives, locate appropriate venues and support facilities, prepare preliminary event budgets, and plan and host site selection teams. The bureau can also help event organizers apply for state or Commonwealth funding to assist an event to come to Sydney. They will make bids themselves or assist associations in doing so. They will also assist in selecting local professional conference organizers for events needing that service.

A Model of the Event Bidding Process

Figure 4.4 (from Getz, 2004) illustrates the bidding process. The destination pursues events that "fit" its goals, while the event owners pursue destinations and venues that will best meet their needs. Continuous marketing and managing stakeholder relationships is obviously very important in this process.

> **Antecedent conditions for owners:** These include needs and preferences for locating their events, and they might include maximizing their profits or revenue, or attracting the most fans or attendees. Mega-events benefit from moving around

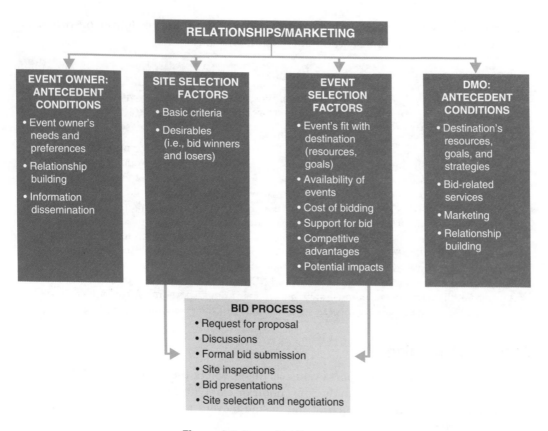

Figure 4.4. Event bidding process.

the globe, especially because their top sponsors want global exposure and brand building. Because these owners tend to be permanent, they have a vested interest in maintaining strong relationships with countries, cities, corporations, and destinations. Most engage in constant information dissemination via websites, publication series, social networking, and their own conferences.

Antecedent conditions for bidders (e.g., the DMO): This box relates to the earlier discussion of bidding strategy, and justifications for bidding on one-time events. The organization's comfort zone will in large part determine what events they can reasonably consider, and this entails consideration of their venues and what "league" they are playing in. Destinations also have to maintain strong, permanent relationships with many external bodies, including event owners and influential stakeholders such as corporate sponsors and politicians.

Site selection factors: Event owners specify what has to be done to even be considered. For sports this includes venues and how the competitions are to be run. For meetings and exhibitions the request for proposals will give these specifications. Bid "losers" are obviously anything that fails to meet the specifications or otherwise seems undesirable to the owner, while bid "winners" will likely be the value adding and unique selling propositions that destinations can offer.

Event selection factors: The notion of a good "fit" for events is really a matter of judgment. A good fit in one place might be completely impossible or inappropriate in another. It could be based on past experience (what has worked well before) or desired positioning (what the destination wants to become). This also relates to the notion of a bidding comfort zone.

Bidding process: If a formal bidding process is required, the major components of the bid document should include the following:

- personalized letter to the client, or sanctioning body;
- letters of invitation/support from all important local organizations and officials (be careful of order, considering proper protocol);
- executive summary;
- profile of the group making the bid and accepting responsibility for the event and its financing;
- support already obtained for the bid;
- summary of the event concept (as it conforms to specifications plus additional, proposed features);
- details of the plan: venue, facilities, investments, timing, scheduling, programming, meeting all the criteria;
- forecast of attendance; marketing plan;
- assertion of financial and economic feasibility; financial plan and budget;
- forecast of impacts; contingency plans;
- highlights of the legacy;
- advantages over competitors for the event.

Creating Your Own Events

Creating and owning events is becoming a rational and competitive choice for many DMOs around the world, and it might be absolutely necessary when there are serious gaps in the portfolio or desirable when opportunities like acquisition occur. It is also more common to see destinations buying or "stealing" events from others! Creation of new events is the wave of the future as this is perhaps the best way to ensure you can control events to meet your goals, especially when it comes to timing, targeting, and obtaining positive images.

Copying from others is an option, as there are many great ideas out there that potentially can be transferred to new locations. But this is not without risks, not the least of which is a failure to understand exactly why some events can succeed in one location and not in another. A community-based planning approach is wiser, especially if the establishment of a permanent, Hallmark event is desired.

Creating a Hallmark Event

Iconic and Hallmark events can be created from scratch, and with effort over much time they can be elevated into the ranks of permanent institutions. The Hallmark event holds special status in Event Tourism so I will use it as an example, but the logic applies to any event that is created within a tourism context. This section borrows heavily from a jointly authored paper (D. Getz, Bo Svensson, Robert Pettersson, & Anders Nordvall, unpublished) and is a result of an action research project in Sweden. The goals was to assist a resort in generating a hallmark event, so a lot of thought had to be put into what that meant and how it could be realized. The basic conclusion was that we are talking about functions, not forms, and that a Hallmark event has to meet a range of goals that are of importance for tourism and the host community. It could be any type of event, but is likely to be a relatively larger and public event. To be accepted as a permanent institution requires a number of special considerations that perhaps are of less importance for some tourism-only events.

The typical Hallmark event is a large, periodic celebration that has become a permanent institution in its community. At that scale, they are undoubtedly co-branded with the city's or destination's brand. But the concept does not imply a particular size or form of event—indeed, it suggests variety—because it is all about the functions, or goals met. These include being a tourist attraction, image making and branding, delivering community benefit, and being sustainable.

In Tables 4.2 to 4.7 specific goals and processes are specified for creating and evaluating the Hallmark event. Each of the six major goals requires separate evaluation, employing a range of specific measures and methods. We start with attraction, as this is the essence of event tourism, but it might make more sense to begin with community engagement.

Attraction

The estimation and forecasting of drawing power is essential to evaluating the feasibility of major events. Research will be needed to test attractiveness and image among target audiences.

Image and Branding

Hallmark events are Iconic in that they stand for (i.e., symbolize and are co-branded with) the city or destination. There is much more power in permanent Hallmark events for image making and co-branding than can possibly accrue from one-time events, no matter how many, although the true mega-events do have a long-lasting halo effect.

Community

Because Hallmark events are traditional and permanent institutions, they cannot exist in any sustainable manner without strong, community support. This entails political support and active support through volunteering, participation, and demand. Over time, the benefits to the community have to be clear, across all dimensions of the triple bottom line. Tokenistic participation is meaningless in this context, as support has to be based on a sense of community ownership and control.

Marketing

Both generic and targeted benefits should be part of the Hallmark event's appeal. It can be large enough, embodying a convergence of forms, to please many segments. For some, it can be Iconic, as the Calgary Stampede is with rodeo lovers or country and western music lovers.

Organization and Ownership

Traditional Hallmark events, the ones that evolved over a long period of time, tend to be not-for-profits and essentially community owned. Often local government is directly involved. In the case of the Calgary Stampede the city owns the land and leases it to the Stampede Board for $1 a year. But creating one from scratch might require a heavy public sector investment, or a public–private partnership. However, it is doubtful that a private, for-profit event can achieve the degree of community support needed.

Sustainability

Permanence, or at least durability over the long term, will depend on achieving the previous sets of goals. In addition, it has to be a green, and socially responsible event.

While it is true that many of the existing events that people have called major or Hallmark are cultural celebrations, this is not necessarily a defining characteristic in assessing drawing power. Sports, overall, undoubtedly attract many more tourists than celebrations, and some sport events have achieved Iconic and Hallmark status—often by surrounding the core competition with a festival. It has to be concluded that any type or

Table 4.2. Attraction Goals and Process for Creating Hallmark Events

Attraction Goals	Process
To attract tourists (preferably long distance and international in origin), generate economic benefits, and combat seasonality of demand	Consider the entire portfolio of events and attractions in the destination, relative to competitors. Prior to event production, demand can only be estimated through comparison to similar events and longitudinal, market penetration studies.
A1: Develop an attractive, unique theme and program that will appeal widely to residents and visitors as well as to targeted segments with special interests	Identify the key target market areas and segments; focus on high-yield, dedicated event tourists. Market area research as well as visitor surveys are required in advance of planning the event and while refining the concept. Test attractiveness and "staying power" with residents (it has to become a tradition for them).
A2: Produce a high-quality event with the potential to become iconic; focus on customer value and satisfaction	Quality can be judged through benchmarking against other successful events; and in the context of the planned theme and program, by experts; constantly monitor customer satisfaction and future intentions to return or spread positive word of mouth.
A3: Develop an attractive and effective community setting for the event(s) including specific indoor and outdoor venues	Involve the community in identifying suitable venues, determining the need for new infrastructure or improvements; plan for a permanent legacy. Consider aesthetic and functional venue requirements and community improvements; set a design capacity for audiences.
A4: Develop high standards and accessibility when it comes to services and consumables	Offer basic needs that matches the visitors' needs.
Evaluation of attractiveness	Measure the fit between program components (or subevents) and the expressed needs/preferences of specific target audiences. Test the theme's generic effectiveness in terms of uniqueness and appeal to broad audiences; evaluating the Unique Selling Proposition has to include benchmarking comparisons with other events and destinations. Evaluate the aesthetic appeal and functional effectiveness of venues and the community setting. Marketing planning will deal with many of these indicators.

form of planned event could become a hallmark. In searching for the primary attraction factor for Hallmark events, it appears that *reputation* is paramount, and this has to be fostered over a long period of time. Therefore, permanence and a tradition of local support (institutionalization) appear to be prerequisites. This goes together with the fact that many Hallmark events possess permanent facilities, and the view that the entire community is a setting or stage for the event.

Servicing Events

Servicing can be thought of as "value adding" to make it a more desirable and satisfactory experience for events, or as an essential part of being in the Event Tourism business (which is what service-dominant logic suggests). The venues, DMOs, the entire host city has an obligation to facilitate great event experiences, not just sell space.

Start with "essential services," those things that must be provided. Many of these are provided at the venues, but others must be added to meet an event's particular needs. The DMO or event development agency will likely have to work with many local stakeholders to ensure adequate provision of:

- transportation (inbound tour operators and destination management companies);
- information (the DMO, venues, hotels and restaurants, attractions);
- police and emergency services (especially for outdoor events);
- cleanup (especially for outdoor events);
- business services (copying, printing, faxing, emailing);
- specialists: audio-visual; mechanical; exhibition design);
- entertainment (local entertainers, booking agencies, and festivals with their networks);
- food and beverage (beyond in-house catering).

Next comes "problem solving," because there is always a need to have someone standing by to answer questions and solve problems. At large venues that is usually the job of event coordinators, and at hotels it is the convention service people or duty manager. Anticipating problems begins with feasibility and risk assessments, before bids are even made, or at least when it becomes known that an event is definitely planned. Past experience is the best starting point, and that might require benchmarking events that were held elsewhere. Using risk analysis consider both the likelihood of a problem arising and the potential severity of its occurrence.

"Hospitality" of some kind is an essential part of hosting events. This is not merely the provision of rooms, food, beverages, and other essential services; it is also making every guest feel welcomed and honored. Volunteers do this job in many cities, including meeting and greeting people at airports. Major events have entire hospitality (and associated VIP services) teams.

In my opinion, every guest to your city or country should have a cultural experience, and that begins with the greeting, then food and beverages, plus entertainment. All forms of host–guest contact are, in fact, cultural experiences. Many international visitors will want memorable, authentic cultural experiences outside the confines of the event venue or program, and that should be facilitated in pre- and posttours, as well as opportunities for more meaningful engagement with residents and institutions.

Finally, true "value adding" starts with the question: "What else can we do to make the event successful and visitor experiences more rewarding and memorable?" These might be bid winners, or simply gratuitous offerings to delegates, participants, or fans. A pleasant surprise will be remembered, and a quality souvenir will be treasured. And what can be done for the meeting planners or exhibition organizers who might be under a lot of pressure during an event? Can you make their job easier?

Some of the specifics of event servicing are included in the Visit Denver and Calgary Sport Tourism case studies.

Table 4.3. Image and Branding Goals and Process for Creating Hallmark Events

Image and Branding Goals	Process
To develop an iconic brand for the event, and to co-brand the hallmark event and destination, taking into account the identity residents attach to their community and the event	Widespread consultation is essential. Residents and other stakeholders must be directly asked to consider place identity and desired image. The band must reflect destination and community strengths and convey a unique and attractive message.
I1: Generate and sustain positive media coverage of the event and destination	Integrate event and destination/community marketing. Plan visuals and other messages at the concept stage and integrate into all aspects of design and production.
I2: Develop and sustain strong media partners	Obtain media input to planning and evaluation. Maximize number and types of media as sponsors.
I3: Develop and constantly monitor brand equity	Conceive of the event as a brand with its own values, co-branded with destination; build brand equity with target segments through coproduction of events and related destination experiences.
I4: Maintain positive event image among all key stakeholders	Monitor media coverage quantitatively and qualitatively. Regular evaluation of image is an input to decision making. Visitor and target market surveys employing measures of awareness, strength (positive or negative), and appeal (desire and intent to visit) among target audiences.
I5: Specifically foster a strong reputation through media communications, quality, uniqueness, and positive word-of-mouth recommendations	Media management to include dealing with image problems and disasters. Managing word of mouth requires attention to product and service quality, cocreation of experiences, and incentives.
Evaluation of image and branding	Media monitoring should be continuous. Implement meaningful consumer and resident feedback. Employ experts to make comparisons and evaluate overall image and branding effectiveness.

Facilitating and Growing the Events Sector

Every community and region has an existing population of events that can be classified by type, season, size, and impacts, but most are largely uncoordinated, existing in a kind of free market for events. Certainly most event populations are not managed, and portfolio management has not yet become the norm. In this state of affairs populations of events are subject to some of the ecological forces that affect all organizations and businesses.

We have already looked at the "legitimation" process by which events have become accepted as instruments of public policy and corporate strategy. That goes hand in hand with "capacity building" through proactive marketing and relationship building to make an integrate approach to Event Tourism acceptable and viable. Also consider the points made by William O'Toole (2011) on building an events industry through concerted, evolutionary policy. And remember the introduction to possible roles and development methods shown in Figure 3.1.

Table 4.4. Community Goals and Process for Creating Hallmark Events

Community Goals	Process
To establish and sustain an event that will directly benefit and be supported by residents, effectively becoming a tradition and a permanent institution	Community participation in the process is essential, allowing for all voices to be heard. Key stakeholders that can support or scuttle the process should be emphasized.
C1: Generate specific benefits for the community	New and better employment (measure direct and indirect jobs created; full- and part-time; wages/benefits). Infrastructure improvements (i.e., parks, leisure facilities, parking, toilets, etc.). Better entertainment (new opportunities; high cultural and popular). Animation and more efficient use of facilities and parks. Improved sense of community pride (measured by community attitude survey). New forms of social interaction and integration (e.g., public concerts, music). Physical appearance and design (lights, public art, decoration, etc.).
C2: Create attractive opportunities for volunteerism and other forms of participation in the hallmark event	Measure volunteer numbers, age/gender distribution, skills that will be learned. Measure other participation (e.g., athletic, artistic, managerial). Improved capacity for community development (e.g., new and improved organizational and decision-making capacity; better networking; demonstrated innovation and vision).
C3: Avoid, and where necessary ameliorate, negative impacts on the community	Avoid traffic and parking problems, noise, and other amenity threats. Avoid rowdy crowds and tourist activities; keep the peace. Avoid negative environmental impacts (adequate waste disposal, recycling, control of movement to avoid sensitive areas).
C4: Sustain political satisfaction and support for the event; ensure effectiveness in securing regulatory approvals	Might require constant lobbying to obtain funding and key votes. Internalizing political support through seats on boards of directors is often necessary.
C5: Implement full and open accountability regarding the event's costs and benefits, its management and planning	Consider setting up a monitoring and advisory group open to residents and other stakeholders.
Evaluation of community goals	Periodic community surveys (e.g., knowledge, attitudes, measures of involvement and participation). Periodic stakeholder forums (e.g., police, elected officials, community groups, industry). Reports from the organizers (on volunteers, etc.). Direct observation of the event(s) with video evidence. Annual visitor surveys (including questions on activities and perceived impacts).

Table 4.5. Marketing Goals and Process for Creating Hallmark Events

Marketing Goals	Process
To professionally and effectively market the hallmark event so that it can achieve all its goals	Consider the relative advantages of internalizing the event's marketing as opposed to consultants or a DMO.
M1: Effectively manage the marketing mix to achieve goals: experiential elements include product, place, programming and people; facilitating elements include price, packaging, partnerships, and promotions/communications	Product = unique, quality experiences for residents and for tourists (programming that is appealing to both generic and targeted benefits); packaging for tourists is essential; the event is the destination for many, but the community/destination is on permanent display; a two-price system might be desirable to ensure resident support; promotions/communications tie in with image making and branding; long-term, strategic partnerships are a key process goal; keeping the event fresh becomes a challenge with age.
M2: Implement a quality control and constant improvement system	Encompassing quality of management, personnel, programs, services, settings, communications. Employ accepted standards for management systems (ISO 9000).
M3: Build and sustain essential relationships to ensure a loyal audience, positive word of mouth, committed staff, volunteers, and sponsors	For the host community implement a permanent outreach and involvement mechanism. Permanent relationships with the tourism and hospitality sectors is required.
M4: Adopt a strong consumer orientation, especially for niche target markets and their social worlds	Institute a learning organization through research and evaluation; seek constant improvement; participate in the social worlds of target market segments.
Evaluation of marketing	Periodic marketing audits will be desirable. Performance measures are needed for each goal and subgoal. Resident and consumer feedback is essential.

Here are two examples of cities that are world-renowned for festivals (Edinburgh) and sports (Melbourne), both of which have won prestigious awards. The criteria for receiving such awards indicate what destinations must do, or possess, to be considered world class or at least leaders in their field.

Edinburgh won IFEA's World Festival and Event City award for 2010 and was declared the "most outstanding global entry" (www.ifea.com). IFEA said "There is a real sense of magic in the transforming power that a truly great festival brings to a city. The intensity of that magic in Edinburgh is not from one festival, but twelve." Here are their criteria:

- infrastructure to host and/or support those producing and attending festivals and events;
- diversity and success of current festivals and events that serve each market's city residents and visitors;
- city/government/community support of festivals and events;

Table 4.6. Organization and Ownership Goals and Process for Creating Hallmark Events

Organization and Ownership Goals	Process
To create an appropriate and feasible business model and organization that will produce and sustain a successful hallmark event	There are choices regarding ownership and organization, so it is critical to deal with this issue among all the stakeholders as early as possible.
O1: Secure adequate capital investment and other necessary resources to launch the new event	This might be the most critical element in planning hallmark events as without adequate financing there is no point in proceeding to detailed planning. Investors and grant-givers might be from outside the community, and not necessarily require an equity stake. Determine the optimal balance between commercial (for-profit), voluntary (nonprofit), and public ownership and responsibilities. Conduct prefeasibility and detailed feasibility studies, as planning evolves. Consider opportunity costs (are there equal or better investments in events, tourism, or other forms of branding and economic development?). Agreement on risks is necessary (i.e., who will underwrite potential financial losses?). Economic impact and cost–benefit evaluations are necessary.
O2: Maximize industry and community investment (fostering a sense of ownership) and ensure permanent support from all key stakeholders	Internalize key stakeholders. Constant lobbying. Assure full accountability to owners and the community. Conduct annual audits.
O3: Ensure a high degree of professionalism in all aspects of the event's planning and management	Professional staff recruitment and development systems must be in place. Implement volunteer training systems and "careers."
O4: Encourage and reward innovation in all aspects of event design and management	Innovation will follow from professionalism of staff and from volunteer and other stakeholder input. Management systems must encourage change and renewal. Comparisons and benchmarking with successful events will reveal weaknesses and opportunities.
Evaluation of organization and ownership	Evaluation: review by an oversight committee of key stakeholders; external expert evaluation and benchmarking-set standards for supplier quality and their conformance environmental and social goals. Value to stakeholders and the community must be measured against targets.

Table 4.7. Sustainability Goals and Process for Creating Hallmark Events

Sustainability	Process
To be a sustainable event in terms of environmental and social responsibility, economic viability, enduring support, and interorganizational relationships Innovation and creativity are necessary, considering that events are likely to follow a life cycle leading to decline in popularity as competition increases and/or the experience gets stale	These goals are in addition to pertinent sustainability goals in the other elements of the model. Sustainability in all its dimensions cannot be guaranteed, nor can permanence, so the owners and community must always be aware of weaknesses, threats, new opportunities, and successes (i.e., conduct regular SWOT analyses).
S1: To be an environmentally green event in all its operations and impacts	Adhere to sustainable event standards.
S2: To be a socially responsible event in all its operations and impacts	Enter into a contract (or license to operate) with the community. This will be based on transparency, accountability, problem solving, and delivery of benefits.
S3: Ensure adequate resources are permanently available for the development and growth of the event; generate surplus revenues to provide both a contingency fund and capital for investment	Periodic financial crises can be expected, so how will they be handled? It should be expected that the event becomes self-sufficient and generates revenue for reinvestment. Business planning and budgets to be approved and monitored for effectiveness in generating surplus revenue (i.e., a focus on specific revenue generation and cost control measures).
S4: Risk assessment performed initially and annually	Monitor and forecast demand-influencing factors/trends, including competitive events and attractions. Perform financial sensitivity analysis (e.g., effects of demand fluctuations on revenue). Forecast risks to the public, customers, participants, environment, staff, and volunteers.
S5: Set and monitor targets to control impacts, using triple bottom line accountability	Be "green" in environmental terms (considering waste, energy, water, recycling, traffic, wildlife effects, etc.). Social and cultural measures (e.g., community attitudes and quality of life; crime; threats to amenity such as noise). Economic measures (e.g., employment, occupancy rates, efficiency).
S6: Ensure the organization and network is able to adapt to changing conditions and renew itself periodically	Strategic planning is a must. All personnel to be strategic in orientation. Constantly reflect on how to adapt the structure, rules, etc.
Evaluation of sustainability goals	Monitor changes in stressors (i.e., visitation numbers, development, traffic) and resident perceptions/attitudes. Establish sustainability criteria (triple bottom line). Research program working with local/regional institutions. Stakeholder input.

- market leveraging of the "community capital" created by festivals and events—helping the judges to understand how the City and its nongovernmental partners maximize the branding and marketing images/opportunities provided by local festivals and events to leverage return in other areas;
- additional programs, services, and event-related resources that were not covered in the areas above (local university degree programs in Event Management, local certified professionals, shared event resource programs, etc.).

Melbourne, Australia won the "Ultimate Sports City" award from *SportBusiness* magazine (www.sportbusiness.com) competing against 24 other cities, for the third time in a row. Criteria included:

- the number of annual sports events held;
- major events held or hosting rights secured between 2006 and 2014;
- numbers of federations hosted;
- facilities/venues;
- transport;
- accommodation;
- government support;
- security;
- legacy;
- public sports interest;
- quality of life.

Later in this chapter the discussion of portfolio creation and management further elaborates on what can be done to assist the events sector and facilitate Event Tourism development.

Leveraging Events, and the Legacy

A lever, in mechanical terms, is a device that gives us the power to do more work. An event can be "leveraged" to gain more from it than merely ticket sales or basic tourist spending; its benefits can be extended in scope and over time through proper planning and management. A portfolio of events can be "leveraged" for even greater benefits, given that the many assets of venues and events in a city or destination can have major, lasting impacts that individual events cannot.

In investment, we can use borrowing to invest and gain a higher rate of return than is needed to meet interest payments—this is also called "leveraging." Applied to Event Tourism this means that debt financing of events and venues is sometimes justified when there will be a known, positive return on investment (ROI). But debt always carries risk—it has to be repaid even if benefits are not realized, and interest rates might go up.

Actual methods are discussed below, but several general leveraging principles can be stated:

- As in mechanics, an event is used as a tool or instrument to increase the destination's ability to do more work and achieve better results; research and experience are needed to learn how best to use events as instruments for wider and greater good.
- Long-term legacies of events are difficult to measure (i.e., by proving cause and effect), but the long-term costs and benefits have to be figured into calculations of ROI and the effectiveness of leveraging.

- When viewed as assets, an event and the existing portfolio of venues and events in a destination should always be yielding benefits (allowing for new infusions of money for maintenance and renewal), otherwise it is like owning a depreciating asset that eventually will have no value.
- It must be certain that the net benefits outweigh the costs of borrowing, otherwise the ROI is negative and the investments cannot be justified (of course, a variety of ROI measures are applicable, it is not always a simple calculation in monetary terms).
- Portfolios of venues and events should be able to achieve "critical mass" and become self-sustaining, dynamically adapting, and growing benefits on their own.

Leveraging Events for Local Business Advantages

Chalip and Leyns (2002) reported on how local businesses could get the most out of a major sport event. These authors noted that the uneven distribution of benefits from events is an important issue, because if local businesses feel little direct benefit they might oppose or fail to support events. Standard marketing practices can be employed (e.g., promotions, theming areas in line with the event, adding entertainment, extending hours), but the key is working collaboratively as a business community.

A study by Pennington-Gray and Holdnak (2002) examined the potential for event leveraging in Florida.

Research Note

Pennington-Gray, & Holdnak, A. (2002). Out of the stands and into the community: Using sports events to promote a destination. *Event Management, 7*(3), 177–186.

Spectators to a drag race event in Florida were examined within the context of tourism impacts and place marketing. In this case it was found that a majority of the sport tourists participated only in that event, while most others spent money in the county only on one activity—dining out. The researchers found this to be disappointing and recommended that the county should work specifically to overcome the "disconnect" between the event (which attracted lots of tourists) and the attractiveness of the area (which had been largely overlooked by the visitors). Destinations employing events as place marketers and wealth creators have to learn how to better leverage their events.

Faulkner et al. (2000) discussed mega-event impacts and the legacy, describing the research Australia did to measure the effects of its leveraging program surrounding the Sydney Olympics of 2000. Generic leveraging strategies included the following:

- using the event to build or enhance destination "positioning";
- enhancing visitor spending at the event;
- fostering longer stays and add-on trips/activities;
- building new relationships.

Delegate Boosting

This term is employed for meetings and conferences where attendance has to be encouraged, as opposed to events where people are required to go. Market intelligence is a key—that is, understanding motivations and constraints (see the research note below). Various techniques are also used by planners and marketers of events, including the following:

- value adding (tours, entertainment, celebrities on the program);
- direct marketing (as opposed to mass mailings);
- using email promotional "blasts";
- advertising in the association's newsletters or website;
- publicity campaigns in trade magazines;
- taking booths at the association's conventions in the years leading up to the year the event will be held.

Social Leveraging

O'Brien and Chalip (2008) suggested how social leveraging could work, starting with event-generated "liminality" (a term borrowed from anthropologist Victor Turner, meaning a time separated from normal life for sacred ritual or secular playfulness). This fosters both "communitas" (belonging and sharing, as equals) and media attention. Communitas is a vehicle for focusing event-goers' and other stakeholders' attention on targeted social issues, meaning that the event becomes a social marketing tool. Media coverage is managed to attempt to set or change the community's agenda, which can be viewed as a social construction. The "means" or methods include typical leveraging actions (lengthening visitor stay) but also enticing the engagement of visitors with the social issues. Media will have to be convinced to connect their coverage of the event to the social issues.

The Legacy

This term has already been used many times in the book, and in the EventScotland case study its full meanings were detailed. One point to remember, a caution really, is that "legacy" usually has positive implications (and that is the way marketers want it portrayed) but there are also many negative legacies of events that can be mentioned. Just think in terms of negative impacts that last a long time, such as the debt legacy, the displacement of lower income housing, or disruption to natural environments.

Professor Holger Preuss is an expert on event impacts and the opportunity costs. In this contribution he explains his approach to analyzing event legacies.

Expert Opinion on the Lasting Effects of Major Sporting Events

Holger Preuss is Professor for Sportsociology and Sporteconomics at the Johannes Gutenberg-University Mainz, Germany and Professor at Molde University, Norway for Eventmanagement. Editor of ESMQ (European Sport Management Quarterly). Reproduced from Preuss, H. (2006). Lasting effects of major sporting events. Retrieved from http://idrottsforum.org/articles/preuss/preuss061213.html.

Benchmarking and the use of macro data do not correctly reveal legacy. Hence a bottom-up approach is introduced which identifies the event legacy by evaluation of "soft" and "hard" event-related changes in a host city. These changes are defined as "event-structures" (infrastructure, knowledge, image, emotions, networks, culture). Many of them change the quality of location factors of the host city in the long-term. The benefits/costs through the transformation of the host city are the legacy of a mega sport event. Here a particular focus is put on tourism legacy.

Infrastructure: Means the sport infrastructure for competition and training, but also the general infrastructure of a city such as airports, roads, telecommunication, hotels, housings (athletes, media and officials), entertainment facilities, fair grounds, parks, etc. All infrastructure left after an event should fit into the city's development. Today temporary constructions can avoid negative legacies such as oversized and extraneous facilities.

Examples are a movable velodrome (Olympics, Atlanta 1996), a temporary 50m indoor pool in a fair hall (FINA World Cup, Fukuoka 2001) or an athletic stadium transformed into a football stadium (Commonwealth Games, Manchester 2002). Szymanski (2002) supports this idea. He claims that all spending should be directed at the most productive activities (p. 3).

Knowledge, skill-development and education: The host population gains knowledge and skills from staging a major sporting event. Employees and volunteers achieve skills and knowledge in event organization, human resource management, security, hospitality, service, etc. Spectators and volunteers learn to use public transportation and are acquainted with environmental projects. They also gain greater knowledge about the history of their city and country, culture and other issues.

Image: Major sporting events have tremendous symbolic significance and form, they reposition or solidify the image of a city, region and country. Usually events create a positive imagery and the city and politicians can "bask in [its] reflected glory" (Snyder, Lassegard, & Ford, 1986). On the other hand, the worldwide exposure of the event, the host city and its culture depends on the media representatives and cannot be entirely controlled by the organisers (Preuß & Messing, 2002). Negative incidences such as a bomb attack, hooligans, organizational shortcomings or just bad weather also influence the image of the host. Not only negative incidents, but also general bad attributes can be transported through a mega event to millions of potential visitors, customers or business partners. Exaggerated nationalism or unfair spectator behavior spoils hospitality, and poverty and crime create doubts about a potential tourism destination.

Emotions: Mega sport events give politicians a common vision to gain international prestige, citizens are emotionally involved and private industry is inspired to welcome an extraordinary and worldwide event. The pride of hosting such an event creates local identification, vision and motivation. An example is the Olympic Games in Seoul 1988 which created a national perspective, a feeling of vitality, participation, recognition, and an international perception of being modern and technologically up-to-date (Denis, Dischereit, Song, & Werning, 1988, p. 229). The Chinese are keen to demonstrate their increasing economic importance through the Olympics in 2008 (Lin, 2004).

Private industry is stimulated by the expected influx of money and a potential positive post-event legacy. This may change the readiness to invest instead of saving (Thurow, 2004). The announcement of the event leads to a programme of anticipatory investment. Directly, or indirectly it is the catalyst for a number of 'piggy-back' events (which in turn promote further investment). And during the event itself, there is a boost to local demand. While all of these boost the local economy in the short-term, the key to any longer-term effects lies in whether and how these leave a permanent legacy in the infrastructure, or in industry competencies (Swann, 2001, pp. 2–3). There is evidence from Olympic Games that these anticipatory investments have taken place. Critically seen, some have created oversupply (Preuss, 2004a; Teigland, 1996).

Negative emotions may also be caused if new event facilities use space of former workers' areas. Then citizens living there suffer from expropriation and relocation, but also from gentrification of their area, which leads to a loss of their social environment (Garcia, 1993, p. 260; Cox, Darcy & Bounds, 1994, p. 75; Lenskyj, 1996, p. 395; Preuss, 2006b).

Networks: International sport federations, media, politics, etc., need to cooperate in order to stage an event successfully. Their interaction creates networks. In general events improve political networks, such as close partnership with the central government. In particular the greater knowledge of sport, networks between politicians and sport federations and the image of being a sport city increase the affiliation to sport. Grassroots coaching programs, facilities for schools, sport for all, and additional sport events may be the result.

Culture: Major sporting events produce cultural ideas, cultural identity and cultural products. Opening ceremonies especially include a cultural-artistic aspect which is a condensed display of the host country's culture. A positive cultural image, increased awareness, new infrastructure and additional tourist products, combined with the soft factor of better service quality have a great potential to increase tourism in the long-term (Solberg & Preuss, 2006). Barcelona for instance used the Olympics to transform its infrastructure to become a "cultural city" (Garcia, 1993). The cultural presentation educates the host population and forces them to address their history. For example, there was increased awareness of aboriginal history in Australia during the 2000 Sydney Olympic Games, and increased understanding of Mormon traditions in the USA during the 2002 Salt Lake Olympic Winter Games. However, it is critical that the cultural awareness betters the situation of these minorities. Another example is "The Spirit of Friendship Festival," which was launched for the Commonwealth Games 2002 and aimed to celebrate the Commonwealth, thus leaving a cultural legacy. "It was a nationwide programme [and was . . .] set out to communicate the visual and performing arts and cultural traditions of countries in the Commonwealth" (Maunsell 2004, p. 24).

Legacy Planning

Leveraging the games requires stakeholder commitment and coordination among many partners. Ritchie (2000) looked at the Calgary and Salt Lake City Winter Olympics and drew 10 lessons for event legacy planning.

1. involve all stakeholders (costs and benefits);
2. understand and build upon local values;
3. include cultural, educational and commercial components, not just athletics;
4. involve and get support from the wider region;
5. because enthusiasm wanes after the event, plans must be solidified in advance;
6. residents have to be "trained" in providing hospitality;
7. develop "satellite" festivals and conferences;
8. use the event to foster social and cultural understanding and cohesion;
9. achievement and impacts of the event have to be preserved and publicized for younger generations;
10. tangibly connect the event to other local events or characteristics for synergy.

Will hosting a mega-event contribute to long-term economic development? Spilling (1998), a Norwegian researcher, concluded that the Winter Olympic Games of 1994 in Lillehammer, had "rather marginal" long-term impacts in the context of the overall economic activity of the region. The benefits that were created included an increased capacity to host events and better tourism infrastructure. No long-term impact on unemployment could be detected, and overall business growth was minimal. Thus, the Games could not be justified in terms of economics, and this is likely true in all lightly populated regions where infrastructure costs will be high and business growth opportunities small. Event tourism was the real winner!

Leveraging starts with the goal of maximizing the benefits of each and every event, and these can range from economic to ecological in nature (Table 4.8).

Leveraging Events for Urban Renewal and Social Development

Carlsen and Taylor (2003) observed that major events in the UK are seen as an integral part of urban renewal and economic development. Specific to Manchester and the Commonwealth Games, goals included:

Table 4.8. Leveraging Goals and Methods

Leveraging Domains and Goals	Methods
Economic: increase backward linkages; foster trade and investment; spread the benefits in time and space; build capacity for future events and development; generate financial legacy for residents and causes	Work with local businesses to ensure they benefit from new direct spending; employ local workers; use local suppliers; host international companies and investors to link with local manufacturers, traders, etc.; hold pre- and postevents, and subevents, outside major cities; package pre- and posttours; new infrastructure and venues for future events; marketing capabilities increased.
Social	Capacity building for community action through training and volunteering; fostering social inclusion, especially by incorporating benefits for disadvantaged and marginal groups; raising money for social causes; creating spin-off events; improved leisure venues and opportunities; bringing diverse groups together; carry messages related to social integration, civic pride, healthy living.
Cultural	Increase arts and sport participation; all events to deliver authentic cultural experiences to visitors.
Environmental	Explicit urban renewal tied to events; infrastructure improvements that benefit residents.
Ecological	Incorporate environmental education in all events to reinforce "greening" policies; incorporate life cycle accounting; stress adaptive reuse rather than new facilities; make public transport improvements

- heighten the city's profile;
- give impetus to urban renewal through creation of major sporting and commercial development;
- create a social legacy of benefits through culture and educational programs associated with the games.

Between 1999 and 2004 an economic and social program was established in concert with preparations for the Games, to improve skills and education, especially among young people; improve community health; enhance business competitiveness. The volunteer component of the Games involved training 3,000 disadvantaged people from the region. As well, the "Let's Celebrate" program aimed to foster increased intercultural understanding around the multicountry games. The city invested little in infrastructure, relying on UK grants and private investment, thereby allowing it to concentrate on social, cultural and environmental legacies.

The Built Legacy

Dimanche (1996) provided a graphical model of how the New Orleans World's Fair or other major events might generate lasting impacts, especially in terms of increased visitor travel to a city. The main initiators of change are:

- leisure visits and other participation in the event, leading directly to repeat visits in the future;
- infrastructure improvements (hotels, transport, other facilities) leading first to increased capacity and visitor satisfaction, then to more tourist demand;
- community benefits leading first to resident satisfaction and word of mouth recommendations;
- increased media coverage leading first to increased awareness and improved tourist image;
- increased tourist promotion leading first to increased awareness and improved tourist image.

Mitigation of Negatives

Weed (2009) argued that Chalip's (2004) approach to leveraging events should be modified to include mitigation. He put it this way (p. 61): "leveraging and mitigation implies a much more pro-active approach to capitalizing on opportunities and ameliorating undesirable consequences, rather than impacts research which simply measures outcomes." As this requires emphasis on the process of change cause by events, and within which events tourism operates, it represents a new paradigm.

Developing and Managing a Portfolio of Events

By "portfolio" I am using the usual business and financial meaning, namely a collection of investments, or assets, that are held for the purpose of generating sustainable yield. Various ROI measures are employed to value portfolios, and these will be discussed. But we should not forget that event portfolios are becoming more common, and important, in other policy domains such as social and cultural, and so portfolios held by tourism and event development agencies are very much likely to overlap with others.

Portfolio management represents a paradigm shift in Event Tourism (and in event studies in general). An emphasis on single events is mostly a supply-side approach, based on sales and bids, or exploiting the events already in existence. Moving to the strategy of developing and managing a portfolio of events opens up many new possibilities, but requires new thinking and involves many broader issues.

Many changes are required in orientation, accompanying a switch to portfolio creation and management, starting with a whole new set of network relationships, broader goals, and different performance measures. This cannot happen overnight, hence the need for a capacity-building strategy. Some destinations or cities might find they are already evolving this way, while others will have to make a conscious decision to expand the scope of their operations and consider carefully what new investments and institutional arrangements are needed to make it work.

Capacity building with regard to portfolio development is an ongoing process of growing the competitiveness and effectiveness of events in the city or destination. This does not necessarily imply growth in numbers or size, but that might be the case in the early years. Yield, competitive advantages and sustainability are top priorities.

Generic Portfolio Strategies

Drawing from conventional investment portfolio advice, several approaches can be taken, from aggressive to hybrid. Are they applicable to Event Tourism? An "aggressive portfolio" seeks high reward (or ROI) and accepts high risks (remember the "comfort zone"). It is difficult to see justification for an entire events portfolio based on this strategy, but perhaps the pursuit and development of a few events might be worth the risk. The idea would be to find new events and grow them, develop your own, or bid on ones that others are overlooking.

In contrast, a "conservative or defensive portfolio" would consist of tried and true events with little risk. Assuming that risk comes from the unknown, then a portfolio based mostly on locally owned and produced events might qualify. One-time events, won through sales or bidding, would have to have proven track records of attracting tourists at reasonable risk and cost levels. What events are resistant to recessions and rising travel costs?

A "balanced portfolio" spreads the risks across a number of diverse investments with the idea that when the market declines in one area the others still perform well. For private investors this might consist of equities balanced by bonds, with cash in reserve, whereas in an events portfolio it will have to be different kinds of events, at different times of year, aimed at different target markets, and with a variety of venues. This only applies fully at the city or wider destination levels, but individual venues can also aim for balance within their possible range of events.

Long-term versus short-term gain is another way to approach construction of a portfolio. Hotels, retailers, and restaurants want instant returns, all-year round, so the events they favor will be different from those that build reputation and brand. In some cities there is ongoing tension between those pursuing a balanced, long-term strategy and those focused on immediate results through constant infusions of conventions and exhibitions. Can all your stakeholders be pleased equally? Are they broad-minded and strategic enough to see the big picture? Perhaps they have to be educated.

This is all new territory in the Event Tourism sector, as little has been written about portfolios. Let's consider how some of these generic strategies might look at the city or destination level.

Model A: Portfolio managed for immediate, maximum tourism/economic gain. While this strategy can hardly be recommended, it might appeal to destinations just getting into Event Tourism, or where serious repositioning is required. The idea would have three parts: boost the marketing of existing events with the highest tourism and branding potential; bid on events with high impact that can be held in the near future; and perhaps create one or more new events for specific target markets. Building events into Hallmarks with long-term benefits requires a different strategy. Model A can be called the "blitz."

Model B: Diverse portfolio managed for long-term, triple bottom line (TBL) sustainability. This has to be the preferred strategy for most cities and destinations. And the most challenging. It requires careful planning and management, a lot of investment in capital projects (both events and venues) and in marketing, and multiple stakeholder involvement. Social, cultural, economic, and environmental goals would be balanced, as would the portfolio of events by type, markets served, and benefits realized. ROI is multidimensional, and complicated in this scenario.

Model C: Focused portfolio managed for increasing long-term benefits. Many cities are into this model, perhaps by default or lack of sophistication. But there is no reason why it cannot generate permanent benefits. The focus will be on the traditional sectors of sport or conventions/exhibitions, or perhaps festivals and cultural events. A strong focus can be useful in generating sustainable competitive advantages, in branding and positioning, and in managing the portfolio. A balanced portfolio within one sector is quite different from a diverse portfolio as in Model B.

For example, a balanced sport-focused portfolio would consist of a mix of one-time and permanent (preferable Iconic or Hallmark) events, appealing to a broad range of target markets, and fulfilling a variety of specific objectives such as venues used, time of year, media exposure, and participant and spectator oriented. Sports can be all-year round, but some cities/resorts will specialize by season. Both indoor and outdoor sports could be the focus.

In terms of business events, there are additional challenges. A focus on this sector will likely emphasize sales and bidding, relying on a few large and many smaller venues. Cities are constantly faced with demands or requests to expand the size and quality of their major convention/exhibition venues, making it an expensive option (though not necessarily more so than for sports). The really difficult challenge in the business events sector is to develop permanent events, owned by the DMO, the venue or a local group which potentially can become Iconic or Hallmark events on their own. What competitive advantages are held that could generate these types of events, such as the nature of local corporate headquarters (energy, finance, resource development?) or local manufacturing (textiles, machinery, food?) that can be exploited?

Permanent, owned events have the greatest potential for sustainable and accumulating benefits, but in any sector these can be complemented by a series of one-time events that generate additional benefits.

Critical Mass

The concept of "critical mass" has not yet been studied in the Event Tourism field, but with the ascendency of portfolio thinking it will become very important. Borrowing from nuclear physics, we can express it this way: *In Event Tourism "critical mass" is the minimum portfolio of events, venues, and related investments that is necessary to achieve a permanent, adaptable portfolio and self-sustaining growth in net benefits.*

Related to innovation theory, it could be expressed as the necessary confluence of stakeholder action, political power, monetary capital, and knowledge needed in a city or destination to get to the point where a sustainable portfolio of venues and events is recognized as being desirable and feasible. This connotation also links to organizational ecology in which the term "legitimation" is used to describe how a population of organizations begins to grow, like festivals as instruments of public policy, as it becomes accepted as being a proper form of government action.

We have no separate theory on Event Tourism portfolios, and nothing to explain how critical mass might actually work. What we can do is look at successful, dynamic cities and destinations through case studies and draw some inferences. Here are some starting points for theory development, stated as propositions in need of empirical testing:

> **P1**: A basic level of event venues is needed to develop critical mass; therefore, critical mass is linked to city size (it cannot be achieved as easily in a small town where large or many facilities are impractical).
>
> **P2**: A basic number and variety of permanent and one-time events is needed to achieve critical mass (because there are many possible synergies, not the least of which is developing the image of an event destination or capital) and this too is linked to size (larger resident populations will have the need for and means to support many more events).
>
> **P3**: Critical mass in Event Tourism cannot be achieved without market intervention by key stakeholders, likely a partnership between government and the private sector (competitive forces probably restrict collaboration among events and venues and industry unless there is policy and incentives to do so).

P4: "Legitimation" will be needed before critical mass can be achieved; this is a process of making investment in events and venues desirable because of demonstrated benefits.

P5: It is likely that a successful track record in bidding and hosting major events is necessary for achieving critical mass (publicity and a positive reputation being an important element in the legitimation process).

While small size and limited resources probably restrict the development of a self-sustaining portfolio of events and venues, this is not to say small towns or resorts, or even venues, cannot or should not pursue a portfolio strategy. Every place has some potential for hosting multiple events. See, for example, the approach taken by the world-famous resort of Whistler (cohost of the Winter Olympic Games in 2010).

Profile of Tourism Whistler (http://events.whistler.com/About-Whistler/Event-Tourism-Strategy/)

Whistler's largest resort partners, Tourism Whistler, the Resort Municipality of Whistler and Whistler Blackcomb Mountains, recognized in March 2007 that there was a need to develop a resort-wide Event Tourism Strategy to help Whistler expand upon its ventures that complement tourism (i.e. events) in an effort to build and stabilize customer visits. This strategy evaluates the role of event tourism (as an economic driver for Whistler, consistent with the Resort's Whistler 2020 vision), explores the impact of event tourism on the Resort's stakeholders, community and its guests, and provides recommendations for Whistler to reach its vision for events ("Whistler is an internationally recognized tourism destination—renowned for its superior quality and diverse events—making it a place to visit again and again"). Specifically, it addresses the following goals for event tourism:

- Grow and promote a portfolio of events that supports Whistler's brand, values and needs, and enhances Whistler's image (focusing on Whistler's existing events).
- Develop the infrastructure to support large events in Whistler.
- Access funding to grow events in Whistler.
- Streamline Community Partner roles & responsibilities to better serve events.

To date, Whistler has hosted a wide range of events from small local gatherings and regional celebrations, to "signature" events attracting national and international attention. In addition to annual festivals and events, animation has also played an integral role in enlivening the Resort and the guest experience. At the other end of the event scale, Whistler will also be a host venue for the 2010 Olympic and Paralympic Winter Games, a "mega" event that is already garnering international attention for the Resort.

Whistler's stakeholders, specialists in the field of event tourism and destinations that are already engaged in event tourism strategies widely accept that it is necessary to adopt a long-term, strategic approach to event tourism in order to realize the full tourism potential of events. The stakeholders interviewed for this strategy also support an integrated approach that considers both the needs of the guest (or "event tourist" or "tourist") and the community. They unanimously agree that authentic, organic events that celebrate the destination and are aligned with Whistler's brand and values have much greater potential to grow and attract new and repeat visitation.

Since the majority of Whistler's most recognized regional and "signature" events have been established over time, it is important that Whistler's Community Partners continue to focus on nurturing existing events and look for opportunities to grow smaller events into economic generators for the Resort (i.e. attract regional, national and international event tourists). Smaller, grass roots events are typically championed by locals and therefore have already established some level of community buy-in and participation. These events are also more likely to reflect the values, community passion and products of the Resort, and provide a competitive edge over other destinations (e.g. other resorts).

It is also recognized that there are some gaps in Whistler's event portfolio (i.e. specific types of events) and event calendar (i.e. times of the year when there are no events). This provides an opportunity for Whistler to attract and develop new events that can potentially fill these gaps and attract new and repeat visitation during key times of the year. Continuing to focus on Whistler's unique and natural attributes and talents as well as the products that Whistler offers will be key to setting the destination apart from its competitors and ensuring that events remain authentic and aligned with its brand, garnering greater community support and tourism appeal.

Portfolio Models for Event Tourism

There are a number of models to consider, and they are not mutually exclusive. In this first model, Figure 4.5 (first published in Getz, 1997) the emphasis is placed on the scale and drawing power of events, plus measures of value to the city or destination. Events within the area can be grouped according to two criteria: demand (measured by trends in the number of tourists attracted) and value in meeting other tourism goals (e.g., media coverage, image enhancement, theme development, sustainability). Sustainability of events should be a primary factor when examining value, as events with long-term community support, financial self-sufficiency (which will stem in part from ability to make surplus revenue), and are environmentally "green" will have more strategic significance.

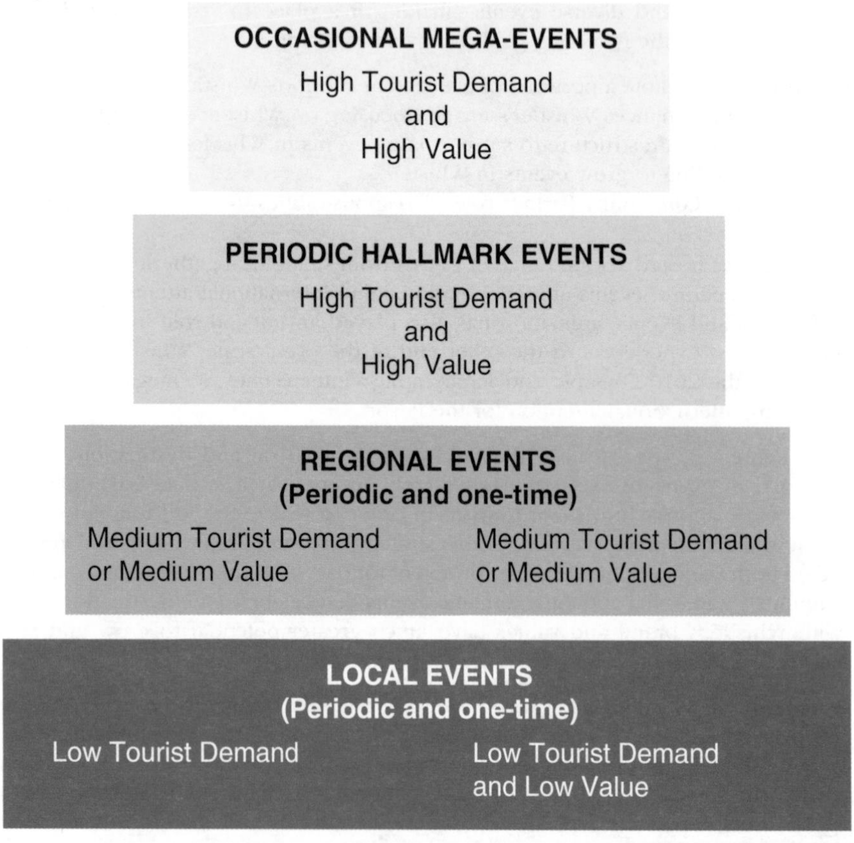

OCCASIONAL MEGA-EVENTS
High Tourist Demand
and
High Value

PERIODIC HALLMARK EVENTS
High Tourist Demand
and
High Value

REGIONAL EVENTS
(Periodic and one-time)

Medium Tourist Demand   Medium Tourist Demand
or Medium Value   or Medium Value

LOCAL EVENTS
(Periodic and one-time)

Low Tourist Demand   Low Tourist Demand
and Low Value

Figure 4.5. Event Tourism portfolio of events by type, season, target markets, and value.

One key underlying principle shapes this approach: almost all events have tourism and community value, but only some are capable of generating major tourism demand. Within any destination there is likely to be evident a hierarchy of events, with the majority having little direct tourist attractiveness, whatever the type. They nevertheless have value in the various roles discussed earlier, and some of them might have potential to become attractions. A smaller number of events will have medium tourism attractiveness and value, which usually means regional in scope. Some will have medium attractiveness but with low value in terms of other criteria, or vice versa.

The smallest number will be those events with high tourism attractiveness and high value in other roles, such as image enhancement. Mega-events and Hallmark events are those that display the greatest value and attractiveness. Mega-events are likely to be occasional, while Hallmark events are periodic. In this model occasional mega-events are not necessarily world-class events requiring major, new investments. The term is relative, so that any venue, town, or destination can host events that are exceptional in terms of demand, cost, or impact.

Ossian's Matrix (Figure 4.6) is taken from the ideas (unpublished) of Ossian Stiernstrand at Goteborg and Company, Sweden. His dynamic model suggests that events can be shifted in frequency and drawing power (combining scale, length of the event, and increased tourist numbers), and I have added the notion of creating permanent Hallmark events. In this view, a balanced portfolio might consist of half local events and half tourist-oriented events, with a mix of permanent and one-time events. Management of the portfolio has to be based on longer term goals. "Growth" in this model is multidimensional and applies both to individual events and the portfolio's overall value to the city.

Based on the well-known Boston Consulting Group Matrix, the next model (new for this book, by the author) suggests management of an events portfolio should always consider asset value on the one side and costs/risks on the other (Figure 4.7). This model does not apply to one-time events.

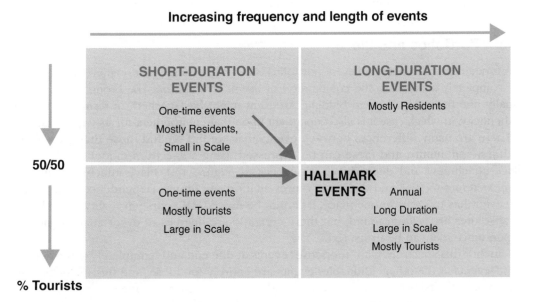

Figure 4.6. Ossian's Matrix.

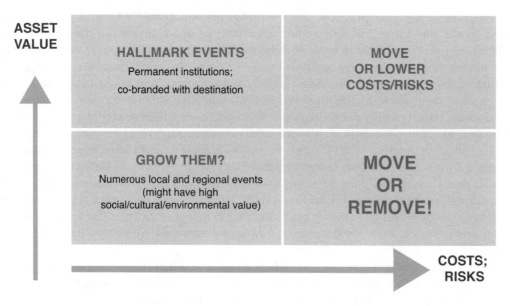

Figure 4.7. Managing an Event Tourism portfolio.

Individual events can be placed, at different points in time, in one of four quadrants. Permanent Hallmark events have high value and low cost/risk [i.e., once they are established as (or evolve into) institutions]. Getting events into Hallmark status will take time and money. Events with potential can be identified and grown for increased value. Where value is low, or costs high relative to value, events can be removed, moved into a different market category (such as by refocusing on tourist markets), or support withdrawn. In reality, many local events will simply be ignored by DMOs and event development agencies. The fourth quadrant is problematic in that value is high but so are costs and/ or risks. Can the costs/risks be reduced? If not, the events have to be repositioned in the portfolio, perhaps by shifting them into the Hallmark event category or turning them over to another organizer.

Event Portfolios and Place

A fundamental distinction in event portfolios is that of "owning" your own events (i.e., they are completely attached to the community) or events that can only be brought to a place, usually one time only, through bidding. An event might be "attached" in terms of cultural authenticity, in which case it is also dependent upon that environment for its legitimacy.

There are many differences between events that are bid on and those that grow from within a community, and these can be expressed using a spectrum model that features place attachment and dependence concepts (see Figure 4.8). Place attachment in this context refers to "fit," and authentic representation of culture. Dependence means that the event has to occur in one place, it cannot be moved. Of course in reality these kinds of absolutes are seldom found, but there certainly are degrees of event attachment and dependence that can be measured.

I anchor this spectrum with "footloose" events at one end and "completely place dependent" events at the other. "Biddable" events are entirely footloose, and this includes one-time mega-events, because this category seldom if ever returns to one destination—their owners can put them anywhere they want. Local and regional events are at the other end, as they exist only when residents support them. Also close to the "completely place

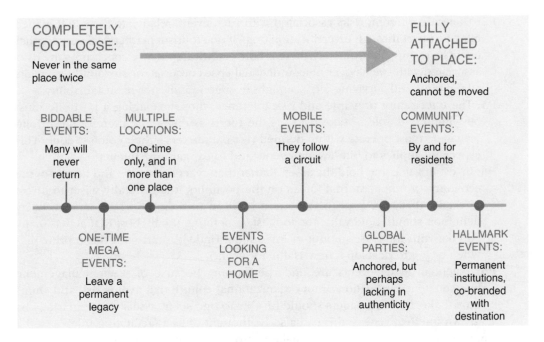

Figure 4.8. Events and place attachment.

dependent" end of the spectrum are Hallmark events that are permanent institutions, co-branded with the destination. Any event that is firmly attached, and/or dependent upon a single location, can be called "anchored."

The essence of place attachment (i.e., "anchored events") is that an event has a permanent home and contributes in one or more important ways to the portfolio. Some of these events are going to be mostly significant in cultural and social terms, notably festivals but also some traditional sport events and fairs or shows. The community takes ownership of these events. Those that become permanent institutions cannot possibly be moved or they lose an important part of their identity, their very reason for being. The more goals that an event meets, the more stakeholders that become committed, the greater an event is embedded in a community.

Iconic events have no particular location in this spectrum, as they are either a Hallmark event or hold symbolic value for a particular interest group or social world. They could be one-time or permanent.

Most mega-events have no dependence on place, and cannot become attached. However, through the construction of new venues, iconic architecture, or a more intangible legacy, they can permanently alter the host city and culture.

Principles of Portfolio Management

Should widely employed principles of financial portfolio analysis be applied to events? The analogy works to a certain extent.

> **P1**: Events have different benefits so the portfolio should treat them as complementary assets, each contributing to the desired whole; this applies to seasonality of demand, with events desired in all seasons; it also applies to geographical spread within a region, with all subareas being covered; it applies to resident versus tourist benefits, and to placing bodies in beds (favoring hotels) versus event tourists who spend more on self-catering and recreation/entertainment.

P2: There are different risks associated with each event, relative to their ROI, which must be offset through diversification (e.g., if one tourism market declines, another might be rising); unfortunately, there is little empirical evidence concerning the risks associated with events over time; individual crises occur at, or surrounding, events all the time, and surviving a crisis might be a good indicator of sustainability.

P3: The uncertainty principle and risk tolerance: those managing a portfolio must be willing and able to take risks, as the future is uncertain; therefore, portfolio managers must operate within defined risk parameters—their comfort zone. This especially applies to bidding on events and to capital investments.

P4: Invest in value and hold the asset: Rather than react to the ups and downs of the economy, or other external forces on the portfolio, it is generally wiser to invest in events that have proven value and hold on to them; the Hallmark event by definition should hold value the longest, generating the highest ROI across many criteria, with the least amount of investment (indeed, start with those principles when trying to develop a new Hallmark event).

P5: Potential: Many events are underperforming because of weak management, inadequate capitalization or an organizational culture that avoids risk and shuns growth. Portfolio managers should be able to find such "assets" that can easily be grown in effectiveness; this can also be thought of as a facilitating role.

P6: Cash flow: some events will make a profit or surplus that can be returned to the portfolio or distributed to owners as dividends; perhaps every event portfolio should contain one or more "cash cows."

P7: Cash cows are often matched by "dogs" in a portfolio, or events that should be terminated because they are both costly and ineffective, with little hope of improvement.

But there are other factors to be considered:

Lumpiness: Each event in the portfolio is not necessarily a discrete asset; indeed, synergies are likely to be at work so that if one fails another might fail, and if some succeed others might follow in imitation or by being free-riders (riding on the coat-tails of success); this can be thought of as a lumpy playing field for events; we have no research evidence on this matter.

Sunk costs: Events cannot easily be converted to cash, and many are created with permanence in mind. Thus, substitution is not always possible, and costs or risks are not completely manageable; some degree of messiness in the portfolio has to be accepted.

Service versus profit: Events have to meet multiple aims, and those pertaining to community service (or culture) are quite different from those pertaining to tangible ROI or profit, so different criteria are required when assessing costs and benefits. Some events should be valued mostly on their service value, but this raises the question of who is actually managing and paying for event portfolios—if it is just tourism, service value might get ignored.

Recommended Process for Events Portfolio Planning and Management

Clearly the complexities of portfolio management are so great that a process is needed to support planning and management. If it was a question of personal financial portfolios an expert would be consulted and perhaps the entire job would be turned over to the pros for a fee, but that is unlikely to happen in Event Tourism. The DMO or Event Tourism agency, hopefully with a lot of stakeholder support, will have to do the job.

- Step one is to develop a strategic event tourism vision, goals, and performance measures; little can be done without purpose and direction.
- Step two is to involve all the key stakeholders, as no one can be expected to deal with all the possible goals, measures, and research necessary to support the portfolio.
- Step three is to establish a permanent monitoring and evaluation system with regular reviews: develop indicators and methods of measurement, both tangible and intangible; again, multiple stakeholder perspectives will be required to cover all possible measures of change and impact.
- Step four is that research and information management will be increasingly important; working with academic institutions is a good option; scenario making, evaluation tools, cumulative impact assessments, all require expertise.

Finally, it is axiomatic to suggest that small portfolios will be easier to plan and manage than large ones, and that incremental changes will be more manageable than major, game-changing developments. Adding the Olympics or other mega-event to a city's portfolio will instantly overload the system and divert attention and resources, and will therefore necessitate a shift to a higher level of policy, financing, and planning (to be cynical, in these cases let the national government take control and responsibility, assuming all the debt).

Case Study: Queensland Events Corporation and Gold Coast Events

"Events Queensland is responsible for identifying, attracting and developing significant events that contribute to the Queensland economy, Queensland industries, enhance the profile of Queensland and foster community pride." Their mandate establishes the following priorities:

- Identify, secure and/or create new events that contribute to the generation of economic, marketing or tourism outcomes.
- Ensure existing events supported by Events Queensland continue to generate economic, marketing or tourism outcomes.
- Provide whole-of-Government leadership for events in the State and promote the importance of the events industry in Queensland.
- Support events across Queensland that build the social, physical and knowledge infrastructure of the events industry.

"Through building a dynamic and diverse events calendar, and strategic investment across a range of major, business and regional events, Events Queensland supports regional economies and showcases Queensland as a place where events shine.

Varying from major international tournaments to small community-run festivals, all these events share a common goal: to boost the social and economic prosperity of Queensland.

Events play a vital role in attracting visitors to Queensland and supporting the state's $9 billion tourism industry—an industry that sustains more than 200,000 direct and

Photo 4.1. Gold Coast Airport Marathon
(Credit: photo courtesy of Queensland Events Gold Coast).

Photo 4.2. Pan Pacific Masters Games, Dragon Boat Race, Gold Coast
(Credit: photo courtesy of Queensland Events Gold Coast).

indirect jobs. It is estimated that events deliver an overall economic boost to Queensland of almost $1 billion a year.

Events Queensland has a subsidiary company, Events Queensland Gold Coast, which owns and operates the popular Gold Coast Airport Marathon and the biennial Pan Pacific Masters Games.

The Events Queensland Regional Development Program also ensures benefits reach far beyond cities and into smaller communities throughout Queensland.

An initiative of Events Queensland, the Asia Pacific Screen Awards promote and acclaim cinematic excellence and cultural diversity of the vast Asia-Pacific region."

Profile: John O'Sullivan, CEO Events Queensland

John O'Sullivan has been the Chief Executive Officer Events Queensland since February 2010. As CEO of Queensland's chief events organization, John is responsible for securing and bidding on new major events that deliver an economic and community benefit to the state.

Since joining Events Queensland, John's leadership has seen an expansion of Queensland's dynamic and diverse events portfolio. His leadership has been instrumental in securing key sporting and cultural events including winning the Rugby Sevens bid for the Gold Coast and securing Ironman Cairns for Tropical North Queensland, as well as exclusive arts and cultural events such as Surrealism and the Cuban Ballet.

Prior to joining Events Queensland John was Chief Commercial Officer of Football Federation Australia from January 2004 to January 2010 where he was responsible for the growth of the game's commercial revenues from $25 million per annum to $90 million per annum. Prior to this, John was Head of Business Development at international television rights distribution firm Octagon CSI and worked for 4 years on the Sydney 2000 Olympic and Paralympic Games where he was Head of Paralympic Integration and Transition.

Origins

Queensland Events Corporation Pty Ltd was created in 1989 following the success of Brisbane's World Expo '88. Queensland Events was given the mission "to develop and support events that are capable of generating substantial economic activity and that lift the profile of Queensland both within Australia and overseas."

World Expo '88—and earlier, the 1982 Commonwealth Games (the most financially successful games of their time)—had increased awareness of the major economic and social benefits that can be derived from events. The Queensland State Government felt that event professionalism had increased substantially as a result of Expo '88 and that a formally established organization could help the state maintain that level of progress. As a result, Queensland Events was established to continue attracting world-class events to the state.

Queensland Events is a limited liability company wholly owned by the State Government and forms part of the portfolio of the head of state, the Premier of Queensland. Queensland Events also owns and operates the Gold Coast Airport Marathon and the Pan Pacific Masters Games through a wholly owned subsidiary company on Queensland's Gold Coast.

Queensland Events major objectives were at first devoted to the following:

- identify and bid on major international events;
- review and develop existing events with the potential to achieve national or international profile;
- develop new events of all kinds that have the potential to promote the state.

The following early priorities for Queensland Events were established:

- identify Queensland's strategic assets;
- identify major events that could be held in Queensland;
- continue liaison on existing proposed events;
- identify existing events with potential to develop a national or international profile;
- develop criteria for funding assistance;
- develop a data base of international events;
- establish priorities for developing new event concepts;
- conduct feasibility studies;
- establish a computer model for evaluating economic impacts of proposed events;
- develop a standardized list of financial criteria to assist event organizers in preparation of their business plans and budgets;
- prepare guidelines to assist event organizers in their submissions to Queensland Events;
- review marketing strategies and tools used by Australian cities in event bidding;
- identify agencies and organizations that can contribute expertise and resources to future bids;
- brief the major companies in the state on Queensland Events role, and determine their sponsorship and marketing policies;
- provide advice to event organizers and introductions to potential sponsors;
- conduct meetings with relevant government departments aimed at offering assistance with their representation at international events;
- upgrade marketing support material;
- produce a brochure outlining the role of Queensland Events;
- assess the viability of a special event newsletter;
- produce a brochure offering advice of use to event organizers;
- produce a high quality publication to promote Queensland's natural attractions and competitive advantages to event organizers, international sanctioning bodies, and potential sponsors;
- update a data base on event marketers and sponsors;
- identify relevant overseas trade exhibitions and events at which the state should be represented.

Their earliest major triumph was attracting the first Indy Car race to be held outside North America. This was held on the Gold Coast in 1991. Queensland Events established a new company to operate the race, which took a 5-year contract with CART (the owners of Indy Car racing) plus an option for five more.

In 2001, the State introduced an events policy and the strategy of investing in major and regional events. The Queensland Events Regional Development Program supports events outside the state capital of Brisbane, taking event tourism throughout the state (see details below).

The year 2003 was a big year for events in Queensland, as 22 major events were supported by Queensland Events, resulting in the "highest level of event-driven visitation from interstate and international markets in the state's history" (Queensland Events The Year in Review, 2003, p.10). Biggest of these was the Rugby World Cup, an Australia-wide event in which Queensland hosted 12 matches involving 14 national teams that attracted over 400,000 spectators. The state's Premier described the media coverage obtained by this globally televised event as "priceless."

Although most major events are sports (see the profiles following), 2003 also brought the Rotary International Convention which attracted over 17,000 delegates from 114 countries and generated over 120,000 room nights in the state. Delegates were surveyed and it was determined that the average spending per-person, per-night was AUD$295.68. It was the first convention to win the Queensland Tourism Award for Major Festivals and Events. Rotary International declared the 2003 event "the best convention in Rotary's 94-year history," stating the assistance the city and state provided with logistical support, venue, city hospitality, transport, and generally its attitude is no doubt the reason behind its success.

Queensland Events Regional Development Program

Events Queensland Regional Development Program (EQRDP) is an investment program designed to extend the flow of economic and social benefits of events to regional Queensland.

In collaboration with local councils and regional tourist organizations (RTOs), the EQRDP supports a diverse portfolio of events that help to attract a continuous stream of interstate and international visitors to Queensland while also raising the profile of the state nationally and overseas, encouraging future tourism and investment.

Events that receive funding through the EQRDP vary in size, theme, and purpose and range from music, art, and food festivals, to sporting events and regional and cultural celebrations. These events showcase regional Queensland, attract visitors and enhance their experience, and retain valuable tourism dollars within the region and state.

Events Queensland has created the most comprehensive portfolio of supported events of any state in Australia with over $18.3 million invested through the EQRDP across 856 events since 2001.

The Events Queensland Regional Development Program offers two funding options for regional events:

- Core event funding: single year event support;
- Significant regional events scheme: multiyear support (up to 3 years).

It is expected most events will apply for and be supported via the Core program, single event funding (1 year). At the discretion of the assessment committee, some applicants may be offered targeted project support.

Events Queensland Gold Coast

Profile: Cameron Hart, General Manager, Events Queensland Gold Coast

Cameron oversees the delivery and presentation of the Gold Coast Airport Marathon and Pan Pacific Masters Games, two of the Australia's leading Sports Tourism events. During his time, the Gold Coast Airport Marathon has doubled in size to become a benchmark participation event. Following nine years in the PR industry, Cameron worked on the Masters Games in 1991, the 1994 World Masters Games, 1996 Queensland Masters Games, inaugural Asia Pacific Masters Games in 1998, and was Event Manager for the 2000 and 2002 Asia Pacific Masters Games.

Gold Coast Airport Marathon

The year 2012 marked the 34th running of this event, in its 10th year under a major title sponsorship by the city's airport authority, attracting over 5,200 marathoners, while all the events involved a record 28,200+ participants from 30+ countries. Of this number over 20,000 are visitors to the city, generating tens of thousands of bed nights for the host city, of which tourism is a major industry.

The Gold Coast Airport Marathon is an annual, 2-day event held on the first weekend in July. The event includes a full marathon, half marathon, 10-k run, 5.7-km run–walk, and a 2-km and 4-km Junior Dash. Given the nature of the sport of marathon, the main focus is on attracting event participants rather than spectators.

Media relations are primarily maintained through the employment of a professional Communications Manager whose role is to create media interest in the event and ensure a continuous feed of stories to the mainstream media and social media platforms. The event website has demonstrated its success as a key marketing tool. Radio, television, and Internet and running magazine advertising are all used to attract participants. The official Gold Coast Airport Marathon website is designed to attract event participants in part by promoting the general attractiveness of the area, technical excellence in event delivery, and attention on the needs of competitors with a host of support activities such as 3-day sports expo, carbo- loading lunches, and marathon running champions and celebrities as guest speakers. Extensive destination information is provided and also accessible via an included link to State and City Tourism Authorities websites. A media monitoring service from traditional and social media is used to archive the national media coverage of the event, and analyzed to evaluation media activities and sponsor branding generated.

The Marathon has international links with other marathons, sport organizations, sports travel specialists, and general travel agents in New Zealand, Japan, Hong Kong, China, and South Korea. The Marathon utilizes these contacts to attract overseas attention and increase interest in the event. This activity, supported by targeted advertising in international running magazines, attracts participants from over 30 countries (including more than 500 from Japan, 400 from New Zealand, and growing numbers from the US).The event was named the state's best major event at the 2011 Queensland Tourism Awards and entered the Hall of Fame category by taking out this award in 3 successive year.

A 1-hour television production is distributed within Australia and internationally to over 30 sports broadcast channel reaching over 100 countries.

The Pan Pacific Masters Games

This event was previously named the Asia-Pacific Masters Games and is a biennial, 9-day-long, multisport event. In 2003 it was renamed to the Pan Pacific Masters Games with the plan to be alternating between the cities of Sacramento, California and the Gold Coast in Queensland. This alliance formed between Queensland Events and the Sacramento Sports Commission did not continue beyond 2003; however, the Gold Coast event continues to be conducted every 2 years. In 2010 the event attracted over 11,000 participants, making it the world's second biggest Masters Games behind the World Masters Games, which is held every 4 years.

Being a complex event encompassing approximately 40 sports, the operation of individual competitions is contracted out to pertinent sport organizations, and acts only as an umbrella organization providing infrastructure and marketing activities. Similar to the Marathon, the Masters Games focuses on attracting participants via range of media including Internet, social media platforms, sports-specific publications, and mainstream press. Media coverage during the event at a local level includes print, radio, and some television. Until recently, national coverage of the event has been limited to regional Australian newspapers featuring human interest stories (e.g., profiling "home town" participants). It is therefore positioned primarily as a lifestyle event. For the 2010 event a professional camera crew was hired to produce a 30-minute broadcast highlights package.

The 2012 Games expects to attract over 12,000 participants due to an increase of the numbers of sports on offer.

Gold Coast and the Commonwealth Games

After winning the 2018 Commonwealth Games Bid, the public was informed of details. The event could generate up to $2 billion in economic benefit with up to 30,000 full-time equivalent jobs created between 2015 and 2020. Over $500 million will now be invested on sport and transport infrastructure as a direct result of the successful bid. Infrastructure upgrades are to include:

- increasing the capacity of Metricon stadium from 25,000 to 40,000 seats;
- new badminton and mountain bike facilities;
- a world-class squash complex;
- development of the Coomera Sports and Leisure Centre;
- upgrades to the Broadbeach Bowls Club, Gold Coast Hockey Centre and the Gold Coast Aquatic Centre.

Summary and Study Guide

"Development" has many meanings, and the relevant ones were explained at the beginning of this chapter. In particular, Event Tourism is normally viewed as economic development, but also connects strongly to urban and rural development, to community development, and other social, cultural, and environmental policy initiatives where events can play a role. Most of this chapter is devoted to detailing the main methods of Event Tourism development, while two related topics (feasibility/risk and sales) have been dealt with in other chapters.

Our process model (Figure 4.1) refers back to the previous chapter when policy and planning were examined, and also incorporates as an ongoing process the marketing and branding functions that are necessary for Event Tourism development. Within that process we looked specifically at how branding, co-branding, image, positioning, and reputation are all interconnected and must be managed as a system. Media management is an essential part of this process.

The first of the main development methods, or actions, is venue development. This is merely introduced here because subsequent chapters look in greater detail at sport facilities and convention/exhibition centers. Again, how public expenditure on these facilities is justified is a major issue. Then bidding on events is closely examined, including the notion of a "comfort zone" that bidding agencies must determine for themselves by balancing potential value against costs and risks. Remember that value, or the "worth" of an event, can be measured in different ways, and has specific meaning within a portfolio strategy where synergistic and cumulative changes are generated.

Of great importance to the five major challenges is the idea that destinations should consider creating and owning their own events, both to seek competitive advantages arising from market intelligence and to realize the benefits of Hallmark and Iconic "destination events." A process is detailed for Hallmark events, showing numerous goals and the main implementation processes. This can be applied to other types of events that will become "anchored" and perhaps achieve "institutional" status. Combine this advice with the material in Chapter 5 on conceptualizing and design "Iconic" events for special interest segments, such as ecotourists.

A large section was devoted to developing the concept and practice of Event Tourism portfolios. A number of portfolio models and strategies were examined, along with the observation that there is precious little empirical evidence available on the subject. It is a research and theorizing frontier. The chapter also looks at facilitating and growing the sector, servicing events, leveraging and boosting, creating a legacy (and related controversy).

Finally, the case study of Queensland Events Corporation reveals much about both state- and city-level development of Event Tourism by one of the earliest and leading event development agencies. Its events in Gold Coast are profiled, but also look at the overall mandate, strategies, and development methods Queensland Events Corporation employs.

Study Questions

- Define "development" and demonstrate how Event Tourism is developed; use a diagram.
- Discuss the importance of branding and co-branding in Event Tourism, and how the management of image and reputation are linked.
- Work through an example of how you would develop a new, Hallmark event, with emphasis on goals and processes; what does it mean to be "anchored" or "attached" to a place?
- In the bidding process, what is a destination's "comfort zone"?
- Explain the "portfolio" approach to Event Tourism development by reference to goals, advantages, and necessary implementation actions; refer to "portfolio models."
- How do DMOs and other agencies "service" events for competitive advantage?
- Define "leveraging" and "boosting" and explain how and why it is done.
- Are all Event Tourism "legacies" positive? What are the main factors affecting long-term costs and benefits?
- Do you think "mega-events" are ever justified? Define the term, then give reasons.
- Compare Hallmark events, Iconic events, and mega-events on value versus costs and risks.
- How does the Queensland case study demonstrate both city- and state-level event AND Event Tourism development?

Additional Readings and Resources

- *Convention Sales and Services.* (Astroff & Abbey, 2011)

Chapter 5

Creating and Marketing Events as Tourist Attractions

Learning Objectives

Upon completion of this chapter the student should understand and be able to explain the following:

1. The tourism marketing audit.
2. A tourism orientation for events.
3. The 8 Ps of the marketing mix for events.
4. Marketing process for events.
5. Marketing planning and measuring demand.
6. Marketing strategies.
7. Positioning and branding.
8. The meaning, design, and marketing of Iconic destination events.
9. Feasibility studies.
10. Risk assessment and management.
11. Segmentation methods and uses.
12. Consumer research, including visitor and market area surveys.
13. Principles of service-dominant logic applied to creation of value propositions.
14. Packaging for event tourists.

Introduction

This chapter covers the individual event as a tourist attraction, and more generally the ways in which events can improve their tourist appeal. Not all events want to, or need to, be tourist attractions, and their wishes should always be respected. However, there are very good reasons for events, including festivals and cultural celebrations, to enter the tourism market and perhaps even to become destination events:

- generating additional revenue (through collaborative packaging, charging higher prices than residents will pay, attracting niche segments that want value-adding benefits);
- broadening the event's appeal in order to reduce dependency on one or a few segments;
- attracting the attention and support of tourist, place marketing, and economic development agencies;
- attracting a different set of potential corporate sponsors (who want to reach tourists or a broader audience);

- extending their communication and education reach (e.g., as authentic cultural traditions or as agents for societal change).

We can distinguish between events that are attractive to tourists, either as something to do while in an area for other reasons, or as a part of a broader destination allure, and "destination events" that are created for the specific purpose of attracting tourists. The term "attractiveness" will be used the same was as "drawing power" to indicate the event's potential to attract tourists from different market area—from regional day-trippers to international, long-stay visitors. So, this definition is important: *A **destination event** is created for the specific purpose of attracting tourists. Participants and/or spectators base their travel decisions mostly on the attractiveness of the event, although overall destination attractiveness is often a part of the decision.*

It also has to be stressed that many events cannot exist without tourists. International conventions and exhibitions, by their very nature, are established and marketed as destination events. Some attendees will go wherever the event is held, because the event is important to them, while others will be tempted to attend by an attractive location.

Now consider world championships in sport in the context of tourism. These events usually attract many tourists, but if they are large in scope (i.e., many games, in many venues, such as the World Cup of Football, or a World Junior Ice Hockey Championship), then it can be necessary to sell most tickets to residents.

The mix of residents and tourists at an event is very important, both for its economic impact and its flavor. If an event is perceived by residents to be "overly touristy," they might stay away. If residents do not want to celebrate, tourists might find a festival to be fake or otherwise uninteresting.

Tourism Marketing Audit

A starting point is the *tourism marketing audit*, conducted with the purpose of determining an event's marketing orientation, attractiveness for tourists, and readiness to serve them. Any event serious about tourism has to have a marketing plan, considering how all elements in the marketing mix relate to residents and tourists, plus sponsor and media issues that link to image and tourism.

A number of indicators can be used to determine if event organizations and periodic events are tourist-marketing oriented:

- Is there a statement of mission, mandate, or vision related to the customer, guests, or clients? Does it assign importance to attracting tourists?
- Have specific marketing and tourism-related goals been formulated? Has a marketing plan been completed?
- What marketing research has been undertaken (on-site surveys; in target market areas)?
- What are the formal links with destination marketing and tourism planning agencies?
- Does the event belong to or work with the various tour associations (especially bus/coach tours)?
- Does the event have a presence, singly or jointly, in foreign or domestic travel trade fairs or consumer shows?
- Does the event have a visible presence at other events and attractions?

- Can event packages be bought through travel agents? Foreign tour companies? Who packages the event? Are blocks of tickets allocated to tour groups and foreign markets?
- Can tickets be reserved? Is there a separate pricing strategy for tourists? Can reservations be made online?
- Does the event have a toll-free number? Does it respond to email enquiries? Use social media?
- Are hosts or guides provided to tour groups? Does the event take part in fam tours and site inspections?
- Has the event Hallmark status, being co-branded with the destination or city? Or Iconic status with particular social worlds? What is its image?
- Are relationships established through social media? Does it have official media sponsors?
- Do corporate sponsors help the event reach wider or targeted audiences?

Marketing Mix

The *marketing mix* consists of those elements that the manager can manipulate or influence to achieve goals. Morrison (1995) said there are eight, each beginning with the letter P, and these have been adapted to events in Figure 5.1. The diagram also classifies the components as being "experiential" and "facilitative." This distinction highlights the fact that some marketing elements directly affect the customer's experience at the event. Implications for Event Tourism have been specified.

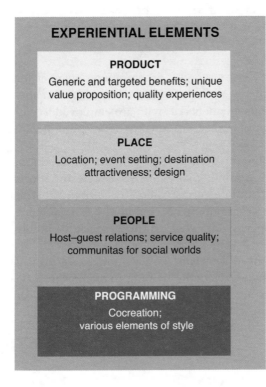

EXPERIENTIAL ELEMENTS

PRODUCT
Generic and targeted benefits; unique value proposition; quality experiences

PLACE
Location; event setting; destination attractiveness; design

PEOPLE
Host–guest relations; service quality; communitas for social worlds

PROGRAMMING
Cocreation; various elements of style

FACILITATING ELEMENTS

PACKAGING
Essential to package for individual and group tourists; value adding

PRICE
Tourists will often pay more; residents need incentives for repeat visits

PARTNERSHIPS
Joint marketing with DMO and other events, sponsors, and hospitality industry

PROMOTION
Targeted to specific tourist segments (advertising, public relations, social media; media management)

Figure 5.1. The marketing mix for tourist-oriented events.

Product or Experience?

Many events suffer from a "product orientation"—that is, they try to sell their event with little or no regard for what potential customers need, want, and will pay for. Many event organizations fail to consider alternatives to their marketing mix because they are committed to a single product concept. This usually happens because of the particular interests of the founders and volunteers, such as those dedicated to a particular style of music, other art form, or a sport. Sometimes there is simply an assumption made that if a good event is produced, the audience will materialize (the fabled "Field of Dreams" scenario).

The Event Tourism product is really a set of experiences (often brought together by packaging) that can be marketed as a value proposition. Experiences cannot be designed, only facilitated, but service and program quality can certainly be designed and delivered. The "product" in this context consists of both generic and targeted benefits, with a destination event having to be very specifically designed and targeted to certain interest groups.

Place

This term refers first of all to the location (destination attractiveness) and setting of the event (its venue) but also to the design of an attractive atmosphere. A major part of this component in the marketing mix is ambience, or atmosphere, and how it is created through design and programming. In some cases (like TransRockies) the outdoor environment is the setting and is all the atmosphere that is needed.

"Place" also refers to the distribution of event products, or how they are sold to customers. This is mostly a facilitative component, but if done poorly can negatively affect the customer's enjoyment. Distribution can be included with packaging.

Also consider "place attachment" as discussed in the previous chapter, as some events are anchored and authentic, while many are footloose and one time only in any given place.

Programming

To a built attraction, resort, or community, events are a key programming element for animating the place. But programming within the event is also a marketing decision, especially by way of creating targeted benefits. Various "elements of style" are employed to create unique, attractive programs, and both program and service quality figure prominently in making the event a success.

"Convergence theory" suggests that the hallmark of any event, whether competition, celebration, or commerce, can be augmented by adding other elements of style and forms of event. A simple sport event gains power in symbolic terms when it is co-branded with a destination through festivities and city-wide programming. A community festival gains attractiveness by incorporating many different types of events, from spectacle to highly targeted concerts.

"Co-creation" of experiences has become the norm, with target audiences involved beforehand in designing the program, or audiences actually helping to shape the form and flow of an event. Many large-scale events are now augmented with "fan zones" or other ways for people to participate when they do not have tickets, including online streaming and social networking. Building fan communities, much like corporations seek to create brand communities, is a hot trend.

People

People are an integral part of the marketing mix. First and foremost, the staff and volunteers are usually essential ingredients in making the event a success—they are literally part of the product and can be referred to as "the cast." This fact gives rise to the need for "internal marketing," which is the process of developing team spirit and a customer orientation among staff and volunteers.

Customers are also part of the product in the sense that most events cannot take place without them! The interactions between customers, the setting, and the staff/volunteers constitute a large part of the event experience and so cannot be left to chance. We call the management of these processes "interactive marketing." Facilitating "communitas" is an important design goal, especially for those events that feature celebration and that attract members of social worlds and subcultures.

Host–guest interactions are important in Event Tourism. Whether at an event, or external, the hospitality received by visitors directly shapes their experience. As a rule, it is suggested that the more engaged is the community with the event the more residents will want to share their experience with outsiders. This has its limits, of course, and cannot work with the smallest of neighborhood festivals.

Packaging and Distribution

Packaging is essential for Event Tourism, if only because so many events sell out within the community before tourists even have a chance to get tickets. Making blocks of tickets available to tour companies, and for nonresidents online, ensures that tourists will be able to attend.

A package is any combination of elements offered for sale at a single price. Packaging seeks to make the event experience more attractive by lowering costs (compared to buying all the elements singly), maximizing convenience, or providing "value added" in the form of extra features that cannot be obtained otherwise. Destinations can package events with other attractions and services, or events can offer their own, either for a specific event or in conjunction with other events, attractions, and services.

Tour companies market diverse packages, so event marketers can seek to influence them to promote specific events more effectively. When selling tickets and event packages the distribution network becomes important. Intermediaries of various types will be required, such as travel agents, tour companies, computerized ticketing agents, and others. Good relationships must be cultivated with packaging partners and intermediaries.

Price

Even events that are nominally "free" impose a price on customers in the form of time, travel costs, or lost opportunities. More specifically, event organizers usually have to set one or more prices for their products, including admission to the event, merchandise, vendor rentals, and sponsorship fees. These latter two categories do not impinge directly on the customer. The price of event-related packages will often be largely outside the control of the event organizers, and this could prove damaging.

Often tourists will pay more, given a strong interest and the fact that it is a special experience for them. Two-price systems are common, with residents given incentives to make multiple visits through whole-event packaging, and by way of promotions with local sponsors.

Partnerships

Marketing, especially in the tourism field, often demands the formation of partnerships to engage in joint marketing initiatives. Single events often cannot, on their own, achieve their marketing goals. The most common partners will be tourist organizations, governmental agencies such as city promotional offices, and other events. Joint marketing will be different from single-event marketing. While event managers might want to promote their event above all else, joint initiatives will generally have to promote the destination first, and then multiple events. This does not have to replace communications by single events, but they can become more targeted. As well, when packages are jointly marketed, event managers might have to modify their price and even their products to make the packages more attractive. Partnerships are also important in the production of events, as many organizations require direct involvement from other groups. Partnerships and relationship marketing are obviously part of the same process.

Promotion (Communications)

Although "promotion" is a commonly used term, it is more accurate to speak of the "communications mix," which refers to the full range of communications tools including advertising, public relations, and sales promotions. Image building for the event and destination is a related element. There is a tendency to emphasize "promotions," or specific campaigns developed to publicize the event. But the communications mix requires ongoing management and relationship building, not just one-off efforts.

Brand and Positioning

Drawing on our earlier discussion (see Figure 4.2), branding is closely related to positioning, image, and reputation management. There are considerable differences between how destinations and individual events go about this process, and it should be easier for a single event.

Branding

Probably one of the best known visual and symbolic brands in the events world is the Olympics and its five-rings logo (owned by the International Olympic Committee). The brand should be an easily recognizable name plus symbol or logo, and in the minds of consumers or the public at large it should ideally stand for the values or qualities the event wants to be known for. The brand reflects your identity, or character, and this in turn must be reflected in all aspects of design.

When a brand is fully developed it can be compared to other brands, so that an event like the Calgary Stampede, with a well-established brand, could be compared not only to other events but to other brands. Why is that useful? One practical application of brand mapping (a comparison very similar in method to the multidimensional scaling illustrated in Figure 5.2) is to find sponsors that are very compatible to the event in terms of public or target market recognition and favor. Both event and sponsors, for example, would want to be perceived as embodying tradition, quality, reliability, and social/environmental responsibility. This kind of brand mapping is illustrated in an article by Green and Muller (2002).

"Brand extensions" are highly desirable for events, assuming the event itself is well received. The Olympic rings, as a case in point, are highly valued by corporations for co-branding and so the Olympic logo appears on many lines of merchandise (under licensing agreements of course). Events can create other events with the same brand, or get into totally different enterprises on the strength of their existing brand.

"Brand equity" is the value of the brand, both in terms of goodwill and tangible returns. In the corporate world it is common for companies to buy well-known brands to add to their portfolio, an example being that of large wine companies purchasing (and keeping) small family winery brands. The only way for an event to realize its equity in monetary terms is to offer itself for sale, but it can be realized over time in other important ways including increased sponsorship and grant revenue, public and political support, and ability to borrow money.

Events that are community oriented might find little need to worry about branding. They are often "product oriented" and their managers tend to believe they are not competing with other local events. That might, in fact, reject anything that smacks of commercialism or a business approach. I think that is as much a mistake as not developing (and following) a sound business plan and budget.

With a tourism orientation in mind, an event's brand and positioning become critical, as the challenge of attracting tourists (especially from abroad) is difficult and potentially costly. Working with the destination, and co-branding, is clearly a good starting point.

Identity and Brand Values

The "brand" must reflect the event's identity and core values, and our TransRockies and Woodford cases show how this works in practice. For Iconic events targeted at social worlds, the brand must have specific and symbolic meaning to the target group.

Brand values can be thought of as expressions of the "personality" of the event, or what makes it different and interesting. Statements about "This is who we are, and what we believe" should emerge from soul-searching and not be fabricated to come up with a clever (but inauthentic) brand. Such statements have to resonate well with target audiences, holding meaning for them; an emotional connection is also desired. The two basic foundation points are: "we are part of your community" and "we know exactly what you need and want," but expressed in ways that can be clearly understood.

The brand values I believe to be of most importance to event tourists:

- uniqueness (for events this is in terms of experiences);
- authenticity (the event is a genuine reflection of local culture or a particular subculture);
- quality (usually this requires building a reputation for quality over time);
- reliability (especially for safety and health);
- value for money (especially important when the cost of long-distance travel is considered).

Adding to these values must reflect the needs of specific target markets, so the more you understand them the better. In the case of amateur athletes I have studied, challenge was very important (i.e., the event is THE most challenging), and the highly involved absolutely required competent management and a well-run event. In the ecotourism event example developed later in this chapter, core values of the event had to match those of dedicated ecotourists in terms of environmental responsibility and a making a positive contribution to conservation.

Research Note on Branding and Image Management

Camarero, C., Garrido, M., & Vicente, E. (2010). Components of art exhibition brand equity for internal and external visitors. *Tourism Management, 31*(4), 495–504.

This paper aims to explore determinants of brand equity for cultural activities from the perspective of internal as well as external visitors. Our analysis advocates four elements for brand equity in artistic and cultural activities (loyalty, brand image, perceived quality and brand values) and assesses them for the case of an itinerant art exhibition staged over the past twenty years in a region of Spain. Building on extensive literature, a model of the relationship is developed and empirically tested using survey data collected from 406 visitors. Data are analysed through Partial Least Squares. Findings suggest that external visitors attach greater importance to brand image as a determinant of value than do internal visitors, whereas for the latter brand values are the main source of value.

Image Making for One-Time and Recurring Events

Both supply and demand factors have to be considered in creating an image to satisfy the needs or desired benefits of the target markets, and for creating an image to highlight the best attributes of the event or destination. Uzzell (1984) advised that the image be constructed in a form that appeals to the potential consumer's emotions and desires: "It is an image of something he wants to be, to have, to experience, or to achieve" (p. 84). In this way, both the push (need) and pull (attraction) factors must be addressed in image making. The tension between wanting to get away from the ordinary or the bad, and finding the extraordinary and the good, can be exploited.

Every event "purchase" should be a special experience in the life of the visitor, and it might be a once-in-a-lifetime spectacular experience. The image of a one-time event has to be constructed in such a way as to make it a "must see" attraction. Emphasizing its uniqueness is essential, but there must be more. After all, many types of events have imitators and television makes it possible to stay at home and witness something unique from anywhere in the world. So the image must combine uniqueness and the rewards that only being there, being part of it, can bring.

For recurring events, it is essential to make the experience so attractive and complete that repeat visits are assured and word-of-mouth promotions will be strong. Thus, the event itself is part of the image-making process. The integrated theme, high quality goods, services and entertainment, the setting, the staff and volunteers are all instruments of image making. Similarly, each and every event is an integral part of the destination region's image enhancement. If the one event attended by the overseas visitor is a bad experience, the entire region suffers the consequences.

Targeted benefits, aimed at the special interests of key market segments, are important for creating "brand loyalty." Those visitors who find exactly what they are after will likely return. The image of the event or destination area should also employ the strengths of festivals and events to establish the image of a sophisticated, exciting place to come back to.

Research Note on Branding One-Time Events

Merrilees, B., Getz, D., & O'Brien, D. (2005). Marketing stakeholder analysis: Branding the Brisbane Goodwill Games. *European Journal of Marketing, 39*(9/10), 1060–1077.

The paper aims to explore a major issue in international marketing: how to build a global brand in a way that makes a strong local connection. Using qualitative research methods on a single case, the Brisbane Goodwill Games, the processes used in the staging of this major sport event are analyzed. In particular, the stakeholder relations employed by the marketing department of the Goodwill Games Organization are investigated and a process model is developed that explains how a global brand can be built locally. . . . The findings demonstrate that stakeholder analysis and management can be used to build more effective event brands. Stakeholder theory is also proposed as an appropriate and possibly stronger method of building inter-organizational linkages than alternatives such as network theory. Previous literature has generally dealt with the global brand issue in terms of the standardization versus adaptation debate, and the extent to which the marketing mix should be adapted to meet local needs in foreign countries. This research provides a unique extension to this literature by demonstrating how the brand itself needs to be modified to meet local needs.

The Role of Sponsors

In addition to providing money, "contra" (i.e., in-kind contributions) and technical support to events, corporate and public sector sponsors alike should proactively augment the event's marketing reach and help refine its targeting. This is especially true for media sponsors with multiple channels available to them.

The "fit" between sponsors and events should in part reflect this desired marketing augmentation, including mutually reinforcing brands (this is also a form of "co-branding") and particularly when the sponsors have been cultivating their own "brand communities."

The Role of Social Media

In today's environment it is essential to work with an array of alternative media including bloggers, E-Zines, other online sites, and to develop your own social network. Consider this quote from Amiando, a company that specializes in ticketing and registration for events:

> To determine the fundamental attitudes on the part of event organizers regarding the importance of social networks, the question was posed to them about how important social media are as marketing tools. The answers to this question were unambiguous: 73% of respondents indicated that social media is "very important" or "somewhat important." Only 10% saw social media as "somewhat unimportant" or "not important at all" as a marketing instrument. Facebook remains the most frequently used social media channel at 84%, followed by the microblogging service Twitter, used by 61% of those polled. XING, YouTube and LinkedIn were also frequently used, with participation levels between 41% and 46%. What's remarkable is the strong interest in Google+, with 36% of respondents reportedly active on the relatively new platform. One sees however that the network has been unable to date to establish itself as a competitor to Facebook, and is used as a supplemental network to Facebook, not a replacement. The values did not change significantly since 2011, excepting that blogs dropped 6 percentage points. (http://blog.amiando.com/; accessed August 1, 2012)

Social networking works best when there are clear target segments and you know how to reach them. Many events are establishing their own "brand communities" and engaging them in "cocreation" of event programming and experiences, even in building new events. Although mostly associated with the under-thirties, social media have attracted widespread use in older generations as well.

Positioning

"Positioning," as a strategy employing the full marketing mix, manages how an event or destination wants to be viewed and understood by specific target markets (or "publics"), relative to competitors (see Figure 4.2 again). This entails "unique selling propositions" that differentiate you from competitors. Obviously, this strategy (or set of strategies in terms of marketing to specific interest groups) must also reflect brand identity and values.

"Iconic" events are positioned with particular social worlds in mind (see Figure 5.2). In the case of TransRockies Challenge, and other events targeted at highly involved, amateur athletes, their iconic status comes from unique attributes such as "most challenging," and their appeal to "communitas" (i.e., socializing with others who share their values and interests).

The diagram shows positioning relative to competitor events on two dimensions: uniqueness and social appeal. Note that symbolic meaning is essential within social worlds, and that all "positions" are perceived by customers or potential event tourists. The strategy has to be implemented with value propositions, targeted and effective communications, pricing, and packaging—all the 8 Ps.

To test the potential effectiveness of a positioning strategy, the perceptions and responses of target markets must be researched. They could be asked to give a score out

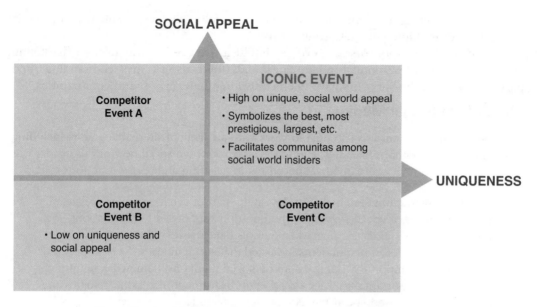

Figure 5.2. Positioning as a destination event. An example of an
Iconic event targeted at highly involved amateur athletes.

of 7 to the event, and to comparable/competitor events, on each of these two dimensions. Results can be plotted on a multidimensional scaling diagram. When the average (mean) scores are calculated, those events perceived to be both unique and appealing specifically to communitas within a social world should be placed in the upper right quadrant. If your event is not there, a positioning challenge is evident.

Creating a Tourist Orientation for Events

Becoming a tourist-oriented event requires much more than adoption of the marketing concept, although that is a prerequisite. Because the needs and motives of tourists are likely to be different from those of residents, and the tourism and hospitality industry must be accommodated, becoming a tourist-oriented event is much more complex.

A publication by Tourism Canada (1994) entitled "Packaging and Marketing Festivals and Events for the Canadian Tourism Industry" outlines the basic elements of a tourist-oriented event, and similar advice was provided in *The Cultural Tourism Handbook* (Lord Cultural Resources Planning and Management, 1993). Key points are:

1. Identifying and meeting the needs of tourists for:

    - more information; in different languages; longer in advance; with easy booking and packaging;
    - assurances about the event and the packages bought;
    - special support services (transport, access, accommodation, food, comfort, communications);
    - a quality product worth the investment; a destination experience in addition to the event;
    - value, or increased perception of value for money;
    - convenience, security and support in group travel.

2. Providing the essential visitor services:

- preferably a toll-free number (for information and reservations);
- reserve seating; a ticketing policy;
- information kits available upon request and distributed to prospects (e.g., individuals and tour companies);
- commitment from residents (as volunteers, participants, hosts, and accommodation or service providers);
- cooperation from the local industry (to ensure rooms are available, provide sponsorships and discounts for packages, to promote the event);
- an easily accessible information, ticketing and service office and on-site facility;
- decoration of the site and community; programming for visitor tastes; creation of the right ambience to attract and satisfy visitors;
- shuttle services to and among venues;
- hosts, guides, and hospitality for arriving tourists, both at the site, at gateways to the community, and at places of accommodation.

Iconic Events

While Hallmark events are also iconic, being symbols of their city or destinations, Iconic events also exist within every community of interest or social world, and might be small and easily overlooked by tourist marketing organizations. Yet their potential is great, especially for destinations that have unique selling propositions and those that want to get more heavily into producing their own events for niche markets.

The core meaning of "iconic" is that of a symbol, or something possessing symbolic value. Levy (2007), referring to news rather than planned events, described iconic events as those that gain mythic status within a culture, related to their newsworthiness followed by extensive interpretation and exploitation in political arenas. Holt (2004) discussed iconic brands in the context of cultural icons; that is, people, places, or things that convey symbolic meanings, gain mythical standing, reflect cultural values, and identity aspirations. The culture industries, according to Holt, want to create and profit from cultural icons, and this certainly includes planned events. By referring to Holt's ideas, I argue that Iconic/Hallmark events must embody valued traditions (which convey cultural meanings and the identity of the host community), and gain "mythical standing" through longevity, media attention, and positive reputation.

Another side to the cultural icon is its relationship with self-expression, or personal identity building, and this leads to the importance of iconic events within specific communities of interest, or social worlds. These will be events with high symbolic value to those affiliated with the special interest, providing opportunities for *communitas* (sharing with others who hold similar values) and self-expression (defining who they are). This status might be derived from size (the biggest), prestige (attributable to being the best or signifying the highest level of attainment), reputation for excellence, or uniqueness. Events within competitive pursuits tend to be hierarchical, with many at the small, local level and only one or a few at the apex.

The logic for developing Iconic events is found in the previous discussion of involvement, social worlds, and the event travel career trajectory. Figure 5.3 provides a conceptual model for ecotourists, with the following discussion also being important to their development and marketing.

The core of this concept is that of symbolic value, expressed as benefits targeted at specific communities of interest or social worlds. Iconic events stand for something of importance, and offering unique experiential opportunities appealing most to people with particular interests. Sharing these experiences with "others" is possible, but usually the most involved will want separate opportunities. Categories of uniqueness include the biggest, best, most prestigious, most challenging, or most unusual. These are context-specific benefits, dependent upon the values and practices of those within the social world. You cannot create them without a full understanding, and probably the active cocreation, of insiders. Levels of involvement have to be considered, as the most highly involved insiders will often want something different from their experience. A common benefit is communitas, or the sense of belonging and sharing with others, and this means socializing is important. The sharing might also be intellectual, as in learning/teaching, or behavioral, as in doing good deeds together. These ideas are incorporated into the ecotourism event model.

Research and Design for an Iconic Destination Ecotourism Event

Enough has been written about ecotourists to understand that they often participate in a global a social world, travel frequently, and represent a prime target market. But little is known about their event travel careers. Based on a literature review and drawing inferences from other types of highly targeted events, the following research and design process for ecotourism events is suggested. The logic and process should apply to most social worlds and all demand-side product development for Event Tourism.

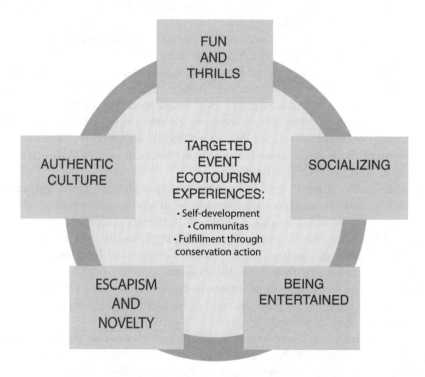

Figure 5.3. Concept for a destination ecotourism event:
Overall destination appeal and activities.

What Is an Ecotourism Event?

According to Singh, Slotkin, and Vamosi (2007), ecotourism is often conceptualized in terms of benefits—that is, what tourism should do for the environment or culture—rather than as activity. Criteria have generally been agreed upon for determining what is ecotourism, according to M. Wood (2002), and these can be applied to the events sector. By inference, ecotourism events should provide the following benefits:

- conserving biodiversity;
- sustaining the well-being of local people (indigenous or not);
- experiential learning;
- responsible action by stakeholders;
- the use, where possible, of renewable resources;
- local participation and ownership.

This set of criteria implies that ecotourists will be looking for these benefits in the program, marketing, and evaluation of events that attract them, whereas their personal experiences will be expected to deliver benefits such as self-development and socializing.

Who Are "Ecotourists" and Why Do They Travel?

Often demographics do not reveal much about special interest groups, although it goes without saying that to be prime targets for international Event Tourism they largely have to have money, time, and strong interests! Usually when I research special interest groups (whether mountain bikers, runners, wine lovers, or foodies) I am completely uninterested in the vast majority of people—they do not constitute a viable "market" and it would be a complete waste of time and effort to randomly sample the entire population.

Instead, I want to narrow my research to those who are most likely to travel, and preferably internationally, because of their involvement. This suggests starting with a sample of people who are known ecotourists because they belong to a club, read specific magazines or blogs, or are attending an event with an environmental theme. Use a survey to ask about motivations and involvement with ecotourism (or related concepts like environmental education, conservation, birds), then travel patterns and preferences. While those who have already traveled internationally for an ecotourism event will represent a prime target group, other highly involved ecotourists might also be lured by the right benefit package.

A number of research studies have examined the economic impacts of birding and wildlife festivals, and in doing so have profiled their visitors. Hvenegaard and Manaloor (2007) reviewed the pertinent literature and concluded that wildlife festivals in North America attract the "very educated," and somewhat more female and older visitors than the general population. The proportion of tourists attracted to the documented events ranged from 10% to 73%. In their own research on two Canadian wildlife festivals, Hvenegaard and Manaloor determined that the one attracting more longer distance, higher yield tourists appealed to the more specialized ecotourist.

Curtin (2010) applied the concept of serious leisure to "serious wildlife tourists," concluding that "the 'culture' of 'serious' wildlife tourism is made up of individuals who differentiate themselves from other tourists in terms of dress, behavior, development of skills, equipment and intellectual capital, illustrated by their desire to scope, identify and photograph wildlife" (p. 1). A closely related concept is that of "recreational specialization" (Bryan, 1977), defined as "a continuum of behavior from the general to the particular, reflected by equipment and skills used in the sport, and activity setting preferences"

(175). This construct postulates that as people become more involved in a leisure pursuit their increasing specialization can be measured by attitude and behavior.

Burr and Scott (2004) found that only a small fraction of participants at a birding festival were highly specialized, and they were less satisfied with the event. Most attendees had an interest in birds but did other things, and enjoyed general festival programming. Maple, Eagles, and Rolfe (2010) examined specialization among birdwatchers, finding that beginners spent less time bird watching, and their trips were shorter and resulted in lower tourist expenditure. Intermediate and expert birders were similar to each other, and were different from the beginners. The more experienced birders required specialized programs.

Eubanks, Stoll, and Ditton (2004) defined the "birding social world" to include "all who watch birds for recreation or consider themselves birdwatchers or birders" (p. 152). They suggested that the birding social world would "contain a diversity of individuals who participate in a diversity of birding forms for a diversity of reasons or motivations" (p. 152). Members were thought to start out as "strangers," while more dedicated "insiders" had birding as a central life interest and a basis for self-identity. This corresponds to what D. Scott, Baker, and Kim (1999) called "serious birders" participating in the Great Texas Birding Classic. McFarlane (1996) used cluster analysis on data from a sample of birders and was able to rank them from low to high specialization. The birding social world ranged from casual birders to advanced birders (7% of the sample) who share their expertise with others, take several birding trips per year, can identify many species, and have a great deal invested in their birding activity.

We can deduce that serious, highly involved ecotourists are the most likely to travel (especially over great distances) to attend an ecotourist event, and therefore should be a primary target segment. These people are engaged in long-term, leisure careers, and involved in one or more related social worlds that generate an interest in attending events that promise to yield the benefits they seek. They might travel to events in the capacity of tourists, volunteers, organizers, or officials. Designing events with this segment in mind presents a number of challenges. They will require separate, experiential programming from lesser involved guests, as they seek different benefits.

Hard and Soft Ecotourism

According to Laarman and Durst (1987) "nature-oriented tourism has hard and soft dimensions in two senses" and these relate to the extent to which the tourism is dedicated or casual on the one hand, and difficult or easy on the other. Weaver and Lawton (2007) concluded that the hard/soft dichotomy is dominant in the ecotourism literature. However, they also identified the "structured ecotourist" who wants a hard ecotourism experience in natural environments but at other times prefers luxury, or soft ecotourism.

Singh et al. (2007) sampled visitors to two US bird festivals, which they called "soft ecotourism events." The market is composed of "somewhat older, educated and affluent ecotourists who participate in these events for entertainment as well as learning" (p. 119). They found evidence that a significant segment participating in "soft ecotourism" "contributed towards enhance sustainability" by way of engaging in conservation and advocacy. However, those researchers also concluded that "little is known about the underlying psychographic characteristics that define ecotourists," and additionally, "whether different categories exist in terms of their level of commitment to sustainable tourism" (p. 12).

Concept for a Destination Ecotourist Event

The core (see Figure 5.3) consists of those benefits desired by dedicated ecotourists, namely self development (through meeting challenges, learning, pursuing excellence), fulfillment (through making a difference, volunteering, assisting in conservation), and the communitas that comes from sharing with others within a social world. Augmentation of this core can consist of many different programmic elements of style that will broaden the audience to those seeking generic benefits and might include the dedicated ecotourists as well. The event and destination can both provide for authentic culture, hedonism (fun and thrills), escapism (getting away from routine, novelty seeking), being entertained (a passive experience of something pleasurable), and socializing (meeting people, people watching, exchanging information).

Feasibility and Risk Management

The feasibility of a single event is one question, but in Event Tourism there is also a need for studying the feasibility of strategies, events to be bid on, venues, and portfolios. Key feasibility issues are generally the same, whatever the application:

- affordability and profitability (including ability to get funding and/or approvals, ROI calculations, demand projections, and risk-to-reward considerations);
- refinement of the concept through market tests and demand forecasts;
- technical feasibility (including meeting the specifications of event owners, having the necessary infrastructure and expertise);
- determining if it can physically be produced (including climatic and weather considerations, venues, accessibility, accommodation);
- capacity to host an event or events (related to venues, volunteers, staff, accommodation, accessibility);
- desirability (linked to branding, political and community support, triple bottom line impact evaluation);
- sustainability (the legacy of each event and cumulative impacts; long-term portfolio health).

Major events should not only play a role in the destination's tourism plan, but be acceptable and supportable by the host community. It must not only be financially sound, but its full costs and benefits should be evaluated. The politics of attracting events, especially mega-events, is sometimes bizarre and frightening. Several authors have noted how irrationality, rather than sound planning, tends to accompany the pursuit of events (Armstrong, 1985; Butler & Grigg, 1987). In such cases there is likely to be tension or outright hostility between proponents and those who insist on detailed feasibility studies and cost–benefit evaluations.

Proponents of major events should demonstrate that the venue, host community, and destination area all have the capacity to absorb the event and its impacts. This requires a detailed forecasting and evaluation of the potential impacts, generally based on experience with other events, and consideration of how positive effects can be maximized and how negative effects or costs can be avoided or ameliorated. Will the event "fit" the proposed venue and area? This matter of suitability is too often ignored, but can be vital in determining the success of the event, as well as its impacts. A number of points can be considered, although every situation is unique:

- is there a track record of hosting successful events?
- the nature of the population (cosmopolitanism; wealth; interests; receptiveness to new ideas);
- availability of volunteers and leaders, sponsors and supporters;
- politics and ideology;
- sophistication in organizing events.

At this stage it should be possible to estimate the likely costs and revenues, and thereby calculate financial feasibility. In other words, can we afford it? The more adventuresome might ask: "If we commit ourselves, can we raise the money?" In fact, this is how many bids proceeded. Even so, a risk assessment is vital. What happens if the grants or revenues fail to materialize, or costs escalate? Who pays? It would be wise to consider the potential for political disruption, the effects of bad weather, and possible organizational failure.

Impact Assessments

A formal social (SIA) and environmental impact assessment (EIA) might be required during the feasibility stage, or perhaps after the decision has been made to proceed. Social and cultural impacts are generally included. EIA legislation varies among jurisdictions, but generally will consist of the following elements:

- specification of all actions likely to have environmental and community impacts (on land, water, and air resources; on the built environment; on social/cultural process and ecological systems);
- determination or forecasting of the likely nature of impacts and related uncertainties and risks;
- determination or forecasting of the likely direction (positive or negative) and severity of impacts;
- plans for avoiding and reducing potential negative impacts, achieving positive impacts, and ameliorating any resultant problems;
- evaluation of costs and benefits of the project in light of impact forecasts and plans.

Economic feasibility is slightly different, and pertains more to the community or destination as a whole. Opportunity costs must be considered, as well as the possibility of adverse economic impacts. Long-term gains and losses must be assessed. The tangible economic costs and benefits to the destination area and host community must be compared, and intangibles considered subjectively. Financial or economic considerations should not predominate, as equal consideration must be given to social, cultural, and environmental factors.

If the benefit-to-cost ratio is favorable, that is still not sufficient grounds to proceed. It might very well be that some costs are not acceptable under any circumstances (such as destruction of heritage or ecological damage). It will also be possible to conclude that the potential benefits, however much in excess of costs, do not justify the effort required, or that the benefits are too concentrated in a few hands to warrant public investment.

Risk Management in Event Tourism

There are many risks associated with the operation of events (see Silvers, 2008) but this discussion pertains specifically to event tourism and the bidding process. Risk assessment will normally be part of the feasibility study undertaken before creating, developing, or bidding on an event. It is a big part of the "due diligence" required before spending money and making commitments.

Just what could go wrong? These are some real possibilities:

- inadequate demand or ticket sales (a major financial risk);
- failure to achieve sponsorship goals lead to financial loss;
- unanticipated costs;

- disruption of travel (e.g., an airline strike or bad weather could prevent participants or fans from attending);
- venues are not ready in time, or are of poor quality;
- disruption of communications, or less than anticipated media interest;
- health issues, such as an outbreak of infectious disease; risk of injuries;
- security threats to people and infrastructure;
- accidents or other bad news lead to image damage.

Bid organizations often have to take calculated risks, and that is part of the business. It largely defines entrepreneurship! Underwriting potential losses is perhaps the greatest risk in terms of both likelihood and severity of political consequences. Often a government body has to take on this burden, but ideally it will be shared among key stakeholders. Event proponents and especially supportive politicians love to say that expensive events will break even, more than pay for themselves through tourism benefits, or "cannot possibly fail!". All of which is usually transparent rubbish, as there are certainly enough event disasters, financial losses, and other problems covered in the mass media to make ordinary citizens aware of the true risks of hosting big events. The ultimate issue from the public's perspective is this: If the event fails to at least break even (as a business venture, considering all its direct costs and revenues), will the taxpayer be responsible? A secondary issue that has to be openly discussed is this: What hidden or indirect costs will the taxpayer be liable for, including security, infrastructure, and marketing? These latter costs are often (and in my view maliciously and irresponsibly) excluded from event accounting.

While the financial losses of an event might or might not cause a political scandal (given that the true accounts are often unavailable and tourism benefits are frequently exaggerated), there is a matter of governmental accountability that simply cannot be avoided. Should local or senior levels of government take these risks, operating as private enterprises do? The answers lie in our discussion of justifications for intervention, and these will have varying appeal to citizens and governments across the globe. The whole process and its justification are seldom explained to citizens.

Losses are not always permanent losses! If the event fails to live up to its revenue projections, and cost estimates are overrun, the organizers incur a loss and the public (or other stakeholders) underwrite this loss. But the hidden benefits (from tourism and increased trade) plus longer term image benefits can easily constitute a credible return on investment that has to be estimated and explained to the public.

Risk Assessment and Management Process

In this section a standard risk management process is adapted to the bidding and development process in Event Tourism.

Identification of Risk Fields

Problems can occur in each of these major risk "fields":

- **Financial**: loss of revenue sources; theft and loss of assets; costs exceeding projections; law suits and other unanticipated costs (who exactly is liable for losses?).
- **Management**: corruption or managerial incompetence can ruin any event, but will also tend to give the host destination a bad reputation—especially if an event is cancelled.
- **Health and safety hazards for organizers, participants, guests, and the general public**: accidents (at and outside the event), health problems, fire,

crime, terrorism, social disturbances and unanticipated emergencies; security has become one of the biggest worries and expenses for major events.

- **Environmental**: negative impacts on the environment, community, and economy; lobby groups will certainly be watching for problems.
- **Community**: social and cultural issues will certainly increase with event scale and cost; increasingly, citizens want full accountability.
- **Natural hazards** (bad weather; earthquakes, floods, etc.).

Identification of Specific Risks, and the Consequences, Within Each Field

Working with experienced event managers, security experts and insurance companies will help in this process. But the risks are not just associated with the event and its production, they relate to broader considerations including the travel and media aspects of Event Tourism. For major events it is normal to employ media professionals to manage the process as best as they can, both to obtain positive coverage and to counter any negative publicity.

Assignment of the Probability of Risks Occurring (e.g., Low, Medium, High)

Evaluate the probability of occurrence. How likely is it that each risk will materialize? Group the risks into high, medium, and low probability categories, but do not assume that low probability hazards will not occur! Without a doubt, in today's world, protesters and possibly anarchist rioters will show up at all international political and state events; security experts will have to assume that terrorists will view media events as targets; even the smallest festival has to assume that accidents and health risks are the norm. Having said that, most events are held without major incident, if only because precautions were taken.

Estimation of the Potential Magnitude of Impacts

Not all risks will necessarily result in losses or problems, so try to anticipate the positive and negative outcomes of each potential circumstance and the magnitude of the consequence. Those with potential negative and severe consequences require special consideration. Within each risk field major disasters could occur, and they should be ranked according to potential magnitude, from multiple perspectives. Protecting the DMO or event organization and its assets might come into conflict with protecting the environment or the public, so beware of bias.

Political implications are also important. Are their ideological reasons why some political parties might oppose the event and look for issues to exploit? How will local, regional, and national politicians each view the event, given the distribution of costs and benefits?

Ranking of Risks, From High to Low Priority

Event managers prepare a matrix to help decide which risks to deal with. They combine the probability of occurrence with evaluation of the potential severity of each, especially those for which the organizers will likely be held responsible. High priority risks have to be dealt with at once. However, in the context of bidding, and Event Tourism in general, some risks will simply be inestimable. Others might be normal to any form of travel, and therefore accepted without much question. All highly likely and potentially severe risks should be dealt with in some manner: further research; experts brought in; comparison to other events, etc.

As a general rule, if you cannot comfortably measure the risk in terms of both probability and severity, why take it? Just whose money or health and safety is being put at risk?

Risk and Cost Versus Reward

When deciding if a bid is worth the costs and risks, there has to be a cost/risk-to-reward calculation. Any number of combinations can come into play, and there should be an approved policy to guide decisions. The following scenarios definitely arise, and the decisions are suggestions, not laws:

- **High risks (both probability and potential severity)**: Do not proceed unless risks can be avoided/reduced or the consequences ameliorated; after-the fact attempts to justify the taking of known high risks that result in huge losses usually result in serious political problems and loss of credibility, if not legal problems.
- **High costs and risks (both probability and severity)**: Not worth it, regardless of rewards! (but there will nevertheless be disputes about the risks, underestimates of the costs, and exaggeration of the imputed benefits, as is often the case with the Olympics and other mega events!).
- **High costs, low risks**: Proceed only if affordable AND the rewards are potentially substantial (i.e., what's your comfort zone?).
- **Low costs, low risks, high rewards**: Does this scenario ever happen? Perhaps the research and calculations should be double checked! My constant advice is that permanent, Hallmark events are best for these reasons.

Remember that somebody always gains when money is spent, and that fact easily leads to arguments over values and priorities, disputes over facts and calculations, and to deliberate obfuscation and misrepresentation of the truth. Call that politics as usual.

Identification of Strategic Options to Deal With Risks: Selection of Appropriate Strategies

Risks can be dealt with in several ways; they are not always absolute and insurmountable. The common strategies to deal with risks are applicable to events and Event Tourism.

- **Avoidance**: Can the development or event be modified so as to eliminate a risk altogether? Can someone else assume liability (as in underwriting potential financial losses)?
- **Reduction**: Some risks can be minimized or kept to an acceptable level through better management, training, or operations. Reduce the severity of damage or losses. Assuming that problems will occur, the manager must be prepared to cope. The event must have emergency response procedures. Thefts occur, but the number and severity can be minimized. Weather is unpredictable, so contingency plans are necessary.
- **Diffusion**: Spreading risks among stakeholders, or over time and space, can be effective. For example, if sponsors or other organizations are involved, it is logical that risks should be spread among all parties, rather than being absorbed by the event organization alone. However, logic might not convince the other parties to accept a share of risks. Vendors and suppliers can usually be required to share in the risk management process and provide their own insurance. Large crowds can be dispersed in time and place through good design.
- **Reallocation**: In some cases the risks can be reallocated completely, as where a parent body or municipality absorbs risks for specific events. Any group under contract to the event can be required to absorb their own risks and take out independent or co-insurance.
- **Insurance**: Insurance is necessary to protect against risks that materialize. Insurance companies increasingly demand that managers demonstrate that they have a risk management strategy in place, and these companies might even give appropriate advice. Liability laws and the need for types and amounts of

insurance vary widely among countries and cannot be generalized. You probably cannot get insurance for a bid, or for a strategy! Mega-events cannot be insured in their entirety, again raising the issue of who underwrites potential losses?

Implementation of Strategies and Evaluation of Results

In a learning organization every decision and action is evaluated, with feedback utilized to make better decisions in the future. Even a failed bid to win an event can yield valuable information to improve strategies and ensure a higher level of success.

Marketing Planning, and Measuring Demand

The marketing planning process generates marketing plans, which are typically prepared every year. The one-time event needs an initial marketing plan as early as the feasibility study, with periodic modifications as the project develops. Figure 5.4 illustrates the marketing planning process for a tourist-oriented event, and the main stages are discussed below.

Purpose, Goals, Objectives

We can assume here that the event has a purpose/mandate that includes tourism, and a vision that foresees the role tourism will play in the future. Goals and objectives can be much like those for a destination (see Table 3.3) or precisely crafted to fit an event's status as Hallmark (see Chapter 4) or Iconic (see the discussion of ecotourism events above).

Situation Analysis and Environmental Scanning

The situation analysis includes future scanning and organizational audits. The major concerns for the marketing process, however, are factors affecting demand for the event or affecting the organization and its resources and capabilities.

At the most basic level, this assessment will be largely qualitative and based on readily available material (including studies of other events). More sophisticated organizations will undertake original research to quantify market potential, including segmentation studies. These key questions must be addressed by destinations and events:

- What is the existing and potential demand for special events of this type, in this area, based on past experience?
- How many customers can be expected, including local, regional, and national/ international origins?
- What types of person/group are most likely to be interested in this event, or can be most easily attracted?
- What are their needs and motives? What benefits will they get from the events?
- What are the anticipated spending patterns of visitors/customers? What will people pay for packages, admission, and merchandise?

Measuring Market Potential (Demand) for One-Time Events

The most difficult forecasting problem is faced by the one-time event. Mules and McDonald (1994) noted that forecasting the attendance or impacts of events is often difficult: "The data on which forecasts are based are often of doubtful quality and their applicability problematic" (p. 45). Furthermore, major events are all different and must be analyzed individually; drawing conclusions from other mega-events could be very misleading. Nevertheless, forecasts are essential for planning, especially when bids are made and mega-events won.

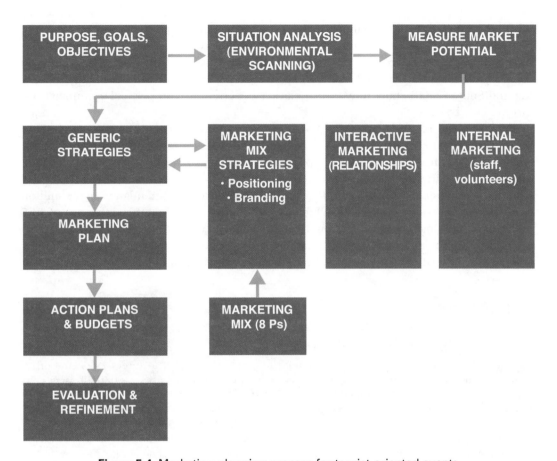

Figure 5.4. Marketing planning process for tourist-oriented events.

Dungan (1984) showed that expected attendance at one-time events could be based on an estimate of market penetration, with other events and comparable attractions, such as theme parks, used as guides. "Market penetration" is calculated as a percentage, so that if every resident in the local market area attended once, the penetration would be 100%; if every resident attended twice, the penetration rate would be 200%. Dungan reported that Expo '67 in Montreal achieved a local market penetration of 618% (i.e., over six visits per capita), whereas the 1964–1965 World's Fair in New York achieved a low penetration of 82%. But all market areas and events are unique, and events are different from theme parks and other attractions, so direct comparisons have obvious weaknesses.

Market area surveys can be used to make better forecasts of market penetration. What is required are "tracking surveys" in the local, regional, and national or international target markets to measure awareness of the planned event, attitudes towards it, and respondents' assessment of their likelihood or actual intent to attend. These periodic samplings can also be used to gather valuable information on other elements in the marketing mix, especially price. Over time, a more refined forecast of attendance can be derived, and the event modified according to market preferences.

The formula for calculating the penetration rate is: $R = P \times F$ (where R is penetration rate; P is percentage of each origin market's population that will attend; F is the mean per capita frequency of visits).

If 40% of a city's 100,000 population visits an event at an average of 2.5 visits per capita, the penetration rate is $0.40 \times 2.5 = 1.00$. This means an attendance of 100,000, but it all comes from 40,000 individuals. If every resident came to the event once, the penetration rate is also 1.00. Thus, it is a measure of drawing power, which can only be based on past experience and/or original market research (such as by asking: are you certain you will attend? if not, what is the probability you will attend? how many times?). Xie and Smith (2000) show how to use market penetration with particular emphasis on income effects.

Blackorby, Ricard, and Slade (1986) undertook an interesting analysis of various World Fairs, using linear regression analysis to detect the key factors affecting attendance. They concluded that three factors—average price in US dollars, size of the site in acres, and the number of foreign pavilions—accounted for 93% of variation in attendance at the World Fairs they examined. Using this conclusion they predicted an attendance of 18 million paid visits to Vancouver's Expo '86, which can be compared to the official forecast of 13.5 million and the final count of 22.1 million site visits (J. Lee, 1987).

Another approach to forecasting attendance at a one-time event was conducted by Louviere and Hensher (1983), using choice theory. In this research survey respondents in

---

Research Note

Xie, P. F., & Smith, S. L. J. (2000). Improving forecasts for world's fair attendance: Incorporating income effects. *Event Management, 6*(1), 15–23.

When applied to major events, such as a world's fair, it is normal to forecast penetration rates from a small number of zones based on proximity, such as: 1) residents of the host city; 2) residents of the day-trip zone; 3) residents of the overnight or vacation zone. The basic assumption, based on almost universal experience with events, is that close-in residents will attend most, and most frequently. For example, much of the success of Vancouver's 1986 expo was attributed to selling affordable season's passes to residents who then used the expo frequently for dining and entertainment (and to external forces and good marketing). Xie and Smith noted that income is a major factor that has to be factored into attendance forecasts, particularly after the lower-than-predicted attendance at the New Orleans World's Fair in 1984 which was partly blamed on being too expensive for locals.

---

one "experiment" were asked to select preferred mixes of event attractions, and those in another survey were required to rank choices by examining alternative locations, prices, types, and sizes of the event. From these data the researchers calculated probabilities of attendance for the population as a whole, specific to a number of event alternatives. Ideally this kind of analysis would be incorporated into a tracking survey.

Trend Extrapolation for Periodic Events

For established events, a trend extrapolation is the easiest way to forecast next year's attendance, but many factors (especially the weather and competition) can intervene. If reliable attendance estimates are available for a period of years, the growth or decline over a period of years can be projected to continue at the same rate, but only if it is assumed that prevailing conditions of supply and demand that affect the event will continue.

Comparisons

Comparison with other events is a reasonable starting point for new events wanting to make a demand forecast. Similar events have to be researched, particularly taking into account market area (e.g., distance to cities), competitive position (are there other events at the same time or in the same area?), and attractiveness (size, quality, and diversity of the proposed event compared to the others). The comparison will be more useful if the origins and growth of comparable events can be traced, focusing on their initial attendance and their promotional efforts.

Destination planners can assist in forecasting by collecting reliable data from many events and analyzing long-term trends. Total attendance at festivals and special events has grown in many regions, so a more refined assessment of demand specific to types of events, and geographic patterns of demand, will help a great deal.

It must be cautioned however, that as the number of events within a market area increases the growth of new events might very well be impeded by established competition. Factors to consider are:

- new, unique events can tap "latent demand" (i.e., unmet demand for specific, new experiences);
- the emergence of multiple events can increase total demand (i.e., the size of the events "pie" gets bigger) through increasing publicity, word-of-mouth recommendations, and greater interest in the event sector;
- new events can achieve market penetration through "stealing" demand from established events, especially if the new ones are perceived to be better or different;
- old events might be declining through lack of new programming, or poor management, giving new events a natural window of opportunity.

Causal Factors (Price and Income Elasticity)

More sophisticated techniques of demand forecasting, especially regression analysis (see S. Smith 1995), require knowledge of "causal factors." For example, tourism demand forecasts consistently reveal that rising personal income leads to rapid growth in travel demand, and this can be used in a regression analysis to forecast demand between specific origins and destinations. Other factors, such as costs and exchange rates, will certainly intervene, and marketing efforts must also be considered. While the factors most responsible for demand changes in tourism are understood, there has been little analysis of event demand. Is it more or less price or income elastic than other tourism products?

"Price elasticity" refers to a predictable relationship between price and demand in which increased price results in corresponding decline in demand. "Income elasticity" is the relationship in which demand rises correspondingly as consumer income (or disposable income) rises. There is no reason to believe that demand for most events is not price and income elastic, but research on specific cases has been lacking. Some events, however, might have sufficient appeal to be considered preferred goods.

Under what circumstances might events be considered "preferred goods" for which residents or tourists will pay more than usual? Mega-events of a once-in-a-lifetime nature might very well encourage many people to spend whatever it takes to attend it, whereas annual events will not usually have this effect unless they contain specific elements of very high appeal. Some evidence from focus groups (Getz & Cheyne, 2002) suggested this is true. A number of respondents in New Zealand considered a possible trip to the Sydney Olympics in the year 2000 to be a once-in-a-lifetime opportunity that would be worth more to them than other desirable foreign, event-specific trips.

Sometimes raising prices and fostering a mystique around an event or program element can elevate them to the status of preferred goods. Snob appeal, exclusivity, and excellence will likely be required.

Qualitative Forecasting Methods

Because of the problems associated with statistical forecasting, a number of qualitative methods have been used in tourism studies. The most basic is "expert judgment," either by individuals or groups. Managers do this all the time in their own planning exercises, but more formal techniques can be applied. The Delphi method involves several rounds of structured consultations among a panel of experts with the usual purpose of identifying trends or future scenarios, and assigning probabilities and importance ratings to them.

A scenario, in the context of strategic planning, is a hypothetical description of circumstances at some point in the future. Planners formulate scenarios for one of two general reasons: to show what might happen and how it will affect the event or destination; to show a desired future state and draw inferences about how to achieve it. Trend analysis and understanding underlying causal factors is essential to good scenario making when the object is to predict a future state and its implications. Working backwards, the planner can then determine how to influence the various forces shaping trends that will likely lead to that future state—either to prevent it, modify it, or develop strategies to adapt to it.

In the second approach, imagination is required. Conjure up a desired future, say one in which your destination is blessed with a rich portfolio of attractive events, then determine how to achieve that goal. It sounds simple, but it is actually difficult. The ideal future state is easy enough to depict in a scenario, but realistically describing the pathways and actions needed to get there requires a considerable amount of real-world expertise.

Willingness to Pay

To an economist, "demand" is the amount of a good or service consumed (i.e., purchased) over a schedule of prices. In other words, what would the demand be for the event, in terms of total attendance, if the price was X? In the absence of direct experience in evaluating the change in demand which results from price changes, the potential customer's "willingness to pay" can be assessed.

Limited research on willingness to pay for events has been undertaken. In a major study of festivals in Canada's National Capital Region (Coopers and Lybrand, 1989) customers at five free-admission events were asked how much they would pay, while at two events with admission prices a sample was asked if the amount was too high, too low, or just right. One useful result was the revelation that tourists would be willing to pay more than residents, which makes sense given that many traveled specifically to attend the event or were already on a pleasure trip.

About 20% of respondents at the free events said they would not pay anything. The consultants suggested that this represented a "contingency valuation" problem, as consumers would fear the introduction of a price. This author's personal experience with similar questions at events supports the conclusion that most consumers will say they are comfortable with prices similar to those already charged. Major increases are likely to be met with considerable negative reaction. This makes it difficult to determine what proportion of the audience might be lost if prices are introduced or raised, and it also suggests that it can be difficult to introduce a charge at free events. Several issues and problems with this technique must be considered:

- people are likely to underestimate what they would actually pay (they do not want to encourage increases!);

- some segments will be able to afford more; increasing prices therefore become an "equity" issue for public services;
- tourists, and those attracted specifically to the event, will likely pay more.

We get back to willingness to pay in the context of use and nonuse valuation, in Chapter 10.

Segmentation and Selecting Target Markets

To better understand the event consumer, and for purposes of more effective marketing, it is necessary to segment the market. "Segmentation" methods normally employ research and analytical techniques to identify relatively homogeneous groups that can be targeted through marketing. An option is to segment people on the basis of their actual and often varying travel or consumption patterns; this is known as "occasion-based" segmentation (Morrison, 1995).

To be useful, a market segment must meet certain criteria (Mill & Morrison, 1985). The group of people being described as a "target market" or "segment" must have common characteristics (i.e., homogeneity). It must be a measurable group (how many are there?), and of a size or characteristics making them worthwhile of attention (e.g., small, wealthy, special interest groups can be important). Finally, the organizers must be able to effectively and affordably communicate with the group. Although the ways to identify target markets are many, and often overlapping, meeting these criteria ensures that target marketing does not get out of control. In practice, each event should focus on one or several easily defined groups. For events and event tourism the following criteria are also important:

- segmentation must identify the groups most interested in attending and/or traveling to various types of events, including those who currently consume event-related products;
- identify travelers with a secondary interest in attending events; pay particular attention to emerging or potential markets and segments;
- determine the segments by reference to variables that can be used to enhance target marketing;
- describe the segments by reference to how they can be reached through the communications mix;
- identify the highest "quality" visitors and event tourists;
- consider the durability of segments (will they last?), their size and quality (are they worth the effort), and the cost-effectiveness of attracting them relative to other targets;
- consider the event's and destination's distinctive competencies and competitive advantages when establishing target segments.

S. Smith (1988) said that segmentation can also answer questions about the size of potential markets, spending patterns, price sensitivity, loyalty, response to changes in the marketing mix, and the potential effectiveness of promotions. Once the segmentation analysis is completed, the most promising groups are selected as target markets, and the marketing mix should be oriented to these groups. In fact, the product and target markets must be continuously matched, as both are likely to change over time.

Below, the major segmentation variables are discussed. Depending on the circumstances, any one or combination of these variables might be used to delimit existing and target markets. However, geographic, demographic, and socioeconomic variables are almost always needed for events. Figure 5.5 depicts the variables grouped according to the main segmentation questions: From where will they come? Who exactly are they? What do they want? Under what conditions will they attend the event? How can we reach them? How often will they visit? If you phrase these questions in the context of special interests or social worlds, as we did earlier with the ecotourism example, then much more research will be needed.

Geographic Variables

Most event visits will be generated within the local or regional market area. Surveys are needed to determine the existing and potential ratios of local, regional, and long-distance consumers, using criteria like distance traveled, name of the home community, or postal code address. A decision will have to be made on what constitutes a resident versus a tourist, and this is often made on the basis of an arbitrary distance traveled (say, 80K or 50 miles) or by reference to local authority boundaries, census-defined metropolitan areas, or delineations of trading or commuting zones.

Telephone surveys in likely market areas can be used to test awareness and interest levels, advertising effectiveness, and other variables that correlate with distance, access, and other geographic factors. Remember that if only visitor surveys are used, no data are obtained on noncustomers.

Combining geographic data with other marketing facts through "encoding" is a valuable technique. For example, in many countries census data can be combined with postal code information to reveal patterns and potential applications such as:

- communities with high-income residents (the kind who travel most or to consume cultural products);
- areas with older residents (who might be most interested in group travel);

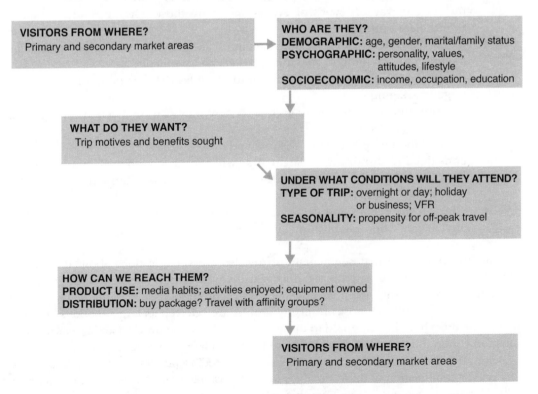

Figure 5.5. Segmentation variables for Event Tourism.

- concentrations of families (most likely to seek low-cost, accessible entertainment and social outlets);
- ethnic neighborhoods (most interested in certain types of music);
- households with boats or other sporting equipment (potential sports show consumers);
- newly settled versus well-established areas (perhaps indicative of interest in local community-building events).

Demographic Variables

Age and gender are usually important factors affecting demand for events, along with marital and family status. Household type and size are potentially useful, such as the distinction between one- and two-parent families, and identification of nontraditional households. Race and ethnicity are becoming more important in many countries, reflecting the increasingly multicultural nature of the population.

Age, gender, family status, and other variables combine in the "life stage concept," which has important implications for all leisure activities and preferences. Young people before marriage have a set of values, desires, opportunities, and constraints that is quite different from those of married couples, "empty-nesters" (i.e., couples whose children have left home), and the elderly who are retired.

Sports and entertainment events are more likely to attract young males, whereas arts and cultural festivals have much stronger appeal to females. Community festivals and celebrations do attract more families, with a more balanced gender distribution. In Saskatchewan, for example, it was found that 60% of visitors at a range of events were with families (Derek Murray Consulting Associates Ltd., 1985). In Dickens on the Strand in Galveston, Texas, the research found that 35% of respondents to the on-site random survey were with a group of adults without children, while 21% were in a single family group with children. Females accounted for 53% of the sample (Ralston & Crompton, 1988a).

The setting, sponsors/organizers, and theme will probably have a marked bearing on attracting different racial or ethnic groups. Ethnic and multicultural festivals are often aimed directly at achieving intergroup mixing and fostering better communications and understanding, whereas it appears that different types of entertainment, cultural, and sporting events have distinct racial and ethnic appeal. For example, in 1987 the Louisville Kentucky Bluegrass Music Festival had an audience that was 96% white. Most surveys do not record this information, and it might be inappropriate to do so in direct interviewing or self-completion questionnaires. It is nevertheless a factor organizers should consider, and nonintrusive measures can be taken by direct observation to determine if certain groups are underrepresented in the audience.

Socioeconomic Variables

This group of variables pertains to an individual's or household's economic status (income, employment) and related factors such as educational attainment. Income is the greatest predictor of travel consumption and entertainment expenditure, although it certainly does not explain everything.

Surveys for Dickens on the Strand festival in Galveston, Texas (Ralston & Crompton, 1988a, 1988b) revealed its customers to be "up-market" in terms of age and income levels. Combined with other data, this revealed a segment of repeat adult visitors without children who traveled specifically for the event and spent a lot of money on accommodation, dining, etc. Sponsors and tourist authorities love these high-yield tourists. But it also suggested the need to appeal to other segments, including families.

Psychographic Variables

These are based on psychological or personal dimensions, such as personality traits, beliefs, values, attitudes, and lifestyle preferences, which can help explain motives and travel behavior. "Psychographic segmentation" has become popular in tourism research (see the discussion in Morrison, 1995), but some have found it to be of limited value if not combined with other segmentation variables.

Plog (1987) identified dimensions used commonly in psychographics-based tourist segmentation:

- adventuresomeness (the explorer types);
- pleasure seeking (related to the desire for luxury);
- impulsivity (will spend a lot, without planning);
- self-confidence (will travel alone);
- planfulness (wants package tours and bargains);
- masculinity (the action-oriented and outdoor groups);
- intellectualism (is lured by culture and history);
- people orientation (wants to be close to others).

Whatever the psychographic factors employed in segmentation, there will be the need to link these to one or more of the other segmentation methods. The psychographic dimensions of these ideal segments, expressed in terms of what event tourism marketers hope to find, could be:

- values, beliefs and attitudes (e.g., belief in the centrality of arts in society; sports valued as character builders; belief that festivals are good for the community);
- personality traits (e.g., conservatives who will buy packages; adventurers and will seek out the authentic and unique);
- lifestyle (e.g., active in a variety or sports, arts, or within the community; already a consumer of similar products).

To me, the ego-involvement framework is a more useful theoretical perspective, especially when we are targeting special interest groups. It embodies some of the psychographic elements, as well as benefits sought.

Benefits Sought

Consumers can usually identify what they want from an attraction or travel experience, such as: to enjoy social and family relationships; to learn about cultures; to have fun or be entertained; to compete or achieve. If asked what benefits visitors derived from an event experience, they are attaching meanings to it, such as: "We had an authentic cultural experience" or "I enjoyed the time spent with others." A great deal can be learned through focus groups or interviews about how people perceive the event experience (Getz & Cheyne, 2002).

Depending on the product, benefits can be defined and consumers or potential visitors can be asked to rank those which interest them most. Segments based on stated benefits will have to be correlated with other factors, especially demographics. Older adults with high incomes, for example, are less likely to seek thrills.

Our distinction between generic and targeted benefits is essential here. Finding out that most people want a pleasant social or family experience, or something entertaining and novel, does not help you in attracting dedicated event tourists (see the earlier discussion and Figure 2.3).

Type of Trip

Are your event visitors most likely to be on an informal day-trip, family touring vacation, visiting friends and relatives, staying at a second home, on business, or traveling primarily because of the event? A number of other segmentation variables can be combined to form useful trip-type segments. For example, the business traveler is often difficult to segment on demographic and geographic variables, but many of them will display common patterns of activity when in a destination. How easy will it be to attract them to an event and add a day to their trip? Events can also be packaged with conferences, and possibly provide an incentive to bring families with the business traveler.

More complicated is consideration of the event tourist career trajectory and its implications for trip patterns and preferences. Go back to Table 2.5 to review how, in theory, increasing involvement in a serious leisure pursuit, or in a business or profession, is likely to lead to different travel choices revolving around one's career. The "highly involved" are quite different kinds of travelers.

Seasonality

This is an often ignored segmentation variable, but has particular relevance to events. Some groups are easier to attract in the off-season, while the largest market potential is likely to be in the summer holiday and tourist season. Another way to look at this method is to ask what would happen to an event's markets if it moved seasons?

To be useful, other segmentation variables must be attached to seasonality. Older, retired people are generally easier to attract in spring and autumn. Busy professionals want to take short getaway trips throughout the year.

Repeat Visits

Numerous festival surveys have detected a loyal group of return visitors, obviously including a high proportion of area residents. But this important group also includes a segment with strong brand loyalty to particular events, returning again and again, and a segment that takes in many different events. Music festivals in particular seem to attract a mobile audience, and sports have dedicated traveling fans.

Research Note on Segmentation

Warnick, R., Bojanic, D., Mathur, A., & Ninan, D. (2011). Segmenting event attendees based on travel distance, frequency of attendance, and involvement measures: A cluster segmentation technique. *Event Management, 15*(1), 77–90.

The purpose of this study was to conduct a postevent evaluation for the Great New England Air Show to apply a cluster segmentation technique using travel distance, purchase decision involvement, and frequency of attendance among its current visitors as measures to improve marketing applications and to further examine the economic significance of the event. A cluster analysis procedure identified four groups of attendees: 1) Locals, 2) Highly involved enthusiasts, 3) First timers/nonloyals, and 4) Fringe attendees. Significant differences were identified across the four cluster segments on individual involvement, number of times attended, distance from the event, length of trip, likelihood to return, expenditures per person, average age, and income. A graphic mapping technique was provided to visually depict the dispersion of the markets. Market applications suggestions were made as these segments were identified and to provide this segmentation method as a strategy to more accurately measure the economic significance of the event.

Product-Related Variables

Those with likely interest in sport events can be identified by the equipment they own, magazines they read, and their recreational activities. An event can also concentrate on persons who are frequent users of certain facilities, and clubs with specialized product demands (e.g., antique car hobbyists). The object is to identify products or services linked to the target segment and the event.

Application of involvement theory has shown that the highly involved spend more on their special interests, including equipment, travel and event related (see the data from our TransRockies case study).

Distribution Channel Variables

Another approach is to identify target groups by the ways in which the event can be linked to potential customers. Tourists might be most easily reached through specialized tour wholesalers who do their own marketing. Links with parks and recreation departments in nearby cities can pay off, as they might organize senior citizen excursions to events. In both cases, the target groups are defined by the way in which they are reached.

Many special interest travelers prefer to make their own travel arrangements, being independent minded and seekers of precise information about desired experiences. They are also most likely to be reachable through social world websites/blogs, and social networking.

Problems and Limitations of Segmentation

Many of the segmentation variables discussed above, on their own, can be misleading or misinterpreted. Often a number of factors must be understood, such as the age, gender, lifestyle, and attitudes of a person, before their demand for events can be predicted. Segments are often not as homogeneous as they might seem, because the cluster or factor analysis used in their formation is subject to manipulation to achieve a certain number of segments.

The biggest failure of segmentation, as currently practiced, is its almost total lack of consistency. Each new study seems to invent new methods and terms, based on different sampling, and based on often untested theory. This criticism is not applicable to simple studies, but is typical of multidimensional and psychographic segmentation. The result is a confusing array of segment labels and an inability to directly compare or combine results.

Targeting Through Theming

An event's "theme" communicates its benefits and can be used as a target marketing tool. All festivals are themed, by definition. They celebrate or commemorate something of importance to the community, such as its heritage or way of life. But the theme is more than the mere object of celebration. As noted by Korza and Magie (1989) the theme unifies an event or festival: "By permeating every aspect of a festival . . . a theme can provide programmatic direction and coherence and provide a hook which is readily understood by the media and audiences" (p. 10). In other words, the object of the celebration suggests a theme, but the realization of a theme is a function of coherent programming and image making.

Event themes can be linked to destination area themes for mutual advantage. In some cases the regional theme is strong, giving rise to events which take advantage of, and reinforce the destination image. Some regions have based their image making and theme on the success of one or more special events. There is no need to try to link all events into a coherent destination theme, however; diversity is to be valued. Rather, packages and tours can be employed to highlight and link the events that most strongly develop the destination image or theme.

Other special events almost always have a specific theme based on the nature of the event, such as a sport or recreation activity. But special events do not always develop a theme fully or integrate it well in promotions. Kreag (1988) advised that all the important elements of an event have to be synthesized "into a cohesive message or statement of purpose" to ensure effective communications. Themes can be expressed in a number of ways:

- in the name of the event;
- through logos and mascots;
- in the setting/design;
- in the activities and attractions;
- in food and beverages;
- in merchandise for sale;
- in consistent advertising format and style;
- by stressing specified (targeted) benefits.

See the ensuing case of the West Coast Whitebait Festival on the subject of theme and programming, related to authentic local culture.

Case Study: West Coast Whitebait Festival, New Zealand (by Dominic Moran, Ph.D.)

Dominic studied social psychology at the University of Canterbury before completing his Ph.D. at Lincoln University in New Zealand. During the past decade he has held senior management positions in regional tourism organizations with responsibilities for destination marketing and the development of local tourism industry. Since 2009 he has operated his own consultancy business specializing in developing tourism strategies, events development, economic development, and local government (for more information visit www. morantourism.com).

Background

The inaugural West Coast Whitebait Festival was held in 2011 to coincide with the Rugby World Cup tournament held in New Zealand in September and October of that year. RWC 2011 attracted approximately 100,000 visitors to New Zealand and the West Coast Whitebait Festival was at the forefront of efforts to attract a share of those visitors to the isolated but ruggedly spectacular West Coast region.

The West Coast of New Zealand's South Island is a thin strip of land approximately 800 km long and bordered by the Southern Alps on one side and the Tasman Sea on the other. Although sparsely populated (30,000 people), it is a stunningly beautiful region boasting subtropical rainforest, mirror lakes, snow-capped mountains, glaciers, and rugged coastline.

West Coast residents are from pioneering stock, self-reliant and strongly independent. They are proud of their environment and communities and are welcoming to visitors. Tourism is a leading industry on the West Coast with 2.5 million visitors recorded in 2009, including 1.2 million international visitors and 1.3 million domestic visitors.

Whitebait Festival

Whitebait is a natural theme for a West Coast-based festival. It is a seafood delicacy that is found and enjoyed throughout New Zealand. However, 90% of whitebait is fished on the West Coast.

The pastime of catching and consuming the delicacy has been described as being less like a sport, hobby, or occupation and more like a religion! Indeed, when the whitebait are "running" in the local rivers, entire communities have been known to take up their nets and join in the fishing. The passion for whitebait was a key promotional message to encourage domestic visitors to travel to the West Coast for the festival, particularly from the South Island and lower North Island regions.

Rugby World Cup 2011 provided an ideal opportunity to promote the region. However, there were no matches or teams scheduled to be played or based in the area. The Whitebait Festival was devised as a way to attract tourists who were visiting New Zealand as part of the tournament. It gained the support of REAL New Zealand Festival as the national body promoting the country as tournament host.

With national level support to help its promotion, the West Coast Whitebait Festival also relied heavily on the pristine scenery of the region, the engaging attitude of local people and the range of activities available such as sightseeing, fishing, hunting, mountain biking, hiking, glacier visits, flight seeing, wining and dining.

Festival Activities

The West Coast Whitebait Festival included a range of activities that were held in many small towns and communities throughout the region. This approach encouraged local "buy in" and participation in festival events. Activities included:

- A "Whitebait Menu Challenge" was organized with local, regional, and finals cook offs to determine who had the best whitebait recipes.
- There was a competition for restaurants where clients could phone text their votes for favorite dishes in the competition.

Photo 5.1. Inaugural West Coast Whitebait Festival 2011 in Reefton, New Zealand (Credit: photo courtesy of Dominic Moran).

- A Whitebait photography competition was held with categories including people, places and whitebait. This allowed tourists and locals to email their favorite snaps while traveling through the region.
- Concurrent local events and activities were also included in the festival program to help add to its critical mass. Examples included street motorcycle races, art exhibitions, conservation activities, and community fun/sports days.

Festival Impacts

The West Coast Whitebait Festival attracted a mix of locals, domestic visitors and international tourists. The numbers of both domestic and international tourists increased as the RWC 2011 tournament progressed. Domestic visitors increased from 30,000 in September 2011 to 39,000 in October. International visitors increased from 29,000 in September 2011 to 38,000 in October 2011. However, these figures were down (–9.4%) compared with September and October 2010.

Overall visitor numbers to the West Coast in 2011 were affected by the earthquakes in neighboring Canterbury during 2010 and 2011. These events had a major ongoing impact on tourist numbers throughout the South Island of New Zealand. Many RWC 2011 visitors stayed in the North Island for most of the tournament. Nevertheless, without RWC 2011 and the supporting Whitebait Festival, the impacts on visitor numbers would have been more dramatic for the West Coast region.

The inaugural West Coast Whitebait Festival was sustainable because it was connected with local communities, adopted a theme that utilized the local environment, a culinary delicacy, and showcased the passion of New Zealanders for whitebait. Promotion of the festival was assisted by aligning it with a major global sports tournament and using connected marketing themes that highlighted spectacular scenery, passionate local people, and community values.

Marketing Strategies

According to Porter (1980) competitive advantage can be gained through three generic marketing strategies: differentiation, price leadership, and focus. Following an introduction to these, other generic marketing strategies are mentioned.

Differentiation

To Porter, only product differentiation assures sustainable competitive advantage. Events must cultivate uniqueness in program, theme, and targeted benefits and use the marketing mix to gain a position of strength relative to competitors. Stressing value is more important than competing on price. Events that imitate others are not differentiated. If there are others just like it in the same market area, some will likely not succeed.

Differentiation is difficult for "community festivals" that offer a wide range of generic benefits, and these have to cultivate a strong sense of community ownership, authenticity, and tradition.

Market Focus (Niche Marketing)

Pursuing one target market segment above all others can be an effective strategy for some events, especially if it is a high-yield segment (see our TransRockies case). The goal is to out-compete all other events for this segment. The risk is that changes in the marketplace can result in a serious threat to event viability.

Most long-standing events, and especially Hallmark Events that have become permanent institutions, are "generalists" with broad appeal. Their stakeholders are diverse, and they seek to meet many goals of importance in the community.

"Convergence" of forms and functions is part of this process, but then there is a risk of becoming "undifferentiated"! A reasonable strategy, therefore, is to package targeted experiences for special interests within the broad program, and to keep adding new attractions to complement the traditional programming.

Cost Leadership

If costs can be kept low through subsidies, economies of scale, or more efficient operations, products can compete through cost leadership. Lower prices, in this strategy, should result in higher demand than competitors. Many events have no direct competition with other events, or are free, and so cost leadership is not applicable. Adding value to the event experience is more likely to be a sustainable strategy, although all managers should strive for greater efficiency.

Market Penetration

This strategy is one of attracting more users to the same event, without necessarily changing the types of users or the market area. Managers of static attractions and resorts can use special events to get patrons returning more frequently, but the challenge for annual events is quite different. It can be accomplished through better promotions, price discounting, better sales to special interest groups, or giving better value for money.

Aggressive marketers might take aim at luring customers from the nearby competition, through direct comparison and boasting of advantages. This has limited possibilities for one-time events, and for community festivals without obvious competition. The uniqueness of events should be a fact, not a promotional fantasy! Another technique is to use visitor and market surveys to identify nonusers within established market segments (organizers should have already identified customer needs and desired benefits) and promote to them more aggressively, such as through direct sales.

Product Reformulation

If established audiences are losing interest, modifying the program or other fundamental elements of the product (e.g., the setting) can stimulate repeat visits. Just as theme parks add new rides or special events regularly, annual festivals can adopt a long-range plan to keep adding new and appealing features. Arts festivals do the same when they upgrade the quality of performances or attract big-name headliners. If the product improvements are consistent in theme, the same market segments can be lured back. Care must be taken to not drastically alter the event program to the point where returning customers are both surprised and disappointed with the changes.

Market Development

This strategy seeks out new target markets for the same product, often in geographical terms or by benefit-defined segments. For annual events, it means tapping the day-tripping market and then going after tours and independent travelers from farther afield. Cooperative efforts with tourist organizations and regional/national promotional bodies are necessary. Most special events find that direct marketing to bus tours is an excellent way to break into new tourist markets.

Product Development

An alternative is to develop new products, such as offering variations of the event, aimed at the same market. For example, an arts festival can add different types of performance throughout the year. Some events have winter and summer versions, catering to different tourist markets, while others have multiple sites.

Diversification

This is the most radical marketing strategy, and is seldom used by event organizers. The aim is to create new products for new markets. It will also require planned organizational change.

Visitor Surveys for Market Intelligence and Evaluation

Whether by self-completed questionnaire, direct interview, or log books, visitor surveys provide essential information for marketing and evaluation of events and event tourism. They are relatively easy and inexpensive to undertake and analyze, at least at a basic level, but they do present challenges of design, sampling, and interpretation.

It is now quite easy to get access to event surveys and professionals capable of advising organizers or tourism officials on how to implement them. But experience in conducting and reviewing numerous surveys has convinced this author that it is a mistake to use somebody else's questionnaire, or to fit bits and pieces from surveys together and call it your own. Instead, it is essential that each visitor survey be formulated for specific purposes, and in such a way that the evaluators or planners get exactly the information they need. The following steps provide a simple guide to this process of custom designing the survey. Table 9.1 specifies data needs and methods that can be incorporated into visitor surveys and evaluations, with appropriate adaptation to the circumstances.

(1) State the General Purposes of the Survey

Different purposes require different methods and measures. It is efficient to accommodate multiple purposes, but only with the resources to do it properly. Joint ventures among event organizers, tourist agencies, and other stakeholder should be pursued for these reasons. A visitor survey can be an excellent, and in many cases essential, method for obtaining data to:

- stimulate off-peak demand through event packages;
- determine visitor needs, motives, and benefits sought;
- permit market segmentation and targeting;
- assess the effectiveness of communications and sponsorship;
- evaluate customer service and program quality;
- determine visitor spending and tourism impacts;
- obtain ideas for product and market development.

(2) Determine the Specific, Ultimate Uses of Data

To avoid becoming overambitious, the evaluators must carefully specify who exactly wants the data, and in what ways it will be used. The interests of tourism and the arts community will coincide in some areas, but conflicting needs are likely. So the group must prioritize the possibilities, and a good way to do that is to ask each stakeholder to rank their key objectives or questions. If there still remain too many questions after accommodating all the top priorities, it might be necessary to launch more than one survey. A master survey can be formulated with inserts of questions (to meet different needs) randomly mixed in, or a short on-site survey can be augmented by a longer take-home form.

(3) List Key Data Requirements, Measures, and Alternative Data Collection Methods

Any goal or question can be converted into specific data requirements. For example, to evaluate the effectiveness of promotions it will be desirable to ask visitors how they heard about the event, or what information sources they consulted. The objective of determining economic impacts requires data on visitor spending. The measures must be developed next. Visitor spending can be measured in a number of ways: on or off site; by place; type of expenditure; by time of day or day of week. The unit of measurement is normally monetary in nature, and can be aggregated by party or kept at the individual level.

To collect each type of data might require different methods, and the visitor survey might not be best for all of them. Log books have been used to measure tourist spending, but they would require very special expertise to attempt at a special event because visitors might only stay a short time and may be difficult to contact in advance. Direct interviews on the site or at exit points will work, as will self-completed questionnaires. An interesting alternative is the conducting of a postevent, random telephone survey in the market area. Each method has merit, and limitations, but the intent at this stage is to screen all the options and determine the list of measures to be covered in the visitor survey.

(4) Assess Feasibility of Methods

Which method will be most cost-effective in obtaining the data needed? Can the organization provide the human resources, funds, and technical expertise necessary to do the job right? It might be a matter of cost or convenience that determines the choice of survey methods. And the comfort and convenience of visitors must not be forgotten. There is no point in giving them self-completion questionnaires without pencils, or forms hard to write on, or that take an hour to read and complete. Are there convenient places to sit and write, or in which to be interviewed? Will questionnaires be picked up, or are there places at exits for drop-offs?

Selecting the sampling method is a crucial decision, and will be an important factor in determining feasibility. Options are presented later, and each has implications for cost, timing, personnel, and ultimate use of the collected data. Quick and dirty surveys, without random sampling, do yield useful insights for minimal cost, but cannot be used to measure impacts or convince sponsors of success.

Another factor to weigh is the need for support data. A random survey of visitors is meaningless without accurate attendance counts or estimates. Log books cannot be used for reliable estimates unless the participants are known to proportionately represent all event-goers.

(5) Survey Design

Some creativity is involved in formulating the questions and formatting the survey, but all designs and questions should be pilot tested. The best tests are at events, but for many organizers that is impossible. Instead, a sample of ordinary people, the organization committee, and some experts could all be asked for feedback. Revisions will likely be in order, and if they are major ones, another test should be attempted. Finally, arrangements for production, personnel and equipment can be made.

Conducting Market Area Surveys

When only visitors are surveyed the event manager learns nothing about why people do not attend, nor about the potential for attracting new segments. There are several basic approaches to market area survey and examples have already been presented. The various foreign pleasure market surveys conducted by Canada, the US, and many other countries are the most ambitious type and clearly beyond the capability of most event managers. Hopefully more destinations will develop event-related questions in this type of foreign research.

In a unique piece of contract research, Wicks and Fesenmaier (1995) attempted to measure the market potential for events within a 5-hour driving radius of an Illinois town. This "catchment area," or area of demand potential, contains over 30 million residents, and this population was found to be very active in traveling for events. There were 94% of respondents who had taken at least one vacation trip within 300 miles of home during the previous year, and 74% had made an overnight trip. Fully 57% of all pleasure trips had included a festival or special event, and 31% of them had traveled more than 50 miles for an event; 55% had included an event in an overnight trip. These and other data enabled the researchers to estimate there were 50 million event attendances in the region annually!

The survey by Wicks and Fesenmaier (1995) is an excellent example of event-related

---

Research Notes on Market Research for Events

Verhoven, P., Wall, D., & Cottrell, S. (1998). Application of desktop mapping as a marketing tool for special events planning and evaluation: A case study of the Newport News Celebration in Lights. *Festival Management & Event Tourism, 5*(3), 123–130.

Declining attendance over 4 years at this holiday event was attributed to increased competition and decreasing novelty. The authors recommended that new attractions be added each year to bring people back. Their mapping technique identified the primary "catchment area" and proved that a "distance-decay function" explained much of the travel to this event. In other words, advertising beyond the primary catchment area would not be cost-effective in increasing attendance. Income was apparently a factor in determining the exact catchment area, as lower-income households could presumably less afford the admission charge or did not have private cars. Offering lower-cost packages with public transport would possibly help overcome this barrier.

Yoon, S., Spencer, D., Holecek, D., & Kim, D.-K. (2000). A profile of Michigan's festival and special event tourism market. *Event Management, 6*(1), 33–44.

Data were obtained from selected questions contained in a market-area household telephone survey funded by Tourism Michigan and Michigan State University. Respondents in Michigan and surrounding states plus Ontario, Canada, were asked about pleasure trips taken to/within Michigan and the included activities. Results showed that 28% of those who had taken such a trip in the previous 12 months had included an event, and these event-inclusive trips were primarily in the summer months. Forty-three percent of the event-inclusive trips were my residents of Michigan, and the primary motive for all pleasure trips taken to/within Michigan was visiting friends and relatives. Those persons including festivals and events were much more action oriented and participated in many different forms of recreation and entertainment, plus their trips involved more nights in the state, thereby resulting in higher expenditures.

---

market area research that is within the capability of most destination organizations such as visitor and convention bureaus. Through telephone or mail-outs, a random sample within the target zone can be asked a series of questions regarding event preferences, visits to events and related trip details, and awareness and interest in specific events. Consultants for the major evaluation of eight festivals in Canada's National Capital region used local telephone surveys to help estimate attendance at events. Two other pertinent surveys have been reported: by Verhoven, Wall, and Cottrell (1998) for a single event and Yoon, Spencer, Holecek, and Kim (2000) for Michigan's event tourism market.

Many destinations conduct "exit surveys" that interview departing visitors. The logistics are difficult and the costs high, but extremely valuable data can be collected on activities, expenditures, likes and dislikes, etc., of visitors to the area. Unfortunately, many exit surveys do not include sufficient data on events. Ideally, all major travel-related surveys should include the following basic data:

- Have respondents traveled specifically/mainly for an event? If yes, what kinds? Where and when?
- Have respondents attended events while on trips for other purposes? If yes, what kinds? Where and when?
- What types of activities and benefits do travelers seek (that could be manifested through events)?
- How important are certain types of events in motivating travel or in selecting a destination?
- What specific benefits are desired from events of various kinds?

Packaging

Events are themselves packages—of activities, venues, and experiences that cannot otherwise be enjoyed. The first principle of packaging, therefore, is to combine elements for the consumer that otherwise are difficult to acquire, or that contain value-added features. The extra value can come from a package price (cheaper than buying the elements separately) or the inclusion of features not available to those not buying the package. Convenience should be maximized through packaging, effectively removing barriers to making the purchase. Assurance or security, the feeling that the trip will be safer and the experience guaranteed, is another key benefit to the customer.

The goals of packaging for events are related both to the event's marketing strategy and the destination:

- attract tourists;
- off-season through event packages;
- reach specific, high-yield market segments;
- generate additional revenue and improve the cash flow through advance bookings;
- enhance the event's image (through related promotions);
- encourage visitation outside the peaks (e.g., weekdays);
- develop partnerships with sponsors, tour companies, etc.;
- combat competitors.

Although the main focus of packaging is likely to be tourism, every event can develop and sell packages. Some ideas follow:

- two or more events for one price;
- two or more elements of the event for one price, or a discounted price;
- the event plus other attractions;
- sponsors' products included in the admission price.

Packaging for Tourists

The group-tour business (in which everyone buys the same tour) provides volume, whereas packages purchased by individuals can serve to attract specific segments.

Packages can be "all-inclusive" in nature, assembling everything the tourist needs and wants for one price, or provide limited benefits as when visitors must separately arrange for their own meals or transport.

Events can form the "core product" (i.e., the major attraction) of the tour package, or can be an added element to give value to other packages and other events. Independent travelers should be able to purchase the event package easily and prior to arrival in the area. Group tours will usually be wholesaled to tour companies from outside the area, but local destination management companies can be valuable partners in selling packages. Events are logical and appealing add-ons to incentive tours and meetings.

Targeting packages is preferable to simply offering one or two for general consumption. They can be customized through market research and cooperation with the tour and hospitality industries. Tables 5.1 provides a framework that can be used as a starting point for event packaging. Across the top are the elements that can be combined in many ways for a good package: accommodation; other activities (attractions and entertainment); dining; and shopping. Transportation will often be added, but this depends on the segments being targeted. In some events the form of transportation can actually be part of the themed experience.

The table shows several event types, each of which will likely attract different market segments. Research will be needed to provide profiles of existing and potential customers. For example, the sport spectator event is more likely to attract younger males whose interests are focused on the event itself. Their accommodation and dining preferences might very well be lower cost. Any add-on activities should fit their profile—possibly nightlife, adventures or amusements. As to shopping, sport souvenirs will probably be popular.

The up-market arts festival tourists attending a performing arts event can be expected to differ substantially from the sport traveler. Accommodations could be of higher quality, and fine dining can be featured. Cultural tourists tend to combine events with visits to galleries, museums, and other cultural attractions.

When it comes to shopping, packages can include "free" souvenirs (costed into the total price), shopping at the event itself, and excursions arranged through merchants or shopping centers. Similarly, dining can be included, at the event, or elsewhere.

Managers should also remember that many events contain elements that will appeal to multiple segments, so that more than one package is likely to be needed. For example, the Olympics appeal to sports fans, but also to cultural tourists, because all Olympics contain arts festivals. A community festival might have a sufficiently diverse program to attract music lovers of different types, athletes for participatory events, and sophisticated urbanites interested in acquiring antiques and sampling down-home cooking.

Caution is required for several reasons. Not all packages might be viable, so reliance on the tour industry is important. Also, trying to attract too many different segments could result in user conflicts and programming headaches. Events can put together and sell their own packages, but this might be risky and difficult. Tourist organizations like visitor and convention bureaus can assist, or actually market the packages. A third option is to work with tour companies to encourage and help them to create and sell packages featuring the event.

Tour Companies

Below is an example of how private tour companies offer packages to sport fans and cultural tourists. These are very popular for professional sports as well as major, international competitions and festivals. Anyone traveling abroad for an event is wise to consider prepurchasing tickets from home (online is an easy option) and perhaps accommodation and transport as well.

Table 5.1. Packaging Framework for Tourist-Oriented Events

	Transport to and Within	Accommodation	Other Activities	Dining	Shopping
Spectator sport	Fans who travel together (group tours)	Block booking by wholesalers	Nightlife	Eating at venues	Souvenirs of the sport and event
Participation sport	Teams and clubs plus individuals with families	Home billeting option	Outdoor pursuits	Dining at venues	Shopping tours for accompanying persons
Arts festival	Independent travelers by car	Make reservations on their own	Museums and galleries	Fine dining; wine and food events	Up-market; on their own
Trade fair	Exhibitors with equipment	Block bookings for the registered	Hospitality suites	At the venue plus on their own	At the venue
Corporate event	VIPs needing security	Special suites	VIP hospitality	Catered	Gifts for attendees
Association convention	International air arrivals	Block bookings for members	Pre- and posttours	Catered and on their own	Coupons and incentives from retailers

Roadtrips Sports Travel Packages (www.roadtrips.com)

Let us build your dream sports travel experience!

At Roadtrips it is our distinct pleasure to create custom travel experiences to the World's most exclusive and desired Sporting Events. We believe that discerning travelers should not have to buy someone else's package, but that they will enjoy lifetime memories when they get to create their preferred trip. Since 1992 we have been providing exceptional travel experiences to top sporting events around the globe. We invite you to give us a call and let us work with you to build your Ultimate Sports Travel Experience.

Experience one of the World's Most Exclusive Events

This is your chance to join stars from all over the world as they gather at Cannes for this prestigious film festival. The incredible Cote d'Azur is the perfect venue to host the beautiful people of the entertainment industry at this exclusive event. You can have your chance to be a critic as films from all over the globe are screened at this festival, vying for the prestigious "Palme d'Or." Every evening famous actors and directors climb the stairways outside the Palais des Festivals while the paparazzi cameras flash, every night the parties go late. You can join the hottest film stars in this famed destination on your customized Cannes International Film Festival travel experience.

Bus Tours

As observed by McConkey (1986), bus tours have many advantages but also tend to be highly price sensitive and often consist of seniors who require extra care and might not be high spenders. Also, the bus tour market is very competitive and committed marketing is needed to secure and keep tours coming.

Getting involved in the bus associations and their marketplaces is a starting point, and offering familiarization tours for operators is often necessary. Destination tourist organizations will do this for events, or at least assist them. Familiarization tours can be used to get the wholesaler to the event, or at least to the setting at a different time.

The wholesalers will typically look for certain elements of attractiveness, from their perspective, including how well the tourists and escorts will be received. Other criteria in selecting events could include:

- distance from their markets;
- cleanliness and safety;
- uniqueness of the event;
- its established reputation;
- suitability of the event and its setting for their markets;
- value for price (to the tourists and to the wholesaler);
- available information, and its quality; promotions by the event itself.

McConkey (1986) said that establishing personal relationships with tour wholesalers and other intermediaries is critical for success in attracting tour groups. The event's marketing people have to work to get to know the intermediaries and their needs or preferences. The attitude of event staff might be as important as the product in maintaining good relations.

Benefits and Costs of Packaging

Events can increase tourist numbers and revenue, both off and on the site, through packaging. Specific target markets can be attracted, and a better match realized between product and visitor demands. For example, group tours provide the opportunity for selling meals or souvenirs in larger quantity under ideal merchandizing conditions, to assemble higher quality entertainment, and to broaden the program. Sponsors might also be easier to cultivate when the numbers and characteristics of tourists present attractive marketing opportunities. Destinations can enhance their overall attractiveness by including events in general packages or making events the focus.

In return, events will usually have to make specific changes to cater to packages (all of which are likely to include reserved tickets) and group tours in particular. In addition to the points listed earlier, events might have to:

- expand the event's duration to accommodate more tourists and a preference for weekend visits;
- change dates to meet tour company demand;
- move or expand the venue to accommodate increased numbers;
- control access and reserve seating/viewing areas;
- add facilities (such as bus parking, more toilets, or reception areas);
- develop ticketing, reservation, and refund systems;
- schedule for group tour arrivals; ensure punctuality within the program;
- work closely with the industry;
- develop a pricing strategy;
- plan and produce programs at least 1 year in advance (so that tour companies can adequately market their packages);
- consider the impacts of, and manage, larger number of visitors with specific expectations and needs;
- provide photographs and other promotional material for tour companies to use in their marketing.

Creating a Package

Packages, aimed at target segments, can accomplish different goals. Determine in advance if the aim is to build attendance, generate revenue, expand market share, provide benefits for sponsors, or boost tourism to the destination. Any combination of these goals is possible.

Market research, and especially segmentation, is necessary. Sometimes this can be done by examining existing data, as described earlier, or by consulting the tourist organizations and tour operators. They know the marketplace. In particular, examples of successful packages to the destination and its events should be examined. The event's own visitor surveys can also reveal segments suitable for target packaging. A package concept should next be formulated, with creativity to make it interesting. Give it a catchy name.

A Tourism Canada (1994) publication (Packaging and Marketing Festivals and Events for the Canadian Tourism Industry) provides a form to evaluate packaging ideas. Elements of the package (e.g., type of accommodation, additional entertainment, meals) are evaluated for their relationship to the theme and whether they are essential or optional to the package. It is important to ask what the Unique Selling Proposition will be, or what gives the package added value. How unique is it? What kind of image will it convey about the event? Will it afford a competitive advantage?

Presumably the event will have a clear theme that is expressed through the package, such as heritage, the arts, or sports. Alternatively, program elements, especially entertainment and spectacle, can provide an effective event package theme. This theme should be used when combining the event experience with other opportunities in the area.

Feasibility must be assessed, including the price and ability to deliver the product at high and consistent standards. Setting the price will likely involve negotiations with suppliers, such as accommodation establishments and bus companies; this also helps determine the marketability of the product. One test is to see if a tour company will be interested in taking over the package. Another test is to compare it directly with existing successful packages.

In the Tourism Canada (1994) publication detailed advice is given on setting the price. This involves determining fixed costs per customer (e.g., rental of one bus and driver, one host/guide) and variable costs (e.g., per meal or reserved seat at the event). Add overhead costs, like marketing and staff time, and determine the break-even point. Add a profit margin, but also allow for contingencies. Other considerations include discounts for large groups, whether or not drivers and guides get free product, and special prices for seniors or youth.

Remember that in selling the package through intermediaries, commissions of 10–15% or higher will normally have to be paid. These can be negotiated, but many travel agents and tour retailers will not touch a package without adequate commission rates.

Hosting Tour Groups

The tourist is an honored guest of the event and the host community, and must be made to feel as such. To enhance the tourist's experience a number of additional benefits can be offered:

- a welcome and departure ceremony that is distinct from that given to other customers;
- easier accessibility, parking, and related directions;
- more detailed and better quality information, including souvenir programs;
- small gifts or "free" extras;
- arrangements with local accommodations, restaurants, entertainment places, etc., to offer discounts, other inducements, and better service;
- emergency and amenity services aimed at the special needs of strangers (e.g., rest areas; food and beverages; medical);
- some tourists will appreciate being identified as guests, while others might prefer anonymity while enjoying the event—give tourists a choice;
- on-site tours or guides; a look at the "backstage" and meetings with performers, organizers, celebrities, etc.;
- price the package to allow adequate profit for the event and the tour operators; check out the competition;
- allow for visitors with special needs; be flexible where practical and important to the customer; otherwise, packages are standardized (e.g., allow for wheelchair seating and special diets);
- vouchers are generally issued to tour companies who reissue them to customers; voucher redemption at the event, hotels, etc., must be prearranged;
- accommodation establishments must be able to reserve blocks of rooms for event patrons;
- inform all visitors and tour companies of special requirements (e.g., are visas needed? currency exchange facilities; prices—especially what is NOT included in packages; what is subject to cancellation or replacement in the package or in the event program);
- exceed customer expectations by providing a bonus (e.g., a welcome gift or goodbye souvenir; meet a VIP or performer);
- establish a refund policy and procedures (e.g., accept cancellations without penalty up to 30 days before the event);
- are taxes included or extra? advise the customer.

Evaluating Packaging

A "conversion rate" can be calculated on the basis of how many people receiving specific information about the package (e.g., in a mail-out or in response to telephone/Internet inquiries) purchased the event package. Package customers should be surveyed to learn about any problems and to measure satisfaction levels. Participating tour companies, hotels, etc., have to be asked for feedback on how the packages could be improved for their target markets. A customer complaint system is needed at the event organization.

Summary and Study Guide

We turned to individual events in this chapter, focusing on how to market events to tourists and create a tourist orientation. A starting point for reviewing this material is to image yourself as a consultant hired to enhance the tourist attractiveness (and hence the marketing effectiveness) of an existing event. You need to do an event audit, so what exactly do you look for? There should be clear signs of a tourist orientation and appropriate use of the marketing mix to appeal to various segments. Does it have a strong brand and is it positioned to establish a clear, attractive image for one or more target segments? Are those segments based on research, and how are they specified (i.e., the six variables)? They need to do market and evaluation research, so also give the organizers advice on conducting a visitor and market-area survey. Now they need new "products," so do a feasibility study for a new event or programming element, including costs and risks. Finally, develop one or more packages targeted carefully at the primary and secondary segments.

The process of doing research for, and designing Iconic destination events for special interests was also emphasized. This cannot be done without detailed understanding of special interests and their values, and it helps to specifically examine how their social networking (social worlds) mediate to shape demand for events and Event Tourism. This has design implications as well, but we only dealt with this conceptually.

Study Questions

- Describe the marketing mix for events, giving examples of experiential and facilitative elements necessary to create a tourist orientation.
- Outline the process for creating and marketing events as tourist attractions, including how to conduct a marketing audit of an event.
- Explain how to brand and position an event in order to attract tourists seeking both generic and special interest benefits.
- Define a "destination Iconic event" and describe the research necessary for its design to attract a specific segment of highly involved leisure traveler.
- Why do a feasibility study? What exactly is included?
- Outline the risk management process for events and give examples of the generic risk management strategies.
- Describe six segmentation methods and how to use them (both singly and together).
- What are the possible event demand forecasting methods?
- How are packages assembled and targeted? Work through an example for an ecotourist destination event.
- What are the purposes and major elements of an event customer/visitor survey?
- When and why do you use market area surveys?
- What does the Whitebait Festival teach you about marketing and positioning?

Additional Readings

- *Risk Management for Meetings and Events* (Silvers, 2008).
- *Events Design and Experience* (Berridge, 2007).
- *Event Marketing: How to Successfully Promote Events, Festivals, Conventions and Expositions* (Preston & Hoyle, 2012).
- *Consumer Behavior Knowledge for Effective Sports and Event Marketing* (Kahle & Close, 2010).
- *Innovative Marketing Communications for the Events Industry* (Masterman & Wood, 2006).

Chapter 6

Sport Event Tourism

Learning Objectives

Upon completion of this chapter the student should understand and be able to explain the following:

1. Sport tourism.
2. Types of sport events and sport tourists.
3. The fan: motivation and desired experiences.
4. Amateur, athletic participants: motivation and desired experiences.
5. The meanings of participation for seniors and subcultures.
6. Patterns and trends, with implications for sport event tourism.
7. Event tourist careers in sports.
8. Development methods for sport event tourism.
9. Bidding on sport events.
10. Venues: trends and justifications for public sector investment.
11. Producing and marketing sport destination events.
12. Variables influencing the impacts of sport event tourism.

Introduction

In this chapter we examine sports event tourism more closely, to be followed by similar examinations of business events, festivals and cultural celebrations, and entertainment plus private functions. These chapters demonstrate how a demand-side approach can work, based on detailed understanding of the event tourist: their motivations, benefits, and experiences desired; decision making; travel patterns; and preferences. Issues relating to each of the main event sectors are also discussed, including venues and impacts.

First we look at sport tourism in general and where sport event tourism fits. Then comes a thorough discussion of motivation and experiences, including references to pertinent foundation theories. There is a fundamental difference between fans as spectators and athletes as participants (even though they can be the same people on different trips), and this will be highlighted. Both professional and amateur sport events draw spectators, many of whom are serious sport fans (e.g., football fanatics) and fans of particular teams (the home team, country team, etc.). Since spectators are a big market it is necessary to understand more about their motivations and experiences, and their event tourist careers differ from those of athletic participants. Just keep in mind that roles do change, so that a highly involved person might at various times compete, spectate, officiate, or organize events.

What Is Sport Tourism and Sport Event Tourism?

Sport tourism encompasses much more than events, as people travel for adventurous activities (e.g., whitewater rafting), to visit iconic sport places (museums, halls of fame, famous arenas, and golf courses), and to learn at sport camps or conferences. But any sport activity you can think of (and more arising every year) translates into events. There are spectator events for fans, put on both by professionals and amateurs, and participatory events for fun and competition by amateurs or a mix of amateurs and professionals. Sport events are found everywhere, in rustic outdoor playing fields and in enormous, luxury stadia. Sports events are found at all levels of organization, from local to international. They are infinite in variety, and are frequently packaged as, or with, festivals, entertainment, and spectacle. Many are produced as media events, involving few participants or spectators.

H. Gibson (1998) classified sport tourism into three main areas: nostalgia sport tourism (including halls of fame and museums), active sport tourism (including activity holidays and active events), and event sport tourism (including passive and active sporting events). She defined sport tourism as "Leisure-based travel that takes individuals temporarily outside of their home communities to participate in physical activities, to watch physical activities, or to venerate attractions associated with physical activities" (p. 49).

Weed and Bull (2004, p. 37) identified five main categories of sport tourism: sports participation; tourism with sports content; luxury sports tourism; sports events; and sports training. They said (p. 204) that motivations for sport tourism are related to the unique experience that comes from the interaction of activity, people, and place.

Gammon (2012) classified sport tourism events with a view to practical and research applications. His framework considered economic activity (high to low), level (local to international), single or multievent (Olympics are multisport), media interest, periodicity (regularly held or not), spectator versus competitive or both, tourism potential, and opportunity for developing sport. This approach is evaluative in nature, allowing destinations and events to consider the roles and effects of sport events in a tourism context, not merely their form or target market.

Research Note on Triathletes as Active Sport Tourists

Miller, A. (2012). Understanding the event experience of active sports tourists. In R. Shipway & A. Fyall (Eds.), *International sports events: Impacts, experiences and identities* (pp. 99–112). London: Routledge.

"The findings indicate that for triathletes, the focus of the holidays on the event and the decision making is all made with a view to enhancing and maximising their personal performance and minimising risk for their health and their sports kit. Their acknowledged selfishness and competitiveness affects their choices as to hotels and transport to be used. Where the triathletes spoke about positive experiences and about wanting to repeat the experience it was mainly due to a well-organized event at a good destination and where both triathletes and spectators had an enjoyable experience. Interestingly the specifics of the event and the layout of the course were not only important for the event itself, but it could also lead to destination loyalty and repeat visits for event participation and training. Notably, the holiday and the event are integral as interviewees see themselves as triathletes engaging in their leisure pursuit in the form of an event whilst on holiday."

The Fan: Motivation and Experiences

Benckendorff and Pearce (2012) discussed the psychology of events and developed a very useful framework for applying theory to event participation, applicable to both fans and athletes. They consider preevent, on-site, and postevent experiences, for spectators, attendees, performers, and elite participants. Psychological theory on personality, motivation, and involvement are important when looking at antecedents, while role theory, identity, liminality, flow, mindfulness, emotional and performative labor, and experience analysis can be applied to the event experience itself. Satisfaction, loyalty, self-actualization, and personal development apply to the postevent. Superior performance is a concept pertinent to the elite athlete.

The review of literature on motives of sport spectators by Benckendorff and Pearce (2012) is a good starting point, and we cover some of the key sources in this section. Key theoretical perspectives on the fan include the following: Wann (1995) and Wann, Schrader, and Wilson (1999), who developed the most frequently cited Sports Fan Motivation Scale; Milne and McDonald (1999) on the motivation of sport consumers; Trail and James (2001) who developed a Motivation Scale for Sport Consumption; Funk, Mahoney, Nakazawa, and Hirakawa (2001), Funk, Mohoney, and Ridinger (2002), and Funk, Ridinger, and Moorman (2003) and their Sport Interest Inventory; James and Ross (2004); Mehus (2004) with an Entertainment Sport Motivation Scale; and Koo and Hardin (2008).

Attending a sport event can be motivated by a desire for entertainment and spectacle (i.e., simple diversion), the desire for emotional stimulation, or having a social outing. Being a sport spectator is a role we can all play, and most spectators know that it is generally more interesting (certainly more emotionally exciting) to be at a live event as opposed to watching on TV. Being a sport "fan," however, is something quite a bit more engaging. Highly involved fans are emotionally attached (Shank & Beasley, 1998) to their sport and/or team.

Wann (1995) and Wann et al. (1999) developed a "sport fan motivation scale," which covers both intrinsic and extrinsic motivation. It consists of eight common reasons for watching sport, and these can also be conceptualized as desired experiences: escape, "eustress" (i.e., stress evoked by emotions or events, here considered to be positive stimulation), aesthetics (appreciation of the beauty of sports), self-esteem, group affiliation, family, entertainment and economic (e.g., betting). Intrinsic motives (i.e., aesthetics, excitement, entertainment) were found to be more important for fans than extrinsic motives like self-esteem, escape, and family togetherness. As shown in the ensuing research note, the type of event makes a difference to motivation.

Chen (2006) provided a review of the literature on sport fans, in an article devoted to a phenomenological study of event sport fans' behavior, experiences, and values. Chen concluded that most studies suggest that personally relevant values (from needs and the benefits sought), and "identifications" (such as social identity) most explain why fans become highly involved and committed to teams. Chen's study determined that "personal balance" and "socialization" were the essential parts of the experiences being sought, and these were obtained through volunteering, being at events, travel with other fans and the team, "pilgrimages" to places with special meanings, and nonrelated social and touristic activities in destinations.

Weed and Bull (2009) elaborated upon and revised a Sports Tourism Participation Model (its origins being with the English Sports Council) for different products, including both spectator and participation sports tourism. Their model for spectating sport tourist (for a one-time event) is presented in their book *Sports Tourism: Participants, Policy and Providers* (pp. 107–123).

A number of studies of sport events suggest that this market is quite different from cultural tourism. Leibold and Van Zyl (1994) noted that sport enthusiasts attending the Los Angeles Olympics in 1984 came primarily to see the Games but generated very little revenue in dining and sightseeing. They concluded that sport tourists might be less affluent and spend less on entertainment than average travelers.

In the following research note from Fairley, group identity is revealed to be a major motive and significant part of the group-tour, sport fan experience. Earlier work by Fairley showed how nostalgia was an important component of the overall sport-event tourist experience.

Research Note on Sport Event Fans

Fairley, S. (2009). The role of the mode of transport in the identity maintenance of sport fan travel groups. *Journal of Sport and Tourism, 14*(2/3), 205–222.

Groups of sport fans continually travel to multiple destinations to follow their favourite professional sport teams. Fan travel can be usefully understood from a group identity perspective. The role of the bus in the formation and maintenance of a group sport tourism experience is examined. Participant observation and ethnographic interviews were used to examine the role of the bus for three supporter groups that travel on a regular basis to support their team in the Australian Football League (AFL). It is suggested that the bus is much more than a mode of transport for these groups and that travel time itself has much positive utility. The bus is key and central to the creation and celebration of a shared group identity and acts to ensure the sustainability of the core supporter group.

Wann, Grieve, Zapalac, and Pease (2008) looked at how fan motives varied with the type of event.

Research Note on Sport Fan Motivations

Wann, D., Grieve, F., Zapalac, R., & Pease, D. (2008). Motivational profiles of sport fans of different sports. *Sport Marketing Quarterly, 17*(1), 6–19.

The current investigation examined sport type differences in eight fan motives: escape, economic (i.e., gambling), eustress (i.e., positive arousal), self-esteem, group affiliation, entertainment, family, and aesthetics. Participants (final sample N-886) completed a questionnaire packet assessing their level of fandom and motivation for consuming one of 13 target sports . . . classified into three different dichotomies: individual (e.g., figure skating, golf) versus team (e.g., professional baseball, college basketball); aggressive (e.g., professional wrestling, professional football) versus nonaggressive (e.g., professional baseball, figure skating); and stylistic (e.g., figure skating, gymnastics) versus nonstylistic (e.g., professional hockey, tennis)." The sample was of young college students, but it revealed there were substantial motivational differences among the types of sports studied—with the exception of the "escape" motive which did not differ significantly.

Athletic Participants: Motivation and Experiences

In this section we focus on the athletic participant, such as those who travel to Masters Games or TransRockies mountain-biking and running events (see the Case Studies). These are active and often serious, highly involved people. I am ignoring the elite competitor here, as they are usually the focus of fan attention and do not constitute a large segment except for very select events.

Active and Serious Sport Tourists

H. Gibson (1998) first described the "active sport tourist," and referred to involvement and concentration theories to help explain motivation and travel behavior. She determined the "active sport tourist" to be primarily male, but also college educated with higher income. Gibson said these active sport tourists are likely to travel for participation in favorite pursuits well into retirement.

Robinson and Gammon (2004) argued there are very specific motives that apply to active sport tourists, namely the need to compete, a desire to win, and the opportunity to improve one's skills. These authors proposed a classification of sport tourists that separates passive and active participation in a competitive sport event, as well as separates casual participation in sports while traveling from trips motivated by sport participation. The term "serious sport tourism" has recently entered the literature, and according to Frew (2006) "serious leisure" had not previously been applied extensively to tourism, and even less to sport tourism.

Green and Jones (2005) explained the relevance of serious leisure and social worlds to sport tourism studies, arguing that "serious sport tourism" (i.e., travel to participate in serious leisure) provides individuals with a positive social identity. They also stressed that event-related travel yields extraordinary, extended contact with other participants including more experienced members of the particular subculture. In this context, sport events provide spaces for social identity formation and reinforcement.

Highly involved recreational runners have been studied more than other groups, perhaps because it is such a huge and international phenomenon. In their research, McGehee, Yoon, and Cardenas (2003) found that highly involved runners traveled more on overnight trips to participate in events when compared to the medium involved. They confirmed the well-established proposition that greater involvement results in higher levels of participation, and for runners this means competitive events. They also found that runners did not attend all the races they would have liked, owing to a number of constraints such as family obligations. Event characteristics and destination choices were not examined.

In another study of runners, Chalip and McGuirty (2004) examined "bundling" and specifically how the athletes could be attracted through augmentations such as other activities and attractions. A sample of 277 adult runners at events in Sydney and Melbourne were asked to consider bundling options for possible participation in the Gold Coast Marathon. Cluster analysis was used to develop four segments that differed in terms of their bundling choices, and these relate explicitly to involvement. "Dedicated runners" were older and only interested in official marathon parties, not the destination. The other segments had varying degrees of interest in destination bundling. "Running tourists" were younger and less "involved" with the sport, so they were less attracted by opportunities to celebrate with other runners. Events, in this context, represent an opportunity to combine running with a holiday at the host destination.

According to Shipway and Jones (2007), amateur distance running is often serious leisure. Applying social identity theory, and employing a quasiethnographic methodology, greater explanation of the running careers of participants was achieved. Those authors have also classified London Marathon runners as "serious sport tourists" on the basis of the level of ability needed to compete in a marathon, length of trip and stay necessitated by participation, and the relatively high cost of training for the event (p. 65). They argued for the existence of a "runners prototype" (p. 67) reflected in the homogeneous look of the participants—clothing and badges as subcultural capital. According to their observations, discussion between participants—often focusing on past experiences—emphasized the importance of travel, with faraway events generating more social capital. Running careers were discussed, and the London marathon, for some, was a "career marker" towards becoming a serious runner. The collection of subcultural capital leads to "the desire to travel and collect places" and a lot of storytelling (p. 72).

The study by Sport England (2005) identifies three concepts related to lifestyle sports: "alternative," "lifestyle," and "extreme," and argues that the new lifestyle forms have led to the development of new cultural and consumption practices. Shipway and Jones (2007) advocate the concept of "sport tourism identity," suggesting that participants focus heavily on the identity they receive from association with certain sport tourism activities, association with like-minded people, and strong desires to participate in an activity and then "return home and talk about it" (p. 200). It is suggested that a strong subculture exists within many sport tourism activities, especially those that are perceived as "lifestyle" sports. These forms of sport tourism challenge mainstream sport in terms of cultural significance.

Funk (2008) employs self-concept in his approach to studying consumer behavior for sports and events, namely as an integral part of the "psychological continuum model" (see also Funk & James, 2001, 2006). Awareness, attraction, attachment, or allegiance are the progressive steps open to consumers and participants. Self-concept connects specifically to identifying with a sport, event or team.

Research Notes on Sport Event Motivation

Funk, D., Toohey, K., & Bruun, T. (2007). International sport event participation: Prior sport involvement; destination image; and travel motives. *European Sport Management Quarterly,* 7(3), 227–248.

"This study utilised the attraction process within the Psychological Continuum Model (PCM) (Funk and James, 2001; 2006) to develop and examine five hypothesis related to motives of international participants (N = 239) who registered for a hallmark Australian running event. Structural equation modelling revealed registration in the event is motivated by prior running involvement; desire to participate in organised running events, favourable beliefs and feelings toward the host destination and perceived travel benefits of escape, social interaction, prestige, relaxation, culture experience, cultural learning, and knowledge exploration."

Funk, D., & Bruun, T. (2007). The role of socio-psychological and culture-education motives in marketing international sport tourism: A cross-cultural perspective. *Tourism Management,* 28(3),806–819.

The authors conducted a survey among international runners at the 2005 Gold Coast (Australia) Marathon. Several well-tested scales were use: Personal Involvement Inventory, Strength of Motivation Scale, Attitude Towards Australia, Knowledge-Learning Scale, Cultural Experience Scale, and Cultural Learning Inventory. "The study found that participants, regardless of cultural background, had a positive attitude toward Australia, a high level of running involvement, and a strong desire to participate in organized running events." Running was the primary travel motive, but Japanese runners in particular also wanted to learn about Australian and Australian culture (leisure activities, music and art and lifestyle).

Sport Subcultures (or Countercultures)

When a special interest group rejects the mainstream it tends toward the status of subculture, rather than social world. A subculture identity means that participants will likely not attend events aimed at a broader audience, they want their own. They will also likely eschew corporate sponsorship and media coverage, and in general they want only to do their own thing. Marketing to subcultures will therefore entail many challenges!

Hinch and Higham (2001, pp. 114–116, in the second edition of their book *Sport Tourism Development*), suggested that subcultures are often characterized by unique relationships to places, such as places where venues or environments are highly conducive to their sport (e.g., windsurfing in out-of-the-way bays), and communities where they can "hang" together (e.g., certain mountain resorts where ski-bums cluster). When such places are discovered and mass tourism encroaches, the counterculture types will move on.

Pitts (1999) reported on the gay and lesbian sport tourism industry, finding this target segment to be large and affluent, with its own sport travel industry, media, and events. The Gay Games are an annual, international participation event with substantial economic impact, and many smaller, sport-specific events are growing in popularity.

Research Note on Sport Subcultures

Green, B. C. (2008). Leveraging subculture and identity to promote events. In M. Weed (Ed.), *Sport and tourism: A reader* (pp. 362–376). London: Routledge.

Green argued that organizers "have had to invent ways to make events more appealing to more people" (p. 362) and that it has become common to augment a sport event's appeal through generic entertainment or festivities. Green argues that for many people attending events is a form of "symbolic consumption" related to their personal or group identity. Three events were analyzed (women's flag football in key West, Florida, a marathon in Gold Coast, Australia, and the Australian Motorcycle Grand Prix). "Taken together, these cases illustrate the significance and utility of subculture and identity as levers for event marketing. The Key West Women's Flag Football Tournament demonstrates the central role that opportunities for subcultural revelry and socializing play in the quality of experience that participants obtain from an event. The Gold Coast marathon shows that event augmentations permit a wider range of opportunities for participants to parade and celebrate the subculture they share. The Australian Motorcycle Grand Prix demonstrates that systematic application of insights derived from attention to subculture and identity is both practical and useful."

Other Types of Participation

Some sport events do not focus on athletic participation, or even on competition. Gillis and Ditton (1998) compared tournament and nontournament recreational bill-fish anglers as to their motives. This sport attracts mostly the wealthy elite and they are highly sought-after tourists. The researchers found the respondents to be mostly interested in the challenge of sport fishing, and the experience of catching large specimens. Raybould (1998) also studied motives for participating in a fishing event, this one a week long in a remote, Australian location. His found that "social stimulation" and "escaping" motives were rated highest, contrary to the competitive aspects and extrinsic rewards stressed by organizers. Most respondents were male, so "family togetherness" ranked lowest. The statement "because the event was unique" achieved the highest individual mean response, and it was included in the "social stimulation" factor. The researcher's conclusion was that organizers should emphasize the social and relaxation benefits and make less of the extrinsic rewards (i.e., prizes) and competitive elements.

Nogawa, Yamaguchi, and Hogi (1996) studied two "sport for all" events in Japan, where the emphasis was on the joy of participation and health or fitness, not on winning. They found that regardless of travel duration, the "health/fitness and challenge" motivators were paramount among participants.

Major Patterns and Trends in Sport Event Tourism

Some of the major trends shown in Table 6.1 are from Hinch and Higham (2011), adapted from P. Bourdeau, Corneloup, and Mao (2002), and some I have added. As well, I have added implications for event tourism.

Table 6.1. Trends in Sport, and Implications for Event Tourism

Trends	Implications for Event Tourism
Increasing development of individual sports as opposed to collective sports	The emphasis on personal development translates into many more highly involved sport tourists seeking knowledge, challenges, communitas, and unique event experiences; participation triumphs over spectatorship; more travel relating to events plus destination experiences. See the TransRockies case study.
Diversification of sports participation models	People try more sports and develop broader portfolios of competitive sports; sports appeal to broader audiences; events can cross-promote at other types of sports.
Exaggerated segmentation of sports disciplines	Unlimited potential for events catering to specific interest groups.
Adaptation of sports activities to the constraints of urban life	Indoor simulation of traditional nature-based sport means new event business for venues; employ urban clubs and events to promote remote events.
Development of a mythology of adventure in a natural environment	Nature takes on new, symbolic meanings as a place for adventure and risk-taking; see the Voss Extreme Sports Festival.
Global media reach; the rise of sport sponsorship	Major sport events reach billions of viewers, attracting huge sponsorship deals. Sport as live communication (i.e., event marketing). Minor sport events have their own niche (but large) audiences. Sport as entertainment.
Virtual sport event experiences through fan zones, live streaming, and social media	The experience is no longer confined to the arena; cocreation of sport tourism experiences is of equal importance as the competition.
Gigantism of events accompanied by equally enormous security issues and costs	Ever-larger sport events come with astronomic costs and risks.
Increasing sport participation by women, people with special needs, but not children	More events for women and special needs groups; in many countries there is an urgent need to get children physically active.
A new wave of arenas and stadia	Sport venues as tools in urban renewal and city repositioning or branding; public–private partnerships; competition with venues and events for world-class sport city status; sport venues becoming multievent facilities.

Specific areas of growth have been identified as being female participation in many sports, active baby boomers well into retirement, and younger generations taking up challenging athletic activities in greater numbers (like the X Games). Corporate sponsorship and global media reach (with numerous sports TV channels) and online broadcasting are all fueling interest in sport events as live and media communications tools.

Major Studies of Sport and Sport Event Tourism

In this section a number of major studies of sport event participation are summarized. Research on this scale is rare, and while valuable for shedding light on whole populations, the studies do tend to get out of date quickly. So use the results with caution, and always try to find current material.

Travel Industry Association of America: Profile of Travelers Who Attend Sports Events

Travel Industry Association of America (TIA) (1999) based its analysis on 1997 survey data that examined travel over the previous 5 years. Sport event tourism was determined to have been increasing in popularity in the US, alongside other forms of special interest travel. Thirty-eight percent of US adults had been sport event travelers (defined as those attending a sport event while traveling at least 50 miles from home), either as event participants or spectators, within the previous 5 years. Seventy-six percent of these travelers listed the sport event as their primary purpose for their most recent such trip. Fully 84% of the most recent sport event trips were to spectate, rather than participate, and one quarter were to watch children or grandchildren play in the event. Sixteen percent of sport event travelers participated in the event (most recent such trip), including a minor portion who both participated and spectated. In total 6% of all resident trips (amounting to 60 million person-trips) in 1997 included a sport event, making it the 10th most popular travel activity.

In the US, 45% of men and 31% of women attended sport events while traveling over the previous 5 years. The dominant segment consisted of parents, especially among those on trips made specifically for a sport event, so there is a very large family market to tap. The average age of the sport event traveler was 45 years, but compared to all US travelers they were more likely to be younger, have children, and be employed full-time. The percentage of sport event parties having children was 30%, compared to 21% overall, but party size was comparable.

The most popular sport events attracting tourists were baseball/softball (17% of adults had done so over the previous 5 years), followed by football (15%), basketball (9%), auto/truck racing (8%), golf tournament (6%), skiing/snowboarding (5%), soccer (5%), and ice hockey (4%), while all other sports events accounted attracted 13% of adults. Professional and amateur sports were attended equally on respondents' most recent trips. Professional sports attracted 50% of the travelers, with the most popular amateur events being high school (14%) and college-level sports (13%). The other categories of amateur sport event were amateur athletic (12%), little league (5%), church/intramural (4%), and other (6%). Summer is the peak season, followed by autumn. It is very interesting to note that men and women identically ranked the top for types of sport events attended, although females were less interested in golf and hockey. Men definitely traveled more for professional sport events (54% of males compared to 45% of females). Mothers do support their children's sporting activities.

Sport event trips involved about the same amount of spending as all types of trips, although the TIA research determined that this segment tended to purchase sport-related equipment or clothes for their trips. It is mostly done by car, although some use air transport. Overnight travel for sport events was high, with 84% of trips being overnight, compared to 82% for all US trips. Just over half (52%) stayed in commercial accommodation, but their overnight trips were shorter than the average US overnight trip (3 nights versus 3.3). Overall, sport event trips were the same average length (3.3 nights) as all trips. Group tours accounted for only 4% of the total person-trips among sport event travelers, which is the same proportion as for all US travelers. Party size for sport event trips was found to be slightly higher (2.1 compared to 1.9 persons).

American Patterns of Sport Event Tourism: Travel Activities and Motivation Survey (TAMS) (Source: TAMS 2006 A Profile Report)

TAMS reports are all available online (www.mtc.gov.on.ca/). The research was conducted for the Canadian Tourism Commission to gain a better understanding of the American market.

Travel to Attend Amateur Tournaments

Over the previous 2 years, 5.9% (for an estimated total of 13,082,310 persons) of adult Americans attended an amateur tournament while on an out-of-town, overnight trip of one or more nights. One half (51.4% or 6,728,338 adult Americans) of those who attended an amateur tournament while on a trip reported that this activity was the main reason for taking at least one trip in the past 2 years.

Relative to the average US pleasure traveler, those who attended amateur tournaments while on trips are more likely to be male, and to be either young (18–24 years of age) or middle aged (45–54) with dependent children (18 and under) living at home. This segment has above average levels of education (68.8% university degree or higher) and household incomes ($84,756). Those who attended amateur tournaments while on trips traveled more often than the average US pleasure traveler.

Those who attended amateur tournaments while on trips were much more active in culture and entertainment activities and outdoor activities than the typical US pleasure traveler. They were especially likely to attend major sporting events (e.g., professional sports, national and international events) and equestrian and western events, to exercise and jog, and to play golf, games, and individual sports and team sports while on trips. They also exhibit above average interest in participatory outdoor attractions (e.g., participatory historical activities, agrotourism) and theatrical and musical performances (e.g., high art performances, theater, film, and music festivals). In addition, they were more likely than average to take tours (e.g., same-day tours, casino tour) and cruises (e.g., sightseeing cruises). Their preferred types of accommodation were seaside, lakeside, or riverside resorts and public campgrounds. Similar to other US pleasure travelers, this segment seeks vacations that give them a break from their day-to-day environment and allows them to relieve stress.

Those who attended amateur tournaments while traveling were more likely than average to use the Internet to plan (80.5%) and book travel (60.5%). They can be effectively targeted through sports-related media, including sports magazines, television programs, all-sports radio stations, and sports websites.

Attending National and International Sporting Events While on Trips of One or More Nights

Over the previous 2 years, 1.4% (3,166,274) of adult Americans attended a national or international sporting event while on an out-of-town, overnight trip of one or more nights. Attending a professional soccer game (0.7%) and a professional figure skating event (0.5%) were the most popular events, followed by a national or international sporting event such as the Olympics (0.4%) and a curling bonspiel (0.1%); 46.7% (1,478,435) of those who attended national and international sporting events reported that this activity was the main reason for taking at least one trip in the past 2 years.

Relative to the average US pleasure traveler, those who attended national and international sporting events while on trips are overrepresented among young (18–24) single males. This segment is relatively affluent with an above average level of education (71.4% university degree or higher) and above average household incomes ($88,675). They are overrepresented among those living in cities with a population of 500,000 or more.

National and international sporting event attendees are more frequent travelers than the average US pleasure traveler and they were more than twice as likely to have taken a trip to Canada in the last 2 years (30.4% vs. 14.6%). The most common Canadian destinations were Ontario, British Columbia, and Quebec. However, they are overrepresented among US travelers to all Canadian provinces and territories, making this an excellent target market for Canadian tourism initiatives.

Travelers who attended national and international sporting events were much more active on their trips than the average US pleasure traveler in both culture and entertainment activities and outdoor activities. They were especially likely to have engaged in sports-related activities both as a spectator (e.g., professional sporting events, amateur tournaments) and as a participant (e.g., games and individual sports, team sports). This segment also exhibits above average interest in live art performances (e.g., high art performances, rock concerts), theater, film, and music festivals and strenuous outdoor activities (e.g., extreme sports, "board & blade" activities) when traveling. They were much more likely than average to take tours and cruises, and especially overnight multi-location tours. They tended to stay at seaside, lakeside, or riverside resorts and public campgrounds. This segment seeks vacations that offer novelty, intellectual stimulation, physical challenge and opportunities to learn.

National and international sporting event attendees frequently use the Internet to plan (79.8%) and book travel (61.1%). They are avid consumers of travel-related media and can also be targeted effectively through sports-related media (e.g., professional sports magazines, television sports programming, all-sports radio, and sports websites).

Attending Professional Sports Events While on Trips of One or More Nights

Over the last 2 years, 12.5% (27,464,064) of adult Americans attended a professional sports event while on an out-of-town, overnight trip of one or more nights. Baseball games were the most popular professional sports event attended on trips (8.1%), followed by football games (4.4%), basketball games (2.5%), ice hockey games (1.9%), and golf tournaments (1.0%); 45.9% (12,602,543) of those who attended a professional sports event reported that this activity was the main reason for taking at least one trip in the past 2 years.

Relative to the average US pleasure traveler, those who attend professional sports events while on trips are more likely to be young, single males 18–34 years of age. They are relatively affluent with an above average level of education and above average household incomes ($86,175). They are overrepresented in Alaska and the West North Central, East North Central, and New England regions of the US.

Over the past 2 years, those who attended professional sports events while on trips traveled more frequently than the average US pleasure traveler and they were more likely to have taken a trip to Canada (22.5% vs. 14.6%). The most common Canadian destinations were Ontario, British Columbia, and Quebec; however, this segment is overrepresented among US travelers to all Canadian provinces and territories.

Those who attend professional sports events as spectators are much more likely than the average US pleasure traveler to also play sports (e.g., games and individual sports, golf, team sports) and to participate in strenuous outdoor activities (e.g., downhill skiing and snowboarding) while on trips. They are also more likely than average to take advantage of nightlife activities (e.g., rock concerts and recreational dancing), the arts (e.g., theater, film, and music festivals) and other sporting events (e.g., amateur tournaments) while traveling. This segment most often stayed at a seaside resort or public campground while on trips and was more likely than average to take tours (especially casino, winery, or factory tours) and cruises.

This segment is more likely than the average US pleasure traveler to use the Internet to plan (80.5%) and book (62.1%) travel. They were particularly likely to have purchased tickets for specific activities or attractions online (presumably for professional sports events).

This segment can be targeted most effectively through sports-related media, including professional sports magazines, television sports game or talk shows, all-sports radio stations, and sports-related websites.

Development of Sport Event Tourism

In Canada's Province of British Columbia, "Sport tourism is defined as any activity in which people are attracted to a particular location as a sport event participant, an event spectator or to attend sport attractions or sport-related business meetings. Sport tourism visitors travel more than 80 km to reach the host community and/or stay overnight" (source: The Langley Advanced Sport Tourism Workshop by Tourism BC, 2011; www.tourism-langley.ca/images/AdvancedSportTourismReport.pdf). Tourism BC estimated that sport tourism "has developed into a major generator for the province's economy, generating $13.2 billion in provincial tourism revenue in 2007. BC residents make up more than half of all visitors to British Columbia, with the rest of Canada and the U.S. each accounting for twenty percent of visitors."

Tourism ministries, DMOs, and cities around the world have come to the same conclusion as British Columbia. They value sport event tourism for a number of important reasons: economic development and job creation, sport development (through infrastructure and enhanced training and competition), and various community legacies including imputed social and health benefits.

Through the 1980s and 1990s, American cities in particular engaged in urban redevelopment schemes that "put a heavy emphasis on sports, entertainment and tourism as a source of revenue for the cities" (Sports Business Market Research, Inc., 2000, p. 167). And according to Gratton and Kokolakakis (1997), in the UK sports events were already the main platform for economic regeneration in many cities. Whitson and Macintosh (1996) argued that countries and major cities compete for mega sport events in order to demonstrate to the world their "modernity and economic dynamism" (p. 279). To those authors, international sport "has become one of the most powerful and effective vehicles for the showcasing of place and for the creation of what the industry calls 'destination image'" (p. 279). In past, this force reflects the growing integration of news, entertainment and promotion. Cities have to "position" themselves as service centers, places for entertainment and shopping, because their manufacturing sectors are no longer vital.

Indianapolis is widely acknowledged as being a sport tourism success story. Rozin (2000) termed it a "classic case" of civic turnaround, based first on the efforts of a newly established Indiana Sports Corporation to attract amateur sport governing bodies after 1978. Massive infrastructure development followed, aided by the private Lilly Endowment, pumping $884 million into sport facilities between 1979 and 1984. This helped make the city attractive for other corporate headquarters. Indianapolis expected to gain some $304 million from sport events in the year 2000.

Numerous cities or regions have established sport commissions or event development corporations that have the mandate to create, bid on, and facilitate sport events, plus most DMOs also engage in bidding. In the US, the Cincinnati-based National Association of Sports Commissions was established in 1992 and pulls together commissions that had their roots in chambers of commerce or visitor and convention bureaus. The national association provides a forum for exchange between commissions, and with national sport governing bodies, event rights holders (i.e., the owners of events), sport marketing firms, and service or equipment suppliers. Their Executive Director is Don Schumacher, who explained to me their rationale: "Increasingly, the value of the sports event industry in terms of tourism, economic development and image enhancement is being recognized. In response, communities are forming sports commissions whose purpose is to attract sports events" (personal communication, 2000). In 2012 Don Schumacher wrote a piece on the Sports Travel Industry, including this statement:

> Many cities have realized sports travel is a specialty. They have created sports commissions or sports authorities staffed by experts who understand these special needs. These experts understand where events can be found and have relationships in place with many event owners. About 110 of these special sports organizations can be found today. Some are affiliated with a CVB or chamber of commerce. Most are independent organizations. The National Association of Sports Commissions, the industry's trade association, estimates that of the 110 sports commissions about 20 are affiliated with a CVB. The other 90 markets have both: a CVB and a sports commission.

Information available from the National (USA) Association of Sports Commissions includes the following, for members (from their website: www.sportscommissions.org):

- **Economic impact template**: This template assists NASC members in predicting economic impact prior to bidding on an event, and provides the estimated economic impact produced by an event.
- **Event calendar**: Member organizations can add BOOKED EVENTS to the calendar. This tool is beneficial for both rights holders and host organizations. The calendar can be utilized to gather historical data on events listed within.
- **Event database**: NASC rights holder members post their events available for bid in the NASC Event Database. NASC active members may search the database by event name, bid deadline, organization name, or sport to find events to bid on.
- **Event owner directory**: Are you looking for new events to bring to your community? Save time researching and gathering contact information for event owners by using the event owner directory, a valuable member resource and time-saving tool. An instant lead sheet with more than 800 unique event owner organization contacts listed, members can search and sort the directory. Find an Event Owner.
- **Models & samples**: Who has time to reinvent the wheel? This collection of models and samples, used by real host organizations, event organizers, and industry partners, is designed to generate ideas and save you time. Feel free to adapt to your needs or adopt it as is!

- **NASC insurance program**: The NASC and Rand Sports & Entertainment Insurance have come together to create a unique and exciting tool for our members. With NASCINSURANCE.com, it only takes a few minutes to put insurance coverage in place for short-term special events, sports, and recreation activities.
- **NASC reports**: The NASC conducts reports each year to provide data for our members that will improve the quality of the events they own and host. Topics of our published reports include: Economic Impact, Site Selection, Salary and Benefits, and the State of the Industry.
- **SGMA reports**: Through a partnership with SGMA, the NASC is able to provide valuable data and annual reports produced by the Sporting Goods Manufacturing Association (SGMA). Reports that NASC members are able to download free of charge include Sports Participation in America and U.S. Trends in Team Sports. NASC members are also able to view the NASC/SGMA 2009 Amateur Sporting Event Study, a co-branded study conducted to analyze the state of the amateur sporting event industry.

Ultimate Sport Cities

Cities might want to be renowned as a sport capital or win an accolade like "SportBusiness Ultimate Sport Cities" (www.sportbusiness.com). SportBusiness provides internationally recognized rankings of the world's top sports hosts, as initiated by independent industry consultant Rachael Church-Sanders in 2006. In 2012 the top city was London, host of the Olympics, while Melbourne was previously top dog.

In order to determine the Ultimate Sports City 2010 overall winner, information was gathered and scored based on the following areas:

- Numbers and importance of events held in the period 2006 to 2009 (including annual events of international interest and continental/national events). How successful has the city been in securing events over the last 4 years and how important are they globally?
- Numbers and importance of events to be held in the period from 2010 to 2014 (including annual events of international interest and continental/national events). How successful has the city been in securing events over the next 4 years and how important are they globally?
- Numbers and importance of international federations based in the city.
- Current facilities and capabilities for major sports events. How many spectators can the venues hold? Where are they located? Are they easy to get to? Are they perceived to be of world-class quality by industry insiders and fans?
- Infrastructure, including accommodation and transport (internal and external). How easy is it to move around a city and actually attend a sports event? What else is there to do in the city and how suitable is the accommodation both in terms of numbers of rooms and prices/quality? Is the airport conveniently located and efficient?
- Government support and major sports event strategy. How supportive does the local government of a city appear to be and does the city have national government support once it has won an event? Has a city made its ambitions transparent by creating an official entity that bids for major sports events and advises on hosting them?

- Legacy planning and impact. How effective has legacy planning been in a city so far? How are cities building legacy into their strategies for hosting? Are some cities better at legacy planning and implementation than others?
- Security. What is the threat from terrorism or other security threats and has there been a major attack in the period of analysis? What security planning is in place?
- Quality of life. Is pollution a problem in a city and how suitable is the climate/weather for a sports event? Is the standard of living in a city both good and affordable and what is it like to be employed by an organizing committee and actually live there? How safe is a city for events and visitors?
- Public interest and attendance of events. How well supported are sports events? Is the local population sufficient to sustain a large sports venue? Are the public fully behind an event and involved in its marketing? How many people take part in sports activities in the city recreationally?
- Web presence and marketing ability. How easy is it to find out who is responsible for sport in a city and how well presented/user friendly are their websites? Once contact is made with the right entity, how effective are they in communicating what they do? How well do they promote themselves?

Melbourne's Claim to World Status

Melbourne, the state capital of Victoria in Australia, remained the best location in the world to hold a sports event in 2010. The 2006 Commonwealth Games host came out on top for the third time in a row, beating new entrant Singapore into second place and London, England into third place. Germany's capital city Berlin took fourth place and Melbourne's Australian rival Sydney took fifth.

Although Melbourne was the clear winner by 55 points, only 24 points separated the cities in second, third, fourth, and fifth places, highlighting how closely fought the competition was. Despite hosting a successful 2010 Winter Olympic Games, Vancouver fell one place to sixth in the table compared with 2008. New entrant Manchester entered the rankings in seventh position, with Dubai, Paris and New York completing the top 10.

Speaking about the findings, Ultimate Sports Cities 2010 author Rachael Church-Sanders, said:

> Bidding for and then hosting sports events is a massive business with a lot of attention given to major events such as the Olympics, FIFA World Cup and Commonwealth Games. Whilst our winner has proven itself as an excellent host for the latter, Melbourne also has a strong track record of hosting major annual events such as a Formula One Grand Prix and Australian Open Tennis Championships. The city's excellent facilities, strong government support, exceptional legacy planning and not to mention fabulous weather make it a worthy winner once again. Meanwhile, second-placed Singapore's position is fully-deserved due to the city's efforts to propel itself to the forefront of event hosting through the 2010 Youth Olympics, World Netball Championships and its Formula One Grand Prix. London, Berlin and Sydney are all top five stalwarts in these Awards and continue to host exceptional events.

Research Note on Sport Events and Destination Brands

Chalip, L., & Costa, C. (2005). Sport event tourism and the destination brand: Towards a general theory. *Sport in Society, 8* (2), 218–237.

Sport events are being used with increasing frequency to build the brand of their host destinations. Events can take different roles relative to the destination brand: as co-branding partners with the destination brand, as extensions of the destination brand, or as features of the destination brand. Which role is appropriate depends on the nature of the event's brand. Since each role presents different opportunities, risks and requirements, events must be incorporated strategically into the destination's marketing plan. Strategic incorporation of sport events into destination branding requires that each event be cross-leveraged with others in the destination's event portfolio, as well as with the destination's other sport activities and attractions.

Case Study: TransRockies Events (www.transrockies.com)

Much of this case study consists of direct quotes from various TransRockies publications and websites. Some of this material has been previously published in Getz and McConnell (2011) and McConnell and Getz (2007).

Introduction

Written in cooperation with Aaron McConnell, President, TransRockies US LP [email: aaron@transrockies.com (see his profile and interview in Chapter 1)].

TransRockies Events, based in Calgary, Canada, is a privately owned event production and management company. In this case study the company and its owner-produced events are profiled, then two major participation sport events are examined in detail through research findings: mountain-biking in Alberta, Canada, and running in Colorado, USA. These are destination events that attract participants from great distances. Every destination needs events of this kind—anchored, profitable, highly targeted, and successfully co-branded. In the case of outdoor events like these, the co-branding covers the image of a mountain playground and spectacular scenery.

Knowledge of their target markets was essential to development these events, and remains critical to attracting and satisfying the customers, most of whom are highly involved amateur athletes.

Profile and Business Model of the Company

TransRockies Inc. was formed for the purpose of producing a for-profit event to be known as the TransRockies Challenge. Ten years after the launch of the first major international Mountain Bike Stage Race, the TransAlps Challenge in Europe, TransRockies was first produced in Canada in 2002. This weeklong event emulates the owners' already established European event, the TransAlps. Heinrich Albrecht, Founder and Vice-President of the events company Plan B (based in Munich, Germany), was a pivotal figure in the sport of mountain biking before inventing TransAlps. Heinrich was responsible for creating the Mountain Bike World Cup series and countless other mountain biking events around the world before creating the TransRockies in 2002.

A "business model" can be thought of as the way in which a company is organized (i.e., governance, ownership, how decisions are made and by whom), its strategies and operations, all directed at creating, delivering, and capturing value. In the case of private businesses, the value is profit, whereas in other organizations it is service or the implementation of policy. In the service-dominant logic, destination events offer a "value proposition" that potential customers or guests want to pay for (in time, monetary expenditure, and effort), otherwise known as the event tourism experience.

Of critical importance to the business model of a private event production company is an intimate, detailed understanding of their markets. This market intelligence provides a competitive advantage, and ideally a "unique selling proposition" and "distinctive competence." "Knowledge capital" has to encompass motivations, experiences, and benefits desired, how quality is perceived and evaluated, how event and travel decisions are made, and the influence of social worlds and media that define and influence niche markets.

How does a private event company generate profit? There are several models, most commonly the selling of tickets for concerts and festivals, shows and attractions. As will be seen in this case, other revenue generators of importance are registration fees, sponsorship deals, the sale of merchandise, and rentals. This makes it absolutely essential to develop relationships leading to partnerships, or at least collaborations, including corporate sponsors or clients, and tourism agencies. Relationships with various levels and agencies of governments can be crucial in terms of moral support and permissions.

The Company's Events

(a) Gran Fondo Highwood Pass

"Gran Fondo Highwood Pass is a 147 km bike ride (capped at 600 participants) created by TransRockies Events. The Gran Fondo is a type of cycling event created in Italy, with numerous classic events drawing thousands of riders to take on spectacular and challenging routes. Now this Italian phenomenon is sweeping North America as well and cyclists from all over the continent are scrambling to find openings in these fast-filling events.

Gran Fondo means "big ride" or "great endurance." These events are different from other recreational rides in that Gran Fondos utilize mass starts and chip timing like bike races, so that riders can measure themselves against others or against themselves. Gran Fondos are like great marathons, rich in character and excitement.

The only distance for Gran Fondo Highwood Pass is 147 km. All riders must complete the ride within the allotted 12-hour time limit. That's an average pace of about 15 km per hour (9 miles per hour). This time limit was established to accommodate cyclists of all fitness levels. The cut-off pace will allow even the most recreational cyclist to complete the full distance and join the party at Stoney Nakoda Resort."

(b) The North Face Rundle's Revenge

"This is a two-day fun-fest that includes mountain biking and trail running. Where duathlons combine the two events into one day, Rundle's Revenge gives you a full day for each event. The distances are longer and more challenging. And if you only want to do the mountain biking on Saturday or just the trail running on Sunday, then you can! There are shorter courses and longer courses, and for you competitive masochists that both bike and trail run, you can participate in both long courses (aka: The Full Donkey) for maximum pleasure. Bring your A-game to the full donkey and you just might qualify for The Iron Donkey Award. Really . . . who wouldn't want to be an Iron Donkey?

There's even a team relay competition where the bonds of friendship will either be cemented for eternity or strained beyond measure—all in good fun, of course! The Canmore Nordic Centre is home to many world-renowned mountain biking events, Rundle's Revenge included. The Nordic center itself was built on the slopes of Mount Rundle, more specifically a peak named East End of Rundle. Locals just call it EEOR—like

Disney's Eeyore, the endearing donkey from Winnie-the-Pooh, known for his persistent but loveable pessimism."

(c) Canadian Rockies Heli Run (New in 2012)

"This is the first race of its kind in the world, with an innovative and unique trail running experience located in the Canadian Rockies. This is a two person team event. Teammates will run in a relay format from the Heliport to a remote alpine lake and back again, but there's a twist. The twist is: the first runner runs in from the heliport to the lake and flies out by helicopter, the second choppers in to the lake and runs out to the heliport. We have partnered with Kananaskis Mountain Helicopters and Icefields Helitours to offer each participant the spectacular six minute helicopter ride as part of this trail running adventure.

Just outside of Banff National Park, located in the beautiful Canadian Rockies, the Cline River Heliport is situated on the banks of Abraham Lake. From here, the run is approximately 19 km for each runner. The net elevation change is 780 m. You and your teammate make the decision of who will run the uphill leg; the stronger runner may choose this portion, and who will run down. If you are struggling with this decision, an easy coin toss will do the trick! Either way, runners can look forward to an incredible and scenic adventure with two vantage points: in the air and on the trail."

(d) Trail Striders Running Vacations by TransRockies ("The Ultimate Vacation for Runners of all Abilities and Experience Levels")

"Whether you're curious about trail running but you've never run except when chased, or you want to stride further or faster in the backcountry, or you're seeking the camaraderie of other Trail Striders, join us for one of our specialized unforgettable camps that will help you achieve your goals. Whether you come alone, with friends, or a spouse, we guarantee you'll leave with a new community of trail running buddies, a deep sense of accomplishment, and an inexplicable desire to run feverishly through the wildlands in your own habitat. (At Trail Striders Camps by TransRockies, people "get you," your outdoor addiction, and your odd habits). Gather with other Trail Striders in one of the unforgettable destinations we've scouted, get access to the best local trails, obtain insider information on all things trail running, and gain inspiration from some of the swiftest and most revered athletes in the field."

(e) TransRockies Challenge—Mountain Biking

- Date: July 28 – August 3, 2012
- Fernie, BC to Canmore, AB
- 7 Stages, approx. 370 km.
- 12,000 vertical meters of climbing (projected)
- Categories: Men, Women, Mixed, Masters Men, Masters Mixed, Veteran Open
- Divisions: TR7 (7 days for teams of two), TR3 (first 3 stages solo), TR4 (last 4 stages solo)
- Field Limit: 500 riders total

This annual, for-profit event, is positioned as the "world's toughest" race for mountain bike enthusiasts, thereby seeking equivalence (in a marketing sense) with ultra marathons or ironman triathlons. Extending over a full week, in this event pairs of mountain bikers compete for prizes and bragging rights by competing in one of several categories defined by age and gender. From its inception in 2002 through 2006, the 7-day race covered over 600 kilometers of trails and back roads and over 12,000 meters of elevation gain, from Fernie, British Columbia to Canmore, Alberta. Starting in 2007, it moved entirely to the

Photo 6.1. TransRockies Challenge 2012, Stage 2 Start, Fernie, British Columbia
(Credit: photo courtesy of Kelvin Trautman).

Province of British Columbia, primarily in reaction to restrictions placed on the number of participants by Alberta Parks (Getz & McConnell, 2008). In 2010, it returned to a course primarily in Alberta, with a different, 400 kilometer course. After a decade of varied routes in Alberta and British Columbia, TransRockies is now balanced evenly between British Columbia and Alberta, with the registration day plus 3 stages in BC, and the remaining 4 days in Alberta.

Although the riders start together each day, the overall results are based on the combined time from each day's stage. The starts and finishes are partly in towns, with the remainder in wilderness camps provided by the event organizers. There are seven categories for ages and both genders, including mixed teams. A cash purse is divided among winners in the various categories.

Marketing of the TransRockies Challenge is focused on attracting paying participants, and on sustaining the event's reputation as the world's most challenging mountain bike race. The event's reputation as an incredible experience and a highly unique race became established early on, and has been strengthened with each successive running. The event regularly receives coverage from a wide array of cycling publications, as well as endorsements from high-profile figures within the cycling community. This word-of-mouth advertising within the cycling community is of key importance to organizers, since most participants must plan and prepare to compete in the event for a year or longer.

A substantial response from Europe was originally sought, but did not quickly materialize. In 2006, for the first time, over 50% of the participants came from outside Canada.

TransRockies Challenge participants make a high personal, financial, and emotional commitment to the event. Financial commitment includes travel, additional equipment costs due to wear and tear from the event (often over $500 per person), accommodation (hotels at start and finish, while some teams also use recreation vehicles during the race), and entry fees ($1,300–$3,000 per person). Personal commitment includes time invested in training for the event (most are not professional athletes), traveling to, and participating in, the event, and enlisting the help of at least one support person during the event, usually a close friend or family member.

The TransRockies Challenge is a grueling and exhausting experience for most participants. According to its organizers, the early days of the race sometimes create feelings of regret and fear in participants. As the race progresses, however, moods elevate and most racers are elated by the end of the week. Overall, there are very high barriers to participation in this event. It is accessible only to those with significant disposable income, time, and interest in the sport. However, completing the event brings a high sense of personal accomplishment and prestige.

Optimizing the participants' experience is a key priority for organizers. They strive to provide good food, showers, bike service facilities, and a high degree of safety and medical support. At the end of each stage, there is an awards ceremony where the stage winners are presented with medals and the race leaders in each category receive leaders' jerseys. This is followed by a video fresh from the day's race, which is intended to lift the spirits of the athletes and motivate them for the next day. The organizers spend a great deal of time communicating with athletes before the event, and strive to create a brand community around the TransRockies Challenge.

Participant Profile

"Along with great international coverage, the heart and soul of TransRockies are the participants. Every year our demographic reach widens and we count triathletes, adventure racers, and committed recreational adventurers as a significant and growing part of our participant base. In 2006, TransRockies recorded a record 45% annual growth, reaching its field limit of 300 teams."

- Average Age: 40
- 80% male
- Median gross annual personal income: over US$100,000
- 38% from Canada, 16% from the US, 16% from UK, 5% South Africa, 4% Australia, 21% other international

Communication Plan

"Prior to the event, the objectives are: 1) to build awareness of the event; 2) to drive team registration interest; 3) to build sponsor value by establishing association.

Print and Internet media partnerships will provide Value In Kind advertising and direct marketing of the event: *Canadian Cycling Magazine*/website; *Outdoor USA Magazine*/website; *Bicycle Retailer Magazine*/website.

Event website (www.transrockies.com). An information-rich resource is required, as the event is a big commitment for participants. The website focuses on the experience and provides a key opportunity for partner exposure and integration.

eNewsletter: A monthly eNewsletter reaches a targeted database of more than 8,000 worldwide friends of TransRockies. The newsletter highlights event and sponsor news, promotes early registration, and provides links to relevant sites of interest, including product and sponsor sites.

During and postevent, the objectives are: 1) to deliver marketing value for event partners; 2) to deliver compelling stories from the event that increase its appeal to worldwide audiences."

Television

"We use our own experienced local camera crew working in partnership with our European agency, Smaragd Medien GmbH. Total worldwide exposure now exceeds 800 hours. We are executive producers of all video materials related to the event. We have a dedicated and professional broadcast crew that deliver the great stories of this seven-day epic to the world. Over ten years, we have accumulated over 800 hours of broadcast time.

We produce broadcast-quality footage for free distribution throughout the world. This model can generate hundreds of hours of cumulative broadcast time throughout the world In addition, there is an opportunity to produce regionally targeted television specials for key markets. In the past we have achieved strong distribution of a one-hour TransRockies show in Germany, the United Kingdom and other markets."

(f) GORE-TEX TransRockies Run

- Date: August 14–19, 2012
- Buena Vista to Beaver Creek, CO
- 6 stages, 120 miles
- 20,000 vertical feet of climbing
- Prize Purse: $20,000 cash + $25,000 product
- Categories: Men, Women, Mixed, Masters Men, Masters Women, Masters Mixed
- RUN3 3-day solo sub-event for Men and Women
- Field Limit: 200 teams of 2 plus 100 solos (500 total)

"Over 40 million people in the United States are trail runners. In 2005, there were over 1.3 billion trail running activities and it was the 2nd most popular outdoor recreation activity in the United States. Trail Running is unique among outdoor pursuits in that it has shown steady growth over the past several years. In addition, research indicates that half of all trail runners are competitive in running or another sport. The media attention that trail running receives has also grown. A search of the New York Times database for "trail running" pulls up over 20 recent related articles including features, gear articles, travel and even real estate choices for committed runners. Media recognizes this sport."

TransRockies use a format they invented, and have shown to be successful, first with the TransAlp Challenge mountain bike race launched in Europe in 1998, then brought to North America with the TransRockies Challenge in 2002. In 2005, they introduced the first running event with this format. In 2007 it was taken to the US with the inaugural GORE-TEX® TransRockies™ Run.

"It is a spectacular geographic journey. Runners move from place to place, as opposed to having a central base or completing loops. Runners make their way over 120 miles and 20,000 vertical feet through the most rugged and majestic terrain the Colorado Rockies have to offer. The experience of starting and finishing in different communities is unique.

By spreading the distance over a number of days, the participants have the opportunity to fully experience emotional highs and lows and come together as a community over the course of the week. The team format is a key safety feature, and place emphasis on teamwork, camaraderie and friendship. Finally, we believe that the highest quality of organization and support, while still maintaining a feeling of wilderness, enhances the runners' experiences.

Today, we know that people are gathering around their interests and creating communities that aren't bound by many of the segmentations of the past. That's why lifestyle

Photo 6.2. GORE-TEX®TransRockies Run 2011, Stage 3 Start, Leadville, Colorado
(Credit: photo courtesy of Klaus Fengler).

based marketing is so important. Smart marketers have learned to develop enduring brand relationships with people by reaching them through the activities that they are most passionate about. Run participants represent the core of the international outdoor active lifestyle market. They are passionate, affluent and adventurous and define the TransRockies brand."

Participant Demographics

"The Run not only draws in committed ultra-marathon runners, but adventure racers, mountain bikers looking for a change of pace and even adventure tourists looking for a supported high speed traverse of the Rockies. Our participants are a little bit older than the overall demographic for the sport, with established careers, and a lifelong passion for sport."

- Average age: 41
- 53% male/47% female
- Median gross annual personal income: over US$125,000
- 75% from United States, 15% from Canada, 10% International

Marketing

Prior to the event, the objectives are: 1) to build awareness of the event; 2) To drive team registration interest; 3) to build sponsor value by establishing association.

Print and Internet media partnerships will provide Value In Kind advertising and direct marketing of the event: US Running Magazine/website (various); US Outdoor Magazine/ website (*Outside Magazine*); Canadian Outdoor Magazine/website (*Impact Magazine*); Running Retailer Magazine/website.

"Through partnerships in 2011 we earned full page advertisements in the *Runner's World* Trail Special, and *Outside Magazine*, with a combined media value of over $100,000. The title sponsor of the event, W. L. Gore & Associates, does an annual media buy for the event of at least $100,000, focusing on popular regional publications such as the Competitor Network, as well as national publications such as *Trail Runner Magazine*. Total bought and sponsored advertising value for the event is typically over $200,000.

Event website (www.transrockies.com): An information-rich resource is required as the event is a big commitment for participants. The website will focus on the experience and provides a key opportunity for partner exposure and integration. We produce monthly e-newsletters sent to our email database of over 3,700 names worldwide.

During and postevent, the objectives are: 1) To deliver marketing value for event partners; 2) To deliver compelling stories from the event that increase its appeal to worldwide audiences.

Working in partnership with our skilled Video Team, we produce broadcast quality footage for free distribution throughout the world. We are increasingly using the Internet as a distribution channel for video coverage at the event, posting video clips on our website, you-tube, and Facebook, which are frequently linked from numerous blogs and twitters. The natural narrative arc and spectacular scenery of the event will lend itself to strong print and Internet editorial.

Media teams who participate in the event come away with moving firsthand experiences, which make for entertaining stories. We can provide media outlets with photo assets to complement any story. Our PR agency, Outside PR (www.outsidepr.com), has worked hard to seed coverage of the event with media outlets worldwide. Feature coverage in all the major running magazines is already secured. In addition to these efforts, the event by its nature attracts journalists and photographers looking for great stories and pictures.

Print and online editorial and feature pages continue to stack up with a print audience of over 35 million and an online reach of over 9 million in 2011, adding to the awareness of our partners and stage communities and building the legend of the GORE-TEX® TransRockies™ Run. Visit the media page on our website to see all the latest coverage: http://transrockies.com/transrockiesrun/news/?page_id=13."

Accolades
- One of America's Top 50 Adventures—National Geographic Adventure April 2009
- Most Scenic Race—Colorado Runner, 2009

Sport Venues

Sport facilities are permanent event venues and constitute a tourism resource for the host community, but if they are purpose built for an event they represent a cost, or at least an investment that has to be amortized over many events. Similar to a convention center, managers of sport facilities can claim tourism-related economic benefits to the community based on the number of tourists who travelled specifically for events.

There are often controversies over sport event venues, particularly when professional teams are involved. Public expenditure on any event facility raises serious issues, and many of those applying to sport venues also apply to convention and exhibition centers, to arts and cultural facilities.

In North America the debate has been dominated by the issue of public subsidies for professional sport teams who regularly demand new, state-of-the-art facilities as a condition of moving to, or staying in, a city. Economists, according to Coates and Humphreys (2008), are unanimous in condemning such subsidies as they represent a public gift to for-profit companies. In fact, that does not seem to matter to many citizens and politicians, as they really want their sport teams!

There are sound reasons for public sector investment in sport arenas and stadia, and other event-oriented facilities, although it is often a controversial subject with lobby groups making conflicting claims about costs and benefits. The main lines of justification for public funding or other forms of intervention (like regulations, direct production of events, or marketing) start with philosophy, or political ideology, namely that expenditures and other interventions generate "public good" (see the discussion in Chapter 1).

Specific reasons for investing in sport facilities include claims pertaining to economic development through event tourism, urban renewal, and tax generation, plus expanded leisure and social opportunities for residents. Increasingly, multiple goals are pursued through major urban development/renewal schemes that include various facilities and public–private partnerships. The following arguments are typically made in support of government-supported sport facilities.

Urban Development and Renewal

In this line of proinvestment reasoning, new (and sometimes improved) sport facilities are catalysts for urban development and renewal. This is a mainstay of the recent emphasis on center-city locations, in contrast to many arenas and stadia that have been built in the suburbs, surrounded by parking lots. The Edmonton case study (see below) makes it clear that many cities want renewal, and incorporate sport facility development into ambitious multifunction designs for districts that feature cultural, entertainment, shopping, residential, and office expansion. Public–private partnerships are the norm in these cases, as cities must, at a minimum, service the new developments. Often cities have to provide, or help assemble the land.

Mark Rosentraub (2009), author of *Major League Winners: Using Sports and Cultural Centers as Tools for Economic Development*, is a leading proponent of inner city development of sport and cultural facilities, using public–private partnerships. He argues that human capital is essential to the creative city, and is attracted by a vibrant downtown. A combination of uses, as opposed to stand-alone sport facilities, can generate positive tax revenues for cities.

Place Marketing and City Image

Facilities of all kinds are instrumental in making cities livable, attracting the "creative class," and stimulating investment or relocations. Cities without sport, recreational, cultural, and entertainment facilities are likely to be saddled with a dull or negative image. As well, major new developments present the opportunity for iconic design features that attract attention and differentiate the city. This applies both to districts (e.g., Toronto's Entertainment District, which directly abuts its iconic domed stadium) and to specific buildings or plazas. When the opportunity arises, cities incorporate festival places into these developments, thereby enhancing their value to residents and for cultural tourism.

Social Benefits and Psychic Benefits

Although intangible, researchers have shown that residents value events even when they do not directly attend. This applies to some extent for sport, recreation, and other experiential opportunities. It is often argued that sport fans support new facilities even if they will seldom or never pay to attend—it is a matter of personal pleasure derived from being a fan.

Smaller facilities generally come under the heading of leisure services and are expected to be provided by government (or not-for-profit organizations) because they are perceived to be "public goods" generating considerable social value in terms of healthy lifestyle, entertainment, and leisure opportunities. But the giant facilities built for mega-events seldom perform well afterwards, and locals often shun them.

Although residents are often reluctant to pay for new facilities if they think taxes will increase or other projects/programs will be sacrificed (i.e., the opportunity costs are too high), equally they will complain about poor facilities—either because they use them, or are embarrassed by comparisons to other cities that have better facilities.

In Europe there is a Capital of Sports Award for cities that stress the health and social benefits of sport, especially the disadvantaged and most in need. This philosophy and related programs should be incorporated into all decisions made about sport facilities and event tourism.

Cultural Benefits

To the extent that sport is a major element of popular culture, cultural benefits are derived from sport facilities and events. If one accepts the argument that every visitor to a city or country should have an authentic cultural experience, then sport is one way to manifest this goal. Another is to ensure that sport event tourists have other cultural experiences, and this can be facilitated through good design (e.g., combining sport and other facilities) and packaging (e.g., event tickets plus meals and cultural productions).

Sport and Events Tourism

Cities compete for events, with both sports and entertainment events making use of indoor arenas and outdoor stadia. Capacity is an important consideration, as is the overall customer experience. Increasingly, stadia and arenas are designed to maximize their flexibility for a variety of events. A large number of events is necessary in order to pay for operating the facilities, leading to pressure on facility owners and managers to be aggressive in creating and attracting events.

Venues need a certain number of events (or, more correctly, revenue generation from events) to at least break even on operating costs. Seldom if ever can major venues recover capital costs. The economic value or worth of a venue can be assessed, in part, by reference to the value of future events that can be held there (i.e., its legacy).

The economic benefits of many events accrue to investors, owners, the hospitality industry, and the community at large, thereby generating public good. Accounting for tourism-related "new money" is easy enough to do, including how the incremental earnings from tourism are distributed through the economy. But measuring tangible and intangible benefits accruing to the public (or taxpayers) is more challenging—government or tourism agencies supporting events and facilities must be able to at least specify what these benefits will be, then seek to estimate them.

Several other factors have to be considered:

- Venues both restrict and facilitate certain types and sizes of events.
- Who manages a venue, and who attracts or creates the events is an important variable (are they separate entities?).
- Is there competition? Can venues be substituted? At what level (local, regional or national/international)?
- Who will underwrite any loss accrued by events or facilities?

Generally the agency bidding on events must accept the risk, or find partners to share it with. Since the legacy value of future events can easily be overestimated, decisions made about facility investments could easily lead to future liabilities.

Venues and Competitive Positioning

Cities fall into categories of competitiveness for certain events based on their venues, both size and quality being considered. For bidding on sports, entertainment, conventions and exhibitions the physical capacity of facilities is critical, and this information is widely available, but frequently changing!

A very basic strategic question in Event Tourism is "What league do we compete in?" By league I mean world-class versus national, regional, or local. Without the infrastructure there is no use competing against much bigger players. Set realistic goals and find your comfort zone, but how?

Several lines of evaluation have to be completed, including a competitive SWOT (i.e., strengths, weaknesses, opportunities, and threats) that considers both capacity and quality, as well as competitive actions being taken or planned—including bidding and funding strategies. Evidence of need can come from benchmarking against known sport cities and particularly by making comparisons with comparably sized and positioned cities. Another approach is to set targets for the kinds and sizes of events you want to be able to host (taking into account what it will also cost to bid on them, and other infrastructure like transport and hotels), thereby generating minimum standards for venues.

A New Arena for Edmonton, Canada

The Edmonton example shows the complexity of issues, and connections to Event Tourism strategies and urban renewal, when new sport facilities are proposed. Edmonton, capital of Canada's Province of Alberta, is a city of about 1 million residents. Its old arena needs major renovations, triggering a review of options. In this way it is similar to many other North American cities that host professional ice hockey teams. The case provides a good illustration of how public–private partnership can work for both sports and urban development. It also provides an up-to-date look at how North American cities go about these projects. The following summary is from the city's website, followed by an excerpt from the developer's website.

City Shaping—The Summary Report of the Leadership Committee for a New Sports/ Entertainment Facility for Edmonton (available online at: http://www.edmonton.ca/ city_government/documents/CityGov/SportsEntFacilityReport.pdf)

Many cities have used major multipurpose facility developments as a springboard to spark rejuvenated downtowns and new entertainment districts, resulting in significant economic, social and cultural benefits. Facilities in many Canadian and U.S. cities provide examples of the ability of these types of developments to spur economic development and community renewal in urban centers. Several factors have converged to make this an opportune time to consider the benefits of constructing a new sports/entertainment facility in Edmonton:

- Edmonton has an opportunity to integrate a new sports/entertainment facility into renewal plans for its downtown.
- Northlands, owners and operators of Rexall Place, looked at the future life and capacity of Rexall Place and commissioned a study by HOK Sports, a leading international sports architecture firm, in February 2007. The study estimated the cost of modernizing Rexall Place at about $250 million. Built in 1974, and home to the Edmonton Oilers as well as the venue for many high-profile sports/entertainment

events, Rexall Place is now one of the smallest and oldest sports venues in the National Hockey League (NHL).

- The Oilers' 10-year lease at Rexall will expire in 2014.

On Feasibility and Opportunity

1. A downtown sports/entertainment facility in Edmonton is clearly feasible.
2. It is not just feasible, it is desirable. It provides a unique opportunity to develop an urban sports/entertainment district downtown to the benefit of the citizens in the city, region and primary catchment areas, such as northern and central Alberta.
3. Downtown Edmonton has a number of appropriate districts and sites that could accommodate a new sports/entertainment facility, supporting a larger community agenda. The downtown could be rejuvenated through such a project.
4. Edmonton has the advantage of having a primary sports tenant in the Oilers. An NHL franchise is a significant opportunity around which to develop a sports/ entertainment facility.
5. At the same time, the facility should be programmed to maximize use through concerts, events, shows and community uses, given the limited numbers of Oilers games annually.

On Financing

Based on the level of analysis and the stated assumptions, a downtown sports/entertainment facility is financially feasible. Given the scale of investment required, and the potential impact a new downtown sports/ entertainment facility would have on the community, the most appropriate funding structure involves both private and public participation.

On Community/Design Components

1. That a sports/entertainment facility within a multipurpose activity district be designed to link the neighbourhood, the City of Edmonton, the Edmonton capital region and central and northern Alberta.
2. That design principles be developed that ensure residential growth supports retail development and encourage businesses to relocate to or expand into the area. Parks, shops, artist spaces, public grass areas, pubs, cafes, meeting areas and water features should blend with the sports/entertainment facility.
3. That linkages to the unique cultural and business communities in the district be developed to foster meaningful contact and a sense of access and comfort within diverse populations of age and culture.
4. That the activity district be seen in context of all its users, residents, tourists and frequent users from across the Edmonton capital region and from central and northern Alberta.
5. That existing parking in the multipurpose activity district be maximized. That any additional parking be considered underground or at the perimeter of the district to enable and encourage walkable spaces, and the creation of a stylized main street where store fronts and play areas are incorporated into the district's design.

The following summarizes a report written by Dr. Mark Rosentraub, entitled "Sports Facilities, A New Arena in Edmonton, The Opportunities for Development and A City's Image: Lessons from Successful Experiences." Dr. Rosentraub is author of two highly pertinent books: *Major League Winners: Using Sports and Cultural Centers as Tools for Economic Development* (2009) and *Major League Losers: The Real Cost of Sports and Who's Paying for it* (1999).

Summary of Lessons From Other Cities

The building of a new sports facility is a 30-year planning decision. What a community decides relative to an arena's fit into an overall development plan and strategy, and where the facility will be located, has very long-term effects on development and land use patterns.

In the competition for human capital that is driving the 21st century economy, vibrant urban cores and downtown areas are vital assets. The companies that will define the future growth of every nation choose to locate where the best and brightest workers wanted to live. Increasingly this is in or near downtown areas of urban centers which have invested to make their core areas vital and unique.

What has been learned from the experiences of numerous U.S. cities across more than four decades of building new sports facilities, is that stand-alone arenas surrounded by acres of open parking lots tend to become lost opportunities for development and the building of a city's image. If a sports facility is not part of an integrated and comprehensive plan to redevelop an area and enhance a city's image, its construction becomes a largely missed planning opportunity. The consequences of that missed opportunity last for several decades.

There are examples, however, where cities made a facility an anchor part of an integrated plan, and their success in terms of development impacts and changes in their image highlight opportunities for Edmonton. The examples of success from Columbus, Indianapolis, Los Angeles, and San Diego identify many of the factors that any community should consider as a major arena facility is being considered and designed.

Beginning in 1974 and continuing through 2009 (spanning the administrations of four different mayors), Indianapolis formed a series of public/private partnerships to use sports to turn a deteriorating downtown area into a commercial, residential, and hospitality center which transformed Indianapolis's identity. In 1974, Indianapolis's leaders paid for a study that disclosed the city had no real identity with Americans—it was relatively unknown and considered a nondescript part of America's Midwest. Dramatic changes would be required to remake the city's image and improve its identity and chances for economic development. Indianapolis's sports and downtown development strategy was comprised of three components.

And finally, to round out the discussion, is this newspaper article entitled "Downtown arena closer to reality" by Gordon Kent, Edmonton Journal (December 29, 2011):

It's been called the key to one of Edmonton's biggest downtown revitalization projects and a billionaire's massive tax-funded gift, but like it or not, a new arena is finally poised for construction.

Edmonton Oilers owner Daryl Katz, who has been angling for years to move his team out of aging Rexall Place into a facility he controls, saw his wish near fruition in October when city council voted to push ahead with the scheme.

Supporters hope an entertainment, housing and office district will spring up around the site and make Edmonton's moribund heart start beating again.

But detractors argue a city-owned arena run by a private company shouldn't receive a public handout, and worry the Oilers could ask for more help in future.

The city, Katz and ticket-buyers will each kick in part of the $450 million needed for the project.

Design work is underway and land for the development has been purchased, but there are a couple of hurdles to cross before shovels go into the ground.

For one thing, the financing is still $100 million short, and despite lobbying, provincial leaders insist they aren't interested in investing. As well, if construction costs come in higher than $450 million, either side can walk away from the deal.

And then debate about the whole contentious issue can start all over again.

Expert Opinion: Sport Arenas Today and Tomorrow (by Harald Dolles)

Harald Dolles is Professor in Sport Management at Molde University College, Specialized University in Logistics, Molde (Norway) and Professor in International Business at the School of Business, Economics and Law, University of Gothenburg, Gothenburg (Sweden).

In the 21st century the stadium has become a center of urban living, incorporating spaces for leisure activities, movie theatres, stores, cafes, restaurants, hotels, and offices, which ensued from a new way to manage the modern facility, regarded as a public area and open 7 days a week. These multipurpose sporting venues also host shows, concerts, and the football (soccer) shares the center space with other sports. The football match or other sports competition, the show or concert itself is the center of a "package event": the prephase, break(s), and postphase are occasions for a variety of attractions, intended not only to appeal to the single spectator or visitor but the whole family, to encourage the spectators/visitors to arrive earlier, leave later, and to consume more in merchandising shops or shopping areas and in bars or restaurants.

Today's modern stadia and large-scale events usually have an extraordinary positive impact on the host region in terms of one or more of the following dimensions: tourist volumes, visitor expenditures, publicity, and related infrastructural and administrative developments which substantially increase the destination's capacity and attractiveness. The additional media-related aspects of hosting large-scale events can rarely be overlooked. Having a modern stadium and hosting large-scale events leads to a heightened awareness and presents the chance for cities to transmit promotional messages to billions of people around the globe via television, the Internet and other developments in telecommunications. The stadia of the current generation are lively 7 days a week and are the centers of attraction in their places. Stadia are classified by the sports governing supranational institutions as main attractions in the bidding documents of cities (regions, nations) to host major international events. Latest-generation stadia must incorporate high safety requirements, feature advanced visitor seating and audio-visual arrangements, high-quality technological communication and TV transmission systems. Their role as architectural urban icons, new points of reference in the city environment and as displays of identity that are easily recognizable all over the world, is widely acknowledged.

Three trends seem to dominate the development of new stadia and/or are of main concern for stadia reconstruction today: 1) preserve or create unique features in the stadium architecture; 2) modular construction elements, able to respond to different types of events, marketing, and media-related requirements; and 3) environmental friendliness and sustainability.

Apart from conserving architectural highlights, like in the reconstruction of the Berlin Olympic Stadium in Germany (build in 1936 and reopened in 2006 to host the Final of the Football World Cup in 2006), cities and clubs as owners or stadia tenants aim to integrate special features to create identity. Especially in the construction of roofs and visual design the creativity of architects is virtually unlimited. For example, roofs with translucent membranes and walls with creative lighting design (see the Allianz arena in Munich, Germany, as an example) will successfully placed a new or refurbished venue in scene. For many years permanently installed sports facilities and single purpose stadia were regarded as the measure of all things—not lastly for reasons of prestige. In the stadia of today other values like modular construction, marketing and media-related requirements take precedence. Modern multipurpose arenas feature steel constructions with modular individual elements making it possible to enlarge or downsize to optimum configuration and the maximum comfort whatever event to take place. Completed in 2009, the Cowboys Stadium in Arlington, Texas

(USA) is the largest domed stadium in the world with a retractable roof offering seats for 80,000–110,000 spectators. Open areas are behind seats in each end zone and on a series of six elevated modular platforms connected by stairways. The stadium can be used for a variety of other activities outside of its main purpose (professional American football) such as concerts, basketball games, boxing matches, college American football, football (soccer) matches, and motocross races. The stadium has the world's largest column-free interior and the world's second largest high-definition video screens—49 m wide and 22 m tall; 53 m diagonal; total 1,070 m²—which hangs in the center above the field.

The stadia planned for the final rounds of the Football World Championships in Russia (2018) and Qatar (2022) might be on the forefront how stadia of tomorrow will look like. The Al-Shamal stadium planned for Qatar 2022 takes its shape from the traditional "dhow," the traditional sailing vessels with one or more masts with lateen sails used in the Red Sea, the Persian Gulf, and the Indian Ocean. It will have a capacity of 45,120 spectators, with a permanent lower tier of 25,500 seats and—an increasingly important feature in modern multipurpose arenas—a modular build additional upper tier of 19,620 seats. Al-Khor will be a brand new stadium with a capacity of 45,330 fans featuring a stunning seashell motif and a flexible roof. The permanent lower tier will seat 25,500 fans and in addition a modular upper tier with seats will be constructed. Due to this construction method the structures of new stadia remain flexible, when necessary reusable, and can be adapted to new requirements with minimal effort—for instance, when different governing institutions require different standards (e.g., standing and seating arrangements). Modular elements will also be used to expand the current Al-Rayyan stadium in Qatar to double the seating capacity to host Football Word Cup matches in 2022. The Al-Rayyan stadium has also been designed to include a "media façade" after reconstruction that includes a membrane that acts as a screen for projections: news, commercials, sports updates, and current tournament information and matches. In all stadia designed for the Football World Cup in Qatar it is planned to use solar technology to power carbon-neutral technology to cool the stadia and to make sure the temperature during match day does not rise above 27°C.

Nowadays the idea of resource conserving and environmentally friendly events and stadia has become the predominant issue in the planning and operation of stadia. The final round of the Football World Cup was hosted by Germany 2006 and apart from the sports, for the first time in the history of the World Cup, environmental concerns have been systematically addressed in the construction and refurbishment of stadia—the so-called "Green Goal" environmental program. Specific measurable environmental objectives for waste treatment and avoidance, water usage and saving, energy consumption and spectator transportation have been developed and since the football stadia in Germany are intensively used throughout the year, considerable effects on the environment are also to be expected as a result of their use in the German First and Second Division Bundesliga matches. For that reason environmental management competence in arena management had to be strengthened (e.g., the arenas in Nuremberg and Munich were the first football stadia in Europe adopting the eco-management and audit scheme, while the football arenas in Hamburg and Gelsenkirchen introduced the ÖKOPROFIT environmental management system).

I might conclude the importance of sustainability, green strategies, and the promise of environmental renewal will become crucial for the competitive bidding for all kinds of large-scale events in the future. It might also be assumed that visitors and fans will increasingly perceive the entertainment process and environmental measures as integrated parts of their very own "entertainment consumption" in the stadium.

Bidding on Sport Events

Meeting the technical specifications for producing and operating sporting events is only part of the job required to bring an event to a destination. The entire bid process would not exist if competition was not high and if decisions were not based on more than the bare specs.

The following outline is for a periodic, international sport event owned by a national-level federation. I have left out the details, as this is to be illustrative of the process, and each one will be different in some important ways. Many such documents are circulated on the Internet, whereas others are sent only to prospective hosts (in the minds of the owners). Sport commissions and bid agencies know which ones they want to bid on, and if they have any doubt about the process or their capability or the feasibility of bidding on a particular event they will probably attend, talk to organizers, and try to develop a working relationship.

1. Overview of the event.
2. The owners, and how a selection decision will be made; key people such as site selection committee.
3. The schedule and process for making bids; how bids will be assessed and when a decision will be made.
4. Organization: In many cases the owner of the sport event will form a partnership with national and local host organizing committees. Only sanctioned bodies will be eligible, not just anyone can bid. A committee structure might be specified, including decision-making processes. For most events, volunteers will be needed and their integration in the organization has to be specified. The host city might very well have to establish a new organizing body for each major event and its goals and performance measures for success should be specified. Many of the following selection criteria have to be in place before a bid is made, with proof submitted of venue availability (e.g., ownership details or rental agreements), contracts for accommodation and other services, and written guarantees of financial capability.
5. Site selection considerations: Host community and its location: anything that makes it special? Is there a track record of successfully hosting events? Accessibility; key venues, hotels, and infrastructure; distances and travel times between venues, airport, hotels.

    *   Venues: must meet specifications; availability and condition; upgrades needed? new ones? costs?
    *   Finances and business plan: including sources of revenues (ticketing, media, sponsorship, souvenirs, supplier rentals, etc.) and expenditures; financial forecasts and budget; break-even analysis and targets for profit/surplus; who is responsible for underwriting potential losses?
    *   Marketing plan including advertising; ticketing and packaging plan, with prices.
    *   Sponsorship plan; targets; unique selling propositions, benefits offered; the owner probably has sponsors with rights, and the host city/country will have to accommodate their needs first while avoiding potential conflicts.
    *   Media plan: including advertising, media as sponsors; media management; webcasting; host broadcaster rights and international distribution (are rights to be sold or are they awarded by the event owner?).
    *   Scheduling and critical path to organize the event; scheduling of the event.
    *   Accommodation for athletes, officials, media, tourists: availability, quality, location, cost: do local organizers have to pay?
    *   Operations and logistics: getting people to the city, within, and between venues; use of local transport companies (i.e., destination managers); managing the venues; guest management.

- Technical services: for officials; record keeping and statistics; lighting; photography/videography; services for the media.
- Risk management plan; security and emergency response; accreditation; health and safety services; insurance.
- Staffing and volunteers: competencies of staff and duties, hours, payments; volunteer recruitment and training, supervision.
- Ceremonies: opening, closing, medals.
- Community events, entertainment; engagement of residents before and during.
- Special services for teams and officials: accommodation, transportation, food, health, training or practice, security, equipment.
- Special services for owners and VIPs: reserved tickets; VIP treatment.
- Languages and translation services.
- The legacy: profit sharing; for the sport; for the community; for the participants.
- Accountability and reporting: what is made public?

Power and Negotiation

Owners of events in high demand have power and they use it to set conditions favorable to them, leaving potential hosts to determine what exactly is left for them to negotiate, if anything. Owners of popular events usually have their own long-term agreements with media and sponsors, and these are automatically brought to the event. Local hosts have to find compatible, lesser sponsors.

Owners can make demands for their own special privileges (much like musicians on tour!). Their technical specifications for the event are likely to be set in concrete, and every detail will be checked. Some expect to be treated like royalty before, during, and afterwards. Of course, they will sing a different tune if competition for the event disappears. That is why many potential hosts will elect not to bid on specific events.

Once the specifications of owners are met, there are considerations that can be called "bid winners." Think of this category as value-adding to make owners more favorably inclined towards a bid. If owners are wise and responsible they specify what is possible and what must not be done, making it clear that payments (bribes, gifts) and other perks will not be tolerated. Ideally, there should never be even a hint of wrong-doing or secret deals.

Case Study of the Calgary Sport Tourism Authority (www.visitcalgarysports.com)

This case study was written in cooperation with Marco De Iaco (see his profile in Chapter 1). Although Calgary hosted the Winter Olympics in 1988, which left a substantial and well-appreciated legacy of new facilities and the money to operate them, the city was very ad hoc in developing and bidding on sport events. Tourism Calgary (its DMO) is a marketing body, but in 2005 it became clear that many other cities in North America were much more competitive, and most cities in Canada already had a sport commission or other event-bidding organization. The necessity for becoming more professional was reinforced by aging Olympic facilities and the fact that two other Western North American cities (Salt Lake City and Vancouver) were also able to boast of being Olympic cities—with more modern facilities. Calgary had to reconsider its strategy.

Calgary Sport Tourism Authority (CSTA) is operated by Tourism Calgary and cofunded by the City and the Calgary Hotel Association. "The CSTA is a dedicated group of community and business leaders passionate about bringing world-class sport events to the city of Calagry. We work with Tourism Calgary, local champions and key stakeholders to achieve a range of sport, civic and tourism objectives. Our goal is to promote and position Calgary as the premier host of sport events in Canada, building a balanced and dynamic portfolio of sport events."

The positions and responsibilities in Sales, Sport, and Major Events are:

> Vice President, Sales, Sport and Major Events (Marco De Iaco)
> Director
> Business Development, Sport
> Manager, Sport and Events
> Assistant, Sport and Major Events

Sport tourism is one of the fastest growing segments of the tourism industry in Canada with approximately $3.6 billion in annual spending by domestic travelers in 2010 and is a powerful tool for increasing economic development, enhancing quality of life, and promoting a community's image on an international stage. As a result, attracting sporting events has increasingly become a sophisticated, strategic, and tactical pursuit. When Marco was hired by Tourism Calgary in 2003 there was no strategic investment made in the pursuit of sport and cultural events for the city of Calgary. Today, sport tourism is a key pillar of the organization and recognized as one of the most important priorities and growth segments for the industry. Further, the segment has produced arguably the most significant return on investment and incremental benefit for key tourism stakeholders in the city of Calgary over the past 7 years.

Organization and Operations of CSTA

CSTA has an annual budget of $1.1 million for operations and bidding, although additional funds can be obtained for some bids from the city and province. Increased core funding from the hotel association reflects their satisfaction with the CSTA's work. In particular, Calgary's business travelers fill up hotels during the week, and sport event bring visitors on weekends, so it balances the demand. As well, both the city center and peripheral accommodation providers benefit, as sport tourism demand is not geographically concentrted in the entre the way business travel is.

"The CSTA mandate is to provide advice and strategic direction in the proactive processes of attracting sport events to the City of Calgary. Based on event seletion criteria, developed by the authority, members will work together to evaluate and recommend sport events to be pursued and/or supported that will achieve a range of tourism, sport and civic objectives."

It does not have the mandate to manage or operate events. There are few "biddable" events outside the sport sector, but CSTA has had some success in bringing major cultural and entertainment events to Calgary, notably the 2008 Juno Awards (Canadian music); 2009 Gemini Awards (Canadian television); Cavalia (2011); and in 2012 the Magnetic North Theatre Festival (see the profile of Cavalia in Chapter 8).

Strategy

In 2012 CSTA was formulating a long-term bidding strategy, including the conducting of a SWOT to see how Calgary is positioned relative to other cities as a potential sport capital.

"Guiding principles of the strategy include: drive economic growth, direct wise spending and strategic investing, create community legacies and enrich quality of life, and instill professionalism and accountability within the evaluation, investment and bidding process."

"Mission: To increase Calgary's capacity for bidding to host sport events."

Goal: to promote and position Calgary as the premier host of sport events in Canada by building a balanced and dynamic portfolio of events.

Activities: To capitalize on major sport opportunities; lead a collaborative process to secure national and international events; develop bidding and hosting capacity through services offered to local organizations bidding on non-major events; support and lead imitative to secure a variety of cultural and special events.

"Bidding on major events:

- lead the collaboration of a proactive bid and evaluation framework;
- recommend events for bid or investment that yields incremental and positive benefits;
- lead the process of establishing working committees for recommended bids;
- encourage public sector support of sport event tourism;
- develop and cultivate private sector sponsorship programs.

Bidding on non-major events, service, and promotion:

- identify and cultivate local champions;
- provide exceptional service and bid assistance to local sport organizations;
- raise awareness of services locally;
- promote value of event tourism to local stakeholders;
- positioning Calgary as the premier host of sport events in Canada;
- through event activation, leverage opportunities to maximize ROI."

Funding

Event bidding expenses are met by CSTA, which also offers funding to organizations for bidding and hosting smaller local, regional, or national events. Events in Calgary are generally funded by municipal, provincial, and federal government sources. The City of Calgary ratified in 2009 its Festival and Events Policy 2010, which recognizes the social, economic, and cultural value that events and festivals bring to the city. This policy cemented the city's commitment to creating a supportive enviroment for festivals and events.

Advice to Organizations

"Your bidding process is our priority. Presenting a bid to a committee or board can be both daunting and time-consuming. The CSTA can help guide you through the process, aligning objectives and coordinating partnerships with key community stakeholders. We'll assist you with all aspects of your bid preparation and can provide your bid committee with help in preparing dynamic bid packages and presentations for event rights-holders. We'll also give you access to our network of suppliers and industry partners.

In addition, Tourism Calgary has created a Sport Tourism Marketing Plan to help develop bidding and hosting capacity through a range of services offered to organizations working on regional events. Once you've secured your event, Tourism Calgary will not only help to market and promote it, but will stand by you as you welcome your guests to our city. Being a great host is what Calgary does best. From the moment your delegates touch down at the Calgary International Airport, Tourism Calgary will roll out the welcome mat—whether it's a White Hat greeting and a personalized message that appears on airport teleprompters, or visitor guides and maps tailored specifically to your audience. Tourism Calgary can also help raise the profile of your event through strategic marketing. The organization can increase visitation through in-market campaigns and leverage opportunities to maximize destination awareness through a network of community stakeholders."

Legacy

"But as we never tire of saying, major events are about more than just short-term economic gain. They also serve to raise Calgary's profile on the world stage. The 2009 Tim Hortons Brier nabbed 6 million viewers across Canada and the 2009 CN Canadian Women's Open received 13 hours of television coverage that was distributed to 126 million households in 100 countries. Other events like the 2009 Viterra Ironman 70.3 Calgary and the 2009 World Water Ski Championship attracted extensive local, national, and international media coverage."

"Major events also deliver legacies that transform communities. Our efforts to bring events such as the 2009 World Water Ski Championship to Calgary helped develop the facilities at Predator Bay into a world-class venue. An annual competition like the Viterra Ironman 70.3 Calgary establishes long-term benefits for the tourism industry and promotes health, wellness, and an active lifestyle in our city. The relocation of Canada's Sports Hall of Fame brings one of Canada's greatest sport tourism attractions to Calgary. And thanks to the 2009 CN Canadian Women's Open, the Alberta Children's Hospital Foundation received a donation of $1.6 million benefiting children and their families right across the province."

"Sport and major events can be powerful tools for promoting a community's image and can play an invaluable role in branding host cities. The motivation to bid for major events is now more about the long term; bidding can be a means of repositioning a city as a place to visit or do business with. Many of the events that CSTA has brought to the city have produced significant media attention, raising Calgary's profile on a national and international stage. The 2009 CN Canadian Women's Open received 13 hours of television coverage that was distributed to 126 million households in 100 countries. The 2009 Ironman Triathlon, 70.3 was sold out in its inaugural year, making it the second largest triathlon in Canada with 1,600 competitors from 20 countries, traveling from as far away as Africa and Japan; and *Triathlete Magazine* has recently declared the event as "One of the Top 10 Most Scenic Races."

"Calgary and Edmonton successfully cohosted a major international event for the first time, setting the stage for the potential of future international co-initiatives between the two cities. The 2012 IIHF World Junior Championship had 23 games broadcast on TSN with the Canada versus Russia semifinal, enjoying 2,947,000 viewers. In fact, the event website had 12.4 million visits and 480 accredited media produced over $2 million in unpaid media coverage. Other highlights are:

- 38,000+ visitors; 18,000+ hotel room nights sold; $92 million+ in gross economic activity;
- A long-term legacy for grass roots sport in Canada through a record profit of $21 million;
- $1 million in legacy investment directly into Alberta-based programs;
- A total of 571,539 tickets were purchased for 31 games, exceeding the previous record of 453,282."

Photo 6.3. World Championship of Junior Hockey, Calgary, 2012
(Credit: photo courtesy of Stefan Schulhof).

Photo 6.4. Chuckwagon Races at the Calgary Exhibition and Stampede
(Credit: photo courtesy of the Calgary Exhibition and Stampede).

Photo 6.5. Bob-sledding at Calgary's Canada Olympic Park
(Credit: photo courtesy of WinSport).

Sport Event Impacts

Much of the literature on event impacts comes from sport events, so there are many examples throughout this book. A few Research Notes in this section provide additional details, and the two Expert Opinion pieces by Holger Preuss should also be consulted.

In addition to the material contained in this book, there are a number of reviews available on sport event impacts: Andersson, Persson, Sahlberg, and Strom (1999); Crompton (1999); Turco, Riley, and Swart (2002); Gratton, Dobson, and Shibli (2000); Hinch and Higham (2004, 2011); Masterman (2004); Preuss (2004a, 2004b, 2007a, 2007b); Higham (2005); Gratton, Shibli, and Coleman (2005); H. Gibson (2006); Weed (2006, 2008b). There a number of chapters of relevance in the 2012 *Routledge Handbook of Events*.

A considerable and disproportionate amount of research has been directed at mega-sport events, which makes sense given their global prominence and huge costs, but is somewhat irrelevant when it comes to providing useful lessons for developing an Event Tourism portfolio in most cities and destinations. Nevertheless, there is sufficient material available to provide major lessons for anyone in the sport tourism business.

Variables Influencing the Impacts of Sport Events

A study of event impacts on local communities by Crompton (1999) revealed the potential significance of amateur, minor sport tournaments in the US. But to be effective such events have to be planned with tourism in mind. Short tournaments (many were 1 day only) generate few overnight stays and little economic impact for the host town. Similarly, more teams involved leads to more participants and accompanying visitors, increasing the potential for local expenditures. For some of the tournaments studied, Crompton found that the events were viewed as family holidays, leading to longer stays and increased spending. And it was observed that some sports generated higher local expenditure than others, connected to the amount of time participants had between competitions, and whether or not they had to buy supplies while in the area. There were also differences in impacts between adult and youth tournaments, and while adults might be expected to generate higher spending, youth events often attract family groups who stay, shop, and eat. In other words, each event and each sport can be quite different.

A comparative study of seven sport events in South Carolina by Daniels and Norman (2003) concluded that regular sport events held great tourism potential for the host, especially when (supporting observations from Higham, 1999) they required little or no bidding expenses, the infrastructure was already in place, there was little or no burden on public funds, and there was negligible impact on residents. For the events Daniels and Norman studied, it was observed that event formats determined the length of stay (overnight in host communities being essential), and spending on entertainment and other non-essentials was often minimal and depended on whether or not the organizers built it into the event program.

Gratton et al. (2005) reported on a comparative UK study of six major sport events that revealed a wide variety of impacts. Economic impacts were greatest when events attracted large numbers of overnight visitors: fans, participants, and others (i.e., accompanying family, media, coaches, officials). Media events attract media tourists, so those with TV audiences can generate long stays and high spending (see the research note by Solberg et al., below). In a finding similar to that of Daniels and Norman (2003), the UK research demonstrated that events attracting seniors (e.g., Masters Games) had high impact owing to the average income levels and daily expenditure of participants, plus their propensity to add holidays. Long events require longer stays, increasing total expenditure (but not necessarily daily).

Sport events attract a variety of tourists, each with different spending patterns. Athletes might get paid to attend, or win prize money; therefore, leakages to the area occur. Spectators, including the friends and relatives of participants, are valuable tourists who will likely stay in commercial accommodation. Officials might also get paid and therefore take money out of the local economy. Media covering sport events usually inject a lot of new money. Gross generalizations are therefore not possible, especially when the scale of events is considered—from tiny regional minor league competitions to the World Cup. This again reinforces the need for a demand-side approach so that you understand the markets.

Research Notes on Sport Event Impacts

Solberg, H., Andersson, T., & Shibli, S. (2002). An exploration of the direct economic impacts from business travelers at world championships. *Event Management, 7*(3), 151–164.

Impacts of various types of sport event tourists were examined by studying two events in Norway and two in the UK. The focus was placed on nonparticipants and nonspectators, or the "business" tourists that accompany major sport events. This category included team officials and officials from governing bodies, staff working for organizers, media workers, sponsors and their guests, and a variety of Very Important Persons such as politicians and celebrities. It was found that visitors from the media were a very small proportion of all travelers at the events, but the media at the two Norwegian events stayed the longest and spent the most money. In the UK the media were of a different type, being mostly freelancers, and they were not big spenders, so international coverage of a sport event makes a big difference. The authors also concluded that sports with a large following in the host country will attract many more tourists.

Dwyer, L., Forsyth, P., & Spurr, R. (2006). Economic impact of sport events: A reassessment. *Tourism Review International, 10*(4), 207–216.

Governments are spending increasing amounts to attract and host sporting events in the belief that they generate significant additional economic activity and jobs. Current practice is to measure the economic impact of events through the use of multipliers that are derived from Input–Output (I–O) models. Computable General Equilibrium (CGE) techniques are now preferred to I–O models because of their superior ability to reflect resource constraints and feedback effects across the economy. The authors have applied a CGE model of the Australian and New South Wales state economies to examine a selected event, the Qantas Australian (Motor Racing) Grand Prix. The results are compared with projections using an I–O approach. The CGE analysis estimates impacts on gross product that are half of those projected by the I–O analysis for the host state and 20% of the I–O projections for the Australian economy as a whole. The article then discusses the distinction between the impacts and net benefits of events. Finally, the article discusses the institutional framework required for a more rigorous assessment of economic impacts of sport events, making some general observations about event strategies and evaluation internationally.

Summary and Study Guide

Sport events are important everywhere, and they generate enormous amounts of travel. This phenomenon is not just about mega and media events; it is also big business for numerous small towns and even rural areas, stemming from small, amateur competitions and iconic destination events. At the beginning of this chapter we looked at the sport tourist, both fans and participants, as to their motivation and experiences. Special note was made of subcultures and of sport events that fall outside the normal types of competition. In other chapters you can read about extreme sport competitors, seniors, mountain bikers, and runners.

There is quite a bit of research available on sport events and sport tourists, including a number of major studies that have been cited. Try to find similar, large-scale research from other countries in order to make comparisons. Remember that these surveys tend to get out of date fairly quickly. All available studies confirm the importance of sport event tourism, and reveal a vast array of sport event types.

The development of sport event tourism is undertaken mostly at the city level where venues are concentrated (they are constantly engaged in selling and bidding) and various organizations including DMOs and Event Development bodies that bid on, and sometimes create, events. The bidding process has been described in detail here and in Chapter 4. Indeed, cities compete to be sport capitals, with Melbourne given as an example. A number of Canadian and American cities are looked at in the special section on Edmonton's New Arena.

Sport venues are crucial, and cities have to decide what "league" they are playing in by reference to their existing and potential venues (mostly size, but also quality). Expert Opinion by Harald Dolles reveals important trends in sport venue development, and factors shaping impacts. You have to be able to critically examine claims made about sport venues and their impacts, including the consideration of public–private partnerships to fund them, and the preference for integrating venues with urban renewal and community development plans.

A major case study of the Calgary Sport Tourism Authority exemplifies how cities and destinations are becoming aggressive, professional, and strategic in their Event Tourism development. This is largely a bidding agency, focused on sports, but they also look at cultural events. The very establishment of such an agency, or sport commission, can propel a city into a higher competitive league, but it must be backed by capital, expertise, and stakeholder commitment.

Enough information and examples have been provided so that we could end the chapter with a summary of factors affecting the impacts of sport event tourism. Because this sector is enormous and diverse, with new opportunities arising all the time out of special interests and social worlds, it is essential that practitioners be able to predict and manage impacts. Not all events are equal!

Study Questions

- Define sport event tourism. Is it only for "active sport tourists"?
- Why do subcultures want their own events?
- Are there any important differences between fans and participants when it comes to sport event tourism? What are they, in terms of motivation and experiences?
- What makes for an ideal "destination" sport event? Discuss "Iconic" events in this context.
- Discuss the issues surrounding sport venue investments by government. How can they be justified?
- Describe the bidding process for an international event. What are likely to be the winners and losers?
- What are the main variables influencing the impacts of sport events? Show how different types of sport events can generate more local benefits; compare mega-events with small, amateur events.
- Summarize lessons learned from the TransRockies case on the following: private sector events; the design and marketing of iconic, destination events; roles of sponsors and host communities.
- Summarize lessons learned from the Calgary Sport Tourism Authority case on: strategies for development of sport event tourism; bidding processes; impacts on the community and sport.

Additional Reading

- *Sport Tourism: Interrelationships, Impacts and Issues* (Ritchie & Adair, 2004).
- *Consumer Behaviour in Sport and Events* (Funk, 2008).
- *Sport Tourism: Concepts and Theories* (Gibson, 2006).
- *Sport and Adventure Tourism* (Hudson, 2002).
- *Sport Tourism Destinations: Issues, Opportunities, and Analysis* (Higham, 2005).
- *Major League Losers: The Real Cost of Sports and Who's Paying for it* (Rosentraub, 1999).
- *Major League Winners: Using Sports and Cultural Centers as Tools for Economic Development* (Rosentraub, 2009).
- *Sport and Tourism: A Reader* (Weed, 2008).
- *International Sports Events: Impacts, Experiences and Identities* (Shipway & Fyall, 2012).
- *Sport Tourism Development* (Hinch & Higham, 2011).
- *Olympic Tourism* (Weed, 2008).
- *Sports Tourism: Participants, Policy and Providers* (Weed & Bull, 2004).

Chapter 7

Business Events
(Meetings, Conventions, Exhibitions)

Learning Objectives

Upon completion of this chapter the student should understand and be able to explain the following:

1. The nature of business events (their purpose and roles).
2. Research themes and trends related to business events.
3. Industry trends and issues, especially technology.
4. Meetings and conventions, both for associations and corporations.
5. Motivation; business event travel career.
6. Impacts of meetings and conventions.
7. Exhibitions (trade and consumer shows).
8. The exhibition industry in China.
9. Convention and exhibition centers.
10. World fairs and state fairs.
11. Impacts, including non-economic.
12. Attracting, leveraging, and boosting business events.
13. Factors affecting destination competitiveness for business events.
14. Sales process for business events.
15. How a CVB (Visit Denver) develops business event tourism.

Introduction

In this chapter we consider the business event sector, specifically meetings, conventions, and exhibitions. Economic exchange underlies all business events; they exist to facilitate sales and marketing, learning, and professionalism—all things pertaining to "doing business"—and are therefore essential to all economies. We can substitute telecommunications and virtual events for some business functions, but people will always want to get together in person, and some forms of exchange can only be facilitated in person.

The "business events" sector is sometimes referred to as the "MICE" sector, for Meetings, Incentives, Conventions, and Exhibitions (or Events). "Incentives" are sometimes focused on events (notably seminars and retreats), otherwise they are tours or holiday trips. A considerable amount of convergence of event forms is evident in this market, especially as exhibitions or trade shows are often attached to association conferences, and trade and consumer shows are frequently combined at the same venue; most congresses or conventions incorporate various social programs and tours. Major sport events are often corporate hospitality events, as that is where business is done. Festivals usually have sales areas, for food and beverages, souvenirs, and the wares of sponsors. Nevertheless, there are distinct motivations and experiences associated with each of the major business event types.

The two largest components are examined first, namely meetings and conventions, as they have different needs and formats. Then exhibitions are profiled—the industry largely consists of trade and consumer shows. We also look at World fairs and State fairs. Information is provided on the motivations for attending, event experiences, and impacts. Data from the US and Melbourne, Australia provide details on attendees and impacts, and some consideration is given to non-economic effects of business events. There is a separate discussion of venues (the convention and exhibition center and related hotels).

We have expert opinion on motivations, technology, how to leverage business travel for maximum benefits, and the exhibition industry in China. The nature of destination competitiveness, or attractiveness for business events, is examined. How destinations conduct sales and in other ways attract business events is examined, but readers should also relate this to other discussions on bidding. A case study of Visit Denver provides details about how the business event sector is developed and the reasons for producing your events.

Meetings and Conventions

Research Trends

A literature review of convention and meeting management articles by J. Lee and Back (2005a) employed content analysis on 147 articles published in tourism and hospitality journals between 1990 and 2003. This revealed five core research themes: economic impact of conventions; site selection; meeting participation processes; destination marketing; and advances in technology. Three of these themes are clearly related to tourism, while the participation processes and technology themes can be important in terms of meeting the expectations and needs of organizers. Yoo and Weber (2005) reviewed convention tourism research, finding that over half the published articles concerned marketing; they were focused on North America, but Asian and Australian studies were increasing.

Mair (2012) also reviewed the research literature on business events, covering the decade of 2000 through 2009. Her article highlighted the continuing difficulty of getting "meaningful statistics on the business events industry." (p. 133). There was also noted a lack of rigor in many studies, and a tendency to employ purely descriptive statistics and analysis. Social and environmental impact studies were lagging, including a neglect of climate change, and few papers had been published on incentive travel. Mair did observe an increase in research concerning the satisfaction of meeting planners, the role of destination image in attracting attendees, and the decision-making process of business-event tourists. She called for more use of qualitative research to gain a better understanding of meanings attached to business events, and their experiences. "Questions of gender, ethnicity, and power relationships at work, for example, have not been addressed to date" (p. 139).

Industry Size and Trends

People assemble for many reasons, and have always done so, but according to Spiller (2002) the modern convention industry grew in concert with industrialization and trade in the late 19th and through the 20th centuries. A parallel movement was the growth of trade, professional, and affinity associations of all kinds. The first convention bureau in the US was established in 1896 in Detroit, and at that time hotels were the main suppliers of venues.

The market for meetings and conventions is usually separated into those held by associations and by corporations. The largest are typically held by associations, such as professional groups (medicine being one of the mainstays), religious organizations, educational and scientific bodies, or political groups. The Rotary International annual convention, for example, regularly pulls 20,000 or more delegates and other participants to the host city.

According to the International Congress and Convention Association (www.iccaworld.com/), from their ICCA 2011 statistics, the international association sector is resilient and showing healthy growth.

> "With the release of the 2011 Top 20 Rankings for cities and countries, ICCA is reporting another year of continued strength in international association meetings market. For the first time ever, more than 10,000 regularly occurring association events which rotate between at least three countries were identified by ICCA members and ICCA's in-house research team as having taken place during 2011, over 800 more than identified a year previously.

The ICCA country and city ranking (measured by number of meetings organized in 2011) showed little change in the top 10 countries, with the top six repeating their rankings, led by the US, Germany, and Spain. The US saw by far the biggest jump in the number of events held, a rebound after years of economic recession. "In the city rankings, Vienna retained its number one status, and below it Paris overtook Barcelona in the 2nd and 3rd place duel. The biggest climber in the top ten was London, with the 2012 Olympics effect pulling them up from 14th to 7th, and Beijing, which led the way amongst the fast growing BRIC destinations by climbing from 12th to 10th." (ICCA represents the main specialists in organizing, transporting and accommodating international meetings and events, and comprises over 900 member companies and organizations in 87 countries worldwide.)

The "corporate" segment is different in a number of ways. Companies hosting large numbers of meetings and conventions are likely to employ their own event managers or meeting planners, although large associations also do this. Corporate events are also likely to be more diverse than those initiated by associations, including training, hospitality, product launches, motivational assemblies, retreats, publicity events, grand openings, and team-building exercises. There is a strong tendency for corporate clients to repeatedly use the same venues, and strong links have been forged between corporations and specific hotel and resort chains for this purpose.

We are interested in the kinds of meetings and conventions (or international congresses) that are large enough to need a venue, and will be held outside their own offices, and therefore can be won through sales or bids. This is not a uniform market. Crouch and Weber (2002, p. 60) emphasized the differences between corporations and associations in convention destination marketing. The corporate segment consists of many more firms that are potential targets, and they hold many more, but smaller, meetings. Decision making is often quick and centralized at headquarters, and some corporations are big enough to have their own meeting planners.

The association segment is smaller in terms of the number of target organizations, but their events are often larger in terms of numbers of attendees. There are many that are local, national, and international in scope. Typically they hold exhibitions or trade shows with their annual meetings and conventions. Decisions are made by groups, but often there is a set formula for moving the convention around a country or internationally that requires a longer planning period, often years in length.

Relationships have to be built with target organizations, and knowledge of their specific meeting needs is essential. Corporate meetings must generate specific ROI such as learning or performance enhancement, while associations might be more concerned with satisfying members on multiple grounds, including socializing and networking.

Professional associations and the tourism industry (including DMOs) watch closely for trends in business travel and business event demand. For example, Meeting Professionals International and American Express team up to produce a periodic report called Futurewatch. It includes insight from more than 450 industry professionals in 20 different countries. Looking at these reports, some major trends and issues can be detected for business travel in general, and various business events, current to 2013.

- competition is high, and competitive pricing is important;
- increasing emphasis on value and ROI to justify events;
- in tough economic times, the number of events declines and business travelers stay closer to home; meeting professionals see less work and more competition for it; some meeting planning companies fail;
- when economies grow, the number and size of events increases;
- venues and organizers have accepted green events and corporate social responsibility principles;
- the latest in technology and communications are required, including online augmentation of events.

"Virtual meetings" are not only technologically feasible in all parts of the world, but rising costs and fears about travel and security have brought renewed interest in alternative delivery systems such as tele- and videoconferencing. Convention centers are increasingly viewed as "information ports" with satellite and Internet broadcasts of meetings in order to extend their reach. Clients are increasingly concerned about the "cost of proficiency" regarding education and training, so Internet-based delivery systems look appealing. Webcasts can be live presentations to a group, video presentations, or include varying degrees of interactivity.

Expert Opinion

Some Key Technology Trends and Issues in the Business-Events Sector (by Dr. Rob Davidson, Senior Lecturer, University of Greenwich, Events Management; Department of Marketing, Events and Tourism).

Technology: On-site Internet access: planners attach very high importance to the availability of on-site Internet access; they're coming to negotiations with the expectation that a hotel, resort, or conference center will have current meeting technology installed. There has been rapid growth in the use of social media by venues and Convention Bureaus, as part of their marketing communications strategies. In moves to appeal to the younger generation of meetings planners and delegates, destinations and venues are increasingly turning to Web 2.0 applications such as blogs, Facebook, and Twitter in order to drive business to their websites and to monitor what the market is saying about them. Social media are growing in importance to planners as they seek information and customer feedback on properties they are considering. Additionally, an increasing number of planners are using Facebook to befriend sales executives from provider properties with whom they have developed a relationship, offering another channel of friendly and casual contact to solidify a business exchange. 2010 saw an evolution in the balance between the use of virtual meetings and the use of face-to-face events, with advances for both sides. On the one hand, a 2010 study published in the Cornell Hospitality Industry Perspectives series provided compelling, science-based arguments that large-group, face-to-face meetings and events are by far the most effective option when a business or organization needs to capture attention for a new or different strategy, relationship, or project or to inspire people and build a positive emotional climate. Nevertheless, for reasons no doubt linked to the state of the economy, the use of virtual meetings to substitute face-to-face events or to complement them has made advances. For example, the MIA Pathfinder Report conducted in Spring 2010 noted that there had been a slight increase in videoconferencing usage, and just over 50% of survey respondents stated that they planned to invest in this technology in the future.

Corporate social responsibility: Incorporating CSR elements into meetings and events has become a "given" for certain types of clients. Being "green" is now generally assumed, but for certain segments, such as federal and state government and education business, it's a requirement. For corporate groups, meeting providers are generally expected to have green programs in place, although this is not yet universally required by corporate America. For federal and state government business as well as the education segment, however, properties must meet basic green hospitality requirements to even be considered for a meeting or event. Including "social legacy" initiatives in meetings and events has also become more prevalent, not only in the corporate market but also for association events, as confirmed by the President and CEO, Orlando/Orange County Convention & Visitors Bureau, who was quoted by MeetingsNet as saying that one big trend he's seeing is medical associations asking for information about community service projects: "They want to connect with the local community in a meaningful way."

Motivations for Attending Meetings and Conventions

It might be assumed that people attend meetings and conventions because they have to (i.e., extrinsic motivators), but personal benefits often get combined with business necessity, and business trips get mixed with vacations; this often means that the spouse and family accompany the attendee.

Research Evidence on Associations

Price (1993) found that education, networking, career path, and leadership enhancement were major factors influencing association members to attend conferences and conventions.

Oppermann and Chon (1997) modeled the decision-making process for convention attendees, concentrating on personal and business factors, the event itself, and its location. One of the major motivational factors they discussed was the level of commitment to an association, as that would influence its value to the participant. Hearing experts in a field, keeping up with developments, learning new skills, and developing valuable new relationships are other specific motives. Destination image is important, but locational inhibitors such as cost and accessibility can counter that attractor.

Ngamsom and Beck (2000) found that opportunities for travel overseas, outdoor recreation, business or political activities, a change of pace, networking, and education were all important motivators for association members. Inhibitors were found to include perceived safety and security risks, inconvenience, unfamiliarity with destinations, time, money, and personal health problems. Deals on travel packages, opportunities to do things with family, and costs covered by employers were all important factors facilitating attendance at international conferences.

Expert Opinion

Why Do We Attend Conferences and Conventions? (by Dr. Judith Mair, Senior Lecturer, Department of Management, La Trobe University, Melbourne, Australia).

Researchers have been considering this question for some time now, and while there are always some factors specific to individual events, it is now generally accepted that there are four–six main motivations for attending association events (for more details, see Mair & Thompson

2009). The top motivation in most studies is networking. Conferences and conventions offer excellent opportunities for attendees and delegates to meet with like-minded people, and seek business and other collaborations. Most conventions include plenty of time for networking—welcome receptions, tea and coffee breaks, relatively long lunches—as they recognize the value of this time. In addition, many delegates meet up for dinner or socializing outside the official convention, and this is where much of the networking is done.

Another key reason for attending is for personal and/or professional development. For some professions, attendance at conventions is an important part of maintaining their professional accreditation, while for others it is an excellent way to find out about new developments in their field. The location of a convention is often one of the deciding factors for potential delegates. Attractive and easily accessible destinations are usually the most popular choice for meeting planners, as these tend to result in greater numbers of delegates attending (and usually for association conferences, maximizing attendance is a vital part of the financial stability of the association).

The cost of a convention is also crucial. In the association context, delegates are often paying for their own attendance, and therefore cost can become a barrier to attendance—once you add up the cost of registration, travel and accommodation, the cost can prove to be prohibitive. Most associations are aware of this, and some are taking steps to choose inexpensive locations, with low air fares. Finally, there are other attendance factors (sometimes known as inhibitors and facilitators) which can have significant influence on the attendance decision, including the time and date of the event (does it clash with other events, or with work or family responsibilities?); whether attendees believe that the location is safe and secure; and whether the destination offers tourist attractions that make it worthwhile adding on a trip pre- or postevent.

Business Event Travel Careers

It might not be as obvious as with sport enthusiasts, both athletes and fans, but business events also engender travel careers. Careers could begin in several ways, each accompanied by somewhat different motivations and results:

- As a student in a professional program (tourism, hospitality, events, business, etc.) going to a student-specific meeting or attending a professional congress as a student delegate; students might want to network with future jobs in mind or simply to learn about what the profession does; fees and travel might be subsidized by the association; going on the cheap will be the norm.
- As a young careerist, employers might send staff to meetings and conventions out of town; now there is an expense account!; a report on the trip will be required; there might be the incentive of working towards certification; meeting colleagues with similar interests or problems is a factor; benefits to the attendee and to the employer will be expected.

It can be hypothesized (with no research evidence available) that as business event travel careers progress, *communitas* becomes more important, with sharing and belonging, meeting old friends, and nostalgia taking over from learning and career advancement.

Academics certainly develop event travel careers, as we are required to attend seminars and conferences related to our research interests. Some are more prestigious than others, and some locations are attractive. Over time, the developing academic might repeatedly attend some events, while occasionally sampling others. There are instances where one is invited to speak, or is involved in event organization because of personal connections or having responsibility within a professional/academic organization. This is not too different from other professionals who belong to associations, each of which presents opportunities for event tourist careers.

Inside corporations are many private meetings and special events, and others that are aimed at the public or external stakeholders (i.e., "business-to-business"). Travel careers might be less evident than for leisure and association/scientific professionals. Here are some cues to look for when examining event travel careers in the extrinsically motivated realm:

- Does the profession/job/business require travel to events? Is it compulsory?
- Is there a progression over time by type of event, benefits offered, etc.?
- Is there a pattern of event travel that changes over time (e.g., in terms of traveling more frequently, or farther from home? combining pleasure with business? taking family or spouse along?)
- Are there Iconic events that are symbolic of the best, biggest, most prestigious?
- Are there events that people find most enjoyable and want to go back to frequently?

Research in the UK suggested that 40% of business travelers and their families or colleagues return to the hosting destination as leisure visitors in the future (Business Tourism Partnership, 2004).

Impacts of Meetings and Conventions

It is conventional wisdom, supported by many studies, that the business event traveler is a high-yield tourist. Whether or not this is true in every case is open to debate, as there are numerous variations available. Also, it is uncertain whether business event tourists are in general higher yield than other event-dedicated visitors. Destinations and venues have to do their own research to answer such questions.

Dwyer (2002), writing about convention tourism impacts in the book *Convention Tourism: International Research and Industry Perspectives*, noted the following key facts:

- Substantial numbers of people accompany convention-goers (in Australia the accompanying tourists add 15–20% to convention-related expenditures).
- Convention tourists are likely to spend more than other types of visitor (in Singapore, about three times as much!).
- International convention tourists stay longer and spend more than domestic visitors.
- Corporate and medical conferences generate the highest visitor expenditure.
- Longer conventions generate more spending in total.
- Pre- and postmeeting tours add considerably to the economic impacts (in one study, up to 50% of total spending by international convention-goers was on tours).
- Substantial economic benefits can also accrue from spending by organizers, associations and sponsors (if it is "new money" to the area).
- International convention tourists (at least in Australia) spend most their money in capital cities and tourist "gateways," while interstate visitors spend equally in urban and nonurban areas.

Conventions and conferences tend to attract mostly tourists who would not otherwise have traveled to the host city and therefore inject mostly new money into its economy. They also tend to be higher yield visitors, as the mostly stay in hotels, and especially if someone else is paying for the trip. When a convention center evaluates its impact on a city it has to specify the number of events that attract mostly local residents for meetings, as these generate little if any new money for the city; they might be justifiable on the grounds that the facility has surplus capacity and needs to generate cash flow, even though convention centers typically have a tourism-oriented mandate.

Research by Grado, Strauss, and Lord (1998) sheds light on the impacts of this sector in a rural region, while a study by Hanly (2012) looked at the Irish association market.

Research Notes on Economic Impacts

Grado, S., Strauss, C., & Lord, B. (1998). Economic impacts of conferences and conventions. *Journal of Convention and Exhibition Management, 1*(1), 19–33.

The researchers assessed the impacts of conventions and conferences in a rural, nine-county portion of Pennsylvania. They determined that a majority of attendees were non-residents and they injected substantial economic benefits. Moreover, their spending was equal to or greater than other types of tourists in this area, including recreationists, and this sector had a high income multiplier because convention-related spending generated high levels of local employment and used local supplies.

Hanly, P. (2012). Measuring the economic contribution of the international association conference market: An Irish case study. *Tourism Management, 33*(6), 1574–1582.

This study assesses the economic contribution of the international association conference market to Ireland and highlights key sectors that demonstrate strong multiplier effects. Primary conference expenditure estimates are combined with sector multipliers to determine direct, indirect and induced effects across a range of monetary aggregates in Ireland in 2007. Total direct conference spending of 131.1 million Euros generated 235.8 million in output, 45.4 million in income, 101.6 million in value added, 52.0 million in imports, and 9.3 million in product taxes. Key conference sectors are highlighted including hotels and restaurants, renting services of machinery and equipment, air transport, and retail shopping.

Report on the Economic Impacts of Business Events in the US

In 2011 the Convention Industry Council released a study entitled "The Economic Significance of Meetings to the U.S. Economy" (www.MeetingsMeanBusiness.com). The study used the World Tourism Organization's definition of a meeting as "a gathering of 10 or more participants for a minimum of four hours in a contracted venue." These are highlights:

- The U.S. meetings industry directly supports 1.7 million jobs, a $106 billion contribution to GDP, $263 billion in spending, $60 billion in labor revenue, $14.3 billion in federal tax revenue and $11.3 billion in state and local tax revenue.
- 1.8 million meetings, trade shows, conventions, congresses, incentive events, and other meetings take place across the country; 1.3 million are classified as corporate or business meetings, 270,000 are conventions, conferences, or congresses, 11,000 are trade shows, and 66,000 are incentive meetings.
- The vast majority of meetings (85%) were conducted at venues with lodging. Meetings generate 250 million overnight stays by 117 million Americans and 5 million international attendees.
- Spending on goods and services resulting from meetings and events in the US totals $263 billion. The majority of direct spending, $151 billion, is related to meeting planning and production, venue rental, and other non-travel- and tourism-related commodities; $113 billion is spent each year on lodging, food service, transportation, and other travel and tourism commodities.
- A total of 205 million people, representing domestic and international delegates, exhibitors, and organizers attend the 1.8 million meetings. The meetings serve as vehicles for job training and education, generating sales revenue, linking

domestic and foreign buyers and developing lasting relationships in personal environments that build trust and unity.

- For the purposes of this study and according to UNWTO, meetings are defined as a gathering of 10 or more participants for a minimum of 4 hours in a contracted venue. Meetings exclude social and recreational activities, certain educational and political activities, and gatherings for sales of good/services such as consumer shows.

Melbourne, Australia, Convention Delegates Survey, 2010

This study surveyed delegates attending eight international association conferences held at the Melbourne Convention and Exhibition Centre (MCEC) between March and November 2010.

A mixture of international, interstate and local delegates participated. Highlights include:

- The majority of international delegates came from Asia (38%), Western Europe (14%), and North America (13%) and were aged between 30 and 59 years old (74%).
- Pretravel planning: 75% sourced information on Australia prior to their visit. The primary sources of this information were travel guide books (45%), the Tourism Australia website (26%), and word of mouth (21%).
- Travel companions: 27% traveled with two other people who did not attend the conference. Accompanying people were generally a spouse/partner and/ or friend(s).
- Modes of transport: 30% flew with Qantas and 11% with Singapore Airlines. The cost and schedule offered were deemed to be a high priority for delegates when deciding which airline to choose; 52% booked their flight to Melbourne with a travel agent and 34% used online booking methods.
- Length of stay: International delegates stayed in Melbourne for 6.0 nights while attending a conference and 6.8 nights in Melbourne overall. On average, international delegates stayed in Australia for 9.8 nights.
- Pre- or postconference travel: 44% planned to undertake pre or post touring in regional Victoria or other parts of Australia prior to attending the conference in Melbourne. The Great Ocean Road was the most preferred Victorian destination. The most popular Australian destination was Sydney; 20% intended to visit other countries before or after their trip to Melbourne; 63% were first-time visitors to Australia.
- Travel intentions: 56% would not have visited Melbourne if the conference had not been held in the city; 75% stated that attending the conference had increased their likelihood of returning to Australia to do business in the future and 71% may return to Melbourne for a holiday.
- Accommodation type: Of the 91% who stayed in a hotel or apartment whist in Melbourne, 59% stated their accommodation was either 3 or 4 stars; 34% booked their accommodation online.
- Sponsorship: 62% were sponsored to attend the conference, primarily by their employer.
- Expenditure: On average, international delegates spent an estimated $799 per day and $4,134 during their stay in Melbourne. Expenditure in regional Victoria was estimated to be $2,205 per trip, per person, and international delegates

spent approximately $3,618 in other parts of Australia pre- and/or postattending conference in Melbourne.

- Main reason for conference attendance: The primary motivations to attend a conference were the conference content and program, the social program and the opportunity to visit Australia.
- Likelihood of recommending Melbourne: 96% said they would recommend Melbourne to their friends and colleagues as a place to visit.
- Key features of the Melbourne experience: International delegates were most satisfied with the safety in Melbourne, friendliness of people and the convention facilities.
- Free time while attending the conference in Melbourne: 38% had free time after the conference each day (5pm onwards) and most of this free time was spent with colleagues; 58% spent time shopping and 56% visited parks and gardens.

In recent years there has been growing interest in the non-economic value of business events to destinations, participants, and other stakeholders. The following research note by Edwards, Foley, and Schlenker (2011) provides some empirical evidence.

Research Note on the Social Legacy of Business Events

Edwards, D., Foley, C., & Schlenker, K. (2011). *Beyond tourism benefits: Measuring the social legacies of business events*. Sydney: University of Technology.

Through a robust and rigorous methodology the findings are representative of the survey population—in this case being attendees at the five congresses surveyed—and clearly demonstrate a direct connection between the staging of business events and a range of benefits and outcomes for delegates, sponsors, exhibitors, and the destination. Business events assist communication that promotes the effective diffusion of knowledge. Over 90% of respondents believe that these congresses have facilitated the dissemination of new knowledge, ideas, techniques, materials, and technologies by providing Sydney/New South Wales (NSW) based educators, practitioners, and researchers with access to a network of international colleagues. This networking affords local delegates with new business and research collaborations, which can generate innovation, ideas and research agendas for many years to come. Business events provide a supporting platform from which the growth of intercultural understandings and international friendships can occur. Sydney's capacities are showcased through the staging of international business events, putting the destination "on the map," fostering Sydney's reputation as a place of highly skilled, capable, world leading researchers.

Exhibitions

Trade and Consumer Shows are primarily considered in this section, plus a short discussion of World Fairs or Expos. There is little evidence available on State Fairs and tourism, but they are mentioned in this section. An Expert Opinion contribution by Karin Weber and Jin Xin provides details of the surging exhibition industry in China and in particular the Canton Fair in Guangzhou.

Trade and Consumer Shows (The Exhibition Industry)

Morrow (1997), in the book *The Art of the Show: An Introduction to the Study of Exhibition Management* (produced for the International Association for Exposition Management—IAEM) emphasized that the core purpose of "trade" and "consumer" shows was to connect buyers to sellers in a temporary market.

The usual differentiation is that consumer shows are open to the public, with the intention of both informing and entertaining customers (e.g., auto, outdoor, and lifestyle shows), while "trade shows" are for invitees only, either based on specific business needs or association membership. "International trade fairs" are a special class. Typically they are at the large end and targeted at a global or multicountry audience, and therefore are usually held in cities with major airports and exhibition halls. The Canton Fair fits into this category. Hybrids exist, with trade/media guests on some days, followed by opening for the public on others.

The Center for Exhibition Industry Research (CEIF) (www.ceir.org) exists to provide data to the industry. According to CEIR, "Attendees rate exhibitions as the number one most useful source of information with which to make a buying decision." Professionals attend trade shows to learn about new products and meet face to face with suppliers.

Exhibitions have a seasonal rhythm, with the lowest month for show starts being December and the peak 2 months being (almost equally) October and March. Summer (July and August) constitutes the second low season. Part of the growth in venues in North America over the last two decades is attributable to the shortfall of space during the two peak exhibition seasons. They are also reactive to world events. The publication *Tradeshow Week* (which no longer exists, as of 2012) (www.tradeshowweek.com) documented major declines in attendance at shows in the aftermath of September 11, 2001. Terrorism and market recession were given as the main reasons.

In 2000, 16 North American cities hosted 46% of all exhibitions, each with over 200 events (CEIR Direct 2002: www.ceir.org). The top three were Orlando (hosted 625), Las Vegas (589), and Toronto (582). Total gross revenue generated by exhibitions in North America was estimated to be $10.4 billion, generating $120 billion in total economic impact. M. J. Lee, Yeung, and Dewald (2010) note that in the US alone, exhibitions contributed US$122.31 billion to GDP.

Mair (2012) found that along with incentive travel, all aspects of exhibitions are notably underresearched. Prominent areas of existing research into exhibitions include: exhibition service quality; trade show managers' use of technology; exhibition site selection; association meeting participants; antitrust regulations; positioning of Asian exhibition host cities; the economic impact of the exhibition industry; criteria for evaluating trade shows; and the exhibition industry at specific destinations, such as Korea, Macao, China, and Thailand.

Trade Show Attendance Motivation

Most studies on exhibition attendance focus on trade shows. Previous studies have examined the motivations for attending trade shows (e.g., Berne & Garcia-Uceda, 2008; Ling-Yee, 2006; Tanner, Chonko, & Ponzurick, 2001). Recently, some researchers have begun to expand this research direction to include attendance motivations at trade and consumer exhibitions (Kozak, 2006; Kozak & Kayr, 2009; M. J. Lee et al., 2010).

Research Note on a Consumer Travel Show

Rittichainuwat, B., & Mair, J. (2011). Visitor attendance motivations at consumer travel exhibitions. *Tourism Management, 33*(5), 1236–1244.

This study identifies the major motivations of visitors for attending consumer travel exhibitions and segments visitors based on their motivations. The findings suggest that visitors to consumer travel exhibitions have multiple motivations: acquiring purchase information, being attracted by the theme, or being encouraged to visit by media coverage. Half of the visitors perceived travel fairs to be an important distribution channel through which they could get special deals on travel to desirable destinations (or at least sourcing information on travel). It seems likely that consumer travel show attendance may be closely linked with the individual leisure desires of the visitor. The study suggests two clusters: 1) Shopper cluster whose major motivation is purchasing and 2) Total Visitors whose motivation is to undertake an ongoing information search and attend seminars to maintain their awareness of new trends with the tourism industry.

The findings of this study suggest that although there are some differences, the broad attendance motivations of consumer exhibition visitors are not significantly different from those of trade show visitors. Consumer exhibition visitors have multiple attendance motivations, including purchasing, gathering information, and keeping abreast of current trends. Similar to Tanner et al. (2001) in the trade show context, this study found that there was a substantial emphasis on learning (about new products, companies and special deals) among consumer exhibition visitors. As M. J. Lee et al. (2010) suggest, "Exhibitions are not just selling/buying tools, but are also networking and search tools" (p. 206).

Expert Opinion

The Exhibition Industry in Mainland China: An Overview (by Xin Jin and Karin Weber).

Dr. Karin Weber is Associate Professor in the School of Hotel & Tourism Management, Hong Kong Polytechnic University. Prior to joining the school in 2001, she taught in marketing and tourism at Monash University, Australia.

Dr. Xin Jin is a lecturer of the Department of Tourism, Leisure, Hotel and Sport Management, on the Gold Coast Campus of Griffith University, Australia. Prior to entering academia she worked as a tour operator in the travel industry in China.

The exhibition industry worldwide has experienced significant growth over the past few years, resulting from a substantial increase in trade and commerce. Owing to the region's economic boom, the focus of the global exhibition industry has shifted to Asia, which in turn creates more favorable conditions for the development of China's exhibition business. China has become a dominant player in the Asia Pacific exhibition market, with its exhibition sector being regarded as a valuable resource in showcasing the country's economic vision and having a tangible positive impact on local revenues. It also plays a significant role in promoting success for Chinese brands in a global market in addition to the direct value of its own commercial success.

In 2011, about 7,000 exhibitions of a diversified nature and scale were held in China, with machinery, building materials, food, and textile, fashion, and leather representing the most frequently exhibited industrial sectors (China Convention and Exhibition Society [CCES], 2012). Indoor exhibition space totaled 4.7 million square meters, accounting for 15% of the world total. Thus, China ranks second among the countries with the highest venue capacity, following the US and preceding Germany (UFI, 2011). In 2011, there were 153 convention and exhibition centers in 36 cities, with 28 of them having more than 80,000 square meters indoor exhibition space (CCES, 2012), yet the average rental utilization rate was only about 20% (Guo, 2012). Compared with the international standardized utilization rate of 40%, space in purpose-built centers is evidently underutilized in China. Table 7.1 shows the largest centers in major Chinese cities, together with their respective size. These venues are usually the ones most recently built, with the most sophisticated facilities and designs, and thus represent the most popular options for exhibition organizers. However, in many of these cities there is more than one exhibition venue.

Based on city size, prestige, economic strength, tradition, and history in hosting exhibitions, and the number of exhibitions hosted per annum, Shanghai, Beijing and Guangzhou are usually classified as first tier cities in the exhibition sector in China, while provincial capital cities or economically developed cities striving to develop the exhibition industry are classified as second tier cities (e.g., Chan, 2007; Guo, 2007). Shanghai, Beijing, Guangzhou, and Hong Kong Special Administrative Region (SAR) dominate the market, and the number of exhibitions in these cities is stable and even increasing. Exhibitions in other cities fluctuate and positioning of these cities is difficult.

Table 7.1. Largest Convention and Exhibition Centers in China

City	Space (m²)	Population	City	Space (m²)	Population
Guangzhou	381,600	7,547,467	Shanghai	226,300	14,230,992
Shijiazhuang	225,000	1,935,553	Dongguan	190,000	3,870,036
Shenyang	155,200	4,596,785	Beijing	153,800	10,300,723
Changsha	150,000	2,122,873	Nanjing	140,000	3,783,907
Qingdao	139,000	2,720,972	Hefei	136,100	1,549,476
Chongqing	132,700	5,087,197	Chengdu	130,000	4,273,218
Zhengzhou	112,000	3,870,504	Shenzhen	105,000	6,480,340
Wuhan	104,000	6,787,482	Xiamen	103,000	1,454,450
Xi'an	96,000	3,870,504	Hangzhou	91,000	1,750,251
Tianjin	89,000	6,839,008	Harbin	86,500	3,627,082

Source: Space of the centers was compiled from CCES (2012). Population was compiled from http://www.citypopulation.de/China.html, with reference to the year 2000. Population was included to indicate the sizes of these cities. Only the urban population of these cities was extracted; the population in suburban areas was excluded.

China's largest trade show in terms of exhibition footage, attendance, and business turnover is the China Import and Export Fair, formerly known as the Chinese Export Commodity Fair and commonly referred to as "Canton Fair." The Ministry of Commerce and the Guangdong Provincial Government in Guangzhou (Canton), the capital of the Southern Chinese province of Guangdong, jointly initiated it in 1957. The fair has been organized and managed by China Foreign Trade Centre, a government affiliation. It was established with the aim to break the blockage and embargo of the capitalist alliances and find new sources to enlarge foreign trade in the 1950s. At that time China had normal diplomatic relations with only about 20 countries, 80% of foreign trade was tally trade with socialist nations, and foreign exchange was scarce (China Foreign Trade Centre [CFTC], 2006). Guangzhou (Canton) was chosen due to its ideal geographical vicinity to Hong Kong and Macao, and close historical and cultural affiliation with overseas Chinese.

Since its inauguration, two sessions of the Fair have been held consecutively each year, uninterrupted even during the years of the Great Leap Forward in the early 1960s, the Cultural Revolution in the late 1960s and early 1970s, and the SARS outbreak in 2003. The first fair witnessed only 1,223 international buyers from 19 countries and regions, 68% of which were from Hong Kong; in contrast, by its 101st session in the spring of 2007 the Fair welcomed 206,749 international buyers from 211 countries. It utilized 285,000 square meters net exhibition space, accommodated 31,682 standard booths, 14,430 domestic exhibitors, and 314 international exhibitors (China Import and Export Fair [CIEF], 2007). A detailed account of the history of the Canton Fair is provided by Jin and Weber (2008).

The development of the exhibition industry in a region is closely related to the state of its economic attributes, such as market leadership, industry fragmentation, and economic concentration (industry agglomeration). Further, the global economic state, competition in the exhibition industry at local//national level, and internal management challenges' impact on exhibition development (UFI, 2012). The 2008 global financial crisis and its repercussions have certainly affected global exhibition industry development. Yet, despite decreases in net space rented in Europe and North America, in 2010, net space rented in China reached 13 million square meters, a 6% increase over the previous year (UFI, 2011). This shows that China remains a strong growth market for exhibitions where the standardization and internationalization of its exhibitions will further boost the country's exhibition industry development.

World's Fairs (Expos)

There is no doubt that a world's fair generates a lot of tourist demand, especially because they tend to be 4–6 months in length. But they are not always successful financially, and they do not always achieve their aims. Typically they are conceived as instruments of repositioning and urban development or renewal. They aim to foster trade and international goodwill.

See the section in Chapter 5 on forecasting demand for several references to world's fairs and tourism generation (Blackorby et al., 1986; Dungan, 1984; Xie & Smith, 2000). In addition, there have been tourism-related papers published by Dimanche (1996), Mendell et al. (1983), and de Groote (2005). The 2010 world's fair in Shanghai generated a huge number of papers, especially by Chinese scholars. (e.g., L. Yu, Wang, & Seo, 2012).

According to an article in Wikipedia (accessed August 1, 2012) Shanghai was the largest world's fair ever held in terms of its cost, site, and the number of countries participating. An overriding aim was to position Shanghai as a "world city." It was reported that 73 million visitors attended, a record attendance, with 250 participating countries or international organizations. About 5.8% of the visitors, or 4.25 million, were foreigners. The legacy is intended to be one of best practices in urban design, plus the Bureau of International Expositions (BIE) and the Shanghai government announced plans to construct the world's only official World Expo Museum on the expo site. Like all mega-events, it was not without mega-controversies, and some of these are covered in the Wikipedia article. They include displacement or residents from housing to make room for development.

Tourism displacement effects can be quite severe for a major event like a world expo, because of its rare and substantial drawing power. According to J. Lee (1987), normal

Photo 7.1. Canton Fair, Guangzhou, China (Credit: photo courtesy of Xin Jin and Karin Weber).

travel patterns were disrupted by the 1986 Vancouver World's Fair so that Vancouver and British Columbia gained, but the rest of Canada lost, traffic. That particular event greatly exceeded its forecast sales, whereas others (e.g., New Orleans) have failed spectacularly to achieve estimated numbers. From a Wikipedia article (accessed August 1, 2012) comes this summary of the New Orleans Expo:

> Plagued with attendance problems, the 1984 Louisiana World Exposition has the dubious distinction of being the only exposition to declare bankruptcy during its run. Many blamed the low attendance on the fact that it was staged just two years and two states from Knoxville's 1982 World's Fair, and also on the fact that it coincided with the 1984 Summer Olympics in Los Angeles. There has not been a World's Fair in the United States since.

Legacies of world's fairs can have permanent physical and symbolic value: witness the Eiffel Tower in Paris (the first great piece of iconic architecture to survive from an expo) and Seattle's space needle. But world's fair sites are not always accessible or identifiable by visitors, given the tendency to fully remove pavilions and other obvious indicators and to encourage private sector or institutional redevelopment. Dimanche (1996) studied the infrastructural developments associated with the New Orleans World's Fair, saying it created a legacy in terms of new hotels, transportation, and other facilities that benefited tourism—and thereby lead to future tax gains.

Research Note on World's Fairs

de Groote, P. (2005). A multidisciplinary analysis of world fairs (Expos) and their effects. *Tourism Review*, 60(1), 12–19.

Since the Great Exhibition of London (1851) approx. 75 Expos have been held worldwide. They are regulated by the BIE in Paris. An Expo is a show case of technological progress, represented in pavilions. Until 1873 a unique building hosted the exhibits. Later the Expo sites were located extramuros, and sometimes afterwards redeveloped into a leisure or science park or a multifunctional urbanised area. Mostly Expos have a positive effect for the city and the region on income, employment and infrastructure. The impact on culture, science, technology and tourism is also very important. However, Expos can generate an increase in prices, overcrowding and even environmental damage. Several Expos were even a financial disaster! The post-event depression was certainly the case for many Expos. Expos still bear witness to their era and that they have tried to maintain the harmony and peace between people. Still they have opportunities for communication, investments, development, trade and tourism. The case study focus on the successful Expo 1992 in Seville.

State Fairs

Despite their enduring popularity and institutional status in many cities across North America (they are called shows in Australia and New Zealand), the tourism appeal and roles of state fairs and similar exhibitions has been an extremely underresearched topic. Mihalik and Furguson (1994) referred to a pilot study by Henry and Robbe (1993) of the Urban Policy Research Center at Georgia State University, which indicated that hundreds of millions of visitors have attended a state fair in the past 12 months making it one of the largest leisure spectator activities in the US.

State Fairs seem to capture the essence of agricultural shows, festivals, and exhibitions rolled into one. In the case of the Calgary Exhibition and Stampede (see Getz, 1993, 2005, for cases on its marketing) it also includes a rodeo, parade, and community events.

In 2012 The Calgary Exhibition and Stampede (the "Stampede" for short) celebrated its 100th anniversary, although its origins as an agriculture fair go back to the late 1800s. According to the newspaper *The Calgary Herald* (July 16, 2012):

> It was a record year for attendance. This year's Calgary Stampede was antici-pated to be the granddaddy of the "grand vision" founder Guy Weadick pic-tured in 1912. And with expectations taller than a 10-gallon hat, the Stampede lived up to its billing as the Greatest Outdoor Show on Earth. The centennial bash will be remembered for sizzling summer days, record-setting attendance and spectacular country crooners. "We knocked it out of the park this year," said spokeswoman Jennifer Booth. Daily attendance records were shattered for most of the 10-day hootenanny. Officials say the 10-day total attendance was 1,409,371, a new cumulative record, outpacing the previous high by 234,674 visitors. (http://www.calgaryherald.com/)

Here is an excerpt from my 2005 case study, as published in *Event Management & Event Tourism*:

> **Visitor Attendance and Origins:** A large majority of attendees every year are Calgarians—65% in 2003; 13% came from another country, 13% were from other parts of Canada, and 9% from other parts of Alberta.
>
> **Visitor Motivations:** Annual visitor surveys track the proportion of people who come to "look around" versus those with specific motivations. The "look-ers" seem to be increasing in numbers, accounting for 61% in 2003 com-pared to 51% in 2002—these visitors are seeking generic event benefits. Of the specific attractions mentioned, the most popular being the rodeo (25%), entertainment (16%), chuckwagon races (10%), and animals (7%).
>
> "Midway" rides and entertainment appeal more to younger attendees, while the rodeo attracts an older audience. Research over the years has also demonstrated that tourists are much more attracted to the rodeo, while rides attract repeat visits from locals.
>
> Perhaps surprisingly, a large part of the motivations specific to attending the rodeo are social (30%), followed by action/excitement/fun (25%), a spe-cific rodeo event (24%), and curiosity (23%). As to the nightly Grandstand Show and Chuckwagon Races, which are very popular with locals, 64% specifically wanted to see both.
>
> **Nonuser Research:** For the first time, the Stampede in 2001 commissioned a study of nonusers. Objectives were to measure the incidence of visitation among Calgarians, assess nonvisitor demographics, examine barriers to atten-dance, measure the appeal of current elements of the Stampede, and quan-tify lifestyle and recreational activities of nonusers. Almost 2,000 "contacts" resulted in 800 telephone interviews with residents who had not attended the Stampede in the previous year. It was found that most nonusers (64%) had in fact attended the Stampede within the previous 3 years. The main reasons for not attending were given as "out of town," "not interested," and "cost."

Research Note on State Fairs and Tourism

Mihalik, B., & Ferguson, M. (1994). A case study of a tourism special event: An analysis of an American state fair. *Festival Management & Event Tourism, 2*, 75–83.

The primary finding of the study was that fair visitors rated the recreation, social, and educa-tion functions as important reasons for attending the fair. The scale item receiving the highest mean score in the survey was "family togetherness." Marketing the fair as a family event will likely appeal to and satisfy the need for this type of social interaction.

Convention and Exhibition Centers

Hotels, resorts, and other venues host enumerable business event and private functions, but most cities also want their own convention and exhibition venues. They are often joined, but sometimes separate facilities. The private sector does build and operate some, for profit, but mostly the public sector and public–private partnerships are created to build and operate them.

These venues are getting bigger and bigger! According to an article in Wikipedia (List of Convention and Exhibition Centers, accessed August 1, 2012), the top 10 American venues in size are as follows:

- McCormick Place, Chicago, Illinois, 2,760,000-square-foot (256,000 m²) of exhibition space.
- Orange County Convention Center, Orlando, Florida, exhibition space: 2,100,000-square-foot (200,000 m²). Total area: 7,000,000-square-foot (650,000 m²).
- Las Vegas Convention Center, Las Vegas, Nevada, exhibition space: 2,000,000-square-foot (190,000 m²), 3,200,000-square-foot (300,000 m²) total space.
- Boston Convention and Exhibition Center, Boston, Massachusetts, 1,700,000-square-foot (160,000 m²) total area.
- Georgia World Congress Center, Atlanta, Georgia, 1,500,000-square-foot (140,000 m²) exhibition area; 3,900,000-square-foot (360,000 m²) total area.
- Cobo Center, Detroit, Michigan: 700,000-square-foot (65,000 m²) exhibition area; 2,400,000-square-foot (220,000 m²) total area.
- Walter E. Washington Convention Center, Washington, DC: 2,300,000-square-foot (210,000 m²) total area.
- Colorado Convention Center, Denver, Colorado: 584,000-square-foot (54,300 m²) exhibition area; 2,200,000-square-foot (200,000 m²) total area.
- Dallas Convention Center, Dallas, Texas: 1,000,000-square-foot (93,000 m²) exhibition area; 2,000,000-square-foot (190,000 m²) total area.
- George R. Brown Convention Center, Houston, Texas, 853,000-square-foot (79,200 m²) exhibition area; 1,800,000-square-foot (170,000 m²) total area.

More subjective lists of top convention centers and cities are readily available on the Internet.

Read the following material about the Colorado Convention Center and its events personnel in conjunction with the Visit Denver case study.

Colorado Convention Center (www.denverconvention.com; accessed August 1, 2012)

Opened in 1990, with more than 100 professional meeting planners working together with architects to design every aspect of the building, the result was simple; a sensible, state-of-the-art facility with easy traffic flow and everything you need in a stunningly beautiful building in the heart of downtown Denver. Expanded in 2005, well-known as one of the most practical and "user friendly" meeting facilities, the Colorado Convention Center is now home to over 400 events annually. The Colorado Convention Center is located within easy walking distance of over 8,400 hotel rooms, 300 restaurants, 9 theatres of the Denver Performing Arts Complex and a wide variety of shopping and retail outlets.

Debbie Welsh, CMP is Director of Event Management. Debbie has over 19 years of event management experience at the Colorado Convention Center.

Currently, she leads a seasoned team of nine Event Managers, an Event Coordinator, and an Event Management Coordinator. She has overseen servicing a wide variety of city-wide conferences including, PCMA, MPI, and ASAE. She also has experience with high profile political events such as World Youth Day, Summit of the Eight, Presidential/Vice Presidential visits, as well as the 2008 Democratic National Convention. Debbie has a strong passion for the hospitality industry and emanates the philosophy that exceptional customer service will, in fact, bring business back to the Colorado Convention Center. The Colorado Meeting and Events Magazine inducted her into the 2011 Hall of Fame under the Meeting Professional category for her years of exceptional service in Event Management.

Justifications and Issues

Justification for public expenditure as a "public good" must deal with the fact that it is difficult to argue that a major convention/exhibition facility serves residents with something they really need or desire—the justification is tourism and business related, not culture or leisure as with sport venues and festival places. As with sport and arts facilities, convention and exhibition centers are often viewed as the catalyst for urban development or renewal, and as being essential infrastructure for major cities.

Clark (2006) wrote about developing convention centers in the book *Developing a Successful Infrastructure for Convention and Event Tourism*. Her chapter is entitled "What are cities really committing to when they build a convention center?" She drew upon expert opinions on the financial consequences of building a convention center in a municipality, finding that many venues are not financially viable on their own. The up-front capital costs require subsequent commitments to marketing, and the venue itself might have to be augmented with many amenities expected by convention-goers. There is a debate about the real economic benefits, and many believe that new venues have to be accompanied by investment in convention hotels. Often the building of centers is justified by overoptimistic feasibility studies, and by reference to urban renewal/development plans, with the event venue being a catalyst.

Clark (2006) says the following are required: additional marketing staff and funding for sales and marketing, including branding efforts; incentives to attract events; augmentations like parking, convention hotels, transport infrastructure including pedestrian access; further city amenity enhancements; and of course eventual improvements, repairs, or enlargement.

Some experts told Clark (2006) that if the city was not already a tourist destination a new convention center would unlikely be successful. In a very competitive US marketplace, many elements are needed to attract meetings and conventions. She concluded that the industry as a whole was mature and very competitive.

Morgan and Condliffe (2006) also authored a chapter on "Measuring the economic impacts of convention centers and event tourism: A discussion of key issues." They said there is a need to separate the impacts of construction, which can generate a lot of temporary jobs and have a high multiplier, from that of the events attracted to venues over a long period of time. And it is important to determine what is in-scope for impact assessment, as extending the area of concern from the city to the metropolitan region can expand the scale of impacts. Sanders (2004) is cited as representing those who believe economic benefits have been overstated, especially because a boom in construction in the 1990s resulted in a big oversupply of exhibition space that was then sold at discounted prices. Sanders also argued the impact studies overestimated visitor spending and used inappropriate multipliers. Many events using venues do not, in fact, attract tourists. The more difficult it is to sell the space, the more likely it will be used by residents and local businesses. Finally, the timing is critical, as any events held in otherwise peak demand periods will displace other visitors (although perhaps with higher yield business tourists). Externalities are seldom considered in decisions to build new venues, said Morgan and Condliffe. These costs can include traffic congestion and loss of amenity for residents, or environmental impacts such as pollution from traffic.

Convention Hotels

Nelson (2006) examined the trend to public sector financing of hotels to support the business events sector. He quoted Hunter (2005, cited in Nelson), who argued that the public sector must get directly involved with the business event sector in terms of venues, hotels, and often adjacent development, visitor attractions, entertainment districts, even food and beverage outlets near to convention centers. The convention hotel offers direct connection (or close proximity) to the venue, and the potential to reserve large blocks of rooms.

Nelson (2006) summarized the benefits to cities of investing in these types of hotels:

- increased tax revenue, in part from room or bed taxes, sales taxes, and property;
- job creation and fostering entrepreneurial activity (lots of value-adding accompanies business events);
- improved quality of life for residents (new entertainment venues and districts, night life, amenities, etc.);
- real estate appreciation.

On the other hand, hotels might object to public subsidies for competitors, especially when room taxes are used for this purpose.

Attracting Business Events

Some destinations have a real advantage because of their location, climate, and accessibility (a combination of comparative and competitive advantages, given our earlier discussion). Others rely on venue development and marketing, including strong relationship building. Cities tend to fall into "leagues" within which they compete, based on a variety of considerations and especially the size and quality of their facilities and services for business events.

How meeting planners and event owners evaluate and select destinations and venues has received a considerable amount of attention from researchers. Key location selection factors have been identified (sources: Crouch & Ritchie, 1998; Opperman & Chon, 1997; Wan, 2011):

- accessibility (travel time considerations; airline schedules; costs and convenience of travel);
- local support (bidding or support groups at the destination; DMO actions and support services; subsidies or grants to attract events);
- extra-event opportunities (local attractions and entertainment; shopping; tours; professional networking);
- accommodation (availability and quality; price and discounts; security; reputation);
- venues and meeting facilities (capacity; layout suitability; ambiance; service standards; security; experience; reputation);

- information and marketing (by the venue and DMO; wireless and other media availability);
- the destination (climate; infrastructure; reputation and image; the immediate setting of the venues; hospitality and friendliness);
- other criteria (known risks; potential to make profits for associations; fit with the corporate or association image/brand; novelty).

Special Considerations for International Business Events

The attraction of international visitors categorically changes the nature of event marketing and services. Krugman and Wright (2007) addressed the special considerations that go into attracting and hosting global meetings and exhibitions. These are some of the key requirements and considerations:

- site inspections are needed in advance (are foreign delegations to make key decisions?);
- passports and visas are required for visitors (some countries are easier to get into);
- shipping and customs (can materials easily enter the country?);
- currency exchange (will exchange rates prevent some from attending?);
- political issues or threats (is there a risk of disruption?);
- language (official languages and the need for interpretation);
- protocol (flags, anthems, seating order, titles, etc.);
- cultural considerations (foods, taboos, customs to honor);
- law (will all contracts be honored?);
- taxes and other regulations (who pays?).

Research Notes on Competitiveness

Jago, L., & Deery, M. (2005). Relationships and factors influencing convention decision-making. *Journal of Convention and Event Tourism, 7*(1), 23–41.

This paper examines the views of key decision-makers in the convention industry as part of a CRC for Sustainable Tourism research project. In particular, it examines the relationships between the main participants, the key factors for a successful convention and the emerging trends within the industry. In order to explore these influences, the research method used structured interviews with international convention associations, professional conference organizers (PCOs) and international delegates. The study revealed that the relationships between the convention bureaus and convention centers were very important. The interviews confirmed the findings of previous studies regarding the key success components for a convention, but also pointed to emerging trends in the convention sector that will impact upon success in the future. These trends included the increasing number of female conference delegates, the increased need for Internet facilities for conventions, and the high priority placed by convention participants on the safety of the convention destination.

Wan, Y. (2011). Assessing the strengths and weaknesses of Macao as an attractive meeting and convention destination: Perspectives of key informants. *Journal of Convention and Event Tourism, 12*(2), 129–151.

Macao's meeting and convention industry has begun to develop in the past few years. The interest in developing this industry is due to the recognition of its significant contribution to the local economy and the belief that it could help to diversify the city's economy and reduce its reliance on the gambling industry. Macao's meeting and convention sector is still at an early stage of development, and research in this area is limited. This article examines the strengths and weaknesses of Macao as an attractive meeting and convention destination by interviewing 16 stakeholders in the industry. Macao's major strengths are identified as sufficient hotel, entertainment, and convention facilities; strong governmental support; a location connecting the European countries and the East; and the passion of local people working in the industry. The weaknesses include the lack of human resources, poor infrastructure and transportation, the lack of attractions, the lack of legal regulation or a government department to coordinate the sector, limited capacity of the border gates, and the absence of an industry base and a poor business climate. Recommendations are proposed to increase the attractiveness and competiveness of the industry.

Sales

Every event venue and most events have sales staff to win business. For a convention center it is primarily a process of bringing in conventions and exhibitions, with local meetings and functions being a secondary market. You cannot allow small, local events to dominate or the tourism benefits will disappear and justification for heavy investment goes with it. For individual events the sales effort is generally aimed at ticketing, or selling to paying customers. There might also be sales efforts directed at potential sponsors, exhibitors, or co-producers.

Just what is being sold? Superficially it is a venue, with some additional services provided, or tickets that give admission to an event. But within the service-dominant logic (discussed earlier), the sales person has to understand much more about what clients and customers need. It is not merely a space that an association needs; it is a package of services (including space) to attract and hold a successful event—with success being defined both by the association and their attendees. If learning and sharing are primary motivators (as they typically are) for people to attend association conventions, then the sales person has to make the case for being able to deliver those benefits. For a sport event or concert, those purchasing tickets are seeking entertainment plus (in many cases) socializing and identity-building opportunities, while participants in amateur competitions need to know in advance that their time and expenses will be rewarded by a high-quality, challenging athletic experience.

In other words, it isn't just about selling, it's about service. And that requires a deep understanding of what the customer or client wants and needs. In a demand-side approach, that is always the starting point. Satisfaction, repeat business, and loyalty are the ultimate measures of success, not just events and tickets sold.

Sales Process

Professional sales people know that it is as much an art as a science. A good salesperson, with strong interpersonal skills and a feel for how to "close the deal," can make a big difference. However, when it comes to selling a convention center or a destination for a sport event it really is more about the team (professionalism), the service proposition (i.e., ability and willingness to meet needs), and the details (including value adding). Below are the key steps in this permanent process of sales.

>   **Organization and staffing:** Most event venues have their own sales team, but it is possible to outsource this work. Knowledge of the industry and clients is important, but so too is training and experience, the right personality and demeanor. Many salespeople in the business (whether working for a hotel, arena, or conference center) are on some kind of salary plus incentive system. The rewards might be a commission (i.e., a fixed or progressive percentages of sales) or bonuses for outstanding performance.

Developing and approaching prospects: Sales people get used to making "cold calls," but there has to be a starting point—typically in the marketing plan where target areas and segments are specified. Qualified leads might be generated by the DMO and passed on to appropriate hotels or other venues. "Qualification" means there is a reasonable fit between the event and the supplier. The National Association of Sports Commissions provides a starting point for sport bidding (www.sportscommissions.org):

Event Owner Directory

Are you looking for new events to bring to your community? Save time researching and gathering contact information for event owners by using the event owner directory, a valuable member resource and time-saving tool. An instant lead sheet with more than 900 unique event owner organization contacts listed, members can search and sort the directory.

Direct marketing will consist of sending material to specific people, and sending the sales force to meet decision makers, including professional meeting planners.

Engagement and relationship building: Staff must understand what potential clients need and how their problems can be solved, including how they measure ROI. In order to effectively provide necessary services and communicate the value proposition background research might be required. It is typical for sales staff to be assigned to particular areas and segments in order to ensure that there is knowledge and empathy before contacts are made. In DMOs it is common to separate the leisure and business event markets, while sport events are often pursued by dedicated sport commissions. The corporate and association markets are different enough to justify separate marketing and sales approaches. In a demand-side strategy, the more one learns about target segments, the better the engagement will be. Once it is known that a venue, city, or DMO is proactive with events, it is likely that permanent relationships can be established with key event owners, corporations, and associations. In fact, events might be brought to the destination because of its reputation.

Responding to requests for proposals: all venues should be fully approachable, and their services searchable, online. This example from Visit Denver is typical (www.denver.org):

Thank you for your interest in having your conference in Denver, the Mile High City. To assist you in finding a suitable location for your meeting or convention we have three quick and easy options to choose from: Fill out the form below with your meeting specifications. If you have your own RFP (request for proposal) click "Upload your RFP" to attach and send. Or contact us . . .

Site visits and familiarization tours: Conducted by sales staff, or others who specialize in impressing visitors; many stakeholders can be involved, including transport, accommodations, attractions, entertainment, and convention centers in putting together a good tour.

Close the sale: negotiation might be required, in which case price and extras will be the hot topics. Value adding at this stage might sway the client. Detailed contracts are absolutely necessary, covering such matters as room rates, venue fees, services provided, and how and when rooms must be booked.

Retention (customer loyalty): Satisfied customers might become loyal clients, and this will generally depend on delivery of promised ROI. That makes it essential to promise only what can be delivered, and to solve all the client's problems. Again, the venue or DMO is providing service, not merely a place to hold an event.

An Online Presence

The information and services available online are now a critical part of the sales process. Here are examples from Visit Denver's website, highlighting web pages aimed at distinct user groups.

MEETING PLANNERS
PLAN YOUR DENVER MEETING: Denver prides itself on going the extra mile for meeting and event planners. In fact, as the city's official marketing arm, visit denver, The Convention & Visitors Bureau, has a full-time, award-winning staff prepared to assist with just about anything you need in planning your corporate events, conferences or convention.

TRAVEL PROFESSIONAL RESOURCES
The Tourism Staff at visit denver works directly with you, the travel trade, to promote Denver worldwide. Partnerships with airlines, travel agents, tour wholesalers and trade organizations are part of our daily business. We can assists domestic and international travel planners in developing leisure programs for individuals and groups, incentive travel programs and student and youth tour opportunities.

GET MARRIED IN DENVER
Whether you're a Colorado native or are planning your dream Denver wedding from 3,000 miles away, this website (and the knowledgeable Bureau staff) can assist you with a wide array of free Denver wedding planning services. Still undecided if a Rocky Mountain wedding is right for you? These 10 reasons to get married in Denver will convince you.

SMALL GROUPS & REUNIONS
visit denver employs a team of specialists in its Tourism Department who can provide you with information and assistance, free of charge, as you plan your trip. From girlfriend getaways and student travel to church groups and reunions, you will find a multitude of tools online that are designed to save you time and money.

In sales, the customers make up their own minds about whether or not your venue offers what they need at the right price. That means they need facts, easy to access and compare, about the facility and the services offered, then about prices and options. Comparisons are the norm, unless of course there is a Unique Selling Proposition (UPS) that is so compelling that alternatives are simply not considered. Is that USP your location? Design? Reputation?

Leveraging and Delegate Boosting

Organizers of events as well as the hosting venues and destination want to optimize (not necessarily maximize) attendance, and to leverage the event with a view to higher yield per attendee. Organizers have a break-even point to surpass, and destinations want longer stays with higher spending. Various techniques to achieve these objectives are often referred to as delegate boosting and leveraging, although we really need to distinguish between methods for boosting attendance and for boosting yield per visitor. The following Expert Opinion by Dr. Rob Davidson covers the expenditure of business visitors to the UK and what can be done to boost the yield.

Expert Opinion on Leveraging Tourism Benefits of Business Events (by Dr. Rob Davidson, University of Greenwich Senior Lecturer, Events Management, Department of Marketing, Events and Tourism)

Research into incremental expenditure by business visitors in the UK shows that currently:

- 17% of conference delegates are accompanied by a guest who is not a delegate.
- Delegates spend on average an extra 0.8 nights at the destination, before or after the business event they are attending, although this figure is higher for those attending association and academic conferences.
- 39% of delegates claim that they would be likely to return to the destination of the conference for a holiday or short break.

But, although these indirect benefits already represent considerable incremental spending for UK businesses, some of our competitor destinations are also achieving great success at reaping the full benefits of business visitors. For example:

- Conference visitors to France spend on average 4.5 days in that country, exactly 1 day longer than delegates to conferences in the UK.
- 42% of delegates attending conferences in Sydney are accompanied by one or more guests, compared to 17% for the UK.
- Foreign business visitors to Paris spend on average £170 per trip on shopping for clothes and gifts.
- 20% of foreign conference visitors to Germany combine the visit to the event with a holiday, meaning that half a million international visitors to conferences in Germany also become holidaymakers in that country.

Improving our own take-up of leisure opportunities by business visitors has the potential to create enormous additional benefits:

- If an additional 10% of the annual 6.8 million business visitors to Britain from overseas were to extend their visit by just 1 day for leisure purposes, then an estimated £50 million more would be earned on accommodation, food and drink, entertainment, and shopping.
- This represents an extra 1,650 jobs on top of those already created by business tourism.
- Add to this the opportunities for encouraging domestic business visitors to spend more time—and money—at their destinations, and the potential benefits to British businesses look even more attractive.

How to give early information, such as in these examples:

- Philadelphia Convention Bureau's motto is "Come early, stay late." They arrange for a brochure promoting the leisure, cultural, and gastronomic attractions of their city to be sent out to every convention delegate with the initial invitation to attend the event. The information in the brochure is tailored to the specific leisure interests of the delegates and carries the name and logo of the association. A reply-paid card in the brochure, which asks if delegates are bringing guests and/or extending their trips, is used to request further tourist information.
- The year before any association's conference is due to be hosted in Glasgow, the Glasgow Convention Bureau sends a member of staff to wherever the association

is holding its conference that year, to set up a mini Trade and Investment Congress promoting Scotland's attractions and pre-/postconference tours.

How to sell the destination:

- In bid documents, Marketing Manchester places considerable emphasis on the options for pre- and postconference tours, selling the destination as a gateway to more classic tourist destinations such as the Lake District, the Cotswolds, and Stratford-Upon-Avon. They also include a section on such tours in any presentations they make to organizing committees.
- Familiarization trips and site inspections provide Convention Bureaus and suppliers further opportunities to impress key decision makers. Again, Marketing Manchester makes full use of these occasions to demonstrate how Manchester's location makes it very easy to reach some of the UK's most beautiful countryside and heritage.

How to package attractive offers:

- The New York City Convention and Visitors Bureau operates a "Convention Delegates Pass Program" in association with American Express, offering discounts and promotional offers at local restaurants, attractions, theatres, and shops to delegates who present their conference name badge and redeemable coupon and pay with an American Express card. Details of the scheme and participating businesses can be sent to delegates in advance, posted on the conference website, or included in registration packs.
- The Detroit Convention and Visitors Bureau's "Let Us Entertain You" scheme provides conference delegates in that city with a book of coupons offering discounts at local shops and attractions, on car hire, and on entrance to special events, if used at weekends. By tracking the number of coupons used in this way, Detroit is able to estimate the volume of business visitors extending their trips over the weekend.

Case Study: Visit Denver (www.visitdenver.com)

Introduction

Denver has achieved the reputation of being an events city that competes well beyond its size, with an extraordinary array of professional sports, a vibrant arts and festival scene, and a major convention center being key elements in its event tourism positioning. Lonely Planet in 2011 named Denver as the sixth best place to visit in the US, and *The Globe and Mail* (a major Canadian newspaper) has named Denver as the best destination for major conventions in the world.

In this case study Denver as an arts-, sports-, and events-rich city is profiled, then details are provided on the organization and work of the DMO, Visit Denver, in the events tourism sector.

Specifics are provided on Visit Denver as an event owner/producer of events, the Colorado Convention Centre and Denver as a major league convention destination, sales and promotions, event impacts within the overall tourism context, and the roles of events in countering seasonality and in branding of the city and state.

An Overview of Events in Denver

Denver Arts

Today, Metro Denver collects and distributes more public money for the arts than any other city on a per capita basis. Through the unique Scientific & Cultural Facilities District, residents in the seven-county Denver metro area have voted three times to approve a

1/10 of a cent sales tax increase for the arts. More than $42 million was collected in 2007 and distributed to 300 arts and cultural organizations. Some highlights are:

- Denver opened three new art museums in a short span. The new Hamilton Building at the Denver Art Museum opened in 2006 to rave reviews. It is renown architect Daniel Libeskind's first building in the US. The new building doubles the size of the museum and gives it the space to host any touring art show that has ever been organized. The $90 million cost was approved by Denver voters.
- Denver has a growing reputation for its collection of art galleries in trendy neighborhoods that include more than 30 art galleries in the ArtsDistrict on Santa Fe; the hip galleries of Rhino (River North); the Golden Triangle Museum District; LoDo (short for Lower Downtown) and Cherry Creek.
- The Denver Performing Arts Complex is the second largest arts center in the nation with 10 venues that seat 10,000 people for Tony Award-winning theater, Broadway road shows (*The Little Mermaid* premiered in Denver in 2007), dance, opera, and symphony. The complex includes a voice research laboratory, acting school, and video production company. Original productions have moved on to successful runs in New York and London.
- The new $90 million Ellie Caulkins Opera House opened in 2006 as part of the Denver Performing Arts Complex and is one of only three in the nation to feature in-seat translation devices.
- The Denver Theatre District has transformed 14th Street in the blocks around the Denver Performing Arts Complex with electronic signage, wider sidewalks, and public art.
- Denver's Red Rocks Amphitheatre won so often as the nation's top outdoor concert venue that it was removed from competition and the award was renamed "The Red Rocks Award." The spectacular 9,000-seat amphitheater has hosted everyone from the Beatles to top symphony orchestras.
- Denver is known as a center for live music with venues that include the legendary Fillmore, the Ogden, and Bluebird, as well numerous jazz clubs and Coors Amphitheatre.

Arts Events

- As a recognition of Denver's increasing role as a cultural center, the American Association of Museums Annual Meeting and Museum Expo was held in Denver in 2008, attracting an estimated 15,000 museum professional and volunteer members and 3,000 institutional members.
- The City of Denver hosted The Biennial of the Americas in 2010, a 2-month long curated celebration of contemporary art from throughout North America. It is planned again for 2013.
- The Cherry Creek Arts Festival is consistently ranked as the largest outdoor-juried arts event in the country and attracts more than 300,000 people every July 4th weekend.
- Denver hosted its first Denver Arts Week in 2007 and its fourth Doors Open Denver in 2008, allowing admission to more than 70 architectural treasures in the city.

Visit Denver called 2010 a "year of blockbuster events," featuring an unprecedented number of shows including Body Worlds, Denver Day of Rock, King Tut, Moore in the Gardens, and the Biennial of the Americas. These were promoted through a $2.5 million integrated marketing campaign, with the theme "Denver's Blockbuster Summer," that generated 400 million impressions through newspaper and magazine ads, radio, billboards, direct mail, publicity, e-blasts, and Internet promotions.

Denver as a Sports Capital

Denver is the only US city besides Philadelphia to have seven professional sports teams [Denver Broncos (NFL); Colorado Rockies (MLB); Colorado Mammoth (NLL); Colorado Avalanche (NHL); Colorado Rapids (MLS); Denver Nuggets (NBA); Denver Outlaws (MLL)], and Denver has a record six new sports stadiums. Denver was recognized by *Sporting News* in 1997 as the #1 Sports City in America and by *Sports Business Journal* in 2004 as the #1 Sports City in America for Fan Loyalty.

Denver as a Convention Destination (www.denverconvention.com)

The Colorado Convention Center is owned and operated by the Division of Theatres and Arenas, a City and County of Denver agency charged with managing and maintaining the City's cultural and public assembly facilities. Theatres and Arenas also oversees the Denver Performing Arts Complex, Red Rocks Amphitheatre, and the Denver Coliseum.

The Colorado Convention Center doubled in size at the completion of a $310 million expansion in 2004. Now the eighth largest public meeting facility west of the Mississippi, the venue began implementing sustainable practices following the expansion and now boasts a range of environmentally friendly policies aimed at increasing energy efficiency,

Photo 7.2. Denver, Live Concert in Civic Center Park
(Credit: photo courtesy of Steve Crecelius and Visit Denver).

Photo 7.3. Denver, Ellie Caulkins Opera House
(Credit: photo courtesy of Steve Crecelius and Visit Denver).

Photo 7.4. Denver, the Colorado Rockies compete at Coors Field
(Credit: photo courtesy of Rich Grant and Visit Denver).

Photo 7.5. Denver, the Colorado Convention Center
(Credit: photo courtesy of Scott Dressler-Martin and Visit Denver).

conserving water, reducing waste, and assisting meeting and event planners with hosting carbon-neutral gatherings. *Colorado Meetings and Events* magazine recently honored the venue with a Reader's Choice Best-Of Award for "Green Meeting Facility."

The website for Meeting Planning (www.visitdenver.com/conventions) was completely rebuilt in 2011, with input from professional meeting planners representing different segments of the industry. Planners are constantly searching for information and want it readily available: meeting facilities, hotels, venues, and much more. Some of the contents:

- Requests for Proposals (RFP): meeting planners can submit their own meeting details or attach documents. The RFP requests the convention center to submit a bid for a specific planned event.
- Colorado Convention Center details: floor plans, exhibit halls, ballrooms, theater.
- Attendance-boosting and promotional tools, including a Digital Marketing Kit that allows meeting planners to download graphic files of material that can be customized for their events.
- Green Meeting Resources: a list of green venues and two carbon calculators (for meeting impact and travel impact); a PDF can be downloaded on Sustainable Events, with case studies.
- Why Denver? This section aims to sell the city and its attractions.

Visitor Numbers and Trends

Visit Denver numbers show that 2010 was the second best convention year in Denver's history with 75 conventions in the Colorado Convention Center and 423 other meetings in 2010, for a total of 371,003 delegates with an economic impact of $652 million. CEO and president Richard Scharf commented: "The increase in marketable visitors in 2010 shows the importance of tourism marketing, and the impact that blockbuster events can have on the city's economy."

In 2010, Denver had a total of 12.7 million overnight visitors, according to Longwoods International (Visit Denver Press Release, June 11, 2011). The study, commissioned by Visit Denver, found that in 2010, metro Denver visitors spent $3 billion, while supporting nearly 50,000 jobs. A breakdown of all visitor spending reveals that accommodation is the biggest (29%), followed by eating/drinking (26%), transportation (20%), retail (16%), and recreation at 9%. "While business visitors and business spending mirrored a national decline, Denver did see an increase in convention business," according to Longwoods.

The Metropoll survey of corporate and association meeting planners is sponsored by 80 US cities and conducted every 2 years. Denver ranked in the top 10 on three of four reputation criteria for city meeting facilities: new or expanded convention center, excellent hotel meeting facilities, and being good for large trade shows. Of 21 measures of reputation specifically for the convention center, Denver ranked in the top five on 13 items including first in helpful staff, second in having a hotel adjacent to the center, and second on being a green-certified facility.

Profile of Visit Denver

In 1908, Denver hosted the Democratic National Convention. Recognizing the economic benefit that came from this meeting, some farsighted businessmen created a new agency that would come to be called Visit Denver.

Visit Denver is a private, nonprofit trade association that is responsible for marketing metro Denver as a convention and leisure destination. The Bureau is contracted by the City and County of Denver to act as the official marketing agency for Denver. It is governed by a board of directors, and employs a staff of more than 60 professionals.

Visit Denver is funded from both private (membership, advertising, and sponsorship) and public sources (voter-approved lodging tax). In 2010, the Bureau had a budget of $16.3 million, which was derived from 2.75% of the lodger's tax in the City and County of Denver, from advertising and private fundraising, and from the membership fees the Bureau collects from its nearly 1,200 business members.

The Convention & Visitors Bureau Mission is: *To bring conventions and leisure visitors to Denver for the economic benefit of the City, the community and our membership.*

The Bureau uses a sophisticated integrated marketing approach to sell Denver as a travel destination, which includes direct sales, sales blitzes and telemarketing, advertising and direct mail, tourism and convention industry trade shows, Internet promotions, e-mail blasts, websites, podcasts, and e-newsletters, visitor guides and brochures, public relations and press tours, client familiarization tours and site inspections, and visitor information centers.

Organization

Of particular interest are the following units, with a description of their roles:

   Tourism: Aims to attract leisure segments; attend tradeshows, conduct sales missions, work with travel companies to increase the number of offering Denver as a destination.
   Marketing: Collaborates with the convention department in creating an integrated marketing campaign.
   Communications: Advertising; generate free publicity in travel publications as well as websites.

Visitor Information Centers: almost 500,000 people received assistance at one of the centers located on the downtown mall, airport, and convention center.

Housing: Made 36,421 hotel reservations for 10 groups in 2010.

Convention Services Department: Conducts site visits and provides services to events held in the city; provides business referrals to members.

The Convention Department: This unit (see the meeting planning section at visitdenver.com) markets Denver as a meetings destination and is contracted by the City and County of Denver to book the Colorado Convention Center and area hotels for national meetings, conventions, and tradeshows. Once a meeting is booked, the Convention Services Department and Housing Bureau work with meeting planners to help them produce events.

Convention sales staff (including sales offices in Washington, DC, and Chicago) undertook the following:

- Participated in over 40 convention-industry trade shows.
- Leads: over 1,000 leads for individual hotel meetings were sent to Visit Denver member hotel businesses in 2010.
- Client events: in 2010 top prospective meeting planners were hosted in Washington, DC, New York, and Chicago, as well as local planners in the Denver area.
- Site visits: 187 meeting planner site visits were hosted in 2010, bringing hundreds of meeting planners to Denver.
- Convention Advisory Board: The board met twice in 2010 and brought 20 of the industry's leading experts to Denver to advise the Bureau on sales and marketing.
- Confirmed Bookings: For 2011 and beyond there were 178 confirmed citywide conventions for the convention center; these should attract nearly 1 million delegates and generate an estimated economic impact of $2 billion.

Visit Denver's Own Events

November to March is the traditional slow time for meetings business, and for room bookings in hotels, so special events and promotions are an attempt to reduce seasonality of demand. Visit Denver has been very proactive in combating this problem, with the following highlights:

Mile High Holidays (www.MileHighHolidays.com) is an annual collaborative marketing campaign to attract visitors before and over the winter holiday season. Running from late November through January, the campaign includes a dedicated website, Internet promotions, radio and television ads, outdoor boards, RTD ads, and newspaper inserts, at a cost of about $500,000. Media partnerships and in-kind services provide substantial additional value. Events held at this time benefit from the campaign. Visitors can watch the parade of Lights, attend the National Western Stock Show & Rodeo, take in a theatrical performance of The Christmas Carol, or watch professional basketball and hockey. Hotels offer special rates and New Year's Eve packages.

Denver Arts Week (www.DenverArtsWeek.com). The fifth annual Denver Arts week was held November 4–12, 2011. Organized by Visit Denver, it is described as "a nine-day celebration of all things art in the Mile High City with more than 300 arts-related events at more than 170 art galleries, museums, theaters and concert halls, and even restaurants." Many of the events are free, others offered at discounts.

Denver Restaurant Week (www.DenverRestaurantWeek.com). Denver Restaurant Week, created by Visit Denver in 2005, is a 2-week celebration of the culinary scene. In 2011 there were 303 participating restaurants offering fixed-price, multicourse dinners; over 360,000 meals were served, up 7% over the previous year. Website traffic increased 54% to 567,243 visits and 8 million page views. While every major American city has a similar event, Denver boasts of being the largest in terms of participating restaurants. Visit Denver believes that tourism marketing begins with local awareness, hence it is important to get residents interested and involved in fine dining.

Denver Beer Fest (www.DenverBeerFest.com). The third annual Denver Beer Fest was held September 23 to October 1, 2011, offering 9 days of beer-centric events. The festival was expected to generate more than 150 events from "Meet the Brewer Nights" and beer-paired dinners to firkin tappings and beer competitions. Many of the events were previewed on the newly launched website, which also has information on brewery tours, Denver's beer history, and features brewer profiles from craft breweries located throughout the state. Denver Beer Fest is presented by Visit Denver, in partnership this year with Westword and the Colorado Brewers Guild. "Just like fine dining, beer has become part of Denver's tourism brand," states Richard Scharf, president and CEO of Visit Denver. "Denver brews more beer than any other city, is home to the largest single brewing site in the world—Coors Brewery—and hosts the annual Great American Beer Festival (GABF), which has been declared the largest beer tasting event in the world," Scharf said. It was to welcome GABF that Denver Beer Fest was created. "We knew that GABF was attracting some of the world's top craft beer writers and aficionados, and we wanted to give them opportunities to sample Denver's beer scene, in addition to tasting all the American beers available at GABF," Scharf said. With GABF selling out 11 weeks early, Denver Beer Fest has given locals another opportunity to be involved in the city's beer culture. Some of the events include:

- Rare Beer Tastings
- Meet the Brewer Nights
- Firkin nights (a cask conditioned beer will be tapped and drained until it is gone)
- Tap Takeovers (a brewery takes over all the taps at a bar or restaurant)
- Beer-Paired Dinners (a restaurant works with the brewery and has a different course paired with a different beer in a fixed-price dinner)
- Beer Competitions (beers are paired off against each other, often with the bar patrons voting for their favorites, until there is one winner)
- Beer Education (special programs or lectures that discuss different aspects of beer tasting or brewing)
- Pub Crawls (two or more bars work together on a pub crawl, or beer walking tour, or beer cruiser bike night)
- Brewery Tours (special theme tours of breweries)
- Beer Games (quizzes, contests, special events)
- Music (music events that take place during Denver Beer Fest and can be tied into it)

Research and Evaluation

Visit Denver press release, Jan. 27, 2011:

"The Snow Show, promoted as the world's largest snow-sports tradeshow, attracts 19,000 delegates over 4 days. Sport retailers, manufacturers, and decision-makers meet at the Colorado Convention Center and generate an estimated $30 million in spending throughout the metro Denver region. An eleven-year deal to host the event began in 2010 and is the largest convention booking ever for the city.

Visit Denver CEO and president Richard Scharf said "This week's Mile High SnowFest, Jan.25-30, which started with Big Air and will run through this weekend with special events throughout downtown, is designed to welcome the Snow Show delegates and get local residents involved in the celebration of Denver as a snow sports capital."

Colorado Governor John Hickenlooper stated: "We want to enlist the 19,000 international delegates at his show to help us brand Colorado as the snow sports capital of the world—a state that welcomes innovation and new investment, offers an unmatched snow sports product, and leads the world in the manufacturing and sales for snow sports equipment."

Summary and Study Guide

Business event tourism is very well established in most cities and destinations. Dedicated convention/exhibition centers and convention bureaus sell venues, alongside numerous hotels, resorts, and other venues, while DMOs stress the attraction of major business events. In this chapter we covered the two main components, meetings and conventions (divided into association and corporate segments) and exhibitions (trade and consumer shows). Other types of events considered were World's Fairs and State Fairs.

Motivations to hold and attend business events were examined, and their impacts.

Expert input from Xin Jin and Karin Weber gave us a look at the exhibition industry in China, and it is noteworthy that China has been investing hugely in Event Tourism infrastructure, bidding, and mega-events. Some cities, like Guangzhou, are focused on exhibitions for competitive advantage.

Attracting business events is partly a sales process, which has been outlined, and partly a matter of ensuring the destination and its venues meet the specifications and expectations of clients and their meeting planners. Factors shaping competitive advantage were given, and it is also useful to look again at the earlier section on bidding, and comparative/competitive advantages for a fuller picture. Obviously venues are required, and some of the issues surrounding convention and exhibition centers (and related hotels) have been explored. Also, delegate boosting and leveraging were examined, with special input from Rob Davidson.

The case study of Visit Denver provides details on how a CVB operates in the Event Tourism sector, with emphasis on why and how it produces its own events. Compare its approach to that of the other cities, states, and countries profiled in this book.

Study Questions

- What are the main differences between the corporate and association segments of the meetings and conventions market?
- Do business events have a future? Why can't virtuality replace such events? Where do technological advances fit into this picture?
- Are all trip motivations for business events extrinsic in nature? How are business event experiences often both leisure and work?

- What are the main variables influencing the economic impacts of business events?
- Are there non-economic benefits to hosting business events? How can they be measured?
- In the exhibition industry, what are the relative advantages and disadvantages of hosting trade and consumer shows, World's Fairs and State Fairs?
- Why has China pursued the exhibition market?
- What unique planning and marketing considerations are associated with the building and operation of convention and exhibition centers? Explain justifications for public sector investment; explain why convention hotels are also needed.
- What do meeting planners look for in a destination and a venue for locating their business events?
- How can cities and destinations increase their competitiveness for attracting international business events?
- Specify the components of a plan to leverage business events for maximum local value; include "boosting" tactics.
- In what ways are business event sales a "service value proposition"? What is the sales process?
- What lessons are revealed about business event tourism from the Visit Denver case study? Why do they create their own events?

Additional Readings

- *Convention Tourism: International Research and Industry Perspectives* (Weber & Kaye, 2002).
- *The Business of Tourism* (Davidson, Holloway, & Humphreys, 2009).
- *Marketing Destinations and Venues for Conferences, Conventions and Business Events* (Davidson & Rogers, 2006).
- *Business Travel: Conferences, Incentive Travel, Exhibitions, Corporate Hospitality and Corporate Travel* (Davidson & Cope, 2003).

Chapter 8

Festivals, Arts, and Entertainment

Learning Objectives

Upon completion of this chapter the student should understand and be able to explain the following:

1. Three discourses on festivals and tourism.
2. Themes in festival tourism research (including authenticity and commodification).
3. Festivals, culture, and urban policy.
4. Motivation to attend festivals and cultural celebrations.
5. Patterns and trends in festival-related travel.
6. Impacts of festival tourism.
7. Greening of festivals; sustainability.
8. Marketing of festivals as destination events.
9. Entertainment events as tourist attractions.
10. Music events as attractions.
11. Other forms of entertainment events (e.g., reenactments; pilgrimage; touring exhibitions).
12. Private events (e.g., reunions, weddings).

Introduction

Many festivals and cultural celebrations spring organically from the needs and desires of communities and interest groups, with little or no desire to be tourist attractions. These wishes should always be respected. But there are good reasons for becoming a tourist attraction and many cultural events have realized their potential in this marketplace. Furthermore, in the age of "festivalization," destinations and cities have been aggressively establishing festivals as tourist attractions and promoting cultural tourism in general, both through creating and marketing festivals, and building iconic cultural buildings such as museums, galleries, theaters, and heritage-themed visitor centers. Much of this impressive investment is directly linked to urban renewal, economic revitalization (in a deindustrializing world), and repositioning (or branding) to place cities and regions squarely into the experience economy.

In large part we are speaking of a subset of cultural tourism. The World Tourism Organization defines cultural tourism as "covering all aspects of travel whereby people learn about each other's way of life and thought." Much of cultural tourism focuses on historic sites and other heritage attractions, many of which produce interpretive events. Another integral dimension of cultural tourism is all forms of cultural festivals and celebrations that give visitors access to local traditions and lifestyles. A third major component is that of performing and visual arts, with theaters, museums, and galleries being the pertinent objects of tourist interest. Native or aboriginal tourism fits into the cultural tourism definition, encompassing events like Pow Wows in North America, or Maori entertainment in New Zealand. Even sports can be considered as a cultural product, especially when combined with festival programming.

This chapter commences with a review of the literature on festivals and tourism, highlighting the main themes and issues. Motivations to attend and travel to festivals and other cultural celebrations are examined, and summaries of several large-scale surveys are employed to shed light on festival tourism patterns and preferences. Impacts are then considered. The entertainment industry is next reviewed, with emphasis on music, touring shows, and theater, followed by short profiles of pilgrimage, reunions, reenactments, and weddings.

Also in this chapter is a profile of what Northern Ireland and Belfast are doing in the realm of cultural tourism and festivals, related to repositioning and urban renewal, and a major case study of the Woodford Festival in Australia—positioned as a green event. A summary of the major Edinburgh Festivals Impact Study provides details from a triple bottom line perspective.

Themes and Research on Festivals and Tourism

Previous reviews of the literature (e.g., Formica, 1998) plus my own review (see the article Festival Studies, Getz, 2011) led to identification and description of three major discourses within festival studies, each of which has a different perspective on festival tourism.

Discourse on the Roles, Meanings, and Impacts of Festivals in Society and Culture

Festivals in society and culture, pertaining to their roles, meanings, and impacts, is the oldest and best developed discourse. The literature review identified the following classical themes within this discourse: myth, ritual, and symbolism; ceremony and cele-bration; spectacle; communitas; host–guest interactions (and the role of the stranger); liminality, the carnivalesque, and festivity; authenticity and commodification; pilgrimage; and a considerable amount of political debate over impacts and meanings. There are landmark works by Van Gennep (1909/1960), Turner (1969, 1974, 1982), Geertz (1973), Abrahams (1987), Falassi (1987), and Manning (1983). Numerous contemporary studies of specific cultural celebrations have been published in literature outside events and tourism (e.g., Cavalcanti, 2001). Two recent books make explicit connections between tourism and the cultural dimensions of festivals: Long and Robinson (2004) and Picard and Robinson (2006a).

Recently, scholars within and outside the traditional disciplines have been examining festivals with regard to an increasing variety of issues: their roles in establishing place and group identity; the social and cultural impacts of festivals and festival tourism; creation of social and cultural capital through festival production; fostering the arts and preserving traditions; and a variety of personal outcomes from participation in festivals, including learning, acquired social and cultural capital, and healthfulness. The value and worth of festivals to society and culture has been addressed, as well as the imputed need for festivity, but research on these important issues has been slim. Festivals are being examined in the context of sustainability, corporate social responsibility, and as permanent institutions.

Discourse on Festival Tourism

"Festival tourism" is an important element in "event tourism," so much so that the term "festivalization" has been coined to suggest an overcommodification of festivals exploited by tourism and place marketers (see, e.g., Quinn, 2006; Richards, 2007). Indeed, a marked trend toward treating festivals as commodities has emerged. In this approach, drawing heavily upon consumer behavior and other marketing concepts, motivations for attending festivals have been studied at length, and more recently the links between quality, satisfaction, and behavior or future intentions have been modeled (e.g., Hede, Jago, & Deery, 2004).

The roles of festivals in tourism include attracting tourists (to specific places, and to overcome seasonality), contributing to place marketing (including image formation and destination branding), animating attractions and places, and acting as catalysts for other forms of development. Dominating this discourse has been the assessment of economic impacts of festivals and festival tourism, planning and marketing festival tourism at the destination level, and studies of festival tourism motivation and various segmentation approaches. The negative impacts of festivals and festival tourism is a more recent line of research.

Festival tourism is essentially instrumentalist, treating festivals as tools in tourism and economic development, or in place marketing and the selling of attractions and venues. Although arts and tourism linkages have been advocated by many (e.g., Tighe, 1985, 1986), and certainly exist, with regard to festivals, concerts, and staged performances, there will always remain tension between these sectors.

Discourse on Festival Management

Much of the literature pertaining to event tourism is of direct interest to festival managers, especially the line of research concerning consumer motivation and evaluation. As well, the literature on event and festival impacts is somewhat pertinent, to the extent that managers might want to know how assessments are conducted and what they contribute to strategic planning. Event and festival management is dominated by generic management concepts and methods (covering the full range of management functions, but especially marketing).

Major Themes in Festival Tourism

The themes discussed in this section all have some relevance to Event Tourism in general, but are particularly well developed in the festival-specific literature.

Political Discourse on the Meanings and Effects of Festivals

In one school of thought, festivals and rituals bind people together in communities and cultures (Durkheim, 1965), while in another they reflect and encourage disagreement and even disputation of the meanings and impacts of events. An early paper by Lavenda (1980) assessed the political evolution of the Caracas (Venezuela) Carnival, including power relationships and the role of political elites. Bankston and Henry (2000) looked at how Cajun Festivals in Louisiana are "invented traditions" that contributed to Cajun identity revival since the 1960s. Gotham (2005) theorized on "urban spectacles" highlighting the conflicts over meanings as well as the irrationalities and contradictions of the spectacularization of local cultures. P. Jackson (1992) explicitly dealt with the politics of carnivals. Waterman (1998, 2004) examined the cultural politics of arts festivals, specifically noting how place marketing influences lead to "safe art forms" and how many arts festivals are dominated by cultural elite.

Authenticity and Commodification

Greenwood's (1972) study of a Basque festival from an anthropological perspective lamented the negative influence of tourism on authentic cultural celebrations. The authenticity of events, their social-cultural impacts, and effects of tourism on events remain enduring themes. MacCannell (1976) is almost always cited in discussion of tourism authenticity. In another early study, Buck (1977) advocated staged tourist attractions, such as festivals, for protecting vulnerable cultural groups.

E. Cohen (1988) addressed commodification and staged authenticity in the context of tourism, and whether tourists could have authentic experiences. He argued that authenticity is negotiable and depends on the visitor's desires. Emergent authenticity occurs when new cultural developments (like festivals) acquire the "patina of authenticity over time." The article is not explicitly about festivals but is highly relevant. In a later article, E. Cohen (2007) addressed the authenticity of a mythical event in Thailand.

A few authors have examined the authenticity of ethnic festivals, including Hinch and Delamere (1993) on Canadian native festivals that served as tourist attractions. Xie (2003) studied traditional ethnic performances in Hainan, China in terms of the relationship between commodification and authenticity. Chhabra, Healy, and Sills (2003) and Chhabra (2005) addressed authenticity issues by reference to goods sold at a festival and the perceptions of visitors. Müller and Pettersson (2006) focused on a Sami festival in Sweden, while Neuenfeldt (1995) took a sociological approach to the study of an aboriginal festival in Australia, viewing the performance as social text.

Community, Culture, Place Identity, and Attachment

Festivals are connected to cultures and to places, giving each identity and helping bind people to their communities. Similarly, festivals and other planned events can foster and reinforce group identity. De Bres and Davis (2001) determined that events held as part of the Rollin' Down the River festival led to positive self-identification for local communities. Derrett (2003) argued that community-based festivals in New South Wales, Australia demonstrate a community's sense of community and place. Elias-Varotsis (2006) considered the effects of festivals on the cultural identity of spaces.

Communitas, Social Cohesion, and Sociability

"Communitas," as used by Victor Turner, refers to intense feelings of belonging and sharing among equals, as in pilgrimage or festival experiences. Research supports the existence and importance of communitas at planned events. Costa (2002) described "festive sociability" at the Fire Festival in Valencia, Spain as being central to the transmission of tradition. Matheson (2005) discussed festivals and sociability in the context of a Celtic music festival. The backstage space is the realm of authentic experiences and communitas. Hannam and Halewood (2006) determined that Viking-themed festivals gave participants as sense of identity and reflected an authentic way of life. As mentioned elsewhere, communitas is a vital part of Iconic events and any event targeted at special interest groups or social worlds.

Festivity, Liminality, and the Carnivalesque

"Liminality," or the temporary state of being apart from the mundane (as in a ritual, travel or event experience), is an enduring theme, with Turner as the greatest inspiration. It is also useful to examine the differences between sacred and profane experiences, with religious rites and rituals on the one hand and the social/behavioral inversions and revelry of carnival on the other extreme. Scholars often refer to the writings of Bakhtin (1984) when discussing the "carnivalesque." A. Cohen (1982) discussed the symbolic structure of the carnival and its potential for generating political positions and statements. Jamieson (2004) examined how festivity permeates Edinburgh, producing spaces and identities. Anderton (2008) explored the V Festival in Britain, which has to varying degrees "commodified, modernized, or subverted" the counterculture and carnivalesque imagery and meanings associated with outdoor rock and pop music festivals.

Rites and Rituals; Religion

From the early writings of Van Gennep (1909) on *rites de passage*, anthropologists have been fascinated by the connection between ritual and festivity, much of which has religious or at least spiritually symbolic significance. Turner (e.g., 1974) has probably had the greatest influence in a classical sense, whereas Graburn (1983) and others have looked at ritualistic behavior in a tourism context, citing festivals as examples. Parsons (2006) studied the contemporary, "invented-tradition" festival of Saint Ansano in Sienna Italy, which is based on long-established rituals. Kaplan (2008) wrote about the rituals and politics associated with a very old Ethiopian festival.

Myths and Symbols

Myths and symbols are embedded in traditional festivals, whereas in modern societies it is sometimes necessary or desirable to invent myths or symbolism with political, religious, or other meanings. Manning (1978) evaluated Carnival in Antigua regarding its symbolism related to nationalism and its commodification as a tourist attraction. Quinn's (2003) study of the Wexford Festival Opera in Ireland analyzed symbolic practices and meanings associated with the festival, including myth making.

Pilgrimage

Some festivals attract pilgrims, and others are an essential part of pilgrimage (in a religious or spiritual sense) to holy places. Ahmed (1992) studied the Hajj in terms of its tourism importance and organizational challenges. Díaz-Barriga (2003) studied a pilgrimage festival in Bolivia, which has become a point for political controversy and contested meaning. Nolan and Nolan (1992) studied religious sites in Europe that act both as festival-pilgrimage and secular tourist attractions, stressing management implications. Ruback, Pandey, and Kohli (2008) compared the differences between religious pilgrims to a festival in India and nonreligious visitors on their perception of the Mela.

Spectacle

MacAloon's (1984) theory of spectacle is important when considering all cultural performance, with the real threat that larger-than-life visual stimulations will replace or render insignificant the more fundamental purposes and expressions of festivity. Foley and McPherson (2004) analyzed Edinburgh's Hogmanay celebration from the perspectives of authenticity, festivity, and televised spectacle. Knox (2008) studied the process by which Scottish song traditions evolved to become public spectacle and tourism performance, in the context of assessing their authenticity.

Marketing

Festival marketing research has examined marketing or consumer orientation, segmentation for target marketing purposes, place marketing with festivals, developing new markets, market area and market potential studies, branding, and image making with festivals. Several researchers have sought to determine the marketing orientation of festivals (Mayfield & Crompton, 1995; Mehmetoglu & Ellingsen, 2005; Tomljenovic & Weber, 2004). It has often been observed, and the research tends to confirm this suspicion, that many arts festivals in particular display a lack of concern for tourism and take a product orientation that tends to ignore customer needs and commercial realities.

Wicks and Fesenmaier (1995) determined the market potential for events in the Midwestern US, while Yoon et al. (2000) profiled Michigan's festival and event tourism market, both through market-area telephone surveys. Barlow and Shibli (2007) explicitly considered festival audience development, while Axelsen (2006b) studied the use of special events to motivate attendance at art galleries. Shanka and Taylor (2004) focused on sources of information used by festival attendees.

Evaluation

Evaluation has emerged as a strong topic, with many citations, although the majority of these research articles pertain to assessments of quality and satisfaction. This fashion has basically adopted consumer marketing to events through application of model building. For example, L. Bourdeau, DeCoster, and Paradis (2001) examined satisfaction levels at a music festival comparing residents and tourists. S. Y. Lee, Petrick, and Crompton (2007) developed a structural equation model to examine relationships between perceived festival service quality, perceived value, and behavioral intentions. K. Kim, Sun, and Mahoney (2008) identified motivational segments of Koreans attending a cultural festival employing factor-cluster analysis, then evaluated satisfaction levels to draw marketing implications.

What is not receiving much attention is evaluation of the effectiveness or efficiency of event operations, or return on investment measures, evaluation of unanticipated outcomes, or learning systems. Along those lines, Getz and Frisby (1991) studied management effectiveness in community-based festivals in Ontario, Canada, while M. Williams and Bowdin (2007) documented how UK festivals employed evaluation and the methods used.

Stakeholders

With so many potential goals to satisfy, and stakeholders to involve, festivals are somewhat unique in the events sector. Stakeholders and stakeholder management have come into the lexicon on festivals, with many citations. Sometimes stakeholders are a secondary topic when discussing planning and the strategic environmental forces affecting festivals. However, a number of recent studies have explicitly used stakeholder theory to examine festival politics and strategies, the festival organizational environment, types and roles of stakeholders, and stakeholder management. Articles on partnerships and collaborations also deal with stakeholders, such as Long (2000), who examined organizational partnerships in the management of a themed festival year in the UK.

Larson (2002, 2009) and Larson and Wikstrom (2001) employed the concept of a "political market square" to examined power and interstakeholder dynamics at festivals. Getz, Andersson, and Larson (2007) used case studies in Canada and Sweden to identify key stakeholders, their multiple roles, and how they were being managed. Crespi-Vallbona and Richards (2007) studied the meaning of cultural festivals through the perspectives of multiple stakeholders in Catalunya, Spain. Stokes (2008) addressed the stakeholder orientation of event tourism strategy makers in Australia, and Johnson, Glover, and Yuen (2009), in studying the Festival of Neighbourhoods in Kitchener, Ontario, Canada, focused on the role of community representatives in creating the event.

Attendance Estimates and Forecasts

Attendance estimation techniques have been scrutinized by several researchers, but forecasting seems to have been largely overlooked. Perhaps the open nature of many public festivals has led researchers to believe that forecasting is unnecessary or too difficult. Brothers and Brantley (1993) documented the use of tag and recapture method for estimating open-festival attendance, while Denton and Furse (1993) described their method for estimating attendance at the open, multievent, and multilocation Barossa Valley Vintage Festival. Raybould, Mules, Fredline, and Tomljenovic (2000) used air photos. Tyrrell and Ismail (2005) also discussed methods for obtaining estimates of attendance and economic impacts at open-gate festivals.

Policy

Few researchers have taken a mainstream political science perspective in festival research. The preferred topics include government funding issues and policies (Felsenstein & Fleischer, 2003; Frey, 2000; Tomljenovic & Weber, 2004), and the nature and justification for public sector involvement with festivals. Some papers cover policy development for festivals and events (e.g., Getz & Frisby, 1991), but on that topic one has to look mostly in books (e.g., Getz, 2007; M. Hall & Rusher, 2004). Specific topics covered include articles by Burke (2007), who addressed the development of cultural policies through the lens of the Caribbean Festival for the Arts, Matheson, Foley, and McPherson (2006) who evaluated festival policy in Singapore from the perspective of globalization, and Peters and Pikkemaat (2005) on the management of city events in Innsbruck Austria, illustrating important success factors and risks within a policy context. Thomas and Wood (2004) studied event-based tourism strategies among local authority strategies in the UK, while Pugh and Wood (2004) looked at local authorities in London as to their policies and strategies for events and festivals. Wah (2004) examined how traditional festivals were influenced by government in China, where a nationalistic outlook has been given to traditions by appropriating official symbols. Whitford (2004a, 2004b) did research on event policies in Australia and their ideological underpinnings.

World or Global Parties

According to MacLeod (2006), "The potential for festivals to construct and express the cultural identities of place and community means that cultural tourists in search of an authentic engagement with the locals can expect to find this within a festival" (p. 229). However, there are now many large-scale celebrations that appeal to international audiences looking for a global, rather than local, communal experience. In other words, although the events might be rooted in tradition, the experience itself is more like a big party that anyone can join. The book *World Party* by Dakota (2002), and related websites, have popularized this term.

MacLeod (2006) views these events as emphasizing spectacle and the carnivalesque at the expense of authenticity, resulting in a sense of placelessness. Ravenscroft and Matteucci (2003) said that global parties stress international norms and conviviality, plus consumption, and not local meanings.

Research Notes on Festivals and Tourism

Anwar, S., & Sohail, M. (2004). Festival tourism in the United Arab Emirates: First-time versus repeat visitor perceptions. *Journal of Vacation Marketing, 10*(2), 161–170.

The United Arab Emirates (UAE) has been making incessant efforts to promote tourism in order to attain the avowed objective of economic diversification and growth. It has organized a number of events, including the oft-quoted Dubai Shopping Festival, to attract tourists in the UAE. The festival has been a prime mover behind tourism marketing, taking advantage of the perceived positive international business image enjoyed by the country far and wide. Using survey data, an attempt is made in this study to analyze the perceptions of first-time visitors and of those repeating their visits to the festival and other related events and sites in the UAE. The results provide interesting insights into an assessment of festival tourism provided by the tourists for policy makers willing to expand the tourism sector in the vibrant and diversifying economy of the UAE. The study shows that tourist perception in the UAE is multidimensional, in line with conventional wisdom, and highlights that it is influenced by all the festival tourism-related facilities and environment.

Chang, J. (2006). Segmenting tourists to aboriginal cultural festivals: An example in the Rukai tribal area, Taiwan. *Tourism Management*, 27(6), 1224–1234.

Festivals are increasingly being used as instruments for promoting tourism and boosting the regional economy . . . very few studies related to aboriginal cultures have been published. The main objective of this study is to profile tourists based upon their motives and demographic characteristics, as these traits are associated with attraction to aboriginal cultural festivals and other related activities. The research reveals that cultural exploration, among other motivational dimensions, is the most important factor attracting tourists to the aboriginal cultural festival. In addition, not all tourists have the same degree of interest in the festival cultural experience. Furthermore, motivational variables are found to be more important than demographic variables in explaining and segmenting visitors to an aboriginal festival.

Festivals, Culture, and Urban Policy

The arts, and cultural tourism, have been prominent in the repositioning of many cities. By the mid-1970s many cities and countries were facing a process of deindustrialization, with many cities suffering in terms of factory closings, job losses, and unemployment. G. Hughes (1999) noted that festivals were viewed as one way to reposition cities into a service economy, and physical spaces had to be reconfigured, or designed from scratch, as festival or sport and entertainment districts. This can be seen as the widespread beginning of the "festivalization" process.

In his book *Events and Urban Regeneration: The Strategic Use of Events to Revitalise Cities*, A. Smith (2012) called this process a form of culture-led regeneration and he emphasized a number of dimensions in a conceptual model (p. 11). "Event-led regeneration" involves new or upgraded venues, while "event-themed regeneration" entails parallel physical regeneration of a city and social regeneration as a process. The entire strategy has to include new directions, notably a tourism strategy, and institutional reconfiguration (who does what, and their capacity to move in new directions). While Smith only examines one-time, major events in this process, it is also firmly connected to recurring, and especially Hallmark or Iconic events.

One region and city in particular stands out, especially in 2012, and that is Belfast in Northern Ireland. Incidentally, Ulster Business School hosted and Tourism and Events congress there in June, 2012, to help mark this special year.

Case Study: Northern Ireland and Cultural Tourism (compiled with the assistance of the NITB)

The year 2012 was "Titanic" for Belfast and Northern Ireland. As described in their "Big Guide to Big Events" (produced by the Northern Ireland Tourist Board), "It's the year we take center stage with new, iconic visitor attractions, unprecedented events and historic anniversaries. It's our chance to go out and shout about how great Northern Ireland is—it's our time to shine."

The packaging of events into a theme year is quite common, although in this case the 100th anniversary of the building and sinking of the *Titanic* provided a wonderful opportunity for Belfast in particular to shine. Other major events held in Northern Ireland, including the Irish Open golf tournament and several other festivals and one-time events made it possible to promote the theme "NI 2012 Our Time Our Place" both as a tourist lure and a message of renewal and hope for residents.

Impressive physical redevelopment of the Belfast docklands, once a world-class shipbuilding hub, was provided a shining, iconic landmark with the 2012 opening of the Titanic Visitor Centre. Accompanying all the surrounding fanfare (including a visit by the Queen) was the 3-week Titanic Belfast Festival. It was described this way in the official brochure (www.belfastcity.gov.uk/titanic; www.ni2012.com): "During the three-week festival, there'll be a fusion of world-class public events to mark the opening of the multi-million pound Titanic Belfast visitor attraction in the newly enveloped Titanic quarter."

Preparing for the 2012 celebrations was an enormous effort involving numerous stakeholders. Part of the process was a design "toolkit" aimed at getting all the participants to use the same themes and messages. A number of key "positioning statements" were formulated, and it should be kept in mind that many other places were capitalizing on the Titanic sinking in 2012:

"Only Belfast can offer the visitor a truly unique, authentic and memorable Titanic experience.

Celebrate Belfast's industrial heritage, the innovation, the pioneering spirit, the quality of craftsmanship and the global ambition.

Use human stories to bring the past, present and future to life. Use humor and charm to endear the audience—but only where appropriate.

Point out the legacy, the renewed spirit in Belfast, the plans for success ahead."

Of the "key messages" attached to positioning, several stand out in explaining the strategy and the inherent value of events:

"Today, Belfast is a vibrant exciting, charming renaissance city.

Titanic Belfast is a world-class visitor attraction and events venue . . ."

Highlights of the Titanic Belfast Festival:

- Successfully delivered with approx. 60,000 people attending events across the month.
- £43 million generated in PR coverage, including a number of high profile BBC programs which were viewed by 12.4 million people across the UK.
- The Titanic Lightshow has been viewed by 353,000 people across the world.
- Titanic Belfast has welcomed 200,000 visitors in its first 10 weeks of opening from over 80 countries, (63% of visitors being from out of state).

Interview with Alan Clarke, CEO of Northern Ireland Tourist Board

Q: How did you go about preparing for this very special year of events in Northern Ireland?

A: In many ways the planning for 2012 started with the development of the Northern Ireland tourism brand in 2009. Unlike many other tourism destinations, we felt the brand needed to be much more than a communication brand and rooted in the visitor experience. The big idea of the brand was a Northern Ireland that was "confidently moving on" and underpinned by two key themes—uncover our stories and experience our awakening. Hence, 2012 presented a once in a lifetime opportunity with a unique set of circumstances: £300m of infrastructure investment coming on stream including the opening of major new attractions such as Titanic Belfast and the new Giant's Causeway Visitor Experience, a series of significant anniversaries including the centenary of Titanic and the 50th Belfast Festival at Queens, the Olympic and Paralympic games taking place in London with Northern Ireland participating in the torch relay and in the Cultural Olympiad events. Together, these presented a one off opportunity. We also looked at, and learnt from, what Scotland had achieved in its Homecoming celebrations in 2009 based around the anniversary of the birth of Robert Burns. Together, these presented us with a series of distinctive events that, when combined, would deliver a year-long inspirational celebration of Northern Ireland more importantly, it presented us with a platform which

Photo 8.1. Belfast, MTV Titanic Sounds Concert
(Credit: photo courtesy of the Northern Ireland Tourist Board).

to reposition Northern Ireland as a place to live, work, invest and study and visit. Hence we developed a series of core aims for 2012 to:

- change global perceptions and present a positive image of Northern Ireland internationally, raise the profile of Northern Ireland as a tourism destination, drive visitor numbers and spend, generate economic impact and, importantly, underpin civic pride and self respect in Northern Ireland residents;
- the year was made up of a series of special events to animate and raise awareness of the new capital investment/anniversaries through a series of 8 major Tier 1 events, supported by over 50 Tier 2 events and a range of other smaller events throughout Northern Ireland. The Tier 1 events had to hit more than one of three targets i.e., visitor numbers, changing the perception of Northern Ireland and inspiring chat. A creative group was instigated to develop the Tier 1 events and a steering group representing wide spectrum of agencies, local councils etc., was set up to coordinate and communicate across all sectors. Within NITB, a dedicated project team was established to progress ni2012, but it was also a corporate objective for the organization.

Q: What were the main challenges?
A: The main challenges were as follows:

- Budget—additional budget was secured for the Tier 1 events and for marketing and promotion.
- Industry buy-in—industry buy-in was secured by the production of a spirit guide and a comprehensive industry development program in the run up to 2012.
- Wider business—key objective was to use 2012 to be a shop window for Northern Ireland, not just for tourism. Support was secured with the main industry

associations such as the Confederation of British Industry, Institute of Directors, and the Northern Ireland Chamber of Commerce and their support was vital to the implementation of the project.

- Coordination—coordination was secured through a series of collaborative working groups, overseeing by a steering group involving all the major players related to delivery.
- Media—briefings were given to the media and some were the key media, especially the BBC and the Belfast Telegraph came aboard at an early stage and were totally supportive of the project.

Q: Are you satisfied with the results?

A: Initial feedback has been incredibly positive—the Titanic Festival was exceptionally well received by public and visitors and the Titanic Visitor Attraction attracted almost 200,000 visitors in its first 2 months, compared to an annual break even figure of 293,000 and an estimated year 1 visitor projections by the operator of just over 400,000 visitors. International media coverage was secured generating in the order of £40 million sterling advertising equivalent value. There has been exceptional positivity across all media to the 2012 'Our Time Our Place' message with high feedback in terms of civic pride objectives. The Irish Open Golf Tournament, held in Northern Ireland for the first time in 59 years, was unique among European Tour events in being a sell out prior to the tournament proceeding and with the record 130,000 visitors over the 4 tournament days, the pro-am day, and the practice day. The 112,000 visitors over the 4 competition days compared with 85,000 the previous year in Killarney and a total this year for the Scottish Open of 57,000.

Motivations to Attend Festivals and Cultural Celebrations

Of all the possible antecedents to explaining participation in festivals, or demand for them, only the study of festival motivation is well established. It has always been strongly attached to mainstream marketing and consumer research. Festival motivation studies were popular right from the beginning (e.g., Backman, Backman, Uysal, & Sunshine, 1995; Formica & Uysal, 1998; Mohr, Backman, Gahan, & Backman, 1993; Uysal, Gahan, & Martin, 1993) of the journal *Festival Management & Event Tourism* (now *Event Management*). Review articles have been published by C. Lee, Lee, and Wicks (2004), R. Li and Petrick (2006), and Wooten and Norman (2008).

Motivational research involves exploration of why people attend festivals, and how they make their choices and decisions. Many researchers have employed market segmentation in conducting motivational studies, and only a few have referred to theory on cultural needs or social identification. Within the event management and even tourism discourses the classical reasons for holding and attending festivals have all but been ignored, opening a great theoretical gulf. Almost entirely, scholars have adopted the positivistic, quantitative paradigm favored by consumer behavior studies, even though this approach fails to consider fundamental social and cultural antecedents.

There is a tendency, I think, for researchers to oversimplify motivation and completely ignore needs. After all, cultural celebration is a basic need in all civilizations. It is also unwise to commodify festivals alongside other entertainment "products" such as going to the cinema or buying a television. Attending festivals and other cultural celebrations is not necessarily rational, it might be socially obligated, and it certainly involves experiences that are unlike other consumer "products."

After many studies it is generally found that the *seeking and escaping theory* (Iso-Ahola, 1980, 1983) is largely confirmed. These are *intrinsic motivators*, with the event being a desired leisure pursuit. Researchers have demonstrated that escapism leads people to events for the *generic benefits* of entertainment and diversion, socializing, learning and doing something new (i.e., novelty seeking). Nicholson and Pearce (2001) studied motivations to attend four quite different events in New Zealand: an air show, award ceremony, wild food festival, and a wine, food and music festival. They concluded that multiple motivations were the norm, and that while socialization was common to them all, it varied in its nature. Event-specific reasons (or targeted benefits) were tied to the novelty or uniqueness of each event. *Serious leisure* (as used by Mackellar (2009a, 2009b, based on the theories of Stebbins) and *involvement theory* (e.g., as employed by S. Kim et al., 1997) offer great potential for exploring event-specific motives.

Kay (2004) reviewed the literature on cross-cultural research in developing international tourist markets, noting how little had been published, especially in the events sector. Since most published work is in English, from the North American or European cultural settings (including Australia and New Zealand), there will always be potential problems when taking our theories and methods into much different cultural environments. Schneider and Backman (1996) examined the issues surrounding the application of festival motivation scales to other cultures than their origin. They concluded that we can use the motivational scale in Arabic countries, while Dewar, Meyer, and Li (2001) concluded the same for Chinese festivals. In other words, there does appear to be a universal set of motivations that lead people to attend festivals, and people are similar regardless of the culture (especially socialization and family togetherness, or what Getz, 2005, 2007, calls "generic festival benefits"). However, that is a very large hypothesis in need of much more systematic, cross-cultural testing.

A number of specific motivational issues have been researched. Junge (2008) looked the motivations explaining heterosexual attendance at Gay events, while H. Kim, Borges, and Chon (2006) employed the New Environmental Paradigm scale to examined motivations of people attending a film festival in Brazil that was created to foster awareness of environmental issues. Yuan, Cai, Morrison, and Linton (2005a, 2005b) studied wine festival attendees on their motivations, while Yuan and Jang (2008) explored the wine festival attendee's satisfaction and behavioral intentions.

Constraints

Event and festival nonattendance, and constraints acting against attendance, have been largely ignored in the literature. Van Zyl and Botha (2004) considered the needs and motivational factors influencing decisions of residents to attend an arts festival, including "situational inhibitors," while Milner, Jago, and Deery (2004) conducted the only study of why people did not attend festivals and events. This is a line of research that deserves greater attention, especially in the context of leisure constraints theory (see, e.g., E. Jackson, 2005).

Research Note on Festival Motivation

Lee, C., Lee, Y., & Wicks, B. (2004). Segmentation of festival motivation by nationality and satisfaction. *Tourism Management, 25*(1), 61–70.

Using a factor analysis of data obtained from visitors to a Korean "Culture Expo," the researchers identified six motivational dimensions: cultural exploration, family togetherness, novelty, escape, event attractions, and socialization. These were consistent with other festival motivation studies reported in the literature. A cluster analysis performed on the six motivational dimensions identified four consumer segments, of which the "multipurpose seekers" were the most numerous and, perhaps because they had the broadest range of motives, were most satisfied. Domestic visitors and foreign visitors responded to different promotions, with foreigners more influenced by friends and travel agencies and domestic visitors more responsive to radio and television advertising. Foreigners were found to be more satisfied, overall.

Large-Scale Surveys

As with sport tourism, large-scale surveys occur infrequently and require longitudinal interpretation to make sense of trends. As well, the ups and downs of economic growth and recession always impact on numbers, and an aging population must also be taken into account. Furthermore, the cultural diversity of North America, Europe, and many other countries is increasing and that is bound to keep changing participation in the arts and entertainment, and cultural tourism, including events.

Nearly 93 million Americans said they included at least one cultural, arts, heritage, or historic activity or event while traveling in 2001, according to a survey conducted by the Travel Industry Association of America. About one in five (21%) of total domestic person-trips (business and pleasure) included an historic/cultural activity. In fact, historic/cultural travel volume was up 10% from 1996, increasing from 192.4 million person-trips to 212.0 million person-trips in 2000. Art and music festivals were the most popular type of festivals attended while traveling.

A study by the Travel Industry Association of America and *Smithsonian* magazine, called The Historic/Cultural Traveler 2003, found that 81% of adult Americans who had traveled in the past year could be considered "historic/cultural tourists" based on their activities and interests. They were found to be high-yield tourists, in terms of lengths of stay and spending, and for 30% their choice of destination was influenced by a specific historic or cultural event or activity. Over half of them had a hobby or interest that influenced their travel. This was not considered to be a passing fad, as cultural tourism in general had been leading the way over the past decade. Older, better educated, and more sophisticated, they concluded that tomorrow's tourists will be even more interested in cultural/historic sites and events.

The National Endowment for the Arts (USA)

National Endowment for the Arts (NEA) conducts regular research, and of particular interests are results of its 2002 and 2008 Survey of Public Participation in the Arts. These are highlights from 2002 (http://www.arts.gov/research/notes/81.pdf):

- Nearly one-third of American adults reported going to at least one jazz, classical music, opera, musical, play, or ballet performance during the 12 months preceding August 2002 (not including elementary or high school performances).
- One-quarter said they had visited an art gallery or art museum.
- Growth in attendance since 1992 had been considerable, but largely due to population growth rather than an increase in the participation rate.
- Counting all forms of participation, 76% of American adults made the arts a part of their lives.
- Art/craft fairs and festivals attracted 33.4% of adults, 7% below 1992 (possibly due to September 11 and a decline in travel).
- Women had higher attendance rates except for jazz, which is about equal; females accounted for almost 70% of ballet goers and 60% of attendees at musicals, plays and arts/craft fairs.
- Non-Hispanic whites had the highest participation rates.
- Non-Hispanic African Americans had the highest attendance at jazz concerts.
- Age, income, and particularly education are better predictors than race/ethnicity when it comes to arts attendance.
- Higher incomes do translate into higher participation, but education is actually more important.

- Those with incomes below $30,000 (in 2002) were underrepresented at art events.
- In keeping with the aging of the population overall, arts attendees grew older between 1992 and 2002; the median age of adults attending classical music was highest, at 49 years; for jazz it was the lowest, at 43 years of age; the proportion of young attending arts was lower.
- Participation rates are highest for those with college and graduate school education (e.g., graduates had 5 times the participation at classical music concerts than high school graduates); jazz has a higher appeal than the other art forms for those with only high school education.

By 2008 the picture had changed somewhat, primarily reflecting economic conditions, but also aging of the population and the rise of electronic entertainment. In the US, and presumably elsewhere, higher levels of education translate into higher participation in the arts, and this includes formal exposure to arts in school and other programs. Also worth noting is the continuing popularity (and for tourism, importance) of outdoor music and arts festivals.

From the National Endowment for the Arts: 2008 Survey of Public Participation in the Arts Research Report #49 (available at: http://www.nea.gov/research/2008-sppa.pdf):

- The 2008 survey results are, at a glance, disappointing. A smaller segment of the adult population either attended arts performances or visited art museums or galleries than in any prior survey.
- Nor were bad economic conditions in 2007–2008 the only factor at work. From 1982 to 2008, audiences for performances in classical music, ballet, non-musical theater, and—most conspicuously, jazz—have aged faster than the general adult population. Even among the most educated, adults are participating less than in previous years.
- The proportion of Americans who had gone to at least one of the seven types of benchmark activities had previously been very stable—39% of survey respondents had attended a benchmark activity in 2002, approximately the same rate as found in 1982. The rate dropped below 35% in 2008.
- 47 million people reported going to an outdoor performing arts festival in 2008, which is more than for any other type of performing arts event included in the survey. About 38 million people went to a musical play. About 11 million people attended a Latin music performance.
- The number of people attending performing arts events declined for most art forms between 2002 and 2008.
- The largest absolute decline in audience size was for non-musical plays and jazz performances. On a relative basis, the decline in people going to opera was most severe.

In 2009 the NEA also conducted original research on outdoor festivals in the US, including seven case studies: National Endowment for the Arts Research Report 51. Live from Your Neighborhood: A National Study of Outdoor Arts Festivals (available at: http://www.nea.gov/research/Festivals-report.pdf). This excerpt is highly relevant as it points out why festivals are so popular, and how they differ from other forms of art productions.

Repeat iterations of the NEA's Survey of Public Participation in the Arts (SPPA) have shown that festivals and fairs collectively attract more unique audience members per year than most arts events.

In 2008 alone, more than 55 million U.S. adults attended at least one arts-and-crafts fair or festival in the past year, and 47 million attended at least one outdoor performing arts festival (approximately 14% of Americans attended both). In sheer numbers, attendance rates for festivals far exceed those for many single types of art activities—classical music concerts, for example, or theater, ballet, or opera. But the size of their audiences is not the only characteristic that merits serious study of arts festivals. Festival audiences, on average, are more diverse than those for many other types of live art events. . . festival audiences seem to more closely resemble the general population than do other groups of art-goers. This finding is notable as arts organizations strive not only to build new audiences but, what may be more important, to actuate potential audiences that already exist among groups who engage in art through a variety of ways not often acknowledged or studied.

In the NEA report "Live from Your Neighborhood: A National Study of Outdoor Arts Festivals, Vol 2: Seven Case Studies" their visitor surveys revealed an important fact:

Almost all of the case study festivals play a role in the local tourism industry. For instance, at many of the case study sites, between 20% and 30% of the festival audience came from outside the local Metropolitan Statistical Area. Audiences from outside the local area were particularly high at Chicago Jazz Festival and Santa Fe Indian Market.

Visiting Fairs and Festivals While on Trips of One or More Nights (Travel Attitudes and Motivations Study [TAMS]; A Profile Report, July 4, 2007)

Over the last two years (i.e., before 2006), 31.7% (69,847,152) of adult Americans visited fairs and festivals while on an out-of-town, overnight trip of one or more nights. A farmers' market or country fair (14.4%) was the most popular, followed by a fireworks display (12.3%), a free outdoor performance such as a play or concert (10.8%), an exhibition or fair (8.3%), a food or drink festival (7.7%), a carnival (6.9%), an ethnic festival (4.2%) and a circus (3.1%). 29.8% (20,824,610) of those visiting Fairs and Festivals reported that this activity was the main reason for taking at least one trip in the past two years.

Those who visited fairs and festivals on trips are similar to the average U.S. Pleasure Traveler in terms of gender, age, marital status and parental status, however, their level of education (61.8% university degree or higher) and household incomes ($78,425) are above-average. They tend to live in large cities with populations of 2 million or more.

Those who visited fairs and festivals on trips were more likely than average to participate in a wide range of culture and entertainment activities while on trips in the past two years. Relative to the average U.S. Pleasure Traveler, they were especially likely to attend theatre, film and music festivals and were more likely to participate in a wide range of outdoor activities on trips (e.g., ocean activities, wildlife viewing), and to take a variety of tours and cruises.

Those who visited fairs and festivals on trips exhibit particular interest in food-related activities. They were more likely than the average U.S. Pleasure Traveler to go fine dining and to visit spas, to have stayed at a country inn or resort with a gourmet restaurant or a cooking or wine tasting school and to have taken a winery tour. They seek vacation destinations that offer novelty, intellectual stimulation and opportunities to learn (e.g., gain knowledge of history and other cultures or places).

The majority in this segment have used the Internet to plan (75.6%) and book travel (54.8%) in the past two years. They are avid consumers of travel-related media (including websites, newspapers, magazines, television). Home and garden-related programming is also an effective method to reach this segment (e.g., house & home websites, home & garden and cooking TV shows, craft, antique & collectible magazines).

U.S. Festival Tourism Enthusiasts (2004) [A Special Analysis of the Travel Activities and Motivation Survey (TAMS); prepared for: The Canadian Tourism Commission (CTC); prepared by: Research Resolutions & Consulting Ltd.]

Festival Tourism Enthusiasts are as likely to be women (51%) as they are to be men (49%).

They span the age spectrum, ave. between 46 and 47 year of age. Most Festival Tourism Enthusiasts live in adult-only households—those with no members under the age of eighteen. These enthusiasts span the income and education spectrums. They are less likely to fall into the lowest education groups and are more likely have at least some post-secondary education.

Local festivals and fairs attract the largest following, with over 8-in-10 Festival Tourism Enthusiast patrons claiming to have included a visit to one on a recent overnight leisure trip. Over two million, or more than half of these festival enthusiasts, went to a **music festival** and slightly fewer or about 1.9 million went to a **theatre festival** on a recent leisure trip.

Festivals that are considerably less popular include **carnivals** such as Mardi Gras at about 1.1 million, **western theme events** such as a rodeo and Pow Wows or other **Aboriginal celebrations** at just under one million (each). **Literary festivals** or events attract about 1-in-5 Festival Tourism Enthusiasts.

Because Festival Tourism Enthusiasts also go to other types of attractions when they travel, those who are packaging tourism products for this market might consider adding local arts and crafts studios and/or history or heritage museums to the package. Approximately 3-in-4 members of this U.S.A. market segment go to these types of events on their leisure trips. Two-in-three claim to visit zoos, farmers' fairs or markets, aquariums and art galleries on their travels.

There is an appreciably higher level of participation in many performing arts and wine/culinary activities among tourists in the festival segment. Perhaps because of their interest in music festivals, more than 2-in-5 festival enthusiasts also go to popular or rock and roll concerts or jazz concerts while travelling. Additionally, approximately 1-in-3 Festival Tourism Enthusiasts seek out classical music concerts or ballet performances and 1-in-5 attend opera performances while on their trips.

Three-fifths of Festival Tourism Enthusiasts are in the market for dining at internationally acclaimed restaurants when they travel and almost one-half spend some of their time on trips touring wineries. These rates of participation in wine and culinary activities are noticeably higher than those evident for American travellers as a whole, suggesting that festivals might benefit from co-packaging with these experiences to lure the festival crowd. Almost 3-in-4 share interests with **Heritage** Enthusiasts; two-thirds are also **Museum & Related Cultural Institution** Enthusiasts; and over 1-in-2 are also **Performing Arts** and/or **Visual Arts** Enthusiasts. Two-fifths share the interests of **Wine/ Culinary** and/or **Soft Outdoor Adventure Enthusiasts**. These overlaps suggest opportunities for cross-market packaging and promotion within cultural tourism products and between festivals and outdoor experiences for the American Festival Tourism Enthusiast market.

Impacts of Festival Tourism

It is sometimes difficult to sort out festival impacts from festival tourism impacts, especially when we go beyond economic impact assessments. Social and cultural effects are more likely to be connected to actual attendance and participation, not the travel to festivals. Nevertheless, Event Tourism practitioners and strategists have to be thorough in examining all potential outcomes. In Chapter 10, see the detailed report on the Edinburgh festivals impact study.

Economic Impacts

Mostly individual events have been studied, but increasingly there is a need to examine portfolios and whole populations of festivals. For example, research conducted for the British Arts Festivals Association in 2003 proved they constitute a major wealth creator for the nation. A total of 137 festivals spent £37.4 million sterling in a year, stimulating a total of £90 million or more elsewhere in the UK economy. These festivals employed over 3,000 staff, plus created income for numerous performers and technicians. Of course, these figures show that arts festivals are big business, but do not say anything specifically about tourism-related impacts.

A case study of the Canadian Tulip Festival (summarized in Getz, 2005) showed very high economic impacts are obtainable by festivals that attract tourists, especially in the non-peak travel season. Festivals also tend to attract lots of visiting friends and relatives who do not use commercial accommodation and who might have visited anyway.

Many community festivals have diverse programs that include specific events that attract real tourists, such as participants in sport events. This is an excellent strategy for adding economic value to a resident-dominated festival. One-day festivals are common, and they do not encourage people to stay overnight, even if they attract tourists. Festivals that extend over two weekends are also common, and at these events there is often a big difference between weekend visitors (more tourists staying overnight) and weekday attendees (more residents). Festivals that attract vendors, such as art and craft sales, can generate substantial economic impacts through their expenditure in the area, but it has to be remembered that they also take money home with them.

Brannas and Nordstrom (2006) used econometric models to determine the extent of increased hotel accommodation versus displacement caused by festivals. Also see Hultkrantz (1998) for evidence of tourist displacement associated with a peak-season event. The potential for invalid assessment and deliberate misuse of event impact assessments has been detailed by Crompton and McKay (1994). Specific topics within this theme include research by Boo, Ko, and Blazey (2007) on how prior festival visitation (and other variables) influenced expenditures. Turco (1995) examined tax impacts.

Surveys such as that undertaken by Crompton, Lee, and Shuster (2001) are needed to determined the net impact for the area.

Research Note

Crompton, J., Lee, S., & Shuster, T. (2001). A guide for undertaking economic impact studies: The Springfest example. *Journal of Travel Research, 40,* 79–87.

This paper provides specific guidelines for conducting economic impact studies of events, as illustrated by an evaluation of Springfest in Ocean City, Maryland. Their interviews revealed a large number of genuine event tourists, time switchers who had changed their plans to accommodate the festival, and casual visitors who had not travelled because of the event. They also found that a portion of "casuals" did extend their visit owing to attendance at Springfest. In total, they estimated that time-switchers and casuals constituted 49% of all visitors.

Social and Cultural Impacts

Although research on social and cultural impacts of events goes back to occasional anthropological studies like Greenwood (1972) and the conceptual overview provided by J. R. B. Ritchie (1984), it can be said that only very recently has there begun a systematic and theoretically grounded line of comprehensive event impact research, including papers by Delamere (2001) and Delamere, Wankel, and Hinch (2001) on development of resident attitude scales as social impact indicators. Fredline and Faulkner (1998, 2002a, 2002b) and Xiao and Smith (2004) have researched resident perceptions of event impacts, while Fredline, Jago, and Deery (2003), Fredline (2006), and Small, Carlsen, Robertson, and Ali-Knight (2007) have all worked on development of social impact scales for events. Arcodia and Whitford (2006) considered the connections between festival attendance and the creation of social capital. A Social Impact Perception Scale was tested by Small, Edwards and Sheridan (2005). E. Wood and Thomas (2006) measured cultural values and residents' attitudes towards the Saltaire Festival in England.

A number of specific social impact issues have been considered, such as Eder, Staggenborg, and Sudderth (1995) on how the National Women's Music Festival fostered lesbian identity but did not achieve its goals regarding racial diversity among women. Snowball and Willis (2006) believed that cultural capital had been created by means of the National Arts Festival in South Africa.

Image and Place Marketing Impacts

Festivals are being employed as tools in destination image making, repositioning strategies, and branding. Articles deal with both the effort being made, and the imputed or tested effects. Harcup (2000) examined how a festival was developed to deliberately help change the image of Leeds. Jago et al. (2003) studied how to build events into destination branding in Australia. X. Li and Vogelsong (2005) compared two methods for assessing the effects of a small-scale festival on destination image, concluding that many visitors did go away with an enhanced image of the host community. Mossberg and Getz (2006) studied stakeholders and the ownership of festival brands, many of which are explicitly but informally co-branded with cities through their names. Boo and Busser (2006) tested how a festival could improve a destination's image.

Only a few scholars have made a connection between festivals and urban development or renewal, and it is accurate to say that this topic is mostly connected to mega-events like the Olympics and World's Fairs. Regarding festivals, Mules (1993) looked at festivals as part of urban renewal strategy for Adelaide. G. Hughes (1999) examined the use of festival in urban image making and revitalization. Gabr, Robinson, Picard, and Long (2004) looked at how the Dubai Shopping Festival utilized historic sites and resident attitudes towards this practice, and Che (2008) examined the branding of Detroit and promotion of a positive image through creation of the Detroit Electronic Musical Festival.

Environmental Impacts

Research on festivals' environmental impacts has lagged, although many articles and several books have been directed at green and sustainable event management. One study that fits this theme is by Shirley et al. (2001), who reported on the effects of a festival on a nearby population of bats. Pertaining to events in general, several other authors have made contributions, according to Sherwood (2007), whose dissertation examined how a triple bottom line approach to event evaluation could be structured and implemented. Topics that should be thoroughly covered but mostly are not, include: changes to ecological systems and the physical environment as a result of festivals and events; the energy consumption and carbon footprint attributable to event-related travel; water production and avoidance; pollution of air, water, and land; effects on wildlife and habitat; reducing, recycling, and reusing materials, buildings, and sites.

The ensuing case study of Woodford "a green festival" is illuminating, as this event is both a destination festival and is iconic for certain audiences because of its sustainability theme.

Case Study: Woodford—A Green Festival (http://www.woodfordfolkfestival.com)

This case study was prepared by David Gration, Lecturer in Event Management at the University of the Sunshine Coast, Queensland, Australia. The cooperation of the Woodford Folk Festival in sharing their research material is greatly appreciated.

The idea to found the folk festival happened, in the words of its Director Bill Hauritz, when "a few folkies who wanted more opportunities to perform got together over a few bottles of red and started talking about possibilities." Pragmatic self-interest combined with genuine community-of-interest aspirations saw those early person-to-person conversations and networking sessions blossom into the first Maleny Folk Festival in 1987 on the relatively small Maleny Showgrounds site. Eight years later, with attendances of approximately 65,000, audience growth and the desire for venue self-determination led to the purchase of a new site near the small town of Woodford, hence the first "Woodford Folk Festival" in 1994. There, 500 acres of farmland are being progressively reclaimed as "environmental parkland." The festival site incorporates a mixture of natural landscape and built components. It achieves approximately 100,000–120,000 attendances (Figure 8.1) from a diverse demographic target market over a 6-day period from December 27 to January 1

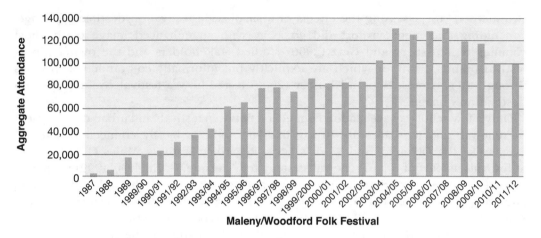

Figure 8.1. Woodford Festival attendance trend.

each year. Of vital importance to the festival are its 2,400 volunteers who contribute both at festival time and, as a smaller group, throughout the year.

This Australian regional festival features concerts, dances, street theater, writers' panels, film, comedy, jams, social dialogue and debates, folk medicine, a distinct children's festival, an environmental program, arts & craft workshops, circus, cabaret, parades, and spectacular mass participation events, all under the title of "folk."

Photo 8.2. Woodford Festival crowd parade
(Credit: photo courtesy of Amanda Jackes, General Manager).

Photo 8.3. Woodford Festival: The Goanna (Credit: photo courtesy of David Gration).

The festival cleverly blends the traditional and alternative, the communal and individual, and the natural and built into a blended festivalscape with wide audience appeal. The festival reflects and reinforces the self-image of its participants. The natural environment and associated environmental programming attracts audiences with a proenvironmental worldview. The built environment has synergy with the natural environment. The sense of community between like-minded people at the festival encourages a positive social experience. This blended festivalscape (Figure 8.2) creates a sense of community, or communitas, that physically comes together on-site once a year but lives as a transportable concept, a type of virtual community, for the time between festivals. Each member of this community becomes an ambassador and promoter for the festival wherever they travel.

The festival is owned by the not-for-profit Queensland Folk Federation (QFF). The site was transferred to the local government authority in 2011 with a long term "peppercorn" lease being granted back to the QFF.

Festival growth has not been built on a massive marketing budget, or extensive advertising. Rather it has been built on delivering quality experiences, building a community of interest and belief, and good old fashioned positive word of mouth. Inclement weather conditions at this outdoor festival, where approximately 70% of attendees camp-out, has led to a decline in overall attendances over the past few years. Significant work has been undertaken on the site to ameliorate the negative impacts of potential severe weather events while still maintaining the "close-to-nature" atmospherics

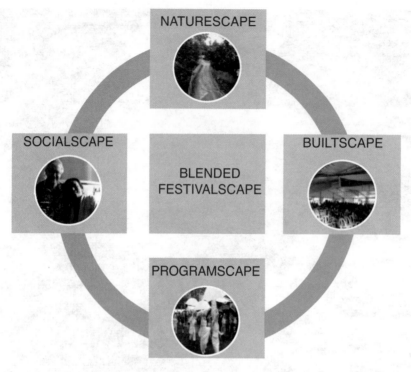

Figure 8.2. Woodford Festival: The blended festivalscape.

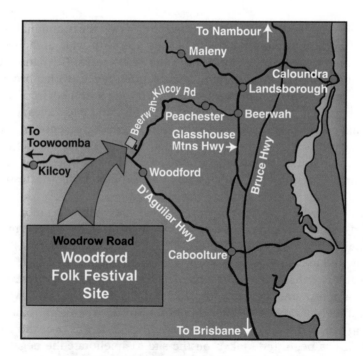

Photo 8.4. Woodford Festival location map.

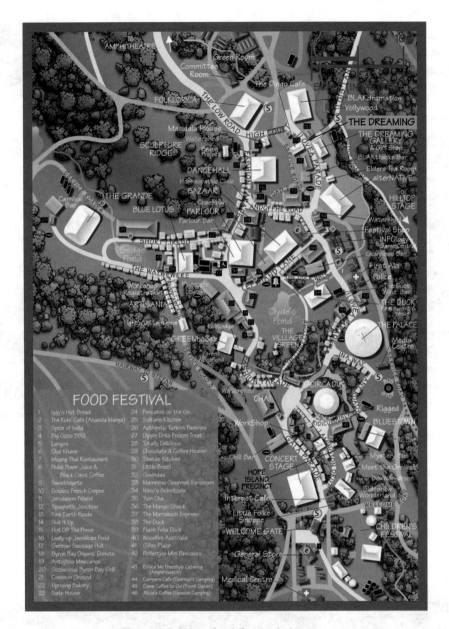

Photo 8.5. Woodford Festival site map.

of the site. Despite challenges, the strong core community of supporters has ensured the festivals survival and revival.

The Woodford Folk Festival site is located a few kilometers from the small township of Woodford on a stand-alone site that has been named "Woodfordia." As such nearly all festivalgoers can be classified as visitors, a title they prefer as opposed to the more commercial sounding "tourist" tag. Unlike most other festivals there are no direct local community out of which the festival has grown. In the case of the Woodford Folk Festival it was artificially imposed, with a temporary community of interest established on-site. As can be seen in Figure 8.3 the major origin of festivalgoers, approximately

Photo 8.6. Woodford Festival reception (Credit: photo courtesy of David Gration).

Photo 8.7. Woodford Festival camping (Credit: photo courtesy of David Gration).

Photo 8.8. Woodford Festival facilities (Credit: photo courtesy of David Gration).

50%, comes from the "local" South East Queensland region (being a 1–2-hour drive from the festival site). The next major source is interstate with approximately 30%. While only a small number are drawn from the international market, this area has shown steady increases in recent years.

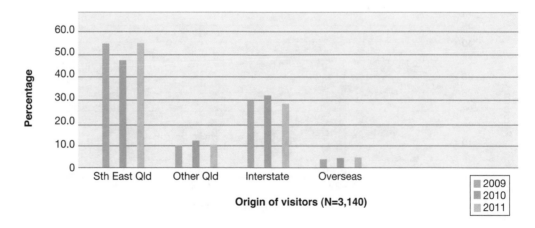

Figure 8.3. Woodford Festival visitor origins.

In terms of demographics, gender is split 60/40 between female and male festivalgoer categories. About 36% of festivalgoers who come from management and professional backgrounds, 20% are students. Over 42% of festivalgoers hold either a graduate or postgraduate degree; 18–29 year olds represent the single largest sector at approximately 40% (Figure 8.4).

The festival has a high return visitation rate of approximately 70% with its long existence leading to examples of second- and third-generation attendees. The likelihood of return visitation is significantly higher for those who have attended the festival before and those who attend more frequently, suggesting that repeat visitation leads to loyalty (Figure 8.5). Ninety percent of festivalgoers cited the festival as their main reason for visiting the area. The festival has an estimated economic impact of $15 million per annum.

The festival spends only a small amount on paid advertising. Its primary investment is in the use of printed materials, such as the festival program, and Internet-based communications, such as their websites (http://www.woodfordia.com/ and http://www.woodfordfolkfestival.com/) and electronic newsletters such as the Woodfordia Mail (http://news.woodfordia.com/). Recent festivalgoer research showed that the top three sources of festival information were friends and relatives' word of mouth (~50%), festival website (~25%), and direct mailing list (~7.5%). High levels of satisfaction with the festival experience are consistently reported in annual surveys.

A wide range of annual incomes have been identified in festivalgoer research with the two largest groups being <$20,000 and $100,000+, with each representing approximately 20% of the total festivalgoer base. The diverse income levels demonstrate the festivals range of appeal and general affordability in the marketplace.

Some interesting festival statistics:

- Covers more than 13,000 sq.m. with tents and built structures.
- Has a closed loop water system and an environmentally innovative waste water treatment plant.
- Presents over 400 distinct performance acts with over 2,000 performers.
- Has 218 named streets on the festival site.
- Sells over 18,000 pints of Guinness and Kilkenny.
- Planted over 100,000 trees and 600 species on the site since 1994.
- Volunteer hours are in excess of 1,400,000 hours.

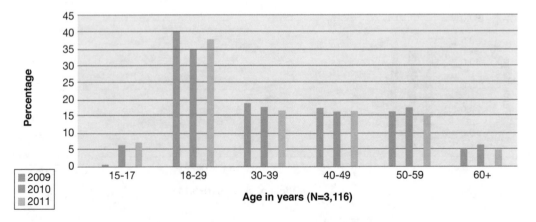

Figure 8.4. Woodford Festival age distribution of attendees.

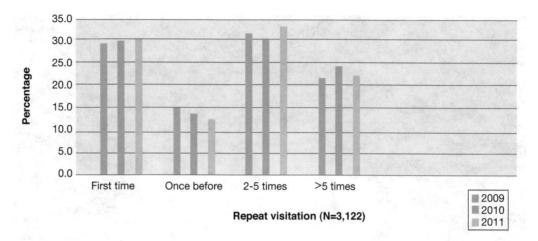

Figure 8.5. Woodford Festival attendees, first-time versus repeat visitation.

- Has a temporary population approximately the size of cities and towns such as Hindley (UK), Laguna Beach (USA), Central Otago (NZ), Harstad (Norway), Forst (Germany), Baarn (Netherlands), or Nambour (Australia).

Entertainment

Entertainment is defined as: (1) The action of providing or being provided with amusement or enjoyment; (2) An event, performance, or activity designed to entertain others.

Although anything can be considered "entertainment," as it depends on one's personal interpretation and enjoyment of an experience, we do associate certain events and elements of event programming with entertainment. Those things we tend to think of as "entertainment" are "social constructs" based on what we have learned, the influence of media and peers, and the nature of particular cultures.

Within event management the designer employs various elements of style, such as music, theatrics, humor, and games, to entertain the audience, whereas in Event Tourism we focus on "entertainment events" that can motivate travel. To a large extent this overlaps with festivals and other cultural events, but there are distinct forms of entertainment

Photo 8.9. Woodford Festival poster (Credit: courtesy of Amanda Jackes, General Manager).

Photo 8.10. Woodford Festival closing ceremony
(Credit: photo courtesy of Amanda Jackes, General Manager).

events to be considered, namely stand-alone concerts, awards and theatrical productions, and traveling shows and exhibits.

Is There an Entertainment Industry?

Many people talk about an entertainment industry, which reflects the fact that entertainment in all its forms is big business. Stein and Evans (2009) defined the entertainment industry as including media (TV, radio), recorded music, video games, film, publishing, theater, sports, theme parks, casinos and gambling, travel and tourism, museums, shopping, and special events.

They emphasized several points about following about American entertainment. First, it generates about $930 billion in total spending, including advertising, each year in the US. Competition for attention and consumer spending has never been greater, and in fact the country is saturated with entertainment options. They argued that for one entertainment sector to grow, another must decline. Americans, according to Stein and Evans (2009, p. 11), have become obsessed with entertainment and celebrities.

Arts and Entertainment

H. Hughes (2000), in his book *Arts, Entertainment and Tourism*, covers performing arts and entertainment, saying that the "arts" are usually associated with refinement and "high culture" while entertainment performances are more mainstream, or popular.

Entertainment is usually provided by the private sector, for profit, but distinctions between arts and entertainment are mostly a matter of judgment. Hughes argued that education is the primary determinant of people's choices, with higher education leading to more participation in the arts. The motivations could overlap a great deal, including relaxation and escapism, but the arts are thought to appeal more to those wishing to learn, and of course for aesthetic appreciation.

Various case studies are presented in the Hughes book, including New York's Broadway, Las Vegas, Atlantic City, and Coney Island (all US); Blackpool, London's West End, the Buxton Festival, the Glastonbury Festival, and Cromer and Bexhill (all UK); the Adelaide Festival (Australia); Mardi Gras (Brazil); and Oberammergau (Germany).

Research Notes on Entertainment

Reid, G. (2006). The politics of city imaging: A case study of the MTV Europe Music Awards in Edinburgh '03. *Event Management, 10*(1), 35–46.

In November 2003 the city of Edinburgh hosted the MTV Europe Music Awards. This article discusses the event's contribution to Edinburgh's reimaging and local involvement. After outlining links between cultural events and contemporary urban policy, an in-depth case study charts the evolution of the MTV Europe Awards Edinburgh 03 and how it became embroiled in local political realities. The event became politicized because MTV was given £750 thousand public subsidy to part-fund the show's temporary structure and the outside broadcast costs of a simultaneous live concert in Edinburgh's city center Princes Street Gardens. Officials argued that, beyond the local economic benefit—estimated initially at £4 million— this was justified as the event offered extensive local inclusion and unique promotional opportunities that would give the city's conservative image a contemporary edge. They believed Edinburgh's reimaging as an exciting short-break destination would occur because of the association with A-list celebrities and MTV's innovative marketing that connected with the global traveling, yet elusive, "MTV generation." MTV found Edinburgh an ideal city as its experienced events team eased production of their complex "live" television show, while its young people and iconic place features gave the show a distinctive narrative. The article's key finding is that MTV's desire for these place features to reimage their television show meant the event primarily benefited them and the local tourist industry. MTV happily fostered local involvement—creating memorable moments for participants—but their celebrity and place focus meant their voices were often marginalized. This was accentuated because the local newspaper, part of a group often critical of public sector organizers, emphasized the event's cost and disruption, the inappropriate actions of public officials, and MTV's ticket allocation to corporate clients.

Che, D. (2008). Sports, music, entertainment and the destination branding of post-Fordist Detroit. *Tourism Recreation Research, 33*(2), 195–206.

Post-Fordist cities have increasingly converted former industrial areas into tourist entertainment districts. Events that can generate tourism income, spur the transformation of event cities into cities of culture, and help reinforce a city's brand have also been used to reinvent so-called post-industrial difficult areas. This downtown tourism and entertainment strategy has been utilized in Detroit, the best-known difficult area in the US. This paper examines the sports and music components of Detroit's plan to address economic and social challenges stemming from deindustrialization, disinvestment, and decentralization. To foster economic growth and improve the city's persistently poor image, Detroit has redeveloped its downtown into an entertainment district anchored by two sports stadia and focused on landing sports mega events. This development, which mirrors that undertaken by other cities, is part of its long-term strategy for dealing with blight and its image problems. Detroit also has belatedly focused on events celebrating its musical heritage. Specifically the Detroit Electronic MusicFestival (DEMF), which centers on techno, an alternative musical form born in the city and intertwined with its post-industrial cultural identity, has been used in differentiating and branding Detroit. The DEMF attracts an international audience and can thus help promote an image of post-Fordist Detroit as creative and cosmopolitan, rather than economically and socially paralyzed. Finally, this paper examines how Detroit's newest destination branding strategy incorporates, both the traditional and alternative, in its focus on cars, culture, gaming, music and sports and sells post-Fordist Detroit as cool, cutting edge, and real.

Public and Private Sector Involvement

Most cities regularly host concerts and other entertainment event, all provided by entrepreneurs working with venue owners. This business does not really need the help of DMOs except, as in the case of Belfast, to promote the destination with a music or entertainment theme. The high arts, on the other hand, are closely linked to public facilities like arts centers, and to heavy government subsidies. Even within the arts there is discrimination, and it has to be asked if it can be justified. For example, Wanhill (2008) observed that opera in the UK received "five times the amount of subsidies per attendance compared to other performing arts establishments while being attended by only 7% of the population" (p. 354).

Destination Music

The term "destination music" comes from a major UK study of music festivals and concerts—"The Contribution of Music Festivals and Major Concerts to Tourism in the UK" by UK Music (available online at: www.ukmusic.org). There is no doubt that music as a theme, and musical performances are a great generator of travel, including pilgrimages to places like Graceland, visits to museums and galleries where music is featured, entertainment districts within cities (often focused on drinking/dining/music establishments), and musical theater. Shows that tour can be considered special events in cities, as can the numerous concerts that promoters place in concert halls and arenas around the world.

In some cities music can be a unique selling proposition, take Belfast for example:

Belfast music: "one of the great musical cities"

Belfast provides a good example of how different agencies can come together to form an organisation that promotes both music and tourism. Belfast Music is a partnership between Belfast City Council and Culture Northern Ireland (a web-based organisation funded mainly by the Arts Council of Northern Ireland). It is supported by the Northern Ireland Tourism Board who also administered the European Regional Development Fund under the European Sustainable Competitiveness Programme for Northern Ireland programme for this project. The main rationale for this project is to bring information about music into one place, the website, and to promote this via e-marketing tools such as Twitter and Facebook. Belfast music also produced a mobile phone app that guides visitors around music venues and activities. (www.belfastmusic.org)

The UK Music study, with data from surveys undertaken in 2009, covers both music festivals and single concerts. Here are some highlights:

- The 2009 data, from analysis of 2.5 million ticket purchases, underestimates true scale of music-related travel because not all events were covered.

- The study estimated that 7.7 million visits were made to over 5,000 festivals and concerts.
- Resultant spending came to £1.4 billion sterling, of which £864 million is added to UK economy by music tourists.
- Music tourists made up 41% of audiences at large concerts and 48% at music festivals (on average).
- Domestic music tourism accounted for 95% of all music tourist visits, but international accounted for 18% of spending.
- Music tourists spent 25% more than other international visitors to the UK, on a per-night basis.
- Those attending festivals tended to spend more than for concerts.
- Spending was 38% on tickets, 17% on site, and 46% off site.

The report noted: "Our research suggests that a generation of young people are already factoring their favourite live music events into their holiday plans" (p. 11).

North American Research on Music and Tourism

The TAMS research conducted in North America allows breakdowns by types of event-related travel. Highlights are from the report: Attending Rock Concerts and Recreational Dancing, TAMS: A Profile Report, August 31, 2007:

- Over the last 2 years, 11.8% (26,005,373) of adult Americans went to rock or pop music concerts or went recreational dancing while on an out-of-town, overnight trip of one or more nights.
- 9.1% attended a rock or pop music concert on a trip while 3.7% went recreational dancing.
- 40.3% (10,470,740 adult Americans) of those who attended a rock concert or went recreational dancing reported that this activity was the main reason for taking at least one trip in the past 2 years.
- Relative to the average US Pleasure Traveler, those who attended rock concerts or went recreational dancing while on trips are equally spilt between males and females but overrepresented among young (18 to 34 years of age) singles. This segment has slightly above-average levels of education (64.7% university degree or higher) and household incomes ($81,480). They are also more likely to live in large cities (population 2 million or more).
- Travelers who attended rock concerts or went recreational dancing are very active on trips and more likely than the average US Pleasure Traveler to participate in a wide variety of culture and entertainment activities, outdoor activities, tours, and cruises. They were especially more likely to engage in sports-related activities, both as a spectator (e.g., professional sporting events) and as a participant (e.g., team sports), to attend live arts performances and theater, film, and music festivals and to participate in physically strenuous outdoor activities (e.g., downhill skiing & snowboarding, sailing & surfing). They also enjoy fine dining, winery tours, and health spas. This segment seeks high-energy, activity-oriented vacation destinations that offer novelty, lots to see and do, intellectual stimulation, physical challenge, great shopping opportunities, and an opportunity to be pampered.
- This segment is an above-average user of the Internet to plan (81.5%) and book travel (61.2%). They can be most effectively targeted through travel media as well as music and entertainment media (e.g., music/video shows or channels, modern rock or Top 40 radio, magazine, and entertainment websites).

Theater

In some cities, notably London, Las Vegas, and New York, theatrical performances and a permanent theater district are huge tourism attractions. Permanence of this kind is clearly different from Event Tourism, but there are overlaps in the form of touring shows and special promotions like the Year of Culture. And certainly many tourists coming to a city for the theater experience consider it to be a special event.

Research Note on Tourism and Theater

Gilbert, D., & Lizotte, M. (1998). Tourism and the performing arts. Travel & Tourism Analyst, 1: 82–96

This study looks at the evidence of the inter-relationship between tourism and the performing arts. It finds that the theatre is an important drawing card for London, but that what might at first sight appear to be a mutually beneficial relationship is not without its problems and critics. Some of the widely-held criticisms include: the belief that too great a dependency on tourism will reduce the quality and artistic integrity of the arts; the view that the tourism industry does not yet adequately understand the role that the arts can play in creating and sustaining demand for a given urban destination; and the objection that the more the arts come to rely on tourism as a source of business, the greater the pressure to reduce public subsidy to the arts.

Annual theater "festivals" have become a staple summertime feature around the world, and a few of these have evolved into permanent arts attractions.

Research Note on Theater Festivals

Mitchell, C. (1993). Economic impact of the arts: Theatre festivals in small Ontario communities. *Journal of Cultural Economics, 17*(2), 55–67.

This paper has demonstrated that visitors to professional theatre companies located in towns and villages of southern Ontario contribute to the economic well-being of the local economy. Furthermore, it has been documented that while all communities receive some monetary benefits, spatial variations are found to exist. These discrepancies are a function of differences in the average expenditures of non-local residents and the total number of visitors attending the theatre event. As expected, average expenditures appear to be highest in communities supporting a large commercial sector which are capable of sustaining a tourist market. Moreover, the number of visitors attending a theatre event appears to be greatest in small communities supporting an established theater company.

Music Festivals in Australia

C. Gibson and Connell (2012), in their book *Music Festivals and Regional Development in Australia*, said "Since the 1980s, in Australia and elsewhere, some music festivals have been linked to local tourism strategies, their growth nothing short of dramatic and their economic potential considerable" (p. 16). They concluded that music festivals are well established throughout the developed world and are extending far beyond that. Their research in 2007 found that music festivals in regional (i.e., rural) areas were "not as numerous as agricultural shows, community festivals or sporting carnivals [but] they were more common than other popular festivals such as arts and food and wine festivals" (p. 16). Over 80% had been established since 1990.

Major music festivals had become co-branded with a number of towns. "This growing economic role has been accompanied by more comprehensive marketing, such that by the 1990s the major festivals were institutionalized, as part of formal tourism campaigns, and sought increasingly national and even global markets" (C. Gibson & Connell, 2012, p. 20). Placing the rise of festivals into the context of rural and small-town development, or in many cases revitalization, they argued: "Festivals are one means to add vitality, generate a sense of community and market a place as caring about fun, pleasure and quality of life, where the arts are present" (p. 37). These events often draw large crowds from major cities, and encourage local investment and in-migration. If a town cannot survive on its traditional economic bases, then building an amenity or lifestyle image can be an alternative.

C. Gibson and Connell observed from their own work that "The majority of visitors to music festivals are there to socialize and have fun, as much as for the musical genre, but all festivals have a certain percentage of dedicated fans and regular, repeat visitors" (p. 53). These are the fans and fanatics as identified by the research of Mackellar (2009a, 2009b).

A number of other researchers have looked at festival audiences and tourism in Australia (Pegg & Patersson, 2010). Also consult the Woodford Case Study in this chapter.

Research Notes

Mackellar, J. (2009a). Dabblers, fans and fanatics: Exploring behavioural segmentation at a special-interest event. *Journal of Vacation Marketing, 15*(1), 5–24.

This paper explores the behavioural segments of the audience at the Elvis Revival Festival in Parkes, Australia. Audiences were observed travelling to, and participating in, this two-day event, held in January 2007, which celebrated the life and music of Elvis Presley. The study highlights differences in fan behaviour, resulting in four behavioural audience segments: social, dabbler, fan and fanatic. The study demonstrates the use of participant observation as a method to understand differing audience segments. As a result, differences in marketing and management strategies may be created to cater for the different needs and expectations of visitors and local communities.

Mackellar, J. (2009b). An examination of serious participants at the Australian Wintersun Festival. *Leisure Studies, 28*(1), 85–104.

Events, such as festivals, have been identified as places in which activities are provided for participants to develop skills and build their leisure careers. This study aimed to explore the leisure and tourist behaviours of serious, and at times fanatical, participants at the Wintersun Festival in Queensland, Australia. The weeklong nostalgic celebration of music, dancing, cars and lifestyles attracts participants from distant communities to travel and participate in the activities that are integral to achieving their leisure goals. This study utilised participant observation to identify nine domains which describe and explain the behaviours of participants including specialised travel, lifestyle, identity reinforcement, pride, fanaticism, social interaction, fixated consumption, competition and skill development. The results highlight the specialised travel experience undertaken by participants and the important role of events in fulfilling their personal and social goals.

Pegg, S., & Patterson, I. (2010). Rethinking music festivals as a staged event: Gaining insights from understanding visitor motivations and the experiences they seek. *Journal of Convention and Event Tourism, 11*(2), 85–99.

Event managers are increasingly under pressure to develop new strategies that will optimize any competitive advantages that their event may have, while, at the same time, minimizing their operation's vulnerability to external threats and emulation. Yet, for all this, little research has been done to date with respect to visitor engagement in events, such as music festivals, in the Australian setting. With this in mind, the principal aim of this study was to profile visitors who attended the Tamworth Country Music Festival to determine their main motivations for attendance and what aspects of the event have differentiated it from others of its type. Overall, over 1,500 visitor surveys were collected, with results showing that there was a significant difference among festival visitors with respect to their activity engagement, reasons for attending the festival, and assessment of it when comparisons across key study variables were determined. These findings provide clear insights into the changing nature of visitor engagement in the experience economy and the importance of servicing the diverse needs of discrete niche groups who might congregate at a particular event.

Touring Art and Museum Exhibitions

When galleries or museums host major touring exhibitions they are often promoted as tourist attractions. The more unique they are the more they can attract cultural tourists from outside the host community. Similar to festivals, they also tend to attract a lot of residents, casual visitors, and time switchers. A study by Mihalik and Wing-Vogelbacker (1992) is one of the few to document the impacts of this type of event, while Carmichael (2002) studied the impact of an art exhibit.

Research Notes on Touring Exhibitions

Mihalik, B., & Wing-Vogelbacker, A. (1992). Traveling art expositions as a tourism event: A market research analysis of Ramesses The Great. *Journal of Travel and Tourism Marketing*, *1*(3), 25–41.

A study of this "itinerant event" emphasized that its value could be measured in terms of educational value, cultural understanding, promoting scientific or technical trade, encouraging tourism, and contributing to place marketing. Museums use them to build community support and memberships as well as their profile. The Ramesses The Great Exhibition at the Mint Museum of Charlotte, North Carolina, was a success in that it generated over 600,000 ticket sales and resulted in museum membership jumping from 3,000 to 9,000. Exit surveys determined that about 73% of visitors came from the defined "secondary market" beyond metropolitan Charlotte and within 150 miles.

Carmichael, B. (2002). Global competitiveness and special events in cultural tourism: The example of the Barnes Exhibit at the Art Gallery of Ontario, Toronto. *The Canadian Geographer*, *46*(4), 310–324.

From September 1994 to January 1995 the Art Gallery of Ontario in Toronto hosted a major art exhibit of French impressionist paintings "From Cezanne to Matisse, Great French Paintings," known as the "Barnes Exhibition." This special cultural event affected the attraction mix of Toronto's urban tourism product and acted as a "magnet" drawing out of town visitors to Toronto with the main purpose of visiting this unique event. This paper explores the spatial impact of the Barnes Exhibit in a segmentation analysis of "out-of-town" Barnes Exhibit visitors. Visitors are segmented by major trip purpose and visitor origin. The pull of the Exhibit is examined using two simple gravity models to describe the distance decay effect. Out-of-town visitors from Ontario are compared with visitors from the United States according to the main purpose of their trip, their demographics and spending patterns. Out-of-town visitors from Ontario tend to be older than US visitors, spend less than US visitors and are more likely to have the Barnes Exhibit as the main purpose of their trip to Toronto. This study illustrates the value-added nature of special events to the urban cultural product both for recreational and tourist travel. It shows the complexity and overlapping of urban fields of a Toronto attraction for different types of visitors to the same event.

Touring Shows

For an earlier generation, in simpler times, the biggest show to come to town was the traveling circus, while the county fair with its touring amusements (the "carnival" or "midway") was a reliable summertime attraction. Now there are many such touring entertainment productions, at a much grander scale, often using existing venues and sometimes erecting their own big-tops.

The show itself is usually the same wherever it is played, but traveling entertainment shows are special events in the communities they visit. Those with drawing power are highly valued additions to a city's event portfolio. Perhaps the best known globally is Cirque du Soleil with its multiple shows and tours. Another example is Cavalia, described below from its visit in 2011 to Calgary.

CAVALIA (from a Tourism Calgary media release, March 10, 2011)

A magical encounter between human and horse will gallop into Canada Olympic Park this spring! An innovative multi-media and multi- disciplinary production created by Normand Latourelle, one of the co-founders of Canada's famed Cirque du Soleil, will have its Calgary premiere on May 25, 2011 under the White Big Top at COP. "Tourism Calgary is proud to bring Cavalia to Calgary," said Randy Williams, Tourism Calgary President and CEO. "The world-class show is an excellent draw for tourism to Calgary enhancing our city's reputation as a dynamic, cultured city while generating economic impact for the community."

The show is performed in the largest tent in North America, a 26,300 sq. ft. big top, and takes 40 people 12 days to build. The event will be staged for 5 weeks (35 Shows) from April 15 to May 20, 2011.

Photo 8.11. Cavalia (Credit: photo courtesy of Cavalia).

In a postevent evaluation, the following data were released by Tourism Calgary (according to postal code data tracked by Cavalia the statistics were provided to Tourism Calgary):

- 15,494 tickets were purchased from out-of-region (a distance of greater than 80 km from Calgary) of which 9,732 tickets were purchased from a distance of 80 kms or more within Alberta: Edmonton 1,069; Red Deer 573; Lethbridge 404; Medicine Hat 251; Other Alberta 7,435;
- 5,762 tickets were purchased from outside Alberta (USA 1,930; BC 1,434; Saskatchewan 310; Other 2,088);
- The performer/crew production block actualized 3,820 total hotel room nights; this exceeded the initial block issued by Tourism Calgary (3,465 hotel room nights);
- Conservative estimates suggest the event generated an additional 2,700 hotel room nights from out-of-region visitation. This estimate is based on the premise that all reservations were single-night-stays, double occupancy bookings, and that only 39% of total out-of-region ticket sales resulted in hotel room bookings;
- 6,520 total hotel room nights booked (*actual official block + estimated out-of-region visitation*).

This example makes it clear that hosting popular touring shows can generate significant tourist demand. Basically, if you want to see this kind of entertainment you have to be in a big city or travel to the host city. Their high costs require large audiences, over a substantial period of time.

Private Functions

Although often nearly invisible, taking place in private, this is a constant business sector of particular importance to hotels, resorts, and catering establishments. Some of it is definitely within the entertainment area, and entertainment figures prominently in the programming, but many functions are *rites de passage* in people's lives, with a more solemn undertone.

We can break this market down into weddings, reunions, parties, and *rites de passage* like *bar mitzvahs* and graduations. Small corporate events and association meetings often fall into this category. Increasingly, professional planners and coordinators are employed to make these occasions special and trouble free. What often goes unmeasured is the enormous amount of travel generated by these small planned events.

The Wedding Market

People are always traveling for weddings, and "destination weddings" where everyone travels to a favored site or resort are more popular than ever. Numerous cities and resorts compete for weddings, and it is big business for hotels, caterers, wedding planners, and other suppliers. Some destinations have comparative advantages, based on location or climate, while others are good at marketing to this segment.

Hawaii has remained popular for Japanese weddings. This article from *Pacific Business News* (October 19, 2004) gives some reasons for its popularity, and an indication of its scale. Note that we are talking about the event itself, with "stag or hen parties" and honeymoon travel bringing additional benefit.

More than half of all Japanese overseas weddings this fall have been booked for Hawaii, reports the Japan Travel Bureau, which books the lion's share of Japanese outbound travel.

For October, November and December, 50.5 percent of Japanese weddings in foreign locales will be in Hawaii, 28.8 percent in Micronesia, and 12.8 percent in Oceania, JTB said in its Autumn Honeymoon and Wedding Season survey.

The Hawaii Visitors & Convention Bureau said Tuesday that JTB attributed the popularity of Hawaii for Japanese weddings to "wide selection of venues for the ceremony, chapels overlooking the ocean, and adjoining facilities for a party."

JTB estimates the average cost of an overseas wedding ceremony at $1,613 (177,460 yen).

Hawaii also ranks as the most popular overseas honeymoon destination for the Japanese this autumn, with 29.8 percent of all bookings, ahead of Oceania with 24.6 percent and Europe with 17.3 percent.

Research Note on Wedding Tourism

Johnston, L. (2006). 'I do down-under': Naturalizing landscapes and love through wedding tourism in New Zealand. *ACME: An International E-Journal for Critical Geographies*, 5(2), 191–208.

This paper examines the importance of place for wedding tourism. A focus on tourist weddings offers a unique opportunity to examine critically the ways in which wedding rituals rely on "natural" landscapes to produce "down-under" weddings. Drawing on material from a New Zealand television documentary "I do down-under," New Zealand wedding tourism websites and brochures, plus interviews with wedding tourism operators, I offer an analysis of New Zealand destination weddings. I suggest that heteronormative tourist weddings and New Zealand landscapes constitute each other as "natural," 100% pure, exotic and romantic. Landscapes such as white glaciers, rugged mountains, lush green subtropical forests, blue water coastlines and golden beaches are promoted as part of the wedding package. In turn these moral geographies of tourist weddings naturalize and romanticize heterosexuality. Furthermore, the landscape takes on the role of family and friends who are "escaping" down-under to marry.

Stag and Hen Parties

Whole groups of friends traveling before a wedding, segregated by gender, to provide a final fling for the still unmarried couple? It sounds a little strange, and is definitely a private function, but has nevertheless generated big tourism business! Here is how one tour company describes it (release travel co.uk)

> If you are looking to arrange a classy Hen Weekend, Release would like to help. We know how to make a hen weekend special with destinations like London, Barcelona, Bath, and Brighton; we guarantee that you will have the best weekend ever.

> For the perfect Stag Weekend come to Release. We have all the best destinations such as Las Vegas, Bournemouth, Prague and Amsterdam to name just a few. Whether it is a luxury stag weekend or just a good value stag do, look no further than Release.

Not all cities want the business, as it has become associated with drunkenness and bad behavior in some places, but of course there are more sophisticated and sensitive options available.

The Reunion Market

Family and class reunions have always been popular (not to mention the stuff of comedic movies), but many affinity groups also hold reunions. Military reunions are particularly common and can be quite large, and so can corporate reunions such as special events for company pensioners.

Research Note on Reunion Tourism

Yun, J., & Lehto, X. (2009). Motives and patterns of family reunion travel. *Journal of Quality Assurance in Hospitality and Tourism, 10*(4), 279–300.

The family travel market is growing and family reunion travel is an unexplored niche within this expanding market. This study uses a series of in-depth interviews to perform a qualitative analysis and to identify patterns and characteristics of the family reunion travel market. The findings from the analysis are classified into two main parts: motivational themes and behavioral characteristics. By exploring family reunion travelers' motivations, researchers can better understand and interpret the behavioral characteristics of family reunion travelers.

Pilgrimage and Other Religious Events

You cannot create religious pilgrimage events from scratch, at least not explicitly as tourist products. Pilgrimage emerges from significant cultural forces and historic incidents that make places (i.e., shrines) and routes attractive for treks or visits. The pilgrimage is a special event in the pilgrim's life, and if people arrive at the same time you have the potential for very large events.

Research Notes on Pilgrimage Events

Nolan, M., & Nolan, S. (1992). Religious sites as tourism attractions in Europe. *Annals of Tourism Research, 19*(1), 68–78.

Europe's religious tourism system is described with emphasis on the fulfillment of the expectations of visitors ranging from devout pilgrims to secular tourists at three types of attractions. These are pilgrimage shrines with strong emphasis on religious devotions, but with few characteristics to attract secular tourists; shrines that function as devotional centers and religious tourism attractions because of various combinations of historical, artistic, and scenic site characteristics; and places where religious festivals are the principal attractions. Problems related to conflicting interests of pilgrims and tourists are discussed along with some examples of management strategies designed to minimize these conflicts.

Henderson, J. (2011). Religious tourism and its management: The Hajj in Saudi Arabia. *International Journal of Tourism Research, 13*(6), 541–552.

Religion and tourism share a close relationship in which the former motivates travel and is a source of assorted visitor attractions. Pilgrimage is one expression of the ties between the two and the paper identifies key pilgrimage tourism issues pertaining to demand and provision that are discussed within the context of the contemporary hajj. The hajj by Muslims to the cities they deem holy in Saudi Arabia is a distinctive illustration that involves the mass movement of pilgrims every year. Numbers are strictly controlled, but set to rise as the government pursues a policy of expanding space at certain holy sites and encouraging an increase in the supply of accommodation and other amenities as well as enhancing supporting infrastructure. Some projects are very ambitious, leading to questions about whether the pace of development is sustainable. The purpose of the study is to improve understanding of the uniqueness and significance of the hajj phenomenon and illuminate the challenges of managing large-scale religious tourism events in the changing world of the twenty-first century.

Secular Pilgrimage Events

Anyone with a special interest can engage in pilgrim-like travel to sites of importance. There might even be a kind of spiritual experience involved, the kind derived from a sense of accomplishment (e.g., I finally played the old course at St. Andrews!), reverence (I got to touch the Stanley Cup!), or deep respect (these vineyards are a thousand years old). Yoga practitioners might want a pilgrimage to an ashram in India, while foodies flock to the cooking classes and retreats offered by celebrity chefs. Visits to sport events can be a combination of interest in the competition itself and the place in which it is held.

All sites of pilgrimage have the potential for being augmented through iconic events—that is, events that will hold special significance. These are equivalent (in terms of being able to draw visitors) to the rituals and festivals held at sacred pilgrimage sites, although not equivalent in meanings, nor the scale of the events.

Ever-more popular are sites associated with celebrities, with Graceland being near the top of the list in terms of global recognition. Strangely, Elvis-themed events flourish in other parts of the world, owing to his popularity combined with nostalgia for that period of time (e.g., the Parkes Elvis Revival in Australia).

> **Research Notes on Secular Pilgrimage and Tourism**
>
> Hall, C. M. (2002). ANZAC Day and secular pilgrimage. *Tourism Recreation Research*, *27*(2), 83–87.
>
> This paper describes ANZAC (Australian and New Zealand Army Corps) Day, arguably the most important national occasion in Australia and New Zealand. Held every 25th of April, it marks the anniversary of the first major military action fought by Australian and New Zealand forces during the First World War. The paper describes the ceremonies and services held during ANZAC Day; the notion of pilgrimage used by the travel industry in promoting travel to Turkey and war graves; and the financial contribution of the Australian and New Zealand governments used to upgrade facilities at commemorative sites due to the increase in numbers of international visitors attending ANZAC Day.

A related phenomenon is that of pilgrimage as entertainment or spectacle for others. This makes pilgrims the object of "tourist gaze" and places the event into two, potentially conflicting mindsets. Such an event is the "Pilgrimage of the Gypsies," which has become a tourist attraction for non-Romanis.

> Wiley, E. (2005). Romani performance and heritage tourism: The pilgrimage of the gypsies at Les Saintes-Maries-de-la-Mer. *TDR*, *49*, 135–158.
>
> Every May some ten thousand Romanies (aka Gypsies) perform a pilgrimage to Les Saintes-Maries-de-le-Mer, a remote fishing village in the south of France. Their annual gathering has developed into a popular festival of Romani culture that spawns its own pilgrimage of tourists and journalists—as well as some tension between the townspeople and the Romani.

Reenactments

Any historical event can be reenacted, often as a heritage celebration and sometimes merely as entertainment. Some are produced by amateur societies (like Civil War enthusiasts in the US) and others by historic sites where the event can be an important animation and interpretation tool. To those who take part, actors and amateurs, there can be a special significance attached to participation, involving communitas and even pilgrimage-like appreciation.

Battle reenactments are controversial, for reasons associated with the depiction of death and destruction as entertainment. Other historic reenactments attract controversy over the meanings attached to the event and how it is interpreted.

Research Notes on Reenactments and Tourism

Carnegie, E., & McCabe, S. (2008). Re-enactment events and tourism: Meaning, authenticity and identity. *Current Issues in Tourism*, *11*(4), 349–368.

Re-enactment events have began to play a significant role in the calendars of individual attractions, regions or even nations to generate media exposure, develop inbound tourism activity and raise the cultural heritage profile of a locality for community development and/ or regeneration purposes. The (re-)presentation of cultural heritage in these forms creates a unique set of interactions between landscapes, local communities, tourists and heritage organisations. In the recent past however, re-enactment events have been subjected to increased debate and criticism as to their educational value and meaning and for their contribution to understandings of cultural heritage in post-modern consumer societies. This paper presents an interdisciplinary review of these debates and draws on small scale research findings to reassess the value of re-enactment events as a means of presenting heritage to audiences.

Ray, N. M., McCain, G., Davis, D., & Melin, T. L. (2006). Lewis and Clark and the *Corps of Discovery*: Re-enactment event tourism as authentic heritage travel. *Leisure Studies*, *25*(4), 437–454.

Heritage tourism has evolved to include study of sub-segments who travel to attend and participate in historical event re-enactments. In the US, the bicentennial of the Lewis and Clark expedition to the Pacific coast and back again is being commemorated from its point of departure to its end. This paper is an exploratory study of a sample of re-enactment tourists who attended three of the Lewis and Clark events. The role that re-enactment tourism plays in heritage tourism is examined and preliminary findings on perceptions of nostalgia and authenticity of the re-enactment products and events are presented. Preliminary managerial benefits and suggestions for host communities are provided.

Wallace, T. (2007). Went the day well: Scripts, glamour and performance in war-weekends. *International Journal of Heritage Studies*, *13*(3), 200–223.

The recent growth of interest in heritage events has relied implicitly upon a modernist ontology in the way assumptions are made about the distinctiveness between visitor and performer identities. This article questions these assumptions through an analysis of the different groups of social actors attracted to war-weekends organised through preserved steam railways. War-weekends bring together in the same locality visitors, volunteers, performers, dressers-up and re-enactors sharing stories, enjoying the present and reflecting on the past—experiences in which each individual's participation is enhanced. Although these and other "events" are crucial to the continued existence of preserved railways in the UK they provide the participants with more than just a nostalgic trip back to the community spirit articulated through the so-called "blitz mentality" of the 1940s.

The Wallace article discusses railway-based "war weekends" in the UK, and the nature of these events is revealed in this publicity piece from the Internet site of the railway company:

> North Yorkshire Moors Railway
> Railway in Wartime
> 12–14th October 2012
>
> We've turned the clocks back to 1943 for our most popular event of the year, with ENSA entertainers, street parades, vehicle displays and re-enactments along the railway, and new for this year at the showground on Malton Road. This year's event promises to be bigger and better than ever! The NYMR is proud to announce

that our ever popular event has expanded to encompass a full programme of 1940's shows, traders, battle re-enactments, dances, historic vehicles and living histories at the Showground, Malton Road, Pickering. This exciting development should benefit the public and the re-enacting community alike—enhancing still further the popular "NYMR Railway in Wartime experience." The extra space will allow us to accommodate more of our re-enactor friends and help the public to safely enjoy an enhanced NYMR 1940's experience.

Case Study: Edinburgh Festivals—Excerpts From the Edinburgh Festivals Impact Study (May, 2011) (www.bop.co.uk)

"BOP (need beginning quotation mark) Consulting was commissioned to conduct an impact assessment of the 12 Festivals represented by Festivals Edinburgh. The Study was commissioned by the Festivals Forum and in partnership with Scottish Enterprise, Festivals Edinburgh, City of Edinburgh Council, EventScotland (also representing VisitScotland), The Scottish Government, and Scottish Arts Council (now Creative Scotland).

While the assessment of economic impact remains a key concern of this study, there was a shared recognition among the Festivals and the commissioning stakeholders of the need for a more rounded assessment of the value of the Festivals. This study therefore set out to take a "360 degree" approach to assessing impact that considers social, cultural, environmental, and media aspects, in addition to the economic effects. The research thus enables the Festivals to demonstrate their value to a much wider range of stakeholders across Scotland and beyond.

The scale and depth of the study exceeds all previous research projects carried out on behalf of the Festivals: more than 50 separate surveys were conducted across the 12 Festivals, involving in total more than 15,000 respondents. This did not only include audiences, but also sought to understand the impact that the Festivals have on a range of other groups and stakeholders (performers and delegates, attending journalists, volunteers, temporary staff, teachers and Festival sponsors).

Cultural Impact

The research finds that audiences are very satisfied with their experience of the Edinburgh Festivals. Indeed, they rate the events as better than other comparable events and activities. Audiences value the Festivals because they give them the opportunity to have an enjoyable social experience with friends and family, but also because they result in a number of specific cultural benefits.

- Audiences value world class and international cultural experiences—and the Festivals provide these.
- Through the Festivals, audiences are able to engage more deeply with the many art forms, including discovering new artists, new styles, and new genres.
- Audiences consider the Festivals to be unique and distinctive—standing out from comparable events.

The study also shows that the Festivals have an impact on cultural participation more widely, in particular on audiences' year-round attendance. For instance, there is evidence that:

- The Festivals are a stimulus to further attendance at similar cultural events subsequently.
- Audiences are more likely to take their children to similar cultural events as a result of their Festival experience.
- Audiences are more likely to take greater risks in their cultural choices and explore new cultural experiences as a result of their Festival-going.

Aside from events for the public, the Festivals also promote, develop and support the cultural, creative, and events sector in Edinburgh, Scotland, and beyond. Most obviously, the Festivals make an important economic contribution to the range of cultural venues that are involved in hosting the Festivals throughout the year. The Festivals also contribute to the professional development of performers and artists. Simply taking part in the Festivals increases artists' reputations and provides them with inspiration for new work as well as the prospect of follow-on sales and new commissions.

The Festivals are also proactive in supporting performers and companies. This includes directly spending a significant proportion of their budget on artists based in Scotland, and by providing tailored delegate programmes that increase practitioners' knowledge and skills, and widen and deepen their peer networks.

The Festivals help to build capacity for the sector long-term. Volunteers and temporary staff who are working with the Festivals are more intensely engaged than in, for instance, the Scottish museums sector (in terms of the average number of hours contributed per volunteer). This wealth of experience constitutes a resource for the sector when looking ahead towards other large scale events such as the Glasgow Commonwealth Games in 2014.

Place-Making and Media Impact

One of the most striking findings from the research is the strong and positive impact that the Festivals have on the way the City of Edinburgh and Scotland are perceived, by locals and external visitors alike. While it might be expected that attendees have a positive attitude towards the Festivals, the results exceed what is known from research on other cultural and heritage activities (including where improving local pride and perceptions have been a major aim of the activities). Our results show that:

- Local residents take great pride in the Festivals and the value they provide to Edinburgh as a city.
- Visitors believe that the Festivals make the city distinctive; they highly value the experience of having multiple Festivals running simultaneously during the summer period, and are more likely to re-visit as a result of attending the Festivals (thus ensuring the continued contribution to Edinburgh's visitor economy).
- The image that the Festivals present of Edinburgh and Scotland is one of diversity and openness; showcasing a positive national identity.

The media attention that the Festivals generate (as recorded through the online monitoring service Meltwater News) is also very significant, and it exceeds that of other comparable events. The data recorded by the online news monitoring tool used in the study does not allow any conclusions to be drawn as to whether this media attention is positive or negative. However, the social media activity generated by the attending journalists has been assessed and it is largely favourable. This suggests that the ultimate media messages that are networked and syndicated from the attending journalists are predominantly favourable.

Social Impact

With the exception of the Edinburgh Mela, achieving social outcomes is not the primary aim of any of the Festivals. Nevertheless, our research shows that the Festivals do have a number of social impacts, in addition to promoting local pride and a sense of belonging. In this study, the Festivals' social impacts were interrogated based on the concept of social capital, which considers the formation of social networks, relationships and links to resources as a first step in achieving longer term socio-economic outcomes. From this perspective, there is evidence that the Festivals help to build social connections between people—whether between family members, or between people from both similar and different communities. Providing opportunities for people to meet people from, and share messages about, different cultures—within the positive and informal context of a cultural event like the Edinburgh Mela—also helps people to increase their understanding of other cultures.

Economic Impact

The study also confirms and further strengthens the key message from the earlier Edinburgh Festivals Economic Impact Study: the Festivals are a major contributor to both the local Edinburgh economy and the national Scottish economy. This economic impact spreads far beyond the immediate cultural economy. In fact, the biggest beneficiary businesses in Edinburgh and Scotland are those in the tourism, hospitality, and leisure sectors. The economic impact was assessed according to the principles of the Scottish Government and HM Treasury's Green Book, which means that only the economic contribution which is genuinely additional has been considered. The overall factors that generate the economic impact of the Festivals are not markedly different from the previous SQW study:

- The economic impact is driven by audience expenditure, but performers and delegates and attending journalists also make significant contributions in absolute terms.
- Audience expenditure is dominated by staying visitors, as they spend more, stay for longer, and their expenditure is more likely to be genuinely additional.
- The large proportion of the overall economic impact is generated by just a small number of the Festivals.

Environmental Impact

The final impact area considered as part of the research is the most challenging for the Festivals, as it consists of assessing the impacts on the environment. Attempting to tackle this issue is a laudable and brave undertaking. The Festivals have already shown leadership in their development of a cross-Festival Environment Strategy. The strategy aims to build awareness and capacity within the Festivals, as well as identify and develop approaches and practice (such as the Green Venue accreditation scheme) to tackle their environmental footprint. Nevertheless, the process of measuring the negative environmental contribution is still difficult and has inherent challenges for organisations' communication agendas.

The Festivals—and the cultural and tourism sectors more generally—are still at an early stage in terms of their thinking around environmental sustainability. This year's research has therefore concentrated on ways of assessing and monitoring the current level of impact (rather than measuring a process of change, as in the other impact areas).

It must be recognised that there are still significant gaps in the Festivals' data (including the impact of most Festival venues, performers and production crew) which means that the figures presented in the report are a considerable underestimate of the overall carbon footprint of the Festivals. From what is known to-date, audiences (and in particular staying visitors) account for the biggest proportion of the impact, but further work is needed in this area.

Economic Impact Data

The average audience expenditure at the Edinburgh Festivals, per person per day, and average length of stay in Edinburgh and Scotland, 2010 are shown in Table 8.1.

Additionality

A key stage of the economic impact calculations is to assess the proportion of expenditures made by all visitor types that would not have been made in the city in any case. This entails converting the gross economic impact into the net economic impact. For example, many residents who attend the Festival might have visited the city and spent money on their trip even if the Festivals had not taken place. Therefore the expenditure incurred on the trip to the Festival is simply deadweight and cannot be considered to be additional.

What is important to note is that additionality varies by the place of origin of the visitors, in connection with the geography of the economy that is being assessed. Thus, a day tripper to the Festival from the rest of Scotland, who would have gone on a trip elsewhere in Scotland if the Festivals had not taken place, would have made expenditure that was not additional to the Scottish economy (as it simply displaced expenditure from elsewhere in Scotland to Edinburgh), but it would be additional to Edinburgh's economy (as it was being made there rather than elsewhere). Similarly, for a Scottish day tripper

Table 8.1. Average Audience Expenditure at the Edinburgh Festivals, per Person per Day, and Average Length of Stay in Edinburgh and Scotland, 2010

Festival	Av. Daily Expenditure per Person (£)	Av. Nights Spent in Edinburgh	Av. Nights Spent Elsewhere in Scotland
Science Festival	£12.5	4.4	0.4
Imaginate Festival	£5.0	4.4	0.0
Film Festival	£39.7	5.4	0.6
Jazz and Blues Festival	£41.1	5.0	0.8
Military Tattoo	£69.0	2.1	3.7
Fringe	£52.4	5.0	0.7
Mela Festival	£11.0	6.3	0.3
International Festival (paid events)	£57.7	7.4	1.5
International Festival (Fireworks)	£46.6	1.5	0.0
Book Festival	£36.5	6.0	1.2
Storytelling Festival	£19.3	3.8	0.5
Hogmanay	£114.0	3.6	0.8

Source: Edinburgh Festivals Impact Study (BOP Consulting, 2011).

who would have gone to work or stayed at home, the expenditure made at the Festivals would not be additional to Scotland (as it is assumed that this expenditure is deadweight, as it would have been made in the local economy at a later date), but it would again be additional to Edinburgh as it was spent in the city at the expense of the day tripper's home town. Lastly, for the Festival organisers' expenditure, we also have to account for any leakage—that is, expenditure made outside Scotland.

In order to quantify these effects, all visitors were asked what they would have done if the Festivals had not taken place. They were given four options:

- "I would have stayed at home or gone to work."
- "I would have done something else in Edinburgh/visited the city anyway."
- "I would have gone elsewhere in Scotland."
- "I would have gone elsewhere outside Scotland."

These responses have been analysed for each of the Festivals, and crucially, for the different visitor types. This is exactly the same question used by SQW in the 2004–5 survey, and the question was has also asked of the other visitor segments included within the economic impact calculation (i.e., the performers, delegates, and journalists).

The effect of applying these additionality criteria is dramatic—almost all of the local visitors answer either option 1 or 2 (stayed home/gone to work, or done something elsewhere in Edinburgh). This means that the expenditure for all but 3% of the locals is not additional to Edinburgh and just 1.1% of the locals' expenditure is additional to Scotland. The vast majority of local visitors therefore get excluded at this stage from the subsequent calculations of net economic value. What this means is that, in addition to the scale of a Festival, simply having a higher proportion of locals attending will significantly reduce the economic impact of a Festival (Table 8.2).

Additionality was also applied to the ticket expenditure. As the data on ticket expenditure was not collected through the surveys, and captured instead from the Festivals' actual box office data, this was achieved through a slightly different method. The average additionality generated through the surveys per visitor type (locals, staying visitors, etc.) was applied to the ticket expenditure, according to the composition of the Festivals' audiences.

Gross Expenditure to Net Expenditure

Gross expenditure in Edinburgh is circa £250m, 89% of which is spent by the audience (£221m). Once the additionality for each Festival has been established, it is possible to convert the gross visitor expenditures made at the Festival into net expenditure (i.e., the proportion of expenditures that is genuinely additional). The difference that the gross to net conversion makes when looking at visitor expenditure is dramatic,

Table 8.2. Proportion of Visitors to the Edinburgh Festivals, by Place of Origin, Whose Expenditure Is Additional to Edinburgh and Scotland, 2010

Visitor Types	Edinburgh	Scotland
Local	3.0%	1.1%
Visitors from elsewhere in Scotland	85.1%	1.6%
Visitors from outside in Scotland	79.5%	71.6%

Source: Edinburgh Festivals Impact Study (BOP Consulting, 2011).

particularly at the individual Festival level. The figures show that Festivals such as Science and Jazz have significant gross expenditures at the Edinburgh level—£1.77m and £2.59m respectively. However, after applying additionality, both shrink to a few hundred thousand pounds. This is predominantly driven by the composition of visitors, with the expenditure of locals not only likely to be smaller, but also far less likely to be additional.

The effect is less pronounced when all the Festivals are looked at in the round, as some of the larger Festivals (e.g., the Fringe, the Military Tattoo and the International Festivals) have significant components of non-locals among their visitors. This means that at the Edinburgh level, more than half of all expenditure (60%) to the Edinburgh Festivals in 2010 was additional to the Edinburgh economy. This is almost identical to the proportion of gross expenditure that was additional in the SQW 2004–5 survey. The figure is reduced for Scotland, but still almost half (48%).

Items of Audience Expenditure

Having established that the audience expenditure is what drives the bulk of the economic impact of visitors, it is important to understand what audiences are spending their money on. The first factor to examine is how important expenditure on tickets is within the overall picture. Looking at the proportion of net visitor expenditure for Edinburgh, ticket expenditure only accounts for 13% of the total. The remaining 87% of audience expenditure is accounted for by expenditure on accommodation, food and drink, entertainment, transport and shopping.

This ably demonstrates the contribution that the Edinburgh Festivals make to the tourist economy, with audiences spending an estimated £41m on hotels, B&Bs, guest houses, (accommodation) etc., and a further £37m in the city's cafes, bars, pubs, and restaurants (food and drink). What should be remembered is that these figures only take into account the net additional expenditure that can be attributed to the Festivals. This means that the major economic impact of the Festivals is not realised in the cultural or events sector, but rather in the city's (and Scotland's) leisure and hospitality businesses.

Shopping: 6%
Transport: 9%
Entertainment: 15%
Food and drink: 34%
Accommodation: 37%

Visitor Types

The amount spent on accommodation already suggests that one of the major factors that generates the large economic returns from the Festivals is the number of staying, paying visitors that they attract. As can be seen from Table 8.3, staying visitors from outside Scotland generate the vast bulk of the expenditure (83%). Although much smaller, the next largest category is accounted for by day visitors from elsewhere in Scotland, who are relatively numerous and have a high average additionality (for Edinburgh).

Multiplier Effects

The last stage in calculating the net economic impact of the Edinburgh Festivals is to account for the secondary effects that the Festivals have on the economies of Edinburgh and Scotland. As the SQW study stated:

The increase in economic activity as a result of the Festivals will have two types of wider "multiplier" effects:

Table 8.3. Proportion of Staying Visitors (Audience Members) From Outside Scotland to the Edinburgh Festivals, 2010

Festival	Staying Visitors From Outside Scotland
Science Festival	5.8%
Imaginate Festival	3.7%
Film Festival	14.4%
Jazz and Blues Festival	10.8%
Military Tattoo	71.3%
Fringe	44.6%
Mela Festival	10.0%
International Festival	31.7%
Book Festival	15.1%
Storytelling Festival	23.1%
Hogmanay	57.9%

Source: Edinburgh Festivals Impact Study (BOP Consulting, 2011).

- supplier effect—an increase in sales in a business will require that business to purchase more supplies. A proportion of this "knock-on" effect will benefit suppliers in the local economy.
- income effect—an increase in sales in a business will usually lead either to an increase in employment or an increase in incomes for those already employed. A proportion of these increased incomes will be re-spent in the local economy.

It is worth quoting the SQW study as we have used the same multipliers in this study (updated for inflation where required). The multipliers in both studies are based on the Scottish Tourism Multipliers, which is currently a standard methodology, which enables comparability with other major cultural and national events and initiatives that have been evaluated using these same multipliers. It also keeps the continuity with the 2004/05 Study. There is, nevertheless, some debate about multipliers and alternative methods are being developed although they are not yet formally adopted by the Scottish Government and wider tourism industry. As is the case for this report, for future iterations the Commissioners of this report and the Festival Directors are committed to using the most widely respected and adopted methodology as it develops, in the interest of best practice.

The Scottish Tourism Multiplier Study (STMS) provides supplier and income multipliers for the tourism sector for Edinburgh and Scotland. The multipliers we have used here are the specific sectoral output multipliers for Edinburgh and Scotland. The employment multipliers come from two different sources. STMS provides information at Edinburgh level while the Scottish Input Output Tables (2000) provide information at Scottish level.

The Festival organisers' expenditure is, as in the SQW study, treated differently from the visitor expenditure as it is not likely to go to tourism related businesses, but instead to suppliers involved in the production of the events. This means that the non-tourism multiplier has been used for the Festival organisers' expenditure. Once the multipliers have been applied, the final overall economic impact of the Edinburgh Festivals in 2010 can be established.

Overall Economic Impact of the Edinburgh Festivals

In expressing the overall economic impact of the Edinburgh Festivals, this can be done in three different ways: by showing the net difference that the Festivals make to output, income, and employment for Edinburgh and Scotland. All three are derived by applying different multipliers for each of the variables to the same net expenditures from the 11 Festivals.

- Output—the net new sales produced by all the sectors of the economy as a result of the various new streams of expenditure.
- Income—defined as income from wages, salaries and profits accruing within Edinburgh and Scotland.
- Employment—measured in terms of Full Time Equivalent (FTE) jobs, which are defined as employment year round for more than 30 hours a week.

Over 2010, the Edinburgh Festivals are estimated to have generated:

- new output of £245m in Edinburgh and £261m in Scotland
- £59m in new income in Edinburgh and £82m in Scotland
- supported 5,242 new FTE jobs in Edinburgh and 4,917 in Scotland

It should be noted that the economic impact of the Festivals is disproportionately concentrated in a handful of the 11 Festivals. In particular, the Festival Fringe accounts for more than half of all the new output (58%), income (58%), and employment (57%). Together with the Tattoo, Hogmanay and International Festivals, these four account for 92% of all new output, and almost the same shares of income and employment (91% and 92% respectively). This concentration of the economic impact within these four Festivals remains consistent from the SQW study."

Summary and Study Guide

Festivals and other cultural celebrations are powerful tourist attractions, and the term "festivalization" has taken hold as a way to express the trend toward developing and exploiting festivals for economic, place marketing, and other strategic purposes. Key themes and issues have been noted, not the least of which is the ever-present danger of commodifying culture and reducing it to an "entertainment product." Clearly, however, culture and festivals are powerful tools in urban development or renewal, and in branding and repositioning cities and destinations, as observed in the Northern Ireland and Belfast example.

We have a considerable amount of research evidence available as to the motivations, experiences, and effects of festival tourism. Some data from large-scale surveys were presented, and research notes, which collectively point to two very important conclusions: there are both generic benefits and special interest benefits that attract people to festivals, and many festivals (especially the typical outdoor, music-filled, summertime, family-oriented events) attract a much more diverse and representative audience than do other forms of the arts. The generic/targeted benefits model is an essential starting point for considering segmentation and target marketing.

Impacts were covered by reference to research on economic, social-cultural, image, place marketing, and environmental effects. There is additional evidence on impacts in the entertainment section. The Edinburgh Festivals study clearly demonstrates the Event Tourism value of festivals (and cultural tourism in general), but it is also essential reading to complement the ensuing chapters on evaluation and impact assessment. In particular, the Edinburgh study employed a triple bottom line approach, matching economic impacts with consideration of social, cultural, and environmental outcomes. In general, we can say that economic impact methodology is better developed than for other impacts.

A major case study of the Woodford Festival illustrates many important aspects of festival tourism, and in the context of "greening" and sustainability. This is an example of a festival as an institution, a destination event, and with subcultural (or at least social world) undertones.

Entertainment tourism was broken down into a number of important categories, with music being the most substantial. While music is almost always incorporated into event programming, and music festivals abound, stand-alone concerts and shows are also major tourist draws. The UK study is the most comprehensive assessment of its value that I have seen. Theater and touring exhibitions/shows were also examined, with the example of Cavalia. Then a number of very special segments were noted, including private functions (weddings and reunions), pilgrimage (religious and secular), and reenactments.

Study Questions

- Why should festival managers be concerned about developing tourism (i.e., should they want to, and what are the issues)?
- Define and explain the process of "festivalization"; how does cultural tourism help branding and positioning? Refer to the Belfast example.
- Discuss major themes in festival tourism research, especially authenticity and commodification, with regard to implications for Event Tourism policy and strategy.
- Compare generic and special interest (or targeted) motivations for attending festivals and other cultural celebrations. What does this have to do with segmentation and target marketing?
- Who is most likely to attend stand-alone music concerts versus festivals? (You need research evidence, and careful attention to generic versus targeted benefits.)
- Refer to the Woodford case study to discuss the importance of festival "greening" and the meanings of festival "sustainability" (you also need the final chapter for this answer).
- Describe key research and data needed to effectively market festivals as destination events.
- Describe the "entertainment industry" and how it connects to festivals and the arts; give examples of specific entertainment events that can be powerful tourist attractions.

Additional Readings

- Festivals and Tourism: Marketing, Management and Evaluation (Long & Robinson, 2004).
- *Festivals, Tourism and Social Change: Remaking Worlds* (Picard & Robinson, 2006).
- *Festival and Events Management: An International Arts and Culture Perspective* (Yeoman, Robertson, Ali-Knight, Drummond, & McMahon-Beattie, 2004).
- *An introduction to the Entertainment Industry* (Stein & Evans, 2009).
- *Sustainable Event Management: A Practical Guide* (Jones, 2010).

Chapter 9

Evaluation and Impact Assessment

Learning Objectives

Upon completion of this chapter the student should understand and be able to explain the following:

1. Purpose and types of evaluation.
2. Uses and misuses of evaluation.
3. Various approaches to measuring ROI (return on investment).
4. Basic data needs and methods for evaluation.
5. Outcomes versus impacts.
6. Measures of effectiveness and efficiency.
7. Research to conduct evaluations.
8. Evaluation of Event Tourism portfolios.
9. Concepts and measures in determining the worth and sustainability of events and Event Tourism.
10. Social, cultural, and environmental impact evaluation.
11. A new paradigm for evaluation of events and Event Tourism.

Introduction

This chapter presents the fundamentals of evaluation, and covers social, cultural, and environmental impacts. Economic impact assessment and cost-benefit evaluation is examined in detail in the next chapter.

The general purpose and three basic types of evaluation are introduced right away, and this first section also shows how evaluation should be used systematically, throughout the formative, process, and summative phases of planning and event production. Because there is so much emphasis placed on ROI in the industry it is also covered right away, including different ways of defining and measuring ROI. This first section also highlights the differences between evaluation and research aimed at determining cause and effect relationships, and the importance of measuring both effectiveness and efficiency. We then examine a very big question: What is an event, or an Event Tourism portfolio "worth"? There is no simple answer, and a multistakeholder approach is likely the best way to deal with it. This issue connects to justifications and policy domains, to stakeholder management and accountability.

In the section Measures and Methods, details are provided on what research is needed to measure and evaluate various processes, outcomes, and impacts. This is also the starting point for developing visitor surveys and other evaluation tools, and for commencing impact assessments. Then our attention turns to special issues that arise when evaluating portfolios. This is a completely new area for theorists and practitioners of Event Tourism, so the advice offered is in need of testing. We look at cumulative and synergistic outcomes first, as the whole point of creating a portfolio is to achieve much more, over a long period of time (in a sustainable manner) than is possible with single events and ad hoc bidding. Suggestions are given as to appropriate indicators for portfolio evaluation, and we deal with the tricky question of "what is a healthy population or portfolio of events?"

The final sections of this chapter provide overviews of social-cultural and environmental impact assessment. There has been more research on social and cultural impacts, and better methodology has been developed, although it has mostly considered resident perceptions of impacts and attitudes towards events. The discussion of social and cultural benefits and costs (or negative impacts) shows clearly what the impacts can be, but cause and effect relationships are seldom demonstrable. This also links into the next chapter where we closely examine use and nonuse valuation of events and full cost–benefit evaluations.

A "new paradigm" for event and Event Tourism evaluation is suggested in the concluding section, although this is really about triple bottom line accounting and social responsibility.

Evaluation Concepts and Return on Investment

Evaluation means to place a value on something (e.g., what is Event Tourism worth?), or to judge (as in "do the customers believe this event delivers high-quality entertainment?"). Evaluation is often a process used to keep a strategy on target, and to determine the outcomes of one's actions. All these apply when it comes to Event Tourism, as we want to place a value on events and event marketing, determine the quality of our events and portfolios, and ascertain the effectiveness and efficiency of our planning and development.

Refer back to the systems model (Figure 1.5) for an introduction to evaluation and some related terminology. "Outcomes" reflect goals—that is, what organizers want to achieve. Typical desired outcomes include making a profit, raising money for charity, ensuring customer satisfaction, generating tourist demand, and contributing to resident well-being. But there can also be unexpected and negative outcomes, including negative environmental and social effects. Unfortunately, many outcomes of an event are not included in evaluations, and have to be looked upon as "externalities," being effects that are beyond the mandate (or interest) of the organizers and evaluators to consider. Air and water pollution, and carbon loading are typical externalities. Evaluation and impact assessment have to be directed towards finding all outcomes, otherwise they are not comprehensive.

I employ a specific meaning for "impacts." People and organizations perceive that they are *impacted* by events, either positively or negatively. Most economic impact studies of events start with the premise that events attract new or incremental money to an area and that constitutes a benefit, so the whole process of economic impact assessment is typically biased. Costs and externalities are not part of the usual calculation of economic impacts, nor of the so-called "legacy." It has to be emphasized that "impacts" and "legacy" cannot be equated with benefits. In social impact assessment we can ask residents how they feel an event (or all events) impacted upon them, such as amenity gain or loss, social integration or disruption, a better entertainment or cultural opportunities, or no impact at all. Similarly, other stakeholders can express perceptions of impacts from their perspective, and these perceptions affect their attitudes towards events.

Purpose and Types of Evaluation

Evaluation steers the entire event and Event Tourism planning and marketing process. It is the way to constantly learn more about the organization's or destination's environment, the intended and unintended outcomes of events, and ways in which to improve strategy and management. Very practical reasons for evaluation can be simply stated:

- to identify and solve problems;
- find ways to improve management and strategy;
- determine the worth of an event or an event portfolio;
- measure success or failure;
- identify and measure impacts, costs, and benefits;
- satisfy sponsors and other stakeholders (accountability);
- gain acceptance/credibility/support.

In a tourism context, evaluation issues multiply, often requiring complex economic impact assessment and cost–benefit evaluation techniques to determine worth. Portfolio management presents yet more complexity.

The science of evaluation begins with realization that this is how organizations (and managers) learn. Without evaluation we do not know if our actions achieve desired results, and therefore we do not know what actions cause what effects. To grow and achieve sustainability, or adapt to change, organizations must institutionalize the learning process. Three basic types of evaluation occur.

Formative evaluations are undertaken during feasibility studies and pre-planning, such as before a bid is made, or in the early stages of strategic planning; they include needs assessments, learning about tourist and resident markets, creating attractive products, setting up effective organizations, and new product or marketing ideas. Generating and testing programming ideas is also formative. Anything that helps with planning and decision making can be called "formative."

Process evaluations can be applied to the organization as a whole (by way of a management audit) to help improve effectiveness, and during the operation of an event, such as through observation and quality control techniques, or during the implementation of a plan. Portfolios can be evaluated at any time (preferably periodically) to monitor progress. The idea is to determine if the plan or event is being implemented as intended, and otherwise to take corrective action. Sometimes improvements can quickly be put in place. Regular internal evaluations of all the management functions (e.g., marketing effectiveness) fits into this category.

Outcome or summative evaluations are conducted after the event or at the end of a program or planning period to evaluate its impacts and overall value; results are fed into the planning process. Many stakeholders want accountability, and they stress specific outcomes and impacts of interest to them. This includes return on investment calculations for sponsors, and environmental audits for the community. A broad and complex outcome evaluation question is "what is this event worth?" and it can only be answered by referring to the mandate and goals of the organization and the interests of all key stakeholders. Answering the difficult question "what is our portfolio worth?" could therefore cause headaches.

Determination of Cause and Effect

Sometimes evaluators want to prove that their event or program was the cause of a desired outcome, such as the creation of jobs or more intangible social and cultural benefits. To do this requires more sophisticated evaluation methods, often employing experimental designs with control groups. The determination of economic impacts of events is a special case, because it does not require an experiment with a control group—nor could that easily be arranged. Rather, it is sufficient to demonstrate through research that "new money" came into the study area because of the event. This is not a simple technical task, however, as will be shown later.

It is often satisfactory to simply determine what the outcomes are, and to use this information to do better the next time. For example, the point of inquiring about visitor satisfaction is to improve event quality, not necessarily to prove what exactly leads to satisfaction. In such cases evaluation asks quite different questions from cause–effect research.

Effectiveness and Efficiency

These terms are used frequently in evaluation. "Effectiveness" is a measure of goal attainment, or how well did we do in reaching our objectives? "Efficiency" is a measure of resource use, as implied in the questions: "did we waste money?" and "what is the optimal use of our resources?"

Measures of effectiveness are required for impact assessment or any summative evaluation. Internally, measures of effectiveness are needed to evaluate the contribution of each person and committee in attaining the goals. Sometimes intangible goals, such as fostering appreciation of the arts or contributing to community development, resist precise measurement. In business, revenue generation and profit are the most common measures. For event portfolios, as argued earlier, effectiveness pertains to long-term sustainability.

Generic and theoretical approaches to evaluating effectiveness were identified by Tzelepi and Quick (2002), but only the first—goal attainment—is frequently employed in the tourism and event sectors. For each of these approaches I have added a comment on related issues.

- **Goal attainment**: Achieving the desired output (but goals are not always clear, and attainment of goals might not make the organization effective in other ways; attainment of 1 goal might prejudice attainment of others).
- **Systems resource approach**: An open-systems approach in which resource acquisition determines outputs; the focus is on measuring outputs, so organizations can be compared without reference to goals; obtaining resource indicates that the outputs are valued (you can start with Figure 1.5 and with stakeholder analysis; specifically, who will give your event or portfolio resources, and what do they want?).
- **Internal process approach**: Internal processes such as information flow and coordination determine effectiveness (this approach is heavy on human resource evaluation; but different processes can still achieve the same ends; again, use the systems model as a starting point and analyze exactly how resources are employed).
- **Competing values**: Internal goals might be in conflict (Who is making the decisions? Is there a strong organizational culture? Goals might be set and effectiveness measured by reference to dominant power blocks, or in an ad hoc manner as an amalgam of individual preferences).
- **Strategic constituencies**: Takes into account critical stakeholders, both internal and external, asking how satisfied are each? (this approach also has to deal with conflicts and the question of which stakeholders have the most power to influence Event Tourism).

To evaluate efficiency, managers will examine the resources consumed to produce a given unit of output, then determine if more can be achieved for less, or if increased inputs can produce a lot more desired output.

This leads to a discussion of ROI, which has various possible meanings and applications, but reflects both the effectiveness and efficiency of an organization and/or strategy.

Return on Investment (ROI)

For such a widely used term, ROI has many possible meanings. To contextualize it within Event Tourism the starting point is a simple proposition: every investment of time, money, and effort has to be rewarded, and if a higher return is possible, then perhaps resources should be reallocated. In other words, every decision about Event Tourism has to be justified somehow, through valid analysis and standard measures.

Unfortunately, every stakeholder is likely to view ROI differently! Calculating ROI for a profit-making business can be simple in concept, nothing more than this formula: ROI = gain from investment minus the cost of investment, divided by the cost of investment.

No private investor wants to just break even, there has to be a surplus. But this is not necessarily true in the world of governmental action and not-for-profit organizations. Outside the realm of for-profit businesses, it is likely that nonmonetary intangibles will be employed to determine if a policy, strategy, or investment is wise and justified, if a program should continue, or if something else should be tried in order to achieve policy aims. That is why ROI is an evaluation concept.

Here are several generic approaches to ROI within Event Tourism, together with related issues:

(1) Standard ROI, as in the for-profit sector, can be used to see if each investment, such as a bid or one-time event, generates more money than the cost, and to compare which events have the highest monetary return.

Issues: The profits or "return" might be difficult to measure, and they often accrue to completely different persons and organizations than the ones who made the investment (giving rise to "free-loading"). Governments have to justify such investments in terms of creating "public good." So it will be argued that if restaurants and hotels are the ones who really see the tourism-related revenues accruing from Event Tourism, this generates tax revenue and jobs that benefit everyone. Event development and bidding agencies usually operate as private companies and use this type of ROI, especially if they are required (or are politically expected) to always generate a positive ROI. Membership-based DMOs do not necessarily have such an issue, as their members collaborate to generate mutual benefits—but the distribution of benefits might become an issue. For an individual event (or program within an event), the monetary ROI is only useful if they explicitly seek a profit or want to decide which program to invest in.

(2) Within tourism the primary measures of impact (as opposed to marketing effectiveness, which looks at conversion rates) are typically visitation numbers and resulting expenditure (i.e., "new or incremental income"). Event Tourism agencies want an overall measure of how successful their efforts are in generating new event-dependent tourism and related expenditure. This leads to the emphasis on economic impact studies that start with the premise that the "return" on investment is measured by the incremental expenditures of event tourists and subsequent multiplier effects.

Issues: As will be discussed in detail in the next chapter, the standard event economic impact assessment is often flawed, and only reveals part of the story. As well, the methodology supporting these impact assessments is open to many mistakes, deliberate or otherwise, and to various interpretations (an especially vexing problem when the full reports are not made public!). Finally, we need better ROI measures and other measures of the impacts and "worth" of portfolios of events, wherein the collective benefit is expected to be greater than the sum of the parts.

(3) Use of intangible measures of effectiveness is common enough, but expressing them as ROI is problematic. For example, if a government agency assists the festival sector, it might want to evaluate its program on the basis of arts development, social integration, or community pride. All of these require development of effectiveness indicators and are probably going to remain subjective in nature. That is fair enough, but calling it an ROI is a different thing altogether. How can the government claim that its investment of so many dollars generated an ROI of much happiness, more community pride, or social integration? It does not work, and I think it is better to stick to the "public good" justifications without resorting to a contrived, quantitative measure called "ROI."

(4) Mixed stakeholder measures are increasingly required, especially for a portfolio of events managed over a long period of time. Simple economic impact measures and revenue-related ROI calculations do not work well in this context. However, if each stakeholder provided their own measures of importance, something collective can be done with them. Furthermore, each stakeholder can periodically evaluate how well the portfolio is doing to achieve its sustainability goals.

Return on Assets (ROA)

An Event Tourism agency or DMO is expected to create a lot of "public good" and/or profit for its members. ROA is a measure of how profitable a company is relative to its total assets, and is therefore an efficiency measure. "Assets" in this context can be capital (such as money to bid on events and to market the area) plus money borrowed (otherwise known as debt, and often this is avoided by DMOs). ROA is calculated by dividing a company's annual earnings by its total assets, and is displayed as a percentage.

This might be a better evaluation tool in the context of a portfolio of events wherein the payoff (i.e., all benefits) is divided among all events in the portfolio. And if some events perform poorly in one year, or change over time, it is factored into the larger ROA calculation. In this way the agency does not have to demonstrate high returns on every event, every year, but it has to perform solidly over time.

Return on Equity (ROE)

ROE measures the rate of return on the ownership interest (shareholders' equity) of the common stock owners. It is an efficiency measure related to the ability to make a profit from every unit of shareholder's equity. Certain DMOs or event development companies with shareholders will be required to realize a high ROE for their investors, but this is uncommon.

ROI for Business Events

The professionals who plan and organize business events are increasingly being required to justify the event, and to demonstrate for clients a solid return on investment. In the book *Return on Investment in Meetings and Events*, Phillips, Breining, and Phillips (2008) deal explicitly with the needs of meeting professionals, as represented by Meeting Professionals International. A paradigm shift is evident, with meeting planners (and therefore those seeking to attract and host events) being required to justify the events up front, and to account for their efficiency and effectiveness afterwards. Previously, it was adequate to merely document what the event programmed, the activities undertaken by attendees, and perhaps satisfaction levels.

The authors of ROI in Meetings and Events provide many measures of impact, not all of which are tangible or measurable in monetary terms. To get the necessary feedback requires detailed research and evaluation. The categories of research and data in their recommended process include the following:

- inputs: what the event actually consists of (number of attendees, what they did, etc.);
- reaction and perceived value (were the attendees satisfied and how do they rate their experiences and the program?);
- learning (what did attendees learn?);
- application and implementation (what was made of the gained/shared knowledge after the event?);
- impact and consequences (effects of the learning on business performance);
- ROI (compares the monetary benefits to the costs of the meeting).

Convention centers, hotels/resorts, and destinations that are competing for, and hosting, business events must be aware of this paradigm shift. It cannot be taken for granted that rapid growth of business events will continue, especially during times of economic downturn, and it must be recognized that increasingly the businesses and associations that hold meetings and conventions want to know exactly what they are worth.

What Is an Event Worth?

ROI calculations do not answer the question, "what is an event (or event portfolio) worth?" There is no absolute answer, so let's examine the different ways of address ing this question, and clearly these are also related to justifications for public sector intervention.

Economic Impact

In this common approach, the "worth" of an event is assumed to be equal to its economic impact (generally from a tourism and development perspective). Tourism agencies investing in events often equate "economic impact" with ROI. It has serious limitations:

- The calculation of economic impact is generally restricted to "new money" coming into an area because of the event, and its "multiplier" effect.
- This estimate is mostly expressed in terms of "income" or "value added" to the area.
- Many authors have used multipliers, which are problematic in both theory and practical application.
- This approach is narrow and often ignores costs and sustainability issues.

Total Event Revenue

A simple calculation of how much income or profit an event makes is sometimes useful. This is usually going to be equal to the revenue or income side of the budget. Consider ticket and retail sales, rents and commissions, donations, grants, and sponsorship revenue. It is too narrow in scope to be a good measure of "worth."

Consumer Surplus and Existence Values

The event is worth the value that consumers assign to it in terms of "willingness to pay." Their "utility value" (i.e., benefits gained from using the event) might be higher than the cost they have to pay or the value of the resources consumed to produce the event. In the next chapter we look carefully at use values and nonuse values, as these are quantifiable measures that might satisfy economists and decision makers.

Existence Value

The theory is that people value things even if they do not see or use them, perhaps because they might attend an event in the future (the "option value") or they think it has value for the community. Researchers could also ask who will support or rescue a threatened event—is it worth enough to the community to bail out more than once, and what might the rescue package legitimately cost? These are examples of nonuse values, and their measurement becomes rather complex when considering portfolios and whole populations of events.

Psychic Benefits

Burns et al. (1986) determined that the Adelaide Grand Prix imposed costs and problems on the resident population, but a large majority still thought the event was desirable and should be held again. In other words, it had "psychic value" for them, which was at least equal to the monetary value of all those personal and community-felt costs. This is another way to conceptualize nonuse benefits or worth.

Sponsorship Potential

How much will the "title" and all other sponsors pay (or commit "in-kind"/"contra") to the event? This is useful because a not-for-profit or public organization can put a commercial value on the event. An event owned by a corporation, on the other hand, might be "worth" the net marketing value, or specifically the net sales value the event generates.

Media Coverage

Many events assign a dollar value to the media coverage they get by valuing the coverage at the same price you would have to pay if it was advertising. But can the viewer or reader "reach" be proven—that is, can a valid estimate be made of the total audience? And is all publicity good publicity? And does good publicity translate into sales or future demand? There are many uncertainties with this measure of "worth."

Multiple Perspectives on Value

A multistakeholder approach is important. What does the community think about the event? Its sponsors and grant givers? Its suppliers, volunteers, staff? The tourism and hospitality sectors, and the arts community? There really is no one measure of value that sums up all these perspectives, so all their views should be solicited. Together, they constitute the community that can help an event be accepted or validated, even becoming a permanent institution. Applied to a portfolio of events, stakeholders can be asked several very important questions about an event or events in general:

- What do you think are the key goals of the portfolio and the events in the portfolio?
- Is the event achieving your goals? How do you measure effectiveness?
- Do you believe the impacts or outcomes of the events and the portfolio of events are positive or negative? What are the key impacts from your perspective (prompting: ecological, social, cultural, economic)?
- Do you support this event? The portfolio strategy? All events in the community? Why or why not?

Sustainability

Principles of "sustainable development" can be applied to evaluating the worth of an event or portfolio. Ask these questions:

- Did the event/do events in the portfolio make it more costly or difficult for future generations to enjoy an equal or better quality of life?
- Are irreplaceable resources being used up?
- Do our events add to global environmental problems, or help solve them?
- Can the long-term impacts be predicted and, where necessary, are preventative and ameliorative actions being implemented?
- Can we measure progress in becoming more sustainable, in a triple bottom line manner?

If you are asked, what is an event worth?, the only possible answer is: it depends! Which of the above-mentioned criteria are most important, and who is to decide? And when it comes to sustainability, are we just talking about the "greening" of events or a process of becoming more sustainable? That issue is addressed later.

Making Evaluation a Permanent Part of the Organization

The "learning organization" (Senge, 1990) requires a permanent approach to evaluation, and so does the "accountable" and "responsible" organization. Evaluation results often get filed and forgotten, especially if they are negative! But nobody learns, and nothing progresses without open and honest evaluation, so the evaluator must try to maximize the usefulness of research and analysis in both practical and political ways. To maximize the effectiveness of all evaluations, the entire process must be firmly institutionalized. In other words, evaluation must not be viewed as an occasional job for solving problems or generating new ideas. It must be a permanent and important responsibility of senior managers.

Misuses of Evaluation

Not all evaluation projects are well intentioned or utilized correctly. Unpopular programs can be "proved" to be too costly or ineffective. Bad performance can sometimes be covered up by evaluations that show positive results in some other area. And managers have been known to conduct time-consuming and expensive evaluations to reinforce or increase their importance. And when results are not shared, there is often the suspicion that results are being managed to further someone's ambitions.

Measures and Methods for Evaluation

The major types of data needed to conduct comprehensive event and Event Tourism evaluations, specific measures used, and an indication of the methods generally required to obtain the data are shown in Table 9.1. For example, the most basic piece of information needed is the attendance at events. This can be broken down into several types of data, namely tourists versus residents, total attendance, attendance at individual sites and attractions, turnover rate, and peak attendance. The measures can be of visitors, visitor parties, total gate or number of visitations. Methods used to obtain these measures include gate counts, crowd estimates, vehicle counts, and market area surveys.

Observation Techniques and Applications

Using standard checklists, event staff and volunteers can gain a great deal of quantitative information as well as an enhanced subjective evaluation of the event. For some organizers, observational research might be a necessary substitute for visitor and market surveys. It should be a formal part of all evaluation strategies. Observations have several advantages over surveys:

Table 9.1. Basic Data Needs and Methods for Event Evaluation

Data Types	Specific Measures	Methods
Attendance: total event attendance; attendance at subevents	Total number of guests, participants, or customers Number of visitations Turnover rate Peak attendance	Ticket sales Turnstile counts Vehicle counts Crowd estimates Market area surveys Registration data
Visitor profile: profile of each visitor; type of party; size of party	Age in years Male or female Employment status Educational level Income level Party type: family only; family and friends; friends only; alone; team; tour group Number of visitors travelling together	Visitor survey Market area survey Direct observation
Market area and trip type: home address; origin of trip; type of trip; mode	Country, state, city or town Origin on day of survey Stops on the trip Accommodation used Number of nights away from home and in the destination Packages used Type of vehicle	Visitor survey Interviews Observation
Marketing and quality management: information sources; reasons for trip; benefits sought; satisfaction; quality of program and service	Media consulted and relative importance (social media, advertising seen, Internet searches, word of mouth) Reasons for trip to the area and to the event (often more than one is given) Importance of event in motivating the trip Desired experiences, activities, goods and services (relative importance of decision-making factors) Things that pleased or displeased Suggestions Intent to return Willingness to recommend the event Importance-performance measures Service quality failures	Visitor survey Satisfaction box Participant observation
Activities and spending: activities at the event; activities outside the event; expenditures	Attendance at specific event activities or venues Activities on the trip and elsewhere in host community Spending on: travel (car, etc.); accommodation; purchased meals; groceries; entertainment, other events, attractions; other shopping	Visitor survey Turnstile count Ticket sales Observation Business survey Financial records

Data Types	Specific Measures	Methods
Economic impacts (area): benefits for the area attributable to the event and to leveraging efforts	Average visitor spending Total incremental visitor expenditure in the area (attributable to the event) Direct, indirect, and induced income or value added (i.e., macro-economic impact) Tax and employment benefits	Visitor survey Local market area survey Attendance counts/estimates Accommodation occupancy survey Business survey Multipliers or econometric models Cost–benefit assessment
Business impacts (event): profit or loss; financial reserves or debt	Cash flow Assets and liabilities	Financial audit
Return on investment: for sponsors and grant givers; for DMOs and tourism organizations; for individual events; for event owners	Sponsor recognition by visitors; attitudes and images held Behavior of visitors (sales, etc.) Sponsors' evaluation Resident perceptions and attitudes Attendee satisfaction	Visitor/attendee surveys Media audit On-site sales records Tax records Sponsors' feedback Resident survey, focus groups, or political feedback
Ecological impacts	Impacts on wildlife Pollution caused Waste generated Carbon and ecological footprints	Observation Audit of environmental practices and outcomes Stakeholder inputs Community resident survey Visitor survey Police, fire, environmental service records
Built environmental impacts	Heritage conservation Housing Transport infrastructure Urban renewal and development	Various stakeholders' inputs Government expenditure accounts
Social and cultural impacts	Amenity loss (privacy, noise) Aesthetics Traffic delays Accidents/injuries Social problems (behavior) Cultural change Positive educational and behavioral effects	Resident and other stakeholder perceptions of impacts and attitudes towards events and tourism Observation (traffic, noise, amenity loss, etc.)
Cost–benefit evaluation: tangible costs and benefits; intangible costs and benefits; opportunity costs; distribution of costs and benefits	Ratio of tangible benefits to tangible costs Evaluation of intangibles Evaluation of net value	Expert analysis Multistakeholder input

- All staff and volunteers can participate, each contributing their own unique perspective on the event, the customers, and the impacts.
- Customer behavior is sometimes a better indicator of problems, preferences and attitudes than are formal responses to surveys.
- Key elements of the event product can only be evaluated by means of direct observation: how people behave under different circumstances; how transport and movement controls actually work; the quality of the experience actually delivered (including food and entertainment); quality of service delivered by staff/volunteers as measured against management criteria; the use of information or directional material and signs; the effectiveness of waste, litter, and pollution controls.
- The atmosphere or ambience of the event, which is a vital but intangible element of the product, can be evaluated best by a combination of direct observation and visitor comments; everyone associated with the event will likely have a valuable opinion on the overall effectiveness of the atmosphere, or at least on specific factors that create atmosphere.

It is a mistake, however, to rely too heavily on casual comments and unsubstantiated observations. Use of an evaluation checklist is recommended, covering several types of measurement:

- items that are present or absent, adequate or inadequate (determined by performance criteria, not subjective opinion) (e.g., are there enough litter bins, and are they emptied frequently enough to avoid spillage?);
- items judged to be good or bad, such as the quality of food;
- items requiring lengthy observation and analysis, such as the behavior of visitors under specific circumstances (e.g., what was the effect of signposting on pedestrian flows?);
- items requiring a summary conclusion, such as the overall quality and visitor satisfaction with entertainment, as determined by observation of visitor reactions and comments.

Some checklists can be completed during the event, though not by all workers, while every volunteer and staff person should complete a form after the event.

Secret Shoppers and Participant Observation

An alternative, or additional, step is to have "secret shoppers" on staff for the sole purpose of making observations. Fast-food chains use shoppers to secretly evaluate food, service, and facility quality, and event managers can do the same. These people should ideally be trained observers, and there are advantages and disadvantages in using known observers as opposed to those who will be strangers to other staff and volunteers.

A major consideration is ethics. Some forms of secret observation can be violations of human privacy or dignity, so observers should be told the limits of their assignments. On the other hand, casual and unobtrusive observers can fit into the crowd without any influence whatsoever. And if staff evaluations are included, there is merit in making them open and obvious so that staff know they are being observed. Everyone subject to evaluation should, of course, have advance knowledge of the criteria being used, and should not be expected to perform duties they are not trained and qualified to handle.

Evaluating Communications Effectiveness and Efficiency

The old marketing adage always applies: if you want to know the value of advertising, stop doing it. On the other hand, if you want to improve its effectiveness and do it more efficiently (i.e., better results for less money), you must evaluate results. "Conversion studies" are widely used to determine the effectiveness of specific communications. For example, when people call for (or receive by mail) a specific event promotion, subsequent telephone calls can be made to determine what proportion (and their characteristics) bought an event ticket.

Conversion rates can only be calculated for targeted messages and promotions, not broadcasting, although market area research can at least determine who heard a given message. The basic validity problem in conversion studies is the assumption that it was the targeted promotion or message that resulted in a sale, whereas in realty many possible factors influence a customer's decision to attend.

Evaluating the Impacts of Events on Image and Place Marketing

Contributing to the formulation of a positive image of a city or destination (or its repositioning) is one of the economic roles of events, but it is difficult to evaluate. This is a special case of ROI calculation, as illustrated by Shibli and Coleman (2005).

Research Note on Media Impact Evaluation

Shibli, S., & Coleman, R. (2005). Economic impact and place marketing evaluation: A case study of the World Snooker Championship. *International Journal of Event Management Research, 1*(1).

This paper evaluates the effects on Sheffield of hosting the World Snooker Championship. The event has been staged in the city since 1977 and has always been thought to be beneficial. The evaluation undertaken on behalf of Sheffield City Council by SIRC, estimated the economic impact attributable to visitors to Sheffield who were attending the snooker and also the place marketing effects associated with the BBC television coverage of the event. The research employed the UK Sport methodology (designed by SIRC) for evaluating the economic impact of sports events and a standard sponsorship industry technique for analysing the television coverage. Results from 1,767 interviews with people in attendance, revealed that visitors to Sheffield specifically for the World Snooker were responsible for almost £2.3m of additional expenditure in the local economy over the 17 days of the event. In addition, the television exposure from almost 100 hours of coverage would have cost more than £3.2m to purchase in the commercial market place. Sheffield has adopted a strategy to attract sports events in order to help regenerate the city, hence it is interesting to note that an annual event that it has not had to bid for, is more significant in economic impact and public profile terms, than all but two events it has bid successfully for and any other event currently on the Sheffield sporting calendar. Consequently, complacency is cautioned against and recommendations are made relative to cultivating the event in order to maximise the benefits to the city. Finally, reference is made to how governing bodies of sport e.g; World Professional Billiards & Snooker Association (WPBSA) might exploit evaluations (such as this) to maximise the commercial value of their event, by using the potential benefits as an incentive to invite competitive tenders from other cities interested in hosting an event.

According to the full report (Shibli, 2002), the cumulative audience of the televised snooker championship within the UK was estimated to be 95 million viewers (i.e., about 18 million individuals watching multiple times), over 17 consecutive days and 100 hours of broadcast. The event's highest television rating (8.2%) was achieved at the final session. The data revealed that viewer interest grew as the event progressed towards the final. More males watched this sport event (57%), and they tended to be aged 55 and older (57%). The volume of clearly visible or audible exposure for sponsors' logos or messages was calculated using specially trained observers and software, then a cash equivalent value was calculated based on how much it would cost to purchase television advertising in the form

of 30-second messages. The same was done for messages about Sheffield. Just over 1%
of the television coverage was devoted to human and place interest stories that included
"postcard" images of Sheffield, for which a monetary value was calculated based on the
commercial cost of the equivalent broadcast time. In total 44 postcards yielding 79 minutes
of coverage were broadcast. However, analysis showed that too much of this "postcard"
exposure featured competitors, or buildings that only residents would recognize. A second
dimension of the evaluation was a survey of spectator perceptions of the city, from which
it was determined that snooker tourists (mostly males) rated Sheffield highly as a place
to visit. The problem is that the profiles of the television audience, spectators, and typical
visitors to Sheffield are all different, raising the question of how best to promote the city.
The study emphasizes that there is no guarantee that such media exposure is effective.

Evaluating Event Portfolios

The problems and pitfalls of event evaluation are magnified greatly when entire
portfolios are considered. The very concept of event portfolio management is new, and
little has been done by way of evaluating them. The starting point has to be the notion
of a portfolio as a set of managed assets. Managed for what purpose? What are the
goals? Individual event owners and producers seldom if ever consider themselves to be
part of a portfolio, let alone complementary to others in the same city or destination.

In Figure 9.1 the transition from single-event to portfolio evaluation is conceptualized,
with an emphasis on capacity building. In the core of the diagram are typical evaluation
and impact measures for single events, reflecting a TBL approach, while in the outer
ring are broad policy domains that portfolios of events might have to be accountable to.
In the most narrow context, only the tourism and economic growth outcomes will be
considered (typically by a DMO). But for portfolios managed at the city or destination
level, or among stakeholders, multiple domains come into play; methods and measures
are needed for all of them.

Capacity building in this context has two meanings, the first being to improve evaluation
and impact assessment capacity, as new methods and measures are required. The second
refers to the overall aim of a portfolio to increase the city or destination's ability to
achieve more benefits, realize more goals, and all the while gain in efficiency.

Within a portfolio a single event can be a valued asset on one or more criteria, including
both tangible and intangible ROI measures. But overall, cumulative impacts measured every
few years are probably more important. The following broad questions can be asked:

- What are the priorities for the portfolio (in a triple bottom line context)?
- Do the events have a cumulative impact that is greater or different from single
  events? How can this be measured?
- Is there evidence of competition or cooperation among the events in the
  portfolio that might alter the portfolio's overall value? Can these behaviors be
  modified? Do individual events consider their place in the portfolio? How can
  complementarities be facilitated?
- Is each event in the portfolio essential? What happens if you remove it?
- Can events be substituted in terms of the roles they play?
- Do we need evidence of ROI from every event, or is an overall assessment of
  impacts adequate?

Is it necessary to manage or monitor all the events in a population, or can it be assumed
that many events will come and go in a free market, with the portfolio being a separate

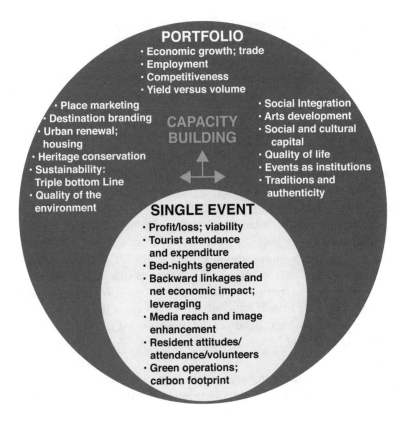

Figure 9.1. From single-event to portfolio evaluation.

concern? This indeed might be a common case, as tourism and event development agencies are most likely to focus on a smaller number that they can control or influence. Within a large population of events, perhaps only a small minority perform substantial roles from the tourism or place marketing perspectives.

Overlapping event portfolios are becoming more common and important. Those managed, or of interest to social and cultural agencies, will often be quite different from those of tourism and place marketing agencies, yet overlapping roles will occur. Take the example of a major, annual cultural festival that also attracts tourists—it fits into at least two important portfolios. The implication is that stakeholders must work out their interests and hopefully employ some standard measures of impact and success. This requires a higher level of policy coordination.

Synergistic and Cumulative Portfolio Impacts

Let's address the issue of measuring synergistic and cumulative impacts, as this is at the heart of the portfolio concept. First, multiple events managed in concert should (hypothetically) be able to achieve much more than the effects of single events. Second, the portfolio over time should be able to realize major, strategic objectives better than (and perhaps faster, and more efficiently) uncoordinated, single events.

A portfolio of events (probably changing in size and composition over time) has to be evaluated repeatedly to determine accumulating outcomes/impacts, plus efficiency-related ROI measurements. Since it is the attainment of overall goals that counts most (not specific event impacts), the variation in portfolio composition and in its management becomes an issue. Does the portfolio in year 3 show a greater cost-effectiveness ratio than at year 1, and can that be attributed to the nature of the portfolio or how well it is being managed? Those are really difficult questions.

With regard to cumulative impacts, there are several additional issues. First, this ongoing evaluation exercise extends well beyond program evaluation (which ideally proves cause and effect) and takes it into the realm of evolutionary theory. How do population ecosystems and individual events as institutions change over time? Are the event's and portfolio's goals also changing along the way?

Second, accumulating outcomes are likely getting more and more complex, affecting more people and organizations, and having possibly hidden effects as well as tangible, measured impacts. By the nature of complex systems, many outcomes will be difficult or impossible to predict the farther we go into the future. Scenario making will have to become part of the process, as "what-if" scenarios will help us find those unpredictable and more complex effects.

As an example, consider a future scenario for a portfolio of managed events in a city. Assume that today's goals stress tourism and place marketing, but a gradual shift to social and cultural priorities will occur, achieving greater balance. In 10 years' time, that might make our current economic impact measures less important than measures of social and cultural benefits—which perhaps have yet to be developed or tested.

Other scenarios that should be considered:

- constantly rising operating costs for a city, owing to today's investments;
- depreciation of tangible assets (the venues) and the eventual need for infrastructural replacements/improvements;
- a possible decline in tourism (affecting demand; perhaps generating more need for marketing);
- a growing, more diverse or sophisticated resident population (affecting needs and preferences for events, as well as perceptions of impacts and attitudes towards desirability).

Indicators Are Essential

Think of a portfolio in terms of sustainability. Managers want their portfolio to sustain its benefits over a long period of time. Although it is useful to make forecasts and generate scenarios, there will always be uncertainty. To ensure the portfolio is at least heading in the right direction, a set of indicators for monitoring the portfolio are essential. The general nature of indicators follows from the logic of evaluation: What are we inputting? How is the portfolio changing? What are the measureable outcomes? Three categories of indicator are required:

- **Input indicators**: operating and capital costs for the entire portfolio, as well as of the individual venues and event assets;
- **Process indicators**: changes that can be measured, such as size, diversity, interdependencies and synergies, competition, failure rates; new starts (i.e., vital statistics from population ecology); political influences and policy shifts; environmental forces acting on the portfolio);
- **Outcome indicators**: TBL evaluation at regular points in time; various ROI measures; independent stakeholder evaluations; overall costs versus benefits (tangibles and intangibles); opportunity costs and alternatives.

What Is a Healthy Portfolio?

How do asset managers know if their portfolio is healthy? Presumably the ROI measures are at the top of their minds, but the "health" of one event or of a population or portfolio of events is a rather subjective evaluation. In theory, a healthy individual organism still dies, whereas for a whole population permanence is feasible. Even if the population possesses the resources it needs for survival, this does not mean every individual event will survive indefinitely or always be healthy.

Good health could mean that events in the portfolio (or population) are able to meet their goals and contribute positively to overall goals for the events sector. Their health is therefore a function of their contribution to the portfolio or population, and they might very well have a defined (or unpredictable) life expectancy. Failures will certainly occur, as will new events be created or brought to an area.

"Planned obsolescence" is a necessary part of portfolio management. This is not to say that individual events are easily expendable, as every event will have its supporters, but that the portfolio managers must at least consider that some events will only have a limited, productive life expectancy.

Managers and evaluators should be looking for signs of *bad health*, or threats to the population/portfolio. For example:

- One sick event might infect others! this could happen by virtue of bad publicity arising from incidents (watch for public opinion and political shifts in attitude).
- Strong events can support weak ones (by collaboration, resource sharing, etc.) or consume so many resources and demand that smaller events suffer.
- Severe disruptions in the economy or political environment can threaten the entire population/portfolio, requiring quick reaction (e.g., financial bailouts; rationalization of the portfolio through sell-offs or suspensions of events; cancellation of bids).

In practice, the field of event portfolio management has not yet progressed to the point where we can say anything for certain about healthy portfolios, nor do we have enough research and theory to make pronouncements about healthy event populations (managed or otherwise).

As a general rule, I would suggest that the aim has to be for long-term health and sustainability of event portfolios and populations, and that means long-term benefits across social, cultural, economic, and environmental indicators. Sustainability is a process of becoming, not an absolute level of achievement.

Social and Cultural Outcomes and Impact Assessment

Why should a DMO or event development agency concern itself with social, cultural, or environmental impact assessment? We only have to look at the justifications for public sector involvement to see the answers, starting with the need to demonstrate that public sector support, whether for event bidding, event production, or venues, generates "public good" in an equitable manner. Next, and equally important, is the near certainty that if residents do not realize benefits, and instead perceive that events cause more trouble or generate more costs than they are worth, then Event Tourism cannot be sustainable.

As already discussed, events and Event Tourism are employed for a variety of social and cultural policy outcomes pertaining to individual and group well-being, urban renewal, community development, social integration, healthy lifestyles, and contributions to the arts and authentic culture. And the potential negative effects of events and tourism have to be prevented or ameliorated, such as hooliganism, crime, and amenity loss attributable to events and crowds. As much as possible, Event Tourism strategists and policy makers need to work with potential partners and attempt to integrate their policies and strategies.

Fredline (2008, p. 396) summarized key variables that affect the social impact of sport tourism on host communities. Many of these are subjective considerations that should be considered when bidding on events and conducting evaluations. The first consideration is whether it is a large or small-scale event, and then whether tourism is well or poorly managed. A series of dichotomous variables, or measures of degree, can then be examined:

- frequency (rare versus regular);
- cost (free to public or expensive);
- location (concentrated versus spatially diffused);
- appropriateness (consistency with local values);
- involvement (active participation versus passive spectators);
- attendee mix (all tourists, all residents, or mixed; elite or open);
- cultural distance (visitors are similar or quite different from locals);
- local population (small and rural or large and urban);
- ecology (robust versus highly sensitive; level of development).

Fredline (2008) discussed two general approaches to examining social impacts. In "extrinsic approaches," general models are formulated to describe how residents react or might change in response to tourism. They consider the stage of development of tourism, destination life cycle, seasonality of demand, host–guest ratio, cultural distance, carrying capacity, or capacity to absorb tourism. "Intrinsic models" of social impact assessment attempt to explain differences in resident opinions and attitudes, or why some groups benefit and others do not. Fredline (2008, p. 400) summarized the key variables that have been explored for attempting to explain such differences, namely:

- financial benefit derived from tourism or events (exchange theory posits that perceived benefits translate into support);
- identification with the theme or event program (residents who enjoy or relate to the theme or activities should be more positive about the event);
- contact or proximity to the action/event (both costs and benefits are typically perceived more acutely and when people are directly impacted);
- values: prodevelopment or ecologically aware values will influence how tourism and events are perceived and evaluated.

Tangibles Costs and Benefits

Some of the social and cultural outcomes of event and tourism are tangible, things that residents and specific stakeholder groups can actually touch and easily measure, including:

- increases in crime, traffic, noise, pollution;
- new opportunities and facilities for entertainment or participation in the arts; new leisure, sport, and lifestyle opportunities;
- decreases in affordable housing, amenities (such as parks), or accessibility to facilities.

These are tangible in the sense that they can be seen, experienced, and measured, although not all of them can easily be given a monetary value. Many would be considered externalities in the usual event or tourism impact assessment, and therefore ignored, unless a comprehensive or TBL approach is explicitly required. Resident and stakeholder input of various kinds is needed to detect and measure these, including perception and attitude questions.

Intangible Costs and Benefits

Intangibles (things not measurable in dollars or other comparable units) can be dealt with in two ways: analyze them subjectively, and separately from the items measured in dollars, or attempt to give them a surrogate monetary value. Some items might actually contain elements that can be treated quantitatively or subjectively. For example, events can have an impact on local housing. The inflation of rents or property values can be measured in dollars, which makes it a tangible cost. But human costs associated with eviction, reduced choice, homelessness or despair require either a surrogate measure (e.g., try to give a dollar value to time spent homeless), or must be treated in a purely qualitative way.

Several intangible costs were dealt with in the Australian Grand Prix research (Burns et al., 1986). Traffic congestion and parking problems experienced by the general population were at times serious. A household survey of residents attempted to measure time lost by residents, and a monetary value was given to this time. Noise disturbances from the races were actually measured (in decibels), and the household surveys determined the degree of public inconvenience caused by noise in several zones around the racecourse. The public was also asked to measure their level of inconvenience arising from crowding. The most interesting intangible cost of the races was that of motor accidents. The researchers analyzed trends in road accidents in the Adelaide area and determined that the Grand Prix did have a psychological impact, which led to an increase in accidents and injuries, over and above that which could be attributed to increases in traffic volume alone. Dollar values were assigned to deaths and injuries, but this measurement will be offensive to some and meaningless to others.

Giving surrogate monetary value to the intangible costs is useful, but fraught with problems. It is also hard to argue that intangible costs are sufficient to neutralize the economic benefits. This line of cost–benefit assessment can only be done in a political forum where values are explicitly stated and weighted. For example, can a tourist-popular motor race be justified if it leads to riots, crime, accidents, or deaths?

Some potential long-term benefits associated with events are very difficult to measure. In the Adelaide case, researchers looked at possible advantages accruing to the region and concluded that the races might have increased local entrepreneurial activity and interest in investment, and an improved attitude of residents toward local products. The analysts concluded: "Perhaps the major long term benefit would be an attitude change on the part of local businessmen and workers, the development of confidence and pride in one's ability" (Burns et al., 1986, p. 28). In this way events can be an "enabling mechanism" for broader and more ambitious changes. Other mega-events have been seen in this light, and even small community festivals could achieve similar improvements in attitude, resulting in real gains for the viability of the economic and social community. Such gains are not easily quantifiable.

Other intangible costs and benefits have been cited in the tourism and event literature, and any of these could be important under certain circumstances. Costs might include an increase in crime and prostitution, which are almost always associated with large crowds. The "demonstration effect" might also come into play, as residents of the host community adopt the values or consumer habits of richer tourists. Or actual hostility toward tourists might arise where residents feel they are being exploited.

"Psychic Benefits" and "Consumer Surplus"

Event proponents often talk about intangible benefits like increased civic pride, social cohesion, cultural significance, happiness, or having a special experience. Do these have any economic value? Can they be included in a cost–benefit evaluation? Andersson and Samuelson (2000) argued that these constitute a "consumer surplus" when people would willingly spend more than the actual cost of the event. Similarly, it was argued by Burns et al. (1986), who attempted to provide surrogate dollar values on a number of intangible costs and benefits associated with the first Australian Grand Prix in Adelaide, that there was a consumer surplus because residents recognized many intangible costs of the event but still supported it enthusiastically.

The "contingent valuation method" has been used to examine people's willingness to pay for events, and this also gets at the notion of "psychic benefits." It is usually found that tourists are willing to pay much more than residents, no doubt because for them the event either the object of their trip or a special experience, whereas residents can presumably enjoy it some other time or have better options for using their disposable income. Capturing higher prices and other economic benefits from event tourists returns some or all of their consumer surplus to the host community.

Measuring Resident Perceptions and Attitudes

Much of the progress made in evaluating the social and cultural impacts of events has been in the form of community or resident surveys, based on the belief that those affected by events know best what the impacts are and whether or not they are positive or negative. Concepts and methods have been documented in papers such as by Delamere et al. (2001) and by Fredline and Faulkner (2002a, 2002b).

Research Notes on Resident Attitudes to Social Impacts of Events

Delamere, T., Wankel, L., & Hinch, T. (2001). Development of a scale to measure resident attitudes toward the social impacts of community festivals, part I: Item generation and purification of the measure. *Event Management*, 7(1), 11–24.

Delamere, T. (2001). Development of a scale to measure resident attitudes toward the social impacts of community festivals, part II: Verification of the scale. *Event Management*, 7(1), 25–38.

In these back-to-back papers the researchers develop and test a scale to measure resident attitudes to social impacts of community festivals. The authors believe that economic and social goals must be balanced to ensure sustainable events. Reliable and valid attitude scales can be an important tool in evaluating events and event development or bidding programs. Their scale was tested on residents of one community in Edmonton, Canada, in the context of local impacts of the annual folk festival, and results were plotted on two expectancy–value grids (similar to importance–performance analysis). The grids graphically reveal the costs and benefits that hold high value for respondents, along with their assessment of the likelihood that each will be achieved (benefits) or inflicted (costs). Respondents were found to be largely expecting positive social benefits, although a number of costs were rated moderate both in terms of value and expectancy: disruption of normal routines; intrusions into their lives; reduced privacy; overcrowding, too much traffic, and unacceptable noise levels. These are clearly concerns that have to be addressed by event organizers and the city.

Also of interest is the researchers' recommendation that community expectations of costs and benefits be managed, as people's expectations might be out of line with reality.

Fredline, E., & Faulkner, B. (2002a). Residents' reactions to the staging of major motorsport events within their communities: A cluster analysis. *Event Management*, 7(2), 103–114.

Fredline, E., & Faulkner, B. (2002b). Variations in residents' reactions to major motorsport events: Why residents perceive the impacts of events differently. *Event Management*, 7(2), 115–125.

In these two articles the researchers examine host community reactions to major motorsport events in Melbourne and Gold Coast Australia. In the first article a cluster analysis was performed which identified the issues of greatest importance to five groups whose attitudes ranged from most negative through ambivalent to most positive about the impacts of the races. By statistically weighting data from the two-city samples, it was estimated that 65% of the populations favored continuation of the races in their current venues. The most negative group (11% of the sample) were older, lived closest to the race areas, were the best educated, were not motorsport fans, and were least likely to work in tourism. In contrast, the most positive group (13%) lived some distance from the events, were the youngest, more interested in motorsports, and more likely to work in tourism. In the second paper additional analysis was undertaken regarding the cluster memberships, with results emphasizing that identification with the event theme (racing plus ancillary activities) was the most important factor separating negative from positive perceptions and attitudes. A number of important issues were considered: relocating the races to permanent venues; involving residents in decision making; ameliorating negatives; and compensating affected people.

The Special Case of Event Tourism and Indigenous People

Events are a traditional way for indigenous people to celebrate and to share their culture. They also make good tourist attractions, and offer economic development opportunities, although not without costs and risks. Several researchers have addressed these issues.

Hinch, T., & Delamere, T. (1993). Native festivals as tourism attractions: A community challenge. *Journal of Applied Recreation, 18*(2), 131–142.

Native festivals are increasingly being regarded as tourist attractions in Canada. While the promotion of these festivals offers the promise of economic benefits for native communities, it also presents challenges, especially in terms of maintaining the integrity of the celebration associated with the festival. The article explores the background and issues associated with the practice of promoting native festivals as tourist attractions. Following a brief discussion of community festivals in general, a description is given of the present status of native tourism and its evolution, and a discussion presented of the existing and emerging issues associated with the planning and management of these festivals, of concerns about authenticity and of considerations related to cross-cultural relationships between the hosts and guests. A case study of the 1992 Dreamspeakers Festival in Edmonton, billed as an international celebration and sharing of First Nations' spirituality, culture, art and film, is used to illustrate and explore these issues.

Whitford, M. (2009). Oaxaca's indigenous Guelaguetza festival: Not all that glistens is gold. *Event Management, 12*(3/4), 143–161.

Guelaguetza is one of Mexico's premiere celebrations of indigenous dance and music. The festival occurs every July in Oaxaca City where it is a premier tourist attraction providing opportunities for socioeconomic growth and development. Yet the festival also creates negative impacts such as commodification and commercialization of the festival, which may lead to the bastardization of culture, including loss of indigenous authenticity and exploitation of local resources. Therefore, the purpose of this study was to critically analyze the positive and negative impacts of the 2007 Guelaguetza in order to determine the extent to which thefestival focuses on becoming a tourist attraction at the expense of community celebration. A qualitative research design utilizing the case study approach was employed to analyze positive and negative impacts emerging from the real-world context of the 2007 Guelaguetza. The results of the study revealed that not all that glistens is gold at the festival. Behind the façade of this visually spectacular festival, the Guelaguetza is at real risk of becoming a colorful, attractive, yet meaningless, commercialized tourist venture if tourist and commercial needs are favored at the expense of the people and their traditions. Consequently, now is the time to revisit and redefine the purpose of the Guelaguetza to ensure it remains a sociocultural and economically viable annual festival for everyone to enjoy, long into the future.

Environmental Outcomes and Impact Assessment

This is the least well-researched or developed element of event and Event Tourism impact assessment. Many articles and several books are devoted to green and sustainable event management, and that is the starting point for anyone wishing to advance this field. It should be accepted that all events and venues are managed according to green practices, and that sustainability is a constant process of improvement. Venues and events should be accredited, and there are now a number of such accreditations available. Guidelines are available from various associations.

The following research note considers new approaches to environmental impact assessment for events. Note that travel is the cause of most of the carbon loading associated with events, leading to repeated calls for more use of mass transit and discouragement of private automobile use in Event Tourism.

Research Note on Environmental Impact Assessment of Events

Collins, A., Jones, C., & Munday, M. (2009). Assessing the environmental impacts of mega sporting events: Two options? *Tourism Management*, *30*(6), 828–837.

At a time when public and private agencies recognise the importance of sustainable development, the environmental impacts of mega sporting events are commanding increasing attention. However, despite event sponsors often flagging the importance of environmental as well as socio-economic legacy components, the environmental impacts of events are difficult to assess quantitatively, being complex and often occurring over extended periods. The general assessment issue is particularly acute with regard to mega events such as the Olympic Games and FIFA World Cup. The practical issues mean that any quantitative techniques seeking to assess environmental impacts are likely to be partial in scope. This paper examines two such approaches for quantitative impact assessment of selected environmental externalities connected with visitation at sporting events. The paper considers the use of Ecological Footprint analysis and Environmental Input–Output modelling. It provides examples of the applications of these techniques to discrete sporting events in a UK region, and discusses whether these techniques are appropriate for exploring the environmental impacts of mega events.

Neither theory nor research practice has yet been developed for evaluating the combined and cumulative impacts of Event Tourism. Portfolio management requires that such tools be available. The larger concerns are associated with tourism in general, namely climate change attributable to fossil fuel consumption, wastefulness with regard to energy, water, and other resource consumption, and a general backlash against conspicuous consumption for leisure purposes in the face of major economic and social inequities. The really big question is if tourism and Event Tourism are going to remain viable.

A New Paradigm for Event Tourism Evaluation

If we want to combine the elements of traditional impact assessment with a more sustainable, triple bottom line approach, plus the key principles of social responsibility, then a new paradigm is required. This new approach also has to consider the "worth" of events, singly and collectively, from multiple perspectives. Event tourism is in many ways exploitive, using events for tourism development and place marketing; both are primarily economic exercises. Therefore, its evaluation can be narrow, focused on a few impact and ROI measures. That is the "business as usual" paradigm.

However, Event Tourism agencies cannot forever operate in a vacuum, divorced from the community and its many stakeholder groups. Whether it is a specific event or cumulative effects that lead to change, Event Tourism inevitably will come under greater political scrutiny. Mega-events tend to do that by virtue of their scale, while many events, over time, will also lead to increased visibility and criticism. Consequently, the old methods will have to change.

Implementing the new paradigm must include the following (see also Getz, 2009):

- bottom-up (arising from needs and consultations) rather than top-down (imposed) planning and decision making;
- less secrecy, yielding to full transparency and accountability;
- matching forecasts of impacts with postevent reality;
- less hype, more discourse;
- narrow measures of ROI (often no more than tourist spending and bums in beds) yielding to broader measures of impact and worth; taking a TBL approach and stressing benefits to residents;
- multigoal perspective involving all stakeholders in setting vision, goals, strategies;
- monitoring, modeling, and assessment of changes caused by events and that affect events;
- from a focus on single events to portfolios and populations;
- less emphasis on mega-events (with their mega-costs and impacts) and more on sustainable events (including institutional Hallmark events).

All this does not preclude the traditional actions of convention and visitor bureaus or event development agencies, as they have members and important external stakeholders to satisfy. Nor will the political emphasis on growth and jobs change overnight. It does imply a new way of thinking about events and tourism, and suggests paths for change and improvement.

Summary and Study Guide

Chapters 9 and 10 go together, with this one commencing our examination of evaluation and impact assessment. Basic concepts and terms were introduced, alongside the purpose and uses of evaluation. Without systematic evaluation there can be no learning organization, and little chance of sustainability. Impact assessment is a subcategory, as are questions such as "What is an event worth?" and "What is a healthy population or portfolio of events?" Many technical evaluation questions deal with efficiency and effectiveness, and with measuring ROI, but overall evaluation of worth or comparison of costs and benefits requires subjective interpretation of the facts, and therefore multiple stakeholder input.

Portfolio evaluation is a new and special application in need of considerable attention. The main challenges pertain to cumulative and synergistic effects that might be hard to predict, let alone control, and require a whole new set of indicators to measure longitudinally. Cities and destinations are increasingly creating events, bidding on more events, and facilitating the event sector, all of which makes for competitive Event Tourism, but also introduces more impact issues. Keeping the portfolio healthy and sustainable will be a permanent challenge, and overlapping portfolios (e.g., with social, cultural, urban domains) adds complexity.

Assessment methods for economic impacts are well advanced (although often poorly implemented), but social, cultural, and environmental methods and theories have lagged. This chapter introduced the nature of resident perception and attitude studies as a way to evaluate event and Event Tourism impacts, but proving cause and effect has seldom been attempted. We simply do not know exactly what aspects of an event experience, or of tourism strategies, will generate specific effects on residents or customers. Environmental impact assessment methods are being developed for the event sector, but so far most of the attention has been given to the "greening" of events and not to cumulative or long-term impacts of Event Tourism. The whole question of "can tourism be sustainable" remains open and controversial.

A "new paradigm" of evaluation is called for, featuring comprehensiveness, responsibility, open accountability, and sustainability. This fits in with the big challenge of developing an integrative, sustainable approach to Event Tourism. However, the concept of triple bottom line accounting, or evaluation, is difficult to implement. The issues and measures of impact are different, and tangibles have to be compared with intangibles. Some of this can be overcome through the use and nonuse techniques covered in Chapter 10, but there will always remain the need for subjective, multistakeholder conclusions.

Study Questions

- Why, and when, should evaluation be conducted for events and Event Tourism strategies (refer to the system model)?
- Explain the various ways to measure and use ROI; give examples of applications to portfolios.
- Specify measures of efficiency and effectiveness for evaluation of an Event Tourism strategy.
- Discuss the policy and evaluation issues pertaining to these two questions: What is an event worth? What is a healthy population or portfolio of events?
- Be able to develop an evaluation instrument, such as a visitor survey, showing appropriate methods, measures, and precise data needed.
- When evaluating an Event Tourism portfolio, how would you measure cumulative and synergistic effects?
- Describe a comprehensive evaluation project to understand the social, cultural, and environmental impacts of a major event on residents.
- What does triple bottom line evaluation mean, and how is it connected to sustainability and accountability?

Additional Readings

- *Return on Investment in Meetings and Events* (Phillips, Breining, & Phillips, 2008).
- *Tourism Economics and Policy* (Dwyer, Forsyth, & Dwyer, 2010).
- *Understanding and Managing Tourism Impacts: An Integrated Approach* (Hall & Lew, 2009).
- *Event Management and Sustainability* (Raj & Musgrave, 2009).

Chapter 10

Economic Impact Measurement and Cost–Benefit Evaluation

Learning Objectives

Upon completion of this chapter the student should understand and be able to explain the following:

1. Why event economic impact assessments are undertaken.
2. Limitations and misleading presumptions.
3. The use and misuse of multipliers; IO versus CGA modeling.
4. How local, regional, and national economic benefits are generated by Event Tourism.
5. Economic impact assessment process.
6. The fallacy of mega-events; why they do not deliver on promises.
7. Cost–benefit evaluation; the distribution of costs and benefits; equity issues.
8. Use and nonuse values.

Introduction

In this chapter we examine in detail the concepts and methods of economic impact assessment and evaluation for events, along with cost–benefit evaluation. There has been enough known about tourism and event impact assessment since at least the year 2000 to prevent mistakes, but nevertheless bad practice and political abuse does continue. Carlsen, Getz and Soutar (2000) reviewed the literature and practice of economic impact evaluation in Australia, then used a Delphi research technique to determine what research directions were needed. They found that some agencies do not make evaluation results public, but release the most favorable findings selectively. This practice continues, and some agencies are not required to make data available for public scrutiny. How this is allowed to continue, in many countries, is a political problem.

There has a great deal of experience in conducting valid economic impact assessments of events, including many published papers about methods and issues. Crompton's (1999) report for the National Parks and Recreation Association, including results from economic impact assessments of sport events across the US, is an excellent reference. Published journal articles by Dwyer et al. (2000a, 2000b) show how to validly conduct impact assessments for a variety of events including conferences, festivals, and sports. The book by Dwyer, Forsyth, and Dwyer (2010) contains everything you need to know, and more.

Probably the most important knowledge to gain from the first part of this chapter is summarized in Figure 10.1, the multiplier model. I do not think the use of multipliers or modeling is absolutely necessary (this is argued in Limitations and Misleading Presumptions), in fact what counts is knowledge of how to maximize the local (or regional, or national) economic benefits of Event Tourism. The supporting discussion indicates the importance of "incremental" or "new money," the "attribution" of expenditure to event tourists, "linkages" and "leakages."

Also of importance is the discussion of mega-events, and why they seldom deliver their promises. When you consider the high risks and costs, the limited number of tourists they attract, and their reputation for a legacy of "white elephant" venues, not to mention consideration of "opportunity costs," it is a real wonder why cities and nations continue to actively seek them. The answers lie in politics and other policy domains, not tourism.

A section on the evaluation of costs and benefits considers tangibles and intangibles, and this leads to the discussion (and case study) on use and nonuse values. Perhaps the most important question in this line of evaluation is *who* gains and *who* pays.

Limitations and Misleading Presumptions of Event Economic Impact Assessments

Limitations

Ironically, it is because they are so limited in scope that event economic impact assessments became so popular! How could that be? Here are the three main reasons.

1. They do not evaluate costs at all, only make claims about the benefits of tourist expenditure and other new money brought to an area because of an event. This enables proponents to focus on supposed benefits while ignoring costs and especially ignoring debt.
2. They say nothing about the distribution of costs and benefits, or who gains and who pays. This enables proponents to hide their vested interests, whether elite sports, profit-making corporations, or politicians seeking fame and reelection.
3. It is very easy to exaggerate the benefits before an event is held by doing a hypothetical economic impact forecast, and to hide the real cost/benefit ratio afterwards, thereby avoiding scrutiny and public accountability.

Most of the misuse of economic impact assessments has occurred surrounding major events that cost enormous sums of money, but it is also a natural tendency for event owners, producers, and others with vested interests to want to make their event look more important than it really is.

Dwyer et al. (2010, p. 406) summarized the main criticisms of event economic impact studies, saying that many critics find that claims of benefits are often exaggerated, costs are ignored, methods are invalid, and it is too narrow in scope. Dwyer et al., and many others, advocate a more comprehensive evaluation process that uses Computable General Equilibrium (CGE) modeling and full cost–benefit analysis (CBA).

Misleading Presumptions About Event Impacts

A number of misleading presumptions persist about event impacts, and this is no longer attributable to the immaturity of event-related research—it is attributable to misuse and ignorance. An article by Crompton and McKay (1994) explored this issue, documenting seven errors encountered in event impact assessments. These are incorporated into the ensuing discussion of presumptions and use of the multiplier.

Presumption 1: To Justify Events, or to Obtain Grants, it Is Necessary to "Prove" Their Economic Benefits

Organizers and supporters of festivals and special events want to obtain grants from public agencies, and they feel that development-minded officials must have "proof" that events create economic benefits. Crompton and McKay (1994) noted: "A scarcity of tax dollars has led to increasing public scrutiny of their allocation. In this environment, producing an economic impact study to demonstrate that economic returns to a community will exceed investment has become almost a *de rigeur* requirement for event organizers. Often these studies are not conducted impartially or objectively," but are done "to legitimize the event's public support by endowing it with an aura of substantial economic benefits" (p. 33).

Unfortunately, I still see this occurring in 2013. It is always wiser to focus on yield and ROI, and in the age of managed portfolios, every event has its roles to play in the bigger Event Tourism policy area.

Presumption 2: All Festivals and Special Events Create Economic Benefits

The cumulative evidence is clear that many events have little economic impact on their community or region, largely because they cater mostly to residents, and sometimes because they are heavily subsidized from public funds. When events attract out-of-region visitors, grants, or sponsorships, they start to create directly measurable economic benefits. Events can also have a significant cumulative impact by improving the destination's image and overall attractiveness, which can be evaluated through studies of perception and trip motivation within target market areas.

The "attribution problem" relates to this question: How much of the spending of event-goers can be attributed as economic impact of the event? To the event organizers the total expenditure of all their customers is an important financial statistic, but in a tourism context the expenditure of visitors who came to the area because of the event is much more important than total revenue. The spending of tourists who travel to an area because of an event is considered to be "new" or "incremental," and therefore is equivalent to the earnings of an export industry.

Presumption 3: Construction of New Facilities for Mega-Events Is a Benefit

For mega-events like World's Fairs and Olympics, and sometimes smaller special events, new facilities or community infrastructure are required. Proponents of the event might claim these additions as benefits to the community, but they are usually costs. The benefit would exist only if capital for the construction is new money to the area, such as one-time grants from central governments. But that represents a transfer of potential spending from other areas.

Also, once the facilities are built—especially cultural and recreational ones—operating costs must be taken into account. Even if the new facilities are considered to be benefits, the permanent operating costs are borne by the host community. But some of these costs can be discounted if the facilities are able to attract new events and new tourist expenditure in the future.

Event Tourism needs venues, that is obvious, but justifying them for one mega-event is not acceptable. This has resulted in far too many "white elephant" facilities that see little or no after-use.

Presumption 4: Festivals Are for Everyone; All Visitors Are Alike

Many event organizers like to believe this, especially if they have a mandate to promote community development and foster leisure or the arts. However, numerous event visitor surveys have revealed that event customers, and particularly event tourists, are a highly segmented market. This has major implications for event impact evaluation, and related demand forecasting or feasibility studies. Some events attract more and higher spending tourists than others, and as reported for the Adelaide Festival (Centre For South Australian Economic Studies, 1990) event tourists spent more per day than average tourists, even when excluding festival ticket sales. The attraction of high-yield tourists, defined in the context of tourism goals for the area, should take higher priority than mass marketing and complex impact measurements.

Presumption 5: Events Create Lots of Employment

Another unfortunate consequence of the use of multipliers and econometric models is the frequent estimate of employment generated by events. The assumption made by using multipliers or other impact models is that so many units of "new" or "incremental" income, created by tourist expenditure, will in turn create employment. Usually this supposed benefit is expressed as full-time job equivalents (FTEs). Crompton et al. (2001) warned that although the IMPLAN model they used for estimating the economic impacts of an event estimated creation of many jobs, in reality, festivals and special events create few full-time jobs and there is available capacity in the workforce to absorb the short-term increase in labor demands.

Successful event organizations typically have small numbers of all-year or part-time staff and most labor at events is done by volunteers. Economists are very reluctant to assign an economic benefit to the contribution of volunteers (Sport and Recreation Ministers' Council, 1991, pp. 2–3) because they create no new income for the area. Under some circumstances volunteer labor might even be considered a cost, such as a case where people work on events for free instead of taking paid employment.

As to the income generated by tourist expenditure, it will usually be dispersed widely among suppliers, accommodation and dining establishments, retail shops, and so on. It helps sustain jobs, and that is very important, but the assumption that tourist expenditure at small events can create new jobs is largely wishful thinking.

Dwyer et al. (2010, p. 425) discuss how economies often have "slack," so that events merely absorb some of it rather than creating new employment. Another consideration is the potential flow of labor into a region because of a major event. Is it from within the same country, or are temporary foreign workers needed?

Mega-events generate construction, and this is where the employment effects are most obvious. But what happens when the construction is finished? A temporary boost in employment might look good to politicians (who are typically fixated on creating jobs), but it could easily be followed by a surge in unemployment.

Presumption 6: All the Expenditure of All Event-Goers Can Be Counted as Economic Benefits

This too is the "attribution problem": of all the money spent by event-goers, how much can be attributed validly to the event as its economic benefit to the area? To determine how much of the spending at events and on event-related trips can be considered "incremental" (i.e., new money for the area), a number of assumptions are typically made concerning the appropriate portion of resident and tourist expenditure. Some economists argue that only the expenditure of true tourists should be counted, while residents' spending must be ignored, yet frequently studies include a percentage of resident spending (called "retained earnings") on the assumption that the events acted to retain money that would otherwise be spent elsewhere, or generated resident spending over and above normal levels.

Note that in the Edinburgh festivals impact study (presented in Chapter 8) attribution is referred to as "additionality." They asked four specific questions of visitors to determine how much of their spending could be attributed to one or more of the festivals they attended.

In the study of eight festivals in Canada's Capital Region (Coopers and Lybrand, 1989), the consultants asked area residents if they spent more than usual during the time of the events they attended, leading them to include a proportion of residents' expenditure. In a study of the Adelaide Festival (Centre for South Australian Economic Studies, 1990) residents attending the festival were asked if they stayed at home, rather than taking a vacation out of the state, because of the event. Researchers in Adelaide concluded that 10.3% of resident visitors were "holidaying at home" and 75% of those would have otherwise traveled outside the state. They also concluded that another 7,000 residents would have traveled outside South Australia more, if it was not for the festival. Accordingly, a proportion of resident expenditure was counted as a benefit for the state.

Researchers who decide to include resident expenditure in the calculation of incremental income should think very carefully about the validity of this practice. First, inclusion of any resident spending is considered to be invalid by most experts. The Sport and Recreation Ministers' Council (1992, p. 2) recommend against it, and the author of this book believes all resident expenditure to be merely an internal transfer—like taking in each others' laundry. The opportunity costs occur because spending at an event likely decreases resident spending elsewhere in the area. It is also difficult to measure, requiring a separate survey or set of questions just for residents, resulting in higher research costs and more complex methods of survey and analysis. Respondents cannot be expected to give reliable answers to such questions as "did you holiday at home because of the event?" or "did you spend more than usual because of the festival?"

Dwyer et al. (2010) considered the "retained earnings" debate and made this conclusion:

> it is perhaps best to include it only when the event held in some destination was selected from a competitive bidding situation or chosen from a particular set of destinations, In such circumstances, the alternative event location is known and the retained expenditure can be estimated on the basis of estimated losses of expenditure by residents who would otherwise have travelled to this successful host destination for the same event. (p. 413)

Most importantly, the object of all such impact evaluation should be visitor oriented. The key questions pertain to the event's ability to attract outsiders and to generate revenue from tourism. The value of an event as a leisure or cultural phenomenon (i.e., having social benefits) is legitimate, but is an entirely different field of inquiry. As an example, Ellis (1990) conducted an evaluation of the Halifax, Nova Scotia, Buskers Festival and concluded that it had a great return on investment for the city because of the large entertainment value generated for residents. Coopers and Lybrand (1989) estimated the "social worth" of festivals by asking respondents about their willingness to pay for free events or to pay more for events having a charge. Burns et al. (1986) described a technique to estimate the "psychic benefit" of an event by assigning monetary value to estimated costs of noise and disruption that residents were willing to bear.

Tourists visiting an area because of an event (or any other kind of attraction) typically spend money getting there and back, some of which is within the destination area being studied, as well as at the event itself. It is tempting to consider all tourist expenditure at the event (usually admission fees, tickets to performances, parking, shopping, dining and drinking) as a benefit to the area—minus, of course, the amounts lost to the area, such as: the costs of all goods and services that were imported; costs of bringing in talent or staff from outside; organizational and marketing expenditure outside the area. But to do so ignores several issues.

What should be done about the expenditure of a tourist who happened to be in town for a convention and incidentally spent money at a festival? It is quite possible that the tourist would have spent money somewhere else, if the event was not occurring, so that all the convention-goer's spending in town should be counted as a benefit of the meeting, not the festival. Attributing the expenditure to both the conference and the event would be double counting, so some sort of allocation is required. The best way to determine the allocation is by asking all visitors a set of questions about their reasons for visiting the destination.

The types of questions commonly employed to solve the attribution problem are twofold: "what proportion of your trip to this area is attributable to the event?"; "would you say that this event was the only (or main, an important, somewhat important, not at all important) reason for your trip here?" From the answers, the proportion of tourist expenditure attributed to a given event or attraction can be estimated. In the example of Winterlude in Canada's Capital region (Coopers and Lybrand, 1989) respondents were asked to give the proportion of their trip motivated by the festival, leading to an estimate that 75% of tourist expenditure could be considered incremental. In contrast, the Festival of Arts attracted only 8% of tourists in attendance, and it was deemed to have no incremental benefit at all (partly because residents attending it said they spent less than normal). Because Winterlude was the dominant tourist attraction of all eight festivals studied, it accounted for $40.6 million of the total $61 million in contribution to the region's gross domestic product.

For the Adelaide Festival (Centre for South Australian Economic Studies, 1990) it was estimated that 900 tourists extended their stay because of the festival, and only the portion of their spending which occurred during the extended stay was included as incremental.

There is a certain arbitrariness in these attribution procedures, which might best be handled by doing a "sensitivity" analysis. Such an approach was taken in the study of nine festivals in Edinburgh (Scotinform Ltd., 1991), where the consultants used different attribution weightings (e.g., from 79% to 100% of the expenditure of residents and from 10% to 27% of day-tripper expenditure was excluded) before concluding that the results were not effected in a major way.

"Time switching" (Burns et al., 1986) is another complication. Some tourists attending events might have simply rescheduled a planned visit to the area, while others might have stayed away because of perceived congestion or expense associated with an event. As well, some residents might actually be tempted to leave town while a major event is held, thereby generating an economic loss for the area. Researchers will find it difficult to take these considerations into account, but at a minimum visitors should be asked if their visit to the area would have been made at another time (say, within a 12-month surrounding period) and had merely been rescheduled to take in the event. The expenditure of time-switchers should be deleted completely from calculations of incremental income.

It can be argued that because events enhance the tourist image of an area there is a "background" economic benefit attributable to events from tourists attracted by this enhanced image. An earlier study of Winterlude (Ekos Research Associates Inc., 1985) found that tourists believed their visit to the event heightened their image of the capital region. This image-enhancing factor could have long-term, positive effects on tourism, but actual measurement of benefits would be very difficult. Some researchers have asked if event-goers plan to return to an area, or would recommend the event or the area to others.

A related line of questioning would be to assess the value of media coverage, either in qualitative terms or by assigning monetary value to free publicity. Even more subjective is the notion that special events make residents feel proud (confirmed by Burns et al., 1986, in their study of the Adelaide Grand Prix), and that heightened civic spirit will have tangible benefits for the area.

Presumption 7: Multipliers and/or Econometric Models Must Be Used to Estimate the "Secondary" Impacts of Events

Although accurate multiplier analysis can add to the evaluation process, multipliers have been greatly abused in economic impact assessments, usually by misappropriating multipliers intended for quite different purposes, larger regions, or other areas (Archer, 1982; Fleming & Toepper, 1990; Murray, 1991). Unfortunately, it appears that the use of multipliers or other models in calculating secondary benefits is often for the purpose of exaggerating the estimate of economic benefits. Multipliers are really intended for use in comparing the economic performance of various sectors of the economy (Archer, 1982). Because of the importance of this topic, and the confusion surrounding multipliers, the ensuing section provides a detailed examination of the applications and pitfalls researchers will encounter.

Multipliers

Economic impact assessments often include a "multiplier" calculation to demonstrate that incremental tourist expenditure has "direct, indirect, and induced" benefits for the local economy. The idea is that "new" or "incremental" money ripples through the economy, changing hands many times, thereby having a cumulative impact greater than the initial amount of tourist expenditure.

Figure 10.1 illustrates the multiplier concept for events. The "direct" income for the area comes from tourists attracted specifically by the event (both at the event and on other goods and services such as accommodation and shopping), plus any new money received from outside by the organization (mostly grants and sponsorships), and other incremental revenue tied to the event, such as money for new infrastructure received from a higher level of government. Keep in mind that tourists spend a lot of money on the trip itself that never reaches the local area, which is why it is important to define the study area boundary. Also remember that not all the new money received by the event organizers circulates in the local economy. Anything they pay for prize money, taxes to higher levels of government, or to import goods and services (including entertainment) cannot be counted in the multiplier calculations—they are "leakages." When looking at the organization's budget it is important to consider exactly where their money comes from and where it is spent.

Most of the economic benefits of events occur at the level of "direct" income, because once the money starts to circulate there are many "leakages." The organizers, as well as other businesses in the local area that receive money from tourists, do business with both local and external suppliers. The money spent on local suppliers is called a "backward linkage," and it creates local profits, taxes, and wages. The overall effect on the economy beyond these first two rounds of monetary flow is called the "induced" income, and is mostly related to higher consumer spending because of increased profits and wages. Indirect and induced income is often lumped together and called "secondary" local area income.

In general, it is desirable to maximize incremental income (new money), maximize internal business linkages, and minimize leakages. Later we examine specific points for increasing the local economic benefits from events.

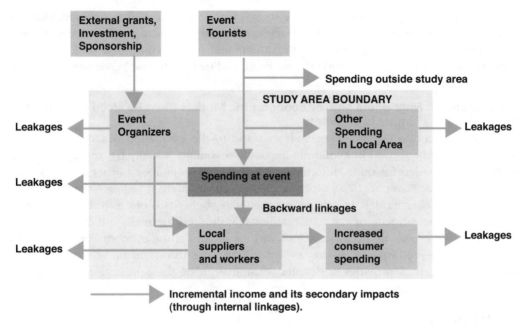

Figure 10.1. The event income multiplier.

Types of Multipliers

A source of much confusion is the use of different types of multiplier and different ways of expressing them. It also appears that some tourism and event boosters use multipliers incorrectly, to exaggerate the benefits. A full discussion is contained in Dwyer et al. (2010, p. 420), who point out that multipliers are based on either input–output (I–O) or CGE models.

The "multiplier" usually used in tourism impact studies is the "income multiplier," which "is basically a coefficient which expresses the amount of income generated in an area by an additional unit of tourist spending" (Archer, 1982, p. 236). For example, if a festival attracts tourists to an area and they spend $100,000 (this is considered to be "new" or "incremental" income for the area), and this spending is found to generate $50,000 of income for the area (after subtracting leakages), then the income multiplier is 0.5.

Archer (1982) cited a number of income multipliers from various studies: for small island countries they ranged from 0.58 to 1.30; for counties and states in the US they were 0.88 to 1.30; for counties in the US they ranged from 0.39 to 1.30. Small town, county, and regional tourism income multipliers in the UK ranged from 0.18 to 0.47. A University of Missouri study in 1986 (quoted in Crompton & McKay, 1994) concluded that 90–95% of US county income multipliers fall in the range of 0.4–0.8, with somewhat higher coefficients for cities. These examples show clearly that the size of the area is an important factor in shaping the multiplier. The same applies for underdeveloped economies—a great deal of leakage occurs owing to imports and other outbound monetary flows.

The "value-added" multiplier, similar to the income multiplier, is preferred by some economists. It represents the wages, profits, and salaries of all the producers in the chain of production begun by incremental tourist expenditure. It cannot exceed a value of 1.0 unless induced consumption is included, and then can have a value up to 1.5 (Burns et al., 1986, p. 14).

Other multipliers are based on the effects of incremental tourist spending on economic activity (sales, transactions, outputs, gross domestic product) rather than income to residents. These can have high values that can be misused to exaggerate the true value of tourism to a local area. Archer (1982, p. 239) gives the example of a small town that was calculated to have a "sales multiplier" of 1.46 and an income multiplier of 0.36 in its hotel sector. This meant that an incremental tourist expenditure of $100 in a hotel would generate $146 of sales activity in the area, but only $36 of local income! Another important point from this example is that sectors of the economy have different multipliers.

Maximizing Local Income Benefits From Events

A number of factors directly determine the multiplier, the most important of which are: amount of leakage/imports (e.g., gasoline for autos is seldom produced locally); backward linkages into the local economy (e.g., how integrated is it? can all supplies and raw materials be obtained in the area?); ownership (which affects the retention or expatriation of profits); labor versus capital intensity (e.g., visitor spending in hotels creates more jobs than in bed and breakfast, but B+B is locally owned and uses mostly local supplies); source of labor (immigrant workers might repatriate wages). These factors have to be considered on a case by case basis.

A coordinated event tourism strategy which seeks to maximize local economic benefits should strive to meet the following objectives:

- attract more tourists to the area specifically for the event;
- attract more external grants and sponsorships;
- make it easier for the visitor to get to the area using local suppliers (e.g., work with local transport companies to package the event) so that more of their total expenditure comes into the area;
- make the event long enough and attractive enough to encourage overnight stays in the host community;
- ensure sufficient accessibility and accommodation so that both tours and individual travelers are able to make convenient overnight stopovers specifically for the event;
- encourage residents to invite guests to stay with them during the event, and to take guests to the events;
- provide sufficient merchandizing to attract visitor spending at the event;
- coordinate events and other attractions to build a "critical mass" sufficient to attract and hold visitors in the area;
- research is necessary to identify and measure the linkages and leakages, and where exactly gains can be realized;
- the event should employ mostly local people for staff and performers;
- require the licensing of merchants/vendors/exhibitors so that locals can be given priority, or a share of profits kept locally;
- make purchases from local suppliers;
- put profits back into community projects;
- make sure that all visitor needs are provided for at the event, or locally (i.e., food, entertainment, souvenirs, accommodation, gasoline).

A few guidelines on types of visitors can also be stated. For creation of local income, the ideal event visitor meets these characteristics:

- stays at least 1 night in the area, preferably at serviced commercial accommodation;
- comes in a group, all of whom spend money;

- consumes merchandise, food, and beverages at the event and in the community;
- prefers local produce, crafts, arts, etc., over imports;
- spends a substantial part of the travel costs locally (gasoline, bus fares, etc.).

Multipliers: I–O Models Versus CGE

Economists Dwyer et al. (2010) argued that "The economic impacts of events are often exaggerated" (p. 406) and I–O economic impact assessment, using multipliers, is flawed. It does not yield an ROI calculation for event funding agencies. Yet multipliers calculated from I–O tables continue to be used, presumably because they are (a) easier and (b) yield more impressive, exaggerated benefits.

According to Blake (2005) "The main difference between input-output and CGE models is that key relationships that input-output models ignore are included in CGE models" (p. 11). I–O models impose no constraint on the amount of extra income that can be earned by labor or capital whereas CGE models impose constraints, and these require that a much higher level of complexity is used in the modeling process. The incorporation of these changes mean a CGE model is more complex than an input-output model but also that it measures impacts more accurately. Blake also argued:

> Two main differences emerge in the way that CGE models and input-output models predict the effects of an event. . . . CGE models, by including (i) the effects of higher prices "crowding-out" tourism demand, and more significantly (ii) the movement of resources into tourism- related industries from other industries, with consequent falls in output of other industries, particularly in other exporting industries, have much lower "multiplier" effects. . . . The second way in which CGE models differ in the impacts that they will predict for events is that construction expenditures are not necessarily positive. (p. 12)

Dwyer et al. (2010, p. 416) emphasized that CGE models take into account many displacement effects and leakages. Some events do not generate much, if any, re-spending in the local areas; in fact, they can reduce local income. They note that events held in peak seasons can simply "crowd out" normal expenditure. Capacity of the economy must be considered when estimating event impacts, and inflation is caused if the local economy does not have surplus capacity. CGE can allow for resource constraints including labor and other inputs—which can cause inflation or alter the economy to the detriment of other sectors. CGE can be calibrated to reflect actual conditions of the economy and particular events. This approach to modeling recognizes that government investment in major events might actually depress consumption. CGE can also account for negative impacts, as tax increases in one sector might be accompanied by decreases in others. CGE can account for where the money comes from, as it might affect exchange rates. Economists use it to run simulations using different assumptions, thereby adding transparency to the estimates.

Economic Impact Evaluation Process

The following steps cover the whole process, including the optional use of multipliers.

Step 1: Formulate Precise Research Goals

Care in formulating research goals will help in avoiding many of the problems and pitfalls discussed above. The researcher or manager must first decide what is of principal interest: for example, knowing that the event attracted a high proportion of out-of-region tourists is extremely important to most event organizers, but estimating regional income and employment benefits is likely to be of interest mainly to tourism agencies.

Rules:

- Define the study area within which costs and benefits are to be calculated.
- Delimit the scope of the evaluation (which costs and benefits to measure; quantitative and qualitative evaluation techniques to be used).
- Define tourists and residents.
- Set criteria for attribution of incremental expenditure (i.e., should resident spending be included?).
- Formulate precise research and evaluation questions.

Recommendations: A great deal of trouble and expense can be saved by avoiding multipliers and other models, and by keeping the whole evaluation process as simple as possible.

- Aim the research at determining the number and types of tourists attracted to the area, with emphasis on high yield; if necessary, and a reliable methodology is available, estimate incremental expenditure.
- Exclude the spending of area residents.

Step 2: Determine Data Needs and Appropriate Methods

Rules:

- Specify types of data needed to answer the research questions; determine the measures needed and the appropriate methods to collect and analyze the data.

Step 3: Determine Attendance at the Event; Calculate Total Number of Tourists and Tourist Visits

Rules:

- Whenever possible, use controlled access and/or ticket sales to estimate attendance.
- For open events, use a systematic observation method which avoids double counting by applying weightings derived from visitor surveys (asking: how many visits have you made, on how many days?).
- Take into account the difference between total number of visitors and total person-visits, and between tourist and resident visits (feasible only if a visitor survey is undertaken).

Recommendations: Avoid estimates based on casual observation.

Step 4: Conduct Visitor Surveys

To obtain event visitor expenditure data, both diary and questionnaire methods have been used. With diaries a sample of visitors is asked to complete a daily record of activities and expenditures. The nonresponse bias of diary methods (i.e., a higher drop-out rate) was found not to be a problem by Faulkner and Raybould (1995) and Breen, Bull, and Walo (2001). However, in both those research studies it was found that questionnaire responses tended to underestimate expenditure, owing to memory lapses, and both found significant differences between males and females. It was suggested by Faulkner and Raybould that males are more likely susceptible to the "social bravado" bias whereupon they report more spending on items influenced by peer pressure (e.g., drinking, entertainment). The Bree, Bull and Walo analysis also found no significant differences in data obtained by those who handed in questionnaires at the end of a multiday sporting event and those who mailed it back later.

Rules:

- An on-site visitor survey is necessary for estimating the number and proportion of tourists at events; their motivations, spending patterns, and whether or not visits were extended or expenditure increased due to the event.
- Ensure that a systematic sample of individuals is taken.
- Include performers, officials, competitors, etc.
- Stratify the sample by applicable factors such as venue, time, and day; use weightings to reflect the true distribution of attendance.
- Guard against sampling bias caused by length of stay and multiple site visits by ensuring that individuals are not mistakenly counted twice; make estimates of average length of stay and number of visits and "weight" the results to reduce the effect of length of stay bias.
- Use past experience or educated guesses to derive a sample size which will yield high confidence limits for statistical analysis, especially ensuring a large enough sample of tourists.

Recommendations: Avoid recall bias by conducting surveys on-site or combining on-site with take-home surveys. Diaries are likely to yield more accurate expenditure estimates. Offer incentives to obtain higher response rates.

Step 5: Conduct Surveys of Other Event Visitors

T. Tyrrell and Johnston (2001) advised that economic impact studies must include the spending of all categories of event visitor: spectators; participants; sponsors and their guests; officials; the media; volunteers; exhibitors and vendors. Theses researchers found that the largest share of economic impacts at certain sport events came from spending by sponsors. Andersson and Samuelson (2000) determined that the media covering international sport events generated the largest per-person impacts (i.e., they generated the highest "yield").

Instead of random samples of event visitors, a complete census of all the special groups might be possible and necessary. For example, in team sports, some might be very heavy spenders and others might get their ways paid by local organizers.

Step 6: Estimate Total Visitor Expenditure (by Tourists and Others)

Frechtling (1994) mentioned eight different ways to make estimates of tourist expenditure, most of which are not applicable to events. Direct observation could be used at event sites, such as recording sales, admissions, and service fees, but this tells nothing of off-site expenditure. Postevent household surveys could measure event-related expenditure, but only in sampled market areas and with the added problem of recall bias. Whatever technique is used, the researchers must pay particular attention to the business traveler who might not know all related trip expenses, and to the package tourist who might not be able to assign the accurate portion of trip expenses to the study area. For these special cases a number of additional questions are needed, or special subsamples will have to be taken to probe more deeply.

Regardless of the survey technique or sample frame, recall bias is a major problem. A number of studies have demonstrated that tourists often underestimate their expenditure, especially after some time has passed (Howard, Lankford, & Havitz, 1991; Sheldon, 1990). Consequently, on-site and exit surveys are likely to yield the best estimates of daily expenditure, and measurement of expenditure for the entire trip is best taken immediately upon completion of the visit. A combination of on-site interviews and self-completed, take-home questionnaires can also be used to good effect (Ralston & Crompton, 1988a, 1988b). As discussed earlier, log books are an alternative for collecting detailed expenditure data.

For the purposes of estimating tourist expenditure, an average amount per tourist visit can be calculated and then multiplied by an estimate of total tourist visits. Or an average amount per tourist can be estimated and multiplied by the estimated number of tourists. In the case of a study of the Barossa Wine Festival (Tourism South Australia, 1991) respondents were asked to itemize their spending on the day of the interviews only. Daily expenditure was then divided by the number of adults covered in the sample, then multiplied by the total number of planned visitor-days. This yielded an estimate of visitor spending per adult.

Sport and Recreation Ministers' Council (1991, p. 4) warned of the problems of using mean versus median tourist expenditure visits. If the sample is random and sufficiently large there is no worry, but in inadequate samples a few large outliers will distort the estimate to total incremental expenditure. Use of medians will result in bias, but lower statistical error. If the outliers are a characteristic of the population as a whole, as well as the sample, use of the mean is proper. Otherwise, the median should be used to enumerate from the sample, but with outlier values added separately.

A special problem occurs when more than one event occurs simultaneously, as in the case of Edinburgh's festival season every August. The researchers (Scotinform Ltd., 1991) found that many tourists and residents went to several events during their stay, giving rise to a serious risk of double counting. To overcome this problem they invented a separate category for the "multiple event visitor" and avoided attribution of their expenditure to specific events.

Normal expenditure categories are: food and beverage; recreation and entertainment; travel; accommodation; retail shopping; admission fees. These should be disaggregated geographically (i.e., on-site, off-site within area, outside the subject area) and possibly by time (before, during, and after the event). If sector-specific multipliers are going to be applied, the expenditure categories must match the definitions of each sector.

Rules:

- Determine average spending per visitor-day, separating on-site from off-site, and within the study area from outside the study area (if total trip expenditure is estimated, the on-site, within-area amounts must be distinguished).
- Include spending by performers, officials, etc., but also account for wages, profits etc., they remove from area.
- Avoid double counting when events overlap; create a multiple-event category of visitor.
- In small, nonrandom samples, avoid using expenditure means if large outliers occur.
- Use expenditure categories that match available classes of multiplier.

- Take into account the special estimation problems associated with package tours (what portion to allocate to the area?) and business or related trips (the traveler might not have paid).
- Minimize recall bias by conducting surveys on-site or as soon after the event as possible.

Recommendations: Use a combination of on-site exit interviews, log books, and take-home questionnaires to get reliable estimates of expenditure per day and for the whole trip.

Step 7: Estimate Expenditure "Attributable" to Tourists

From questions on trip motivation, timing, and spending, an estimate can be made of "new" or "incremental" income derived from all event visitors. Only the spending of persons who traveled because of the event and who would not have visited the region otherwise can be counted totally. The spending of time-switchers has to be eliminated, as that of multiple-purpose travelers must be discounted. For those staying longer or spending more because of the event, a portion of their expenditure can be included. With regard to event visitors who had other reasons for traveling but definitely planned to attend an event, Y. Yu and Turco (2000) argued that their event-specific spending should be considered new money and included in economic impact estimates. The inclusion of any amount of resident spending is controversial, but could only be justified if was demonstrated that the event prevented residents from spending money on travel outside the area (and this is extremely difficult to prove).

Rules:

- Determine the importance of the event in motivating the trip, an extended stay, or increased spending.
- Subtract time-switchers, who would have visited the area anyway (say, during the same year).
- Do not confuse total incremental expenditure with economic impact.

Recommendations: Ask several motivational questions to obtain a valid measure of the importance of the event.

Step 8: Calculate Net Income and Macroeconomic Impacts

Gross visitor expenditure attributed to the event does not equal net income for the area, because of leakage and the multiplier effect.

At this stage it is usual to apply a value-added or income multiplier to account for all the direct and secondary effects of incremental expenditure. An econometric model can be used instead of multipliers to account for macro impacts over time. Government revenue, in the form of taxes at all levels, is usually taken into account when value added multipliers are applied; otherwise it must be estimated separately.

The advance of CGE offers a clear alternative when it comes to calculating appropriate multipliers, most of which are still based on traditional I–O tables for nations and regions.

Recommendations: "Yield" should be emphasized rather than macro impacts, by examining the number and types of tourists attracted and their activity and spending patterns. Consult experts on using CGE modeling.

Step 9: Do a Cost–Benefit Evaluation

Cost–benefit analysis has the added advantage of being able to draw conclusions about the net benefit of the event after costs have been subtracted, and of incorporating intangibles and non-economic measures.

Why Mega-Events Fail to Deliver the Promise

In general, and in principle, this author does not support mega-events that generate enormous expectations matched by enormous costs. Several elite groups in society do benefit from mega-events, namely builders/land developers, corporate sponsors, politicians, and the sport elite, but the taxpayer keeps on paying. Residents will never get the full, promised benefits of new sports stadia built for Olympics, World Cup events, etc., and these supersized facilities are often expensive "white elephants." To be sustainable, reuse and multiuse of venues is desirable; permanent, rather than one-time, events generate a much higher benefit to cost ratio and can become permanent institutions.

This anti-mega-position is supported by a growing body of research on sport event impacts, but is controversial. Those in favor will always have arguments about long-term, beneficial legacies that fall into the pubic-good domain, but these legacies are seldom if ever documented in the future—they remain as promises. Many costs of mega-events are hidden and full accountability is not delivered. Many promises of intangible benefits, such as increased sport participation, have been disproven. Students of events, and residents, should always be skeptical of claims made by mega-event proponents.

Blake (2005, p. 20) used CGE to estimate the likely impacts of the London 2012 Summer Olympic Games, concluding they would be positive. However, certain issues were raised that all mega-event proponents need to take into account. First, debts must be taken into account—raising the specter of Greece in the aftermath of the Athens event and the complete failure of this country to manage its debt. Second, there is a major diversion of money into infrastructure that would not otherwise have been constructed (after all, who actually needs Olympic-sized venues?). This represents opportunity costs for the nation as a whole. Blake, after studying past Olympics, noted that full costs are often ignored, including increased security. The length of the event is too short for employing new people; therefore, unemployed do not necessarily gain (which is a false assumption of I–O models). Who gains and who loses is generally ignored (e.g., from changing real estate values), and if taxes are raised, many people start to pay for the games while lottery diversions from other causes represents an opportunity cost. Residents have often been displaced for new mega-event construction. The positively affected businesses and sectors take away labor from others. Often construction impacts and visitor numbers/expenditures are exaggerated, while environmental costs are often ignored or downplayed (e.g., carbon loads and pollution).

In the following research note, Mills and Rosentraub (2012) document key problems with mega-event claims of benefits. Then, in an Expert Opinion section, Holger Preuss gives a detailed explanation of opportunity costs pertaining to mega events.

Research Note on Mega-Events and Mega-Impacts

Mills, B., & Rosentraub, M. (2012). Hosting mega-events: A guide to the evaluation of development effects in integrated metropolitan regions. *Tourism Management, 34,* 238–246.

Every time a city or country seeks to host or is the location for a mega-event such as the Olympics, World Cup, or Super Bowl, boosters proclaim that substantial financial benefits will result. These claims are rarely, if ever, realized. Independent analysts have long-noted four major errors that lead to the dramatic overestimation of the economic benefits predicted or touted by advocates. First, major events are usually held in large metropolitan areas or well-established resorts that are already tourist destinations. As a result, there is the potential for a substantial displacement or substitution effect. Second, the numbers used to extol the benefits from hosting a mega-event typically report aggregate spending, even though a substantial portion of what is bought is imported into the area for resale. Third, the presence of a mega-event creates a temporary demand for part-time labor. As an example, labor needed only for construction or when the event is under way would qualify as temporary. Those temporary workers who live outside the region will take a portion of their earnings back to their home area and their purchases will lead to growth in other regional economies. Fourth, there is a level of intraregional substitution spending that also occurs. The aggregate spending projected to occur when a mega-event is hosted includes purchases made by people who live nearby. Had those individuals not attended the mega-event or complementing activities, they would have spent a similar amount of discretionary funds for other forms of local entertainment. As a result, those expenditures produce no new economic activity for a region. These criticisms help explain why the projected aggregate spending reported for a mega-event is usually overestimated relative to the local benefits.

Expert Opinion: Holger Preuss on Opportunity Costs. Are Investments in Mega-Sport Events Useful and Efficient?

Economic analyses of mega-sport events often only focus on the positive effects and legacies while ignoring opportunity costs and the efficiency of using scarce resources. Event opponents argue that decisions to invest public resources should also consider alternative uses for the money. This research note aims to clarify the most important issues surrounding the efficiency of event investments and opportunity costs.

To be able to value opportunity costs the alternative investment must be valued against a target. This can be (1) the overall political aim to use all public resources for the most productive activity (Szymanski 2002, p. 3) to maximize income. Alternatively (2) a particular political aim—such as increase of tourism—can be achieved that indirectly also increases the public welfare. While in the first case all thinkable alternative investments have to be compared to the event investment, in the second only the projects that have the same target system have to be considered as alternative. For example the particular political aim to reposition the country's image by staging the Olympic Games has to be compared with alternative investments in worldwide image campaigns.

> Learning: We can value projects only towards a political given target system.

To calculate opportunity costs it is important to consider the strategy politicians use to develop the host city. In case the political target system is to strengthen particular "location factors," a mega sport event may be a very efficient vehicle (Preuss, 2007b).

To measure the efficiency (E) of an event investment we need to set the output (Y) (all benefits minus all costs) of an event in relation to the input (X): $E = Y/X$. However, the input and output differs for each stakeholder. Mega-sport events create a variety of outputs. As displayed in Figure 10.2, events not only change the cities' location factors but also consumption-based economic activity. Both outputs, other location factors, and economic activity in particular branches are differently valued by different stakeholders and they can even be conflicting due to diverse interests. In other words, the same event can be very differently "efficient" for each stakeholder.

> Learning: The efficiency of an event is different for each stakeholder due to different inputs and outputs.

Exemplarily we take a spatial differentiation of the stakeholders in three groups. The input $X_{a,b,c}$ for an event has to be provided by the three stakeholders: international resources (e.g., IOC contribution) (a), national resources from outside the host city (e.g. government, sponsors) (b), and city resources (c). Beneficiaries of a mega-sport even—here also defined special—are the International Sport Federations and the IOC (a), the host nation (b), and the host city (c). Figure 10.2 shows the input and output of a mega-event.

To determine the general efficiency (E) of an event all primary costs (input) ($X_{a,b,c}$) and all output ($Y_{a,b,c}$) have to be considered. However, for a local political decision whether to stage

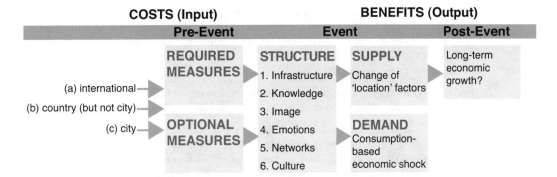

Figure 10.2. Input and output of a mega-sport event. Source: Preuss (2007a).

an event or not, only the ratio between input X_c and output Y_c for the city is of interest. The local efficiency is $E_c = Y_c/X_c$. Since cities often have most of the benefits but only a small part of the costs, mega-events are very efficient for this stakeholder group. The so-called "event strategy" has therefore become a common tool for cities to attract autonomous money.

> Learning: When discussing opportunity costs and the efficiency of event investments the stakeholder perspective and spatial differentiation have to be considered.

There are five aspects to be considered in each discussion about opportunity costs and efficiency of event investments:

1. Indirect and intangible effects of the mega event need to be considered when comparing to the benefits for an alternative project. For example, the decision against staging a mega sport event from a government's perspective—such as Rome 2012 withdraw from bidding for the 2020 Olympics—also means that the other stakeholders (sport federations, citizens, etc.) cannot apply for the event due to the missing share of resources from the government. The decision of the government (which may be obvious from a financial cost–benefit consideration) is a clear political signal and may negatively affect future cooperation with the other stakeholders. Some stakeholders contribute to the input but do not necessarily benefit from the output. Vice versa, the city's input also supports the output for the other stakeholders who have other targets systems. This phenomenon can be called "linked production." It is a prerequisite to assure the input of resources from all stakeholders ($Y_{a,b,c}$) to be able to stage the event. To get all stakeholders to take their share of costs, the expected output for each stakeholder must be greater or equal than its individual input. The whole must be seen and single nonefficient projects may be accepted to reach the overall output. For example the output for the city Y_c can only occur through the total input $X_{a,b,c}$, which is the input from international, national, and city resources.

> Learning: The staging of a mega-sport event cannot be seen isolated from other projects that need to be organized jointly.

2. When arguing that the mega-event costs should better be invested alternatively it has to be considered that, for example, only the input of a city (X_c) can be alternatively invested but not the total investments of the mega-event ($X_{a,b,c}$). Furthermore, only the alternative investment of public resources can be considered, because private resources may not be available for the alternative project.

> Learning: The often claimed alternative use of the money is limited to the input a stakeholder gives and cannot expect the input of other stakeholders.

3. The diversity of targets from different stakeholders leads to the next phenomenon which is partly "forced inefficiency." A complex project such as a mega-sport event may sometimes require an inefficient investment from one stakeholders' point of

view while the same investment maximizes the output for another stakeholder. For example, it may be inefficient for the host city (Y_c) to invest in a state-of-the-art velodrome but is very efficient from the UCI's (international cycling union) point of view (Y_a). This inefficiency cannot be avoided from the cities perspective due to conflicting target systems.

> Learning: The variety of outputs and conflicting interests of different stakeholder necessarily make single investments looking inefficient for stakeholders while the same is efficient for other stakeholders.

4. Event-related input of one stakeholder often results in output for stakeholders not involved in the event. These so-called externalities can be both negative and positive. A positive externality would be the general upgrade of the region's traffic system; a negative externality would be the displacement of neighborhoods. If public resources are used the public welfare of all citizens is on stake and therefore positive/negative externalities have to be considered in discussions about the overall efficiency.

> Learning: The efficiency considerations have to weight-out all stakeholders by also considering externalities.

5. Concerning the long-term development of an area "synergy effects" should be considered in efficiency calculations. The input into events highly depends on the "event structure" (see Figure 10.2, infrastructure, knowledge, image, emotions, networks, culture) that is existent in a city before staging a mega-event. Cities that follow an "event strategy" have already built up "event infrastructure" and therefore reduce their necessary input (X_c) for the next event to be staged. Efficiency becomes greater the more events are staged in a row and therefore the opportunity costs reduce for following events.

> Learning: It is wrong to expect that all investments for an event have to be calculated into this one event when other events follow. A kind of depreciation should be considered when calculating efficiency.

By using the measure "efficiency" (output–input) of alternative investments it became clear that the decision to stage a mega-sport event cannot be taken in isolation and that there are many factors that need to be considered. The argument put forward is based on a stakeholder perspective and a spatial differentiation of interest groups. Opportunity costs are often only argued from one stakeholder's perspective towards a particular output of the event (e.g., the tourism industry argues with the positive image effect of a mega-event). Due to the complexity of stakeholder interests towards a mega-sport event and the variety of different outputs created by a mega-event the argumentation for or against staging an event based on opportunity costs cannot match the reality. Therefore, it may have become clear that the popular statement "We would be better to use the Olympic funding for investments in hospitals" has to be qualified.

When Can a Mega-Event Be Justified?

Some would say "never!", but we should always allow for exceptions and encourage open discourse. As defined in Chapter 1, the term "mega-event" has to be considered in a relative sense. They are not necessarily the biggest in the world, so the first requirement is to be specific about what we mean. Now, consider the following possible justifications:

- Somebody else is paying! If a senior level of government is paying the bulk of costs, then local residents might very well gain (at someone else's expense, of course); the redistribution effects of large capital projects are well known.
- Capital costs will be minimized as we plan to mostly use existing facilities (but beware of project scope creep and the constant, upward revision of cost estimates).

- The project will beneficially reshape an area in need of renewal, or be a catalyst for an otherwise unattainable development. Fine, but get the full cost–benefit evaluation, and remember to consider opportunity costs—there might be better ways to achieve these goals.
- The mega-event is needed for reasons of national pride, reunification, global legitimacy, or some other high ideal. Mostly, these arguments appeal to politicians for their own selfish reasons, but given that host populations usually come out in support, is that not good enough? Maybe, but after the party is over, said supporters have to swallow the costs. How do they feel then?

In my portfolio model, ideally the occasional mega-event is one that utilizes existing capacity to its fullest. If the event stretches supply to the limits, some incremental investment might be needed, and this is fine if it is part of an overall, long-term strategy. If the event is so truly large that enormous costs (and debt) must be contemplated, then my advice will always be to forget it. There simply is no rational, valid justification.

Evaluation of Costs and Benefits

There is a tendency to use the multiplier to demonstrate only macroeconomic benefits, without consideration of economic costs, and without evaluation of intangibles and non-economic items. That makes the multiplier a tool for generating misleading conclusions. Cost–benefit analysis has the added advantage of being able to draw conclusions about the net benefit of the event after costs have been subtracted, and of incorporating intangibles and non-economic measures. It can be used in postevent evaluations, or in feasibility studies to help determine the overall worthiness of a proposal. It is not a method without difficulties. Several general problems always arise:

- how to measure or compare tangibles, such as revenue, with intangibles such psychological benefits;
- how to subtract intangible costs from tangible benefits;
- determining the parameters of the calculations: what area to cover? what time period?;
- measure benefits and costs for the whole community or just the public sector?

In addition, events give rise to special problems. A landmark study of the Adelaide (Australia) Grand Prix by The Centre for South Australian Economic Studies (Burns et al., 1986) highlighted these issues:

- Demand is primarily for related services, not the event itself; therefore, data acquisition must be broad.
- Peaking of demand is typical of short-term and occasional events; the impacts might therefore be difficult to isolate from general trends.
- Peaking also affects the level and distribution of benefits.
- Special attention must be given to the reallocation ("switching") of funds locally, which is not a real benefit.
- The benefits of events might occur over a long time period (e.g., heightened tourism image leading to increased travel), but investments will often be short term; therefore the "discounted present value" of benefits must be compared with costs.

- Justification of costs for event infrastructure might have to be made by considering future use (e.g., the facility legacy).
- Major beneficiaries of events are both the customers and, potentially, the entire host community; therefore, "externalities" are of major interest.

The methods used in the Australian Grand Prix cost–benefit analysis provide a good model, although circumstances and resources will be important factors in shaping methods for different events. One final product of the analysis was a chart showing an upper and lower estimate of the benefit to cost ratio, from the State of South Australia's perspective (see Table 10.1). Two ratios for tangible economic benefits and costs are shown: an upper estimate of 3.8:1 and a lower estimate of 3.1:1. These ratios can be interpreted as follows: for every dollar of cost (or investment in the event), between 3.1 and 3.8 dollars of benefit to the State of South Australia were realized. Intangibles were treated separately, as "psychic" benefits or costs. For a more up-to-date treatment, see the discussion of "use and nonuse values."

Tangible Costs

The Grand Prix researchers (Burns et al., 1986) had to wrestle with the very definition of costs, as applicable to an event like the Grand Prix. Typical of many "mega-events," different levels of government were involved. Grants from the Commonwealth of Australia were counted as benefits, as they were new revenue made available only because of the event. But grants by the State to the event were counted as costs, because that money could have been used for other State purposes (i.e., it had an "opportunity cost"). If the city of Adelaide had been the area for which the cost–benefit evaluation was undertaken, then State grants might have been considered benefits—if they were not simply diverted from some other payments to the city.

The Grand Prix costs were of the following types:

- grants from within the State that could have been used for other purposes;
- construction and demolition expenditure (minus applicable grants);
- amounts written off as depreciation;
- planning, marketing, and operating costs (minus applicable grants);
- cost of borrowing (interest payments);

Table 10.1. Benefit–Cost Ratios for the 1985 Grand Prix in Adelaide, South Australia (Tangible Economic Benefits and Costs Only)

	Benefits	Costs
Upper estimate (benefit to cost ratio: 3.8.1)	Visitor expenditure (including multiplier effects): $ 9,865,000 Event and construction costs funded from outside the State, including multiplier effects: $14,941,000 Total benefits: $24,806,000	Event and capital costs funded within the State: $6,571,000
Lower estimate (benefit to costs ratio: 3.1:1)	Visitor expenditure: $ 9,865,000 Event and construction: $13,765,000 Total benefits: $23,630,000	Event and capital costs: $7,520,000

- externalities: costs to other government agencies (police, fire, health, transport, waste disposal, etc.) that can be attributed to the event as being above and beyond the norm; costs of damage to private property caused by the event; economic losses to businesses adversely impacted by the event.

One could also include the costs of crime associated with events, inflationary costs to housing, property, food, etc., if caused by the event and related development.

Tangible Benefits

External grants are benefits to the region only if they constitute new, and not diverted, sources of funds. Spending by residents is mostly a redistribution of local wealth and not a benefit. The Australian Grand Prix researchers (Van der Lee & Williams, 1986) concluded: "The once in a lifetime character of the first Grand Prix and the relatively limited time to change consumption and savings habits leads to the suggestion that it was likely that some increased expenditure was financed from existing savings, thereby providing some additional economic stimulus in the short term" (p. 46). But they did not include any resident spending in their calculations of tangible benefits, yielding conservative estimates.

Benefits of the Grand Prix attributed to the State of South Australia included:

- grants received from outside the area to construction or event operations;
- private investment attracted by the event (most events by themselves lack the ability to attract new hotels, etc., but might have the effect of accelerating developments; any development "boom" might also result in a subsequent "glut" with weaker businesses experiencing actual losses);
- tourist expenditure attributable to the event; the value-added multiplier was used to estimate total impact on the State.

Multipliers derived from state input–output tables for various industry sectors were used. These ranged from 1.109 for expenditure in the food sector to 1.212 for transport, with a weighted average for all sectors of 1.192. This approach is more accurate than using a gross regional or national multiplier.

Employment

Most events generate little in the way of permanent employment, although the larger annual ones require at least a small full-time staff. Mega-events requiring a lengthy planning, operating, and shut-down period can have a more substantial impact, particularly if major construction projects are necessitated. Hatten (1987) reported that Expo '86 in Vancouver generated 29,000 on-site jobs over the 6-month event and increased employment 7.6% overall in the metropolitan area.

The income created by small events, regardless of direct job creation, does create support jobs, both in tourism and in other sectors as well. The "employment multiplier" is often used to estimate the number of jobs created for every direct job in tourism or, more appropriately for events, the number of jobs created per unit of tourist spending. These jobs are expressed as person-years of employment, or "full-time equivalents" (FTEs), as many of the jobs are temporary (e.g., site construction and site staff) or part-time. For example, the study of eight events in Canada's National Capital Region estimated that tourist income from the events generated 1,881 person-years of employment in the region, including only 20 full-time jobs (Coopers and Lybrand 1989). In the Edinburgh events study it was estimated that 1,319 FTE jobs were created in the region, and 3,034 in Scotland.

Estimates made with multipliers must be treated with extreme caution, as the FTE jobs they "measure" do not really exist—they are mostly bits of existing jobs. It is highly probable that tourist expenditure at events (except the largest ones) will be mostly absorbed by existing labor (i.e., through overtime and more part-time work) rather than through creation of new jobs.

Taxes and Other Public Sector Revenues

Many event impact assessments include an estimate of the tax benefits accruing to government from tourist expenditure at events and related travel. Additional indirect impacts can be created through local property taxes or corporate and income taxes.

One example was given by Taylor and Gratton (1988), who reported that public authorities gained an income of $125 million from the 1984 Los Angeles Olympics. A Coopers and Lybrand study (1989) found that of the $61 million contribution of eight festivals and events to Canada's National Capital Region, $8.8 million was direct tax income to governments.

Turco (1995) provided data on the economic impacts of the 1993 Kodak Albuquerque International Balloon Fiesta. It was estimated that both the city and the state gained substantially from tourist expenditure, as follows:

City revenue from lodging taxes: $987,277
City revenue from sales taxes: $1,234,443
State revenue from sales taxes: $1,323,237
State revenue from gasoline taxes: $900,041

When estimating public revenue from taxes it is essential to consider a number of qualifiers. If local taxes are based on property values alone, then events will contribute little. It is through lodging/hotel taxes that the greatest benefit can accrue, but only when it can be demonstrated that the event attracted tourists who would not otherwise have visited the area, or they stayed longer and in commercial accommodation because of the event. Local business taxes might also increase through the added volume of event tourism, but this will often be difficult to demonstrate.

From the perspective of senior levels of government the tax revenue question is more difficult to evaluate. Travel within a state or country does not generate incremental benefits; only inbound travelers should be counted. It must usually be assumed that events are simply one of a range of leisure opportunities and that any related travel is a substitute for other internal travel. Senior levels of government might, however, be interested in altering the regional pattern of travel in order to bolster the economies of depressed areas.

Events that stimulate tourist spending on highly taxed goods and services obviously generate high public sector revenues, so the presence of room and sales taxes is an important variable, as is the nature of the event attractions and spending outlets. Andersson and Samuelson's paper (2000) can be consulted for additional insights and methodological details.

The Distribution of Costs and Benefits

The question of WHO benefits and WHO pays the costs is often more important than determining and measuring the actual costs and benefits. It is partially an issue of scale, as tourism is often promoted by senior levels of government and by the industry, with local governments and communities picking up many of the costs. And it is an issue of values, as in the case where the severity of some costs is seen to outweigh anticipated benefits.

Unfortunately, these distributional questions are often not asked in impact assessments or in feasibility studies which forecast the costs and benefits of a proposal.

Regarding events, we have already listed some of the key distributional issues in the earlier discussion of the multiplier concept. There it was argued that the multiplier is a planning tool, to be used to help maximize benefits to the host community. By tracing the linkages and leakages that determine the multiplier, the evaluator can learn where the costs and benefits lie, and then take measures to correct problems or realize opportunities. The goal should be to modify the event or its organization to achieve widespread benefits for the community and to minimize costs and disruptions.

Externalities are the most difficult problem. Is it justifiable for event organizers to attain their goals/profits at the expense of property damage, noise, traffic congestion, or other disruptions to uninvolved residents? And can ecological damage or pollution be accepted? What about changes in the social fabric of a community, as a result of annual exposure to large influxes of tourists? The tourism industry gains, but the community is forced or encouraged to change. These are not easy issues to resolve, but they should be considered and debated.

Use and Nonuse Values

When conducting impact assessments the core requirement is to determine what new expenditure or income for the in-scope area is attributable to the event. This is one way to look at benefits, but it is very narrow. As we have already seen, there are potential benefits to individuals, groups, and society as a whole that accrue from events. The concept of "psychic benefits" was introduced in the study of the Adelaide Grand Prix, and that brings us to nonuse values.

Expert Opinion and Case Study (by Professor Tommy Andersson, Ph.D.. The School of Business, Economics and Law at the University of Gothenburg, Sweden; for more detail see Andersson, 2012; Andersson, Armbrecht, & Lundberg, 2012)

The benefits of events can be expressed in a simple, graphical way that separates categories of benefits along two dimensions: (a) benefits to society or benefits to individuals; and (b) intrinsic (occurring within) versus extrinsic (occurring in a tangible way). The quadrant defined by a high degree of both extrinsic and societal benefits includes economic impacts from tourism as well as potential public health and welfare, "social capital" (a sense of interconnectedness), and environmental benefits. Where there is a high degree of both societal and intrinsic benefits we can situate image and "cultural capital" (aesthetic, scientific, and spiritual in nature). Where individual benefits meet the intrinsic dimension are placed identity (self and group) and happiness. And where extrinsic benefits meet the individual dimension we have expenditure, health, conduct, and attitudes. Social marketing works to influence this quadrant in particular, whereas tourism development and place marketing aim to affect mostly the upper-right quadrant. Event designers are particularly interested in creating happiness and fostering identity (often through communitas).

The above conceptualization of benefits is adapted from the publications of Armbrecht (2009) and McCarthy, Ondaatje, Laura, and Brooks (2004) and it leads to the question of how some of these benefits can be measured and assigned value in an economic sense. This is where use and nonuse values are important.

Use and Nonuse Values

The value that festival and event experiences create, for event visitors as well as for local residents, can be described in terms of use value and nonuse value. *Use value* takes into account the benefits during the actual festival. Concert experiences generate an obvious use value during a music festival, but social and other cultural experiences during the festival may for some visitors be equally important. Use value can be further differentiated into direct use value and indirect use value.

Direct use value is created primarily by the festival entertainment and is a reflection of the appreciation of experiences at the festival premises. Direct use value represents the value of the core experience. Indirect use value is also experienced by festival participants but not within the festival area. Indirect use value is an important concept for the tourism industry since it describes the value of tourism activities at the destination apart from the direct activities within the festival premises.

Festivals and events also cause positive and negative impacts by its mere existence and these impacts are not accounted for in traditional financial assessments. People who do not attend an event may still be affected by it through traffic congestion, littering, a positive image, etc. In order to assess the total costs and benefits of a festival, these impacts can be accounted for through nonuse values.

Nonuse value can be estimated in monetary terms as a value that accrues to all residents, also residents who do not participate in the festival. This value can be further analyzed in terms of:

- Option value that represents the value residents attach to the fact that they have an opportunity to visit the festival.
- Bequest value describes the value residents ascribe to providing culture and entertainment for younger generations.
- Existence value is related to the value residents attach to the effect that the festival has on the image and on the developmental direction of the city.

Research on Way Out West Festival, Gothenburg, Sweden

Applied to an urban music festival in Sweden, the results are both interesting and surprising. Surveys were undertaken among festival-goers (who paid admission) and a sample of residents from the city of Gothenburg. *Direct use value* in economic terms was measured by asking attendees: "How much would you at the maximum pay for your festival ticket and still think it was worth the money spent?" This is the essence of the Contingent Valuation Method (CVM), and gives an estimate of willingness to pay. *Indirect use value* was captured by asking: "How much would you at the maximum pay for all the experiences that you have had in Gothenburg and still think it was worth the money spent?" Note that this is intended to reflect touristic experiences beyond the actual event.

Measuring *nonuse values* is a little more difficult. Respondents were told: "If Way Out West needed public funding from the municipality of Gothenburg in order to survive would you then think that the municipality should grant this? If yes, what would be the maximum yearly increase of your local tax that you would accept in order to support Way Out West?" "If no, do you think that the festival should pay a disturbance tax to the municipality, and if so how much?"

Respondents indicating they would accept a tax increase were asked to divide it among three categories of benefits, reflecting what they through was important to them: *option value* ("it gives me the possibility of attending WOW"); *existence value* ("the image and development of Gothenburg is affected positively"); and *bequest value* ("it gives the younger generation access to entertainment and culture").

The results from this study indicate that use value was more than twice the nonuse value and represented 70% of the total value. Most of the festival attendees came not from the city of Gothenburg but from other areas of Sweden and they brought a value of 5.4 million Euros home with them in the form of good memories. But to be able to attend the festival, these visitors spent 4.7 million Euros in Gothenburg. The difference (5.4–4.7) 0.7 million Euros is known as *consumer surplus* for festival visitors from outside the city, which is an indication that these visitors generally speaking were satisfied and considered the festival good value for the money spent (Figure 10.3).

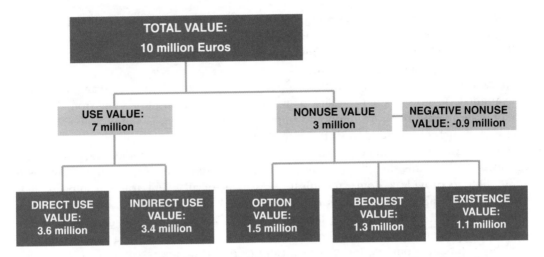

Figure 10.3. Components of use and nonuse value for Way Out West Festival.

Negative nonuse value was found to be comparatively small (0.9 million Euros), reflecting a general acceptance of WOW not only among the attendees but also among the local residents of Gothenburg that did not attend the festival. In fact 58% of the local residents were prepared to pay higher taxes to save the festival from a hypothetical financial failure.

There are a number of issues to consider when contemplating use of this method. First, it attempts to quantify in monetary terms some intangible benefits, and that is always problematic. While providing policy makers and event organizers with a more comprehensive valuation of an event, it is complementary to, and cannot replace a full evaluation of benefits versus costs.

And can it be applied to an entire population of residents regarding all the events in their area, or to a specific portfolio or type of event? That has not been attempted.

Summary and Study Guide

A review should begin by returning to the earlier discussions of the roles of events in tourism and development, to the goals pertaining to economic impacts, the ways in which tourists are attracted (motivation and experiences), and to evaluation principles and methods. Return to the Edinburgh festivals study after reading this chapter to look again at details of economic impacts arising from Event Tourism. Other examples, research notes, and cases in this book add to the knowledge base of how tourism generates impacts—both costs and benefits.

Study Figure 10.1 with a view to being able to discuss and illustrate the entire economic impact evaluation process, beginning with the tourists attracted (are they high-yield, dedicated event tourists?) and the attribution of their spending to the event itself as opposed to "casuals." Consider displacement effects and opportunity costs. How can leakages be minimized and internal linkages maximized? What about the event organizers and their income and expenditure; what part of that constitutes local benefits? If you return to the section on sport event impacts, and the actual data presented on different events, you will be able to see exactly what kind of event and event tourists you want for "destination" and "Iconic" tourist events.

My views on mega-event have been expressed in several places, and again in this chapter I emphasize the high costs, risks, equity issues, and frequent disappointments associated with the biggest events. When they are justified on the grounds of tourism benefits it simply does not hold water; mega-events actually serve other political and elite interests. My own interpretation of mega-events is that they are occasional events that fully utilize existing capacity, and if investment is required it has to be justified through the long-term, "public good" created.

In the contribution by Holger Preuss opportunity costs and the use of scarce resources is examined. He stresses the necessity to evaluate an event against goals and from different stakeholder perspectives. An important impact of a mega-event is shown to be "location factors," as such events tend to shift economic activity.

Regarding costs and benefits, you must understand how tangibles and intangibles are measured, as this directly influences the triple bottom line approach and makes it impossible to provide a single, technical assessment of all Event Tourism impacts. It is vital that costs never be stated as benefits, although the expertise, infrastructure, and venues created for events do have long-term value. This discussion leads directly to the example from Tommy Andersson on use and nonuse values, which is a new method for valuing events in economic terms, specifically to put a monetary value on some of the indirect and intangible benefits accruing to both tourists and residents.

Study Questions

- Is it always necessary or important to conduct an event economic impact assessment?
- At a minimum, what do you need to know about the effectiveness of Event Tourism strategies?
- What is the attribution problem?
- Work through an example of how you expect an event to deliver, and maximize, local economic benefits from tourism?
- Give examples of linkages and leakages related to the economic impacts of events.
- Why should a cost–benefit evaluation be conducted? What are tangibles and intangibles?
- Regarding investment in mega-events, what are the risks and opportunity costs? How can the legacy of mega-events be optimized?
- Discuss the equity issue, and the distribution of costs and benefits, with a full Event Tourism portfolio as the context.
- How can intangibles or "psychic benefits" be measured?
- Describe the research and analysis necessary to undertake use and nonuse valuation of an event.

Additional Resources

A number of pertinent books were listed at the end of Chapter 9. The following are online resources.

- The eventIMPACTS Toolkit (www.eventimpacts.com) has been developed by UK Sport, Visit Britain, Event Scotland, the London Development Agency, the North West Development Agency, Yorkshire Forward, and Glasgow City Marketing Bureau. It comprises some key guidance and good practice principles for evaluating the social, economic, environmental and media-related impacts associated with staging major sporting and cultural events.
- ISO 20121:2012—Event sustainability management systems. To harmonize the event industry's global efforts to tackle this challenge, ISO developed an

International Standard promoting the sustainable management of events. ISO 20121 was planned to be finalized in 2012 to coincide with the London Olympics (www.iso.org/iso/catalogue_detail?csnumber=54552)
- BS 8901 is the British Standard that has been developed specifically for the events industry with a purpose of helping the industry to operate in a more sustainable manner (www.bsigroup.co.uk/)

Chapter 11

Summary and Conclusions

Rather than repeat a lot of details, this summary takes each of the five main challenges as a theme and traces it (all the supportive material) through the book. This enables a pulling together of the relevant terms, concepts, examples, and conclusions.

Five Big Challenges

1: Moving From a Supply-Side to a Demand-Side Approach

As long as the emphasis remains on building and selling venues, and bidding on a limited range of events (sports and conventions or exhibitions) we can call it a supply-side approach. A major emphasis of this book has been to encourage demand-side thinking and strategies, based on research and market intelligence. The leisure and sport markets offer virtually unlimited potential for competitive advantages, if only more is known about the motivations and social worlds of people with special interests.

This represents a paradigm shift that will necessitate adjustments on the part of many practitioners. Yes, we still need venues and they have to be sold and marketed. There will always be events wanting to attract tourists. And bidding for one-time events will undoubtedly remain important. But the demand-side approach opens up numerous avenues of development and marketing that have little if anything to do with the prevailing emphasis on sports and business events.

Of special relevance in the book is all of Chapter 2 plus these topics and sections:

- Table 1.4 and the discussion of special-interest tourism.
- All the discussion of motivations, and data on event tourists (festival, sport, business).
- Case studies and examples: Senior Games, TransRockies, Triathletes, Woodford.
- Hallmark and Iconic event development and design process.
- All references to social worlds, serious leisure, involvement.
- The Event Tourist travel career trajectory.
- Positioning, branding, image, and reputation management require similar market intelligence.

2: From Top Down to Bottom Up (Liberating Innovation)

To make event tourism planning and development more integrated, sustainable and demand oriented will require a shift from centralized, top-down action to the facilitation of bottom-up initiatives. A top-down approach is typical, and is associated with one agency (say, a government tourism department) or organization (e.g., a DMO) preparing strategies and expecting everyone to implement them. It seldom works that way; it's far too simplistic. We do not want to abandon strategic thinking, including visioning exercises, but top-down initiatives have to be in balance with, and support, bottom-up initiatives taken by the numerous entrepreneurs (social and private), organizations, events, and other stakeholders in Event Tourism who are much more likely to adapt quickly, to innovate, and to see new opportunities.

A major goal is to liberate entrepreneurship and innovation, particularly in creating event and other experiences for niche markets. In a highly competitive world, liberating innovation is the key to success. By definition we cannot say what the next great idea will be, or how competitive advantages will be found in the future. Any strategy that attempts to move all the stakeholders in one direction is doomed to failure. Flexibility and adaptability are essential. DMOs and event development agencies will therefore have to expand their operations to encompass more stakeholders, helping them to identify opportunities and to succeed.

This theme is not specifically mentioned in very many places, but its directly connected to the following discussions:

- Chapter 3: who does planning and development in Event Tourism; development roles; strategic planning process.
- All discussions of stakeholders and their input.
- Case studies of TransRockies (private entrepreneurship) and the Whitebait and Woodford Festivals (social entrepreneurship) representing innovation and bottom-up development.
- Bidding, as conducted by and with local organizations (see the Calgary case).
- Community development and capacity building.
- Local and regional events in the portfolio model.

3: From Single Events to Portfolios

Another relatively new idea developed in this book is already being picked up by leading destination marketing and event development agencies. The focus has always been in single events, selling venues to them, bidding on them, developing and marketing them. The future lies in portfolios of events, all managed together as assets achieving multiple goals for the host cities and destinations. If you think it's a challenge to organize or market one event, imagine the complexity involved in managing dozens or hundreds of events to satisfy numerous stakeholders! Within this new portfolio approach it becomes quite evident that the highest value assets are events anchored in the destination or city, particularly Hallmark events with long-term, institutional status, and Iconic events that attract niche markets. One-time events, usually one through sales and bidding, come with higher costs and sometimes dubious value. This especially applies to one-time mega-events that can incur enormous costs. Therefore, sustainability enters the picture as a major theme.

There are many threads running through the book that elaborate upon the portfolio approach:

- The core discussions are in Chapter 4.
- Key models: Figures 4.6, 4.7, 4.8, and 9.1.
- The discussion in Chapter 4 concentrates on evaluation of portfolios.
- Bidding to fill gaps in the portfolio.

4: Create Your Own Destination Events

The destination perspective dominates in this book, as that is where most of the Event Tourism action takes place (by that I mean strategy, policy, funding), but the book also covers single events and how they can be developed and marketed as tourist attractions. And we deal with entrepreneurial possibilities as well, featuring in a case study one company that creates and markets destination events—events you have to travel to. In this context, the book presents new ideas on developing and marketing Hallmark and Iconic events. These two special categories of planned events represent some of the best potential for creating long-term, sustainable benefits and for tapping into the virtually unlimited potential within the sport and leisure markets.

Hallmark Events are, in my opinion, the best in terms of value compared to risks and costs. A detailed process, with goals, for creating Hallmark events is in Chapter 4 (see Tables 4.2 through 4.7).

Iconic events: Hallmark events are "iconic" in one sense, in that they are co-branded with destinations and provide a high degree of visibility and positive image making. But a much larger category of Iconic events exist within social worlds and for special interest groups. They are therefore essential ingredients in the demand-side approach. The specific example of ecotourism events was developed in Chapter 5, and illustrated in Figure 5.3.

Also of specific relevance are the Visit Denver and Queensland/Gold Coast cases, as they provide examples of events owned by Event Tourism agencies. TransRockies provides a private sector view on developing and owning destination events.

5: An Integrated, Sustainable Approach

The fifth big idea, or challenge, is to move from a narrow, supply-side approach stressing sports and business events (both heavily dependent upon expensive venues) to a fully integrated and sustainable development model. DMOs and event development agencies are largely marketing bodies, and therefore not well equipped to act more comprehensively and to develop long-term, integrated strategies. They will have to evolve, taking on new mandates and people with different areas of expertise.

Principles of sustainability can best be applied when portfolios of events and related facilities are managed together, and when the emphasis is broadened to include other types of events and venue-free strategies. This incorporates festivals and celebrations more fully, and also encompasses the basic ideas behind the demand-side, bottom-up approach. One new way of thinking is to avoid the traps presented by gigantism (venues and events getting bigger and bigger) and constant bidding on mega-events.

While sustainable events is a hot topic, sustainable Event Tourism presents us with a fundamental quandary. How can any activity or industry be "sustainable" when it depends so heavily on energy consumption, built facilities, and the luxury of spending great sums of money on nice trips to faraway places? Is that sustainable? Academics and activists go on and on about sustainability, yet the "industry" and government continuously collaborate to develop tourism and push the Event Tourism agenda to the fore. Much contemporary controversy is generic to tourism, including the idea that leisure travel is unnecessary and contributes to pollution, social and environmental issues in the destination, consumes too much energy, and has a high carbon footprint. Tourism, from this perspective, not only contributes to global climate change but is largely indefensible. Unless, of course, you consider the impact of eliminating tourism on jobs and livelihoods!

Two approaches to sustainability have been discussed in this book: sustainable competitive advantage, and sustainable development within a triple bottom line context. While competitive advantages come from a variety of sources, one of them has to be the idea of green and responsible events. If events and tourism are not accepted by the host community, sustainability is in doubt.

My argument is that event tourism, alongside other forms of special interest, niche marketing, is more sustainable than mass tourism ever can be. The focus should be on yield, not numbers, and on attracting visitors who want to experience your destination, not merely those who can afford to get there. Events have the advantage of being controllable, with limits imposed, and manageable for maximum "greening." Event Tourism has many advantages, unless the emphasis is placed on short-term, maximum economic impact. My whole approach is to stress long-term, portfolio management, within a sustainable development paradigm.

Mega-events, and the trend towards event gigantism, have to be singled out for special consideration within the sustainability debate. Numerous scholars and political pundits rightly condemn mega-events for their enormous costs (leading to national debt), disruption of communities, environmental negatives (including a heavy carbon footprint), and the building of white-elephant facilities (rather than maximizing the efficiency of existing venues that are largely for residents). As well, such mega-events clearly serve the interests of elite groups in society, and not the needs of residents who have to be "sold" on supporting mega-events with usual exaggerated if not downright false promises of an enduring, positive legacy (and a great, jingoistic party). All this is accepted by many wise observers, yet the trend continues, reflecting power politics rather than rational planning.

C. M. Hall (2012), writing in an article entitled "Sustainable-Mega Events: Beyond the Myth of Balanced Approaches to Mega-Event Sustainability," scrutinized mega-events from the perspectives of three frames of sustainability. In the "economic" approach, policy is narrowly focused on economic growth and image enhancement, with insufficient attention given to opportunity costs and long-term impacts. In the "balanced" approach, in line with triple bottom line thinking, Hall claims little attention is given to equity issues and decisions to hold mega-events are still largely based on purported economic gains. Thirdly, in the "steady-state" approach to sustainability, grounded in ecological considerations, more emphasis is given to natural capital and quality of life. In this paradigm, or world view, mega-events are not justifiable.

C. M. Hall (2012) concluded that "Mega-events are symbolic of an unsophisticated approach towards sustainable development. They provide substantial corporate benefits with the costs accommodated by the wider public" (p. 128). I can readily agree with Hall that "Instead, sustainable events are more likely to be found in the smaller localized community based events that run over the longer-term or at least help maximize the use of existing infrastructure" (p. 129).

While I recommend the occasional "mega-event" in a portfolio approach, I do not mean the Olympics or other gigantic events requiring massive infrastructure developments and the accumulation of public debt. Mega-events should be viewed as those that achieve extraordinary levels of tourism demand, impact, or effort given the current capacity of the destination. If new infrastructure is required, the event cannot be used as an excuse, it has to be justifiable with other "public good" arguments.

Future Scenarios

All change presents opportunities, and entrepreneurs are often able to realize profit out of chaos. Innovators work in areas of uncertainty, not obvious, fast-growth sectors.

If we can speculate on the future of events and travel, we can suggest opportunities for Event Tourism. Let's look at what some futurists have said, and try to draw out the Event Tourism opportunities. Note that all the implications are made by this author.

Tourism 2023

Tourism 2023 is a project involving future scenarios (www.forumforthefuture.org), coordinated by Forum for the Future in the UK. They believe the pace of change is accelerating, catching many companies and destinations unprepared. Various scenarios were developed to help shape the future discussion on UK tourism. Critical uncertainties were detected in relation to growing domestic demand, resource scarcity, climate change, legislation, population growth, and emerging economies. "Vivid details bring the world of each scenario to life and are designed to provoke debate. Will mass tourism, swollen by the Chinese and Indian middle classes, cause huge overcrowding in popular destinations? Will soaring oil prices make air travel so expensive that families have to save for years to fly abroad? Will we see 'Doomsday tourism,' with visitors rushing to see glaciers and coral reefs before they're gone for good? Or will household 'carbon quotas' see Britons go back to holidaying at home?"

> *My implications:* While continued population growth in Asia (mostly China and India) will both put additional strains on the planet (especially food and water supplies, energy, and air quality), the rise of a huge middle class with disposable income presents tremendous marketing opportunities. Event Tourism will shift to Asia in terms of numbers and sizes of events and related travel, as domestic and interregional demand is certainly going to exceed international demand, so professionals and companies can find many opportunities in the East. But a countermovement will occur, as Asians desire travel to events in the rest of the world. What event experiences will they want most?
>
> Climate change, and rising energy costs or shortages seem to impose nothing but constraints, especially if we assume that the golden age of cheap, mass tourism is coming to an end. The opportunities lie first in repositioning destinations to stress local and regional markets, with competitive advantages coming from accessibility, cost, and convenience. Second, green travel and events will be absolutely essential, not nice options. Events will have to combine opportunities for travel with targeted virtual experiences.

David Tow on the Future of Travel and Tourism (Future Planet — The Future of Tourism, Tuesday, November 16, 2010. Blog Site: http://futureplanetblog.blogspot.com)

David Tow is Director of the Future Planet Research Centre, and was drawing on a speech given at the TTRA 40th conference. "The heart of the program focused on 4 converging forces driving the future, and 4 emerging trends in travel and tourism. As a futurist speaker who tries always to see the 360-degree view of future forces, I began with a run-down on the primary forces shaping our time and which I see converging into one grand pattern—economic disparity and frugality, expensive energy, demographic destiny related to aging, young and diverse populations, and environmental imperatives with associated changes in life styles." The implications for tourism were described as "keeping it local," "alternative transport," "destination evolution," and "new ways of travel."

My implications: The approach taken in this book reflects much of Mr. Tow's arguments, particularly when it comes to the necessity for cities and destinations to get smarter about tourism. Event Tourism will play an ever-more important part, as opposed to mass tourism. Being green and sustainable are imperatives. Market intelligence is the key, and it should be theoretically based. People will want very specific and important reasons to travel; virtuality (i.e., electronic connections) can substitute for some of what we do today, but certainly not all.

Mr. Tow foresaw continued ecological decline, even crises in many ecosystems. While this might mean more no-go zones in which tourism is forbidden (or simply undesired) it presents many opportunities for ecotourism and adventure travel that adhere to sustainability principles. Events fit into that scenario, either to replace travel to protected areas or to interpret them and help raise awareness and money for the conservation cause.

If coastal areas around the world are threatened or destroyed, directly impacting upon mass beach tourism, replacement experiences must be found. There will be more emphasis on events in cities.

I am reluctant to look as far ahead as Mr. Tow, but readers should consider the really pessimistic scenarios presented, related to affects of climate change: mass migration; large uninhabitable areas of the planet; mega-cities; the disappearance of outdoor recreation, and hence of outdoor sport events. Such radical change would impose a paradigm shift well beyond the scope of this book. Ironically (and something I argued in *Event Studies*) if we take tourism out of the equation, events become even more important. Add mega-cities and remove outdoor recreation, and the need for community-based events of all kinds is further exacerbated.

Mr. Tow continued: "By 2050 tourism will have fragmented into myriad primarily urban exotic experiences, often transacted in virtual and augmented realities; simulating extraordinarily realistic and personal immersive experiences, involving all the senses. Gradually such lifestyle scenarios will be indistinguishable from the previous natural realities, allowing unlimited generated options, as well as surreal trips into space and under the oceans, back in time to historic events and forward into future cosmic civilizations."

The Future of Travel by Justin Francis

Justin Francis is Managing Director of responsibletravel.com Ltd (www.responsibletravel.com). He asked "How can we align a desire to visit other cultures in a thoughtful way alongside a conscience that calls for the reduction in our everyday carbon emissions? It's this dilemma that inspired us to start a debate around the future of tourism. If we're serious about pursuing a sustainable future for travel, it's essential that we have a vision to which we can aspire." What he suggests is "travel with a purpose," such as: "When deciding what my next holiday will be, I try to place the focus more on what I need from the holiday and what I can give back to destinations and local people." The more expensive and restricted travel gets, the more important it will be for people to justify their trip. This is in contrast to the current state where cheap air travel permits people to go wherever they want for the most mundane and often unnecessary reasons.

My implications: What better purpose for travel is there than to attend an event essential to your profession or business, to your social world participation and group identity, to your life-long interest? And if the event is green, educational, responsible, and accessible, guilt should not apply as a constraint! Remember also that highly involved people with serious leisure travel careers have, almost by definition, the money and the will to travel internationally.

Mr. Francis went on to say: "This new way of travelling could be described as 'deep' travel. It will be about getting under the skin of a place. We already seek out authenticity—real experiences rather than fake culture packaged up for tourists—but travel in 2020 will go further. It will be about the appreciation of local distinctiveness, the idiosyncrasies and the detail, the things that make a place unique and special. Other future trends will include 'Keeping it local,' both in terms of people staying closer to home and the industry sourcing mostly local supplies. Alternative transport will be the norm, and slower." Think trains instead of planes.

> *My implications:* Think about more 'slow' events that connect people to places (sometimes called "Geotourism"). Try gastronomic festivals and fairs with interpretation and direct links between tourists and producers; think ecotourism events that educate and engage visitors to aid in conservation efforts; imagine local festivals that are authentic enough that residents do NOT want to share them with tourists. As to business events, I repeat something I have said many times: every visitor should have a cultural experience, and that has to start with the locals they meet and then what they eat.

A Research Agenda

Hopefully many research needs and possible topics have occurred to readers while reading this book. Event Tourism as a subfield is quite immature, and as a professional field or business sector it remains quite limited in scope except in exceptionally competitive cities and destinations. Neither can progress without research, continuous evaluation, market intelligence, and a demand-side orientation.

These suggestions for future research on Event Tourism are partially derived and adapted from my 2008 review article in *Tourism Management*, and from the book *Event Studies* (2012). The sections are explicitly connected to the Event Tourism framework model presented in Chapter 1 (see Figure 1.4). Major research questions and problems identified in this book are incorporated into this discussion.

Event Tourism Experiences and Meanings

The fundamental question is: "How do people describe, explain, and assign meaning to various event tourism experiences, within each of these dimensions: conative (behavior), affective (emotional), and cognitive?" Little attention has been given to the event tourist experiences as an integrated whole, including pretrip, event, and postevent travel. The event tourist career trajectory tries to deal with this in terms of evolutionary changes. More research is also needed at the group level, such as has been conducted on sport fans. And what makes event tourism experiences memorable and transforming?

There is a big distinction between generic Event Tourism benefits and those sought by special interest groups. A demand-side approach requires greater attention to the particular experiences or benefits sought by those engaging in serious leisure, whether sports, the arts, hobbies, or lifestyle pursuits. We will need to learn much more about the creating and marketing of Iconic events that appeal symbolically to special interests and subcultures, and how Hallmark events achieve and sustain their status within host communities. This connects to image and reputation.

Almost all research and theory pertains to single events, yet Event Tourism is all about multiple events and portfolios. How are experiences and meanings in a community shaped by aggressive development and marketing of many events, including both the one-time and permanent? Do tourists have different experiences when there are multiple events to enjoy, or do they ascribe different meanings to experiences when they know they are attending a tourism-oriented event?

Antecedents to Event Tourism

When it comes to influences on Event Tourism, we are only beginning to examine how social worlds shape demand and supply, and in particular how participation in social worlds mediates choices and experiences. Since there are potentially an enormous number of special interests and social worlds, many more must be studied and compared systematically. One key question is: "What are the differences between competitive versus noncompetitive and individual versus inherently social pursuits when it comes to Iconic events and Event Tourism patterns and preferences?"

As events and Event Tourism expand in terms of development and impacts, how does this change the way people view events? We have discussed legitimation in terms of the growing acceptance of events as instruments of policy and corporate/industry strategy, but are there similar legitimation effects at work in society? Could a city suddenly stop funding events without repercussions? What happens to residents' expectations when a destination develops a full portfolio of events? One hypothesis is that people will get bored and constantly want more, newer, different events, or perhaps the delivery of a full spectrum of event opportunities becomes institutionalized and permanent. Also consider my conjecture (a future scenario) that if you take tourism out of the equation, events become even more important to communities.

Planning and Managing Event Tourism

Two major challenges loom, for which evaluation and theoretical research are needed. The first is the trend (actually a necessity) to move towards portfolio management, by multiple and overlapping policy domains. Many specific questions were raised about the cumulative effects, sustainability, and how to evaluate portfolios. What, for example, constitutes a healthy population or portfolio? Agencies creating and managing portfolios must evaluate and develop appropriate indicators of performance and health. Theorists must look at the potential applications of organizational ecology and institutionalization.

The second big challenge concerns organizational development and the scope of Event Tourism. Currently it is mainly the purview of DMOs (the typical convention and visitor bureau) or agencies that stress bidding (and on sport events, mainly), plus the often separate efforts of convention centers and bureaus to market, sell, and bid on events for their events. Many other stakeholders are involved, including sport and entertainment venues, festivals, and local organizations. There really are few if any examples to draw upon where the full, integrated potential of Event Tourism is practiced. I think organizations will have to be created specifically for this purpose; otherwise, the existing ones have to evolve with broader mandates and the addition of different areas of expertise.

Some of the specific questions to address are the following. What leadership, planning and decision-making styles and processes are most effective for Event Tourism development? What strategies are most effective in achieving Event Tourism competitiveness and sustainability? How can bidding on events be made more effective? Which stakeholder management strategies work best for Event Tourism? Case studies and cross-case analysis of events and destinations will be desirable, as will benchmarking among destinations.

Policy

Events are now well established as instruments of various policy domains, and Event Tourism must interact with them: from urban renewal to social and cultural development. How can these various policy fields work effectively together, especially when it comes to overlapping portfolios of events? This is largely a matter for stakeholder theory and power politics. Specifically, what are the ways in which stakeholders exercise power, and negotiate, to develop Event Tourism and related policy? Who gets excluded or marginalized? How do we know when Event Tourism policies are effective and efficiently administered? What are the ideological foundations of event tourism policy?

Justifying public sector involvement, from mere assistance to active investment in venues, bidding, and production of events, requires a lot of thought and supportive research. Which justifications for public involvement in event tourism are supported by the public, and why? How do citizens, taxpayers, and other stakeholders form opinions about events and Event Tourism? Will people support events even if they do not attend or see a direct benefit?

Outcomes

Evaluation and impact assessment theory and methods are sufficiently advanced for there to be no excuse in not implementing a triple bottom line approach, encompassing cost–benefit evaluation, at least for single events. But when it comes to populations and portfolios of events, techniques have not been established. Nor has sufficient attention been given to long-term sustainability and how evolving goals and cumulative, synergistic effects can be taken into account. What performance measures exist, and are needed, for the social, cultural, and environmental policy domains?

One question of particular importance will always arise: How are the benefits and costs of events and Event Tourism distributed through the population? This goes well beyond the matter of adopting strategies best for maximizing local economic benefits; it requires consideration of how various elite and private sector groups in society can exploit events for their purposes, while the ordinary, nonattending taxpayers end up paying. Within the public-good justifications this is the fundamental equity issue. Personally, I believe far too many mega-events benefit the few while the many end up paying.

A city's or destination's entire approach to Event Tourism should focus on this equity issue, which is related to the question of what is an event (and portfolio) worth? To whom?

Final Study Questions

Each of the following study questions should be answered by and integrative essay related to the five big challenges. You need to go back to the introduction of each of these five challenges in Chapter 1 and then trace the various elements through the book. I have provided hints for each!

1. How does the demand-side approach differ from the supply-side approach to Event Tourism planning and development? In particular, explain how the typical methods of developing Event Tourism reflect one or both of these strategic approaches. (Hint: while building facilities, marketing existing events, selling space, and bidding reflect supply-side thinking, you still need them! Emphasize market intelligence and the search for competitive advantages through niche marketing.)

2. Is the standard top-down approach to planning and development completely wrong? Contrast top-down thinking with bottom-up thinking and show the relevance to innovation in Event Tourism. (Hint: you have to explicitly link bottom-up approach to the demand-side, stakeholders, innovation, and special interests.)

3. Explain and illustrate the portfolio approach to Event Tourism planning and development. Include your personal recommendations for a particular city or destination. (Hint: contrast the portfolio approach with typical supply-side event tourism; be sure to explain all terms and give an illustration of a portfolio that makes sense in a particular setting.)

4. What justifications are there for cities and tourist/event agencies to create their own events? Place this discussion in the context of strategy, portfolios, and impacts. (Hint: both Hallmark and Iconic events should figure prominently in your answer, but also reflect on the demand-side approach as it leads to this issue.)

5. Is Event Tourism sustainable? Give arguments on both sides, with examples of how research supports the claims. (Hint: take a personal position on this, as I have done by stressing sustainability as a process, and by emphasizing the value versus cost/risks approach.)

Bibliography

Abrahams, R. (1987). An American vocabulary of celebrations. In A Falassi (Ed.), *Time out of time, essays on the festival* (pp. 173–183). Albuquerque: University of New Mexico Press.

Ahmed, Z. (1991). Marketing your community: Correcting a negative image. *Cornell Hospitality Quarterly, 31*(4), 24–27.

Ahmed, Z. (1992). Islamic pilgrimage (Hajj) to Ka'aba in Makkah (Saudi Arabia): An important international tourism activity. *Journal of Tourism Studies, 3*(1), 35–43.

AIEST. (1987). *The role and impact of mega-events and attractions on regional and national tourism* (Editions AIEST Vol. 28). St. Gallen, Switzerland: Author.

Andersson, T. (2006). The economic impact of cultural tourism. In T. Andersson, B. Holmgren, & L. Mossberg (Eds.), *Cultural tourism: Visitor flows, economic impact and product development* (pp. 33–46). Published for the European Cultural Tourism Network at the School of Business, Economics and Law, University of Gothenburg, Sweden.

Andersson, T. (2012). Triple impact assessments of sport events. In S. Söderman & H. Dolles (Eds.), *Handbook of research on sport and business.* Cheltenham: Edward Elgar.

Andersson, T., Armbrecht, J., & Lundberg, E. (2012). Estimating use and non-use values of a music festival. *Scandinavian Journal of Hospitality and Tourism, 12*(3), 215–231.

Andersson, T., Persson, C., Sahlberg, B., & Strom, L. (Eds.). (1999). *The impact of mega events.* Ostersund, Sweden: European Tourism Research Institute.

Andersson, T., & Samuelson, L. (2000). Financial effects of events on the public sector. In L. Mossberg (Ed.), *Evaluation of events: Scandinavian experiences* (pp. 86–103). New York: Cognizant Communication Corp.

Anderton, C. (2009). Commercializing the carnivalesque: The V Festival and image/risk management. *Event Management, 12*(1), 39–51.

Anwar, S., & Sohail, S. (2004). Festival tourism in the United Arab Emirates: First-time visitors versus repeat visitor perceptions. *Journal of Vacation Marketing, 10*(2), 161–170.

Archer, B. (1982). The value of multipliers and their policy implications. *Tourism Management, 3*(4), 236–241.

Arcodia, C., & Whitford, M. (2006). Festival attendance and the development of social capital. *Journal of Convention and Event Tourism, 8*(2), 1–18.

Armbrecht, J. (2009). The value of cultural institutions: A conceptual development of value categories. *(Kulturinstitutioners dolda värden. Kultur och samhällsnytta: Hur kan vi mäta värdet av kultur och vill vi göra det?; red Inga-Lill Söderberg. s. 105: SparbanksAkademins skriftserie.)*

Armstrong, J. (1985). International events: The real tourism impact. In *Conference proceedings of the Canada chapter* (pp. 9–37). Edmonton: Travel and Tourism Research Association.

Atkinson, M. (2008). Triathlon, suffering and exciting significance. *Leisure Studies, 27*(2), 165–180.

Axelsen, M. (2006). Using special events to motivate visitors to attend art galleries. *Museum Management and Curatorship, 21*(3), 205–221.

Backman, K., Backman, S., Uysal, M., & Sunshine, K. (1995). Event tourism: An examination of motivations and activities. *Festival Management & Event Tourism, 3*(1), 15–24.

Bakhtin, M. (1984). *Rabelais and his world* (Trans. H. Iswolsky). Bloomington: Indiana University Press.

Bale, J. (1994). *Landscapes of modern sport*. Leicester: Leicester University Press.

Barlow, M., & Shibli, S. (2007). Audience development in the arts: A case study of chamber music. *Managing Leisure, 12*(2–3), 102–119.

Baum, T., Deery, M., Hanlon, C., Lockstone, L., & Smith, K. (2009). *People and work in events and conventions: A research perspective*. Wallingford, UK: CABI.

Beard, J., & Ragheb, M. (1983). Measuring leisure motivation. *Journal of Leisure Research, 15*, 219–228.

Benckendorff, P., & Pearce, P. (2012). The psychology of events. In S. Page & J. Connell (Eds.), *Routledge handbook of events* (pp. 165–185). London: Routledge.

Bergsgard, N., & Vassenden, A. (2011). The legacy of Stavanger as Capital of Culture in Europe 2008: Watershed or puff of wind? *International Journal of Cultural Policy, 17*(3), 301–320.

Berne, C., & Garcia-Uceda, M. (2008). Criteria involved in evaluation of trade shows to visit. *Industrial Marketing Management, 37*(5), 565–579.

Berridge, G. (2007). *Event design*. Oxford: Butterworth-Heinemann.

Blackorby, C., Ricard, R., & Slade, M. (1986). The macroeconomic consequences of Expo '86. In R. Anderson & E. Wachtel (Eds.), *The expo story*. Madeira Park: Harbour Publishing.

Blake, A. (2005). *The economic impact of the London 2012 Olympics*. Nottingham, UK: Christel DeHaan Tourism and Travel Research Institute, Nottingham University Business School.

Boo, S., & Busser, J. (2006). Impact analysis of a tourism festival on tourists' destination images. *Event Management, 9*(4), 223–237.

Boo, S., Ko, D., & Blazey, M. (2007). An exploration of the influence of prior visit experience and residence on festival expenditures. *Event Management, 10*(2), 123–132.

Bourdeau, L., De Coster, L., & Paradis, S. (2001). Measuring satisfaction among festivalgoers: Differences between tourists and residents as visitors to a music festival in an urban environment. *International Journal of Arts Management, 3*(2), 40–50.

Bourdeau, P., Corneloup, J., & Mao, P. (2002). Adventure sports and tourism in the French mountains: Dynamics of change and challenges for sustainable development. *Current Issues in Tourism, 5*(1), 22–32.

Bowdin, G., Allen, J., O'Toole, W., Harris, R., & McDonnell, I. (2011). *Events management* (3rd ed.). Oxford: Elsevier.

Brannas, K., & Nordstrom, J. (2006). Tourist accommodation effects of festivals. *Tourism Economics, 12*(2), 291–302.

Breen, H., Bull, A., & Walo, M. (2001). A comparison of survey methods to estimate visitor expenditure at a local event. *Tourism Management, 22*, 473–479.

Bricker, K. S., & Kerstetter, D. L. (2000). Level of specialization and place attachment: An exploratory study of whitewater recreationists. *Leisure Sciences, 22*, 233–257.

Brothers, G., & Brantley, V. (1993). Tag and recapture: Testing an attendance estimation technique for an open access special event. *Festival Management & Event Tourism, 1*(4), 143–146.

Brown, G., Chalip, L., Jago, L., & Mules, T. (2001). The Sydney Olympics and Brand Australia. In N. Morgan, A. Pritchard, & R. Pride (Eds.), *Destination branding: Creating the unique destination proposition* (pp. 163–185). Boston: Butterworth-Heinemann.

Brunson, M., & Shelby, B. (1993). Recreation substitutability: A research agenda. *Leisure Sciences, 15*(1), 67–74.

Bryan, H. (1977). Leisure value systems and recreation specialization: The case of trout fisherman. *Journal of Leisure Research, 9*(3), 174–187.

Buck, R. (1977). Making good business better: A second look at staged tourist attractions. *Journal of Travel Research, 15*(3), 30–32.

Burgan, B., & Mules, T. (2001). Reconciling cost–benefit and economic impact assessment for event tourism. *Tourism Economics, 7*(4), 321–330.

Burke, S. (2007). The evolution of the cultural policy regime in the anglophone Caribbean. *International Journal of Cultural Policy, 13*(2), 169–184.

Burns, J., Hatch, J., & Mules, T. (Eds.). (1986). *The Adelaide Grand Prix: The impact of a special event*. Adelaide: Centre for South Australian Economic Studies.

Burr, S., & Scott, D. (2004). Application of the recreational specialization framework to understanding visitors to the Great Salt Lake Bird Festival. *Event Management, 9*(1/2), 27–37.

Business Tourism Partnership. (2004). *Business tourism briefing: An overview of the UK's business tourism industry*. Retrieved from http://www.businesstourismpartnership.com/pubs/briefing.pdf

Butler, R., & Grigg, J. (1987). The hallmark event that got away: The case of the 1991 Pan American Games in London, Ontario. In *PAPER 87, People and Physical Environment Research Conference*. Perth: University of Western Australia.

Camarero, C., Garrido, M., & Vicente, E. (2010). Components of art exhibition brand equity for internal and external visitors. *Tourism Management, 31*(4), 495–504.

Cameron, C. (1989). Cultural tourism and urban revitalization. *Tourism Recreation Research, 14*(1), 23–32.

Carlsen, J., Getz, D., & Soutar, G. (2000). Event evaluation research. *Event Management, 6*(4), 247–257.

Carlsen, J., & Taylor, A. (2003). Mega-events and urban renewal: The case of the Manchester 2002 Commonwealth Games. *Event Management, 8*(1), 15–22.

Carmichael, B. (2002). Global competitiveness and special events in cultural tourism: The example of the Barnes Exhibit at the Art Gallery of Ontario, Toronto. *The Canadian Geographer, 46*(4), 310–324.

Carnegie, E., & McCabe, S. (2008). Re-enactment events and tourism: Meaning, authenticity and identity. *Current Issues in Tourism, 11*(4), 349–368.

Catherwood, D., & Van Kirk, R. (1992). *The complete guide to special event management*. New York: Wiley.

Cavalcanti, M. (2001). The Amazonian Ox Dance Festival: An anthropological account. *Cultural Analysis, 2*, 69–105.

Centre for South Australian Economic Studies. (1990). *The 1990 Adelaide Festival: The Economic Impact* (Vol. 1: Summary; Vol. 2: Methodology and Results: Details). Adelaide: Author.

Chalip, L. (2004). Beyond impact: A general model for sport event leverage. In B. Ritchie & D. Adair (Eds.), *Sport tourism: Interrelationships, impacts and issues*. Clevedon, UK: Channel View Publications.

Chalip, L., & Costa, C. (2005). Sport event tourism and the destination brand: Towards a general theory. *Sport in Society, 8*(2), 218–237.

Chalip, L., & Leyns, A. (2002). Local business leveraging of a sport event: Managing an event for economic benefit. *Journal of Sport Management, 16*, 132–158.

Chalip, L., & McGuirty, J. (2004). Bundling sport events with the host destination. *Journal of Sport Tourism, 9*(3), 267–282.

Chan, C. (2007). *On spatial distribution of China's exhibitions.* Retrieved from: http://www.cnki.net

Chang, J. (2006). Segmenting tourists to aboriginal cultural festivals: An example in the Rukai tribal area, Taiwan. *Tourism Management, 27*(6), 1224–1234.

Chang, S., Kang, S., & Gibson, H. (2007). *Physically active in mid and later life: Senior Games, involvement, motivations and social worlds.* Abstracts from the 2007 Leisure Research Symposium, held in conjunction with the National Recreation and Parks Association's National Congress CD 3p Indianapolis, IN, September 25–29.

Che, D. (2008). Sports, music, entertainment and the destination branding of post-Fordist Detroit. *Tourism Recreation Research, 33*(2), 195–206.

Chen, P. (2006). The attributes, consequences, and values associated with event sport tourists' behavior: A means–end chain approach. *Event Management, 10*(1), 1–22.

Chhabra, D. (2005). Defining authenticity and its determinants: Toward an authenticity flow model. *Journal of Travel Research, 44*(1), 64–73.

Chhabra, D., Healy, R., & Sills, E. (2003). Staged authenticity and heritage tourism. *Annals of Tourism Research, 30*(3), 702–719.

China Convention and Exhibition Society. (2012). *Statistics and analysis report of China's exhibition industry 2011.* Retrieved from http://www.cces2006.org/report/

China Foreign Trade Centre. (2006). 100 Sessions Glory: Memorial of 100 sessions CECF. *Nanfang Daily Press*, Guangzhou.

China Import and Export Fair. (2007). *The 101st session of China Import and Export Fair achieved a complete success.* Retrieved from http://www.cantonfair.org.cn/

Clark, J. D. (2006). What are cities really committing to when they build a convention center. In R. Nelson (Ed.), *Developing a successful infrastructure for convention and event tourism* (pp. 7–27). Binghamton, NY: Haworth Press [also published in *Journal of Convention and Event Tourism,8*(4), 2006].

Coates, D., & Humphreys, B. (2008). Do economists reach a conclusion on subsidies for sports franchises, stadiums, and mega-events? *Econ Journal Watch, 5*(3), 294–315.

Cohen, A. (1982). A polyethnic London carnival as a contested cultural performance. *Ethnic and Racial Studies, 5*(1), 23–41.

Cohen, E. (1988). Authenticity and commoditization in tourism. *Annals of Tourism Research, 15*(3), 371–386.

Cohen, E. (2007). The "postmodernization" of a mythical event: Naga fireballs on the Mekong River. *Tourism Culture & Communication, 7*(3), 169–181.

Collins, A., Jones, C., & Munday, M. (2009). Assessing the environmental impacts of mega sporting events: Two options? *Tourism Management, 30*(6), 828–837.

Coopers & Lybrand Consulting Group. (1989). *NCR 1988 Festivals Study Final Report, Vol 1. Report for the Ottawa-Carleton Board of Trade.* Ottawa: Author.

Costa, X. (2002). Festive traditions in modernity: The public sphere of the festival of the 'Fallas' in Valencia (Spain). *The Sociological Review, 50*(4), 482–504.

Cox, G., Darcy, M., & Bounds, M. (1994). *The Olympics and housing. A study of six international events and analysis of potential impacts of the Sydney 2000 Olympics.* Macarthur: Housing and Urban Studies Research Group, University of Western Sydney.

Crawford, D., Jackson, E., & Godbey, G. (1991). A hierarchical model of leisure constraints. *Leisure Sciences, 13*(4), 309–320.

Crespi-Vallbona, M., & Richards, G. (2007). The meaning of cultural festivals: Stakeholder perspectives in Catalunya. *International Journal of Cultural Policy, 13*(1), 103–122.

Crompton, J. (1979). An assessment of the image of Mexico as a vacation destination and the influence of geographical location upon that image. *Journal of Travel Research, 17*(4), 18–23.

Crompton, J. (1999). *Measuring the economic impact of visitors to sports tournaments and special events*. Ashburn, VA: Division of Professional Services, National Recreation and Park Association.

Crompton, J., & Lee, S. (2000). The economic impact of 30 sports tournaments, festivals, and spectator events in seven U.S. cities. *Journal of Park and Recreation Administration, 18*(2), 107–216.

Crompton, J., Lee, S., & Shuster, T. (2001). A guide for undertaking economic impact studies: The Springfest example. *Journal of Travel Research, 40*(1), 79–87.

Crompton, J., & McKay, S. (1994). Measuring the economic impact of festivals and events: Some myths, misapplications and ethical dilemmas. *Festival Management & Event Tourism, 2*(1), 33–43.

Crouch, G., & Ritchie, J. R. B. (1998). Convention site selection research: A review, conceptual model, and propositional framework. *Journal of Convention & Exhibition Management, 1*(1), 49–69.

Crouch, G., & Weber, K. (2002). Marketing of convention tourism. In K. Weber & K. Chon (Eds.), *Convention tourism: International research and industry perspectives* (pp. 57–78). Binghamton, NY: Haworth Press.

Curtin, S. (2010). The self-presentation and self-development of serious wildlife tourists. *International Journal of Tourism Research, 12*(1), 17–33.

Dakota, D. (2002). *World party*. Chicago: Big Cat Press.

Daniels, M., & Norman, W. (2003). Estimating the economic impacts of seven regular sport tourism events. *Journal of Sport and Tourism, 8*(4), 214–222.

Davidson, R., with Holloway, C., & Humphreys, C. (2009). *The business of tourism* (8th ed.). Ontario, Canada: Pearson Canada.

Davidson, R., & Rogers, T. (2006). *Marketing destinations and venues for conferences, conventions and business events*. Oxford, UK: Butterworth-Heinemann.

Davidson, R., with Cope, B. (2003). *Business travel: Conferences, incentive travel, exhibitions, corporate hospitality and corporate travel*. Harlow, UK: Pearson Education.

Davidson, R. (2010). *EIBTM 2010 industry trends & market share report*. Retrieved from http://www.eibtm.com/files/2010_eibtm_industry_repor.pdf

De Bres, K., & Davis, J. (2001). Celebrating group and place identity: A case study of a new regional festival. *Tourism Geographies, 3*(3), 326–337.

Deery, M., Jago, L., & Fredline, E. (2004). Sport tourism or event tourism: Are they one and the same? *Journal of Sport Tourism, 9*(3), 235–246.

de Groote, P. (2005). A multidisciplinary analysis of world fairs (=Expos) and their effects. *Tourism Review, 60*(1/3), 12–19.

Delamere, T. (2001). Development of a scale to measure resident attitudes toward the social impacts of community festivals: Part 2: Verification of the scale. *Event Management, 7*(1), 25–38.

Delamere, T., Wankel, L., & Hinch, T. (2001). Development of a scale to measure resident attitudes toward the social impacts of community festivals: Part 1: Item generation and purification of the measure. *Event Management, 7*(1), 11–24.

Denis, M., Dischereit, E., Song, D.-Y., & Werning, R. (1988). *Südkorea. Kein Land für friedliche Spiele*. Reinbeck: rororo.

Denton, S., & Furse, B. (1993). Visitation to the 1991 Barossa Valley Vintage Festival. *Festival Management & Event Tourism, 1*(2), 51–56.

Derek Murray Consulting Associates Ltd. (1985). *A study to determine the impact of events on local economies*. Report for Saskatchewan Tourism and Small Business. Regina.

Derrett, R. (2003). Making sense of how festivals demonstrate a community's sense of place. *Event Management, 8*, 49–58.

Dewar, K., Meyer, D., & Li, W. (2001). Harbin, lanterns of ice, sculptures of snow. *Tourism Management, 22*(5), 523–532.

Díaz-Barriga, M. (2003). Materialism and sensuality: Visualizing the devil in the Festival of Our Lady of Urkupina. *Visual Anthropology, 16*(2–3), 245–261.

Dimanche, F. (1996). Special events legacy: The 1984 Louisiana World Fair in New Orleans. *Festival Management & Event Tourism, 4*(1), 49–54.

Dungan, T. (1984). How cities plan special events. *Cornell Hotel and Restaurant Administration Quarterly, 25*(1), 83–89.

Durkheim, E. (1965). *The elementary forms of the religious life* (written in French in 1912; translated by J. Swain 1915). New York: The Free Press.

Dwyer, L. (2002). Economic contribution of convention tourism: Conceptual and empirical issues. In K. Weber & K. Chon (Eds.), *Convention tourism: International research and industry perspectives* (pp. 21–35). Binghamton, NY: Haworth Press.

Dwyer, L., Forsyth, P., & Dwyer, W. (2010). *Tourism economics and policy.* Bristol, UK: Channel View.

Dwyer, L., Forsyth, P., & Spurr, R. (2006). Economic impact of sport events: A reassessment. *Tourism Review International, 10*(4), 207–216.

Dwyer, L., Mellor, R., Mistillis, N., & Mules, T. (2000a). A framework for assessing 'tangible' and 'intangible' impacts of events and conventions. *Event Management, 6*(3), 175–189.

Dwyer, L., Mellor, R., Mistillis, N., & Mules, T. (2000b). Forecasting the economic impacts of events and conventions. *Event Management, 6*(3), 191–204.

Economic Planning Group and Lord Cultural Resources. (1992). *Strategic directions for the planning, development, and marketing of Ontario's attractions, festivals, and events.* Toronto: Ministry of Culture, Tourism, and Recreation.

Edensor, T. (1998). The culture of the Indian street. In N. Fyfe (Ed.), *Images of the street: Planning, identity and control in public space.* London: Routledge.

Eder, D., Staggenborg, S., & Sudderth, L. (1995). The National Women's Music Festival: Collective identity and diversity in a lesbian-feminist community. *Journal of Contemporary Ethnography, 23*(4), 485–515.

Edwards, D., Foley, C., & Schlenker, K. (2011). *Beyond tourism benefits: Measuring the social legacies of business events.* Sydney: University of Technology.

EKOS Research Associates Inc. (1985). *EKOS report on Winterlude: Executive summary. Report for the National Capital Commission.* Ottawa: Author.

Elias-Varotsis, S. (2006). Festivals and events—(Re) interpreting cultural identity. *Tourism Review, 61*(2), 24–29.

Ellis, J. (1990). *The application of cost–benefit analysis: The 1987 Busker Festival—a case study.* Master's thesis in Development Economics, Dalhousie University, Halifax.

Emery, P. (2002). Bidding to host a major sports event: The local organising committee perspective. *International Journal of Public Sector Management, 15*(4), 316–335.

Eubanks, T., Stoll, J., & Ditton, R. (2004). Understanding the diversity of eight birder sub-populations: Socio-demographic characteristics, motivations, expenditures and net benefits. *Journal of Ecotourism, 3*(3), 151–172.

Fairley, S. (2009). The role of the mode of transport in the identity maintenance of sport fan travel groups. *Journal of Sport and Tourism, 14*(2/3), 205–222.

Falassi, A. (Ed.). (1987). *Time out of time: Essays on the festival.* Albuquerque: University of New Mexico Press.

Faulkner, B., Chalip, L., Brown, G., Jago, L., March, R., & Woodside, A. (2000). Monitoring the tourism impacts of the Sydney 2000 Olympics. *Event Management, 6*(4), 231–246.

Faulkner, B., & Raybould, M. (1995). Monitoring visitor expenditure associated with attendance at sporting events: An experimental assessment of the diary and recall methods. *Festival Management & Event Tourism, 3*(2), 73–81.

Felsenstein, D., & Fleischer, A. (2003). Local festivals and tourism promotion: The role of public assistance and visitor expenditure. *Journal of Travel Research, 41*(4), 385–392.

Fleming, W., & Toepper, L. (1990). Economic impact studies: Relating the positive and negative impacts to tourism development. *Journal of Travel Research, 29*(1), 35–42.

Florida, R. (2002). *The rise of the creative class, and how it's transforming work, leisure, community and everyday life.* New York: Basic Books.

Foley, M., McGillivray, D., & McPherson, G. (2011). *Event policy: From theory to strategy.* London: Routledge.

Foley, M., & McPherson. G. (2004). Edinburgh's Hogmanay in the society of the spectacle. *Journal of Hospitality and Tourism, 2*(2), 29–42.

Foley, M., McPherson, G., & McGillivray, D. (2008). Establishing Singapore as the events and entertainment capital of Asia: Strategic brand diversification. In J. Ali-Knight et al. (Eds.), *International perspectives of festivals and events: Paradigms of analysis* (pp. 53–64). Oxford: Butterworth-Heinemann.

Formica, S. (1998). The development of festivals and special events studies. *Festival Management & Event Tourism, 5*(3), 131–137.

Formica, S., & Murrmann, S. (1998). The effects of group membership and motivation on attendance: An international festival case. *Tourism Analysis, 3*(3/4), 197–207.

Formica, S., & Uysal, M. (1998). Market segmentation of an international cultural-historical event in Italy. *Journal of Travel Research, 36*(4), 16–24.

Frechtling, D. (1994). Assessing the impacts of travel and tourism. In B. Ritchie & C. Goeldner (Eds.), *Travel, tourism and hospitality research* (2d ed., pp. 359–402). New York: Wiley.

Fredline, E. (2006). Host and guest relations and sport tourism. In H. Gibson (Ed.), *Sport tourism: Concepts and theories* (pp. 131–147). London: Routledge.

Fredline. E. (2008). Host and guest relations and sport tourism. In M. Weed (Ed.), *Sport and tourism: A reader* (pp. 393–409). London: Routledge.

Fredline, E., & Faulkner, B. (1998). Resident reactions to a major tourist event: The Gold Coast Indy car race. *Festival Management & Event Tourism, 5*(4): 185–205.

Fredline, E., & Faulkner, B. (2002a). Residents' reactions to the staging of major motorsport events within their communities: A cluster analysis. *Event Management, 7*(2), 103–114.

Fredline, E., & Faulkner, B. (2002b). Variations in residents' reactions to major motorsport events: Why residents perceive the impacts of events differently. *Event Management, 7*(2), 115–125.

Fredline, E., Jago, L., & Deery, M. (2003). The development of a generic scale to measure the social impacts of events. *Event Management, 8*(1), 23–37.

Freeman, R. (1984). *Strategic management: A stakeholder approach.* Boston: Pitman.

Frew, A. (2006). Comedy festival attendance: Serious, project-based or casual leisure? In S. Elkington, I. Jones, & L. Lawrence (Eds.), *Proceedings, Serious and Casual Leisure: Extensions and Applications, Annual Conference of the Leisure Studies Association* (pp. 105–122), Luton, Bedfordshire, UK.

Frew, A., & Hay, B. (2011). The development, rationale, organization and future management of public sector tourism in Scotland. *Fraser of Allander Economic Commentary, 34*(3), 63–76.

Frey, B. (2000). *The rise and fall of festivals: Reflections on the Salzburg Festival* (Working paper No. 48). Zurich: Institute for Empirical Research in Economics, University of Zurich.

Funk, D. C. (2008). *Consumer behaviour for sport & events: Marketing action*. Jordon Hill, Oxford UK: Elsevier.

Funk, D., & Bruun, T. (2007). The role of socio-psychological and culture-education motives in marketing international sport tourism: A cross-cultural perspective. *Tourism Management, 28*(3), 806–819.

Funk, D. C., & James, J. (2001). The psychological continuum model: A conceptual framework for understanding an individual's psychological connection to sport. *Sport Management Review, 4*(2), 119–150.

Funk, D. C., & James, J. (2006). Consumer loyalty: The meaning of attachment in the development of sport team allegiance. *Journal of Sport Management, 20*(2), 189–217.

Funk, D. C., Mahony, D. F., Nakazawa, M., & Hirakawa, S. (2001). Development of the Sports Interest Inventory (SII): Implications for measuring unique consumer motives at sporting events. *International Journal of Sports Marketing & Sponsorship, 3*(3), 291–316.

Funk, D. C., Mahony, D. F., & Ridinger, L. (2002). Characterizing consumer motivation as individual difference factors: Augmenting the Sport Interest Inventory (SII) to explain level of spectator support. *Sport Marketing Quarterly 11*(1), 33–43.

Funk, D. C., Ridinger, L., & Moorman, A. J. (2003). Understanding consumer support: Extending the Sport Interest Inventory (SII) to examine individual differences among women's professional sport consumers. *Sport Management Review, 6*(1), 1–32.

Funk, D., Toohey, K., & Bruun, T. (2007). International sport event participation: Prior sport involvement; destination image; and travel motives. *European Sport Management Quarterly, 7*(3), 227–248.

Gabr, H., Robinson, M., Picard, D., & Long, P. (2004). Attitudes of residents and tourists towards the use of urban historic sites for festival events. *Event Management, 8*(4), 231–242.

Gammon, S. (2012). Sports events: Typologies, people and place. In S. Page & J. Connell (Eds.), *The Routledge handbook of events* (pp. 104–118). Oxon: Routledge.

Garcia, S. (1993). Barcelona und die Olympischen Spiele. In H. Häussermann & W. Siebel (Eds.), *Festivalisierung der Stadtpolitik. Stadtentwicklung durch große Projekte* (pp. 251–277). Leviathan. Zeitschrift für Sozialwissenschaft, vol. 13, Opladen.

Geertz, C. (1973). Thick description: Toward an interpretive theory of culture. *Culture: Critical Concepts in Sociology, 1*, 173–196.

Getz, D. (1983). Capacity to absorb tourism: Concepts and implications for strategic planning. *Annals of Tourism Research, 10*, 239–263.

Getz, D. (1991). *Festivals, special events, and tourism*. New York: Van Nostrand Reinhold.

Getz, D. (1993). Case study: Marketing the Calgary Exhibition and Stampede. *Festival Management & Event Tourism, 1*(4), 147–156.

Getz, D. (1997). *Event management & event tourism* (1st ed.). New York: Cognizant Communication Corp.

Getz, D. (2004). Bidding on events: Critical success factors. *Journal of Convention and Exhibition Management, 5*(2), 1–24.

Getz, D. (2005). *Event Management & event tourism* (2d ed.). New York: Cognizant Communication Corp.

Getz, D. (2007). *Event studies: Theory, research and policy for planned events* (1st ed.) Elsevier: Oxford.

Getz, D. (2008). Event tourism: Definition, evolution, and research. *Tourism Management, 29*(3), 403–428.

Getz, D. (2009). Policy for sustainable and responsible festivals and events: Institutionalization of a new paradigm. *Journal of Policy Research in Tourism, Leisure and Events, 1*(1), 6178.

Getz, D. (2010). The nature and scope of festival studies. *International Journal of Event Management Research, 5*(1). Retrieved from http://www.ijemr.org/docs/Vol5-1/Getz.pdf

Getz, D. (2012). *Event studies: Theory, research and policy for planned events* (2nd ed.). Oxon: Routledge.

Getz, D., & Andersson, T. (2010). The event-tourist career trajectory: A study of high-involvement amateur distance runners. *Scandinavian Journal of Tourism and Hospitality, 19*(4), 468–491.

Getz, D., Andersson, T., & Larson, M. (2007). Festival stakeholder roles: Concepts and case studies. *Event Management, 10*(2/3), 103–122.

Getz, D., & Cheyne, J. (2002). Special event motives and behaviour. In C. Ryan (Ed.), *The tourist experience* (2nd ed., pp. 137–155). London: Continuum.

Getz, D., & Fairley, S. (2004). Media management at sport events for destination promotion. *Event Management, 8*(3): 127–139.

Getz, D., & Frisby, W. (1988). Evaluating management effectiveness in community-run festivals. *Journal of Travel Research, 27*(1), 22–27.

Getz, D., & Frisby, W. (1991). Developing a municipal policy for festivals and special events. *Recreation Canada, 19*(4), 38–44.

Getz, D., & McConnell, A. (2011). Serious sport tourism and event travel careers. *Journal of Sport Management, 25,* 326–338.

Gibson, C., & Connell, J. (2012). *Music festivals and regional development in Australia.* Farnham, Surrey: Ashgate.

Gibson, H. (1998). Sport tourism: A critical analysis of research. *Sport Management Review, 1,* 45–76.

Gibson, H. (Ed.). (2006). *Sport tourism: Concepts and theories.* London: Routledge.

Gibson, H., Ashton-Shaeffer, C., Green, J., & Kensinger, K. (2002). "It wouldn't be long before I'd be friends with an undertaker:" What it means to be a senior athlete. *Abstracts for the Leisure Research Symposium of the National Recreation and Park Association Congress* (p. 13), Tampa, FL, October 16–19.

Gibson, H., Ashton-Shaeffer, C., & Sanders, G. (2002). The role of leisure in the lives of retirement-aged women living in Florida. In L. Doty, L. S. Lieberman, M. Flint & K. Grant (Eds.), *Successful aging: Women's health and well-being in the second fifty years* (pp. 174–192). Proceedings of the Fourth Meeting of National Leaders in Women's Health Research, Gainesville, FL, March, 2001.

Gibson, H., Chang, S., & Ashton-Shaeffer, C. (2007). "You get to travel:" A look at the touristic aspects of Senior Games participation. *The Gerontologist, 47*(1), 828–829. (Special issue: Program Abstracts for the 60th Annual Scientific Meeting.)

Gilbert, D., & Lizotte, M. (1998). Tourism and the performing arts. *Travel & Tourism Analyst, 1,* 82–96.

Gillis, K. S., & Ditton, R. B. (1998). Comparing tournament and nontournament recreational billfish anglers to examine the efficacy of hosting competitive billfish angling events in southern Baja, Mexico. *Festival Management & Event Tourism, 5*(3), 147–158.

Goeldner, C., & Ritchie, J.R.B. (2012). *Tourism: Principles, practices, philosophies* (12th ed.). Hoboken, NJ: Wiley.

Goldblatt, J. (2011). *Special events: A new generation and the next frontier* (6th ed.). New York: Wiley.

Goodall, B. (1988). How tourists choose their holidays: An analytic framework. In B. Goodall & G. Ashworth (Eds.), *Marketing in the tourism industry: The promotion of destination regions* (pp. 1–17). London: Croom Helm.

Gotham, K. (2002). Marketing Mardi Gras: Commodification, spectacle and the political economy of tourism in New Orleans. *Urban Studies, 39*(10), 1735–1756.

Gotham, K. (2005). Theorizing urban spectacles. *City, 9*(2), 225–246.

Graburn, N. (1983). The anthropology of tourism. *Annals of Tourism Research, 10*(1), 9–33.

Grado, S., Strauss, C., & Lord, B. (1998). Economic impacts of conferences and conventions. *Journal of Convention and Exhibition Management, 1*(1), 19–33.

Graham, S., Goldblatt, J., & Delpy, L. (1995). *The ultimate guide to sport event management and marketing*. Chicago: Irwin.

Gratton, C., Dobson, N., & Shibli, S. (2000). The economic importance of major sports events: A case study of six events. *Managing Leisure, 5*, 14–28.

Gratton, C., & Kokolakakis, T. (1997). *Economic impact of sport in England 1995*. London: The Sports Council.

Gratton, C., Shibli, S., & Coleman, R. (2005). Sport and economic regeneration in cities. *Urban Studies, 42*(5–6), 985–999.

Green, B. C. (2008). Leveraging subculture and identity to promote events. In M. Weed (Ed.), *Sport and tourism: A reader* (pp. 362–376). London: Routledge.

Green, B. C., & Chalip, L. (1998). Sport tourism as the celebration of subculture. *Annals of Tourism Research, 25*(2), 275–291.

Green, B. C., Costa, C., & Fitzgerald, M. (2008). Marketing the host city: Analyzing exposure generated by a sport event. In M. Weed (Ed.), *Sport and tourism: A reader* (pp. 346–361). London: Routledge.

Green, B. C., & Jones, I. (2005). Serious leisure, social identity and sport tourism. *Sport in Society, 8*(2), 164–181.

Green, B. C., & Muller, T. (2002). Positioning a youth sport camp: A brand mapping exercise. *Sport Management Review 5*(2), 179–200.

Greenwood, D. (1972). Tourism as an agent of change: A Spanish Basque case study. *Ethnology, 11*, 80–91.

Guo, J. (2007). *The report on development of China's convention and exhibition economy 2006–2007*. Beijing: Social Sciences Academic Press.

Guo, J. (2012). *Annual report on China's convention & exhibition economy 2012*. Beijing: Social Sciences Academic Press.

Gwinner, K. (1997). A model of image creation and image transfer in event sponsorship. *International Marketing Review, 14*(3), 145–158.

Gyimóthy, S. (2009) Casual observers, connoisseurs and experimentalists: A conceptual exploration of niche festival visitors. *Scandinavian Journal of Hospitality and Tourism, 9*(2/3), 177–205.

Gyimóthy, S., & Mykletun, R. J. (2009). Destinations as gadgets: Co-creating a sportive identity for Voss. In M. Kozak, J. Gnoth, & L. Andreu (Eds.), *Progress in tourism marketing* (pp. 89–110). New York: Routledge.

Hall, C. M. (1989). The definition and analysis of hallmark tourist events. *GeoJournal, 19*(3), 263–268.

Hall, C. M. (1992). *Hallmark tourist events: Impacts, management and planning*. London: Belhaven.

Hall, C. M. (2002). ANZAC Day and secular pilgrimage. *Tourism Recreation Research, 27*(2), 83–87.

Hall, C. M. (2012). Sustaibale mega-events: Beyond the myth of balanced approaches to mega-event sustainability. *Event Management, 16*(2), 119–131.

Hall, C. M., & Lew, A. (2009). *Understanding and managing tourism impacts: An integrated approach.* Oxon: Routledge.

Hall, M., & Rusher, K. (2004). Politics, public policy and the destination. In I. Yeoman et al. (Eds.), *Festival and events management* (pp. 217–231). Oxford: Elsevier.

Hanly, P. (2012). Measuring the economic contribution of the international association conference market: An Irish case study. *Tourism Management, 33*(6), 1574–1582.

Hannam, K., & Halewood, C. (2006). European Viking themed festivals: An expression of identity. *Journal of Heritage Tourism, 1*(1), 17–31.

Hannan, M., & Freeman, J. (1977). The population ecology of organizations. *American Journal of Sociology, 82*, 929–964.

Hanusch, H. (1992). *Kosten-Nutzen-Analyse.* Munich: Oldenbourg.

Harcup, T. (2000). Re-imaging a post-industrial city: The Leeds St. Valentine's Fair as a civic spectacle. *City, 4*(2), 215–231.

Hassan, G., Mean, M., & Tims, C. (2007). *The dreaming city and the power of mass imagination.* Demos Report.

Hatten, A. (1987). *Economic Impact of Expo '86.* Victoria, BC, Canada: Ministry of Finance and Corporate Relations.

Havitz, M., & Dimanche, F. (1997). Leisure involvement revisited: Conceptual conundrums and measurement advances. *Journal of Leisure Research, 29*(3), 245–278.

Havitz, M., & Dimanche, F. (1999). Leisure involvement revisited: Drive properties and paradoxes. *Journal of Leisure Research, 31*(2), 122–149.

Hede, A., Jago, L., & Deery, M. (2004). Segmentation of special event attendees using personal values: Relationships with satisfaction and behavioural intentions. *Journal of Quality Assurance in Hospitality and Tourism, 5*(2/3/4), 33–55.

Heeley, J. (2011). *Inside city tourism: A European perspective.* Bristol, UK: Channel View.

Helkkula, A., & Kelleher, C. (2011). Experiences and practices: Challenges and opportunities for value research. In E. Gummesson, C. Mele, & F. Polese (Eds.), *The 2011 Naples Forum on Service—Service Dominant Logic, Network & System Theory and Service Science: Integrating Three Perspectives for a New Service Agenda,* June 14–17, Capri, Italy.

Helkkula, A., Kelleher, C., & Pihlström, M. (2012). Characterizing value as an experience: Implications for service researchers and managers. *Journal of Service Research, 15*(1), 59–75.

Henderson, J. (2011). Religious tourism and its management: The Hajj in Saudi Arabia. *International Journal of Tourism Research, 13*(6), 541–552.

Higham, J. (1999). Commentary—sports as an avenue of tourism development: An analysis of the positive and negative impacts of sports tourism. *Current Issues in Tourism, 2*(1), 82–90.

Higham, J. (Ed.). (2005). *Sport tourism destinations: Issues, opportunities and analysis.* Oxford: Elsevier.

Higham, J., & Hinch, T. (2009). *Sport and tourism: Globalization, mobility and identity.* Oxford: Butterworth-Heinemann.

Hiller, H. (2012). *Host cities and the Olympics: An interactionist approach.* London: Routledge.

Hinch, T., & Delamere, T. (1993). Native festivals as tourism attractions: A community challenge. *Journal of Applied Recreation, 18*(2), 131–142.

Hinch, T., & Higham, J. (2004). *Sport tourism development.* Clevedon, UK: Channel View Publications.

Hinch, T., & Higham, J. (2011). *Sport tourism development* (2nd ed.). Clevedon, UK: Channel View Publications.

Hitters, E. (2007). Porto and Rotterdam as European Capitals of Culture: Toward the festivalization of urban cultural policy. In G. Richards (Ed.), *Cultural tourism: Global and local perspectives* (pp. 281–301). New York: Haworth Press.

Holbrook, M. B. (1999). Introduction. In M. B. Holbrook (Ed.), *Consumer value: A framework for analysis and research* (pp. 1–28). London: Routledge.

Holbrook, M. B. (2006). Consumption experience, customer value, and subjective personal introspection: An illustrative photographic essay. *Journal of Business Research, 59*(6), 714–725.

Holbrook, M. B., & Hirschman, E. C. (1982). The experiential aspects of consumption: Consumer fantasies, feelings, and fun. *Journal of Consumer Research, 9*(2), 132–140.

Holt, D. (2004). How *brands become icons: The principles of cultural branding*. Boston, MA: Harvard Business School Publishing Corporation.

Howard, D., Lankford, S., & Havitz, M. (1991). A method for authenticating pleasure travel expenditures. *Journal of Travel Research, 29*(4), 19–23.

Hudson, S. (Ed.). (2002). *Sport and adventure tourism*. New York: Haworth.

Hughes, G. (1999). Urban revitalization: The use of festival time strategies. *Leisure Studies, 18*(2), 119–135.

Hughes, H. (2000). *Arts, entertainment and tourism*. Oxford: Butterworth-Heinemann.

Hultkrantz, L. (1998). Mega-event displacement of visitors: The World Championship in Athletics, Goteborg 1995. *Festival Management & Event Tourism, 5*(1/2), 1–8.

Hunt, J. (1975). Image as a factor in tourism development. *Journal of Travel Research, 13*(3), 1–7.

Hvenegaard, G., & Manaloor, V. (2007). A comparative approach to analyzing local expenditures and visitor profiles of two wildlife festivals. *Event Management, 10*(4), 231–239.

Ingerson, L., & Westerbeek, H. (2000). Determining key success criteria for attracting hallmark sporting events. *Pacific Tourism Review, 3*(4), 239–253.

Iso-Ahola, S. (1980). *The social psychology of leisure and recreation*. Dubuque, IA: Brown.

Iso-Ahola, S. (1983). Towards a social psychology of recreational travel. *Leisure Studies, 2*(1), 45–57.

Jackson, E. (Ed.). (2005). *Constraints on leisure*. State College, PA: Venture Publishing.

Jackson, E., Crawford, D., & Godbey, G. (1993). Negotiation of leisure constraints. *Leisure Sciences, 15*, 1–13.

Jackson, P. (1992). The politics of the streets: A geography of Caribana. *Political Geography, 11*(2), 130–151.

Jago, L., Chalip, L., Brown, G., Mules, T., & Shameem, A. (2003). Building events into destination branding: Insights from experts. *Event Management, 8*(1), 3–14.

Jago, L., & Deery, M. (2005). Relationships and factors influencing convention decision-making. *Journal of Convention and Event Tourism, 7*(1), 23–41.

Jago, L., & Mair, J. (2009). Career theory and major event employment. In T. Baum et al (Eds.), *People and work in events and conventions: A research perspective* (pp. 65–74). Wallingford, UK: CABI.

James, J. D., & Ross, S. D. (2004). Comparing sport consumer motivations across multiple sports. *Sport Marketing Quarterly, 13*(1), 17–25.

Jamieson, K. (2004). Edinburgh: The festival gaze and its boundaries. *Space and Culture, 7*(1), 64–75.

Janiskee, R. (1996). The temporal distribution of America's community festivals. *Festival Management & Event Tourism, 3*(3), 129–137.

Jawahar, I., & McLaughlin, G. (2001). Toward a descriptive stakeholder theory: An organizational life cycle approach. *Academy of Management Review, 26*(3), 397–414.

Jin, X., & Weber, K. (2008). The China import and export (Canton) Fair: Past, present, and future. *Journal of Convention and Event Tourism, 9*(3), 221–234.

Johnson, A., Glover, T., & Yuen, F. (2009). Supporting effective community representation: Lessons from the Festival of Neighbourhoods. *Managing Leisure, 14*(1), 1–16.

Johnston, L. (2006). 'I do down-under': Naturalizing landscapes and love through wedding tourism in New Zealand. *ACME: An International E-Journal for Critical Geographies, 5*(2), 191–208.

Jones, C. (2012). Events and festivals: Fit for the Future? *Event Management, 16*(2), 107–118.

Jones, M. (2010). *Sustainable event management: A practical guide.* London: Earthscan.

Jones, I., & Green, C. (2006). Serious leisure, social identity and sport tourism. In H. Gibson (Ed.), *Sport tourism: Concepts and theories* (pp. 32–49). London: Routledge.

Junge, B. (2008). Heterosexual attendance at gay events: The 2002 Parada Livre Festival in Porto Alegre, Brazil. *Sexuality & Culture, 12*(2), 116–132.

Kang, Y., & Perdue, R. (1994). Long term impact of a mega-event on international tourism to the host country: A conceptual model and the case of the 1988 Seoul Olympics. In M. Uysal (Ed.), *Global tourist behavior* (pp. 205–225). Binghamton, NY: Haworth Press.

Kaplan, S. (2008). Finding the true cross: The social-political dimensions of the Ethiopian Masqal Festival. *Journal of Religion in Africa, 38*(4), 447–465.

Kaplanidou, K., & Gibson, H. (2010). Predicting behavioral intentions of active event sport tourists: The case of a small scale recurring sports event. *Journal of Sport and Tourism, 15,* 163–179.

Kay, P. (2004). Cross-cultural research issues in developing international tourist markets for cultural events. *Event Management, 8*(4), 191–202.

Kim, H., Borges, M., & Chon, J. (2006). Impacts of environmental values on tourism motivation: The case of FICA, Brazil. *Tourism Management, 27*(5), 957–967.

Kim, K., Sun, J., & Mahoney, E. (2008). Roles of motivation and activity factors in predicting satisfaction: Exploring the Korean cultural festival market. *Tourism Analysis, 13*(4), 413–425.

Kim, S. S., & Morrison, A. (2005). Change of images of South Korea among foreign tourists after the 2002 FIFA World Cup. *Tourism Management, 26*(2), 233–247.

Kim, S., Scott, D., & Crompton, J. (1997). An exploration of the relationships among social psychological involvement, behavioral involvement, commitment, and future intentions in the context of birdwatching. *Journal of Leisure Research, 29*(3), 320–341.

Knox, D. (2008). Spectacular tradition Scottish folksong and authenticity. *Annals of Tourism Research, 35*(1), 255–273.

Koo, G. Y., & Hardin, R. (2008). Difference in interrelationship between spectators' motives and behavioral intentions based on emotional attachment. *Sport Marketing Quarterly, 17*(1), 30–43.

Korza, P., & Magie, D. (1989). *The arts festival work kit.* Amherst, MA: University of Massachusetts Arts Extension Service.

Kotler, P., Haider, D., & Rein, I. (1993). *Marketing places.* New York: The Free Press.

Kozak, N. (2006). The expectations of exhibitors in tourism, hospitality and the travel industry. *Journal of Convention and Event Management, 7*(3), 99–116.

Kozak, N., & Kayar, C. (2009). Visitors' objectives for trade exhibition attendance: A case study on the East Mediterranean International Tourism and Travel Exhibition (EMITT). *Event Management, 12*(3/4), 133–141.

Kreag, G. (1988). *Festival, fair, and event marketing*. Paper presented at Festival and Events Seminar, University of Minnesota.

Krugman, C., & Wright, R. (2007). *Global meetings and exhibitions*. Hoboken, NJ: Wiley.

Krysztof, K., & Davidson, R. (2008). Human resources in the business events industry. In J. Ali-Knight (Ed.), *International perspectives of festivals and events—paradigms of analysis* (pp. 241–252). London: Elsevier.

Kurscheidt, M. (2005). Finanzwissenschaftliche Analyse des Sports: Empirische Befunde und allokationstheoretische Erklärungen zur staatlichen Sportpolitik. In H.-G. Napp (Ed.), *Finanzwissenschaft im Wandel* (pp. 211–229). Frankfurt: M. Lang.

Kyle, G., Absher, J., Norman, W., Hammitt, W., & Jodice, L. (2007). A modified involvement scale. *Leisure Studies, 26*(4), 399–427.

Kyle, G., & Chick, G. (2002). The social nature of leisure involvement. *Journal of Leisure Research, 34*(4), 426–448.

Laarman, J. G., & Durst, P. B. (1989). *Nature travel and tropical forests* (FREI working paper series). Southeastern Center for Forest Economics Research, North Carolina State University, Raleigh.

Lade, C., & Jackson, J. (2004). Key success factors in regional festivals: Some Australian experiences. *Event Management, 9*(1–2), 1–11.

Ladkin, A., & Weber, K. (2010). Career aspects of convention and exhibition professionals in Asia. *International Journal of Contemporary Hospitality Management, 22*(6), 871–886.

Lamont, M., & Kennelly, M. (2011). I can't do everything! Competing priorities as constraints in triathlon event travel careers. *Tourism Review International, 14*(2), 85–97.

Lamont, M., Kennelly, M., & Wilson, E. (2012). Competing priorities as constraints in event travel careers. *Tourism Management, 33*(5), 1068–1079.

Larson, M. (2002). A political approach to relationship marketing: Case study of the Storsjöyran festival. *International Journal of Tourism Research, 4*(2), 119–143.

Larson, M. (2009). Joint event production in the jungle, the park, and the garden: Metaphors of event networks. *Tourism Management, 30*(3), 393–399.

Larson, M., & Wikstrom, E. (2001). Organizing events: Managing conflict and consensus in a political market square. *Event Management, 7*(1), 51–65.

Lavenda, R. (1980). The festival of progress: The globalizing world-system and the transformation of the Caracas Carnival. *The Journal of Popular Culture, 14*(3), 465–475.

Lee, C., Lee, Y., & Wicks, B. (2004). Segmentation of festival motivation by nationality and satisfaction. *Tourism Management, 25*(1), 61–70.

Lee, J. (1987). The impact of Expo '86 on British Columbia markets. In P. Williams, J. Hall, & M. Hunter (Eds.), *Tourism: Where is the client*. Conference papers of the Travel and Tourism Research Association, Canada Chapter.

Lee, M. J., & Back, K. (2005a). A review of convention and meeting management research 1990–2003. *Journal of Convention and Event Tourism, 7*(2), 1–19.

Lee, M. J., & Back, K. (2005b). A review of economic value drivers in convention and meeting management research. *International Journal of Contemporary Hospitality Management, 17*(5), 409–420.

Lee, M. J., Yeung, S., & Dewald, B. (2010). An exploratory study examining the determinants of attendance motivations as perceived by attendees at Hong Kong exhibitions. *Journal of Convention and Event Tourism, 11*(3), 195–208.

Lee, S., & Crompton, J. (2003). The attraction power and spending impact of three festivals in Ocean City. *Event Management, 8*(2), 109–112.

Lee, S. Y., Petrick, J., & Crompton J. (2007). The roles of quality and intermediary constructs in determining festival attendees' behavioral intention. *Journal of Travel Research, 45*(4), 402–412.

Leibold, M., & van Zyl, C. (1994). The Summer Olympic Games and its tourism marketing—city tourism marketing experiences and challenges with specific reference to Cape Town, South Africa. In P. Murphy (Ed.), *Quality Management in Urban Tourism: Balancing Business and the Environment, Proceedings* (pp. 135–151), University of Victoria.

Lenskyj, H. J. (1996). When winners are losers. Toronto and Sydney bids for the Summer Olympics. *Journal of Sport & Social Issues, 20*(4), 392–410.

Levy, P. (2007). *Iconic events: Media, politics, and power in retelling history.* Latham, MD: Lexicon Books.

Li, R., & Petrick, J. (2006). A review of festival and event motivation studies. *Event Management, 9*(4), 239–245.

Li, X., & Vogelsong, H. (2005). Comparing methods of measuring image change: A case study of a small-scale community festival. *Tourism Analysis, 10*(4), 349–360.

Lin, X. (2004). Economic impact of Beijing Olympic Games 2008. *Proceedings of the 2004 Pre-olympic Congress* (Vol. 1), August 6–11, Thessaloniki, Greece.

Ling-Yee, L. (2006). Relationship learning at trade shows: Its antecedents and consequences. *Industrial Marketing Management, 35*(2), 166–177.

Long, P. (2000). After the event: Perspectives on organizational partnership in the management of a themed festival year. *Event Management, 6*(1), 45–59.

Long, P., & Robinson, M. (Eds.). (2004). *Festivals and tourism: Marketing, management and evaluation.* Sunderland, UK: Business Education Publishers Ltd.

Lord Cultural Resources Planning and Management, Inc. (1993). *The cultural tourism handbook.* Toronto: Author.

Louviere, J., & Hensher, D. (1983). Using discrete choice models with experimental data to forecast consumer demand for a unique event. *Journal of Consumer Research, 10*(3), 348–361.

Lusch, R., & Vargo, S. (2006). Service dominant logic: Reactions, reflections, and refinements. *Marketing Theory, 6*(3), 281–288.

Lusch, R. F., Vargo, S. L., & O'Brien, M. (2007). Competing through service: Insights from service-dominant logic. *Journal of Retailing, 83*(1), 5–18.

MacAloon, J. (1984). Olympic Games and the theory of spectacle in modern societies. In J. MacAloon (Ed.), *Rite, drama, festival, spectacle: Rehearsals towards a theory of cultural performance* (pp. 241–280). Philadelphia: Institute for the Study of Human Issues.

MacCannell, D. (1976). *The tourist: A new theory of the leisure class.* New York: Schocken Books.

Mackellar, J. (2009a). Dabblers, fans and fanatics: Exploring behavioural segmentation at a special-interest event. *Journal of Vacation Marketing, 15*(1), 5–24.

Mackellar, J. (2009b). An examination of serious participants at the Australian Wintersun Festival. *Leisure Studies, 28*(1), 85–104.

MacLeod, N. (2006). The placeless festival: Identity and place in the post-modern festival. In D. Picard & M. Robinson (Eds.), *Festivals, tourism and social change* (pp. 222–237). Clevedon, UK: Channel View.

Mair, J. (2012). A review of business events literature. *Event Management, 16*(2), 133–141.

Mair, J., & Thompson, K. (2009). The UK association conference attendance decision-making process. *Tourism Management, 30*(3), 400–409.

Mannel, R., & Iso-Ahola, S. (1987). Psychological nature of leisure and tourist experiences. *Annals of Tourism Research, 14*, 314–331.

Manning, F. (1978). Carnival in Antigua (Caribbean Sea): An indigenous festival in a tourist economy. *Anthropos, 73*(1/2), 191–204.

Manning, F. (Ed.). (1983). *The celebration of society: Perspectives on contemporary cultural performance.* Bowling Green, OH: Bowling Green University Popular Press.

Maple, L. C., Eagles, P. F. J., & Rolfe, H. (2010). Birdwatchers' specialisation characteristics and national park tourism planning. *Journal of Ecotourism, 9*(3), 219–238.

Marris, T. (1987). The role and impact of mega-events and attractions on regional and national tourism development: Resolutions of the 37th Congress of the AIEST, Calgary. *Revue de Tourisme, 4,* 3–12.

Maslow, A. (1954). *Motivation and personality.* New York: Harper and Row.

Masterman, G. (2004). *Strategic sports event management: An international approach.* Oxford: Elsevier.

Masterman, G., & Wood, E. (2006). *Innovative marketing communications: Strategies for the events industry.* Oxford: Butterworth-Heinemann.

Matheson, C. (2005). Festivity and sociability: A study of a Celtic music festival. *Tourism Culture & Communication, 5*(3), 149–163.

Matheson, C., Foley, M., & McPherson, G. (2006). Globalisation and Singaporean festivals. *International Journal of Event Management Research, 2*(1), 1–16.

Maunsell, F. (2004). *Commonwealth Games benefits study: Final report.* Manchester: North West Development Agency.

Mayfield, T., & Crompton, J. (1995). The status of the marketing concept among festival organizers. *Journal of Travel Research, 33*(4), 14–22.

McCabe, V. (2008). Strategies for career planning and development in the convention and exhibition industry in Australia. *International Journal of Hospitality Management, 27*(2), 222–231.

McCabe, V. S., Poole, B., Weeks, P., & Leiper, N. (2000). *The business and management of conventions.* Brisbane: John Wiley Ltd.

McCarthy, K., Ondaatje, E., Laura, Z., & Brooks, A. (2004). *Gifts of the muse: Reframing the debate about the benefits of the arts.* Santa Monica: Rand Corporation.

McCarville, R. (2007). From a fall in the mall to a run in the sun: One journey to Ironman triathlon. *Leisure Sciences, 29*(2), 159–173.

McConnell, A., & Getz, D. (2007). Case study of TransRockies Inc. In U. Wuensch & P. Thuy (Eds.), *Handbuch Event-Kommunikation.* Berlin: Erich Schmidt Verlag.

McFarlane, B. (1996). Socialization influences of specialization among birdwatchers. *Human Dimensions of Wildlife, 1*(1), 35–50.

McGehee, N., Yoon, Y., & Cardenas, D. (2003). Involvement and travel for recreational runners in North Carolina. *Journal of Sport Management, 17*(3), 305–324.

McKonkey, R. (1986). *Attracting tours to special events.* Paper presented at the annual conference of the Canadian Association of Festivals and Events, Hamilton, Ontario.

Mehmetoglu, M., & Ellingsen, K. (2005). Do small-scale festivals adopt "market orientation" as a management philosophy? *Event Management, 9*(3), 119–132.

Mehus, I. (2005). Sociability and excitement motives of spectators attending entertainment sport events: Spectators of soccer and ski-jumping. *Journal of Sport Behavior, 28*(4), 333–350.

Mendell, R., MacBeth, J., & Solomon, A. (1983, April). The 1982 world's fair—a synopsis. *Leisure Today,* 48–49.

Merrilees, B., Getz, D., & O'Brien, D. (2005). Marketing stakeholder analysis: Branding the Brisbane Goodwill Games. *European Journal of Marketing, 39*(9/10), 1060–1077.

Mihalik, B. (1994). Mega-event legacies of the 1996 Atlanta Olympics. In P. Murphy (Ed.), *Quality Management in Urban Tourism: Balancing Business and Environment, Proceedings* (pp. 151–162), University of Victoria.

Mihalik, B., & Ferguson, M. (1994). A case study of a tourism special event: An analysis of an American state fair. *Festival Management & Event Tourism, 2,* 75–83.

Mihalik, B., & Wing-Vogelbacher, A. (1992). Travelling art expositions as a tourism event: A market research analysis for Ramesses the Great. *Journal of Travel and Tourism Marketing, 1*(3), 25–41.

Mill, R., & Morrison, A. (1985). *The tourism system: An introductory text.* Englewood Cliffs, NJ: Prentice-Hall.

Miller, A. (2012). Understanding the event experience of active sports tourists. In R. Shipway & A. Fyall (Eds.), *International sports events: Impacts, experiences and identities* (pp. 99–112). London: Routledge.

Mills, B. M., & Rosentraub, M. S. (2013). Hosting mega-events: A guide to the evaluation of development effects in integrated metropolitan regions. *Tourism Management, 34,* 238–246.

Milne, G. R., & McDonald, M. A. (1999). *Sport marketing: Managing the exchange process.* Sudbury, MA: Jones & Bartlett Learning.

Milner, L., Jago, L., & Deery, M. (2003). Profiling the special event nonattendee: An initial investigation. *Event Management, 8*(3), 141–150.

Mintzberg, H. (1994). *The rise and fall of strategic planning.* New York: The Free Press.

Mitchell, C. (1993). Economic impact of the arts: Theatre festivals in small Ontario communities. *Journal of Cultural Economics, 17*(2), 55–67.

Mohr, K., Backman, K., Gahan, L., & Backman, S. (1993). An investigation of festival motivations and event satisfaction by visitor type. *Festival Management & Event Tourism, 1*(3), 89–97.

Morgan, M. (2009). What makes a good festival? Understanding the event experience. *Event Management, 12*(2), 81–93.

Morgan, A., & Condliffe, S. (2006). Measuring the economic impact of convention centers and event tourism: A discussion of the key issues. In R. Nelson (Ed.), *Developing a successful infrastructure for convention and event tourism* (pp. 81–100). Binghamton, NY: Haworth Press [also published in *Journal of Convention and Event Tourism, 8*(4), 2006].

Morgan, M., Lugosi, P., & Ritchie, J. R. B. (Eds.). (2010). *The tourism and leisure experience: Consumer and managerial perspectives.* Bristol, UK: Channel View.

Morrison, A. (1995). *Hospitality and travel marketing* (2nd ed.). Albany, NY: Delmar.

Morrow, S. (1997). *The art of the show: An Introduction to the study of exhibition management.* Dallas: International Association for Exhibition Management.

Morse, J. (2001). The Sydney 2000 Olympic Games: How the Australian Tourist Commission leveraged the Games for tourism. *Journal of Vacation Marketing, 7*(2), 101–107.

Mossberg, L. (2000). Effects of events on destination image. In L. Mossberg (Ed.), *Evaluation of events: Scandinavian experiences* (pp. 30–46). New York: Cognizant Communication Corp.

Mossberg, L., & Getz, D. (2006). Stakeholder influences on the ownership and management of festival brands. *Scandinavian Journal of Hospitality and Tourism, 6*(4), 308–326.

Mules, T. (1993). A special event as part of an urban renewal strategy. *Festival Management & Event Tourism, 1*(2), 65–67.

Mules, T., & Dwyer, L. (2006). Public sector support for sport tourism events: The role of cost–benefit assessment. In H. Gibson (Ed.), *Sport tourism: Concepts and theories* (pp. 206–223). London: Routledge.

Mules, T., & McDonald, S. (1994). The economic impact of special events: The use of forecasts. *Festival Management & Event Tourism, 2*(1), 45–53.

Müller, D., & Pettersson, R. (2006). Sámi heritage at the winter festival in Jokkmokk, Sweden. *Scandinavian Journal of Hospitality and Tourism, 6*(01), 54–69.

Murray, J. (1991). Applied tourism economic impact analysis: pitfalls and practicalities, In *Building Credibility for a Credible Industry, Proceedings of the TTRA 23rd Annual Conference* (pp. 19–31), Long Beach, California.

Mykletun, R. (2009). Celebration of extreme playfulness: Ekstremsportveko at Voss. *Scandinavian Journal of Hospitality and Tourism, 9*(2–3), 146–176.

National Endowment for the Arts. (2002). *Survey of public participation in the arts.* Retrieved from http://www.arts.gov/pub/ResearchNotes.html

National Endowment for the Arts. (2009). *2008 survey of public participation in the arts* (Research report #49). Retrieved from http://www.nea.gov/research/2008-sppa.pdf

National Endowment for the Arts. (2010). *Live from your neighborhood: A national study of outdoor arts festivals* (Research report #51). Retrieved from http://www.nea.gov/research/Festivals-report.pdf

Nelson, R. (Ed.). (2006). *Developing a successful infrastructure for convention and event tourism.* Binghamton, NY: Haworth Press [also published in *Journal of Convention and Event Tourism, 8*(4), 2006].

Neuenfeldt, K. (1995). The Kyana Corroboree: Cultural production of indigenous ethnogenesis. *Sociological inquiry, 65*(1), 21–46.

Ngamsom, B., & Beck, J. (2000). A pilot study of motivations, inhibitors, and facilitators of association members in attending international conferences. *Journal of Convention and Exhibition Management, 2*(2/3), 97–111.

Nicholson, R., & Pearce, D. (2001). Why do people attend events: A comparative analysis of visitor motivations at four South Island events. *Journal of Travel Research, 39,* 449–460.

Nogawa, H., Yamaguchi, Y., & Hagi, Y. (1996). An empirical research study on Japanese sport tourism in Sport-for-All events: Case studies of a single-night event and a multiple-night event. *Journal of Travel Research, 35,* 46–54.

Nolan, M., & Nolan, S. (1992). Religious sites as tourism attractions in Europe. *Annals of Tourism Research, 19*(1), 68–78.

O'Brien, D., & Chalip, L. (2008). Sport events and strategic leveraging: Pushing towards the triple bottom line. In A. Woodside & D. Martin (Eds.), *Tourism management: Analysis, behaviour and strategy* (pp. 318–338). Wallingford, UK: CABI.

Oppermann, M., & Chon, K. (1997). Convention participation decision-making process. *Annals of Tourism Research, 24*(1), 178–191.

O'Toole, W. (2011). *Events feasibility and development: From strategy to operations.* Oxford: Elsevier.

Page, S., & Connell, J. (2012). Introduction. In S. Page & J. Connell (Eds.), *Routledge handbook of events* (pp. 1–23). London: Routledge.

Parsons, G. (2006). Civil religion and the invention of tradition: The Festival of Saint Ansano in Siena. *Journal of Contemporary Religion, 21*(1), 49–67.

Pearce, P. (1993). Fundamentals of tourist motivation. In D. Pearce & R. Butler (Eds.), *Tourism research: Critiques and challenges.* New York: Routledge.

Pearce, P. (2005). *Tourist behaviour: Themes and conceptual schemas.* Clevedon, UK: Channel View.

Pearce, P., & Lee, U. (2005). Developing the travel career approach to tourist motivation. *Journal of Travel Research, 43*(3), 226–237.

Pegg, S., & Patterson, I. (2010). Rethinking music festivals as a staged event: Gaining insights from understanding visitor motivations and the experiences they seek. *Journal of Convention & Event Tourism, 11*(2), 85–99.

Pennington-Gray, L., & Holdnak, A. (2002). Out of the stands and into the community: Using sports events to promote a destination. *Event Management, 7*(3), 177–186.

Persson, C. (2002). The Olympic games site decision. *Tourism Management, 23*(1), 27–36.

Peters, M., & Pikkemaat, B. (2005). The management of city events: The case of Bergsilvester in Innsbruck, Austria. *Event Management, 9*(3), 147–153.

Philips, J., Philips, P., & Breining, T. (2008). *Return on investment in meetings and events.* Oxford: Butterworth-Heinemann.

Picard, D., & Robinson, M. (Eds.). (2006a). *Festivals, tourism and social change: Remaking worlds.* Clevedon, UK: Channel View.

Picard, D., & Robinson, M. (2006b). Remaking worlds: Festivals, tourism and change. In D. Picard & M. Robinson (Eds.), *Festivals, tourism and social change: Remaking worlds* (pp. 1–31). Clevedon, UK: Channel View.

Pine, B., & Gilmore, J. (1999). *The experience economy: Work is theatre and every business a stage.* Boston: Harvard Business School Press.

Pitts, B. (1999). Sports tourism and niche markets: Identification and analysis of the growing lesbian and gay sports tourism industry. *Journal of Vacation Marketing, 5*(1), 31–50.

Plog, S. (1987). Understanding psychographics in tourism research. In J. Ritchie & C. Goeldner (Eds.), *Travel, tourism and hospitality research* (pp. 302–213). New York: Wiley.

Pomfret, R., Wilson, J., & Lobmayr, B. (2009). *Bidding for sport mega-events.* Proceedings of SERC 2009 (pp. 1–19). Retrieved from http://trove.nla.gov.au/work/156366894? selectedversion=NBD47729750.

Porter, M. (1980). *Competitive strategy: Techniques for analyzing industries and competitors.* New York: The Free Press.

Preuss, H. (1998). Problemizing arguments of the opponents of Olympic Games. In R. K. Barney, K. B. Wamsley, S. G. Martyn, & G. H. MacDonald (Eds.), *Global and cultural critique: Problematising the Olympic Games* (pp. 197–218). London, ON, Canada: International Symposium for Olympic Research.

Preuss, H. (2004a). *The economics of the Olympics. A comparison of the Games 1972–2008.* Cheltenham, UK: Edward Elgar Publishing Limited.

Preuss, H. (2004b). Calculating of the regional impact of the Olympic Games. *European Sport Management Quarterly, 4*(4), 234–253.

Preuss, H. (2006). Winners and losers of the Olympic Games. In B. Houlihan (Ed.), *Sport & society* (2nd ed.). London/Thousand Oaks, CA/New Dehli: Sage.

Preuss, H. (2007a). The conceptualisation and measurement of mega sport event legacies. *Journal of Sport & Tourism, 12*(4), 207–228.

Preuss, H. (2007b). Signaling growth—China's major benefit from staging the Olympics in Beijing 2008. *Harvard Asia Pacific Review, 9*(1), 41–45.

Preuss, H., & Messing, M. (2002). Auslandstouristen bei den Olympischen Spielen in Sydney 2000. In A. Dreyer (Ed.), *Tourismus im Sport* (pp. 223–41). Wiesbaden: Deutscher Universitäts-Verlag.

Preuss, H., & Solberg, H. A. (2006). Attracting major sporting events—the role of local residents. *European Sport Management Quarterly, 6*(4), 391–411.

Price, C. (1993). *An empirical study of the value of professional association meetings from the perspective of attendees.* Unpublished doctoral dissertation, Virginia Polytechnic and State University, Blacksburg, VA.

Pugh, C., & Wood, E. (2004). The strategic use of events within local government: A study of London Borough councils. *Event Management, 9*(1/2), 61–71.

Quinn, B. (2003). Symbols, practices and myth-making: Cultural perspectives on the Wexford Festival Opera. *Tourism Geographies, 5*(3), 329–349.

Quinn, B. (2006). Problematising 'festival tourism': Arts festivals and sustainable development in Ireland. *Journal of Sustainable Tourism, 14*(3), 288–306.

Queensland Events Corporation. (1991). *QEC corporate plan: 1991 and beyond*. Brisbane: Author.

Queensland Events Corporation. (2003). *The year in review*. Brisbane: Author.

Raj, R., & Musgrave, J. (2009). *Event management and sustainability*. Wallingford, UK: CABI.

Ralston, L., & Crompton, J. (1988a). *Profile of visitors to the 1987 Dickens on the Strand emerging from a mail back survey*. Report #2 for the Galveston Historical Foundation.

Ralston, L., & Crompton, J. (1988b). *Motivations, service quality and economic impact of visitors to the 1987 Dickens on the Strand emerging from a mail back survey*. Report #3 for the Galveston Historical Foundation.

Ravenscroft, N., & Matteucci, X. (2003). The festival as carnivalesque: Social governance and control at Pamplonas San Fermin Fiesta. *Tourism, Culture & Communication, 4*(1), 1–15.

Ray, N. M., McCain, G., Davis, D., & Melin, T. L. (2006). Lewis and Clark and the *Corps of Discovery*: Re-enactment event tourism as authentic heritage travel. *Leisure Studies, 25*(4), 437–454.

Raybould, M. (1998). Participant motivation in a remote fishing event. *Festival Management & Event Tourism, 5*(4), 231–241.

Raybould, M., Mules, T., Fredline, E., & Tomljenovic, R. (2000). Counting the herd: Using aerial photography to estimate attendance at open events. *Event Management, 6*(1), 25–32.

Reid, G. (2006). The politics of city imaging: A case study of the MTV Europe Music Awards in Edinburgh 03. *Event Management, 10*(1), 35–46.

Richards, G. (2007). The festivalization of society or the socialization of festivals? The case of Catalunya. In G. Richards, (ed.), *Cultural tourism: Global and local perspectives* (pp. 257–269). New York: Haworth Press.

Richards, G., & Palmer, R. (2010). *Eventful cities: Cultural management and urban revitalisation*. Oxford: Butterworth Heinemann.

Ritchie, B. W., & Adair, D. (Eds.). (2004). *Sport tourism: Interrelationships, impacts and issues*. Clevedon, UK: Channel View.

Ritchie, J. R. B. (1984). Assessing the impacts of hallmark events: Conceptual and research issues. *Journal of Travel Research, 23*(1), 2–11.

Ritchie, J. R. B. (2000). Turning 16 days into 16 years through Olympic legacies. *Event Management, 6*(2), 155–165.

Ritchie, J. R. B., & Beliveau, D. (1974). Hallmark events: An evaluation of a strategic response to seasonality in the travel market. *Journal of Travel Research, 13*(2), 14–20.

Ritchie, J. R. B., & Crouch, G. (2003). *The competitive destination: A sustainable tourism perspective*. Wallingford, UK: CABI.

Ritchie, J. R. B., & Smith, B. (1991). The impact of a mega-event on host region awareness: A longitudinal study. *Journal of Travel Research, 30*(1), 3–10.

Rittichainuwat, B., Beck, J., & LaLopa, J. (2001). Understanding motivations, inhibitors, and facilitators of association members in attending international conferences. *Journal of Convention and Exhibition Management, 3*(3), 45–62.

Rittichainuwat, B., & Mair, J. (2011). Visitor attendance motivations at consumer travel exhibitions. *Tourism Management, 33*(5), 1236–1244.

Robinson, T., & Gammon, S. (2004). A question of primary and secondary motives: Revisiting and applying the sport tourism framework. *Journal of Sport Tourism, 9*(3), 221–223.

Rosentraub, M. (1999). *Major league losers: The real cost of sports and who's paying for it*. New York: Basic Books.

Rostenraub, M. (2009). *Major league winners: Using sports and cultural centers as tools for economic development*. New York: Basic Books.

Rozin, S. (2000). The amateurs who saved Indianapolis. *Business Week, 10*, 126–130.

Ryan, C., & Trauer, B. (2005). Sport tourist behaviour: The example of the Masters games. In J. Higham (Ed.), *Sport tourism destinations: Issues, opportunities and analysis*. Oxford: Elsevier.

Sanders, H. (2004). *"A lot of hooey": Heywood Sanders on convention center economics*. Retrieved July, 2006, from http://www.fieldofschemes.com

Schneider, I., & Backman, S. (1996). Cross-cultural equivalence of festival motivations: A study in Jordan. *Festival Management & Event Tourism, 4*(3–4), 139–144.

Scotinform Ltd. (1991). *Edinburgh Festivals study 1990–91: Visitor survey and economic impact assessment, final report*. Edinburgh: Scottish Tourist Board.

Scott, D., Baker, S., & Kim, C. (1999). Motivations and commitments among participants in the great Texas birding classic. *Human Dimensions of Wildlife: An International Journal, 4*(1), 50–67.

Scott, N., Laws, E., & Boksberger. P. (2009). *Marketing of tourism experiences*. Oxon, UK: Routledge.

Senge, P. (1990). *The fifth discipline: The art and practice of the learning organization*. New York: Doubleday.

Shank, M. D., & Beasley, F. M. (1998). Fan or fanatic: Refining a measure of sports involvement. *Journal of Sport Behavior, 21*(4), 436–450.

Shanka, T., & Taylor, R. (2004). A correspondence analysis of sources of information used by festival visitors. *Tourism Analysis, 9*(1–2), 55–62.

Sheldon, P. (1990). A review of tourism expenditure research. In C. Cooper (Ed.), *Progress in tourism, recreation and hospitality management* (Vol. 2). University of Surrey and Belhaven Press.

Sherwood, P. (2007). *A triple bottom line evaluation of the impact of special events: The development of indicators*. Unpublished doctoral dissertation, Victoria University, Melbourne.

Shibli, S., & Coleman, R. (2005). Economic impact and place marketing evaluation: A case study of the World Snooker Championship. *International Journal of Event Management Research, 1*(1). Retrieved from http://www.ijemr.org/docs/shibliandcoleman.pdf

Shibli, S., & the Sport Industry Research Centre. (2002). *The 2002 Embassy World Snooker Championship, an evaluation of the economic impact, place marketing effects, and visitors' perceptions of Sheffield*. For Sheffield City Council.

Shipway, R., & Fyall, A. (Eds.). (2012). *International sports events: Impacts, experiences and identities*. London: Routledge.

Shipway, R., & Jones, I. (2007). Running away from home: Understanding visitor experiences and behaviour at sport tourism events. *International Journal of Tourism Research, 9*(5), 373–383.

Shipway, R., & Jones, I. (2008). The great suburban Everest: An insider's perspective on experiences at the 2007 Flora London Marathon. *Journal of Sport and Tourism, 13*(1), 61–77.

Shirley, M., Armitage, V., Barden, T., Gough, M., Lurz, P., Oatway, D., South, A., & Rushton, S. (2001). Assessing the impact of a music festival on the emergence behaviour of a breeding colony of Daubenton's bats (*Myotis daubentonii*). *Journal of Zoology, 254*(3), 367–373.

Singh, T., Slotkin, M., & Vamosi, A. (2007). Attitude towards ecotourism and environmental advocacy: Profiling the dimensions of sustainability. *Journal of Vacation Marketing, 13*(2), 119–134.

Silvers, J. R. (2008). *Risk management for meetings and events*. Oxford: Butterworth Heinemann.

Small, K., Carlsen, J., Robertson, M., & Ali-Knight, J. (2007). Social dimensions of community festivals: An application of factor analysis in the development of the social impact perception (sip) scale. *Event Management, 11*(1/2), 45–55.

Small, K., Edwards, D., & Sheridan, L. (2005). A flexible framework for evaluating the socio-cultural impacts of a (small) festival. *International Journal of Event Management Research, 1*(1), 66–77.

Smith, A. (2012). *Events and urban regeneration: The strategic use of events to revitalise cities.* London: Routledge.

Smith, S. (1988, November). The festival visitor: It may not be who you think it is. *Feedback,* the Official Publication of the Waterloo (Ontario) Chamber of Commerce, p. 1.

Smith, S. (1995). *Tourism analysis: A handbook* (2nd ed.). Harlow, UK: Longman.

Snowball, J., & Willis, K. (2006). Building cultural capital: Transforming the South African National Arts Festival. *South African Journal of Economics, 74*(1), 20–33.

Snyder, C. R., Lassegard, M. A., & Ford, C. E. (1986). Distancing after group success and failure: Basking in reflected glory and cutting off reflected failure. *Journal of Personality and Social Psychology, 51*(2), 382–388.

Solberg, H., Andersson, T., & Shibli, S. (2002). An exploration of the direct economic impacts from business travelers at world championships. *Event Management, 7*(3), 151–164.

Solberg, H. A., & Preuss, H. (2006). Major sporting events and long-term tourism impacts. *Journal of Sport Management, 21*(2).

Spiller, J. (2002). History of convention tourism. In K. Weber & K. Chon (Eds.), *Convention tourism: International research and industry perspectives* (pp. 3–20). Binghamton, NY: Haworth Press.

Spilling, O. (1998). Beyond intermezzo? On the long-term industrial impacts of mega-events: The case of Lillehammer 1994. *Festival Management & Event Tourism, 5*(3), 101–122.

Sport and Recreation Minister's Council. (1991). *Sports Economics: A newsletter and information service covering the economic aspects of sport and sporting events* (No. 2). Adelaide: Centre for South Australian Economic Studies.

Sport and Recreation Minister's Council. (1992). *Sports Economics: A newsletter and information service covering the economic aspects of sport and sporting events* (No. 3). Adelaide: Centre for South Australian Economic Studies.

Sport England. (2005). *Lifestyle sports and national sport policy: An agenda for research.* London: Author.

Sports Business Market Research. (2000–2006). *Sports Business Market Research handbook.*

Stebbins, R. (1992). *Amateurs, professionals, and serious leisure.* Montreal: McGill-Queen's University Press.

Stebbins, R. (2001). *New directions in the theory and research of serious leisure.* Lewiston, NY: Edwin Mellen.

Stebbins, R. (2007). *Serious leisure: A perspective for our time.* Somerset, NJ: Aldine Transaction Publications.

Stein, A., & Evans, B. (2009). *An introduction to the entertainment industry.* New York: Peter Lang.

Stokes, R. (2008). Tourism strategy making: Insights to the events tourism domain. *Tourism Management, 29*(2), 252–262.

Swann G. (2001). *When do major sports events leave a lasting economic legacy?* (Draft working paper), Manchester Business School, University of Manchester.

Szymanski, S. (2002). The economic impact of World Cup. *World Economics, 3*(1), 1–9.

Tanner, J., Chonko, L., & Ponzurick, T. (2001). A learning model of trade show attendance. *Journal of Convention & Exhibition Management, 3*(3), 3–26.

Taylor, P., & Gratton, C. (1988). The Olympic Games: An economic analysis. *Leisure Management, 8*(3), 32–34.

Teigland, J. (1996). *Impacts on tourism from mega-events: The case of winter Olympic Games*. Sogndal: Western Norway Research Institute.

Thomas, R., & Wood, E. (2004). Event-based tourism: A survey of local authority strategies in the UK. *Local Governance, 29*(2), 127–136.

Thurow, L. (2004). *Die Zukunft der Weltwirtschaft*. Frankfurt/New York: Campus.

Tighe, A. (1985). Cultural tourism in the USA. *Tourism Management, 6*(4), 234–251.

Tighe, A. (1986). The arts/tourism partnership. *Journal of Travel Research, 24*(3), 2–5.

Tomljenovic, R., & Weber, S. (2004). Funding cultural events in Croatia: Tourism-related policy issues. *Event Management, 9*(1/2), 51–59.

Tourism BC. (2011, May 6). *Advanced sport tourism workshop, Langley workshop report*. Retrieved from http://www.tourism-langley.ca/images/AdvancedSportTourismReport.pdf

Tourism Canada. (1994). P*ackaging and marketing festivals and events for the Canadian tourism industry*. Prepared by MGB Tourfest Inc., and The Economic Planning Group of Canada, Ottawa.

Tourism South Australia. (1991). *Barossa Valley Vintage Festival Visitor Survey April 1991*. Adelaide: Author.

Trail, G. T., & James, J. D. (2001). The motivation scale for sport consumption: Assessment of the scale's psychometric properties. *Journal of Sport Behavior, 24*(1), 108–127.

Trauer, B. (2006). Conceptualizing special interest tourism—frameworks for analysis. *Tourism Management, 27*(2), 183–200.

Travel Industry Association of America. (1999). *Profile of travellers who attend sports events*. Washington, DC: Author.

Travel Industry Association of America (2001). *Partners in tourism 2001*. Washington, DC: Author.

Travel Industry Association of America, and Smithsonian Magazine. (2003). *The historic/cultural traveller*.

Turco, D. (1995). Measuring the tax impacts of an international festival: Justification for government sponsorship. *Festival Management & Event Tourism, 2*(3/4), 191–195.

Turco, D., Riley, R., & Swart, K. (2002). *Sport tourism*. Morgantown, WV: Fitness Information Technology Inc.

Turner, V. (1969). *The ritual process: Structure and anti-structure*. New York: Aldine de Gruyter.

Turner, V. (1974). Liminal to liminoid, in play, flow and ritual: An essay in comparative symbology. In E. Norbeck (Ed.), *The anthropological study of human play* (Vol. 60, pp. 53–92). Rice University Studies.

Turner, V. (Ed.). (1982). *Celebration: Studies in festivity and ritual*. Washington, DC: Smithsonian Institution Press.

Tyrrell, B., & Ismail, J. (2005). A methodology for estimating the attendance and economic impact of an open-gate festival. *Event Management, 9*(3), 111–118.

Tyrrell, T., & Johnston, R. (2001). A framework for assessing direct economic impacts of tourist events: Distinguishing origins, destinations, and causes of expenditures. *Journal of Travel Research, 40*, 94–100.

Tzelepi, M., & Quick, S. (2002). The Sydney Organizing Committee for the Olympic Games (SOCOG) "Event Leadership" training course—an effectiveness evaluation. *Event Management, 7*(4), 245–257.

UFI. (2011). *Global exhibition industry statistics, 2011*. The Global Association of the Exhibition Industry. Retrieved from http://www.ufi.org/Medias/pdf/thetradefairsector/2011_exhibiton_industry_statistics.pdf

UFI. (2012). *The global exhibition barometer—Survey of the exhibition industry.* The Global Association of the Exhibition Industry. Retrieved from http://www.ufi. org/Medias/pdf/thetradefairsector/surveys/ufi_global_exhibition_barometer_july_ 2012.pdf

UK Sport. (n.d.). *eventIMPACTS toolkit.* Retrieved from http://www.eventimpacts.com

USM Events. (2011). *Media release: A great Australian tradition.* Retrieved November 9, 2011, from http://www.usmevents.com.au/Triathlon___Multi_Sport/Noosa_Triathlon_ Multi_Sport_Festival/Media___Gallery/Media_Release_-_A_great_Australian_tradition. htm

Unruh, D. (1979). Characteristics and types of participation in social worlds. *Symbolic Interaction, 2,* 115–129.

Unruh, D. (1980). The nature of social worlds. *The Pacific Sociological Review, 23*(3), 271–296.

Uysal, M., Gahan, L., & Martin, B. (1993). An examination of event motivations: A case study. *Festival Management & Event Tourism, 1*(1), 5–10.

Uzzell, D. (1984). An alternative structuralist approach to the psychology of tourism marketing. *Annals of Tourism Research, 11*(1), 79–99.

Van der Lee, D., & Williams, J. (1986). The Grand Prix and tourism. In J. Burns, J. Hatch & T. Mules (Eds.), *The Adelaide Grand Prix: The impact of a special event* (pp. 39–57). Adelaide: Centre for South Australian Economic Studies.

Van Gennep, A. (1909). *The rites of passage* (1960 translation by M. Vizedom & G. Coffee). London: Routledge and Kegan Paul.

Vanhove, D., & Witt, S. (1987). Report of the English-speaking group on the conference theme. *Revue de Tourisme, 42*(4),10–12.

Van Zyl, C., & Botha, C. (2004). Motivational factors of local residents to attend the Aardklop National Arts Festival. *Event Management, 8*(4), 213–222.

Vargo, S., & Lusch, R. F. (2008a). Why Service? *Journal of the Academy of Marketing Science, 36,* 25–38.

Vargo, S., & Lusch, R. F. (2008b). Service-dominant logic: Continuing the evolution. *Journal of the Academy of Marketing Science, 36,* 1–10.

Verhoven, P., Wall, D., & Cottrell, S. (1998). Application of desktop mapping as a marketing tool for special events planning and evaluation: A case study of the Newport News Celebration in Lights. *Festival Management & Event Tourism, 5*(3), 123–130.

Wallace, T. (2007). Went the day well: Scripts, glamour and performance in war-weekends. *International Journal of Heritage Studies, 13*(3), 200–223.

Wah, P. (2004). Refashioning festivals in republican Guangzhou. *Modern China, 30*(2), 199–227.

Wan, Y. (2011). Assessing the strengths and weaknesses of Macao as an attractive meeting and convention destination: Perspectives of key informants. *Convention and Event Tourism, 12*(2), 129–151.

Wang, P., & Gitelson, R. (1988, August). Economic limitations of festivals & other hallmark events. *Leisure Industry Report,* 4–5.

Wanhill, S. (2006). Some economics of staging events: the case of opera festivals. *Tourism, Culture and Communications, 6*(2), 137–149.

Wanhill, S. (2008). A night at the opera festival: The economics of opera. In Á. Matias, P. Nijkamp, & P. Neto (Eds.), *Advances in modern tourism research* (pp. 345–365). New York: Springer-Verlag.

Wann, D. L. (1995). Preliminary validation of the sport fan motivation scale. *Journal of Sport & Social Issues, 19*(4), 377–396.

Wann, D., Grieve, F., Zapalac, R., & Pease, D. (2008). Motivational profiles of sport fans of different sports. *Sport Marketing Quarterly, 17*(1), 6–19.

Wann, D. L., Schrader, M. P., & Wilson, A. M. (1999). Sport fan motivation: Questionnaire validation, comparisons by sport, and relationship to athletic motivation. *Journal of Sport Behavior, 22*(1), 114–139.

Warnick, R., Bojanic, D., Mathur, A., & Ninan, D. (2011). Segmenting event attendees based on travel distance, frequency of attendance, and involvement measures: A cluster segmentation technique. *Event Management, 15*(1), 77–90.

Waterman, S. (1998). Carnivals for elites? The cultural politics of arts festivals. *Progress in Human Geography, 22*(1), 54–74.

Waterman, S. (2004). Place, culture and identity: Summer music in Upper Galilee. *Transactions of the Institute of British Geographers, 23*(2), 253–267.

Weaver, D., & Lawton, L. (2007). Progress in tourism management twenty years on: The state of contemporary ecotourism research. *Tourism Management, 28*(5), 1168–1179.

Weber, K., & Chon, K. (2002). *Convention tourism: International research and industry perspectives*. New York: Haworth Press.

Weed, M. (2006). Sports tourism research 2000–2004: A systematic review of knowledge and a meta-evaluation of methods. *Journal of Sport and Tourism, 11*(1), 5–30.

Weed, M. (2008a). *Olympic tourism*. Oxford: Elsevier.

Weed. M (Ed.). (2008b). *Sport and tourism: A reader*. London: Routledge.

Weed, M. (2009). *Leveraging social, cultural and health benefits from London 2012: Conclusion report*. ESRC Grant No. RES-451-26-0403.

Weed, M. (2012). Towards an interdisciplinary events research agenda across sport, tourism, leisure and health. In S. Page & J. Connell (Eds.), *The Routledge handbook of events* (pp. 57–71). Oxon: Routledge.

Weed, M., & Bull, C. (2004). *Sports tourism: Participants, policy and providers*. Oxford: Elsevier.

Weed, M., & Bull, C. (2009). *Sports tourism: Participants, policy and providers* (2nd ed.). Oxford: Elsevier.

Westerbeek, H., Turner, P., & Ingerson, L. (2002). Key success factors in bidding for hallmark sporting events. *International Marketing Review, 19*(3), 303–322.

Whitford, M. (2004a). Regional development through domestic and tourist event policies: Gold Coast and Brisbane, 1974–2003. *UNLV Journal of Hospitality, Tourism and Leisure Science, 1*, 1–24.

Whitford, M. (2004b). Event public policy development in the Northern Sub-Regional Organisation of Councils, Queensland Australia: Rhetoric or realisation? *Journal of Convention and Event Tourism, 6*(3), 81–99.

Whitford, M. (2009). Oaxaca's indigenous Guelaguetza festival: Not all that glistens is gold. *Event Management, 12*(3/4), 143–161.

Whitson, D., & Macintosh, D. (1996). The global circus: International sport, tourism, and the marketing of cities. *Journal of Sport and Social Issues, 20*(3), 275–295.

Wicks, B., & Fesenmaier, D. (1995). Market potential for special events: A midwestern case study. *Festival Management & Event Tourism, 3*(1), 25–31.

Wiley, E. (2005). Romani performance and heritage tourism: The pilgrimage of the Gypsies at Les Saintes-Maries-de-la-Mer. *TDR, 49*, 135–158.

Williams, D. (2008). Events review—Queensland. Retrieved July 13, 2012, from http://www.premiers.qld.gov.au/publications/.../reviews/events-review.aspx

Williams, M., & Bowdin, G. (2007). Festival evaluation: An exploration of seven UK arts festivals. *Managing Leisure, 12*(2–3), 187–203.

Wood, E., & Thomas, R. (2006). Measuring cultural values—the case of residents' attitudes to the Saltaire Festival. *Tourism Economics, 12*(1), 137–145.

Wood, M. (2002). *Ecotourism: Principles, practices and policies for sustainability.* Paris: United Nations Environment Programme.

Wooten, M. H., & Norman, W. C. (2008). Differences in art festival visitors based on level of past experience. *Event Management, 11*(3), 109–120.

Xiao, H., & Smith, S. (2004). Residents' perceptions of Kitchener-Waterloo Oktoberfest: An inductive analysis. *Event Management, 8*(3), 161–175.

Xie, P. (2003). The Bamboo-beating dance in Hainan, China. Authenticity and commodification. *Journal of Sustainable Tourism, 11*(1), 5–16.

Xie, P. F., & Smith, S. L. J. (2000). Improving forecasts for world's fair attendance: Incorporating income effects. *Event Management, 6*(1), 15–23.

Yoo, J., & Weber, K. (2005). Progress in convention tourism research. *Journal of Hospitality and Tourism Research, 29*(2), 194–222.

Yoon, S., Spencer, D., Holecek, D., & Kim, D. (2000). A profile of Michigan's festival and special event tourism market. *Event Management, 6*(1), 33–44.

Yu, L., Wang, C., & Seo, J. (2012). Mega event and destination brand; 2010 Shanghai Expo. *International Journal of Festival and Event Management, 3*(1), 46–65.

Yu, Y., & Turco, D. (2000). Issues in tourism event economic impact studies: The case of Albuquerque International Balloon Fiesta. *Current Issues in Tourism, 3*(2), 138–149.

Yuan, J., Cai, L., Morrison, A., & Linton, S. (2005a). An analysis of wine festival attendees' motivations: A synergy of wine, travel and special events? *Journal of Vacation Marketing, 11*(1), 41–58.

Yuan, J., Cai, L., Morrison, A., & Linton, S. (2005b). Segmenting wine festival attendees: A factor-cluster approach. *Tourism Review International, 8*(4), 297–309.

Yuan, J., & Jang, S. (2008). The effects of quality and satisfaction on awareness and behavioral intentions: Exploring the role of a wine festival. *Journal of Travel Research, 46*(3), 279–288.

Yun, J., & Lehto, X. (2009). Motives and patterns of family reunion travel. *Journal of Quality Assurance in Hospitality and Tourism, 10*(4), 279–300.

Index

Event Tourism Related Journal from Cognizant Communication

EVENT MANAGEMENT:
An International Journal

Editor: Kenneth Backman
ISSN: 1525-9951; E-ISSN 1943-4308
Softbound   4 issues per year

AIMS & SCOPE

Event Management, an International Journal, intends to meet the research and analytic needs of a rapidly growing profession focused on events. This field has developed in size and impact globally to become a major business with numerous dedicated facilities, and a large-scale generator of tourism. The field encompasses meetings, conventions, festivals, expositions, sport and other special events. Event management is also of considerable importance to government agencies and not-for-profit organizations in a pursuit of a variety of goals, including fundraising, the fostering of causes, and community development.

Event Management aims to be the leading source of research reports and analysis related to all forms of event management. This journal publishes refereed and invited articles, book reviews, and documentation of news and trends. It also invites opinion pieces, profiles of organizations, and management case studies.

Full text available online: www.ingentaconnect.com/content/cog/em